The New Temperance

The New Temperance

The American Obsession with Sin and Vice

David Wagner

Routledge
Taylor & Francis Group

New York London

First published 1997 by Westview Press

Published 2019 by Routledge
52 Vanderbilt Avenue, New York, NY 10017
2 Park Square, Milton Park, Abingdon, Oxon OX14 4RN

First issued in hardback 2019

Routledge is an imprint of the Taylor & Francis Group, an informa business

Library of Congress Cataloging-in-Publication Data
Wagner, David.
   The new temperance : the American obsession with sin and vice /
David Wagner.
      p.   cm.
   Includes index.
   ISBN 0-8133-2568-4 (hc). — ISBN 0-8133-2569-2 (pbk.)
   1. United States—Moral conditions.   2. Temperance—United States.
3. Behavior modification—United States.   4. Political correctness—
United States.   5. Conservatism—United States.   I. Title.
HN90.M6W34   1997
306′.0973—dc21   96-51514
                                                                          CIP

ISBN 13: 978-0-367-31879-6 (hbk)
ISBN 13: 978-0-8133-2569-9 (pbk)

*To the millions of Americans in jail, prison,
or under correctional surveillance, a large number
of them victims of the bipartisan "war on drugs"*

Contents

Acknowledgments

Writing affords me the chance to reflect on continuities and changes over the course of my life. Although I alone must accept any blame for this work, I would like to thank some people who have been crucial to me in the writing process.

The first continuity is the aid of Marcia B. Cohen of the University of New England, my wife and colleague. Although this is my first book in which she is not actually a direct participant in the events of the text, the book bears her influence as my first reader and editor. Moreover, she continues to be a strong source of support at a time when having radical ideas is not very common or easy to maintain.

A second continuity for me is the wonderful staff of Westview Press. Dean Birkenkamp was my editor for my last book, *Checkerboard Square*, and steered this project through its early and middle stages. I was sorry to lose him as an editor last year, but Jill Rothenberg has done an exceptional job at bringing this project to fruition. Melanie Stafford, the project editor, has done a great job of putting together the book and Christine Arden, the copy editor, also did excellent work.

A third continuity for me is the environment of the University of Southern Maine, where I teach. The university not only helped me complete this book by providing a sabbatical leave but also provides a tolerant and open atmosphere in which to be a faculty member. This is something to appreciate because environment so shapes our ability to think and raise critical questions.

There are four people I would like to thank whose aid was invaluable to me, who I either did not know when I started this project or did not know how important they would be. First, Jenn MacAuley, a former student at my university, did a great job as research assistant, not only checking facts and getting library material but positively enjoying the process of thinking about and talking about social issues. Two Swedish colleagues, Thomas Knoll of Halmstad University and Ingrid Sahlin of Lunds University, thoroughly read several drafts of this manuscript and provided a wonderful cross-cultural viewpoint. Although this book focuses primarily on the United States, it has benefited greatly from their comments and views. Dennis Must, my brother-in-law and partner in crime in the new literary journal for poor and other disenfranchised people, *Flying Horse,* has not only been an important reader but a great source of support about the actual process of writing. Although we have known each other for years, our recent collaboration has come as a strong positive surprise that has influenced my thinking and writing.

Finally, since this book is about controversial subjects—the repression of pleasure in America and the constant mantra of danger—I feel I should say a word or two about the text. I find that having an author's personal likes and dislikes, memories and wishes, sins and virtues cast throughout a text is boring and annoying. So, for the most part, I have not discussed my own habits or vices. (Of course, those who are friends either know them or are welcome to ask me.) Moreover, I find contemporary Americans' obsession with the personal to be a sort of "Catch 22": If one pleads guilty to sin, of course, one is discounted or stigmatized; but curiously these days, if one has not sinned enough, he or she is disregarded as a person with no experience of the particular issue or problem. The best stance, I suppose, is that of "recovered": To admit to a long-ago, far-off vice now repudiated (perhaps one never really inhaled anyway).

I will say that the book is in some ways ironic for me. In the late 1960s, when I was a student radical at Columbia passing out flyers, I looked over at some of the hippies smoking dope and tried to figure out how to lure them into political demonstrations. In other words, I was not one of those baby boomers in the 1960s and early 1970s who thought "sex, drugs, and rock 'n' roll" were actually going to do much to "liberate" America. I held quite the reverse position and sought to politicize the cultural rebellion. Yet now, decades later, a funny thing has happened: Not only is a defense of sex, drugs, and rock 'n' roll necessary but it is almost revolutionary because of the repressive climate in America. Only now do I think I realize how radical the 1960s really were, and this in part explains why we have become so intent on repudiating these times since then. I plead guilty to what is perhaps the ultimate crime in the eyes of the establishment: a certain radical nostalgia for the 1960s and early 1970s, since in many ways American society was more alive and vibrant then.

David Wagner

one

The New Temperance

The last decades of the twentieth century may well be remembered as a time when personal behavior and character flaws dominated the American mind. As prominent political figures from Gary Hart to Robert Packwood were brought down by personal scandals, even death seemed to provide no respite from examination of behavior and morality. The media reported on the deaths of the Grateful Dead's Jerry Garcia and baseball star Mickey Mantle as exercises in moral diagnosis. Mantle was said to have died from too much "partying"; and Garcia, from assorted drugs, cigarettes, and food. Constant public service announcements, political speeches, and public health pronouncements urge us to "just say no" to drugs, cigarette smoking, fatty foods, teen sexuality, non-monogamous sex, and violent TV shows and music lyrics. Typically, the media have applauded such changes as reflecting the new mood of the times:

New Age on Campus: Can the Keg

Campus social life no longer revolves around the keg party. . . . "The whole culture is more wellness-conscious. Certainly our students are. The promotional stuff does sink in after a while about what alcohol does to your body," said Earl Smith, dean of Colby College. "We've got a fearful generation that's come of age now between AIDS, dating violence and the much more serious repercussions of driving drunk," said Mike O'Neil, coordinator of a Vanderbilt University program that shelled out $60,000 this year to students who agree to run nonalcoholic parties.[1]

New social problems, from eating disorders to "codependency," were discovered in the 1970s and 1980s, while older unmentionable problems such as child abuse and domestic violence continued to draw public attention. The 1990s, meanwhile, are witnessing the emergence of still newer problems of the personal:

Is a Waft of Fragrance Poisoning Your Space?

"It's sort of like cigarette smoking," she [Schmidt] complains. "They are invading my privacy." Whether she realizes it or not, Schmidt is part of what could be the next big nationwide battle that pits individual rights against public health concerns: the push for fragrance-free environments.

Support Group Helps People with "Messy" Problems

A walk through Judy's house used to mean stepping over piles—piles of magazines, piles of catalogues, piles of letters. . . . So Judy started a chapter of a support group—"Messies Anonymous" for slobs. . . . After the group was written up in the *Miami Herald*, "I got 12,000 letters saying, 'Help!'" Felton said.[2]

The Coercive Consensus

Although the New Temperance is in part a matter of national mood, and of a turning inward since the 1960s away from broader social and political concerns, the focus on personal behavior is not only a matter of style. The new mood in America also reflects a coercive strategy of punishment for those who fail to conform to the new norms.

Beginning in the 1980s, no amount of control, however personal or onerous, was considered excessive to stamp out the ingesting of drugs. By the 1990s, the "war on drugs" was leading to more than 1 million arrests a year, the majority of them for possession of small amounts of illicit substances. The drug war—complete with mandatory drug testing in many workplaces, mandatory criminal sentencing, and constant surveillance, particularly in ghetto areas—has been the major factor responsible for filling American prisons to record numbers. The drug war almost ensures that African-American males driving in poor neighborhoods will be stopped and searched[3] and, in some areas, that white, middle-class high school students will have their lockers and possessions searched. Mothers have been arrested, charged with ingesting drugs into their fetuses; medically ill people have been denied access to drugs for medicinal purposes; and even religious rituals such as the American Indian use of peyote have been halted—all because of the war on drugs.

The drug war now includes among its targets legal drugs such as alcohol and tobacco. The charge of hypocrisy by public health and liberal critics of the drug war has spawned an almost equally virulent war against these substances. As a result of recent legislation, many people with alcoholism or drug addiction are being cut from the Social Security disability rolls as a punitive measure. Youths unlucky enough to be caught with alcohol at a sports event or behind the school building incur charges tantamount to treason, leading at times to suspension or expulsion from school. In many New England towns, police are ticketing and even arresting youthful cigarette smokers. And some companies and public employers are refusing to hire cigarette smokers, whether their smoking is on or off the job.

Yet such repression never seems quite enough, as new calls for surveillance and punishment continue to appear. Consider this recent report from my local paper:

Plan Enlists Community in Drug War

Police would conduct searches of school lockers at a moment's notice. Store owners would routinely call police when they suspect a customer of buying alcohol for minors. Residents whose homes are used for teen parties with drugs and alcohol would be warned of the legal consequences. Clergymen would speak about substance abuse during church services. Those deterrents were part of a Community Wide Substance Abuse Policy being proposed.[4]

Rivaling the alarm over substances is the panic over sex and sexual displays. Beginning with the rise of the New Right in the 1970s, wars have been waged against promiscuity, pornography, and teen pregnancy. Democrats soon joined Republican enthusiasts in promoting "family values" and condemning out-of-wedlock births and teen sex.[5] A key ingredient of conservative attacks on welfare benefits has been the pathologization of the single mother and teen parents. But not to be outdone, President Clinton fired his first Surgeon General for talking about masturbation, while his secretary of Health and Human Services called out-of-wedlock births "morally just wrong."[6] By the 1990s, the consensus against sexuality had reached the point where politicians were competing with one another to support measures to control movies and TV, approving "v-chips" for parents to control children's television, advocating censorship on the Internet, and pressuring advertisers (such as Calvin Klein) to withdraw sexy ads.

Conservatives are sometimes outperformed by putative liberals on the New Temperance issues. Washington Mayor Marion Barry, a Democrat, only recently released from prison for his conviction for crack use, has called for mandatory Norplant implants for young women who are sexually active.[7] And liberal columnist Ellen Goodman has suggested that government fight the war against teen pregnancy by tracking down older male teens who are having sex with younger teens: "A substantial number of the men are what can only be called sexual predators. A substantial number of teen-age mothers are what we once called jailbait. . . . Maybe statutory rape is an idea whose time should return."[8]

The line between health warnings and moral suasion, on the one hand, and force, on the other, is a thin one. Even the new food moralism—touting the avoidance of fat or meat, promoting correct eating—sometimes turns into social control. For instance, my local "alternative" paper recently featured an article about a welfare recipient who was followed around and charged with (among other things) spending her money on "junk food."[9] Conservatives who criticize any pleasurable use of taxpayer money are joined by liberals who disapprove of such dietary excess: In a letter to the same paper, a person complained that "a meat market is soon to move into . . . [name of] Street. What kind of message will this send to the neighborhood, including the kids across the street at [name of] School?"[10]

The present book explores how the America of "sex, drugs, and rock 'n' roll" of the 1960s and early 1970s became so consumed with personal behavior and social control by the 1980s and 1990s. Elements of the Left as well as the Right now vie with each other to stamp out drugs, nonmarital sex, and unhealthy habits, differing only, it seems, on the question of which groups to punish more.[11] As politicians no longer rail against communism but emphasize their toughness on crime, drugs, sexual abuse, and violence in the media, this book asks "Why?" What some have called the "new sobriety," others have termed the "new puritanism," and still others have praised as the new health consciousness or "healthism," I will define here as the "New Temperance."[12]

Defining the "New Temperance"

For most Americans and certainly the majority of the educated public, a large percentage of daily human behavior has become pathologized in the last two decades. Whether the topic is cigarette smoking or fatty foods, teen pregnancy or excessive television viewing, we have been constantly bombarded with messages about health and morality. My intent is not to argue that any or all of these behaviors are healthy or wise, nor do I advocate that the reader smoke cigarettes, drink alcohol to excess, take illegal drugs, or engage in violent behavior. Of course, health messages contain some friendly advice.

But to acknowledge risks, is, from a sociological perspective, not to explain very much about the American obsession with personal behavior. This book argues the constant focus on personal behavior in America serves as a tool of political power as well as a popular social movement. Temperance is a national ideology. That is, Americans of the last two decades seem to have become rigidly focused on problems of personal behavior, as if such issues explain all of life and provide meaning to all events. To say something is an ideology is not to argue that *all* of its observations and ramifications are negative or undesirable. Temperance ideology has much basis in real life; indeed, life has many risks and dangers, and it is good to be warned of them. But ideologies are highly culturally and politically contextual. What one culture sees as risky, others would not. Many Indian tribes saw tobacco as a god, whereas for some Americans today it evokes only concerns about secondary smoke and death. The members of most indigenous cultures are shocked upon first observing Westerners driving around in huge steel boxes that frequently crash (and always spew off smoke). They regard cars as bizarre and quite dangerous. Even in the industrialized world, though, temperance is an especially *American* ideology.[13] For example, when I visited Hungary, I couldn't explain to my hosts why many Americans would be surprised at their high-fat diet, their heavy smoking, and the easy availability of drink and pornography at virtually each corner. I found similar opinions in Sweden, where people laughed at these American obsessions, along with our new taste for decaffeinated coffee and our dismay over teen sexuality. Nor is temperance only a matter of national or cultural boundaries. America has not *always* been consumed by temperance ideologies, as anyone who grew up in the 1950s, 1960s, or 1970s can affirm.

America has long witnessed moralistic popular movements against citizens' sins and vices (see Chapter 2). Because the most famous was the Temperance Movement, lasting from the 1820s to the passage of National Prohibition (against alcoholic beverages) in 1919, I draw upon this name. Although I mean to define *temperance* as being far more than a movement against alcohol, there are persuasive reasons to recall this earlier movement. First, as we shall see, although American temperance activists saved their sharpest denunciations for the "demon rum," temperance organizations and activists in the nineteenth and early twentieth centuries had close links with many long-forgotten movements including the Vice and Vigilance Movement and the Social Purity Movement, which campaigned against prostitution, promiscuity, pornography, and "white slavery"; the Anti-Cigarette Movement; the Social Hygiene Movement aimed at preventing venereal diseases; and a variety of popular health movements stressing proper diet, sexual rectitude, and proper exercise, such as that typified by cereal inventor Dr. Harvey Kellogg (whose popular health movement joined water cures, vegetarianism, and exercise with temperance and sexual chastity).[14]

Second, it makes sense to discuss today's behavioral control movements in terms of temperance because, like the old (anti-alcohol) Temperance Movement, they produce similar political alignments. As in the nineteenth and early twentieth centuries, rural fundamentalists and conservative traditionalists have become allied with urban middle-class "progressives," uniting some elements of the Right and Left.[15] Such movements focus not on broad economic, social structural, or cultural failings of American society but, rather, on individual behavior (though liberal temperance activists criticize a few sectors of corporate power such as the liquor and tobacco industries). And as with the Temperance Movement of old, today's universalist claims about the harms of "immoral" behavior hide major subtexts of anxieties about social class, race, and ethnicity. Temperance activists of the past saw rum as corrupting immigrants and other poor people, whereas today the ghetto "underclass" is the locus of American fears. The writers of old temperance tracts warned their middle-class readers against the evils of whisky, whereas today's middle class seems to have an almost bottomless pit of anxiety, focusing on everything from street crime to secondary smoke to teen and child sexuality. Although I would not reduce all of these anxieties solely to economic causes, Barbara Ehrenreich's imputation of a "fear of falling" in the American middle class, leading this class to constantly examine behavior as status cues, does explain some of the paradoxes of middle-class angst.[16] For example, how do we reconcile the rising middle-class fear of drugs and cigarettes with evidence of sharp declines in these behaviors over the past many years? One possible answer is that temperance ideology helps distinguish the anxious "respectable classes" from grungy "lowlifes" who may still smoke cigarettes or marijuana, much less use crack cocaine, and that such boundary markers have salience only when the middle class is able to differentiate itself from other classes based on behavioral norms.

My approach differs somewhat from other sociological treatments of these concerns (see Chapter 3). I understand temperance to be an ideology, but also an *elite strategy*, on the one hand, and a popular *social movement*, on the other. Most social science treatments stress only one part of the equation. For example, some social scientists—especially proponents of the "medicalization of social problems" thesis—tend to focus exclusively on professionals and related experts as shapers of social problem definitions. Others stress only the media's influence or the popular appeal ("moral panics") of certain problem formulations. These are certainly aspects of the New Temperance, but they don't completely explain it. Accordingly, the present book builds on social constructionist theory while also integrating this approach with other theories. The work of French philosopher and social critic Michel Foucault is particularly helpful toward this end, as his understanding of power strategies and their diffusion throughout society helps us to comprehend how elites develop strategies that are then used by a variety of other forces in society and how power mechanisms may originate at the bottom but become useful for elites.[17]

With this introduction, I can now define today's temperance ideology, movement, and strategy as reflecting a belief in the responsibility of the state and private powers (e.g., corporations) to regulate and restrain personal behavior. Although public health and public education workers hope to instill successful individual efforts at self-control, the failures of self-regulation justify society's more coercive role for the presumed "own good" of the individual. Of course, activists involved in one aspect of behavioral concern do not always support suppression of other behaviors. Nevertheless, the New Temperance can generally be seen as focusing on the following four areas:

- *Substance Abuse:* I refer here to the movements to villainize and repress or punish drug users. These movements take many forms today, from campaigns to prohibit the use of tobacco in public to those punishing and preventing drunk driving, from campaigns telling kids to "just say no" to drugs to those requiring drinking-free zones in sports arenas.
- *Sexual Behavior:* Despite the publicity about "culture wars,"[18] some broad convergences in American thinking over the last two decades have once again appeared. For example, temperance warriors now pathologize and strategize against teen sex and pregnancy, against promiscuous sex (which was deemed an evil even before the AIDS epidemic), and at times, it seems, against all nonmarital sex.
- *Food and Fitness Movements:* As noted above, not only the current American obsession with diet (particularly as it relates to the dangers of cholesterol and fat) but also current health fads from fitness to running exhibit parallels to the healthist movements that originated as far back as the 1830s.
- *Improper Speech and Other Portrayals:* Adherents of temperance ideology often see speech about or portrayals of violence, hate, or sex as being dangerous or potentially dangerous. At times, the Left and Right have joined forces to rid the nation of pornography, television violence, and lewd or violent music lyrics. To some extent, the Left's focus on speech and private behavior ("political correctness"), though somewhat exaggerated by critics, can be seen as an element of the New Temperance.

Owing to the vastness of this subject matter, I will not describe every aspect of temperance. For reasons of space and emphasis, then, I will focus on substance use and sex as examples of the "behavior wars." In particular, I hope to provide a sociological interpretation of events in the last two decades based on my reading of recent history, of cultural events and texts, and of secondary sources about various forms of "deviance" and ill health.

Questioning the Behavior Wars

A reader might ask, "Even though there are excesses, aren't the wars against bad behavior worth fighting?" Or, "Isn't it obvious that America has a drinking/drug/smoking/sexual behavior/eating/aggression problem?"

Yet these questions raise some interesting issues. First, it is not at all clear that temperance movements *follow* an increase in the behavior being criticized. Often quite the opposite is true. We know, for example, that cigarette smoking was far more widespread two decades ago than it is now, yet smoking did not arouse public anger in the 1960s or early 1970s. Further, Stanton Peele argues that Americans drank far more alcohol in the eighteenth century than at any time in the twentieth, and Troy Duster notes that more Americans took illicit drugs (primarily morphine) in the late nineteenth century than during the 1960s.[19] These examples raise sociological questions as to when and why issues of behavior have come to be of such great concern to people; and, indeed, this is a subject on which the book focuses.

Second, to view health and moral admonitions as simply benevolent would be to ignore considerable latent functions in both the older and contemporary versions of temperance. One such function, as previously noted, is the development of a social control machinery that, along with detecting personal problems, systematically buttresses the power of corporations and government over Americans' daily life. Mandatory drug testing in the workplace confirms the ability of employers to control the most basic personal habits of the employee. And government efforts to control smoking, monitor computer communication, register sex offenders, and mandate psychological treatment for a variety of offenses strengthens the state's control over everyday life. Another major problem with all such measures is that, despite their proclaimed goal of fairness, social control—from criminal sanctions to the educational and social service systems' identification of "high-risk" youngsters—seems always to target the behavior of some people and not others. The wars we conduct—whether against drug users, teen parents, or "at risk" students—are wars against primarily the working class, ethnic and racial minorities, and poor people, usually young.

Finally, I argue that temperance is a diversion from the critical issues facing America, that it is doomed to failure even on its own terms.

Rather than insisting that the personal behavior of Americans is "out of control," we could understand the fundamental reasons why many people feel alienated and, in turn, why many Americans are anxious about the personal behavior of their young. First, vast economic changes have sharply reduced the standard of living for many Americans. This historic downturn since 1973 has led not only to increased poverty and misery in the lower classes but also to increased anxiety and fear in the middle and working classes. Remedying the economic situation—particularly the endemic poverty for millions—would likely achieve more of a reduction in child abuse or alcoholism than a thousand educational campaigns. Second, many of the presumed solutions to our "misbehavior" only aggravate the fundamental cultural problem facing our country—namely, the lack of community that has accompanied modernization, technologization, deindustrialization, and geographic mobility. In commenting on Americans' fears about missing children, Halloween food poisoning, child sexual abuse, and so forth, Peele notes that efforts at social control (increased fingerprinting of children, computerized information networks on suspects, stronger efforts by parents to restrict their children) are misguided because "the campaigns and the spirit underlying them directly attack community life."[20] In other words, the very forces that helped protect children in bygone days—such as the involvement of neighbors in one another's lives—have been eroded by rising levels of suspicion and punishment, and by the pressure on parents to become further isolated from other adults and their children. Most of the social problems so emphasized by temperance movements can be linked to cultural alienation; yet, as Peele suggests, the solutions usually proposed by the various "helping" systems are often just the opposite to improving community.[21] By calling for isolation and increased surveillance of "deviants" in the community, we may (to paraphrase General Westmoreland) be destroying our communities to save them.

Organization of the Book

Chapter 2 begins with a discussion of the paradox common to those of us who are "baby boomers": namely, that in the 1960s a vast array of previously "deviant" behaviors were seemingly becoming acceptable. What happened to confound not only our expectations but many social theorists' expectations that American society was becoming freer and more tolerant of such behaviors? I will then go back to the past to review some social movements from the Victorian era and the Progressive period in America (from roughly 1870 to 1917) in order to discuss certain similarities between these times and the period from the mid-1970s on. For a variety of reasons, these older movements against alcohol, cigarettes, and sexual impropriety (involving even the covering up of nude statutes) are rarely discussed today even by social scientists.

From this historical perspective on the New Temperance I shift to a review of theoretical perspectives in Chapter 3. As examples, I begin with questions such as, Who tends to support temperance movements, and why? Why is drunk driving considered a social problem, but not the auto itself, despite the thousands of deaths it causes? Why was masturbation regarded as a severe social evil until about seventy-five years ago? For answers, I draw upon current work in social constructionist theory, coupled with the analysis of power best provided by some Marxist and conflict traditions. In Chapter 4, I examine in greater detail several behaviors pathologized by the dominant American media and political elites: the feared illicit drug, the maligned cigarette, the stigmatized teen mother, and the specter of multiple-partner sex. Although I acknowledge the risks associated with these behaviors, I argue that temperance ideology de-contextualizes behaviors from their actual social environment. I question whether temperate behavior is always logical and desirable. For example, I consider such paradoxes as the finding that drugs help some people work harder, that cigarettes help some depressed people feel better, and that bearing a child while young may be functional for low-income women. Yet these paradoxes are rarely discussed; evidently it is easier to assume that the eradication of such "immoral" or unhealthy behaviors will somehow bring a utopian happiness to the public. The very language of temperance misrepresents the concreteness of our knowledge: "Smoking-related deaths" are about as meaningful as saying a death is "eating related," despite the scientific sound; warnings about "promiscuous sex" intentionally confuse morality with the dangers of sexual transmission of disease under certain circumstances; and references to "drug dependence" or to "drug-crazed" people are moral judgments, not scientific ones. (Why, for example, do we not describe businesspeople as "profit-dependent" or "money-addicted"?)

The remaining chapters of the book develop a historical argument for the great changes in America's view of behavior since approximately the mid-1970s. In particular, I stress the social class and political dimensions of the New Temperance. In Chapter 5, I develop the argument that a combination of factors led to the popularity of social conservatism by the late 1970s. The radical democratization affecting clothes, hairstyle, language, drug use, and sexual norms that occurred in the 1960s and early 1970s came close to reversing the status markers that earlier American society struggled to construct. The result was a severe crisis in social class reproduction, accentuated by the dramatic economic downturn that began with the recession of 1973–1974. In the context of these new "lean and mean" times, during which uncompetitive workers were discarded and a new "underclass" developed, status markers have returned with a vengeance to divide the middle class and other classes seeking respectability from the poor and the downwardly mobile.

In Chapter 6, I argue that the New Temperance is also a political strategy. As such, it has primarily aided the Right, but also, to some degree, the moderate and liberal residue of the 1960s movements. As was true of the older temperance movements, the political "consensus"—for "family values," monogamy, home protection, and the work ethic—most favors conservatives. Indeed, the Right is far more skillful in using temperance symbols, and has a more consistent record of social conservatism and Puritan morality, than the Left. But neither the older turn-of-the-century Temperance Movement nor the movements of today would have gained popularity without support among urban middle-class liberals. Accordingly, I briefly review the Republican strategy on sin developed in the 1960s and 1970s while also noting the support given to healthism by some leftists, the call for stricter social control measures over personal behavior by some activists in the women's movement, and the embrace of the end of the sexual revolution even by some leaders of the gay movement. Although there are many specific reasons for these developments, I note that temperance ideologies retain their great usefulness in American culture *precisely because* they produce convergent or consensual political results.

In the final chapter, I suggest that, symbolically, the New Temperance has served as a vehicle through which the remnants of the "60s" have been conquered and expunged. As with the McCarthyism of the 1950s, one purpose of the new social conservatism is to repress all positive memories of dissent and social unrest. Whereas McCarthyism aimed to dismantle all opposition emanating from the social movements of the 1930s, the New Temperance villainizes the 1960s. It demands an active renunciation, particularly on the part of baby boomers and former activists—just as the suppression of social unrest in the late 1940s to 1950s required people to purge themselves by "naming names." Finally, on a more optimistic note, I raise questions about the idea of totally administering the behavior of citizens and argue that behavioral controls and repression are rarely "successful" even on their own terms. In fact, power has limits and resistance, and the New Temperance will most likely be defeated in the future, just as the movement to prohibit alcohol eventually went down to defeat in the past.

two

Déjà Vu All Over Again

At the risk of some simplification, I suggest that the resurgence of moralism in the late twentieth century aimed at substances, sex, food consumption, and other behavior was a stunning reversal of mid-century trends, harkening back to Victorian America.[1] This chapter places the New Temperance in context by situating it in the American historical tradition that, during the nineteenth and early twentieth centuries, marked off the "respectable classes" from the poor, the lowlife, and the disreputable. In particular, the "behavior wars" of the last two decades most resemble the period from about 1870 through World War I in American history.

Remembering When

For those readers between thirty and sixty years of age, the New Temperance stands in remarkable contrast to the social norms of our youth. The "baby boom" generation grew up with TV ads beckoning them to "walk a mile" for a Camel cigarette and to use Brylcreem for sexy hair that "she would love to rub her fingers through". Boys grew up reading *Playboy,* with its consumerist view of sex, and both boys and girls read *Mad* magazine, with its irreverent attacks on conformity and the dull white-collar world. We took seriously film heroes such as "Murray," who, in *A Thousand Clowns,* quit working on Madison Avenue to "hang out" and "Captain America" and "Billy," who, in *Easy Rider,* traveled across America getting stoned and engaging in orgies. As Barbara Ehrenreich has pointed out, the cultural rebellion against the traditional work ethic and prudery of Puritanism preceded the cultural and political rebellions of the 1960s, starting with critiques of conformity in books of the 1950s such as *The Organization Man* and *The Man in the Grey Flannel Suit.*[2] A combination of postwar prosperity in America and the growth of a consumer-oriented culture that associated products with pleasure helped start a cultural rebellion long before the hippies, the counterculture, the New Left, women's liberation, and the gay and lesbian movement.

To put it mildly, the 1960s movements further challenged the cultural norms of the day. Retrospectives of the 1960s that focus only on the civil rights movement and the anti-war protests minimize that decade's rebellion against the central tenets of the culture—the work ethic, the family ethic, monogamy, prudery, even rational consciousness. The counterculture challenged the point of working at dull routine jobs; of maintaining rational, linear thinking rather than the "drop in, drop out, tune out" drug mantra proposed by Timothy Leary and others; and of upholding individual property rights (rather than "liberating" goods, as Abby Hoffman, for example, proposed in his books). In addition, radicals of the New Left and early feminists saw "smashing monogamy" as representing a rebellion against the "bourgeois values" of the repressive family.

Although care must be taken not to exaggerate the impact of the 1960s, there is empirical evidence not only of a dramatic rise in the middle class's use of drugs during the 1960s and 1970s but also of the reality of the sexual revolution of the 1960s and 1970s.[3] It is doubtful that a movie like Paul Mazursky's *Bob, Carol, Ted, and Alice* (1969), in which middle-class suburban couples engaged in partner swapping, could be made today, at least not without the imposition of severe penalties on the characters such as a violent death or a deadly disease.[4] Moreover, during the early 1970s soft-pornography classics such as *Deep Throat* and *The Devil in Miss Jones* became box-office smashes for the first time in American history. Nor is it likely that popular heroes of the period would be perceived the same way today. Consider, for example, Ken Kesey's popular play and, later, Milos Foreman's Academy Award–winning movie of the same name, *One Flew over the Cuckoo's Nest*, about the horrors of life in a mental hospital. The lead character, P. J. McMurphy, has been sent from a work farm to a mental hospital because he is a sex offender. Not only has McMurphy committed statutory rape, but he is a proud malingerer (recall that he feigns mental illness to escape the work detail), a boozer, a gambler (he promptly arranges an assortment of high-stakes card games at the institution), a smoker, and a procurer of prostitutes (whose entry to the hospital leads to the tragic death of fellow-patient Billy Babbitt). Millions of people saw the play and movie, and cheered for McMurphy in his struggle with the villainous Nurse Ratched. Today, however, it is hard to imagine a play or film portraying a similarly unsavory male and strong female nurse enjoying our sympathy in the same way: Would anyone cheer a 1990s McMurphy? More likely a modern-day Ratched would be the hero instead of the McMurphy character.

Of course, many Americans rejected the counterculture and other radical changes of the 1960s and 1970s. In fact, as we shall later see, the cultural rebellion of that period can be argued to have led, paradoxically, to the success of the New Right and other anti-sin politics.

Declaring Temperance Dead

It is interesting to note that social theorists at the time generally also believed that the moralistic politics of the past—the kind that provided status to the "drys" who campaigned against alcohol for a century—was on its way out. Joseph Gusfield, one of America's most renowned sociologists and an important historian of the older Temperance Movement, began his 1963 book by noting that the "time of temperance is long past" and associating it exclusively with lower-middle-class Protestant evangelicals: "Sobriety was virtuous and, in a community dominated by middle-class Protestants, necessary to social acceptance and self-esteem. . . . As Americans are less work-minded, more urban, and less theological, the same behavior which once brought rewards and self-assurance to the abstainer today more often brings contempt and rejection."[5] Sociologists of deviancy concurred that the days of moralism were over:

> Western man [*sic*] has, on the whole, developed increased tolerance and compassion for problems that were previously dogmatically treated as moral issues.[6]

> [T]he general pattern in American society seems to be one of decreasing stigmatization of behaviors once considered reprehensible.[7]

> A slow but steady transformation of deviance has taken place in American society. . . . Deviant behaviors that were once defined as immoral, sinful, or criminal have been given medical meanings.[8]

In fact, this view was not limited to American theorists. Radical philosopher Michel Foucault made a similar point in a 1975 interview: "I believe that the great intolerance of the population for the delinquent, which the morality and politics of the nineteenth century set out to establish, is in fact now being eroded. Certain forms of illegality or irregularity are becoming more and more accepted . . . for example, . . . stealing something from a shop."[9]

It now seems clear that contrary to Foucault, stealing from shops is regarded as pathological and criminal, and that contrary to Gusfield, temperance both as personal behavior (i.e., abstinence) and as a political slogan is a status enhancer, not a stigma. Nor does the increased tolerance and compassion discussed by these social theorists reflect attitudes today toward the unwed mother, the pregnant teen, the cigarette smoker, the street person, the drug user, the welfare recipient, or the alcoholic.

This is not to suggest a complete lack of important social progress for some groups coming out of the 1960s social movements. The civil rights movement not only radically altered conditions for people of color in the United States but also stimulated the growth of numerous other movements from women's liberation to the gay and lesbian movement to the disability rights movement. Despite deep pockets of resistance among large parts of the population, gay and lesbian people are no longer viewed as sinners or diseased people but, rather, have become accepted and, in some places, legally protected groups in society. Physically and mentally disabled people have also gained powerful legal rights in recent years. Even homeless people have been granted statutory rights to vote, to receive benefits, and, in some areas, to panhandle. Only two decades ago, societies around the Western world were opening up and dumping long-held laws regarding vagrancy, commitment for insanity, sodomy, prostitution, drug use, even the age of sexual consent. At the time, it seemed logical to predict a continuation of such a trend.

Yet in the historical short term, this was not to be. Many Americans, and even the social movements fighting for rights, seem to have adopted the classic sociological distinction between "ascribed" and "achieved" statuses. The statuses socially constructed as "ascribed" are those a person is said to be "born with" (such as race, sex, age, and some developmental and physical disabilities) or to have involuntarily acquired (such as disabilities resulting from accidents). "Ascribed" statuses are statuses that have increasingly become legally protected and socially accepted. Conversely, those statuses associated with groups seen as voluntarily deviating (such as drug users, child molesters, teen parents, and cigarette smokers) are considered either "immoral" or "pathological" and are based on behaviors. These behaviors, in turn, are seen as "achieved" because the dominant Western cultural view of them is that they are freely chosen acts of "deviance." To a great degree, the battle over gay rights concerns the question of whether sexual orientation is an "achieved" (freely chosen) or "ascribed" status.

The presentation of gay sexuality provides an example of the historic change we are examining. The Gay Liberation Movement of the late 1960s and early 1970s strongly affirmed the right of all people to "make love with anyone, anyway, anytime" (in the words of the Gay Activists Alliance).[10] The idea that one was born with a fixed "sexual orientation" ("gay" or "straight") that one "had no choice about" was strongly opposed at that time by the theory of polymorphous sexuality. Since the late 1970s, however, the struggle for gay and lesbian rights has usually posited an "ascribed" status. That is, gays are argued to be either a biological category ("born that way") or members of a finite social minority who have little or no choice about their sexual orientation. Although there is internal controversy over the genetic-difference argument within the gay community, most pro–gay rights political campaigns do support a notion of a fixed sexual orientation, a strategy developed in light of the success of ethnic minority organizing in America.[11]

In this light, the new "don't ask, don't tell" policy of the military toward gays can be taken as paradigmatic of the contradiction between the limited success of the civil rights movements and that of the New Temperance. American society appears to be grudgingly accepting of some rights for those who are deemed "ascribed" to a category, yet it has simultaneously moved to enforce controls over *behavior* that is seen to be up to the individual. In theory, then, it is all right to be "gay," but the practice of gay sex or the public discussion of it is still stigmatized. The medicalization of problems such as mental illness is arguably seen in the same light. The ascription of mental illness provides legal protection for some disabled people at the workplace and elsewhere; but at the point where a person *acts* "mentally ill" (e.g., hears voices or perhaps laughs inappropriately), he or she may then be stigmatized or discriminated against.

The New Temperance's scrutiny and control over behavior may actually make perfect sense in light of the increased legal protection of previously excluded groups (racial minorities, women, etc.) in the workplace and elsewhere. For example, now that employers are unable to sort their workers by ascribed characteristics (such as race and gender), they are increasingly turning to accountings of achieved behavioral statuses: The employee was fired *not* because he is African-American but because he has a drug problem; the company decided against hiring the woman *not* because of her gender but because she acted inappropriately at the job interview. These accountings are not primarily about covering up racial, gender, and age discrimination (though, of course, such discrimination does occur); rather, they reflect the needs of businesses and others to judge human capital in a period of economic competition and downsizing without appearing to violate the law.

Back to the Past: The Old Temperance Movements

Historically, a case can be made not that the "1960s" revolutionized social norms but that dominant American norms at century's end have simply returned to older conservative patterns. In other words, the period from the late 1950s to the early 1970s was an exception rather than a rule. I will develop this argument in more detail later on. For now, however, it is interesting to consider that throughout much of the nineteenth and early twentieth centuries, campaigns led by middle-class Protestants demanded behaviors similar to those I have defined as the New Temperance. The Temperance Movement and the Anti-Cigarette Movement dramatically parallel today's battles over drugs, cigarettes, and alcohol. And three other historical movements—the Social Purity Movement, the Vice and Vigilance Movement, and the Social Hygiene Movement—roughly parallel today's movements focused on chastity and teen sex, promiscuity, child sexual abuse, sexually transmitted diseases, and censorship in art, media, and popular culture.

A discussion of these historical movements requires some caveats. First, popular movements undergo many stages and have many wings; some activists avow extreme ideas, whereas others are more moderate. Some of these movements had a "Left" and a "Right," and, as we will see, temperance ideologies are particularly subject to the combining of repressive and more liberal ideologies. The (anti-alcohol) Temperance Movement, for example, encompassed conservative churchmen and businessmen, but also leading feminists of the time and some Christian and Fabian Socialists.[12]

Second, the language of the nineteenth and early twentieth centuries was not "politically correct" but, rather, relied on religious and moral metaphors. It was also usually intended for "respectable" audiences, not for the "dangerous classes." And although these older movements had overlapping memberships and similar constituencies, and seemed to peak at similar times (between the 1890s and World War I), they were not necessarily coordinated with one another nor did all supporters of one form of behavior control support the others.

These caveats aside, the Victorian and Progressive Period movements were characterized by what scholarly observers consider an exaggerated (described by Gusfield as "utopian") notion of their ability to change behavior, by a huge faith in government's ability to regulate every aspect of private life, and by a strong ethnocentric belief in the correctness of white, Protestant, middle-class social norms (called the "white life" in some Women's Christian Temperance Union and Social Purity propaganda, with an intentional pun on race and purity).[13] In simplified terms, the conservative supporters of temperance feared the "dangerous classes'" political and industrial unrest, seeing lower-class behavior as emblematic of social danger to their way of life. In addition, Progressives and early feminists hoped to socialize immigrants and the lower class to middle-class norms in order to tame this social unrest, while also reducing the personal and social strife that the habits of the "dangerous classes" were presumably wreaking on innocent women and children.

The Old Substance Wars

Followers of both the Temperance Movement and the Anti-Cigarette Movement were fully aware of the harms of the bottle and weed long before any Surgeon General's reports. Like today's anti-drug, anti-smoking, and anti–drunk driving movements, these earlier causes appealed to the nation's health, to its concern for safety, profitable industry, and the future of its children, and to its desire for successful social mobility and status. However, one difference between the earlier movements and today's anti-smoking and anti-alcohol movements was the former's confidence about banning the use of the substances themselves. The common English usage of the word *temperant* is misleading, of course, inasmuch as these reformers eventually became abolitionists, not supporters of limited or moderate usage. Whereas early temperance proponents aimed at limiting alcohol (by defining age restrictions, limiting where it could be sold, licensing bars, etc.), by the 1890s the militant Anti-Saloon League and Prohibition Party had developed a fully prohibitionist program. In 1919, activists succeeded in gaining the passage of the Eighteenth Amendment prohibiting the consumption of alcohol.[14] The Anti-Cigarette Movement, although it accepted limitations on sales and production in some states, was also prohibitionary. By the first decade of the twentieth century, it had succeeded in banning cigarettes from fourteen states (as well as many municipalities and county jurisdictions).[15]

Like the anti-drug movement of today, whose stern "just say no" message is meant to conjure up visions of immediate physical harm from the use of marijuana, heroin, cocaine, LSD, and so on, temperance supporters vilified "demon rum" and the "soot weed" in the harshest terms:

Alcohol ... [is] the most subtle, the most far-reaching, and, judged by its ultimate effects, incomparably the most virulent of poisons. Regular moderate drinking ... lowers the grade of your mind, dulls your higher esthetic sense, and takes the finer edge off your morals (from *McClure's* magazine, 1908).[16]

It is the devil in solution, distilled damnation, more destructive than war, pestilence, and famine; a cancer in human society; and the saloon a rathole for men's wages, a prolific hotbed of anarchy, vile politics, and profane ribaldry (from *Railway Conductor*, 1919).[17]

Many and many a bright lad has had his will power weakened, his moral principle sapped, his nervous system wrecked, his whole life spoiled before he is 17 by the detestable cigarette. The cigarette fiend in time becomes a liar and a thief. He will commit petty thefts to get money to feed his insatiable appetite for nicotine. He lies to his parents, his teachers, and his best friends. He neglects his studies and, narcotized by nicotine, sits at his desk half stupefied, his desire for work, his ambition, dulled if not dead (comment by New York School Commissioner Charles Hubbell, 1893).[18]

Temperance became a popular movement by the latter part of the century, not only a powerful political movement with hundreds of active chapters but also a major cultural presence involving the production of popular plays, songs, and novels. The nation split regionally, racially, ethnically, and socioeconomically between "wets" and "drys"; indeed, it was not until after the repeal of Prohibition in the 1930s that the "wet/dry" issue ceased to be a factor in national, state, and local elections.

Generally, upper- and middle-class Protestants were "dry," as were most rural dwellers. Temperance held a strong base in the Midwest, in New England, and, more gradually, in the West and parts of the South. The "wets" were mostly Irish, Italian, Eastern European, and German immigrants as well as African-Americans and other people of color. Class was a critical factor as well, inasmuch as poor and working-class people opposed temperance, as did most voters in the major urban areas. Religious groups split, with Roman Catholics and Jews more likely to be "wet" and Protestants "dry." Business became strongly supportive of temperance. Some employers fired or refused to hire workers who drank; others discharged workers who smoked; and still others demanded pledges of abstinence from both substances. In contrast, labor unions (except for a few locals composed of highly skilled native-born workers) opposed temperance, as did the Socialist party of Eugene Debs and the Wobblies (the International Workers of the World).[19] And Emma Goldman, an early-twentieth-century radical, had nothing but contempt for the "drys":

> As to Prohibition, everyone knows what a farce it really is. Like all other achievements of Puritanism, it, too, has but driven the "devil" deeper into the human system. Nowhere else does one meet so many drunkards as in our Prohibition towns. . . . The fact that some great geniuses have seen their reflection in the goblet too frequently, does not justify Puritanism in attempting to fetter the whole gamut of human emotions. . . . Puritanism, in whatever expression, is a poisonous germ.[20]

The leaders of the Anti-Cigarette Movement frequently overlapped with those of the Temperance Movement, though on a national level the pragmatic leaders of Women's Christian Temperance Union (WCTU) and the Anti-Saloon League wisely concluded that an official endorsement of too many issues might cause political losses. Nevertheless, on a municipal and state level, Protestant churches, businessmen, ministers, professionals, and reformers led the Anti-Cigarette Movement. They in turn were generally opposed by workers, the poor, and immigrants. Despite the fact that smoking had originally arisen as an upper-class habit,[21] anti-cigarette propaganda targeted the "cigarette fiend" as young, male, and lower class (in fact, the movement never opposed cigar smoking, which was associated with respectable men). Even more outrageous to social reformers, however, was the specter of women smoking. As women took up "the habit," more and more governments rushed to prohibit women from smoking. In New York City in 1908, twenty-nine-year-old Katie Mulcahey "was arrested and jailed for lighting a cigarette in front of a policeman and then compounding the crime by asserting 'No man shall dictate to me.'"[22]

The passage of laws against alcohol and cigarettes was met by exaggerated claims of "heaven on earth" by supporters, who believed that these laws heralded a new day in America. When national Prohibition passed, the famous minister Billy Sunday told a live audience of 10,000 along with a huge radio audience: "The reign of terror is over. The slums will soon be a memory. We will turn our prisons into factories and our jails into storehouses and corncribs. Men will walk upright now, women will smile and the children will laugh. Hell will forever be rent."[23]

It soon became clear, however, that poverty and slums would not disappear (in fact, after World War I conditions worsened for the poor) and that jails would get even more crowded with bootleggers and other violators of Prohibition. The passage of Prohibition coincided historically with a strong rightward political shift that included the famous "Palmer Raids" against immigrants and suspected leftists; the passage of anti-immigrant legislation; and the Harding, Coolidge, and Hoover presidencies.

Efforts to restrict the use of alcohol and cigarettes failed, collapsing from the onus of enforcing public morality on millions of people. Prohibition began losing favor only a few years after its passage, and many repeal activists were former supporters. Many businessmen and legislators feared that disrespect for law was becoming so widespread and acceptable that the example would spread to other issues and cause general lawlessness.[24] And so after the rise of organized crime and the pain and suffering of the Great Depression, repeal finally came to America in 1933.

Anti-smoking legislation was even harder to enforce. Laws usually prohibited production or sales of cigarettes within a state, but interstate commerce could not be prevented without national legislation. By World War I soldiers were demanding tobacco, and opposition to cigarettes became equated with opposition to the "fighting men."[25] Further, when states did try to enforce cigarette bans, officials were often met with hostility. Utah, with its strong Mormon strictures against smoking, was one of the last states to prohibit smoking. In 1923, when police tried to enforce the ban by arresting people, mass rallies were held, steam whistles were sounded in protest, and national press coverage heaped ridicule on state leaders.[26]

Until the recent wars on drugs, cigarette smoking, and alcohol, temperance agitation seemed relegated to an association with "dour, cadaverous, puritanical fellows who were obviously not enjoying life very much."[27]

The Old Sex, Censorship, and Health Wars

The older movements to control sexuality that dominated white Protestant culture in America and England between 1870 and World War I were in many ways as prudish and conservative as the word *Victorian* implies. Some activities, especially those practiced by the vice societies and the WCTU—such as the covering up of nude statues and the banning of ballet because of the pink tights worn by ballerinas—would strike many as absurd today. Other activities—such as the "chastity pledges" taken by millions of American and English men—are quite similar to those practiced by today's Christian fundamentalist organization, the "Promise Keepers."[28] Yet, as with the substance wars, it would be a mistake to believe that the sex wars were only conservative campaigns. The leaders of the vice societies, the Social Purity Movement, and the Social Hygiene Movement were linked, in America, with Frances Willard's Christian Socialism, the women's suffrage movement, the social settlement house movement, and other early forms of social work, and, in England, with Fabian Socialists such as Sydney and Beatrice Webb.[29] Further, although some actions taken by these activists parallel modern conservatism, as D'Emilio and Freedman point out,[30] others parallel twentieth-century liberalism. For example, the frankness with which the Social Purity leaders (and later the Social Hygiene leaders) discussed sex shocked many Victorians. This fact, combined with the firm belief of many of these leaders in sex education, more closely links them with modern liberals in the field of sex education, the health professions, and the AIDS education movement than with contemporary conservatives.

Censorship Wars: The Vice Societies

Although movements against graphic portrayals of sex and lewdness had arisen before, the American history of censorship,[31] vice squads, and repression of overt sexual displays into segregated "red light districts" was a product of the vice movement that began in the 1870s and lasted, to some extent, well into the 1940s. Associated with the bombastic Victorian Anthony Comstock, who founded the New York Society for Suppression of Vice, vice activists went to such extremes that George Bernard Shaw coined the term *comstockery* as a commentary on American censorship and prudery.[32]

The vice societies were dominated organizationally by affluent Protestant men. According to historian Paul Boyer, New York's Vigilance Society and Boston's Watch and Ward Society "read like a Who's Who of the day"[33] and included J. P. Morgan, copper magnate William Dodge, and the Abbott, Cabot, Endicott, Leverett, Lodge, Lowell, Saltonstall, Weld, and other Boston Brahman families. The vice societies were also linked to the WCTU, the Young Men's Christian Association (YMCA), the Salvation Army, the Boy Scouts, the Episcopal Church, Friends societies, state charity society groups, and others. In addition, the vice societies gained the support of Dr. Elizabeth Blackwell, the first female physician and an early feminist, Susan B. Anthony and other suffrage leaders, Jane Addams, Josephine Shaw Lowell and other social service leaders, and former abolitionists such as Wendell Phillips.[34] As Boyer reminds us, purity in speech and representation, protection of the young from sin, and conversion of poor people, immigrants, and nonwhites to civilization through purity were very much a liberal, Progressive mission: "Surprising as it may seem to a later generation, the vice society movement was initially welcomed as a natural and valued expression of late 19th Century philanthropy. . . . [I]t aroused . . . broad and enthusiastic support."[35]

According to the philanthropic and Progressive reformers of this period, the postcards and playing cards picturing naked ladies, or the graphic paintings hanging in many bars, reflected the symbiosis of sin between saloon and brothel (which, in turn, were jointly opposed by the Temperance and Social Purity forces). The reformers also believed that such material produced in the unknowing and undiscerning poor, "feeble-minded," or uneducated a compelling desire to sin. The connection between the representation (through art, literature, and books) of sex or violence and the commission of crime and sin, which today still rings true for both conservatives and anti-pornography activists in the feminist movement,[36] was axiomatic at this earlier time:

> While others endeavor to remedy the effects of crime, we strive to remove the causes. . . . [E]very successful blow at immoral literature, the brothel or gambling-hell goes far to remove the necessity for the hospital, the asylum, and the charity home (Boston's Watch and Ward Society, 1888).[37]

> Literature must bring pure and beautiful ideas to the human mind. The brutal, the violent, the excessive, do not need to be increased and multiplied in the pages of a book. . . . It becomes the guardians of society to keep a watchful eye on the press (reformer Julia Ward Howe, 1870s).[38]

The vice movement had profound effects over a lengthy period of American history. Beginning with the passage of the Comstock Act of 1873, which banned the use of the U.S. mail for all sexual information (including contraceptives and information about contraception), and continuing through the censorship of movies by the vice squads and Legions of Decency of the 1930s, censorship of prurient, lewd, and violent representations held its grip as late as World War II.[39] The following is only a partial list of the forms of art and recreation that were censored: major books, major plays, films (known early on as "living pictures"), music hall entertainment, nude modeling for artists, advertisements, public statues of nudes, waxworks that included nudity, dance halls, illustrated newspapers, seaside photographs, the ballet, and, owing to their violence, football and boxing.[40] The most dramatic example came when members of the WCTU campaigned to cover up naked piano legs!

Sex Wars: The Social Purity Movement

The Social Purity Movement against prostitution, against sexual exploitation of young women, and for a single rather than double standard of morality united the late-nineteenth-century feminists and early Progressive leaders with conservative businessmen and political leaders. Whereas some aspects of this movement—its support of the vice societies, its chastity pledges, and its opposition to masturbation—seem quite conservative, its crusade against the double standard, sexual abuse of children, and domestic violence are comparable to many contemporary liberal feminist concerns.

The American Social Purity Movement had its roots in the early 1870s battle against the "reglementation" system of prostitution. European doctors in the mid-nineteenth century had lent their support to a legalized system of prostitution because of the spreading danger of venereal disease. Paralleling the current controversy over the dissemination of clean needles to addicts to prevent the spread of HIV/AIDS, doctors and political leaders in Europe felt the moral wrongs of prostitution were less important than the gains to the populace generated by legalized regulation of prostitution. The "reglementation" system aroused broad opposition in Europe and America, from both conservatives and from feminists and progressives. Susan B. Anthony, Elizabeth Cady Stanton, and other feminists in the 1870s began lecturing against this system, collecting petitions and organizing public protests. For them, "reglementation" was the institutionalization of the double standard; it was a license to exploit women, particularly young women. Further, they felt that it provided police with a legal excuse, under the guise of regulation, to stop and halt any woman walking alone.[41]

The issue of prostitution, like that of alcohol a century ago, was complex and symbolic. Prostitution was far more prevalent in the nineteenth century than it is today, and certainly there were cases of involuntary servitude ("white slavery"), as discussed later. Because laws governing "age of consent" (for sexual activity) either did not exist or, in some states, gave ten-year-olds the right to legally have sex or marry,[42] the luring of young girls (and sometimes boys) into prostitution or forced sex was rarely prosecuted. Prostitution along with sexual abuse and harassment (though such terms were not used in those days) were clearly problems that contributed to women's oppression. The attitude toward prostitutes maintained by at least the feminist/Progressive wing of the Social Purity Movement was in theory not a punitive one. These "fallen women" needed rescuing, after all. Reformers favored opening up institutions to house and rehabilitate such women. They placed the major blame for prostitution on men.

Nevertheless, the Victorians' obsession with "fallen women" and sex had many repressive aspects. The Social Purity Movement ultimately had little concern for the economic survival of prostitutes, who, in a labor market far more restrictive against poor and working-class women than it is today, often had little choice but to be sex workers. Many prostitutes did not wish to be "saved" and resisted the constant efforts of upper-class do-gooders to "rescue" and institutionalize them. Paradoxically, the repression of prostitution in this period (1870–1920) weakened women's control over the sex industry and forced them into the modern model of control by a male pimp, since strong protection against vice squads and other forms of repression became necessary.[43] Moreover, because the reformers refused to believe that *any* woman would consent to prostitution, they constructed a sexuality that placed all responsibility for sex on the insatiable appetites of men, while insisting that females were asexual. This construction was symbolically held in place by constant "white slavery" scares, during which men (almost always foreign) were said to have forced women into wicked dens of iniquity. These scares led to the passage of new age-of-consent laws and, in 1910, to the passage of the Mann Act prohibiting the crossing of state lines with women for immoral purposes. The scares also coincided with the lynchings of thousands of Southern black men on charges of rape.[44] In addition to maintaining the rigid sex norms of Victoriana, the focus on foreigners and "out" racial groups suggests that, like the Temperance Movement, anxieties about issues other than sexuality were at work.

Led by the same mix of conservative and Progressive churchmen, feminists, temperance leaders, popular health leaders, and social service leaders as those in the vice societies,[45] the Social Purity Movement formed a White Cross Movement modeled after the English counterpart begun by the Episcopal Church. In the 1880s and 1890s, crowds of young men, numbering perhaps in the millions, took the White Cross pledge illustrated in Figure 2.1.

A key aspect of the pledge involved listening to purity lectures and speeches, which were often laced with images of graphic sexuality. Speeches by ministers, in particular, stressed the dangers of masturbation. One minister, for example, "always [told] a harrowing story of an

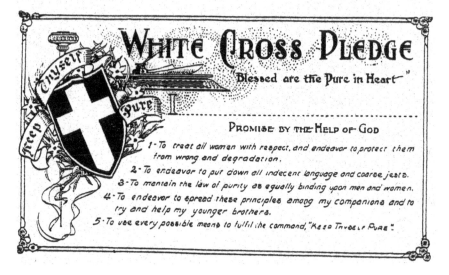

FIGURE 2.1   The White Cross Pledge
Source: D'Emilio and Freedman, *Intimate Matters*, after p. 274.

Elton boy, son of a colonel in the army, a brilliant lad, always head of his class . . . who had been reduced to drivelling imbecility as the result of secret sin, the sight of an obscene photograph exhibited by a scoundrel whom he met in a railway train."[46]

The Social Purity Movement successfully worked to promote the raising of age-of-consent laws and the discovery of "white slavery." Between 1886 and 1895, most states raised their age-of-consent laws dramatically. Purity reformers were disappointed, however, because they had hoped the states would raise the age to twenty-one when in fact most went no higher than sixteen or eighteen.[47] It is important to note that whatever the social gains from raising the age of consent, it was Victorianism (not abstract human nature) that constructed a "childhood" defined as nonsexual. The continuing effort to exclude adolescents from sexuality continues to this day, as I will discuss in later chapters.

Some historians regard the constant "white slavery" scares as "moral panics," describing them as racist and xenophobic. These scares not only dominated the U.S. and English press but were the subject of repeated international conferences and incidents between 1890 and 1920. In this connection, Bristow writes:

> The constant use of the term "white slavery" and the permanent search for victims had predictable consequences. Through Britain and North America it finally generated a series of hysterical panics. . . . [B]y 1914 it was claimed

that over one billion pages were written on white slavery in North America. By then absurd drugging and abduction reports had become endemic. In this climate of opinion . . . 42 states passed their own so-called white slave measures.[48]

Claims that millions of women, particularly young girls, were being held against their will began to proliferate. Often the public was warned by prurient and sensationalistic tracts displaying pictures of naked or partially naked women being held by Asiatic despots or Eastern European monsters. One wonders whether these tracts were designed to eliminate sexual fantasy or to stimulate it. Further, "white slavery" never seemed to originate with native-born Americans but, rather, was always brought in by immigrants disrupting American culture:

> "The vilest practices are brought here from continental Europe," a report to the Senate in 1909 warned, including "the most bestial refinements of depravity." Federal investigators claimed that "large numbers of Jews scattered throughout the U.S. . . . seduce and keep girls. Some of them are engaged in importation . . . [and] they prey upon young girls whom they find on the streets in dance halls, and similar places." . . . Diseased alien women, through their male clients, had infected "innocent wives and children" and "done more to ruin homes than any other single cause."[49]

Racial conflicts were exacerbated by the sex wars of the time. In a famous 1912 incident, the first African-American boxing champion, Jack Johnson, was charged under the new laws for abduction, but the "abductee" turned out to be his willing white wife. After this charge was dropped, Johnson's enemies managed to get him prosecuted and sentenced to a one-year prison term for an old dalliance with a white prostitute in violation of the Mann Act.[50]

Such anti-foreign and racial attacks were not inconsistent with the views of Temperance/Social Purity activists. Typified by their Progressive hero Theodore Roosevelt, they were extremely apprehensive both about the "race suicide" they believed would be the result of racial intermixing and about the growing immigration of swarthy Eastern Europeans. Undoubtedly, much of their sexual anxiety reflected class, race, and ethnic fears—the same kinds of fears that motivated the anti-alcohol crusade. Moreover, the Progressives' concern about poverty, the immiseration of the working class, and the growth of dependent populations led them to support not only political reforms but also a program of eugenics and curbs on immigration. In short, temperance statements about race, drink, and sex certainly do not seem very different from those of white Southerners who lynched African-Americans at the time. For example, Frances Willard of the WCTU blamed "the grogshop . . . the Negro's center of power. 'Better whiskey and more of it,' she wrote, 'is the rallying cry of great, dark faced mobs,' whose drunken exploits menaced 'the safety of women, of children [and of] the home . . . in a thousand localities.'"[52]

Sex and Health Wars:
The Social Hygiene Movement

Shortly after the turn of the century, a New York physician, Dr. Prince Morrow, formed the Society of Sanitary and Moral Prophylaxis. His organization, which aimed at controlling the spread of venereal diseases through the marriage of medicine and morality, captured the imagination of Social Purity forces. Within several years, dozens of similar societies existed throughout the nation. Loosely known as the Social Hygiene Movement, this movement essentially replaced the Social Purity Movement.[53] It soon involved most major Progressive figures, including Theodore Roosevelt and Jane Addams, as well as such organizations as the newly formed Travelers Aid Society, the Parent-Teacher Association (PTA), and the National Education Association. Of interest for our purposes is the ease with which the new social medicine and public health models were wedded to social purity through the use of venereal disease as a moral warning against prostitution, promiscuity, masturbation, and vice, at the same time that health and sex education were being promoted.

In some respects, the Social Hygiene Movement presaged the modern construction of public health and social medicine: Among its positive features were an increased willingness to discuss sex and to confront the reality of sexually transmitted diseases as well as the insight that disease and health were social, not just individual, issues and hence had to be tackled at the environmental level. However, the Social Hygiene Movement was limited by a moralistic and elitist bias that led it to define health risks as emanating from the "Other" (the lower classes, racial minorities, prostitutes, etc.). Moreover, like contemporary public health movements, it had a penchant for exaggeration and spreading panic.

Venereal disease (VD), in existence at least since the fifteenth century, had long been a cause for moralization. Indeed, D. H. Lawrence suggested that the rise of Puritanism in England may well have stemmed from the particularly violent strain of syphilis that befell the country in the sixteenth century.[54] "Disease" does not exist in a neutral sphere distinct from morality; rather, the response and construction of human disease (as well as of other life risks) are greatly dependent on their moral meaning. Thus, although far more people were killed by cholera and the plague than by venereal disease, the moralistic lessons of VD were thought to be critical to proper education, so more attention accrued to sexual diseases.[55] Moral and social objectives were frequently tied to an interest in syphilis. As Bristow notes, "Syphilophobia [was] a well-known phenomenon in the 19th Century. Moralists did their best to reinforce it and French fathers sometimes took their sons through the local VD ward to complete their moral education. . . . [A]s with masturbation, the purity reformers merely promoted anxiety about VD when it would otherwise die down."[56]

The Social Hygiene Movement was consistent with other healthist movements in that it vastly exaggerated the number of people with venereal disease and the ease with which it could be spread. In writings and speeches, Dr. Prince Morrow claimed that huge numbers of people had venereal disease—upwards of "60% of all men."[57] But historians of the disease consider such rates to be fanciful and implausible.[58] Morrow's claim reminds us of the apocalyptic predictions about the AIDS epidemic made throughout the 1980s and early 1990s, some of which specified that a quarter or more of the world's population would die.

In addition, even the physicians of the Social Hygiene Movement were content to allow the public to believe that syphilis could be contracted at public water fountains, park benches, and public restrooms. A recognized historian of venereal disease, Allan Brandt, suggests that this panic paralleled the fears of the Protestant elites about the city: "Progressive unease about hygiene, contagion, and cleanliness was evoked in the belief that in the brief encounters of everyday life—at the grocery, in the park, at the barber shop—these infections . . . could be passed to middle class 'moral' Americans. Fear of contagion justified a distaste for social contact with the urban masses."[59]

Brandt quotes a supporter of the Social Hygiene Movement as noting that panic about venereal disease was widespread:

> Many people today have a very exaggerated idea as to ease of infection and especially the symptoms of syphilis. Gonorrhea, which used to be likened to a cold in the head, is now-a-days likened to leprosy or cancer; while the innocent victim of acne, shingles or poison ivy is shunned as an infectious syphilitic. And whereas only from five to eight percent of syphilitics develop grave lesions of the nervous system, every luetic [syphilitic] now-a-days looks upon himself as doomed to locomotor ataxia.[60]

Why did this exaggeration and fear mongering occur? First, public health leaders and physicians have a vested interest in promoting health crises; doing so allows them the challenge of discovering disease and warning about it as well as treating it. Thus health anxiety has played a major, if rarely acknowledged, role in the growth of modern medicine, particularly in public health bureaucracies. Second, the fear and panic facilitated two agendas: the repression of sexuality and the stigmatization of the "Other," primarily immigrants and native-born "deviants" (such as prostitutes and "feeble minded" persons) being excluded from American life at the time. As with HIV/AIDS seven decades later, it was ideologically more palatable for the Social Hygiene Movement to blame the "Other" than to see disease in a more neutral, scientific way. And indeed, in the late twentieth century, the HIV/AIDS disease has been alternately blamed on gays, Haitians, Africans, and prostitutes rather than seen as a viral disease with numerous means of transmission. Chastity and sexual morality were likewise the key components of the anti-VD war:

> Education about sex should include as a cardinal feature a correction of the false impression instilled in the minds of young men that sexual indulgence is essential to health and that chastity is incompatible with full vigor (Prince Morrow).[61]

> In all previous efforts to safeguard the morality of youth, the ethical barrier was alone available and the situation seemed hopeless. . . . [S]exual morality, long an ethical ideal, became grounded upon the most convincing scientific facts (Reverend William Lawrence, a Social Hygiene leader).[62]

The great fear of Morrow, Roosevelt, and other Progressives was that venereal disease, if not confined to immigrants, would lessen the reproduction rate of the white race, hence allowing swarthy immigrants to dominate America. In short, they saw their movement as linked to eugenics. For example, Brandt quotes Morrow as saying that "[t]he function of eugenics is to produce a race healthy, well-formed and vigorous by keeping the springs of heredity pure and undefiled. . . . [T]he effects of venereal disease is to produce a race of inferior beings, by poisoning the sources of life and sapping the vitality and health of the offspring."[63]

The impact of the Social Hygiene Movement included increased repression of prostitutes (or women who, to officials, looked like prostitutes), increased accusations of white slavery, and increased anti-immigrant and anti-foreign sentiment. During World War I, 30,000 prostitutes and suspected prostitutes were detained by federal troops and held in detention camps because of the fear that VD would spread to the fighting men.[64] The Social Hygiene Movement also succeeded in securing state-mandated blood tests at marriage, mandatory reporting laws, and, in some regions, compulsory examination and quarantine of suspected carriers. Interestingly, all of these proposals were again made in the 1980s to combat the spread of HIV, but they were generally defeated by an alliance of civil libertarians and gay activists.

Although the Social Hygiene Movement certainly promoted health and, through its public education message, may have saved lives, it also helped construct an approach to professional public health management linked to Victorian morality—a link that to some extent continues to this day. Further, although public health officials are far more sophisticated now than during the Progressive era, current public health models are neither "apolitical" nor neutral. The "war"-like metaphors promoted by even liberal public health officials have often suggested social repression "at odds with civil liberties."[65] The health morality associated with the turn-of-the-century movement is still consistent with American society's penchant for blaming contagion on the sexuality of the "Other." The Social Hygiene Movement, and its successors today, demonstrates the paradox that those who campaign to talk constantly of "sex" may only represent the flipside of Victorian morality, as Michael Foucault noted in his *History of Sexuality*.[66] That is, although aspects of the Social Hygiene Movement parallel conservative efforts in our own era around sexually transmitted diseases, its constant discussion of disease and sex, and its exaggeration of risk, has many similarities with today's "progressive" sex activists. Movements around sex continue to make for strange bedfellows.

Themes: Hyperbole, Social Control, Class, and Political Power

I do not question the idealistic motivations of those who campaigned in the nineteenth and early twentieth centuries against alcohol, tobacco, prostitution, nude pictures, or sexually transmitted diseases. Like the New Temperance, the older movements attracted many reformers who believed that changing the norms of personal behavior is key to human progress and the diminution of violence and ill health. However, claims of altruism are not sufficient to prove the overall positive value of a social movement or of major cultural trends. After all, the Ku Klux Klan (a strong supporter of the temperance movements of the Victorian and Progressive eras) made the claim that it championed and protected the virtue of (white) women and children. But the fact that the Klan campaigned against alcohol, extramarital sex, and child molestation hardly leads us to view it as altruistic.[67]

Two important aspects of temperance movements (both old and new) thus deserve serious examination, quite apart from the positive motives that many participants bring to these movements. First, we must question the degree to which the hyperbolic language used by temperance movements is helpful to clear thinking. For example, opponents of "demon rum" (see Chapter 4) actually believed that one drink would send a man into a perdition of immorality and vice; anti-cigarette advocates claimed that children died as early as age eight from smoking the "soot weed"; and participants in movements against vice and prostitution warned that girls who masturbated were destined to become "fallen women." These notions were not merely odd beliefs of the old days; they impelled policy. They brought about intolerance and repression of *ac-*

tual people. Early beliefs about the harms of masturbation led to spiked penile rings and circumcision for some boys and clitoridectomies for some girls. Moral campaigns against "fallen women" led to the incarceration of suspected prostitutes in workhouses, prisons, and detention camps. And thousands of people were arrested during Prohibition for drinking or patronizing "speakeasies."

As we shall see in subsequent chapters, the New Temperance is characterized by hyperbole as well. Having pathologized such actions as drug taking and youthful expressions of sexuality, the New Temperance (albeit in modern language) makes its own overwrought claims about behavior. Likewise, its opposition to the use of substances, sexual behavior, and certain consumption patterns has led to social control measures usually undertaken against poor people and racial minorities. The demonization of "crack" has resulted in hundreds of thousands of arrests as well as the removal of children from families; the construction of an immoral underclass has prompted attacks on welfare benefits for poor women; and attacks on violence in rock music seem to target the lyrics of black rap stars more than those of other musicians. Granted, many reformers do not seek repressive measures but, rather, attempt to use educational or public health approaches to alter behavior. But the fact remains that throughout American history, hyperbole and moralizing have led to severe social control measures.

A second concern arises with the ascription of altruism to temperance movements. As discussed in the following chapter, every social or politicized issue is a *choice* made from among many potential (possibly limitless) social issues. There is nothing "natural" about viewing behavioral issues as the most critical ones for society to confront. During the period of the older temperance movements, for example, were alcohol and prostitution the most important issues confronting America? Most historians would maintain that they were not. This was the era of the "Great Barbecue," the Gilded Age in which massive wealth and monopolies were built up while starvation and poverty reached dramatic levels, particularly during economic depressions. The frequent and bloody class conflicts waged between industrialists and incipient unions caused far more deaths and injuries than most of our overseas wars. After Reconstruction ended, African-Americans were deprived of their rights of citizenship by Jim Crow laws in the South, suffering vicious repression and repeated lynchings well into the first half of the twentieth century. And women were denied not only the right to vote but most other rights of citizenship as well.

The fact that middle-class reformers stressed the harms of alcohol or vice rather than those of, say, capitalism or racial inequality suggests to some critics that the temperance movements were often the result of *displaced symbols.*[68] In other words, the *social-class* position of the reformers themselves as well as the *political viability* of issues of personal behavior made these symbols (the "demon rum," the "fallen woman") more salient to the white middle class than, for example, racial equality or socialism. The Victorian quest for perfectibility and the Progressives' "search for order" were political responses to the perceived need to control the social unrest of the immigrants and native "dangerous classes" of this period. Although the more liberal reformers of the Progressive Period did seek social reforms such as child labor laws, the eight-hour workday, and women's suffrage, their deep anxieties about the decay of white Protestant hegemony prevented them from condemning the social structural arrangements of American society. In particular, they feared that growing labor unrest, radical ideologies, and the diluting of the U.S. native Protestant population by millions of immigrants could lead to revolution or, at a minimum, major losses of status and power.[69] In this sense, "demon rum," picture postcards of nudes, and prostitution were not just moral evils but *symbols* of the decline of old values. Again, I am not suggesting that the behaviors campaigned against (e.g., excessive drinking) were harmless; but it is ironic that reformers from Carry Nation to Theodore Roosevelt were far more horrified by alcoholism and prostitution than they ever were by the lynching of blacks or the shooting of unarmed strikers.

This book will develop the argument that in many (though, of course, not all) respects, the period since the mid-1970s parallels the late Victorian era and the Progressive Period. First, the new wars on use of substances and sexual and other personal behaviors reflect a new middle-class status anxiety, in part comparable to that experienced at the turn of the century. These new wars have occurred in the context of economic decline and the loss of racial and cultural hegemony experienced by many in the white middle class since the 1970s. Second, even within the social movements that have sought broader political and social change, it appears that the symbolism of behavioral controls has facilitated the development of political coalitions. Both turn-of-the-century Progressive reformers who endorsed the temperance movements and many ex-activists of the 1960s would certainly have preferred more significant social change than actually occurred. But given the power of deeply held conservative social norms in the United States, it is ultimately not surprising that alcohol prohibition and strict controls over immigration—rather than the eight-hour workday or the minimum wage—came out of the earlier middle-class movements. Nor did the social movements of the 1960s succeed in their more radical demands. The views of modern "progressives" regarding personal behavior and its control (as manifested in, say, laws against domestic violence, hate crimes, and smoking in public places) have succeeded far more than efforts at, say, "comparable worth in pay for women," "wages for housework," or "a guaranteed income for everyone" (all of which were leftist slogans that readily fell by the wayside). One can conceptualize social movements, particularly of the middle class, as making both social structural demands—for legal and economic reforms, for example, that alter power—and demands on their fellow citizens that they change their behavior—alcohol prohibition or use of appropriate speech, for example. In each period, character reforms are far easier to achieve because, as I shall argue further later, they are less threatening to those who hold power and more conducive to achieving a middle-class consensus than are social structural changes.

Finally, we need to ask why it is that, except during unusual circumstances (such as times of international conflict), behavior "wars" are so popular in America, whereas attempts to change power relations are so difficult. This issue will be addressed later in the book.

three

Temperance and the Social Construction of Risk

To situate temperance as ideology, strategy, and movement, we could explore broad areas of theory; but for our purposes, it is the social construction of personal behavior as *the* major risk of life that is of interest. After all, life poses numerous risks, including the possibility of natural disaster (earthquakes, global warming), technological failure (nuclear plant meltdowns, plane crashes), economic collapse (personal bankruptcy, economic depressions), and political crisis (warfare). In Western society, it is usually personal risks that state officials and a variety of professionals warn against, rather than natural or economic risks.

In the present chapter I explore this issue through discussion of the social constructionist perspective in sociology, using two examples: the automobile and masturbation. Drawing on a number of social theories, I also propose that temperance as an ideology and strategy appeals to political and corporate elites, and, at times, to large sectors of the public as well. Through the use of a historical sociological method, I suggest an ongoing dynamic between temperance strategies and movements and the forces that tend to resist them.

Constructing Social Problems

Many Americans, including social scientists, view social problems or issues as "objective" matters, subject to empirical verification. Whether the issues of concern are those dealt with in this book or others (e.g., the behavior of foreign leaders), the assumption is that these issues have a clear, "real" existence that we can discover. Although we may sometimes doubt the accuracy of certain things we see or hear (e.g., commercial advertisements), most of us trust scientific and official reports about reality. For instance, we accept the truth that Saddam Hussein is a "dictator" partly because we ourselves have no way of verifying this "fact"; but, more important, most of us are also conditioned to accept the authority of political leaders, news media, science, and the professions.

The social constructionist perspective in sociology can be traced back to phenomenology, the sociology of knowledge, symbolic interactionism, and the work of Berger and Luckmann.[1] It also shares some features with recent movements in literature and cultural criticism known as "deconstructionism."[2] Although social constructionist theories vary widely (indeed, the sociologists who identify as "social constructionists" differ among themselves),[3] they have in common the questioning of society's "truths," thus suggesting that our knowledge is historically, culturally, and temporally contextual.

The claim that anything is "good" or "evil" in moral terms, or healthy or diseased in medical terms, is based on subjective and cultural understandings of these terms. In the 1990s Saddam Hussein was constructed by Western mass media and political leaders as "evil" and "dangerous," but this construction was not "truth" to his followers in Iraq or to the millions of his other supporters elsewhere. Social constructionists would interpret the media coverage of and political attacks on Saddam as consisting of "claims" about the truth—that is, rhetorical "frames"— intended to convince the American people of Hussein's villainous nature. In short, no clear good/evil, sane/insane, or other distinction can be made in the abstract: Our beliefs about Saddam are mediated by many different variables, including, of course, our political views and our (American) nationality.

The construction of Saddam as enemy was accomplished not only through "truth claims" made about his behavior but also through a classificatory scheme that sociologist Joel Best calls a "typification."[4] We know that Hussein was an invader of Kuwait; but we are also told that he is to be classified as a "bloodthirsty dictator" along with Hitler, Noriega, Castro, and other enemies of the U.S. government. Such a typification helped construct Hussein as a suitable target for warfare. Yet note that it is possible both to disagree with the "truth claims" about Hussein and to disagree with the classificatory scheme. That is, some people have argued that Hussein's actions were not so terrible or incomprehensible as presented, thus disputing the claims about him, whereas others have concurred with some or all of the claims made but have refused to accept the typification of Hussein as resembling Hitler, thus disputing the classificatory scheme. The latter observers consider him a typical Third World dictator of the sort the United States has been on good terms with.

Social constructionist theorists have been particularly interested in criticizing "social problems" definitions, including many of the topics explored in this book. They have studied aspects of the recent alcohol and drug wars as well as such issues as missing children, child abuse, AIDS, and crime waves. Generally, these theorists question the classificatory schemes by which we label "deviance" or "social problems" as abstract moral, legal, or scientific problems. For example, Howard Becker, in his well-known treatment of the marijuana scare of the 1930s,[5] saw the development of an aggressive campaign by the Federal Bureau of Narcotics at that time as key to the acceptance of the "danger" of marijuana. In his study, Becker noted that although no new scientific information about marijuana had emerged in this period, then Commissioner of Narcotics H. J. Anslinger and others led a campaign to illegalize the drug. Dubbing them *moral entrepreneurs*, Becker described their use of atrocity stories and their association of the drug with Mexicans to convince the public (and Congress) that marijuana was evil, leading to the passage of the Marihuana Tax Act of 1937. In a similar vein, Best's work on the missing-children scare of the 1980s challenged the objective existence of the new social problem of "missing children." Rather, he located this problem formulation in the success of *claimsmakers* in influencing the media and in developing an alliance of lawmakers, police, social service, and other interested parties concerned with bringing recognition and legitimacy to this issue.[6]

According to social constructionists, claimsmakers or moral entrepreneurs, though often political leaders or medical and other experts, increasingly are ordinary citizens who have come together in social movements. Many theorists see an increase in claimsmaking in America; they see a veritable army of competing reformers, demanding that we direct our attention to countless sets of issues. Obviously some claimsmakers are unsuccessful, or only briefly successful, at getting our attention, whereas others draw our attention more consistently.

For a further illustration of the social constructionist view, compare Box 3.1, which concerns the automobile (an issue most Americans clearly would *not* consider a social problem), and Box 3.2, which examines masturbation (a behavior that for centuries *has* been viewed as a major medical and social problem).

Limitations of Social Constructionism

Challenging the "naturalness" and everyday reality of events is a strength of sociological theory, particularly of social constructionism. Using the social constructionist approach, we can strip from our modern thoughts about the car Box 3.1) any preconceived notions about its necessity and somewhat vaunted status. From the same perspective, the construction of masturbation as a "social problem" Box 3.2) is seen to be

BOX 3.1   Is the Automobile a "Social Problem"?

Social constructionists generally analyze and theorize about issues that are already widely viewed by society as "social problems"—that is, those issues that have been successfully transformed into public issues. Conversely, they rarely analyze issues that have failed to elicit successful "truth claims."

The issues that become defined as social problems are usually those presented as grave dangers to the health and safety of individuals or of society as a whole. Claimsmakers warn us that drugs or teen pregnancy will lead to x number of deaths, that y amount of productivity will be lost to industry, or that z number of families will become destitute. Yet arguably the automobile in American society—usually not typified as a danger like drugs or AIDS—causes far more fatalities, injuries, and diseases than do many of the risks we are constantly warned about.

With the exception of accident statistics, data on death and disability caused by autos are quite incomplete. Researchers would need to include figures on automobile production, repair, use, disposal, and respiratory problems related to the breathing in of exhaust fumes to get anywhere near an accurate total. But partly because the auto is *not* regarded as a serious public issue, data are not collected in a way that allows for a cumulative total. Nevertheless, I have presented some of the available data below:

- *Auto accidents:* Accidents are the most publicized health risk associated with the auto, accounting for 43,500 deaths and 1.6 million disabling injuries in 1991 alone.[7]
- *Occupational deaths and injuries in the production of autos:* In 1991, officially at least 1,300 of a total 9,900 occupational deaths occurred during the production process of automobiles (a proportion that would be even higher if all ancillary industries were included in the calculations). In the same year, 140,000 workers were injured.[8]
- *Household and other nonoccupational injuries as well as accidents with autos and auto-related products:* The National Safety Council does not provide a breakdown of the number of accidents that occur at home or in the community as a result of people working on their cars, children swallowing oil or other auto products, or other incidents involving autos. Yet at least nine accident categories—poisoning, fire and flames, inhalation and ingestion, hot substances, electric current, explosive gases, machinery, falling objects, and falls—include deaths and injuries involved in mishaps with auto parts or products. Some portion of the 38,500 deaths and 5.4 million injuries at home or in public are due to auto products.[9]
- *Cancer deaths from auto exhaust:* The Environmental Protection Agency (EPA) has taken a conservative approach to this topic, but its data suggest that between 1,500 and 30,000 cancer deaths a year have been due to vehicle exhaust.[10] Although emissions controls and other reforms are now in place, past estimates figure as high as 2,000 premature deaths a year in New York City alone.[11]
- *Noncancer deaths from auto exhaust:* The EPA has presented no quantitative finding on this issue despite the fact that it reports

the following consequences from long-term exposure to benzene, formaldehyde, butadiene, acetaldehyde, and gas and diesel particulates (all chemical emissions associated with autos): blood disorders, immune system diseases, developmental and reproductive diseases, respiratory and lung diseases, heart disease, and genetic diseases. The EPA does conclude that a percentage of noncancer deaths are associated with auto emission.[12]

Critics have also noted numerous other health and social consequences of automobile use that are hard to quantify: the impact of the auto on our lifestyle, which since the 1920s has become increasingly sedentary, leading to the growth of heart disease, stroke, and other modern diseases; the impact of junking and disposing of autos and auto parts on the environment, including the costs of this pollution; the environmental damage done both by autos themselves and by the huge changes in the ecosystem resulting from the building of highways; stress produced by long commutes, greater traffic, smog, and congestion; and, finally, even violence. Not only have we seen shootings on freeways, but the auto has also played a role in the general hostility and agitation that characterizes modern culture; consider, for example, the impact of traffic, of people "beating each other out" for parking spaces and competing to pass each other on the highways.[13]

My purpose here is not to propose that the auto be banned but, rather, to raise the *theoretical* question as to why the auto is *not* classified or "typified" as a social problem (as a disease or dangerous substance would be). In all probability, the car is seen as too politically and economically indispensable to modern industrial society for claimsmakers to mount a successful campaign against it. Calls to ban autos in America are usually branded as "nutty" or "radical." Claimsmakers would have to wage a massive struggle against a large number of auto-related lobbies, including the auto companies, the highway lobby, the energy industry, and others with a vested interest in the car.

Of course, problems *related* to autos have been accepted as "social problems": Especially since Ralph Nader's 1960s campaigns about auto safety, issues ranging from safety testing to seat belts and air bags have been in the news; the public has accepted controls over drunk driving, limits on highway speed, and efforts to reduce air pollution. But what has been defined as the issue is not the auto *itself* but only its inappropriate use (speed, driving while intoxicated) or its inefficient technology (the need for better emission devices, or for further safety improvements). It is implicitly assumed that the automobile is critical to American life and, hence, that reform efforts must focus on *minimizing its risks,* as balanced against the enjoyment/necessity of driving.

This, of course, is not the American approach to problems such as illicit drug usage. Claimsmakers here acknowledge no necessity for drugs, nor any need for the pleasures associated with them. And since there is no "worthy purpose" to the use of drugs, social policy supports their *elimination* rather than the possibility of reducing their harm or risk—even though far more people die or are injured on American highways than from taking illicit drugs.

BOX 3.2   Is Masturbation a "Social Problem"?

Until relatively recently in our Western history, masturbation (also referred to as onanism) was considered a major social evil, the focus of educators, doctors, philosophers, lawmakers, and religious and political leaders. Between the early eighteenth century and the 1920s, it was believed to cause insanity, sterility, a lowering of intelligence, a weakening of the nervous system, idiocy, and even early death.

Though such fears may seem ludicrous to many today, the social definition of masturbation in Europe and America was not "an old wives' tale" or folk wisdom but was upheld by the principal elites of the society. Voltaire and Kant philosophized against it;[14] America's father of psychiatry, Benjamin Rush, wrote about its dangers along with those of alcoholism and mental illness;[15] schoolmasters expelled students from schools for masturbating;[16] the Boy Scouts, the Purity Movement, the YMCA, and the Temperance Movement combated it;[17] and the medical profession lectured against it. By the mid–nineteenth century, physicians were "designing douches to cool the genitals and devices to restrain them like the spiked penile ring; they then took the ultimate step to clitoridectomies and circumcisions as treatment for masturbation."[18]

Foucault notes that not only did "the sex of the schoolboy become, in the course of the 18th Century, . . . a public problem" but also that the architectural design of secondary schools was influenced by the battle against the evil habit.[19] Space for classes, the shape of tables, and the monitoring of bedtime and sleep periods at private schools originated from this concern. Masturbation was made illegal by the sodomy laws of the time, and the anti-masturbatory campaigns lasted well into the twentieth century. Maurice Bigelow, a professor of biology at Columbia University and a leading Social Hygiene Movement activist, warned in the 1910s that "the habit will weaken the nervous system and indirectly affect all general health." The doctors of the movement recommended sports and recreation as an antidote: "[T]he lad who plays vigorously . . . possesses a great bulwark of defense against sexual vice, especially its secret forms."[20]

A harbinger of modern times was a 1921 meeting between the White Cross Society in England and Ernest Jones, a colleague of Freud who was regarded by many as a dangerous radical at the time. Dr. Jones told the White Cross Society that the worst psychiatric problems he had seen "resulted from the intolerable burden at present heaped on the auto-erotic by clergy, doctors, and schoolmasters alike." Although the White Cross Society attacked Jones's "vague knowledge of Christian ethics," the dangers of masturbation had evidently receded enough that they subsequently withdrew their most fearful pamphlet, *The Perils of Impurity*. One English politician even commented in 1931 that, after all, "if masturbation was so destructive, how could Britain have won the war?"[21]

The historic claims about masturbation raise many fascinating questions. How is it that this "social problem" could have been defined and typified for so long as a danger, with the vast majority of the intelligentsia supporting such a definition, and yet now be regarded as a normal behavior? How is it that this "social problem" has almost vanished, but without a word of apology to the thousands of youngsters expelled from school or forced to undergo surgery as a result of their private moral violations? To what extent can these past "truth claims" be separated from the Western construction of sexual morality and medicine to which they were bound? Shouldn't the old war against masturbation cause us to question other aspects of Western morality and science?

problematic; we cannot say simply that this episode was "history" or that scientific inquiry was less sophisticated in those days. Social constructionists do not assume that today's science is either "value neutral" or "accurate." In fact, theorists are increasingly treating science itself as a "social problem" connected with a modern Western discourse in which certain definitions and claims are privileged whereas others are discarded.[22]

Despite the power of the social constructionist orientation to reframe our day-to-day reality as problematic, several issues in social constructionist theory remain unclear and prevent totally satisfactory answers to such questions as why neither the car nor masturbation is considered a major social problem today. Social constructionism brings us to the door of the problem, but each theorist who has opened it seems essentially on his or her own. Several areas of inquiry or evaluation are suggested.

First, almost all social constructionist inquiries involve a case study approach that provides little basis for comparing phenomena. Second, although many authors provide some proximate history of various social problems, they do not adequately situate them in historical context. Third, many social constructionist inquiries are characterized by a tendency to deny their implicit value scheme rather than to explicate it.

Most social constructionist inquiries are based on a case study approach (e.g., as with the marijuana issue or the missing-children problem discussed previously). However, social problems are usually composed of "clusters" and thus are "bundled" together. As we have seen, historic wars against substance abuse, for example, are not waged in isolation from broader issues. By using the concept of "Temperance," I have sought to identify a group of bundled values, symbols, and defined knowledge. The examples in this chapter (Boxes 3.1 and 3.2) also cannot be viewed in isolation from other issues. The auto retains its cultural hegemony and insulation from social and political attack because it is part of a broader cluster of American technological symbols and achievements, which, though not immune from attack, require a major disaster (of the magnitude of the Three Mile Island nuclear disaster) to provoke popular critique. A broader analysis of the auto would require an exploration of the American view about many types of technological changes and "advances."

The issue of masturbation can hardly be studied in the abstract either. Attitudes toward onanism were integrally bundled with attitudes both toward other "nonproductive" pleasures and toward work and discipline from the eighteenth through the early twentieth centuries. Some social theorists are now coming to use this approach. Philip Jenkins, for example, has made a similar argument. As discussed in the next section, he has noted the "interdependence" of social problems, many of which he links together as "moral panics."[23]

Further, we cannot understand the construction of social problems without gathering historical evidence and using such material to develop theory. Yet most case studies, though they provide brief historical background on the particular social problem, do not fully develop the social embeddedness of the claims being studied. As Best has noted, "[T]here is a tendency among social constructionists to 'finesse' the historical pre-conditions of the rise and fall of social problems or at least [to] fail to account for periods of high claims-making activity."[24] To understand the construction of masturbation as a central "problem" for the eighteenth and nineteenth centuries, we require historical evidence as to its symbolic meaning during this period in Europe and America. Although sexual taboos are still sufficiently powerful to lead to the firing of a Surgeon General, panic over masturbation does not completely jibe with the "truth claims" of our time. In the example of the auto, we need to develop evidence about how opponents of the car or of highway construction (potential "claimsmakers") have been characterized and portrayed ("typified") since the early days of the automobile. If my hunch is correct, historical evidence would show that potential claims were met with organized derision and discrediting by a broad array of forces within American society—forces that have helped dissuade other reformers from challenging the popularity of the car.

In this book I have attempted to situate the historical context of what Best calls "periods of high claimsmaking."[25] As noted in Chapter 2, our own time is not unique but, rather, harkens back to the American obsession with drug use, sex, and other personal behaviors in the nineteenth century. Historical treatments of such issues call our attention to the impact of major events on many different social problems. For example, the defeat of the first Temperance Movement meant that the strategy of "moralization" (and strong claims against some behaviors) would also suffer a general defeat. That is, the repeal of Prohibition, in combination with events such as the Great Depression (which brought the issues of economic equity and social class to the fore), is theorized to have led to a general weakening of American Puritanism as a political force well into the post–World War II period. In contrast, it is well documented that the anti-communism and McCarthyism of the late 1940s had serious social impacts beyond their more manifest aims, leading, for example, to increased repression of sexuality and other personal behaviors.[26]

Finally, we must confront the unspoken issue of values and perspective. Social constructionism, which clearly provides a critique of American society, is sometimes charged by critics with "debunking" in a way that exposes hidden causes and structures that are not obvious to the parties and hence may only be imputed.[27] For example, social constructionists privilege the latent functions of the wars on alcohol and drugs rather than their manifest aim of improving the nation's health and welfare; they look beyond the narrow framing of "crime" to raise questions about broader economic or cultural components of our crime wars. Yet social constructionists often do not acknowledge the *critical* nature of their sociological theory: Typically, they tend to justify their critique only by the argument that the "claims" of moral entrepreneurs are "exaggerated."

In an excellent treatment of the demonization of "crack" cocaine, for example, C. Reinarman and H. Levine critique the social construction of crack, primarily on the basis of the exaggerated nature of its effects and the differential treatment this drug has received in comparison with other drugs (e.g., non-crack cocaine). This empirical demonstration of exaggeration serves the authors' critical sociological stance, in that it provides a vehicle for exploring the many symbolic racial, class, and political overtones of the issue. The critique can thus be conducted along with obligatory bows to the harm of drugs.[28]

Such determinations of "exaggeration" or empirical comparison of problems have been criticized by some sociologists as "ontological gerrymandering."[29] But in my view what is problematic about these sociological treatments is not so much their methodology as the obfuscation of the worldview they represent. In other words, which is the real issue for Reinarman and Levine: confronting the relative harm of crack (versus heroin or other drugs) or confronting the American drug wars? A close reading of the article cited suggests that their main project is the latter. The critique of many social constructionists is hidden behind specific measurements and comparisons. Rather than apologize for a critical social view or refrain from such analysis, social constructionists should simply admit their biases. True, challenging popular beliefs about drugs or criminals will not make such theorists popular; it might even greatly reduce chances for government funding. Clearly, in conservative times there is a tendency among social scientists in general to "toe the line" in terms of what social problems governments and private funders will support. But social scientists cannot be limited to staying within the boundaries and ideologies of their own time and culture. In fact, they need to do the opposite. Years ago C. Wright Mills noted how limited people are in the ability to see, within their own times, the social structural, cultural, and other issues raised by daily life:

> Yet men [*sic*] do not usually define the troubles they endure in terms of historical change and institutional contradiction. The well-being they enjoy, they do not usually impute to the big ups and downs in the societies in which they live. Seldom aware of the intricate connection between the pat-

terns of their own lives and the course of world history, ordinary men do not usually know what this connection means for the kind of men they are becoming and for the kinds of history-making in which they might take part.[30]

Mills's words remind us that social theorists often privilege explanations that transcend the current style of the times. In this book, I argue that temperance is in part an elite ideology and strategy or, in Gramscian terms, a hegemonic project of our times. Indeed, it is because the cluster of symbols surrounding temperance is most valuable for the maintenance of power that I oppose the temperance wars. I also believe that some problem formulations help people see the inequities in a social system or the problems within a culture, whereas others lead them away from such insights. I suggest that rallying against drugs or child molesters in the community will move American society not in a positive direction but only toward the illusion that society's ills will be cured by increased repression. These are my biases. As I shall discuss in Chapter 6, history suggests that the rhetorical flourishes of "the personal is political" (a slogan of the New Left and women's movement) were probably unnecessary in our society. Instead, Americans usually turn the "political" into the "personal," and they do so in a way that is often politically and culturally conservative. Rather than embracing "value neutrality," this book is critical of dominant power structures, social control strategies, structured inequality, and privatized views of social problems.

Medicalization and Moral Panics

Two theoretical constructs that can be seen as partial remedies to the limitations of social constructionism are "medicalization" and "moral panics." Although these constructs have different origins, they both represent attempts to conceptualize the social treatment of "deviance" and help move us beyond the case study approach.

The term *medicalization* originated in critical opposition to the *medical model* in the work of such social critics as Thomas Szasz, Ivan Illich, and Michel Foucault, as well as in the women's, New Left, and gay movements of the 1960s and 1970s.[31] It also found its way into American sociology through both sociology-of-the-professions literature and social constructionism.[32] Essentially, medicalization traces the historical movement of Western society from an explanatory model of behavior based on morality to a medical classification system based on scientific classifications—or, as P. Conrad and J. Schneider succinctly put it, from the label of "badness" to that of "sickness."[33]

In brief, behavior held to be "sinful" in earlier times is currently held to be progressively absorbed into a "medical" or at least professional classificatory model. "Madness" has become "mental illness"; drinking or using drugs has been transformed from immorality into "addiction"; unruly children are now suffering from "attention deficit disorder"; excessive eating or dieting are now "eating disorders"; and excessive desire for sex is now declared to be "sexual addiction." Although the medicalizing of behaviors can be seen as beneficial in some respects, especially when compared to punishment of "deviants" (e.g., most current forms of treatment of the mentally ill are preferable to chaining the "mad" in cells, as was done in earlier centuries), medicalization is also viewed by theorists as intertwined with bourgeois ideology and thus as a new, more efficient form of social control. Many critics of medicalization have questioned the accuracy of defining so much behavior in "medical"- or "disease"-related terms, seeing this construction as having more to do with the imperialism of medicine and other professions than as being a form of "help." And many activists have organized in opposition to the medicalization of some forms of behavior, most notably the construction of homosexuality as a psychiatric problem, which was overturned by the American Psychiatric Association only in the 1970s.[34]

Whereas social and political movements opposing the dominant professions combined with a critical sociology in the United States to develop a critique of medicalization, British social constructionists seem to have been drawn more to the metaphor of "moral panic." Critically deconstructing the broad societal fears in the 1960s provoked by juvenile gangs ("mods" and "rockers") in England, Stanley Cohen described this great hubbub of publicity and anxiety as follows:

> A condition, episode, person or group of persons emerges to become defined as a threat to societal values and interests; its nature is presented in a stylized and stereotypical fashion by the mass media; the moral barricades are manned by editors, bishops, politicians, and other right thinking people; socially accredited experts pronounce their diagnoses and solutions; ways of coping are evolved or (more often) resorted to.[35]

Whereas many American theorists saw the medical labeling of personal behavior (alcoholism, homosexuality, eating disorders) as being the dominant force in naming and hence constructing behavior, many British theorists followed Cohen in highlighting the mass media, politicians, and broader public opinion in shaping the construction of "deviancy" in case studies of crime, child abuse, AIDS, drugs, and pornography.[36] Although most of the work in this vein shares the limitations of case studies noted earlier, Jenkins has recently grouped together a set of "moral panics"—specifically, child abuse, sexual abuse, pedophilia, and Satanism—and defined them as interdependent.

As metaphors, both medicalization and moral panic have made important contributions to recent sociological theory and are relevant to the subject matter of this book. Medicalization helps explain the transformation of behaviors previously judged "normal" into behaviors now deemed "medically" problematic. (Three examples that come to mind are attention deficit disorder, codependence, and learning disabilities.) Societal obsessions with medical metaphors have even crept into places where they are not meant to be taken as literally medical. (Consider, for example, "sick building syndrome" or "workaholism.") Yet medicalization is not the sole cause of this increased tendency to label deviant behavior. In the process of reviewing *The Readers Guide to Periodical Literature*, I found more than 100 new terms for "deviant" or undesirable behavior listed in 1992 that were not present in 1970.[37] Granted, medicalization has sparked dozens of new words (*acrophobia, addiction behavior,* and *attention deficit disorder* are among just the words beginning with *a*), and Oprah Winfrey and others constantly bombard us with talk of new medicalized problems; but panics about moral and criminal behaviors have also triggered many new classifications of behavior. Twenty years ago such phrases as *passive smoking, serial murders, hate crimes, custody kidnapping, enabling,* and *elder abuse* did not exist. The mass media present the world as an increasingly dangerous place, subject to new and growing disorders. Some social critics have even described panic "as the environmental mood of post-modern culture,"[38] suggesting that our entire worldview has become shaped by "fear and trembling."

Yet, despite their usefulness as metaphors, both constructs have limitations. One difficulty that emerges in all discussions of social problems is the problem of "agency." That is, who or what is primarily responsible for the naming, classifying, or enforcing of social problem classifications? Medicalization theory and moral panic theory tend to provide very different answers, although these answers are not mutually exclusive.

Medicalization as a term privileges physicians and associated professionals, excluding large sectors of the population who have an interest in defining "deviant" behavior. For example, in the transformation of "madness" into "mental illness," why privilege only medical actors by the concept of medicalization? Social reformers such as Dorothea Dix and social movements such as the Mental Hygiene Movement of the early twentieth century are at least as important to the acceptance of "mental illness" as any medical classificatory achievement (they also preceded the ability of medicine to actually treat the disorders of the mind). Even where medicine or expert personnel are involved in naming, why is their role more critical than that of, say, the political and eco-

nomic elites who ultimately may accept or reject medicalized definitions, such as "mental illness"? Medicine has no monopoly over problem
definitions; it has played a key role in the naming of many forms of "deviance" but only a minor role in dozens of other "deviance" designations
(e.g., domestic violence, rape, elder abuse, homelessness, and school
dropouts).

If medicalization gives the impression that professional elites control
"deviance" designations, some forms of moral panic theory give the impression that popular opinion, or at least opinion shaped by the media,
completely shapes views of "deviance." Moral panic theory begs the historical and theoretical questions as to how the "criminal," the "mentally
ill" person, or the teen mother became so villainous to begin with. Neither construct necessarily incorporates a critical understanding of how
power relations at the top of society may play a role in privileging abstinent behavior or norms of self-control over behavior regarded as wasteful, frivolous, or dangerous. Why, then, do some issues become the subject of moral panic whereas others (such as driving) are understood to
carry risks but do not lead to stigmatization (e.g., of the driver or even
the auto racer)?

Both constructs have other limitations as well. Medicalization theory
already seems a bit dated, inasmuch as it implied that the harsh attitudes toward personal "deviance" of the past would diminish. Medicalization suggests that when a moral problem is reframed as a medical
problem, the treatment of the offender is altered; yet there is little support for this contention. Does the understanding of most Americans
that smoking tobacco or taking illicit drugs is a physical "addiction" dramatically alter the view of the smoker or drug user? Arguably not. Most
Americans are also familiar with the argument that sexual abuse and pedophilia are "sicknesses"; yet, terminology aside, the new medical labels
have not much affected the angry crowds seeking to keep child molesters out of their neighborhoods. Hence, medicalization may really be a
"fig leaf" for what Foucault has described as the "moralization" of behaviors.

It is likely that medicalization has a broader relevance to middle-class
"purification rituals" in which relatively educated and cosmopolitan
people confess their weaknesses: the alcoholism of a president's wife, a
movie star's bout with an eating disorder, an affluent college student's
memory of her "dysfunctional" family, or a politician's admission of a
psychiatric depression. These "sins" are ritualistically forgiven, and the
media often praise the victim for his or her "openness." However, behaviors that are (actually or perceived as being) "lower class" in nature, from
crack use to cigarette smoking, from delinquency to child abuse, often
tend to be viewed not as medical problems free from blame but as moral

sins worthy of punishment. It is also true that the same behavior that would lead to a medicalized "sick role" in the case of a middle-class person (e.g., psychiatric depression or alcoholism) would lead to severe repression in the case of a lower-class person. Not only is the actual impact of any problem greater for the latter (the same case of psychiatric depression may lead to poverty or homelessness without proper insurance for treatment) but it is also more likely to be judged in moralistic terms (e.g., the "street drunk" and "bag lady" are not viewed through a medicalized lens).

If medicalization as a theoretical construct works less well today in describing how behavior became restigmatized in recent years, the concept of the "moral panic," though highly compelling in capturing the popular nature of today's temperance movements, suffers from vagueness. What brings about a moral panic? And in whose eyes does it become so? In an incisive critique of moral panic, P.A.J. Waddington asks, What would constitute a "sober realistic appraisal" of problems that are labeled "panics"? Sharing my criticism of social constructionism, she argues that there is little definitional agreement about what should be considered an exaggeration of a problem as opposed to an accurate characterization; and, since this lack of agreement is often the *key* claim of the critics, she asks, How do we assess whether mugging (for example) is being overreacted to or not? She also notes the hidden political agenda of moral panic theory. Noting the tendency of British theorists to label reactions to some behaviors (such as crimes committed by the poor and minorities) as "panics," she suggests that these theorists would be reluctant to give the same label to movements closer to the hearts of the Left (e.g., movements against rape, hate crimes, or police brutality).[39]

The medicalization and moral panic constructs have moved social constructionist theory forward by grouping together social phenomena and providing us with valuable metaphors. Yet they are limited in two ways. First, they focus our attention only on selected groups (medicine, media, etc.) in society, rather than accounting for the dominant role that "personal problems" appear to play in the economic, political, and symbolic culture of modern American and English societies as a whole. And, second, though implicitly critical of the labeling of personal problems as either sinful or diseased, they stop short of providing a clear argument as to why the tendency toward pathologizing personal behavior should be viewed critically.

Toward a Theory of Temperance

In the remainder of this chapter I situate temperance ideology within a historical sociological perspective that buttresses the social constructionist project with contributions from a variety of theories. I begin with a set of theses that attempts to specify the role of power elites in the shaping of social problem definitions. Rather than attributing social problem designations only to "moral entrepreneurs" or medical professionals, temperance arguably follows from the specific power needs of modern capitalist societies (as well as state socialist ones).[40] Hence the ideology of "personal problems" may serve key symbolic power needs of the state and elites. This is not to suggest that paradoxes and contradictions are not at work. For example, capitalist advertising often seems to link pleasure with buying, thereby encouraging *intemperance.*

A second set of theses suggests that temperance also tends to become a popular social movement at times, succeeding in secular form the appeal of religious revivalism. Finally, I propose that there is a historical dynamic between popular temperance movements and continued resistance by segments of the population. Concern with temperance rises and falls with the needs of the powerful as well as with the rises and falls of social movements themselves.

The Tendency for Political and Social Elites to Support Temperance

1. *Bourgeois society emerged historically on the basis of its claims to asceticism and meritocracy. Despite the fact that individual members of elites (or perhaps sometimes even a majority) often do not live up to these standards in their own lives, the claims of the bourgeoisie to power rest on this meritocratic ideology, which includes personal behavior. Hence violations of personal behavioral norms are violations of the fundamental ideology of modern industrial society.*

Although all human societies enforce some social norms through patterned social control, many human societies have tolerated considerable freedom in sexual or consumptory activities or have exempted large portions of their societies from strict behavioral rules. At one time, most indigenous cultures throughout the world were viewed by Europeans as "savage" in part because their customs seemed to countenance less discipline in behavior than European social norms did. We need not leave the Western tradition to see variation: Ancient Rome allowed considerable sexual and other freedoms to its freemen, and many European aristocracies were known for their overconsumption of food and drink, and for their general sexual abandon. Martin Luther's rebellion against the Catholic Church was greatly justified by the church's toleration (even encouragement) of almost all human frailties, as long as the church had the power to adjudicate the sin by penance or the sale of indulgences. Prior to the modern state, ruling elites needed no meritocratic or behavioral justification for their dominion. Kings and queens, emperors, nobles, and chieftains ruled through hereditary right and/or charismatic authority. Such God-given power did not require behavioral control by elites. Most of the time it mattered little whether kings or chiefs had an ascetic or bawdy lifestyle *unless* other external events (such as defeat in war or mass pestilence) undermined the ruler's claim to legitimacy.[41] In contrast, as noted a century ago by Max Weber, the bourgeoisie (along with modern Protestantism) arose as a rebellion against the excesses and perceived vices of the luxurious and lazy ruling classes of earlier days. Puritans associated the British aristocracy with sin; and the Cromwellian Revolution quickly prohibited drinking, gambling, theater, and sports, "which were the prized leisure of upper-class Roman Catholics against whom they rebelled."[42] The French Revolution produced a similar mood. Whereas the Puritans emphasized enforcement of a moral utopia, the French revolutionaries hoped that education in the new ideologies of reason and science would lead the average citizen to moral rectitude. Foucault quotes one revolutionary leader as follows: "By training citizens in frugality, by means of simple dietary laws, by showing young people above all the pleasures that may be derived from even a hard life, by making them appreciate the strictest discipline, . . . how many ills would be prevented . . . ? [Let us] undertake the splendid task of establishing in men's lives the positive role of health, virtue and happiness."[43]

The utopian goals of the bourgeois revolution rested on an understanding of the perfectibility of human nature—an understanding that held productivity and control to be virtues, while associating all wasteful luxuries or idleness with the feudal or the "primitive." Even today, bourgeois societies posit a meritocratic individualism that enshrines chieftains of industry and political elites with a claim to power based on their self-control and moral rectitude. A Rockefeller or a Trump, a Roosevelt or a Reagan, is not given a hereditary, natural claim on power but only a contingent one. This acceptance of their power hinges in part on their ability to accumulate capital or to exercise political authority while still complying with the *moral aspects* of bourgeois ideology, including a commitment to the work ethic, to the norm of proper-appearing family life, and to proper public displays of devotion.

Sociologist Werner Sombart, following Weber, characterized temperance as a feature of the life of the shopkeeper or trader "who must be thrifty and sober and industrious and chaste if he does not want to jeopardize [his] existence. To succeed, this class must believe [that] wasting time, love affairs, etc. would lead to beggary."[44] And Gusfield described the nineteenth-century Temperance Movement as reflecting class, status, and religious warfare whereby "abstinence as a symbol of middle-class membership" became also "a public affirmation of the abstemious, ascetic qualities of American Protestantism," triumphing over the poor immigrant's cultural traditions.[45]

Temperance as a bourgeois hegemonic project is intimately bound with the ideology of individualism. The bourgeoisie generalized from their own experience that "anyone could make it" in capitalist society by availing oneself of opportunities. Such an ideology then points to those who fail to "make it" in terms suggesting that personal deficits stand in their way: The poor are alleged to have failed to strive due to laziness or through their own faults such as alcoholism or sexual excess. Although the ascetic style of the early bourgeois has passed, the basic behavioral messages remain. Although we all know that leading industrialists and political elites act pretty much like everyone else (or worse) in their personal lives, the revelation of sin committed by politicians from Charles Parnell in the nineteenth century to Gary Hart in the twentieth is enough to lead to their disgrace. Nor does the capitalist usually advertise his or her gluttony, luxurious lifestyle, or extravagant affairs.[46] The power of the political leader or capitalist is undermined by the revelation of sin since the fact of sexual incontinence, intemperance, or personal instability threatens bourgeois ideology by the *discrepancy* between the notion that the leader or business owner is *entitled* to his or her power and the notion that those who are failures are poor as a result of their own sins. Though we all suspect that this ideology rests on a fiction, those who hold power and are found to be misbehaving usually must abandon their position for their *open* violation of these bourgeois norms.[47]

2. *Beginning in the late eighteenth century, the modern bourgeois state developed a power strategy in the form of classification—specifically, in its invention of categories of deviant persons such as the "mad" and the "criminal." Such categories increased the power of political elites by serving as important tools of social control. They also gradually came to reflect extremely popular ways of seeing the world.*

Whereas Weber made an association among capitalism, individualism, and Protestant asceticism, Michel Foucault, the French philosopher, has significantly added to our understanding of how bourgeois society developed a classificatory system to separate out the poorer classes (and other "deviants") while eventually creating a highly popular appeal for "moralization."

Until well into the nineteenth century in both Europe and the United States, poor people and society's "misfits" were not classified or studied, nor was their misbehavior understood as having resulted from clearly defined behavioral traits ("delinquency" or "alcoholism" for example). Sin, personal deviance, and pauperism were all conceptually mixed together, and few people were interested in sorting through the great mélange referred to as the "rabble." The early almshouses of America, for example, indiscriminately lumped together the pauper, the mentally ill and mentally retarded, the criminal and delinquent, the widow, orphan, and elderly poor, the intemperant, and even the fiddler, palm reader, gambler, and blasphemer.[48]

It was the invention of bourgeois society to develop a classificatory system that divided social outcasts (primarily the poor) into "allegedly universal moral categories"[49] such as the "mentally ill," the "criminal," the "delinquent," the "drunkard," the "wayward woman," and the "orphan." Beginning in the 1830s, separate institutional arrangements were developed for each group of deviants, and eventually special personnel were put in charge of different groups of deviants.[50] Key to developing these classifications was the rise of the professions—medicine, psychiatry, corrections, social work, sociology, criminology, psychology, and so on. One could trace the whole development of Western society since the early nineteenth century as a movement to develop ever more precise measurements of the properties of various deviants: Today, more than ever, social scientists as well as a host of natural scientists (biologists, medical researchers, geneticists) are increasingly specifying new labels and classifications that claim both predictive value (Who carries what gene?) and prescriptive value (How do we deal with those who are "dually diagnosed?").

Most salient in Foucault's work was his understanding of this process as reflecting the power interests of the bourgeois class and state authority, which arose simultaneously. Knowledge, said Foucault, is not independent of power. We know someone to "be criminal" not through a neutralistic application of principles but, rather, through a "power/knowledge" that privileges some types of behavior over others. The "norm" for deviancy was a bourgeois norm of behavior that, during the nineteenth century, contrasted with many popular sentiments.

For example, Foucault reminds us that many criminals were popular among the poor in European societies; in fact, they were seen as rebels or heroes. The robber, highwayman, pickpocket, and con artist were a danger primarily to the rich. The development of both a penal system and the ideology of crime and criminality in the late eighteenth and nineteenth centuries was in part an effort to prevent the lowest ranks of the working class and the drifting poor (who were then seen as the most potentially rebellious segments of society) from having any legitimacy among the more stable ranks of workers:

> The . . . role of the penal system: to make the proletariat see the non-proletarianized people as marginal, dangerous, immoral, a menace to society as a whole, the dregs of the population, trash, the "mob." For the bourgeoisie it is a matter of imposing on the proletariat by means of penal legislation, of

prisons, but also of newspapers, of "literature," certain allegedly universal moral categories which function as an ideological barrier between them and the non-proletarianized people. All the literary, journalistic, medical, sociological and anthropological rhetoric about criminals . . . plays this role.[51]

According to Foucault, the development and spread of a popular moral ideology not only split the poor from the working masses (at a time when mass riots and unrest were fairly commonplace) but also helped protect the bourgeois' property:

How was wealth to be protected? By a vigorous morality, of course: hence the formidable layer of moralisation deposited on the nineteenth-century population. Look at the immense campaigns to christianize the workers during this period. It was absolutely necessary to constitute the populace as a moral subject and break its commerce with criminality and hence segregate the delinquents and to show them to be dangerous not only for the rich but for the poor as well, vice-ridden instigators of the gravest social perils.[52]

Although Foucault separately addressed the "power/knowledge" of crime, madness, and sexuality, not examining a cluster of "temperance" values, his identification of "moralisation" as a critical nineteenth-century feat parallels the rise of organized temperance movements in America. It also helps explain how the viewpoint of the bourgeois of the early nineteenth century came to be gradually ingrained in much of the society. Whereas detective literature and police gazettes were popular staples of the mid-nineteenth century, today countless television shows and films, newspaper and television news stories, and "show trials" give us the vantage point of the "judge" gazing at the criminal deviant. We usually see TV news stories (and movies) about crime events not from the perspective of the "perpetrator" (in fact, the old movie codes prohibited this perspective) but from that of the criminal justice, police, psychiatric, and medical establishments. Thus we usually root for the heroes of *N.Y.P.D. Blue* or *Law and Order* or *LA Law* or *Miami Vice*, not for the drug dealer, burglar, or murderer.

The constant societal focus on the sins of the deviant is, in Foucault's terms, a "colonization" device, which is meant to infuse us all with an identification with power—the power of the police, the courts, and, ultimately, the state.[53] The state has achieved legitimacy to replace the church as the arbiter of morality: Although a loosening of moral norms occurs at times, it does so always within limits, particularly where the poorer classes are concerned.

3. *As Antonio Gramsci has argued, temperance (or "Puritanism," as he called it) became essential to industrial development in the process of*

capitalist development.[54] *The extraction of the maximum labor power of each individual worker places a premium on personal behavior both as a means of productivity and as an assurance that the worker will use his or her wages for subsistence.*

The economic interests of the bourgeoisie in temperant morality were not the primary focus of either the Weberian or the Foucaldian analysis. Weber thought of Puritanism as an ideology of the bourgeoisie primarily based on the status temperant behavior conferred on the individual and its ability to politically justify the rise of this new class; Foucault considered "moralisation" to be primarily a political strategy of the newly emerging elite. But the emerging industrialists of the late nineteenth century supported temperance movements for *economic* reasons as well. The argument was made that alcohol consumption, cigarette smoking, sexual vice, venereal disease, and other social problems interfered with production. To this day, a key argument (at times even the *primary* argument) against some forms of behavior is that they decrease the nation's economic productivity. On an almost daily basis, magazine and news articles quote experts' estimates of the "cost" to business of drugs, alcohol, smoking, teen pregnancy, sexually transmitted disease, high cholesterol, and so on.

Gramsci, an Italian Marxist intellectual, offered one of the clearest explanations for the role of temperance as an adjunct to the extraction of surplus value from the worker. He believed that modern civilization itself was "a continuing struggle . . . against the elements of 'animality' in man," inasmuch as all forms of advanced labor involved "coercion" and "rationalization" whereby the ease of life in earlier times was brutally transformed by industrialism. What was new about *American* capitalism (in the late nineteenth and early twentieth centuries) was unprecedented productivity based on a combination of power (the destruction of craft unions and the breakdown of labor through Taylorization), on the one hand, and (relatively) high wages and other benefits (dubbed "Fordism"), on the other. "The American phenomenon," said Gramsci, "is also the biggest collective effort to date to create, with unprecedented speed, and with a consciousness of purpose unmatched in history, a new type of worker and of man."[55]

Who is this "new type of worker and of man," and why does he require personal control? Although not completely fleshed out by Gramsci, the new man seems to be committed to production and available to constant exploitation through a longer, healthy life that is free of the "animal instincts" derived from pleasures such as drinking or sexual excess. The opposition of the capitalist to drinking and excessive sexuality seems to have two roots: one in the productive process and the other in the reproductive process.[56] In the production process, alcoholism or sexuality stands in the way of both extraction of the maximum labor power available in each worker and the necessary compliance to the discipline of the new production. As Gramsci noted: "In America rationalization of work and prohibition are undoubtedly connected. The enquiries conducted by the industrialists into the workers' private lives and the inspection services created by some firms to control the 'morality' of their workers are necessities to the new methods of work. . . . A forced selection will ineluctably take place; a part of the old working class will be pitilessly eliminated in the world of labor."[57]

But capitalists also have a strong interest in the personal behavior of workers *outside* of the workplace. In particular, the workers need to stay physically fit and healthy, get sufficient rest, and consume a diet sufficient to maintain energy. Thus, as Gramsci further notes,

> Puritanical initiatives simply have the purpose of preserving, outside of work, a certain psycho-physical equilibrium which prevents the physiological collapse of the worker, exhausted by the new method of production. . . . It is necessary for the worker to spend his extra money "rationally" to maintain, renew, and, if possible, increase his muscular-nervous efficiency and not to corrode or destroy it. Thus the struggle against alcohol, the most dangerous agent of destruction of labouring power, becomes a function of the state. It is possible also for other "puritanical" struggles as well to become functions of the state if private initiative of the industrialists proves insufficient. . . . The sexual question is again connected with that. . . . Abuse and irregularity of sexual functions is, after alcoholism, the most dangerous enemy of nervous energies, and it is commonly observed that "obsessional" work provokes alcoholic and sexual depravation. . . . It seems clear that the new industrialism wants monogamy: it wants the man as worker not to squander his nervous energies in the disorderly and stimulating pursuit of occasional sexual satisfaction.[58]

In addition to suggesting powerful reasons for capitalist support for temperance, Gramsci makes the point that modern capitalism (or perhaps all industrialization) increases the desire for substance use or sexual release to the extent that the human mind and body become constrained throughout large portions of daily life. Although hard to prove empirically, this association makes historical sense, in that industrial society does appear to generate a sense of deprivation, dullness, and barrenness that often leads people to seek compensation through the obsessive pursuit of pleasure.

Gramsci's notion that large elements of the old working class would be thrown out of the workforce ("the weak and non-conforming into the limbo of the lumpen classes") parallels Foucault's idea about moralization as a political strategy to divide the "solid workers" from the unruly ones. But it suggests another dynamic as well: Having divided the workforce in this way (i.e., on the basis of morality), the process becomes symbolic and self-fulfilling; that is, although the promiscuous worker may be as productive as the monogamous one, the ideological belief that the former is less productive rewards sexual conformity and punishes deviation. Hence, over time, the elites and employing classes come to *associate* productivity with clean living. (In a similar fashion, discrimination against fat people historically occurred because they were believed to be unable to control themselves.)

4. *There is a historical paradox in the fact that the consumptive needs generated by capitalism require businesses to sell more goods. Advertising, through which pleasure is constantly associated with products, may itself lead to intemperance. However, critics on both the Left and the Right have, in my judgment, somewhat overrated this factor, which may well be a time-limited phenomenon.*

Although much of Gramsci's analysis was prescient, his view of capitalism may have underemphasized the need to sell products (which could arise only after the initial stage of accumulation had occurred) compared with the need for labor productivity. Beginning in the post–World War II period of prosperity, but becoming particularly prominent in recent decades, a successful mass marketing of all sorts of goods to the public has occurred along with the constant promotion of pleasure. Leftist as well as rightist critics have suggested that much intemperance can be located not only in the marketing of specific potentially unhealthy products (cigarettes, alcohol, pornography) but also in the association of sexuality with other consumer goods (cars, perfumes, clothes, music, etc.). The consumer, then, is led not only to smoke and drink but to develop an insatiable need to buy the latest products, to garner the rewards of attractiveness and sexuality promised explicitly or implicitly by ads. In an addictive way, the consumer wants more and more.[59]

As I will discuss in Chapters 5 and 6, this development was undoubtedly *one* cause in the growth of middle-class intemperance in the twentieth century, democratizing habits such as alcohol consumption and cigarette smoking, which previously had been more limited to certain ethnic, class, and regional strata. Television and cinema probably helped spread the sexual revolution of the 1960s and 1970s as well. Nevertheless, I suggest that such a strong accent on capitalism's role in promoting intemperance is exaggerated. First, it relies on a passive "judgmental dupe" view of the consumer as being easily manipulated, while failing to account for the high levels of intemperance in countries (such as socialist ones) that lack such advertising. And, second, critics of media intemperance have overestimated the advertisers' need for appeals to excess. True, advertisers promise pleasure. But they have also been quick to adopt their sales pitches to, say, healthy foods that "lead to a long life" and are low in fat; they have eliminated references to cigarettes and hints of drugs from commercials; and, for the most part, they have even provided a more measured and "politically correct" personification of gender roles in ads. True, some companies continue to promote products that are not healthy, but they are arguably in the minority. Temperance products are, in fact, "hot": Stocks in companies that provide alcohol and drug treatment, in the diet and fitness industries, and in firms marketing the many products claiming to help prevent crime (such as security systems) are all excellent investments. As the New Temperance presses wayward advertisers and media moguls back into the more culturally conservative aspects of modern capitalism, the critique of advertising as a main source of intemperance is partly vitiated.

5. *Historically, some claims about "risk" (whether technological, environmental, political, or economic) are potentially antithetical or challenging to power holders; in contrast, a sociology of risk that focuses on personal taboos located in individual behavior is not a political challenge but, rather, can easily be managed by elites.*

Not only do modern elites often preach the desirability of temperant behavior, but political and civic leaders as well as professional experts usually stress the risk of immoral or unhealthy behavior. Although these leaders rarely accent the risks of war, nuclear disaster, or daily employment, they continually emphasize statistics on drug use, alcohol consumption, teen pregnancy, and high-fat diets.

Douglas and Wildasky attempt to account for the differential assessment of risk in various societies from an anthropological perspective. They begin with the assumption that risk is cultural, arguing that "each social arrangement elevates some risks to a high peak and depresses others below sight." Thus, for example, some African tribes are calm in the face of deadly tropical diseases but view events that have moral or supernatural connotations as major risks. (Examples of the latter include barrenness in women and lightning strikes.)[60] Douglas and Wildasky further argue that all risks are moral and political, not independent of blame and explanation. Primary among cross-cultural fears, they say, is "pollution" or defilement—that is, a contagious, harmful state caused by outside, mysterious forces that "represent a moral defect usually [caused] by the dangerous impurity attributed to moral transgressions of one kind or another."[61] From this viewpoint, certain behaviors, such as those relating to sexual taboos, have always been a key pollution fear. When a disaster of some kind struck tribal peoples—famine, flood, poor harvest—it was usually social deviants or those in low castes who were blamed for the pollution because they had supposedly defiled the group in some way.

Like Foucault, Douglas and Wildasky link the concepts of pollution and power: "Pollution ideas are an instrument of control. When the central establishment is strong, it holds a monopoly of explaining the natural order. Its explanations of misfortune make social outcasts carry the stigma of vice and disease. From the point of view of the central political establishment, the socially inferior are morally and physically contaminating, to be segregated and formally confined."[62]

In a similar vein, Douglas and Wildasky saw in the United States during the 1960s and 1970s the rise of a new kind of risk assessment emerging from the "sectarians" (rather than from central authorities or capitalists). These sectarians were the intellectuals and new professionals who perceived risk in technology, environmental crises, and many other features of the modern society that had previously been taken for granted. Despite the authors' prejudice against this new view of risk, their analysis can be helpful in comparing the differing politics of risk. Many of the environmental and consumer movements of the 1960s and 1970s challenged industrialists and state power, and demanded more accountability and regulation. In contrast, Douglas and Wildasky themselves note that the "defenders of industry in the 1970s constantly pointed out that much ill health [is] life style related."[63]

This conflict is key, I believe. Risk assessments that challenge technological, economic, political, and environmental systems also challenge those in power, primarily the corporate and political sectors. From Ralph Nader's campaigns for auto safety to demonstrations against nuclear power plants, there was a time not so long ago when it looked like the "margins" of society (to use Douglas and Wildasky's term) might alter the shape of the debate about risk, and attach the charge of "defilement" and pollution to the corporate giants and governmental leaders in America.

It is thus not simply insurance liability and health-care costs that have led the corporate sector to promote "healthy lifestyles" and to fight smoking, high-fat diets, and drugs (though these factors have certainly played a role); also implicated has been a reconstruction of risk that is politically efficient for the return of corporate domination of American life after the turbulent 1960s and 1970s. "Lifestyle" illnesses, which began to be trumpeted by government, medicine, and business in the 1970s, cast the moral blame back at the *individual*—the smoker, the drinker, the overeater—rather than attributing the potential defilement to corporate greed, government inefficiency, or the failure of our culture to satisfy human needs. Further, most constructions of personal risk center on social outcast groups; examples include the drugs of the ghetto, the smoking of the lower classes, and the diseases attributed to sexual or social deviants.

To reassert this older construction of risk (in the polluting behaviors of individuals), capitalists had to co-opt aspects of movements that Douglas and Wildasky saw as more radical, such as environmentalism. For example, the current fashion among corporate officials is to accept some blame for isolated sectors of the economy (such as tobacco companies) for their role in creating ill health, thus to some degree incorporating an earlier "marginal" criticism. Most of the effects of the social movements of the 1960s and 1970s, the challenges to risk that Douglas and Wildasky so feared, have been absorbed by symbolic acts such as the "color me green" message in corporate commercials. The more dominant construction of risk is now that in which individual behavior is faulted.

The Tendency Toward a Populist Temperance

The origins of temperance in bourgeois ideology and as a power strategy do not contradict the popularity of temperance movements among sectors of the public at certain historical points. At first glance, this observation may seem paradoxical; after all, we are all supposed to be unable to resist the joys of ice cream, intoxicating spirits, or untamed sexuality. But what we often lose sight of is the fact that people also *enjoy* the ability to righteously resist and refrain from sin and vice. Having sex or eating ice cream may give pleasure, but it is also true in America that abstinence or control over behavior can be fun. The successful dieter or ex-smoker feels a sense of control and mastery, perhaps even moral superiority over obese people or smokers. People enjoy campaigns for safe sex and AIDS activism, and adults and children seem to like the camaraderie in DARE (Drug Abuse Resistance Education) programs. Many people spend countless hours doing nonpaid labor for these causes in their communities. Commitment and solidarity certainly emerge from these social movements, and aspects of religious revivalism can be found in much of modern American life, from self-help groups to "Take Back the Night" rallies.

Moreover, as we shall explore further in Chapter 6, the political realm seems uniquely situated for discourse about control over behavior rather than discourse about pleasure. Pleasure is considered frivolous and nonpolitical; even when it is acknowledged or supported, the public sphere is not usually believed to be the place to make known one's desires for sex, food, or intoxication. In contrast, the state has long had an acknowledged role (across the political spectrum) as the protector of public safety. For political leaders, temperance wars, like foreign wars, are mobilizations that can serve as strategies to excite the masses of people and, for this reason, enjoy continued use.

Temperance movements generally take the form either of voluntary purification rituals or coercive moral-indignation movements. That is, either they aim at improving the *self* or perhaps those nearest the self, or they seek enforcement of temperant norms over rule violators through the power of either group pressure or state action.

1. *Many temperance movements are modern secular forms of confession and purification rituals in which individuals overcome various personal problems through collective acts of redemption based on their admission of sin (alcoholism, overeating, smoking, taking drugs, etc.). Such strategies also provide respectability and integration for individuals and groups that might otherwise be charged with defilement.*

It may seem odd that Americans, in large numbers, are confessing in self-help groups, in magazine and news articles, and on television talk shows to a wide variety of sins and transgressions (drug use, eating disorders, sexual deviancy, "dysfunctional" families, etc.). But the current period differs from the past only in the *secularization* of such rituals. The power of confession as a bond of solidarity and redemption was first developed by Christianity and has had a place in America since its earliest days. Social control in Puritanical New England, for example, was primarily tied not to punishment but to religious confession and penance. For example, as D'Emilio and Freedman note with respect to New England towns, the fornicator or adulterer, though *theoretically* punishable by hanging, most often "had to publicly repent, . . . to stand in front of the congregation, confess, and publicly weep." Only those who failed to confess were excommunicated or further punished.[64] Of course, we do not know how people actually felt during these confessions; but the norm violators were presumably reintegrated into the community and, having admitted to the violations in question, experienced some degree of relief while strengthening community cohesion.

The earliest American temperance movements (in the 1820s–1840s) coincided with the "Second Great Awakening" of Protestant revivalism in America, and the later surge coincided with the new Social Gospel in Protestant revivalism.[65] Yet the weakness of these movements throughout the nineteenth and early twentieth centuries hinged on their religious association with Protestantism (thus partly explaining why most Catholics and Jews opposed the temperance movements). What eventually occurred in America was the diffusion of a power strategy (in Foucaldian terms) from religious ritual to secular movement. One direct link is the initially small group named Alcoholics Anonymous, or AA (which was founded in 1935 and affiliated with the Protestant Oxford Group). AA pioneered a secular form of confession and purification ritual that has evidently worked for millions of people in numerous self-help groups; it also spawned the "12-step" model, which is popular enough to be considered a social movement.

AA and other forms of ritual confession function as power strategies in two ways. First, there is the power that the collective model brings to bear on the actual behavior of many group members (in terms of social control over drinking or other problems). Second, ritual purification models offer a redemptive quality that reintegrates the person into respectable society. To become a "recovering" drinker is to acquire a new status that can exert a powerful claim on others, a claim to time and prestige and trust that the norm violator might previously have lacked. The new status is respectable not only because the person has overcome a problem behavior but also because, prior to recovery, the class and social status of the person may have limited the claim that he or she could place on others. Regardless of whether groups like AA actually lead to upward social mobility, they do provide the trappings of respectability to some who may not have been capable of such claims in the past.[66]

As with any power strategy, however, the distinction between voluntary confessions and coerced ones lessens, as Foucault notes, because power strategies diffuse themselves throughout society. Beginning as a purely voluntary model, AA and other 12-step programs have increasingly been appropriated by the state as a strategy of coercion: The drunk driver now gets released *if* he or she agrees to attend AA meetings, the alleged child abuser is *required* to attend a therapy group, and the teenager found with drugs in his or her locker is given the "choice" between suspension and counseling. The state has found that this strategy of "voluntary compliance" (if the "deviant" truly "accepts treatment" and repents) is superior in many ways to pure punishment.

The secularization and popularity of confession and ritual purification in the post-1960s period may represent a generational and social class response to the "60s" political and cultural unrest in which baby boomers (in particular) have come to repent for the excesses of youth, whether sexual, consumptive, or political. As the model diffused throughout society, it became available to a variety of age and class groups that could then attempt to gain power and respectability (although the poor and people of color are still least entranced with it).

2. *A more coercive form of temperance attempts to demand of others some behavioral change or to exclude others on the basis of their behavior. As a "movement of indignation" it carries forward both an evangelical tradition and a populist attack on elites. Accusations of sin are also a power strategy that often derives from victimhood. By focusing on others' sins, victims derive power that they might lack in the absence of such claims.*

Temperance movements have historically aroused moral indignation, attempts at conversion, and coercive measures. Whereas voluntary temperance movements can be seen as purification rituals, conversion movements reflect evangelical roots. In fact, the movements discussed in Chapter 2 paralleled the "new social gospel" aimed at "purifying" secular American society and moving it to moral perfectionism. Evangelical approaches seek to give the uninitiated the word of God, and to teach them ways of purifying themselves and correcting their behavior. Yet individuals' failure to accept the "light" may also bring calls for coercive action. In today's society, many movements still follow religious leaders who advocate behavior change (witness the tremendous success of Christian fundamentalists in organizing since the 1970s). Other behavioral change movements have become more secular, led by claimsmakers from politics (anti-drug and anti-crime movements), from health and medicine (anti-smoking and anti-teen pregnancy campaigns), and from social service organizations (campaigns against child abuse, rape, and domestic violence).

The interesting thing about the coercive power strategies of today's anti-drug, anti-smoking, and anti-crime initiatives is their ability to elide power relationships by appearing to be anti-elitist and democratic. They accomplish this in two ways. First, they utilize the link between moral coercion and the historic role of the crowd in promoting social control. In eighteenth- and nineteenth-century England, for example, the crowd was frequently aroused to violence by such issues as prostitution, homosexuality, and child sexual abuse.[67] American history has also been fraught with reports of crowd hysteria, from the witch trials of Massachusetts to lynchings in the South "justified" by charges of rape of white women made against black men. The crowd often demanded that elites or political leaders change their own behavior or enforce their own laws. Such indignation calls to mind the frequent exposures of moral impropriety among political leaders and cultural heroes today. To oppose the sexual behavior of the English Tory leaders (as in the Profumo scandal) or the American Gary Harts, Clarence Thomases, or Robert Packwoods seems anti-elitist, going well with our tendency to doubt the morality and truthfulness of leaders. Of course, such moral arousal does not change much about the system itself, and it is arguably a mere social safety valve for the masses. Moreover, populist indignation obscures the extent to which the day-to-day social control apparatus of the state actually forces norms upon the poor or outcast rather than upon elites. Many nineteenth-century English workers, for example, supported the Social Purity Movement because they associated sexual deviance (particularly homosexuality, pedophilia, and white slavery) with the aristocracy.[68] Not surprisingly, however, the Social Purity Movement did not really harm many members of the elite, but it did lead to numerous arrests among the poor.[69]

Second, coercive temperance movements serve as an elision of power in that they turn otherwise privileged people into *victims*, who then have a claim on the use of moral indignation. Concerns about secondary smoke, for example, are uncommon among the poor but prevalent in the middle class. Ordinarily a business executive or lawyer would not be seen as a *victim*, but moral indignation against the cigarette smoker can suddenly bring legitimacy to the demand that a blue-collar worker or poor person stop smoking near the lawyer or executive. "Political correctness" among liberal middle- and upper-class individuals arguably serves a similar function. In a recent essay Marilyne Robinson recounts an incident in which the old "snobbery," as she terms it, was converted into political zealotry:

> Recently I saw a woman correct a man in public—an older man whom she did not know well—for a remark of his she chose to interpret as ethnocentric. What he said could easily have been defended, but he accepted the rebuke and was saddened and embarrassed. This was not a scene from some guerrilla war against unenlightened thinking. The woman had simply made a demonstration of the fact that her education was more recent, more fashionable and more extensive than his, with the implication, which he seemed to accept, that right thinking was a property or attainment of hers in a way it never could be of his. To be able to defend magnanimity while asserting class advantage! And with an audience already entirely persuaded of the evils of ethnocentricity, therefore more than ready to admire.[70]

Some middle-class social movements assert claims to victimization, relying on the possibility of personal rebuke or assault. That is, the possibility of being a crime victim, an aggrieved listener, or a potentially harassed person is made central to life's condition. Katie Roiphe's critique of the "sexual correctness" movement on campus (concerning date rape and speech codes, for example) questions how "voiceless" the "Princeton women, future lawyers, newspaper reporters, investment bankers . . . are, by most people's definitions," when they claim the mantle of oppression.[71] I do not defend or deny harassment or hateful speech when I note that liberal political correctness movements have often elided social power in presenting affluent women (or racial minorities) as poweless. Many Americans, particularly working class and poor people, have some trouble visualizing either Clarence Thomas or Anita Hill, Hillary Clinton or Leona Helmsley, as victims. Yet the combined logic of moral indignation and political correctness movements presents being a woman or an African-American (or other group protected by moral indignation movements) as a potential victim.

As I discuss further in Chapter 6, victim status as a result of behavioral pollution (cigarette smoke, drug use, pornographic images, fear of crime and violence) made for a particularly good fit between the growing New Right movement of the 1970s and the increasingly less radical remnants of the 1960s social movements. By the 1980s, a consensus on behavioral control around a host of issues seemed to have crossed political lines. I do not deny that violent or hurtful actions are committed by individuals when I suggest that the *symbolic* value of the issues of indignation (such as smoking or date rape) are ones that easily evoke an American consensus across political lines. It is far more difficult to move Americans with cries for economic or social justice than to oppose the sins of pollution and defilement.

Historical Change

Temperance, as both an elite strategy and a popular movement, is subject to rapid rises and falls, owing not only to popular resistance but also to external historic events (e.g., economic change, wars, and social movements). In the remainder of this book I aim to explain why personal behavior wars have been waged so often since the 1970s in the United States.

Despite its achievement of "common sense" logic, temperance has at times aroused widespread resistance. It has been subject to rapid declines in popularity due both to its own instability and to historic events that have dramatically altered social norms. In the twentieth century, the most obvious generalized defeats of moralization were the collapse of Prohibition in the early 1930s and the widespread cultural changes in the 1960s and 1970s that temporarily overturned sexual mores and other patterns of behavior.

Even when dominant, Temperance or Puritanism has entailed resistance, particularly from the lower classes, from the young, and from racial and ethnic groups holding low status. Prohibition, for example, was always unpopular among these groups. The "60s" cultural rebellion certainly involved young people and, despite its perceived association with the middle class, was arguably stimulated by aspects of both black culture and Southern lower-class culture (consider the origins of rock 'n' roll, for example). Today, despite the dominance of the "just say no" wars against drugs, cigarettes, premarital sex, and other social behaviors, professionals constantly complain that too many young people (particularly poor and racial minority children) are doing drugs, drinking, smoking, having promiscuous and early sex, or behaving aggressively.

Partly at issue here is the general culture's ambivalence about pleasure. Temperant messages about sex, food, drugs, and so on compete with aspects of the capitalist cultural market that sell commodities, so that even if industries with an obvious interest in sin (pornography) or substances (tobacco companies) were banned, the general cultural message of consumption wouldn't change. That is, rich food, legal prescription drugs, and goods advertised with sexy models would continue to send the message of "just say yes." But while many leftist activists and liberal professionals emphasize capitalism's call to overconsume or consume obsessively, they underrate the symbolic nature of intemperant behavior as a form of resistance. That is, they tend to treat young working-class or poor kids as if they are "judgmental dupes" who don't "know" they shouldn't smoke, drink, or have premarital sex, when in fact it may be their very "knowing" of authority's position that contributes to their resistant behaviors.

As I will discuss in Chapters 4–6, social class and status are intertwined with personal behavior. Young people, poor people, and racial and ethnic outgroups are overrepresented among those charged with misbehavior. I suggest that this fact is intimately bound to stigmatization of behavior. The stigma of cigarette smoking and drug use is directly tied to the prevalence of these behaviors in the middle class. When the middle class changes its norms, it does so in part to disassociate itself from classes below it, as a status marker.

Less clear historically is the degree to which popular resistance should be credited with major changes as opposed to certain external "signal" events. For example, many historians see the Great Depression as the final downfall of Prohibition. Moreover, they usually view wartime as periods of looser moral strictures. The social control needed for mobilization seems to require governments to loosen up on the more minor restrictions of life, such that cigarettes and alcohol are made available to soldiers along with some time for blowing off steam. Even when governments seek behavioral control—as occurred during both world wars when they battled the spread of venereal disease—wars lead to changes in sexual norms. Not only do men separated from partners frequently stray, but cultural historians have seen even more profound changes in women's lives during wartime, when they left isolated households and came to work in war industries within the cities, often breaking with conservative social norms as they did so.[72] Obviously the cultural changes of the 1960s are hard to imagine without the political unrest sparked by the civil rights movement and the anti-war movement. Nor can the symbolic meanings of one period be detached from the next; the cultural movements of the 1960s and 1970s were, at one level, a reaction to the middle-class conformity and Puritanism of the 1950s. And as I argue in Chapter 6, the New Temperance of the 1980s and 1990s has been shaped by negative attitudes toward the mores of the dreaded "60s."

It is the difficult task of this book to develop the links between events at the macro level (involving the economy and the political system) and the changed meaning of many forms of personal behavior in the last two decades. I suggest that elite political strategies were at work; one example is the strategy of moralization that emerged during the Nixon administration as a way of developing a Republican Party majority. These strategies were paralleled by corporate America's drive to compete by getting "lean and mean." Yet the strategies could not have succeeded from the mid-1970s on without popular support. Their appeal was largely based on the intense economic and social anxieties besetting the American middle and working classes, and on the convergence of political symbols between aspects of the "Middle America" strategy and the rightward direction of other social movements that had occurred by the late 1970s. Both the increased attention to personal behavior and the prescriptions regarding misbehavior can be seen as a drive to repudiate the aspects of "60s"-style movements that were culturally threatening.

four

"The Slippery Slope," or Scaring Them Straight

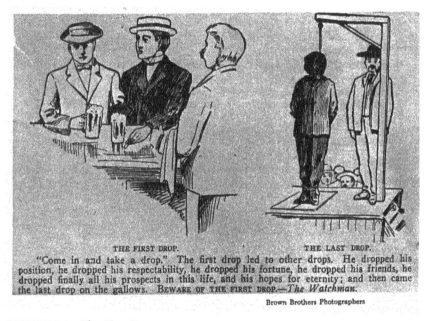

THE FIRST DROP. THE LAST DROP.
"Come in and take a drop." The first drop led to other drops. He dropped his position, he dropped his respectability, he dropped his fortune, he dropped his friends, he dropped finally all his prospects in this life, and his hopes for eternity; and then came the last drop on the gallows. BEWARE OF THE FIRST DROP.—*The Watchman*.

Brown Brothers Photographers

FIGURE 4.1 The First Drop
Source: A. Sinclair, *Prohibition: The Era of Excess* (Boston: Little, Brown, 1962), p. 17.

"Dry Logic"

Lest the older Temperance Movement notion (see Figure 4.1) of health education seem dated, our popular "zero-tolerance" campaigns against

drugs today should remind us that the "slippery slope" of "dry logic"—
one drink (or toke) leads to perdition—is still very much alive. As Stanton
Peele comments: "Ads on drug and alcohol abuse combine the direst
possible predictions: if you think you have a drinking problem—*you do;* a
drinking problem can only grow *worse;* a drinking alcoholic ends up either dead or institutionalized."[1] In a similar vein, Lester Grinspool, a Harvard psychiatrist, remarks that "Partnership [for a Drug-Free America]
ads about marijuana scare the hell out of a high school senior. This student then goes off to college, where his roommate smokes marijuana
with no apparent adverse effects and without going on to shoot heroin.
He begins to wonder if he's been lied to, and winds up trying pot for himself. He lives!"[2]

The "slippery slope" characterizes much of our thinking about sexuality as well. Commenting on the "Scared Chaste" trend in sex education,
Leslie Kantor of the Sex Information and Education Council points out:

> Students are told that teens develop a sort of "tolerance" to sexual activity
> and that it takes increasing amounts of stimulation to achieve the same
> arousal over time. Sexual activity, in the exercise entitled "The Woo Scale,"
> is likened to the analogy of a frog which is boiled to death without knowing
> it when the heat is turned up gradually. Another idea promoted by this con-
> cept is that any sexual activity will eventually progress to intercourse.
> . . . The message [is] that sexual activity always gets beyond the control of
> the people involved.[3]

Nor are "slippery slope" scare tactics that catastrophize behavior limited to conservatives or religious traditionalists. Overwrought and
calamitous attacks on cigarettes as a "poison" and "mass killer," warnings against fatty foods as "America's deadliest missiles" or as "a heart attack on a plate," and descriptions of sexuality in the era of AIDS as "a
deadly miasma of contagion and death" are characteristic of much liberal discourse.[4] A Martian visiting America might well be terrified into
believing that everyone who ever smoked a cigarette, ate a hamburger,
or had sex without a condom would inevitably become a victim of disease and early death. Most likely he would turn his spaceship around
and return home.

That many young Americans resist such totalistic rhetoric surprises
moralists and health advocates, but their resistance is not surprising. In
this chapter I examine how the "scare them straight" strategy of temperance contradicts much of what we know about drugs, fatty foods, cigarettes, teen pregnancy, multiple-partner sex, and other risks. Though
purporting to be scientific, the power strategies of temperance actually
de-contextualize and misstate risk by taking real-life events out of daily

context. Such magnification of risk supports the argument made in the previous chapter that our society privileges almost all claims about intemperate behavior for reasons of power and morality.

"Dry Logic" As De-Contextual

The key ontological device that effectively catastrophizes much of human life is the de-contextualization of isolated behaviors (smoking a cigarette, eating a hamburger) from both the *person, including his or her characteristics* (age, social class, gender, race, ethnicity, culture, etc.), and *his or her situation* (being lonely, angry, sad, aggressive, euphoric, etc.). "Dry logic" (or the general logic of temperance) seems natural to us only because Western science and knowledge routinely de-contextualizes behavior (including life's most intimate activities such as giving birth and even dying) from personal, social, and cultural experience and presents them to us as large-scale data sets (such as statistical correlations). Such data become reified as they are conveyed to us daily through media sound bites. These reifications succeed because they build on a historical tradition of other "knowledge" such as Western religious lore and its pronouncements against sin. The reinforcement of our cultural/moralist/traditionalist agenda with secular rationalistic support by professionals results in a kind of consensual fog, leading to anger against inanimate objects (e.g., a drug or a cigarette) or certain behaviors (a teenager having sex). This anger, in turn, buttresses any claim, no matter how exaggerated, made about some behaviors.

A power *language* about stigmatized behaviors then develops. We may describe people arrested for involvement with drugs in a ghetto neighborhood as "drug-crazed," but we do not speak of corporate chiefs as "profit-crazed." We hear about "smoking-related deaths" but not about "overwork-related deaths" or "sports-related accidental deaths." We discuss "sexually transmitted" diseases (STDs), but we don't often refer to illnesses as "airborne transmitted," "water transmitted," or "food transmitted."

The marriage of morality and public health allows for several types of risk distortion. First, claims about health, even with little empirical support, gain immediate media attention and evoke public anxiety. Yet when new or contradictory information calls into question such fears, these latter reports rarely have as much impact. For example, serious questions have recently been raised as to whether the health advisories about fat and cholesterol have validity for the general public. Even experts who support arguments about the dangers of fat admit that diet alone may account for a mere few months' difference in life expectancy on average.[5]

Second, the language of popular health risk reifies and de-contextualizes life by universalizing a problem. Even where health data are fairly convincing *on average,* we cannot conclude that a particular behavior has the same impact on all people, because none of us is the "average" person. Once *actual people* are brought back into the picture, even the most hearty moralist must pause a little before passing judgment. For example, since the factor of *social class* interacts with all behavior, it complicates all arguments about addiction, risk, and health. In other words, much of what is described as the ill effects of unhealthy or risky behavior may well be caused or affected by social class. For example, the vast majority of homeless people I met in my study of street people in a city in northeastern America used substances (illicit drugs, alcohol, and cigarettes) to get them through each day—to dull hunger, pain, and suffering, and to pass the time more quickly in the face of great difficulties.[6]

In the context of *homelessness* or, for that matter, of *life in the inner-city,* where there are few or no opportunities, it is hard to imagine how drugs or cigarette smoke could be *the major danger* to health. "Dry logic" assumes a middle-class perspective. For a ghetto resident or a street person with a low life expectancy, the advice to avoid drugs, fatty foods, or cigarette smoking is actually questionable because the real threats to longevity are poverty, violence, and general hardship. If anything, substances arguably buffer and mitigate these circumstances.

"Dry logic" also assumes a middle-aged perspective. Media and professional spokespersons continually tell youngsters that "Abstinence Makes the Heart Grow Fonder" and that "Virginity Is Not a Dirty Word."[7] But the youthful recipients of these dicta not only face a very different context for sexual activity but may even doubt whether they'll ever make it to middle age or have a long-term partner. Perhaps even more interesting is the response of elderly people to all these health admonitions. Are we to label as "promiscuous" the many elderly people who are having out-of-wedlock sex in retirement centers, condominiums, and nursing homes? Should they be worried about practicing safe sex or "reducing their number of partners"? Are they at serious risk of disease? Since temperant pronouncements are aimed at the young, similar questions can be asked about the relevance of most behavioral admonitions. Is it really critical for those who are sixty-five or seventy to worry about smoking cigarettes or cigars or eating fatty foods? Nor is it clear that habits that start when one is young are irrevocable; witness the millions of people who have given up cigarette smoking, alcohol, or drug use, usually by middle age. In short, many health and lifestyle pronouncements depend on a host of demographic factors and genetic and environmental vulnerabilities that are obscured by simple "just say no" advice.

Finally, both "dry logic" and traditionalist morality de-contextualize risk by taking the person *out of his or her situation* in life. For example, the smoking of tobacco is weighed against a clean bill of health (presumably exhibited by the nonsmoker). But the rabid attacks on smoking obscure the fact that many people smoke to cope with anxiety and depression (including serious psychiatric illness), which, if they were *not* using tobacco, might lead to even more severe psychiatric illness, to violence, or to substitute substances such as illicit drugs, alcohol, or prescription pharmaceuticals. Prozac, for instance, seems to help people cope with smoking cessation, a finding that suggests some underlying common chemical factors may be involved in substance use. But public health pronouncements accept no "reason" for smoking as worthy, not for those who are terminally ill or severely upset, not for those who are grief-stricken, not for the prisoner or the unemployed, the angry discharged worker or the bored homeless person. It is not only that the low life expectancy of the poor makes health pronouncements less relevant. Indeed, just as cigarettes are given to soldiers to steel their courage and bind their anxiety, people living on the streets and in violent areas of the inner-city may rely on substances while trying to survive in what is essentially a war zone.

"Dry logic" depends on a model of life that assumes no anxiety, boredom, worry, pain, sorrow, suffering, joy, or excitement. Rather, it regards life as a purely rationalistic utilitarian venture. Although this view may correspond with stereotypical Western rationalism, we must question whether it describes anyone's reality. Most certainly it does not for those people who are neither middle aged nor middle class.[8]

Tactics of De-Contextualization

In the remainder of this chapter I provide examples of how the universalistic judgments of "dry logic" de-contextualize behavior in order to magnify risk. Although I have chosen to focus on four issues—illicit drugs, cigarette smoking, teen pregnancy, and multiple-partner sex, I believe the same tactics are true of other presentations of risk such as warnings against high-fat diets, TV violence, and pornography. These tactics fall into the following categories:

1. *Blurring Boundaries:* "Dry logic" catastrophizes phenomena by blurring the boundaries of a problem. It categorizes human behavior in such a way as to cluster together all activities with a vague connection and suggest only the *worst* possible consequences (disease, death, etc.) while at the same time including in the problem statement all possible related forms of behavior in

order to *maximize* its extent. For example, the "war on drugs" sustains its drama through images of "crazed" crack addicts who are violent and engage in bizarre behavior, but the majority of drug users who go to work, sleep, eat, and live altogether less dramatic existences are rarely presented to us. Further, the drug war is directed against *all* those who use *any* drug (including that one toke of marijuana), since the drug war seems to require a typification of very large numbers of miscreants.

2. *Imposing a False Concreteness:* Diseases, deaths, casualties, and sorrows are presented to us with the inference that *only* the personal misbehavior of the user has caused the problem—that the result cannot be etiologically random, multicausal, or complex. For example, heart-attack and lung-cancer deaths are classified as "smoking deaths" if there is any indication that the deceased once smoked tobacco. Not only are these deaths thereby dissociated from other causes (occupational, environmental, accidental), but one must wonder how death came to be so categorized in the first place. Is there any one "reason" that each of us dies? And at what age is a death "premature"?

3. *Falling into Ecological Fallacies:* "Dry logic" makes much of *associations*, which themselves may be by-products of other factors. That is, warnings about health, safety, or well-being may mistake certain behavioral or demographic characteristics for social class or cultural differences. Or admonitions may call forth alarm about a behavior when that behavior has little intrinsically to do with the danger at hand. Two illustrations follow. First, the impact of social class on life chances is usually ignored. For example, inner-city teen parents are held responsible for their own and their children's downward mobility; but we are led to believe that, absent this transgression (i.e., pregnancy), both mothers and children would be affluent and healthy. Second, the identification of HIV and other sexually transmitted diseases with moral characteristics such as "promiscuity" is based on the historical tradition of finding moral wrong in disease sufferers (e.g., lepers). Humans, regardless of their behavior, have always been awed by dread disease, believing that someone is to blame for the disease. But truly we are all "innocent" victims. Even critics of the dominant brand of morality-based AIDS and STD education tend to substitute their own brand of behavioral admonitions, which associate new categories of sexual "deviancy" with disease.

4. *Creating Judgmental Dupes:* "Dry logic" treats the individual as weak, passive, and dumb. Substances, sexual desire, and food, even television and rock music, are portrayed as all-powerful so that the

subject is seen as becoming "addicted" without knowing it or as being simply incapable of managing life's risks. Of course, once the subject is troubled by addictions or unhappiness, only professional help can assist him or her in leading a healthy life. For example, "dry logic" presents humans, particularly youth and poor people, as cognitively impaired. The apparent assumption: If only they had paid attention to the proper lecture, adolescents would not have sex or become pregnant. Overeaters would diet, cigarette smokers would quit, and television watchers would read more books.

Blurring Boundaries:
Drugs, Fear, and Trembling

Just as the Temperance Movement of the nineteenth and early twentieth centuries associated *any* and *all* drinking with inebriation, the poorhouse, prison, and the gallows, the late-twentieth-century discourse on "drugs" presents a picture of an unmitigated evil. Conservative leaders, of course, are most clear in their insistence that drugs are the work of the devil. Consider this statement by William Bennett, former U.S. "drug czar": "Drugs are the great lie, the Great Deceiver. . . . I've seen what I can only describe as the face of evil. Those people who doubt there is evil in the world need to travel a few weeks with me on the drug circuit."[9]

Although media and professional imagery is less religious in tone, it is no less totalistic. In the 1980s and 1990s, it was routine to see drugs touted as the root of evils ranging from low economic productivity to urban decline and educational failure:

> Illegal drugs have become so pervasive in the U.S. workplace that they are used in almost every industry. . . . Their presence on the job is sapping the energy, honesty, and reliability of the American labor force even as competition from foreign companies is growing even tougher. . . . [T]he costs of drug abuse on the job are staggering.[10]

> Drug abuse is at the heart of what many people think has gone wrong with America . . . urban blight, the destruction of families, the failure of schools, the loss of economic productivity. . . . The horrors of drug abuse have become depressingly familiar: crack-addicted mothers abandoning their babies; young children dealing drugs instead of going to school.[11]

One technique for sustaining the mythology of a "drug crisis" in this country is to lump together *all* substances conceivably called "drugs," whatever their uses, whether casual or long term, and then to impute only the most *serious effects* to each of them. Since studies indicate that most drugs are not harmful to most users (as we will see later), drug warriors must manipulate the boundaries not only between specific drugs (tobacco, alcohol, marijuana, cocaine, heroin, etc.) and their respective dangers but also between people who are dependent on drugs but lead regularized lives and those whose lives are harmed by drug use (or who may harm others because of it).

Only by including *all* "drugs" of all types can the "crisis" atmosphere be maintained. For example, Robert DuPont, former director of the National Institute on Drug Abuse, asserts that more people are drug dependent today than in the past: "Never before in world history," he says, "has so large a segment of a national population used such a large number of dependence-producing drugs."[12] But this statement is probably untrue. We know that Andean peasants chewed coca leaves centuries ago, that Asian natives smoked opium from poppies for thousands of years, and that indigenous peoples throughout the Americas have always used drugs. Between 1865 and 1900 in the United States, at least 3 percent of the population was addicted to morphine,[13] and cocaine—a key ingredient in patent medicines and soft drinks—was routinely imbibed by millions of Americans. In fact, in 1885 Parke, Davis & Company introduced coca-leaf cigars and cigarettes whose active ingredient, cocaine alkaloid, when smoked, provided the same sensation as smoking crack.[14]

Yet no morphine or cocaine "crisis" occurred during this earlier period. Morphine and cocaine were legal then, and their users were chiefly middle- and upper-class citizens. The stigmatization of a drug thus appears to follow its association with ethnic minorities (as in the case of Chinese users of opium) and the lower classes (as when cocaine and heroin were used by poor people and racial minorities and subsequently made illegal).

The lumping together of all illicit drugs, from cocaine and heroin to marijuana and hallucinogens, both exaggerates the number of "drug users" and allows the imputation of the most dangerous usage to the least harmful use. For example, despite the large publicity given to drugs like "crack," most violations of drug laws are for marijuana usage.[15] Further, claims are no longer limited to illegal drugs. Beginning in the 1970s, activists and some health professionals began accusing the government of hypocrisy for not including harmful legal substances—alcohol and tobacco—in its warnings about drugs. The paradoxical result was that rather than liberalize punishment for use of illegal drugs (as advocated by most liberals), the New Temperance has added campaigns against legal "drugs" to its broad claims about drug use. Not to be stopped there, many advocates suggest that large numbers of people are hooked on prescription drugs, and some anti-drug activists believe that Americans should be free of *all* substances—including even caffeine.

Such conceptual broadness leads to hyperbole. For example, in 1983 then-Senator Dan Quayle made reference to "53 million illegal drug users in America," while glossing over the fact that 90 percent of this total principally used marijuana.[16] Meanwhile, experts have categorized 20–25 million Americans as "alcoholics," as many as 80 million Americans as "codependents," and more than 50 million American cigarette smokers as "substance abusers."[17] Congressman Peter Stark, among others, argues that more emergency room visits and other health-care costs are related to legal prescription drug problems than to other drugs, and that millions of people are "addicted or at risk of addiction to minor tranquilizers."[18] And if these numbers are not large enough, educators and public health officials have developed the broad category of "at risk" people, particularly youngsters, so that no person need ever ingest a drug in order to become subject to anti-drug surveillance. If the wide definition of drug abuse prevention specialists is to be believed, there are probably few (if any) Americans who are neither drug users nor "at risk" of being abusers.

The blurred boundaries of the drug war also provide political leaders and the media with the flexibility to shift the focus of public attention from one drug to another, from one statistical "blip" to another, without ever having to account for what exactly happened to the last drug "emergency." For example, sociologists James Orcutt and J. Blake Turner demonstrate how, in 1986, *Newsweek* magazine (along with other major media outlets) referred to a statistically insignificant rise in reports of cocaine use among high school seniors as an "epidemic."[19] In fact, cocaine use peaked in the 1970s, *as did the use of most other drugs;* (yet this "good news" was not emphasized by *Newsweek*). When the statistics on all drug use continued to free-fall later in the 1980s and in the 1990s, *Newsweek* turned "the good news of declining prevalence estimates . . . [into] 'bad news' of a new drug crisis" by headlining an "alarming rise" in LSD use—actually just a statistically insignificant one-year jump from 4.9 percent to 5.4 percent in LSD use among high school seniors.[20] The skillful use of numbers by politicians and the media suggests that the flexibility provided by the many drugs of the "drug crisis" has been helpful in fueling the anti-drug campaign, because otherwise "success" would have to be admitted and the "war" metaphor weakened.

Nor is there much scientific justification for lumping all illegal drugs together or for grouping all illegal drugs with legal drugs. Some may suggest that a physical addictive process supports such classifications. Although it is clear that *some* heavy users of alcohol, cocaine, or tobacco become physically addicted, there is no evidence that drugs such as marijuana, PCP, solvents, and hallucinogens are physically habit-forming. Moreover, a majority of users of all substances seem not to become physically addicted to the drug. Is it the change in consciousness that critics of drug use object to? Some have argued that what we really fear about drugs is their ability to alter our sense of logical time and space. Yet even if this argument works for hallucinogens or cocaine, it certainly does not support lumping tobacco with "drugs," nor does it explain why we don't campaign against psychoactive medications, including the new "wonder" anti-depressants, given that these medications are claimed to produce personality changes.[21]

"Drugs," then, may have nothing in common with one another, except for our beliefs about them—what Gerald Klerman calls Americans' "pharmacological Calvinism." Klerman points out that in America, if "a drug makes you feel good, it must be morally bad," since it violates theological views of salvation through "good works" rather than through pleasure. Hence, he argues, many Americans resent even the use of medications to treat depressed or otherwise troubled psychiatric patients rather than having them "work out" their problems through therapy or some other form of secular redemption.[22] Substances that originate in the natural world (marijuana, tobacco, opium poppies) could be grouped with foods, such as coffee and chocolate (both of which are extracted from plants). And chemically produced substances such as LSD and Prozac, as well as over-the-counter medications, could be grouped together. It is only our political, strategic construction that unites these very diverse "drugs."

We Americans subscribe not only to "pharmacological Calvinism" but also to what C. Reinarman and his associates have called a "pharmoeconomic determinism."[23] That is, we seem to believe, or have been led to believe, that *all* users of substances turn into "addicts." Casual use is often equated with long-term use, whereas addiction is assumed to occur despite evidence that even the most demonized drugs are not physically habit forming. Typically, the most fear-inducing headlines are about *one-time* or *experimental* use of a substance. Printed within the borders of an exaggerated spiked graph in the *Newsweek* issue critiqued by Orcutt and Turner is the phrase "A Coke Plague," followed by a caption reading "Within the next 2 years, more than 20 percent of high-school seniors may have tried cocaine." In addition to the altered graph drawn by *Newsweek*'s artists, the failure of the predicted number to reach 20 percent, and the vague reference to students who "*may* have tried cocaine," note that the big scare here is about kids having *ever tried* cocaine, as if experimental use could constitute an "epidemic."[24]

Like opium in the late nineteenth century, heroin in the 1920s, marijuana in the 1930s, and hallucinogens in the 1960s, "crack" cocaine is now the demon drug. Described as "instantaneously addictive" and as the "most addictive drug on earth," it has been made to shoulder the blame for almost all the social problems of the 1980s and 1990s. According to M. Falco: "Crack makes users aggressive, violent, and paranoid.

. . . As one young mother who had sold her baby for crack explained, 'This drug will make you do anything. There's nowhere it won't make you go.'"[25] Yet evidence suggests that most crack users *do not become addicted* to the substance. Recent studies in support of this conclusion report the following findings:

- "Approximately one in six users of crack becomes addicted."[26]
- "The data from surveys, self-selected user studies, and clinical studies . . . provide no evidence that cocaine in any form has a high addictive liability or that an epidemic is under way."[27]
- "Despite the attribution of many deaths to cocaine and crack, a careful study of the official government reports and available medical literature found that none of these deaths [in the first half of 1986] could be confirmed."[28]
- "[R]esearchers found no evidence that crack is instantly addictive or violence inducing, and that the percentage of users who get in trouble with crack is about the same as with other drugs."[29]
- "One could also conclude that only 3% of those between 18 and 25 who ever tried the drug [cocaine] fell into this category [problem users] and that only 10% of those who used cocaine monthly were at risk."[30]
- "The estimate that there are now one million cocaine addicts suggests a one in thirty chance of addiction to cocaine through experimentation."[31]

Whether there is statistical validity in speaking of only 3 percent of users, or whether 20 percent of users become "addicted," is really unknowable—in part because we are dealing with a stigmatized and illegal activity. The key point is that most experts *do* agree that, despite the hype, there is nothing "instantly addictive" about drugs, including the much-vilified "crack."

Even among the smaller number of people who do become "drug dependent," the catastrophization of drug use is unsupported. Most "addicts" are not violent, nor do they behave bizarrely. Studies suggest that most addicts are able to go about their daily activities. For instance, Reinarman and his associates found that despite all the media claims of lost productivity, many heavy cocaine users reported that drug use enhanced their work—for instance, by allowing them increased productivity and tolerance for overtime.[32] Faupel and Klockars's study of heroin addicts found that "most worked in conventional jobs, . . . performed household and child rearing tasks, [and engaged in] leisure activities and . . . altogether unremarkable" behavior.[33] And a study by Phillipe Bourgeois found that crack users managed their schedules so as to be more active users on weekends but less active users during the work week.[34]

None of the foregoing is meant to minimize the harm that *some* drugs do to *some* people. Overall, however, the boundary blurring and catastrophization of drug use obscures more than it elucidates. Peele argues persuasively that it is "pseudo-science" to see murder, theft, or prostitution as resulting from drugs: "It is a mark of naiveté—not science—to mistake the *behavior* of some drug users with the pharmacological effects of the drug."[35] He also notes that drugs' behavioral effects are *linked to cultural interpretation*. In many societies, drug use is not considered to be causative of violence or aberrant behavior. But the cultural interpretation in the United States has always been that violence, aggression, hostility, and so forth can be explained by the use of, say, alcohol. Provocatively, Peele implies that it is the cultural legitimacy of the claim of drunkenness (i.e., the claim made by wife beaters and other assailants that they behaved as they did "because they were drunk"), not the chemical properties of drugs like alcohol, that accounts for America's use of the addiction paradigm as an explanation for all sorts of behavior.[36]

Finally, the totalization of drug use as evil obscures the *situations* in which people seem to *need* drugs. J. Henningfield of the National Institute on Drug Abuse (NIDA) notes that 90 percent of the Vietnam veterans hooked on heroin were able to "kick their habits once free of the stress of battle."[37] This finding supports the argument that drugs (including cigarettes) often serve to ease stress and fear in dangerous circumstances and, hence, are frequently used by socially victimized groups as well as by young people.

False Concreteness: The "Smoking Death"

If government officials, health-care professionals, and other opinion makers have exaggerated the effects of drug use to "scare them straight," conjuring up visions of violence, criminality, and addiction, the "Cigarette-Speak" of the late twentieth century minces even fewer words. Very simply, cigarettes are equated with death:

Cigarette exports are disease, disability, and death.[38]

No drug can rival [the cigarette]; . . . the carnage perpetuated by its purveyors; the merciless irreversibility of destiny once the victim contracts lung cancer or emphysema. . . . [D]*eath is in a cigarette.*[39]

I do not suggest that the repeated ingestion of tobacco through smoking, with particles and chemicals passing through one's throat and lungs, is healthy. The ill effects of this substance were known soon after Sir Walter Raleigh introduced it to England and, as cultural critic Richard

Klein notes, "probably by every schoolboy when they take up smoking to begin with." What constitutes *ideology* in contemporary anti-smoking messages is, first, the insistence (against the weight of evidence) that cigarettes are always a *killer* rather than a *potential* health risk (a distinction that is more than just rhetorical, akin to charging that all gun owners are murderers or that all those with swords will cut themselves) and, second, the refusal to acknowledge tobacco's positive benefits for the many people whose lives are actually enhanced by it (and who, if denied access to tobacco, might replace it with substances or activities posing equal or greater risks to their health).

The health case against smoking should be stated as follows: "Continuous, long-term, heavy cigarette smoking over many years *may* lead to illness and disease." Yet in the 1970s, particularly under the leadership of then HEW Secretary Joseph Califano, in the anti-smoking campaign, health warnings became marked by a statistical head count of "excess deaths" (and, more recently, "smoking deaths") attributed annually to the smoking of cigarettes. We are constantly bombarded with concrete figures—314,000 deaths in 1980, 395,000 in 1985, 500,000 in 1992, and so forth (interestingly, the numbers have risen as smoking has declined)—leading us to conclude that between a fifth and a quarter of all deaths are "caused by smoking."[40] These figures are then broken down state by state, county by county, and so on, such that deaths (at least from smoking) appear to be a known quantity, all tied up in a scientific package.

But such statistics, as Peter Berger puts it, are "a fanciful combination of epidemiology and econometrics,"[41] reflecting both hyperbole and the use of science as a political weapon. First, since we all die eventually, the meaning of "excess deaths" is unclear. Even in an age when (paradoxically for temperance warriors) life-expectancy figures have been rising rapidly, such figures are only averages. That is, none of us is guaranteed a long life simply because some people are living until the age of ninety or ninety-five. If we use such a standard, men, for example, could make a political issue out of their significantly lower life expectancy than women. In any case, regardless of whether we smoke, drink alcohol, or eat right, some of us will die "young" for a variety of genetic, chance, or environmental reasons that we may or may not be able to influence.

The anti-smoking war applies to diseases whose causes are multiple or unknown a quantitative concreteness that would be appropriate to events like wars (which, after all, permit actual death counts). The modern industrial era has seen a dramatic increase in diseases having less identifiable causes such as cancer, heart disease, and stroke. Death certificates, of course, do not list "smoking" as a cause of death, as even the most virulent opponent of smoking knows, because they cannot link individual cases of heart disease or cancer to smoking. Yet, by attributing a percentage of cancer, heart disease, emphysema, and even fire-related deaths to smoking (55,000 or one in seven "smoking deaths" in 1985 were the result of fire), government and health officials are making a political statement. Thus, for instance, a percentage of, say, the lung-cancer deaths of blue-collar workers who smoked (even for only a part of their lives) are declared to be "smoking deaths" even when the work settings, living conditions, environment, genetic makeup, and other circumstances of these workers may have contributed to or been the "cause" of their deaths. A percentage of the deaths of people who are poor and exposed to the elements, inadequate nutrition, and harsh environmental and living conditions are also termed "smoking deaths." The classification of many fire deaths as "smoking related" is a political choice as well, placing responsibility on *smokers and fire victims* rather than on, say, landlords who have neglected to install smoke detectors or sprinklers or have failed to attend to electrical systems. In the social construction of risk and death, someone now must take the blame in our society: But who is it to be? Consider the smoker who is distracted while driving because she is looking for a match, but whose car has poor brakes because of a defect in the vehicle: Should we exonerate the auto company and blame the smoker for her death in the event of a fatal crash? The New Temperance statistically blames the smoker in this instance. It seems to do so whenever a possible link between tobacco and misfortune can be found.

Opposition to cigarette smoking is politically easy and noncontroversial. As Douglas and Wildasky noted in relation to the politics of risk, leaders can deflect attention from their own inability to satisfy significant economic and social human needs by developing consensual sources of pollution and defilement.[42] Republican administrations engage in this practice:

In 1990, [Secretary of Heath and Human Services] Sullivan is making an impassioned anti-tobacco speech, while his boss [George Bush] is trading off environmental reforms in Congress to weaken the law. . . . In an administration that has been faulted for not vigorously addressing problems of the inner-city, its minister of health and well being seeks to mobilize indignation of the citizenry against the traditional luxury of the poor [the cigarette].[43]

Democratic leaders do so, too:

Congressman Waxmen [former Congressional Committee chair and a fervent anti-smoker] may not be able to do much else about the living conditions of people in his fine city of Los Angeles . . . and Robert Reich [Clinton's secretary of labor] may be at a loss on how to improve the labor conditions of the American worker, but when it comes to smoking, Mr. Waxmen is as righteous as he is polite, and Mr. Reich is as principled as he is tall."[44]

The false concreteness of the cigarette = death equation contains several logical fallacies. First, as with any product or substance, the danger of tobacco is subject to amount, just as many products that are "good" for you can kill you if overconsumed. In the case of cigarette smoking, it is assumed that the poor addict is trapped from the time of his first puff until his death from a two- or three-pack-a-day habit. But this assumption is not valid. Many people smoke an occasional cigarette, many people smoke for a while and quit, and many people smoke only when under personal strain or in times of crisis.[45] Even the many people who do "quit" smoking, it turns out, have occasional cigarettes without necessarily returning to the habit. Further, given that more than 40 million Americans have quit smoking since the Surgeon General's report of 1964 (most without any professional assistance), the inevitability of addiction is questionable. Nor is there evidence that smoking a small number of cigarettes over many years is harmful. Scientists do not even agree as to how many cigarettes "cause" cancer or heart disease or combine with other predispositions to possibly lead to these illnesses.

A second problem with the catastrophizing of tobacco smoking is that even if the government's statistical extrapolations are accurate, most smokers will not die from "smoking-related" causes. Some figures indicate that two-thirds of those who smoke a pack of cigarettes or more a day do not die of smoking-related deaths (as broadly defined as they are).[46] W. Kip Viscusi, an expert on risk assessment, argues that most Americans have an *exaggerated sense of risk* of getting lung cancer from smoking because of all the publicity.[47] The lung-cancer numbers themselves are not dramatic. Ginzel, the anti-smoking physician quoted previously, says that smoking risks *may* combine to create as much as a one-in-ten chance of getting lung cancer; others cite a 5 percent figure.[48] From an epidemiological perspective, these are indeed high numbers, but they are still a far cry from the way cigarette smoking has been presented to the public, as if every person who ever lights up is killing him- or herself!

Another troubling aspect of "Cigarette-Speak" is that it confuses correlations based on *smokers* with data about *smoking*. Since people are not lab rats, experiments isolating our various behaviors from real life cannot be conducted. The only way scientists can study the impact of tobacco on humans is to use correlational data that compare cigarette smokers with nonsmokers. This is done through a computer program called Smoking Attributable Morbidity, Mortality, and Economic Cost (SAMMEC), which is based on assumptions, called smoking attributable fractions (SAFs), about each putative smoking-related disease.[49] Several issues need to be addressed here, however. First, we do not know how people are classified, since smoking status is fluid (some people are occasional smokers, some are continuous long-term heavy smokers, some are episodic heavy smokers, etc.). Second, since the causes of illnesses such as cancer or heart disease are not certain, nor are these illnesses necessarily unicausal, we cannot reliably attribute any disease or death to cigarette smoking. Government officials often cite an American Cancer Society study of its membership that compares smokers with nonsmokers, but this study, in addition to being dated, is based "primarily on affluent, white, Protestant, urban, married, college graduates not exposed to hazardous environments or occupations" and thus, on the whole, is "not a valid cross-section of Americans."[50]

Even a more randomized study population of *smokers* and *nonsmokers* would entail a large number of confounding problems. For example, smokers compared to nonsmokers are (1) largely from lower- and working-class backgrounds, and more likely to be downwardly mobile than upwardly mobile; (2) less educated on average; (3) more prone to depression and other psychological illnesses; (4) more likely to be divorced; (5) more likely to engage in other risky behaviors such as drinking, taking drugs, being "impulsive," and being sexually active; and (6) less likely to wear seat belts.[51]

Such confounding factors undermine the reliability of all statistical projections, including the smoking attributable fractions noted previously. Recall that some statistics suggest that 10 percent of smokers but only 4 percent of nonsmokers die of lung cancer: We do not know how much of this difference is due to *smoking itself* and how much is due to the poor nutrition, toxic environments, inadequate health care, and severe stress besetting poor and working-class smokers. Nor do we know how much of the difference is due to the presence of hazardous products and materials at the workplace, how much is due to differential genetic predispositions, and how much is due to some combination of these various behaviors and environmental factors.

Our medical knowledge of heart ailments is probably even less clear than our understanding of cancer etiology. We don't know if a heart attack in a sixty-five-year-old man who drank alcohol heavily and was depressed (but also a smoker) can be attributed to smoking. It is possible that a "cause" of the heart attack was stress or a combination of genetic predisposition, heavy alcohol use, and depression, or a combination of still other factors. Conversely, it is possible that smoking *helped* this man cope with the stress of unemployment or divorce. Whatever the proposed explanation, the problem with these statistics is that they confuse correlations about *people* with correlations about *behaviors*.

The temperance paradigm assumes that the substance or the behavior is *causative* of a problem—for example, that the "rotten weed" causes death or illness. But if it is true that many smokers are depressed or psychologically troubled or undergoing stress because of their class status or personal problems (such as divorce), we must also acknowledge that, for many people, cigarette smoking mediates these stressors. This issue has come to the fore in studies of schizophrenic and depressed psychiatric patients who are disproportionately heavy cigarette smokers. Experts have found that smoking improves patients' "underlying psychopathology by enhancing concentration and redirecting discomfort," reducing anxiety, diminishing the side effects of medication, and easing Parkinsonian symptoms.[52] These experts have speculated that cigarettes bring about an anti-depressant effect "through the modulation of dopamine."[53] If it is true, then, that people are "self-medicating" with tobacco (there is extensive evidence suggesting that illicit drugs and alcohol are used in this way as well), what happens if they are prevented from smoking? "It all depends," says Alexander Glassman, a Columbia University psychiatrist. Glassman goes on to explain "that people who are 'psychiatric casualties' of smoking cessation could, at the very worst, commit suicide, while in the throes of a depressive episode."[54]

That substance substitution is a common way to deal with underlying problems is also supported by evidence from studies demonstrating that many addicted people obtain abstinence only by "adapting other compulsions" (e.g., they stop drinking and start smoking or vice versa),[55] as well as from studies of psychopharmacologists who have successfully treated people addicted to illicit drugs by switching them to psychoactive drugs.[56] Even for those who are not depressed or troubled, cigarette smoking has notable benefits as well as negative health effects: It is frequently used to facilitate weight loss, to aid concentration, and to reduce anxiety and aggression levels. Cigarette smokers have also been shown in studies to be more sociable, to have better memories, and to be more efficient at many tasks than their nonsmoking counterparts.[57]

Rather than insisting on abstinence from illicit drugs and cigarettes, government officials *could* develop a strategy of harm reduction that would allow people to benefit from nicotine, cocaine, heroin, and other drugs, while minimizing the ill effects. One observer, Ronald Siegal, makes exactly this point. Calling all drug use our "fourth drive" (after hunger, thirst, and sex) and describing it as a natural part of our biology, he asks: If "former drug czar William J. Bennett can switch from smoking tobacco to chewing nicotine gum, why can't crack users chew a cocaine gum that has already been tested on animals and found to be relatively safe?"[58] Unfortunately, however, the politics of both smoking and drugs, along with the moralism of "dry logic," precludes the implementation of harm-reduction strategies (such as efforts to make tobacco use safer) that would probably also be more efficient than continually "scaring the bejeezus out of people" with cigarette = death warnings.[59]

Reversing Cause and Effect?
The Teen Pregnancy "Problem"

At first glance, it is difficult to understand why teen pregnancy became such a concern in the 1980s and 1990s. Teen pregnancy actually peaked in 1957, and the birthrate of teens has been declining ever since.[60] Moreover, the health risks that very young girls experience in pregnancy cannot be the key reason for concern since only 2 percent of teen mothers are under fifteen years of age, whereas more than two-thirds of "teen" parents are eighteen or nineteen—not a notably young age to give birth from a biological, historical, or cross-cultural perspective.[61] The idea of "children having children" does not really jibe with the facts either, inasmuch as only one in seventeen pregnancies actually involves partners still in school; indeed, the girl is often of post–high school age, and the male partner, even more often, is in his twenties.[62]

Teen pregnancy is not so much a health hazard, then, as an issue embodying the following potent symbols: (1) youthful female sexuality, (2) nonmarital sex (a major change in the last thirty years has been the rise in "out-of-wedlock" births), and (3) race, class, and poverty. In this sense, teen pregnancy is the modern equivalent of the "fallen woman" of the nineteenth century, a symbol that motivated the Social Purity Movement (see Chapter 2). As before, female sexuality is held to be running rampant, destroying the lives of families and children, leading to poverty, ruin, and immorality. Neither conservative nor liberal observers hide their moralistic perspective on this matter:

> It was once called 'bastardy.' Then 'illegitimacy.' Then 'out-of-wedlock birth.' And, now frequently, wholly sanitized, 'non-marital birth.' Whatever, it's called, it's at the root of our social problems. . . . [M]ore voluntary out-of-wedlock birth yields more dependency, more welfare, less parental control, which yields more crime, drugs, unemployment and poor education.[63]

> Girls termed 'sexually active'—that has replaced the word 'promiscuity.' . . . [N]o one seems to mention morality as playing a part in the subject of sex. Is all the Judeo-Christian tradition wrong? Are we to believe that something so sacred can be looked upon as [a] purely physical thing?[64]

> I don't like to put this in moral terms, but I do believe that having a child out of wedlock is just wrong.[65]

> It is parents and reasonable adults who are left to literally counter the culture, to do combat with the incessant messages of mainstream films, music, t.v.— the conglomerate known as Hollywood—as best we can. . . . It will take all their [media] creativity to make a successful pitch against *irresponsible* sex and teen pregnancy.[66]

Although the impetus of the teen pregnancy "crisis" is morality, particularly the increase in out-of-wedlock births and female-headed households since the sexual revolution of the 1960s, political leaders, media
spokespeople, and social science researchers are generally more comfortable arguing against teen sexuality and pregnancy from a "scientis-
tic" perspective, again using correlational data. Teen parenting is presented as a form of economic and social suicide. Like cigarettes and
drugs, teen pregnancy is statistically correlated with everything negative, from poverty and child abuse to drugs and gang membership:

> Teen mothers, 70% of whom are unmarried, are likely to end up impover-
> ished and dependent, ill-equipped for motherhood. These teens are likely
> to rear children who themselves end up trapped in the same mire of depen-
> dency.[67]

> Children of children are less healthy and more abused than children of
> older parents. They're more likely to drop out of school, become drug ad-
> dicts and move into a life of crime. Two-thirds of teenage mothers aren't
> married. Most gang members are the children of single mothers.[68]

Like drugs and cigarettes, the issue of teen pregnancy has been cata-
strophized and misrepresented as a "crisis." But there is reason to believe that many of the economic and social sequelae of teen pregnancy
reflect a reversal of cause and effect. That is, since young parenthood is a
class- and race-linked phenomenon, the correlations that social scientists draw between teen pregnancy and a host of social problems may be
fallacies, as they are likely to be artifacts of low social-class membership,
poverty, and racial differences.

To accurately compare the impacts of any behaviors or actions, one
requires comparable human actors and environments. But the average
age at which sexual activity is initiated, as well as the age of parenting,
has historically varied by social class and racial and ethnic background.
As several studies (including cross-national ones) have shown, the lower
the social class, the higher the rates of childbearing at younger ages.[69]
This fact has been publicly bemoaned in Western society since Thomas
Malthus's writings in the eighteenth century. Constance Nathanson
points out that prior to about two decades ago, the association among
"illegitimacy" (as it was then called), poverty, and the need for birth control was openly made. Even in the 1960s, the issue was not so much
"teen pregnancy" as one involving the birthrate of poor people and
blacks. In her provocative book *Dangerous Passage*, Nathanson argues
that, ironically, it was the very success of the civil rights movement and
some liberal legislation (such as family planning) that created a false
universalism about teen pregnancy: "[T]he emergence in the 1970s of

'adolescent pregnancy' as the dominant metaphor for women's problematic sexual behavior was due in part to the success of birth control
advocates in blurring the distinction between the 'acceptable' sexual behavior of young women who were white and middle class and the 'unacceptable' sexual behavior of women who were poor and Black."[70]

Because birth control, sexuality, and pregnancy were now to be discussed as mainstream, "universal" issues (those ugly words *race* and *class*
were not to be mentioned), the fact that a vast majority of teen mothers
have always been poor is obscured and, strangely, presented as an *effect*
of teen pregnancy. A typical example of such a contradiction can be
found in the rhetoric of Marian Wright Edelman, president of the Children's Defense Fund. Edelman asserts that teen pregnancy is "epidemic
among all races and classes of American youth." But only paragraphs
later, she notes that *actually* most teen parents are poor, and that black
teens are five times more likely than white teens to give birth. She also
cites a study comparing single parents under twenty-five with young
women under twenty-five who have no children and finds (remarkably!)
that the single parents are *nine* times more likely to be poor.[71]

There are two important fallacies in implying a cause/effect relationship here. First, no one would dispute that, given American social policy
(i.e., the lack of family allowances and universal child-care policies as
well as the low wages for women and for young workers generally), a
woman raising a child alone *will be poorer* than a single woman. Yet it is
not clear that this observation makes a case against *teen* parenting. A
thirty- or forty-year-old single mother also will be poorer than her child-
less counterparts. So it is not a function of teen pregnancy or childrearing
itself that an eighteen- to twenty-one-year-old woman with a high school
degree or less is likely to make only the minimum wage or a bit better to
support herself and her child(ren). Second, most affluent girls and young
women either avoid pregnancy altogether or avoid childbirth (through
abortion) or childrearing (through adoption). Once these women are excluded from our analysis, we have a primarily affluent sample being
compared with a significantly poorer one. It should come as no surprise
that, as time goes by, these middle- to upper-class women will increase
their income even further relative to that of poor young women. Thus the
data reveal nothing more than that the child of, say, a manual laborer will
on average make less money than the child of a physician!

The Alan Guttmacher Institute estimates that 85 percent of children
born to teens are born to low-income women.[72] Moreover, early childbearing has long been a cultural norm in the African-American community.[73] Hence it appears that the statistics about teen pregnancy show only
that the rate of *most* social problems are correlated with social class. In
other words, crime, drug addiction, health problems, psychiatric depression, child abuse, and school dropout rates correlate with social class, not

with the *act* of teen childrearing. The earlier quote suggesting that "[m]ost gang members are the children of single mothers"[74] reflects, in all probability, a class correlation to the effect that all poor children are statistically more likely to become gang members than middle-class kids (whether they have two parents or a mother- or father-headed family, and whether parented by a teen or not). Similarly, Cynthia Tucker's notion that the "children [of teen parents] . . . end up trapped in the same mire of dependency"[75] can also be applied (if one wishes to subscribe to this culture-of-poverty language) to the children of any family in poor areas. Their statistical chance of escaping poverty (in this era, at least) *is* quite small.

As with many other social problems, the teen pregnancy "crisis" is in part a product of the middle class's view of the poor. As Charlotte Low Allen has put it:

> Adolescent childbearing is a phenomenon of the poor and the very poor, of young women who grow up early and look their best when they are young, have little interest in higher education, do not see themselves as having careers and live in communities where health starts deteriorating quickly. The "opportunity costs"—foregone earnings potential—of having a child early are close to nil, and life expectancy is short . . . [Quoting researcher Arline Geronomius:] People project on poor teenagers what a middle-class teenager would want—going to the senior prom, getting into the best colleges.[76]

In other words, it makes more sense for a young middle-class girl to stay in school and prepare for college or other career opportunities than to leave school to have a child.[77] By way of contrast, researchers are finding that for young girls or women of the lower classes, the following advantages may accrue to early childbearing and childrearing as a strategy:

- The lowest earning capacities for young women exist when they are young, allowing intensive parenting demands to coincide with a period when they have fewest employment opportunities. Moreover, since young poor women are usually isolated in low-paying jobs, they lose little earning capacity by taking time off for childbirth and childrearing.
- In many poor communities, particularly those in which African-Americans predominate, the greatest access to free child-care assistance from relatives occurs when the mothers are young. Since young mothers still sometimes live in extended families with high mortality rates and poor health, their access to networks of kin support and child care is likely to be better when younger.
- From the physiological standpoint of both mother and child, early motherhood—assuming that adequate prenatal care is available—may be healthier than delaying parenting because many medical

problems associated with poverty (e.g., lead levels in blood, stress-related diseases) increase with age. Age also increases the chances that violence, suicide, substance use, AIDS, tuberculosis, or other diseases will affect the mother, the male partner, or the child.

- The whole specter of life in poverty areas reinforces the strategy of young parenting both as a survival tactic and as a way of securing some pleasure from life. In an environment where there are few marriageable males, where divorce and separation rates are high, unemployment is rampant, and life expectancy is low, the "need" to wait is often not clear to poor kids.[78]

I am not arguing that there are no tragedies in low-income communities where babies are abandoned, abused, or neglected because they were unwanted or because environmental or psychological pressures simply became too great on families, including young mothers. But many of the reasons for these problems should be blamed on our social policies and social structure. As argued earlier with respect to drugs and cigarettes, it is easier to place the blame with personal behavior than with structural or cultural issues. As one critic suggests: "The poor got poorer in the Reagan-Bush years. Yet it was far more convenient for Washington policy-makers to blame young women for the teen pregnancy rate than to blame themselves. Teenage girls make perfect scapegoats. For one thing, they have no political clout."[79]

As with other temperance issues, the consensus among liberals, conservatives, media spokespersons, and social scientists on the problem statement (i.e., that teen pregnancy causes almost every conceivable problem, particularly high school dropout rates, poverty, and welfare dependency) obscures contradictory evidence that teen parenting may *not* lead to significant long-term problems. For example, one of the few longitudinal studies comparing poor black women over time *with one another* (rather than with middle-class women) has shown that there were few negative long-term consequences associated with early childbirth. Although some women were indeed disadvantaged in the short term, a substantial majority of teen moms in the study cohort finished high school and found regular employment. Moreover, those who had been on welfare were usually off within a period of years.[80] A series of studies by Arline Geronomius and her colleagues at the University of Michigan has focused on similar within-cohort groups, comparing, for example, teen mothers with their sisters who delayed childrearing. These studies, too, found only minimal differences in economic standing, education, and careers between those who had children early and those who waited.[81] Another study has found that, contrary to the conventional wisdom that one of the key risks of teen pregnancy is dropping out of school, most teens who got pregnant were already out of school. In short, the greatest predictor of completing high school successfully was not whether a teen got pregnant but, rather, whether she was having trouble in school or preparing to drop out of school to begin with.[82]

Discussing teen pregnancy as "a trip down the economic scale to poverty"[83] or in terms of "resist[ing] the messages of rap lyrics and the bullying of peers . . . to prepare for success rather than settle for pregnancy and poverty"[84] must seem like "jive" to poor kids whose chances of "success" are not very high, whether they are mothers or not. Given the long history of teen sexuality and young childbearing in many poor communities, and the lack of "moral panic" in some European nations where teen sexuality is high,[85] I suggest that the moralistic "just say no" campaigns in America echo a version of the old Social Purity campaigns, which also targeted the immorality of the poor as a key cause of social ills.

Science as Morality: The "Multiple-Partner" Risk

Young people must be told the truth—that the best way to avoid AIDS is to refrain from sexual activity until as adults they are ready to establish a mutually faithful monogamous relationship.

—Joint statement by Secretary of Education William Bennett
and Surgeon General Everett Koop[86]

It is well known that a mutually faithful relationship is the best means of preventing [HIV] infection.

—Surgeon General Antonia C. Novello[87]

In the late 1970s and early 1980s, the AIDS epidemic reinforced an already growing movement in the middle class to call a halt to the sexual revolution of the 1960s and 1970s. As Susan Sontag has written:

There is a broad tendency in our culture, an end-of-an-era feeling that AIDS is reinforcing, an exhaustion for many, of purely secular ideals— ideals that seemed to encourage libertinism or at least not provide any coherent inhibition against them—in which the response to AIDS finds its place . . . part of a larger grateful return to what is perceived as "conventions" . . . the reduction of the imperative of promiscuity in the middle class, a growth of an ideal of monogamy, of a prudent sexual life.[88]

Indeed, science-as-ideology came to structure the AIDS crisis; but it could do so only because of public receptiveness. Before AIDS, the media were already trumpeting the end of the sexual revolution, which they would repeatedly do each year since 1980. In that year *Time* magazine, for example, declared that herpes had ended the sexual revolution in an article entitled "The New Sexual Leprosy": "The herpes counter-revolution may be ushering in a reluctant, grudging chastity back into fashion. . . . [P]erhaps not so unhappily, it may be a prime mover in helping to bring to a close an era of mindless promiscuity. . . . [F]or all the distress it has brought the troublesome little bug may inadvertently be ushering in a period in which sex is linked more firmly to commitment and trust."[89]

What is most interesting is the easy support for such moralism in the scientific community as well as among political leaders. Throughout the AIDS crisis, a wide variety of temperance warriors have called for abstinence and monogamy, as well as sometimes repressive actions, against gays, bisexuals, and prostitutes under the rubric of public health supported by the new "AIDS-Speak" concerning sex with "multiple partners."

As noted in Chapters 2 and 3, science's claim to a neutral stance separate from the dominant morality has always been weak. It was only a while ago that experts began moving away from warnings about the harms of masturbation. And for hundreds of years many physicians and experts promoted an intentional policy of "syphilophobia" in which (despite the availability of treatment and prophylactics) moralism was dispensed along with medicine. Theodor Rosenberg, a medical historian writing ten years before the appearance of AIDS, captured the dominant medical paradigm for diseases associated with sex: "In the absence of anything better to tell the young, we keep repeating the old injunction against sex before or outside marriage. . . . [I]t is a legacy tracing back to Puritanism, to a doctrine of original sin and beyond. The idea has no roots in hygiene or in a knowledge of human behavior. Maybe for that reason . . . the prohibition has never worked."[90]

Historians of disease point out that it is humans' need to construct meaning that transforms microbes into moral or political entities. As human evolutionary progress halted the earlier ability of microbes to spread from person to person far more easily than today, sexual contact gradually developed as one of very few ways for certain diseases to spread. (Rosenberg notes, for example, that humans' adoption of clothing, settlement in less dense quarters, and improved sanitation cut off some routes of disease transmission.) Although the decreased ability of disease to spread is hardly consolation for those who have suffered the impacts of sexually transmitted diseases, it is important to keep in mind that there is nothing *intrinsic* about sex acts (or types of sex acts or numbers of sex acts) that breeds disease. Nor, overall, does sexual contact appear to be the *major* route for most bacterial or viral disease transmission. Even though more germs are spread by the simple act of breathing, our lack of interest in this mundane activity of life prevents us from developing a category of "breath-transmitted diseases."

Despite this rather dry scientific reality, plagues and epidemics generate panic, causing us to develop a moral accounting for them that is almost always a variant on the biblical "Sodom and Gomorrah" theme. Humans often attribute disease not to microbes but to their own actions: blasphemy, religious disbelief (recall that Jews and Moslems were blamed for the Black Death), witchery and sorcery, the immigration of despised foreigners, or the habits of the poor. As Douglas and Wildavsky note, the modern construction of causation is not terribly different from that of tribal people, since we impute immorality as the cause of suffering and usually try to erect boundaries between the "normal" and the "defiled."[91] As Simon Watney puts it, the general public "is held to be threatened by the 'leakage' of HIV infection, which, like nuclear fallout, is widely and erroneously perceived to be everywhere about us."[92]

In the nineteenth century, cholera was blamed on drunkenness and tuberculosis was connected to the "miasma" of the poor (the air was said to be contaminated in the impoverished areas of the cities). More recently, AIDS has been blamed on sinners of one sort or another (the sexually immoral, drug users, etc.) or on racial and ethnic minorities (Haitians, the urban underclass, etc.). Sociologists Stephen Murray and Kenneth Payne argue that if HIV/AIDS had not initially been discovered in the gay ghettos of the major cities, the "promiscuity paradigm," as they call it, would not have taken hold as an explanation for AIDS. They further argue that because AIDS was "forced into the theoretical procrustean bed of an acute, discrete sexually transmitted disease rather than being conceived as a chronic illness (triggered by introduction of a virus into the bloodstream)," many victims of the disease (from African heterosexuals to American IV drug users and hemophiliacs) were ignored at first. Moreover, the etiology of the disease was obscured for several years as victims of the "gay disease" (as it was initially labeled) were interrogated about the "*number of partners* they had."[93]

As the Center for Disease Control (CDC) developed its obsession with numbers of sex partners, the explanation that promiscuity caused AIDS took hold. For unknown reasons, the first cases of AIDS reported to the CDC occurred among people with large numbers of sex partners. Randy Shilts, author of *And the Band Played On*, played a major role himself in the myth making about the early course of the epidemic by promoting the story of air steward Gaetan Dugas ("Patient Zero") who, like "Typhoid Mary," supposedly spread the disease among his hundreds of partners. We still don't know (and perhaps will never know) whether the early cases of HIV transmission in the United States were chance occurrences (since the disease has had a different epidemiological vector elsewhere) or had something to do with the "lifestyle" or health status of those infected early on. Yet even if we could agree on some definition of "promiscuity," and on the contention that many of the early cases of HIV/AIDS occurred among gay men with many sexual partners, the sexual promiscuity link to AIDS would again be a matter of *association*, not causation.

Uncertainty did not stop political, medical, and even some gay activists (such as Shilts) from initiating a campaign against gay bathhouses as "dens of iniquity" in which the disease was supposedly being spread. In the 1980s these moralistic campaigns proceeded in cities such as San Francisco, New York, and Los Angeles, despite the lack of evidence indicating any link between the disease's spread and the bathhouses themselves. Studies have also shown little difference in sex practices between bathhouse patrons and other gays such as those in bar-going samples.[94] Repeating the path of both the Social Purity and the Social Hygiene movements, some states attempted to jail prostitutes or to force them to undergo mandatory HIV testing—once again, because of the assumption that only the vilified "Other" who was having "promiscuous" sex could be responsible for the epidemic. Counterintuitive to the "promiscuity" link is the fact that prostitutes have sometimes tested *lower* in rates of HIV-positive results than other American women. Yet occasional scare stories about their role in the epidemic continue.[95]

Interestingly, as AIDS was universalized and made to seem a threat to everyone (particularly after Rock Hudson's revelation in 1985),[96] the scrutiny of sexuality intensified rapidly, shifting from prurient interest in gay sex and prostitution to sexuality in general. According to one observer: "[O]nce doctors are convinced that a disease is transmitted [through] sexual contact, many assume that any patient with the disease must have acquired it by promiscuous sexual activity. Those affected are presumed to be guilty until they can prove their innocence."[97]

A retrospective method developed by the media and others involved a "constant surveillance" of sexuality, which seemed to impose on each HIV-infected person a moral stigma unless proven "innocent." In 1991 this obsessive scrutiny of sexuality reached perhaps its greatest height with the announcement of basketball star Magic Johnson that he had HIV. Sociologists Cheryl Cole and Harry Denny noted the moralizing that occurred in response to this event:

> [Magic] Johnson's body was placed under an immediate, *retroactive* surveillance that attempted to make visible earlier evidence of HIV. Photographers kept him under constant surveillance waiting to document the hidden sexualities and/or sexual practices as they become visible on the body. . . . [T]he popular fixation on Magic's sexual practices motivates a series of strategies meant to situate Magic and HIV outside the general public. . . . Magic's sexuality is made suspect and skepticism is invited by invoking

the authorial voice of science and the statistical-AIDS-imaginary to suggest taken-for-granted transmission patterns.[98]

I do not mean to suggest that the appearance of the AIDS epidemic should not have resulted in public health efforts to control the spread of the disease. Rather, my point is that from the early days of the epidemic, warnings to check the spread of AIDS were confused with an attribution of sexuality as the disease's "cause." Moreover, health warnings aimed at checking the spread of disease often consisted of the tactic of "scaring them straight" by repeatedly stressing *numbers* of sex partners. This strategy continued well after the low infectivity potential of the HIV virus (as discussed below) and evidence that condoms and other preventive measures (e.g., needle-exchange programs for drug users) had been fully documented.

Health warnings became so broad and, in some cases, so confusing that their intended targets could not have known what to do. First, there were slogans such as "Reduce your partners." The logic here was that the more sexual partners you had, the greater would be your statistical chance of having sex with someone who was HIV-positive. But there's a problem with this logic: What does "Reduce your partners" actually mean? If Wilt Chamberlain really did have 1,000 sexual partners, would he have increased his health benefits by reducing them in number to 995 or even 895? And what of the person who meets another partner after ending a monogamous relationship: Should that person reduce the number of his or her partners from two to one (forever) because of the threat of HIV? Further, does the proposed reduction last a month, a year, or, as some have promoted, a decade or a lifetime? A second problem is that the equation of partner reduction with monogamy meant that for most people (since few people think in terms of a lifetime of sexual plans) the ideal would be to have one relationship *at a time,* rather than one relationship over a lifetime. As Andy Humm and Frances Kunreuther have noted, many teenagers "believe that they can't 'get AIDS' from someone with whom they are in a monogamous relationship, even if they may have several monogamous relationships over a relatively short period of time. It is hard to counter these myths when the messages on t.v. and from the government reinforce the idea that monogamy, marriage and love are equated with health while 'promiscuity' and drug addiction cause AIDS."[99]

Whereas the advice to "Reduce your partners" suffered from vagueness, the next popular idea was to "Know your partner." Yet this slogan was also of little value from a practical health standpoint. As a prominent physician in the fight against AIDS put it, "This *know your partner* business makes no sense since most people with HIV don't even know they have it themselves." She further argued that, rather than assume that both partners know their HIV status and that each partner is being truthful, we should use condoms and practice safe sex.[100] Evidence suggests that many people, rather than using condoms, have turned the "Know your partner" advice into a reason to select their partners on the basis of status, class, and race. In a study of Canadian adolescents, for example, Eleanor Maticka-Tyndale found that subjects relied on their own identification of "safe partner by appearance," such that "the primary protection strategy was selecting partners who were not the 'wrong kind of person.'"[101] In an ironic twist, her study subjects were arguably safer with *strangers* because condom use was *greater* in their casual relationships than in their long-term relationships; indeed, women, in particular, felt that they couldn't question the truthfulness or infected status of their long-term male lovers.[102]

But even though activists criticize some health warnings for not going far enough ("Everyone is at risk for AIDS"), in actuality, evidence increasingly suggests that many of these catchy phrases are scare tactics. The oft-repeated "When you're having sex, you're having it with everyone they have had sex with in the last 10 years" is typical. A. Brandt comments that this "aphorism turns each sex act into promiscuity, each relationship into anonymity, and each heterosexual act into the possibility of a homosexual act."[103] Indeed, disease is a binary state: Either one has it or not, either one is unlucky enough to get it or not. On the one hand, if the partner you are with has the disease (whether you are a married monogamous heterosexual or someone who engages in sex with a variety of partners), it doesn't really matter whether he or she slept with *one person or 200 people;* either way, you are at some *risk* of infection. On the other hand, if your partner slept with 500 people but does *not* have the virus, the last ten or twenty or thirty years of his or her life makes little health difference.

We have had evidence, at least since the late 1980s, that the HIV virus is of extremely low infectivity, particularly when safe sexual practices are used (I am leaving aside here issues of drug use, blood transfusion, and other transmission routes).[104] Because the HIV virus is far less infective than other STDs during any single act of sex, and because people tend to have sexual contact within their own social networks (by class, race, locale, etc.), predictions about the AIDS epidemic were greatly overblown; in fact, the disease has not spread beyond of the "risk groups" earlier identified.[105] According to evidence summarized in the 1994 national sex study, the infectivity of the HIV virus for heterosexual vaginal intercourse has a probability of 2 out of 1,000. Thus, without condom use, the risk of transmission per encounters is as follows: For one sexual encounter, .00000; for 100 encounters, .00002; and for 1,000 encounters,

.00009. For the same encounters *assuming* condom use, the figures are
.00000, .00000, and .00002, respectively.[106] To put this in plain English,
within a random population of Americans there is an infinitesimal
chance of contacting the HIV virus. (Of course, in some areas of the
country, the chances of infection are far higher than this average.)

Another interesting fact about risk is that our chances of infection are
increased (though only mildly) by our *frequency* of sexual encounters
(even with the same partner). Yet even the most strident AIDS warriors
and moralists have not urged us to reduce the number of *sex acts*. Presumably because certain forms of sex, such as marital sex, are not to be
discouraged or made to seem fearful (even though there is some scientific justification for it), this strategy was avoided. But a woman who has
four "one-night stands" in a year may actually entail less risk than if she
were married and had an affair, and had frequent sex with both men.
The "promiscuity" argument tends to obscure this possibility. The authors of the aforementioned sex study have criticized the "promiscuity
paradigm" as follows:

> Knowing only the number of partners is not knowing very much. Whether
> partners are simultaneous or sequential, what the social networks are from
> which they are recruited, the frequency of sex, the practices engaged in, the
> protection employed—all can dramatically affect the likelihood of infec-
> tion. We suggest that . . . the nearly exclusive focus on the number of sex
> partners that is sometimes found in the public health literature provides a
> very limiting and potentially distorting lens through which to view sexual
> conduct and the risk of disease.[107]

Of course, low risk is not no risk; but if the statistics noted previously
are valid, they suggest that far more risk is involved in driving on the
highway than in having sex. The widespread acceptance of AIDS panic
and of the "promiscuity" paradigm of the 1980s and 1990s is deeply
rooted in "dry logic." I return to this issue in Chapter 6, where I discuss
how the response to the disease united various strands of American
thought across the political spectrum. Both the heavy symbolic meaning that sexuality must carry in American culture and the appeal of
apocalyptic rhetoric to Americans seem to be responsible for this coa-
lescence.

The Judgmental Dupe:
"For They Know Not What They Do"

"Dry logic" has historically relied on the presentation of miscreants as
immoral, addicted, uninformed, or misled. In other words, it has been
assumed that drinkers, smokers, drug users, or overeaters would not *ra-*

tionally choose such behavior. Hence they must be directed by bad morals, have the wrong information, or lack self-control over their impulses. Until the progress of medicalization in the twentieth century, misbehavior was mostly seen as reflecting lack of proper Christian morals. To say that this perspective is still with us today is an understatement.

Richard Nixon, late in his life, still blamed the bad morals of liberals and radicals for the drug problem: "[F]or years the elite class accepted and even celebrated 'recreational' drug use. . . . Drug users in the leadership class helped create a climate of social, cultural, and political acceptance that permitted the drug plague to take root."[108] In a similar vein, religious conservatives blame the sexual revolution and its evident fifth column, sex educators, for promiscuity, AIDS, homosexuality, and teen pregnancy. According to J. Sobran, for example, "What the sex educationists are really doing is burning the cultural bridges back to Christendom—the West's traditional ground of community and public morality. The sexual revolution is really a revolution in our conception of man, a denial of the immortality of the soul. Under color of mere instruction in sexual hygiene, a whole cosmology is being smuggled in."[109]

Conservative moralists maintain the fiction that if it were not for the evil role models of radicals, "deviants," and various leftovers from the cultural revolution of the 1960s, Americans would be living like Ozzie and Harriet did in their TV world of the 1950s. Hence, as I discuss further in Chapter 6, the Right's continued war against what it perceives to be the remnants of the dreaded "60s."

With rare exceptions, however, the professionals, media spokespersons, and social scientists who constitute a large part of the New Temperance movement, along with various other components of the movements for temperance (such as self-help groups), eschew moralism in order to adopt one of two views of judgmental dupe-ism. One popular view is the addiction/denial paradigm, which medicalizes the problem behavior. Recently, however, another view has been catching on as well as an explanation for "deviance": It relies on imputing to the mass media an all-powerful capacity to shape the behavior of its audience.

Beginning with alcoholism, then spreading to other at least arguably "physical" dependencies such as drug and cigarette habits, the addiction paradigm has expanded to the point where Americans now speak of being "addicted" to sex, to food, to work, to love relationships, to television viewing, and to a host of other behaviors for which a physical dependence constitutes at best only a metaphor. Magazines and television shows have trumpeted the addiction metaphor since the late 1970s, acknowledging "America's addiction to addictions." The addiction/disease metaphor allows professionals and self-help movements to reduce the moral stigma of miscreants, but only at the cost of their admission that they are unable to control their own lives. The victims of addiction then must turn to a professional, a self-help group, and/or a "higher power" for assistance in providing this missing control. For example, drug users, contrary to some of the evidence presented previously, are said to be "enslaved" and irrational: "Drugs abridge the freedom of the individual by enslaving him in a habit which he may no longer control."[110]

Yet, as noted, millions of people are *not* physically addicted to drugs; and of those who are, millions are able to control their habits and manage their lives. Furthermore, millions of people have quit smoking, cut back on drinking, lost weight, or gotten off drugs *on their own*, without the aid of professionals or treatment centers or self-help groups. Alcoholism expert Herbert Fingarette argues that the very success of people who quit on their own, and of groups like AA, actually disproves the disease/addiction paradigm. If a person were actually out of control of his life and his drinking, he would not be able to simply cease drinking at some point in time and accept the demands of treatment programs or self-help groups that he abstain henceforth. (Of course, this is not to say that stopping a drinking problem or other serious habit is an easy thing to do.)[111]

Closely related to the addiction paradigm, and so popular that it might be called the American word of the late twentieth century, is the catch-all term *denial*. Although it is true that people with severe problems sometimes don't see them or admit to them, the idea that each substance user or overeater has *no* awareness of his or her actions or *no* control over them is probably a cultural fiction. Moreover, the broad term *denial* removes all power and attribution of rationality from the affected person or group of persons, and places *true* awareness and rationality only with higher-power actors, usually professionals. The use of the concept of denial as a subterfuge for the repression of young people, as well as a means of generating profits for the treatment industry, has become endemic in recent years. As Stanton Peele notes, in 1985 *CBS Evening News* got a teenage girl (who had no drug problem) into a treatment center as a ruse to reveal the profit-generating nature of such facilities; "when she claimed she didn't have a drug problem, a counselor was heard saying that this is the response inmates always give . . . [it was] denial."[112]

Given that the young and poor in particular, but also most consumers, have low power relative to professionals and social institutions, how are we to judge what is an irrational "denial" of facts, and what is a realistic assessment within the context of a person's life? For example, it has become fashionable to speak of denial in reference to AIDS. Sara Nelson, echoing the phraseology of self-help books (i.e., referring to women "who love too much" and make foolish choices), worries that women are denying the reality of AIDS: "Whether you call it cognitive dissonance or denial, now, more than 10 years into the AIDS epidemic, it seems that smart women are making foolish choices when it comes to AIDS prevention."[113]

What is interesting about this charge of "denial" is that the author elsewhere in the same article notes that most women *accurately* perceive little risk of getting the disease. Yet Nelson displays little self-consciousness; somehow she believes herself to be better able to gauge the risk of the disease than most women who are inextricably stuck in "denial." Yet, based on what we now know about the virus as well as on surveys concerning the perceived dangers of AIDS throughout the 1980s,[114] the public at times seems to have more accurately gauged the disease than the experts. Indeed, the latter may have engaged in considerable misstatement about the disease.[115]

Competing with the moralistic views of the miscreant as misled, and with the medicalized view of the miscreant as "addicted" and in "denial," is the new trend, across the political spectrum, toward blaming the media and the "culture." Consider the following examples.

- *Concerning fatty foods:* "[We have] an establishment that wanted us passive, blissed out in front of televised sports, too impacted by beer and junk food to prevent the robbery of our health and country."[116]
- *Concerning teen pregnancy:* "When . . . a Baltimore school principal [was asked by an interviewer] the one thing she'd do to reduce teen pregnancies, the principal had an immediate . . . answer for her: 'Shoot Madonna.' . . . It's a language shared by parents, teachers, policymakers, the whole range of frustrated adults whose voices of reason are drowned out by a culture that sells kids sex as successfully as it sells them sneakers. Just Do It, . . . our culture offers. . . . Sex without consequences."[117]
- *Concerning cigarette smoking:* "[O]ne furious puff from the intense Winona's [Ryder] enticing lips, one wispy smoke-ring hooding the profound Ethan's [Hawkes] poetic eyes, overcomes a thousand pages of Surgeon General's prose. It obliterates the Food and Drug Administration's threat to regulate tobacco as an addictive drug. It stymies the earnest efforts of legislators, social activists, classroom health teachers."[118]

Just as the saloon and the bawdyhouses were blamed in the nineteenth century for luring unsuspecting citizens into drinking, and young girls into prostitution, today's television, films, and superstars are portrayed as leading the young and innocent down the primrose path to sin. There are several ironies here. First, spectators are judged as somehow intelligent enough to understand the countless public service announcements against cigarettes or for condom use, yet they are supposedly not intelligent enough to retain these messages. At least not when they see Winona Ryder or Ethan Hawkes smoking cigarettes on their screen. Second, one wonders how media activists and health critics can blame the "culture," perhaps the most puritanical in the West, for the sexuality of Madonna without the least bit of irony. True, the entertainment industry sells titillation, but most other institutions—from schools, churches, and workplaces to the huge wellness industry—sell temperance. The fact that American consumers prefer Madonna to the "just say no" messages they are exposed to daily does not make our culture libertine. Indeed, a better social psychological theory might argue that Puritanism produces both repression and release. It is not, then, Madonna who leads kids to sex or Darryl Strawberry who leads them to drugs, but human desire. Moralists, evidently unable to admit this human capacity, seek to attribute "sin" only to the "bad influence" of poor "role modeling."

I suggest that there are at least two alternatives to seeing ourselves and our children as mere judgmental dupes, as either "addicts" or pawns of Madonna and other Hollywood forces beyond our control. First, although people sometimes do act impulsively and regret their actions, humans are also often rational actors acting in their own self-interests, even when outside experts disagree. Second, it is the very onslaught of just say no "dry logic" that leads some people—particularly the young and the poor—into a cultural resistance whereby the object (cigarette smoking, drugs) or the activity (eating, sexual behavior) becomes symbolic of their outsider status and defiance.

To take one example of rationality: Recall the earlier discussion of how the decision by poor young women to carry a child to term can be seen as a rational survival tactic given the odds of life in the ghetto (as well as the lack of joy and satisfaction otherwise available). Leon Dash, a reporter who studied poor black teens in Washington, D.C., admits that upon starting his research he expected to find a lack of contraceptive knowledge and of sexual sophistication to be the main reason why "children were having children." But what he found, in the words of one of his subjects, was that "even when kids are 12, they know all about birth control. Girls out here get pregnant because they want to have babies."[119] Surveys conducted in Denver and Atlanta have confirmed that many teens do not regard the prospect of having a child as a negative event.[120] And according to a recent SIECUS survey, although teens agreed that some kids have children too early, they stated that seventeen was not too early, that "few felt pressure to have sex from their peers, partners or media," and that most knew about and used birth control.[121]

Despite such evidence, both conservatives and liberals minimize the role of deliberate choice in adolescent sexuality and pregnancy. For liberals in particular, as Nathanson notes, seeing early childbearing as a deliberate choice would disrupt their view of teen pregnancy as "a problem in preventative medicine . . . [that] leads them to focus on the *unwilled* consequences of 'premature' childbearing, and on the *inevitability* that sexual intercourse, once initiated, will be continued."[122]

The more people are told *not* to do something, particularly something that feels good, the more their desire may be provoked. Historically, as Foucault pointed out, the prohibition of pleasure has increased its attractiveness. In addition, since symbols of collectivity and solidarity often evolve around pleasures, behaviors that are without intrinsic political or social content (e.g., cigarette smoking, alcohol consumption) come to be seen as having meaning.

Two examples of how substance use came to be associated with specific groups will support the view that people, far from being judgmental dupes, tend to gravitate toward a behavior or habit as a result of the very injunction against it.

First, it is of interest that the drinking of alcoholic beverages among American Indians was banned long before the Temperance Movement against "demon rum." This prohibition was legislated for reasons of moral paternalism but also out of the fear that intoxication would lead Indians to rebel and kill settlers. (A similar logic applied to slaves—and, in some states, to white apprentices and servants—all of whom were prohibited from drinking.) Not surprisingly, for many Indians the drinking of alcohol became symbolic of resistance to the white man's cultural edicts and laws, even though, ironically, it had been the white man who introduced the Indians to booze. In a study of Northwest Coastal Indians in the 1950s, sociologist Edwin Lemert found that "the drinking party was [still] a symbol of political rebellion and cultural loyalty" that demonstrated group cohesion and pride.[123] Of course, such symbolism is hardly unique to Indians: In the nineteenth century, alcohol also came to be linked to resistance among a variety of white ethnic groups and, arguably, within the working class in general. The men of these groups typically used alcohol while expressing camaraderie, solidarity, and opposition to their employers and to elites.[124]

Social critic Richard Klein notes that many societies—including almost all totalitarian ones—have fought tobacco use and often banned smoking. As Klein argues, "[C]igarettes become resistance to society [because] people know that since moralists no less than doctors have disapproved of tobacco from its introduction, its use constitutes a form of defiance to authority."[125] In particular, Klein says, many young people begin smoking illicitly behind their parents' backs, and in those countries where they cannot purchase cigarettes, tobacco becomes the object of petty theft. Starting in the nineteenth century, it was the very illicitness and secretiveness of smoking that built solidarity among the young male roughnecks who were labeled "cigarette fiends" by moralists. Likewise, for many adolescents today, smoking serves as a symbol of growing up and, at least among working-class and poor kids, often as a common group activity intended to kill time and perhaps arouse the ire of adults.

Considerable truth was also contained in Benson and Hedges' "You've come a long way, baby" ads of the 1960s, aimed at women. What romanticized cigarette smoking was, in part, the fact that it had been harshly repressed among women, and was associated with "the demonic or sexualized female," particularly gypsies, actresses, and prostitutes.[126] Many women who lit up in the old days were aware of this association, and many who smoked (particularly prior to the 1920s) were either of the lower class or intent on expressing rebellion. (Recall the Bohemians of Greenwich Village in the early twentieth century.) To this day, as Klein points out, the closer women get to achieving gender equality, the more their rates of cigarette smoking resemble those of men.[127] The fact that cigarette smoking has been sexualized in advertising is often attacked by critics of the media. But paradoxically, it was Puritanism and temperance movements themselves that sexualized the cigarette to begin with, by making it illicit. Even the sex appeal of men has been linked to the cigarette. For example, as columnist Hal Piper notes: "Humphrey Bogart died at 54 of throat cancer, probably by cigarettes. A pity, but maybe it was worth it to have been Bogart. I can't imagine Bogie without the cigarette at the corner of his mouth."[128]

The fact that smoking or drinking or any other intemperant activity is a symbol, for some, of resistance or illicitness does not, of course, mean that such behavior is either healthy or, for that matter, the best way of voicing one's resistance to authority. However, understanding the psychology of resistance does provide us with a more sophisticated understanding of the motives and lifestyles of people, particularly of those whose lives afford few other outlets for pleasure and collective expression than the answers supplied by the clichés of "dry logic."

five

Getting "Lean and Mean": The Middle-Class Return to Respectability

The remainder of this book returns to the question of how personal behavior came to be viewed as such a "crisis" in the last few decades of the twentieth century. Of course, my answers will be incomplete, as there are so many issues at hand. Some readers may reject my conclusion that the behavioral crises in America beginning in the 1960s (e.g., drugs, sexuality, "permissiveness") were primarily socially constructed, preferring to believe that we were (or are) "going to hell in a handbasket." Nevertheless, I focus on two central arguments. First, in this chapter, I contend that the 1960s revolts threatened the boundary markers between the classes in America and, hence, that the New Temperance is, in many respects, a reassertion of the ideology of middle-class respectability. Second, in Chapter 6, I contend that the politics of sin, fear, and danger led to a convergence between the strategies of elites and some elements of popular social movements.

For many years, probably for most of American history, "respectability" was successfully constructed along the lines of native, white, middle-class behavioral norms. Although these norms were challenged at times, it was only in the 1960s and early 1970s that a sustained political and social attack on middle-class respectability was briefly successful. I refer here to the radical attack by some baby boomers, characterized by B. Ehrenreich as "class treason,"[1] which in turn led to a sharp middle-class reaction against "permissiveness" by the late 1970s. The New Temperance is also in part a middle-class reaction to its severest economic setback in American history. It also represents a collective effort on the part of the middle class to differentiate itself from the growing numbers of poor not only culturally and politically but also to distance itself geo-graphically and physically.

The Dilemmas of Being Middle Class

As noted in Chapter 3, historically the middle class arose as a class of self-discipline. The English Puritans, the French artisans of the Revolu-tion, and American rebels of the eighteenth century attacked the monarchy and nobility as decadent classes whose claim to legitimacy was undermined by their lack of seriousness and hard work. As a general rule, achievement and self-discipline marked the ideology (if not always the practice) of respectable middle-class people, differentiating them from the extremely rich and the poor. As Margaret Mead once noted: "The member of the upper class rests upon his birth; born a gentlemen, only his [sic] act can take from him something that birth and breeding have given him. The member of the lower class rests in a sense on his birth also. . . . [B]ut the true member of the middle class denies this fix-ity to which both upper and lower are committed. Life depends, not upon birth and status, not upon breeding or beauty, but upon effort."[2]

Of course, many Americans of all classes are wedded to what might be called the "achievement ideology," whereby deferred gratification, long years of schooling, lengthy preparation for and induction into profes-sions, movement up corporate ladders, and saving money to buy homes are held to be necessary for a satisfying life. But the very rich still have less need than others to defer gratification and to be self-disciplined. Some can still live off accumulated wealth while maintaining a life of in-temperance (the comical character in the film *Arthur* comes to mind), whereas others can still get by on their "connections." As for the poor, they often have little gratification to defer and may perceive that there is little to be gained from acting temperantly. But the middle class must *visibly achieve*. No one becomes a doctor, lawyer, or educator without having impressed teachers at some point in time, and without maintain-ing the self-discipline to defer gratification long enough to achieve at least sixteen years of schooling. Then one must get a license, a wardrobe, a home, a suitable business partner, and, often, a suitable mate. Once employed in a profession, corporation, small business, or other posi-tion, the middle-class person cannot cease maintaining his or her repu-tation or achievement because others on the competitive rung always threaten that status. So the middle class must be continually vigilant, sensitive to new norms and behavioral cues.

However, the need for vigilance, for preparing, saving, sobriety—in short, for the Protestant Ethic—conflicts with the need in a capitalist so-ciety for mass consumption of goods. After all, the raison d'être of achievement is accumulation: nice cars, good food, nice homes, good clothes. The genius of American capitalism has been to tie success to pleasure, largely through advertising that leads us on a continual search for new pleasurable products. The contradiction between the need for deferred gratification (so that one can enter a profession, management, or the white-collar workforce) and the need and desire to consume creates the anxiety and insecurity of the middle class. There are no obvious answers to the question as to when middle-class people can "let down their guard" and just enjoy life.

Rather, as Ehrenreich so well describes, the middle class is constantly in "fear of falling." Its status is always insecure: The lawyer who drinks too much may lose everything, the small-business person with a bad reputation may lose his customers, the accountant accused of fraud may lose her license, and the executive who does not "fit into" a company because of "loose morals" or poor perceived performance may lose her job or career. Ehrenreich notes that if the middle class is an elite, as some believe, it is at the same time a deeply troubled one: "It is afraid, like any class below the most securely wealthy, of misfortunes that might lead to a downward slide. . . . [But it also has] a fear of inner weakness, of growing soft, of failing to strive, of losing discipline and will. Even the affluence that is so often the goal of all this striving becomes a threat, for it holds out the possibility of hedonism and self-indulgence."[3]

A second dilemma the middle class faces is how to socially reproduce itself as a class. Of course, unlike aristocracy or elites based on inherited wealth, a small-business person, social worker, or accountant usually cannot transmit huge monetary sums to his or her children. The children of the middle class must learn either to achieve status and income based on a meritocratic achievement in business or the professions or to develop the acquisitive skills needed for business success. Even then, these children require a good deal of luck to succeed. There is no reliable way to reproduce class status from generation to generation. Not only might the child of a doctor fail to become a physician, but he or she could fall into poverty; and the child of an administrative assistant is perhaps even more likely to fail to secure a good job. Thus, says Ehrenreich, "[a]ll that parents can do is attempt, through careful molding and psychological pressure, to predispose each child to retrace the same long road they themselves once took. Hence the perennial middle-class preoccupation with the problems of childrearing."[4] In short, the middle class attempts to reproduce itself by transmitting to children, first, the need to defer gratification—that is, to avoid the dangers of pleasure, which may interfere with education and work—and, second, the need to associate socially with one's own kind (or preferably, one's betters) so that a suitable set of colleagues, contacts, and marriage partners can be obtained.

Middle-class parents have traditionally feared drinking, drug use, and sexual promiscuity not only because they threatened to take the child away from studies, work, and (potentially) the middle-class way of life itself, but also because they knew that such behaviors served as "class cues," which historically have interfered with one's chances of meeting the proper mate and colleagues. Such behaviors caused one to "*fall in with the wrong crowd.*" In other words, who one associated with was critical to one's social status. Such associational parts of status are highly important. Children present themselves to one another at school not as the offspring of doctors or lawyers or steelworkers but simply as kids. A teenager at a dance may fall for an attractive person of a lower social class—the son or daughter of an unemployed person, perhaps, or even a welfare recipient. For most of American history, the "proper" people came to identify themselves through, among other things, their respectable conduct. They did not drink alcohol heavily, if at all; the "proper" woman did not smoke tobacco; the "proper" gentleman did not make sexual advances to a woman before marriage; and the "proper" woman did not accept such advances.

Since class (more than race or gender) can be invisible, boundary markers (or status and class markers) are necessary. The middle class "uses consumption to establish its status,"[5] particularly to distinguish itself from the working class and the poor. Indeed, the middle class has become extremely sensitive to the ever-changing boundary markers by which proper conduct is associated with success. Describing food choices in the 1980s, for example, Ehrenreich notes that "[t]he trick was to understand the language [of status] as it changed month to month, leaving behind the ignorant and less than affluent. As soon as an affordable fad—the example is often given of pita-bread sandwiches—sedimented down to the general public, it would be rendered useless as a mark of status and abandoned by the cognoscenti."[6]

Some status markers, particularly those affordable to poorer people, may go from being "in" or "hip" to "déclassé" and even "grungy" (one thinks of cigarette smoking or eating inexpensive cheeses). But the cluster of behaviors I have identified as part of temperance ideology is not arbitrary either. Marriage is a key part of social-class reproduction; and the more wealth one has, the less cavalier one is about what happens to it. After all, the history of the middle and upper classes since feudalism has been very bound up with the idea of legitimacy for children and proper partner selection because of the danger that a poor choice of partners could lead to downward mobility. Hence issues of teenage sexuality and pregnancy, and the whole cluster of mores around sex, are a continuing concern for the middle and upper classes. The key issue at least until the 1960s (when birth control and the women's movement came to the fore) was whether the wealth of these classes' families would continue or, conversely, whether female sexuality in particular would cause their downward mobility through poor (or no) partner choice.

Unfortunately for social-class reproduction, there is a contradiction, again, between the middle class's desire to avoid downward mobility through careful partner choice and appropriate status cues, on the one hand, and its need to be the avant-garde of capitalist consumption on the other. That is, at the same time that middle-class elders may be exhorting their young to engage in temperant behavior, middle-class status (particularly the upward-moving sectors of the class) requires consumption of necessary items to maintain or improve status (a matter of "Keeping Up with the Joneses"). So the values of capitalist advancement, particularly in prosperous times, require that class markers be expensive enough to attract the like-minded. This mind-set encourages spending, not saving; exhibition of luxuries, not reticence; and conspicuous displays of wealth, not Puritanism. In other words, if upwardly mobile middle-class people must attend the right clubs and wear only the most fashionable clothes and jewelry, they will find it difficult to maintain the stricture against their being trendsetters with respect to, say, consumption of the latest drug in supply at the time. The push toward consumption has spillover effects.

The middle class thus finds itself in a double bind: It must exhibit enough savvy to consume the right goods to attract others with wealth to remain middle class or (better yet) to gain status, yet it must also avoid the dangers of hedonism that are attached to consumption since these pleasures might weaken the sound business and social judgment that is needed for success under capitalism.

I suggest that the norms of respectability stressing the sobriety of the bourgeois life began to break down in this century and, indeed, came close to being overturned in the 1960s and 1970s, due both to economic prosperity and to political unrest. Many events since the mid-1970s can be seen as efforts by members of the middle class (and others)[7] to reassert respectable status boundaries in order to again clearly separate the classes physically and socially, and to prepare their children to reproduce some vestiges of middle-class life under the highly adverse economic conditions of the late twentieth century.

The Achievement of Respectability in America: 1830–1920

Social norms do not just develop naturally; rather, they must be communicated over a long period of time and enforced by rewards and sanctions. Because Americans lack a feudal heritage, they have had few symbols of visible status (such as the titles and sumptuary laws available to Europeans) by which to identify others. Perhaps for this reason as well as because America has been flooded with one of the most ethnically diverse populations in the world, behavioral norms have taken on a much stronger role in the development of status markers here than in other countries.

It is true that the religious tradition of Protestantism from Colonial times on as well as the aphorisms of Americans like Ben Franklin seem fairly consistent with much of what was encoded as a bourgeois morality. And many norms about behavior have remained fairly stable. As historian John Burnham points out, "In the 19th Century, all commentators agreed that a number of common vices . . . embodied some level of sinfulness . . . and they identified . . . a single constellation that included drinking, smoking, gambling, sexual misbehavior."[8]

Yet it is a bit simplistic to assert that American bourgeois values have always been temperant. After all, if most Americans, including the emerging middle class, had always adhered to moderation in life, there would have been no need for a Temperance Movement, a Social Purity Movement, or the other movements described in Chapter 2. It makes more sense to view the cluster of values and personal behaviors that came to be identified with "respectability" as a set of shifting patterns resulting from middle-class social movements that emerged between the 1830s and the passage of Prohibition in 1919. These movements paralleled the rise of Protestant revivalism, the first (anti-alcohol) Temperance Movement, and what came to be known as the Popular Health Movement, and they reemerged periodically through the century. Like all social movements, the temperance movements sought cohesion. Many Americans of that time drank a great deal of alcohol, far more than today. Initially, moral reform was, as J. Gusfield puts it, an "assimilative reform," persuasive and educational in nature—in short, a form of moral uplift.[9] Members of the middle class and the respectable, skilled, native working class were the very groups most proselytized to become abstinent, and early temperance pamphlets and plays always stressed the conviction that drunkenness led to economic ruin. Clearly, the intent of these movements was to control middle-class people (mostly men) rather than the poor or the heathens, who were assumed to be immoral by nature.

It was only in the late nineteenth century, through organizing and proselytizing, that most native-born Protestant Americans came to accept as marks of status a temperant approach to pleasure, an emphasis on saving and hard work, and a gender division of labor resting on the notions of monogamy and purity (at least in theory) for men as well as women. It was this process in particular that combined the features of social movement and elite power strategy, as discussed earlier.

Of course, the more these burgeoning movements succeeded among the middle class, the more nonmarital sexuality, gambling, alcohol consumption, and other intemperate behaviors were pushed into working-class and poor immigrant districts of the city. As Burnham notes: "In urban centers, the [Victorian] underworld had a real, largely geographical experience . . . in which houses of prostitution, drinking places, gambling dens, opium dens, and disreputable people in general tended to locate. . . . In the cities, poor people and people with dubious intentions lived alongside each other in the slum and boardinghouse areas."[10]

The gradual denial of status to those who frequented the tavern or the brothel did not extinguish such behaviors. Rather, such activity became associated with poverty, immigration, and "deviance." The association encompassed not only sexual display, pornography, prostitution, "demon rum," drug use, and the "cigarette fiend" but also consumption of ethnic foods, coarseness of speech, and the political and union organizing that often occurred in places like the tavern. These issues were joined together because, from the standpoint of white middle-class Americans, they all reflected the alien and undesirable character of poor people and immigrants. Temperant beliefs also encoded political fears (social unrest and even revolution) and fears of contagion (the spread of disease and ill morals to middle-class children from the poor). As misbehavior began to be policed primarily among the poor and immigrants, the temperance movements shifted from being "assimilative" to being "coercive," as the symbols of intemperance (the tavern, for example) came to represent not only the potential downward mobility of the affluent but also all the dangers represented by the poor.[11]

Respectability triumphed at a time of strong unrest in the United States amid massive waves of immigration in which an emerging middle class sought desperately to make its place. The chief need of both the upper and middle classes in the late nineteenth and early twentieth centuries was accumulation—of wealth and labor, of a proper educational system, and of a reformed political system (free of immigrant control through political machines)—all of which were somewhat problematic. Consumptive goals, although beginning with the purchase of mansions by the rich and the start of vacation taking at the turn of the century, were much less critical at this time.

The very successes of the movements described in Chapter 2—the eventual passage of prohibitionary laws, age-of-consent laws, Comstock statutes, anti-smoking laws, the Harrison Act of 1914—reflected the fact that the majority of white upper- and middle-class people had come to some consensus on "proper" behavior. Moreover, they were willing to forgo certain pleasures themselves for the sake of stability and control of the poor. Only now did "universal" categories come to exist. Although not all behaviors or practices followed the same route, prior to the success of the coercive movements members of the upper and middle classes simply maintained that when they behaved a certain way (drank, smoked, gambled) they did so respectably, for, after all, they could handle such activities properly. But whereas earlier in American history the same or similar activities carried out by the "respectable" were distinguished from the objects of choice of the "nonrespectable" (the cigar smoking of the rich as opposed to the stigmatized cigarette of the poor, the use of morphine by some respectable people as opposed to the dreaded opium of the Chinese), the idealism of the late Victorian and Progressive eras began to make such hypocrisy difficult to maintain.

By the early decades of the twentieth century, there could be no doubt about what constituted respectable conduct. Both religiously based rural conservatives and middle-class urban liberals endorsed the moves against alcohol and other forms of intemperance as well as sexual regulation, and these symbols helped the members of the middle class identify *one another* as respectable marriage partners, employees, and friends and colleagues. Although the achievement of respectable bourgeois norms in the late nineteenth and early twentieth centuries is commonly minimized, I would argue that the historical development of status markers based on temperant behavior still helps to account for some of the differentials in behavior between the social classes today.[12] Of all the countries in the world, America has one of the highest percentages of people who abstain totally from alcohol, for example. Historically, middle-American Protestant families in particular have been associated with abstinence from both alcohol and tobacco.[13] Although the complex cluster of beliefs and behaviors of "Middle America" broke down somewhat later, the stereotype of the righteous American (as parsimonious, sober, thrifty), from Ben Franklin to Norman Vincent Peele, is not simply a myth. Nor is there evidence for dismissing this stereotype as mere hypocrisy. We have every reason to believe that the millions of "drys" in, say, Midwestern America really did abstain from alcohol, that those who fought prostitution and promiscuity really did practice chastity outside of marriage, and that those who opposed gambling abstained from rolling the dice on the side. Nor did those people who transgressed these norms disprove the class and status boundaries. Those who violated the norms knew they were social "deviants" and were ashamed of their actions.

The Partial Democratization of "Deviance": 1920s–1960s

Although overrated by some observers, some breakdown in the lines of respectability unquestionably occurred in twentieth-century America before the 1960s. The passage of Prohibition reduced alcohol consumption among the poor and working class, but not among the rich and so-phisticated urban middle classes.[14] Even more upsetting to some was the tendency of the affluent to flaunt the new law by carrying open flasks and conspicuously appearing in speakeasies. The prosperity of the 1920s undermined the old styles. Women began openly smoking cigarettes and wearing short skirts. Gradually, between the 1920s and the 1960s, moderate consumption of alcohol as well cigarette smoking were detached from their "deviant" definitions. In addition, food habits converged, particularly during periods of prosperity, as the distinctiveness of immigrants' diets declined and more and more Americans came to accept steak, hamburger, breakfast cereal, and soda pop as basic staples.[15]

The prosperity of the 1920s and, again, during the 1941–1973 period made it hard to restrain consumptive impulses. As advertising and buying on credit triumphed in the "roaring twenties," an ethic of "spend" coincided with having fun. Particularly affected were members of the urban middle class, who were becoming increasingly sophisticated trendsetters thanks to the new mass media of movies and radio. The more open the class structure (as in the post–World War II period), the less the ethic of deferred gratification and stoicism could be maintained. Of course, middle-class parents always preferred that their children marry well; but in 1950s and 1960s, the daughter of a stockbroker who married, say, a mechanic was likely to live adequately in a suburban house with two cars. In short, she could reasonably expect to enjoy the mundane pleasures of consumption.

Two other factors weakened the tight social control characteristic of earlier times. First, open immigration to the United States, so fearful to white, native-born Americans of the nineteenth and early twentieth centuries, was virtually shut off in the 1920s, thus reducing a source of anxiety. Second, for a variety of reasons the social classes mixed more than they had in earlier days, allowing for some diffusion in habits and mores. For example, many historians note that the world wars caused dramatic changes in the habits of Americans, particularly rural Protestant soldiers who did not drink or smoke before the wars but came back behaving less temperantly.[16]

Nevertheless, the decline of respectability was not politically or economically threatening, nor was it as broad based as some have conjectured. The sexual norms, substance-use norms, and even dietary norms of middle-Americans did not change dramatically in these years. Rates of cigarette smoking, heavy drinking, and diet continued to vary by class. To take just two examples: In the 1930s and 1940s, exercise and "correct eating" were already a focus of executives and other middle-class families, but not among poorer classes; and rates of cigarette smoking among the general public reached a peak right after World War

II, yet they were still lowest among farmers, teachers, lawyers, and other professional, managerial, and small-business classes. The rate of smoking in the middle class began to recede as early as the 1950s.[17] Of course, many of the behavioral norms challenged during the 1960s were strongly upheld in this earlier period. Drugs were far more stigmatized after World War I than before. Moral panics over heroin in the 1920s, marijuana in the 1930s, and all narcotics in the late 1940s through the 1960s targeted minorities and the poor.[18] Sexual norms and repression of illegitimacy, homosexuality, pornography, promiscuity, and pre- and extramarital sex were not only strongly enforced but became the subject of moral panics. (For example, J. Edgar Hoover led a much-publicized campaign against "sexual criminals" in the 1930s and 1940s, and periodic campaigns against gays and lesbians became especially fierce during the McCarthy era and up until the late 1960s.)[19] In fact, some of the most brutal repression of "deviance" occurred in the 1950s as crime and vice came to be associated with "difference." Anything "un-American" during the Cold War period was considered dangerous, including jazz and rock 'n' roll, nonconformity to strict sexual roles, and foreign-sounding names and reading matter.

It was not until the 1960s that respectability as an ideological construct was attacked. Between the passage (and subsequent defeat) of Prohibition and the mid-1960s, there occurred only some "loosening up" of the strictures that had been most associated with rural Protestantism and the old middle class (farmers, small traders, shopkeepers). These strictures—including abstinence from alcohol and cigarettes—were altered by the new, more consumptive-oriented urban middle class, which saw itself as more cosmopolitan and sophisticated. However, there were no groups arguing for personal freedom as an ideological principle. Even the leftist radicals of the 1930s and 1940s were unconcerned with issues of personal behavior. They were more likely than not to be socially conservative. Their key concerns were the Great Depression and the War Against Fascism, and they would have considered drugs, sexuality, music, and dress to be, at best, frivolous matters.

The Radical Attack on Respectability: 1960s–1970s

Although many individual aspects of the political and cultural revolution known as the "60s" were not unique in American history, the link between personal behavior (i.e., the rejection of many, if not all, of the norms held by the respectable middle class) and ideology (i.e., the rejection by some of the entire political underpinnings of the "system") was most unprecedented. Through a combination of demographic factors (especially the huge cohort of baby boomers), economic factors (the greatest period of prosperity in U.S. history), and political factors (the civil rights and other social movements), America entered an era of massive social and cultural unrest between approximately the mid-1960s and the mid-1970s.

Beginning with the cultural revolt of a small number of "beatniks" and expanding to the student and civil rights movements, the hippies, the counterculture, the anti-war movement, and, by the 1970s, active women's and gay and lesbian movements, "respectable" cultural norms were strongly challenged. This fact was not lost on conservative spokespeople (and still isn't today). For example, Jerry Falwell commented: "If ever there was a time when God needed a job done, it was during the 1960s and 1970s. The future of our nation was at stake. . . . I sincerely believe that Satan had mobilized his own forces to destroy America by negating the Judeo-Christian ethic, secularizing our society, and devaluating human life."[20] But as leftist social critics Ralph Larkin and Daniel Foss remind us, many aspects of the 1960s movements now presented as trivial or self-indulgent (long hair, drugs, rock 'n' roll), had cultural and political meanings at the time: "[T]he 60s . . . youth movement was not merely against racism, the war or school administrations, but against the *totality of bourgeois social relations.* It is easy to forget [now] . . . that many took drugs not to ease the pain of reality, but to experience a reality that superseded and opposed bourgeois reality. Dissident youth had visions and lived myths."[21]

For our purposes, what was critical about the cultural transformations of the 1960s—the open sexuality, the proud use and even political endorsement of drugs, the changes in dress and appearance, the rejection of the work ethic by the counterculture—is that they took place first among children of the middle class. Whereas up to this point most "deviant" behaviors in the areas of appearance, sexuality, and consumption were associated with racial outgroups and the poor, here were the sons and daughters of doctors, professors, executives, and salespeople thumbing their noses at bourgeois norms. As Ehrenreich notes: "To join the counterculture one had only to drop out . . . and pursue one's chosen path to liberation, which might be through drugs, sex, spirituality, communal living, subsistence farming, music or any combination. . . . [E]verything about the counterculture—the easy nudity, the drugs, the disdain for careers, the casual approach to dress and personal hygiene— was an affront to middle-class values."[22]

These behaviors held a long-term danger. If middle-class youth held on to their anti-establishment cultural as well as political patterns, they simply would not obtain middle-class jobs, eventually falling into the working class or even lower. Quoting an anxious cultural observer in the

1970s, Ehrenreich suggests that what most concerned the older generation of middle-class parents was that "the radical children have not
joined their own class; they have sunk into occupations as 'pushcart
vendors, taxi drivers, keepers of small neighborhood shops . . . house-
painters, housecleaners and movers of furniture.'"23

A second development further complicated the task of repressing the
cultural rebellion of the 1960s and 1970s. Spiro Agnew, George Wallace,
and others could easily and successfully attack the "permissiveness" of
middle-class parents and the "pointy headed intellectuals," gaining political capital. But by the early 1970s, the working class, the poor, the
rich, and the rest of society—all seemed to be aping the avant-garde
middle-class radicals, initially a fairly small group. Long hair and jeans
were everywhere; blue-collar workers began smoking marijuana and
hashish; and the sexual revolution—not to mention the sexualization of
song lyrics, movie screenplays, television programs, and fashion
trends—extended upward and downward in the class structure. Among
the other problems with this new diffusion of previously unconven-
tional behavior throughout society was the collapse of class markers
that the affluent had always depended on for social reproduction. For
example, young people dancing in a disco now faced each other with a
new democracy of style: similar dress and language, similar habits and
norms. How could anyone tell who was a high school graduate or a
dropout, who was the daughter of a stockbroker or a truck driver, who
was the son of a janitor or a psychologist, when everybody looked and
acted pretty much the same?

The middle-class anxiety over the events of the 1960s and 1970s crystallized into a theory of "permissiveness" that heavily emphasized the
dangers to social-class reproduction. Although even at the height of the
counterculture actual behavior still varied considerably by social class
(e.g., intemperant behavior was more common in the lower classes),24 a
discourse of universalism began to have appeal (with such slogans as
"Drug use can happen to anyone" and "Teen pregnancy cuts across all
lines"). From the standpoint of the middle class, it was the spread of
problems such as drugs *to their own class*, to their sons and daughters,
that was the threat. As long as drugs or intemperance in general stayed
in the ghetto, it posed little concern. Similarly, the new sexual hedonism
threatened middle-class reproduction since almost all aspects of the
new revolutions (e.g., the detachment of sexual relations from monogamy and the movements to legitimize gay and lesbian relations) threatened the way in which partner choice allowed for cross-generational
transmission of social-class position.

Finally, there was an irony about the 1960s cultural patterns that
would not become apparent until the late 1970s, when the attack on

"permissiveness" was in full swing. Radicals or hippies countered criticism about their own behaviors with an increasing reliance on criticism of conventional middle-class norms as hypocritical. For example, when their drug use was attacked, New Leftists questioned "straights'" use of alcohol and tobacco. And later, when radicals in the women's movement were attacked for promoting political separatism or lesbianism, they often replied by critiquing dominant heterosexual norms and behavior. Most important, the identification of hypocrisy was meant rhetorically and defensively: Hardly any activist in the 1960s would have proposed more state controls on cigarette smoking or drinking, for example. And few, if any, of the leaders of the early women's movement would have thought of opposing "promiscuity" or pornography as a danger to women. Yet critiques of hypocrisy always allow for two possibilities: the acceptance of new radical norms and behaviors previously excluded by the alleged hypocrites, or the gradual excluding from respectability of old norms that made the establishment seem hypocritical. In other words, it ultimately became more politically feasible to attack alcohol and tobacco and reduce their acceptability than to affect drug legalization. Likewise, it was more politically feasible to attack pornography or sexual abuse than to attack monogamy or the powerful legal and normative codes upholding heterosexual marriage.

The New Temperance and Economic Decline: 1970s–1990s

It is, of course, analytically difficult to disentangle changes in cultural norms from other social changes and to account for complex interactions among the economic, political, and cultural spheres. One can argue that the countercultural trends of the 1960s and 1970s that so shocked the nation were untenable over the long haul and, hence, would eventually swing back toward the old respectable norms of the middle class. Politically, any threat posed by "60s"-style cultural radicalism actually had been turned into its opposite, a convenient symbol for political candidates to run against (as I discuss further in Chapter 6). By the late 1960s both Republican and some conservative Democratic political strategists had tied the rebellious young radicals to the poor and ghetto underclass through a successful construction of the notion of "permissiveness." It was Nixon, after all, who declared the (first) war on drugs in 1969. The issue of drugs served as a masterful symbolic code precisely because it linked the disorder on campuses and among youth with what was beginning to be seen as a dysfunctional "culture of poverty" in the ghetto. In fact, most of the intemperance issues that became popular by the 1980s were already part of the older generation's bill of complaints against the young by the late 1960s: sexual promiscuity, lack of a work ethic, "softness" or permissiveness, and hedonism.

I suggest, however, that the political campaigns against intemperance did not succeed in altering behavior and cultural norms until *after* the economic conditions of the nation had deteriorated, affecting all social classes but (most important for our purposes) the middle class especially. Despite the considerable political success of conservatives (e.g., surveys showed widespread opposition to drugs and other "deviant" activities, whereas liberals were suffering overwhelming electoral defeats by the late 1960s and early 1970s, hardly suggesting much support for countercultural ideas), the actual incidence of "misbehavior" throughout the American population continued to increase despite the political defeat of the counterculture.[25] That is, although the New Left and the hippies were now a thing of the past, widespread use of drugs and non-marital sexual behavior were diffusing throughout society. This was true as well for other forms of intemperance from pornography to increased portrayal of violence in the media. The pattern of respectability had been at least temporarily broken; young blue-collar workers, children of the middle class, and children of the poor shared generational symbols including dress, language, drugs, and sexual behavior. As class markers blurred, not only drugs and sexual license but even criminality (such as widespread support among the New Left and hippies for pilfering and other minor crime) became perceived as a threat to middle-class norms.

Only in the aftermath of the economic slide that started with the severe recession of 1973–1974 and continued throughout the next two decades would a gradual consensus reemerge around respectability, at least in the middle class and (what remained of) the working class. The new consensus occurred during a period that paralleled the greatest decline in economic fortunes for middle America since the Great Depression. At first, it was possible to believe that the economic slowdown was temporary, and that everyone would return to the prosperity of the 1950s and 1960s. But by the late 1970s, deindustrialization was well under way. Phenomena such as plant closings, the rise of homelessness, and labor givebacks (wage cuts and benefit concessions) brought back a language unknown to those who had not lived through the Great Depression. New phrases such as *corporate downsizing, mergers and acquisitions*, and *corporate raiders* came into vogue. In the 1970s, while the decline of America as the dominant world power showed in the "misery index" of constant high inflation and high unemployment, a merciless attack on trade unionism and labor in general began with wage cuts, concessionary bargaining, and the imposition of two-tier salary scales. These factors helped to shape the political sphere, as the New Right arose from the ashes of the old New Deal coalition's collapse, and

Ronald Reagan rose to power in 1980, at a time when voters were fed up with energy crises and Jimmy Carter's calls for sacrifice. What lay ahead was little better. As the president led the attack on organized labor with the smashing of the Professional Air Traffic Controllers Union (PATCO), a new, more severe recession hit in 1981–1982. The 1980s would bring no economic relief to the middle class, as only the rich got richer, prices climbed (albeit at a somewhat lower rate than during the 1970s), and wages stagnated. Social benefit cutbacks and a massive rise in housing costs helped squeeze out those parts of the working class that had barely been hanging on.

The last good economic year the nation had was 1973, a time when a thirty-year-old man could meet the mortgage on a median-priced home with a fifth of his income; by 1986, paying for a home would require double that percentage of income.[26] Lillian Rubin reports that for all but the top fifth of Americans, median family income dropped slightly from 1973 to 1990, even with the increased entry of more family members into the workforce.[27] Per capita income has also fallen since 1973. Of course, much has been written about the most extreme victims of America's economic decline—about the tremendous rise in the number of homeless people and poor female-headed households; the increased rates of poverty among blacks and Latinos, leading to the social construction of a so-called underclass; and the radical change in the working class from blue-collar unionized industrial workers to two-wage service-employees making $5 or $6 an hour each, sometimes with no benefits and often with no union representation.[28]

Although middle-class baby boomers were hardly the most victimized, there are numerous reasons to emphasize their "fear of falling." As Katherine Newman notes, the newly lowered standard of living can be viewed in terms of generational cohorts. Because the baby boomers constituted the largest generation ever to enter the workforce at one time (between the late 1960s and the late 1970s), they faced unique problems:

> Born during a period of growing prosperity, this generation developed high expectations for their adult living standard. However, because theirs is an exceptionally large generation, boomers entering the labor market have had a much harder time. ... Downward mobility is therefore likely to plague baby-boomers because (1) many will find career mobility blocked even as their financial needs and family responsibilities increase; (2) competition for the best jobs creates a glut of talent, making employers confident that they can dismiss and replace employees relatively easily; (3) competition for jobs will retard wage growth; and (4) because of the weaker career prospects for this generation, families need two income-earners, pushing more people (mainly wives) out to work. This places even more

pressure on the job market. To cap the scenario, the size of the baby-boom cohort creates shortages in everything from homes to child care, thus pushing prices for these partly age-specific commodities to unprecedented heights.[29]

Moreover, the Pax Americana of the post–World War II period had created the largest middle class in American history, one that was self-confident about its status, which it passed down to its children as an entitlement to consumer goods and job security. It is important to recognize that even as the news media of the past two decades have reported dramatic stories about middle-class people falling into poverty and homelessness, many middle-class children who did not by any measure *actually become poor* have still felt the anger, bitterness, and anxiety that accompany loss of confidence in the future. In fact, often the most bitter expressions of loss reported in the press in recent years have come not from homeless people or welfare recipients but from middle-class baby boomers employed as reporters, social workers, administrative assistants, and salespeople. For example, in a 1989 article entitled "The Great Boomer Bust," writer Katy Butler spoke for many of her peers when she declared that "the competition with our parents is over. We lost."[30] Contrasting the home and cars of her parents (who were average, suburban, middle-class people) with her own lack of goods and security, she plaintively stated: "I felt shame, resentment, confusion settling out in me. By the standards of their generation, my parents were only comfortably middle-class. Why, then, were they living so much better on one income than Bob and I, who, nearing 40, had no children and were living on two?"[31]

Butler also reported her friends' and peers' anger and resentment:

> In our 20s, my friends and I hardly cared. We ate tofu and hung Indian bedspreads in rented apartments. We were young; it was a lark. But in our 30s, as we married or got sick of having places sold out from under us, we wanted to be grown-up, we wanted money, we wanted houses. . . . [T]he stagflation of the 70s and 80s begot in its victims a sense of individual failure—and its survivors, a sort of chumpish pride, as though they'd come up in the world by paying $100,000 for a house that would have cost their parents a fifth as much.[32]

Against the backdrop of the many poor and working-class people who have fallen into unemployment, poverty, and even homelessness, it is easy to be critical of middle-class baby boomers who feel sorry for themselves for not being able to have both a new house and a new car while also having children (as Butler complains). But the middle class, as Ehrenreich and others note, sets the cultural tone in America; and to some extent, what happens to it, not to the rich or poor, is what the media are concerned with. Although the downward mobility of the middle class has probably been exaggerated, since the mid-1970s economic fear and anxiety have been facets of daily life for most Americans (except the very rich), to an extent not seen since the 1930s.

As the baby boom generation aged and found itself in a world of fierce competition both for jobs and for the income needed to pay for high-priced consumer goods, those who hoped to achieve professional and managerial positions needed new strategies of retaining their class position or at least to avoid "falling." As in a game of musical chairs, it was as if someone said to the middle-class baby boomers, "Each time the music stops, another one of you won't be here (in the middle class) anymore." One strategy that developed in the light of these trends was temperance. Indeed, by the mid-1970s, a period of "fashionable austerity" or "voluntary simplicity had begun."[33]

By the 1980s, the phrase "lean and mean," coined by corporate downsizers to describe their strategy of cutting labor and other costs of doing business, could also be used to describe the aggressive set of values that was shaping middle-class taste. Consumption (especially by so-called yuppies) increased, but it had to be "upscale" and tasteful to contrast with those who were "downscale." Health and fitness regimens, anti-smoking campaigns, and eventually anti-drug, anti-sexuality, and anti-aggression movements came to be integrally connected with the striving of the middle class to regain and reassert the norms of respectability so threatened in the 1960s and early 1970s. The fact that this return to middle-class respectability crossed political lines from "Left" to "Right" reflects the class-based nature of temperance as ideology rather than purely political power strategy.

The New Middle-Class Imperatives

The cultural prescriptions of the 1960s to "do your own thing," "hang loose," and "drop out" were based in the material conditions allowing for social tolerance ("I'm O.K., you're O.K."). These conditions included the family, economic, or social supports for those who did temporarily "drop out." For example, in the late 1960s and early 1970s traveling across the country or living in a commune for a year or two without earned income was "no big thing" for young people in an economy where they could get a job when they dropped back "in" and/or could rely on middle-class or blue-collar working-class parents for support. They could even receive food stamps or other benefits while living in a commune.

Accompanying the sharp economic changes of the 1970s were more gradual changes in the middle class, which shifted from some tolerance for "deviancy" and even political dissent in the 1960s to a moralistic outlook closer to its older traditions. Yet its return to the imperative to maintain self-discipline, and to more temperate class markers to ensure social reproduction, made good sense in terms of the changed economy. The other social trend that had strong political consequences also flowed in part from changed economic conditions—namely, a new social distance from the poor and working class that in turn led to support for (or at most only mild dissent from) the new wars against social "deviants" and the poor. A case in point would be the "war on drugs" in the 1980s and 1990s.

By the phrase "lean and mean," I mean some of the obvious trends, such as fitness, good eating, healthy living habits, and abstinence from smoking, that took hold in the middle class in the 1970s—trends that really did suggest personal "leanness." By the later 1970s, however, parts of American society were moving from "assimilative" reform to more "coercive" reform. From the New Right's successful attacks on sexuality to "welfare dependency," from the anti-smoking and anti-alcohol movements (e.g., MADD) to anti-pornography campaigns, there was a growing sense across the political spectrum that certain people required control or even "meanness" ("tough love") for their own good. The most dramatic example of the acceptance of force as a dominant behavioral paradigm is the drug war that started in the 1980s. Expanding from drugs to various sexual transgressions (e.g., underage sex, for example) and even to speech acts (e.g., politically incorrect speech), the "lean and mean" paradigm most often uses the language of psychological intervention in dealing with "deviants" from the middle class (these perpetrators are likely to be sent into treatment or to sensitivity training), whereas it most often takes the form of criminal intervention in dealing with those from lower classes.

Self-Control and Deferred Gratification

As I noted at the beginning of this chapter, a number of conditions of American life, particularly for the middle class but also increasingly for what is left of the working class, dictate a certain amount of self-control and deferred gratification both to prepare and qualify for certain work and to continue to reproduce a certain level of income and status. I also noted that, particularly during periods of prosperity, temperant norms in the middle class weakened as mass consumption increased. Both the practice of self-discipline (aided more and more by state and corporate force) and that of careful attention to class reproduction returned in the 1970s.

Even during the 1960s, few middle-class people succeeded in obtaining long years of schooling and career credentials without a great deal of self-control. Yet even though some violations of social norms considered "personal" were punished in cases of extremely manifest behavior (e.g., extreme alcoholism), there was no routine personal scrutiny in most American workplaces. Production boomed in the 1960s, when a war economy was in force, and few factories could afford to turn away willing and qualified labor. Under these economic conditions, even a criminal record or a psychiatric history was not necessarily a barrier to employment.

Conversely, what has occurred since the economic downturn has simply been the increased power of employers to select "leaner and meaner" employees. In a tight economy, competition favors employers and lowers the ability of the weakest parts of the labor force to survive (as Gramsci predicted). Ironically, the Civil Rights Act and succeeding legislation and its enforcement have assisted in this process, by shifting employer discretion from the long-term practice of discrimination by ascribed characteristics (race, gender, age, etc.) to discrimination by behavior (drug use, cigarette smoking, weight and health status, criminal status, ability to get along, etc.). In this era during which democratization had forced capital to cease using visible status characteristics to sort labor, a behavioral code of discipline now developed to sort out workers.

But in the 1970s at least, norms that encouraged self-discipline and self-control had to flourish in the middle class before employers and other institutions could actually develop more coercive policies. But these policies were not hard to come by because they built on a preexisting, historically based tradition of middle-class respectability. Being overweight may not have been held against an employee in the 1960s, but trimness was certainly considered a virtue of respectability and fat a symbol of laziness. Many people smoked, drank, and took drugs in the 1960s and early 1970s, but middle-class people knew that these were not productive activities, and that they could interfere with work.

And so, as cultural observers have noted, by the mid-1970s cigarette smoking and high-calorie, fatty foods were "out" and fitness was "in." Hamburgers, twinkies, white bread, and cigarette smoke came to be associated with those lower in class and thus were markers of status. These status differences coincided with the creation of an "upscale" market of taste, symbolic of the elite's ability to resist temptation, to defer the gratification of immediate pleasures in order to be ready, able, and always willing to work.

Metaphors of "health" and of "austerity" in the later 1970s further reinforced asceticism among the educated classes. It was not just that more health information had become available or that the success of the environmental movement in conjunction with hard economic times had led to the popularity of "lean and mean." By the mid-1970s, health-care costs were becoming an issue, and governments and public interest groups were competing in their efforts to place the "blame" either on consumers or on broader social forces. Although environmental groups attacked industry and government negligence, the ultimately more successful argument came from people who blamed personal indulgence: As Joseph Califano put it, "Indulgence in private excess has results that are far from private."[34] The growth of corporate employee assistance programs and wellness programs in the late 1970s as well as increased attempts to screen workers by personality (e.g., through polygraph testing),[35] combined with a concern for reducing health-care costs, reducing theft, and eliminating undesirable workers altogether.

By the 1980s, self-discipline and self-control were not merely symbolic acts that would impress employers or colleagues. Rather, in these new "lean and mean" times, jobs came to depend on behavior. So many variables were now related to getting a job that, in 1986, *Newsweek* could run a cover story asking "Can You Pass the Job Test?" Citing mandatory drug testing, psychological and polygraph tests, health and genetic screenings, the columnist wondered whether "1984" had indeed arrived.[36] Drugs, the bugaboo of the New Temperance and new corporate dominance, served as a metaphor of two failures of self-discipline. First, alleged users were unable to defer gratification, thus failing to demonstrate that they were productive and trustworthy employees. Second, in the aftermath of the defeat of social or labor unrest, drug use became symbolic of *any* resistance to corporate and government power. Now that the country had been told to "just say no," the fact that miscreants continued to say "yes" was particularly irksome, to say the least. As certain behaviors became more and more stigmatized, it is difficult to know whether the initial social-control aims (e.g., for a temperate workplace) were predominant or whether any behavioral deviation had become the issue. (For example, as time went on, drug users were increasingly referred to simply as "lawbreakers," as if explanations were no longer necessary for their persecution.)

In the competitive squeeze of the 1980s and 1990s that emphasized more and more compliance to behavioral norms, corporate culture co-opted some visions of control of the "Left" as well as those of the "Right" and "Center." Today, drug and alcohol use (and, in some companies, cigarette smoking) can lead to job loss; and the increased stricture around issues such as sexual harassment means that the private space of lockers or desks is now policed in some companies. Although corporate tests

generally screen for psychiatric or criminal histories or labor union proclivities, inappropriate speech to coworkers or superiors that might be
linked to intolerance or "political incorrectness" is also policed in a
growing number of workplaces. What is most important about the new
social control is not its content but, as Foucault would argue, its *strategic
power*. Corporations, governments, and other institutions have assumed
the right to police aspects of life previously seen as "personal," and this
power seeps across traditional political lines. In turn, the individual has
little or no social power with which to back up his or her own personal
rights, given the decline of countervailing forces at the workplace. The
accommodation of the corporate world to political and sexual correctness is in part a reflection of the success of the 1960s social movements;
yet it is also true that insistence on "proper" and respectable speech and
actions in the workplace is consistent with earlier visions of social control that employers have always maintained.

Social Reproduction: The Pressure on
Partnering and Childrearing

Ironically, the changed conditions of middle-class life since the mid-
1970s have occurred in response to a brief period of time when perhaps
the least amount of pressure was exerted on young people to "stick to
their own kind." A variety of changes from the easier availability of abortion and divorce to the advent of the birth control pill had helped seed
the sexual revolution, radically changing sexual habits by the 1960s. This
combined with the affluence of the period and even some cultural glorification of the poor and "deviant" led to an increase in class mixing during these years. It is exactly this trend that the New Temperance has reversed. In a climate in which *overt* racism and classism could no longer
be used successfully to mark boundaries ("Don't play with black children" or "with poor children" sounds "tacky" to most of the middle class),
particularly among the more liberal reaches of the middle class, new
types of status markers (which were ostensibly neutralistic) had to become available as a way of reerecting barriers to prevent social mixing.

As noted earlier, heterosexual partnering and marriage are the chief
means by which social class is reproduced from generation to generation. In prosperous times, although parents did not want their children
to "marry down," it still was not "the end of the world" if their daughter
hitched up with a factory worker. In the 1960s, even less concern would
have been expressed about a son's dating habits or marriage choice, although the wife was expected not only to serve as a proper caretaker of
children but also to be educated and able, if not to work, then at least to

represent the family well when the boss came over for dinner. But the pressure on dating and partner selection became far more intense in the 1980s and 1990s. The tremendous changes in gender roles and female workforce participation combined with the changed economic times to produce a new set of difficult imperatives for young people entering the world of relationships.

Recent years have witnessed major changes that suggest the relation of temperant norms to partner selection. First, the mass entry of middle- and working-class women into the workplace, while providing them with new freedom and power, has also commodified their potential class contribution in a qualitatively different way than was historically the case. In the old days, the American "Cinderella" fantasy had some real-life potential: A poor or struggling woman, if she had good looks, charm, or intelligence, could actually find a "prince" who would fall for her. But this story now has a new twist, as Ehrenreich observes in her analysis of the movie *Working Girl* (1988). Here the old Cinderella tale is impossible if the secretary is, after all, only a secretary. There is simply no way that the corporate executive would ever fall for the Staten Island–accented, working-class character played by Melanie Griffith. Only when Griffith is able to deceptively replace her female boss (played by Sigourney Weaver), and to mimic her speech, style, and business acumen, is she considered appropriate as a match (as opposed to perhaps a one-night stand) for the leading man played by Harrison Ford. Noting the reluctance of today's men to marry women "beneath them" in income and status, Ehrenreich suggests the following new social-class rules for women: "[T]he professional middle class has simply become a more impregnable fortress. Once only men had to scale its walls, devoting their youth and young adulthood to preparation and apprenticeship. Women could drift in on the strength of their charm. . . . Today, however, almost no one gets in—male or female—without submitting to the same discipline and passing the same tests."[37] Yet this bad news for secretaries may be good news for the female executives:

> But upwardly mobile young professional women had much to gain from the tightened "pattern of marriage" within the class. Seen as economic partners as well as helpmates, women are more likely to be equals within their marriages. They are also less likely than in the past to be displaced by any of the far more numerous women—secretaries, flight attendants, cocktail waitresses—who lack professional credentials and impressive resumes.[38]

How is the male executive to tell the difference between the secretary and the female boss? In *Working Girl*, after all, the secretary not only pulls off a ruse but is far more appealing than the executive she replaces (Weaver). However, the tension the movie plays on proceeds from the audience's knowledge that the secretary really has a working-class accent, lacks higher education, chews gum, and has a brasher, more open sexuality than the upper-middle-class characters in the film. The social class of the secretaries who ride together on the Staten Island ferry to Manhattan now tends to disqualify them from being upwardly mobile.

In the real world, not only are there few Cinderellas, but class cues such as language, substance use, dress, sexuality, food, and fitness are needed because "bank accounts and resumes are not visible attributes" at a time when, as Ehrenreich notes, "a 'nice girl' or a 'good looking gal' would no longer do." Women who smoke cigarettes, drink Budweisers, eat cheeseburgers, and wear clothes from downscale department stores are easy to identify as "tacky" (i.e., lower in class), and those deemed "promiscuous" or "druggie" are even less acceptable to the single executive or professional as suitable partners.[39]

But the other part of the equation is the changed emphasis on male behavior. Left out of Ehrenreich's account of *Working Girl* is the incident in which the secretary leaves her crude working-class boyfriend from Staten Island before commencing her liaison with the male executive. Whereas Harrison Ford (as the executive hero) is viewed sympathetically in the film, the working-class boyfriend receives extremely negative treatment, although his action of cheating on Griffith is exactly what the Ford character has done to the female executive (Weaver). The gender and class politics of *Working Girl* mimic those of the 1970s film *Saturday Night Fever*, inasmuch as both movies suggest that the only escape from the tackiness and downward mobility that attach themselves to the ethnic working class (at least in the outer boroughs of New York) is to move to Manhattan and secure a more affluent, educated lover or peer group.

Although the 1970s and 1980s brought new pressures on women workers, most of the downturn in per capita income and unemployment resulting from deindustrialization hit male workers hardest (since they occupied most of the blue-collar jobs). Whereas potential male partners like Melanie Griffith's Staten Island boyfriend were once of respectable (if modest) status, perhaps employed as construction workers or steelworkers, the same men today would more often be unemployed or low-paid service workers such as gas station attendants. As William Julius Wilson notes in his discussion of the profound impact of deindustrialization on the African-American community in the 1970s and 1980s, female-headed families at least partly reflect the "low marriageability pool" of available men in the ghetto.[40] Although Wilson is correct in emphasizing the tragic consequences of economic decline for African-American families, his argument need not be limited to the ghetto, as there are "low marriageability pools" of men in many other areas of the United States as well.

It is not simply that an unemployed or underemployed male is a poor partner because of his low income alone. In American society, the inability to be an adequate breadwinner has dramatic psychological effects on most men, and these effects are usually detrimental to self-esteem. Unemployment, job stress, and the economic dislocation itself feed a self-fulfilling prophecy among many poor and working-class men: Indeed, the worse things are, the more likely they are to drink heavily, to be violent and abusive, to engage in crime, even to smoke cigarettes.[41]

Add this reality to the focus of the women's movement after the mid-1970s on issues of male misbehavior, from domestic violence to date rape, and it is not surprising that many middle-class single women complain that there are "very few good men" around. Indeed, with the advance of more women into corporate and professional fields, more men seem declassé, a process complicated by simultaneous economic downturns and changed gender relations. The working-class man is now seen as more likely not only to drink, smoke, take drugs, or eat pork rinds but also to become violent. Although many of the recent show trials on male abuse or sexual harassment have focused on prominent men—such as Clarence Thomas or William Kennedy Smith—in actuality, there is little evidence that middle- and upper-class women are avoiding well-dressed, polite, affluent men. More likely, the new, more temperant norms and strictures against substance use as well as increasingly ritualized forms of regulating sexuality (movements against pornography, against sexual harassment, for dating codes on campus, etc.) are leading to and legitimizing class discrimination. A sole focus on, for example, male violence reaffirms for many middle-class women the historic association between "male brutishness" (as the nineteenth-century reformers put it)[42] and low social status or racial outgroups. The class mixing that did occur in the 1960s and 1970s has probably already become a thing of the past. As E. Maticka-Tyndale's research on safe sex shows (see Chapter 4), middle-class women frequently judge the prospective behavior of a date by his status cues: the way he talks, handles feelings, and manages impulses.[43] Yet, although these protective impulses make good sense, they also tend to reinforce class divisions; as research shows, men of low status are more often seen as potential abusers and rapists than are men of high status.[44] K. Roiphe makes a similar point about the middle-class social movements at universities (such as those against date rape and for speech codes) that may end up inadvertently targeting racial minorities or lower-class men in the process of walling off the campus from "outside" intruders.[45]

If partnering became perilous for most people by the 1980s and 1990s, childrearing produced even more pressure. Even college graduates who formed couples and struggled to advance up the corporate and professional ladders found that their children were about to inherit a world with few easy avenues to success. Their chances of becoming doctors, lawyers, or college professors were—and are—probably even lower than those of their parents. For many middle- and upper-class families, a move out of cities (teeming with growing numbers of poor people) was in order by the 1980s, while millions of others remained in urban areas but abandoned the public schools. Early therapy and counseling for children became common to correct all sorts of ills. By the 1980s, the drug war's tentacles had extended to the point where getting caught with even a marijuana cigarette in school was tantamount to treason; and for many children, psychiatric care, school suspensions, even criminal charges were the order of the day. And now, in the 1990s, smoking a cigarette, having underage sex, being in possession of pornography, and a host of other acts are deemed betrayals of middle-class status itself.

As noted by sociologists such as J. Best and P. Jenkins, who have studied "moral panics," many of the fears expressed by people of the 1980s and 1990s have involved children. We have witnessed the missing-children crisis, the sexual abuse and pedophilia crisis, the ritual abuse and Satanism crisis, the child pornography crisis, the television violence crisis, even a new focus on learning disabilities and other childhood learning problems.[46] Like juvenile delinquency in the 1950s, these issues have become symbolic of a society fearful that it will be unable to reproduce the "good life" of earlier generations for its children. My purpose is not to suggest that these issues lack reality but, rather, that both their incidence and their importance as political issues have been exaggerated by our anxieties.

In sum, the tight labor market of late-twentieth-century America has sent the message to prospective families that they must be "lean and mean" or else they will fail, and likely decline in class. One set of protective strategies involves increased care in selecting mates (and, to some degree, friends as well); another involves increased care in preventing children from straying beyond the "straight and narrow" and "falling in with the wrong crowd."

Social Distancing, Avoidance, and a Self-Fulfilling Prophecy for the Poor

There is, finally, another social trend that links class reproduction since the late 1970s with the New Temperance: the social and physical distance that the middle class has put between itself and the poor, particularly the urban "underclass." The "white flight" from the city is arguably one response to the racialization of the last few decades' moral panics over crime, drugs, sexuality, and disease.

Ehrenreich's work on the inner life of the middle class reminds us that in the 1960s this class had "rediscovered" the poor. Of course, the poor themselves were not lost except in the sense that academics, intellectuals, and journalists had convinced Americans that, in an "affluent society," issues of poverty and inequality had disappeared. A variety of events beginning with the publication of Michael Harrington's book *The Other America* in 1962 and including the civil rights movement and numerous ghetto riots put poverty (as well as issues of race) back on the agenda of the middle class.[47] Much 1960s activism can be traced to the melding of civil rights and poverty issues with the issues of middle-class youth. In addition, association across racial and class lines increased during this period as large numbers of suburban middle-class children reentered urban neighborhoods, actually moving into areas inhabited by the "Other."

The paradox is that no sooner had the 1960s movements taken hold, and some white baby boomers had actually begun to socialize with racial minorities and live in integrated areas, this cross-fertilization was short-circuited. A variety of complex economic and political reasons for the resulting class polarization can be cited. For example, middle-class baby boomers themselves contributed to this polarization by raising housing costs in cities where "gentrification" often expelled the indigenous poor. Nevertheless, the most important cleavages between those lower in the class structure and those higher, and between the middle class (including blacks) and those left behind in the inner cities, occurred as a result of economic changes in the deindustrialization period of the 1970s on.

William Julius Wilson as well as D. Massey and N. Denton[48] are among the social scientists who have demonstrated how the economic downturn of this period coincided with increased racial and class segregation in housing, jobs, and public services. Ironically, the gains of the 1960s were lost in the economic changes of the 1970s and 1980s. For example, both white and black middle-class professionals have left the inner city, either for suburbia or for enclosed sectors of the city armed with security against intrusion by poor people and/or the homeless. This geographical distancing has been paralleled by the political distancing between the middle class and the people who have remained in the inner city, less than fondly referred to as the "underclass."

As just one illustration of this change, consider what happened in (previously) liberal New York City between the mid-1960s and the late 1970s. In the period from 1960 to 1969, especially, liberal whites saw themselves as allies of blacks and the poor, and for the most part supported civil rights as well as New York's relatively generous social welfare provisions. When the fiscal crisis of 1975 occurred, however, little support for social welfare remained in New York, leaving the poor and their advocates, along with besieged municipal unions, to fend for themselves against a combination of bankers and political leaders of both parties. Then, in 1977, when mass looting broke out after a power blackout, mayoral candidate Ed Koch found new popularity by referring to the riot as the "night of the animals." It would have been unthinkable a few years earlier for a Democratic candidate to refer to thousands of mostly racial minority citizens as "animals," but by 1977 this rhetoric had become highly popular and helped propel Koch to the mayoralty.[49]

This social construction of "animality" has a great deal to do with our topic. By the late 1970s, a constellation of behavior identified with the "culture of poverty" was being accepted by a majority of the middle class (as well as by both political parties and many academics) as causative of poverty. Prominent within this "animal" "culture of poverty," of course, were drugs, crime, out-of-wedlock births, teen pregnancy, and "welfare dependency." All of these issues have also been racialized, thus effectively associating them with blacks and Latinos in the "underclass." Meanwhile, middle-class parents have responded to the presence of these "animals" by moving out of the city, placing their children in private schools, and/or supporting increased police surveillance in poor areas of cities.

I do *not* mean to suggest that there is no basis in reality for the fear of crime or urban disorder. There are complex reasons why the politicization of the 1960s turned at times toward more destructive cultures of resistance in the slums from the 1970s on. Rather, my point here is that as middle-class people (of all races) came to accept the notion that the inner cities were drug- and crime-infested and plagued by immorality, elements of self-fulfilling prophecy were at work. Ehrenreich captures this process well:

> [C]lass polarization . . . develops a perverse, self-reinforcing dynamic of its own. As the professional middle class withdraws from public services, those services lose their most adamant advocates and critics. The schools deteriorate into holding bins. The parks are abandoned to the purveyors of drugs. . . . Of course, as the poor become dangerous—addicted, short-tempered, diseased—the middle class withdraws still further from contact. Better to *close* the park, as some affluent lower-Manhattanites have argued, than risk mingling with those who have no other space in which to sleep or pass the time. Better to block off public streets, as some Miami neighborhoods have concluded, than allow free passage to the down-and-out. . . . And the more the poor are cut off or abandoned, the less they are capable of inspiring sympathy.[50]

In other words, *if* the middle class had not abandoned the poor both geographically and politically at a time when the economy was destroying the basis of survival for large numbers of people, this self-fulfilling prophecy might not have occurred. For as conditions worsened for the poor and racial minorities, the triumph of right-wing ideology (often with the nodding agreement of centrist and liberal politicians) was to associate immorality with poverty and the influence of the 1960s:

> The New Right's analysis of poverty and welfare became the conventional wisdom. The War on Poverty had failed; welfare had failed. In fact, they had backfired, inflicting on their intended beneficiaries "divorce, alcoholism, drug abuse, psychosomatic illness, neurosis, suicide," and, of course, more poverty.... [L]iberal social-welfare policies had frayed the fabric of American family life, bringing increased crime, illegitimate birth, drug use, teenage pregnancy, divorce, sexually transmitted disease and poverty.[51]

Ironically, once the middle class accepted this social construction, it provided a political and cultural wedge not only between the middle class and the poor but, often, between adults and their own children as well. As the New Temperance became a coercive movement in the 1980s, exemplified by mandatory drug testing and wholesale arrests of drug users, even sectors of the middle class were swept up in the police net, albeit to a lesser degree than the poor. The social-control paradigm linked a "threat from without" the middle class—the contagion of drugs, sexuality, crime, even secondhand smoke—to a "threat from within"—those who still did drugs, were sexually promiscuous, were soft on pleasures from food to illegal substances, or who committed child sexual abuse or other sins.

By the 1980s, most of the middle class, though fearful of social contagion from the poor and, hence, supportive of various wars against them (e.g., the wars on drugs and crime), had become absorbed in its own problem of social reproduction. In embracing the New Temperance as ideology, the middle class attempted to erect a cultural barrier between the classes, adding to the geographic and political barriers that were already in place.

Social Class, Behavioral Norms, and Temperance

The return of much of the middle class to temperant status markers in the 1980s and 1990s, after the historically brief rebellion of the 1960s, suggests a fair degree of consistency in the patterned social norms that accompany behavior by social class. Although periods of prosperity reduced the social distance between rich and poor in terms of their behavior (particularly in the postwar Pax Americana), patterns of behavior among the poorer classes (particularly of young men) are generally perceived to be, and often are driven toward, patterns that differ from the dominant middle-class norms.

This argument is a complex one: Not only are poor (and often working-class) people socially constructed as "deviant," but behavioral differences have a structured reality as well. Although there are many caveats to consider, historically and currently, rates of substance use (i.e., long-term and heavy use of alcohol, most illicit drugs, and tobacco), rates of felony crime, and rates of wife and partner abuse are overwhelmingly higher among young men from poor or working-class backgrounds than among those from middle-class ones. Moreover, historically and cross-nationally, rates of teen pregnancy are higher among poor women, and rates of teen sexuality and poor diet are higher among the poor of both sexes.[52]

The reasons for the structuring of these often stigmatized behaviors among those in the lower classes, and (in cases of substance abuse, crime, and aggression) among young males, are too numerous for a complete discussion here.[53] Rather than support either an essentialist view of male predisposition toward violence or a moralistic view that blames society's victims, I stress the following explanations.

First, the stigmatization of this behavior, as discussed, *often follows* middle-class social movements that lead to the illegalization of certain markets, relegating these markets to the poor and other outgroups. As we have seen, the use of alcohol and drugs, and the construction of the issue of sexuality, *cannot easily be separated out* from their historic associations with social class. For example, when the nineteenth- and early-twentieth-century Temperance Movement targeted alcohol, drugs, and prostitution, these markets become illegal ones. True, some enterprising businesspeople have trafficked with criminals, managed brothels, and developed lucrative drug routes. However, for the most part, the illegalization of a product or trade has meant that those who risk arrest are mostly the ones excluded from society's more rewarded roles. Few drug sellers or prostitutes—and, likewise, few robbers or muggers—have ever hailed from the middle or upper classes. Of course, this fact is explained *not* by the better morality of the upper classes but by the latter's ability to secure income in an easier way than suffering police repression, personal and sexual exploitation, and other dangers of the "underground" street life.

Second, many observers have cited the tremendous impact of miserable living conditions on the poor and the working class of Western societies. The social stress of growing up poor is almost unfathomable to those who grow up in the middle class or above. Constant anxiety over a parent's ability to feed and clothe a child is transmitted directly to the child, whose own anxiety may lead the parent to become frustrated and begin hitting or slapping the child. Living in crowded conditions without privacy, amusement, or relief from boredom has always compelled children to take to the streets in poor areas, where sexual behavior, aggression, and substance use tend to occur early in life. Unemployment, at least among men, also correlates with substance use and violence. We do not fully know the degree to which these behaviors are responses to diminished self-esteem, increased anger, boredom, worry, anxiety, or the lack of being tied to a conventional role. But there is no question that unemployment and underemployment lead men to smoke more, drink more, and/or assault others more than they would when they have well-paying work. And, again, excluded racial minorities are prominent among those charged with crime, physical abuse, or drug usage because of the economic stress confronting them, compounded by the diminished esteem caused by racism and discrimination.

An understanding of social stress and the pain of lower-class life is critical to understanding violence and, to some extent, substance use and youthful sexuality; but it is only when we also include the factor of culture that we can begin to account for differences in response to living situations. Some ethnic and racial differences interact with class, as I indicated in the earlier discussion of teen pregnancy. Experts on the family and sexual behavior describe a long history of differences in kinship patters between African-Americans and American Indians, on the one hand, and whites, on the other.[54] Generally, blacks and Indians have exhibited freer attitudes about sex than have white Protestants, and the prohibition against early sexuality as well as the sanctions for violating monogamy appear to have been less strong. The norms associated with lower-class culture are also arguably different from those of middle-class culture. Many people who are poor and working class adapt a conventional attitude, but as D. Schneider and J. Smith observed more than two decades ago: "[Members of] the lower class both envy and defer to middle-class values without necessarily embracing them. Members of the lower classes frequently explain their position in terms of the vicissitudes of their daily lives which prevent them from following middle class patterns. . . . [A]ll classes pay symbolic deference to [these] values while adhering to their own."[55]

As I have also argued, the cultural resistance of the poor usually does not take the form of open rebellion or even that of an ideological or value construction openly antagonistic to middle-class norms. The more one is subject to personal surveillance and visibility, the more one will "go along" at least on the surface with what middle-class experts say one should do. As Schneider and Smith note, though, verbally "going along" is a bit different from the reality of one's life.[56] In my experience with a community of street people, for example, substance use and non-marital sexuality were mostly just the "way of the street." Although these behaviors were not glorified—in fact, they were often regretted by those seeking respectability from social agencies or job programs—they were usually not seen as a sign of deviancy or lack of fellowship, unless some other norm of the street had been violated (as when substance use was followed by violence or sexual behavior interfered with someone's "steady" relationship, leading to conflict).[57]

We can further elucidate these structural and cultural arguments about social class by drawing on Travis Hirschi's classic formulations about control and delinquency.[58] Hirschi's argument, in a nutshell, was that without a stake in conventional society, poor or working-class people simply have less reason to control their behavior. For example, a poor person is offered some drugs on the street. What does he or she have to lose by taking them? The lower people are in the social order, the less a lack of linear thinking or rational clarity will interfere with their work roles. Nor will being a drug user destroy a rich future career. Conversely, a high school student planning on going to college, or hoping to make a name for him- or herself someday, would probably think it wise to refuse the drug (at least if there is any chance of being caught by authorities). Or consider the man who is angered by someone, whether by a spouse, a rival, or an employer. The middle-class man may want to hit his wife, kill his rival, or assault his boss. But much of the time, he is likely to think better of it and *control* himself. He does so *not* because he is a "better person" than his poorer counterpart but because middle-class socialization is different:

[H]igher-class members are caught in a net of relatively suppressed affect woven by social organization. A more effective socialization, a greater access to secondary means of anger enactment (e.g., the legal suit), a greater vulnerability to the undesirable consequences of direct acting out of anger that goes hand in hand with a greater investment in maintaining a smooth and equable facade interpersonally and in the community all contribute to the management of anger. . . . "Anger-in" is the major middle-class mode of "reflection" when provoked. . . . Middle-class socialization focuses earlier on control of anger and on self-control in general.[59]

Although, to some people, Hirschi's control theory may appear to mirror conservative explanations about the poor or others failing to live up to behavioral norms, the idea can also be applied quite differently. Using social structural arguments in combination with cultural and control theories, I maintain *not* that the poor are behavioral "deviants," and hence morally responsible for their own poverty or low status, but that "proper behavior" on the part of most poor Americans would not *make* them middle class in any case (no matter how temperantly they behaved!). Thus, the reality testing of those who believe they "ain't gonna make it" anyhow is quite accurate. And although some behaviors of the poor (e.g., violence) are reprehensible, others (e.g., drug use) are stigmatized more because of their association with low class than because they necessarily hold people back from a middle-class lifestyle.

If I am correct in arguing that a combination of legal, environmental, cultural, and social psychological factors tend to cluster "deviance" in the lower classes, it is not surprising that as economic and political anxiety increases among the middle class, the emergence of temperance movements becomes more likely. During periods of confidence, such as the 1960s, respectable classes tend to show more tolerance for, and may even embrace, social norms that are associated with the poor. But once such confidence erodes or the diffusion of behaviors between the classes begins to seem excessive, movements of separation and control arise to assert social boundaries once again. Together, the economic structure and social movements of the middle class act as a kind of "self-fulfilling prophecy": Since the poorer classes, denied other advantages, have so little chance of meeting the dominant culture's conditions for "acting appropriately," they continue to serve as object lessons for middle-class rule makers.

six

Manufacturing Consensus: The Politics of Puritanism

The New Temperance of the last two decades, though a class and cultural phenomenon, succeeded foremost as political strategy. Presidents, members of Congress, Surgeon Generals, state legislators, judges, and grassroots activists came to embrace the politics of Puritanism. This was most clear in the "war on drugs," which saw the development of a powerful state apparatus of control over citizens' private lives, including mandatory prison terms and widespread drug testing. In this chapter, I explore how the American political system tends to support conservative cultural politics. Ironically, some of the slogans of the social movements of the 1960s, such as the "personal is political," may have backfired on its proponents, since longer-term power alignments in the United States favor a "personal politics" of repression and self-control.

Although the New Temperance can be seen as a victory for the New Right, much of what remained of the "Left" by the 1980s and 1990s came to embrace aspects of Puritanism as well. Even when liberals and feminists held to their original ground (e.g., with respect to abortion and gay rights), they did so only by finding narrower (nonsexual and nonlibertarian) rights through which to defend these issues from assault. I argue that although the right wing can claim the mantle of New Temperance, its success is also a victory for moderate and liberal activists in the new social movements who have supported a "politics of danger" rather than the libertarian politics originally voiced by the New Left, Feminism, Gay Liberation, and related movements.

American Electoral Conservatism and the Politics of Puritanism

There is, of course, a major difference between the politics of protest and the politics of governing. The leftist radicals and early feminist and gay leaders of the 1960s were not very concerned about how calls for sexual liberation, "smashing" the family, and ending the bourgeois state "played in Peoria" (or even in the suburbs of New York City, for that matter). By contrast, governing coalitions in America have tended to be culturally and socially conservative. That is, even when power has been held by parties that accept the "liberal" label, such liberalism has rarely supported intemperance or even pleasure seeking.

First, the demographics of the American electorate (actual voters) is somewhat different from that of the American population as a whole. Relatively few Americans routinely vote, and those who do are most likely to be middle class (the poor, particularly, vote in smaller numbers), white, and significantly older than the average American.[1] All of these factors (as reflected, for example, in data about who uses illicit drugs, who smokes cigarettes, and who engages in youthful or multiple-partner sex) generally favor conservatism in personal behavior. Those who hold political and judicial office, of course, are even more likely to be older, "whiter," and of a higher-class background than the average American. They are also more likely to be male. It is hard to think of a politician or judge in the last half-century who has publicly supported intemperance, regardless of his or her personal peccadilloes. The demographics of those who govern—namely, older white men of the middle and upper classes— is one factor mitigating against a politics of pleasure.[2]

Most Americans, particularly office holders and voters, consider themselves to be religious. And regardless of whether they attend church or other religious services, they take the Ten Commandments seriously (even if they violate some in practice). The strong cultural traditions of Puritanism, combined with the natural reluctance of most citizens to organize on the basis of "immoral" behavior (e.g., use of drugs or pornography), have focused the political debate on an idealized Judeo-Christian ethic. On the one hand, office holders, their campaign funders, and organized citizen groups are likely to react strongly to attacks against the nuclear family, monogamy, biblical teaching, and other cultural pillars of society. On the other hand, even when millions of citizens take drugs (as they did during the 1960s and 1970s) or engage in illicit sexual relations, not only are they reluctant to admit it, but they are rarely mobilized to *vote on that basis*. In response to the pollster, the adulterer is usually contrite, the cigarette smoker says he wants to quit, and the overeater says she wants to lose weight. The sinners, as often as not, are ready to vote *against* intemperance even if they themselves have engaged in the illicit activity. In short, religious and cultural traditions exert a powerful pull against endorsement of intemperate behavior.

Even when governing coalitions change dramatically on a given issue (support for gay rights provides perhaps the most vivid example of how millions of voters and some politicians have come to support rights for behavior that only two or three decades ago had been regarded as "deviant" or immoral), they do so only along certain lines. The easiest route to political success is to cite "family values" of hearth and home, children, church, and the 3 R's. Of course, the Right and Center are far more at ease with such appeals than the Left. But the Left, liberals, and feminist and gay activists have increasingly turned to this appeal as well. Typical of the new mainstream appeal of gay rights is the nonsexual, demure, professional, long-term gay partner played by Tom Hanks in the film *Philadelphia*. Stripped of sex, countercultural symbols, and any dangerous attacks on gender or family stereotypes, this new sanitized appeal for gay rights has succeeded in increasing its political support. In a similar vein, liberal politicians denounce drugs as they call for more drug treatment facilities, and many feminists present themselves as defending real "family values" as they denounce family violence or sexual abuse.

American politics is pragmatic. Politicians do respond when enough pressure or social unrest occurs; but even then they usually do so only in a way that provides the most minimal basis of radical demands and reshapes them into a compromise with the dominant order. By corroding radical demands, the political system discourages militant activists and usually rewards only the most moderate of leaderships.

The "Personal Is Political"

Prior to the late 1960s, the dominant issues of national politics for several decades (i.e., since the repeal of Prohibition) had been the economy, foreign policy, social welfare, and civil rights. The Left was generally associated with civil rights, labor unionism, a pro-Socialist or at least pro-détente position on communism, and increases in social benefits to the working class and poor. Yet one of the contradictions of history is that the political symbolism embraced by the Left and its related social movements of the 1960s and 1970s stimulated the development of a New Right that, in many respects, was more skillful in its assertion of the "personal is political" than the Left was.

The history of this phrase remains to be written,[3] but, briefly stated, it appears to have originated in the New Left during the 1960s. Initially it stressed the necessity of personal commitment to broader political goals (e.g., taking action against the draft, "putting one's body on the line" against the war or racism). Later, after the phrase had been filtered through the women's movement, it was interpreted as requiring a deconstruction of the split between the public life of "politics" and the "private" life of sexual, cultural, and familial life. The public/private split in bourgeois society was said to be a creation of capitalism and patriarchy that, on the one hand, oppressed women and others (children, sexual minorities) by casting them into the private, domestic sphere, while, on the other hand, minimizing issues of personal life such as sexuality and aggression in the family. The result was advancement of the political theory for the many "social issues" of the 1970s: abortion and reproductive rights, gay and lesbian rights, domestic violence, children's rights, anti-rape and sexual abuse legislation, and so forth. However, the "personal is political" was also quite ambiguous, in that many viewed it as a kind of imperialistic concept in which all human behavior could be evaluated in a "political" way. In what would become a much-disputed notion of "political correctness," some activists sought to view each individual's patterns of personal relationships and each nuance of personal life (from a joke told at a party to one's physical appearance) as being "political."

Initially, the politicization of the "personal" coexisted with the libertarian spirit of "sex, drugs, and rock 'n' roll." In the late 1960s, drugs were still seen by many radicals as a challenge to conventional consciousness and bourgeois rationality, untamed sexuality as a challenge to family norms, and even "ripping things off" as a challenge to bourgeois property norms. For example, as feminist writer Jean Tepperman recalls, in the early 1970s "among left feminists, it was almost assumed that the desire for sexual fidelity was a bourgeois hang up."[4] That attitude was captured in the phrase "smash monogamy." Of course, the irony, as we will see later in this chapter, is that these norms would change dramatically. Whereas in 1969 "living the revolution" for some meant "liberating" food from stores and residing in communes, by the late 1970s many leftists and feminists had begun to reject intemperate behaviors. For example, certain segments of the women's movement rejected the entire sexual revolution as "male inspired," and some would agree with Ti-Grace Atkinson that "the institution of sexual intercourse [itself] is anti-feminist,"[5] recommending the best personal course in relationships to be celibacy.

Several problems would ultimately emerge with the Left's embrace of the idea of "personal politics." One problem was the indeterminacy about which behaviors were "radical" or "correct." Many behaviors deemed revolutionary in 1970 might be considered downright reactionary now. Is there, then, really a "politics" of smoking cigarettes, of driving a car, of having friendships, or of disposing of garbage? Were those who failed to live up to some established norm—using correct words or recycling or treating the earth well—to be ostracized or rebuked? Activists were always split on these issues, but it seems clear that a large number of people did not remain in many leftist movements because of their fears (or actual experiences) of being upbraided about some aspect of their personal lives. When righteousness about personal habits or speech replaced substantive positions, considerable battles occurred within the movements themselves as activists attacked each others' habits and predilections.

A second problem was that many activists turned the phrase on its head: If all behavior was "political," then a politics of personal improvement (therapeutic and recovery groups, Spartan commune life, vegetarianism) was as much "politics" as picketing, boycotting, or petitioning. Feminist historian Alice Echols describes the "personal is political as one of those ideas whose rhetorical power seemed to work against or undermine its explication. It could encourage a solipsistic preoccupation with self-transformation [and] subordinated politics to lifestyle."[6]

Such politics, moreover, could be very self-serving for middle-class activists who in the context of the 1970s and later had lost much interest in protesting, yet (as noted in Chapter 5) had increasingly become absorbed in adopting the symbols of respectable middle-class life (even if their speech, dietary, and other behavioral patterns had transformed middle-class life somewhat).

Before we further examine how the new social movements of the Left moved it toward the New Temperance, it is important to note that the Right (quite intentionally) froze its view of the Left in the late 1960s and early 1970s. Well into the 1990s, many spokespeople on the Right treated activists on the Left as if they were still rebellious anarchists intent on undermining Western civilization by urging an end to the family, the church, and the state. According to Jerry Falwell, for example, the Left was promoting "free use of pornography, legalizing prostitution and gambling, and free use of drugs."[7] This characterization is amusing because it came at a time when many leftist activists were opposing drugs and pornography, whereas few leftists were expressing any position at all on prostitution or gambling. Whatever slogans or discussions about "smashing" the family, the state, or other dominant institutions might have emerged in the 1960s, by the 1980s they were confined to extremely small sectors of the Left.

But if the symbolic meanings of personal behavior changed radically for what remained of the Left after the late 1970s, new actors in the political arena would skillfully use the symbols of daily life to win adherents among the broader public. Prior to the 1960s, right-wing movements had also emphasized foreign affairs, communism, economic, and social welfare issues. Richard Viguerie, one of the founders of the New Right, highlighted this strategic change in his book recounting its origins: "For the past 50 years, conservatives have stressed almost exclusively economic and foreign policy. . . . We feel that conservatives cannot become the dominant political force in America until we stress the issues of concern to ethnic and blue collar Americans, born-again Christians, pro-life Catholics and Jews. Some of these issues are busing, quotas, crime, abortion, pornography, education, and traditional Biblical moral values."[8]

Whereas the Old Right was associated with wealthy elitists like William Buckley, a new populist Right emerged; "bold and innovative," it attempted to capitalize on the racial, sexual, and countercultural politics of the 1960s. One historian of the New Right suggests that the construction of politics as "personal" was as new to the Right as to the Left: "No longer, in their eyes, should politics be limited to bread and butter issues such as inflation, jobs, taxes, and business issues. Now the government . . . had a constitutional right and duty to be the custodians, or keepers, of *a specific moralistic worldview and set of behaviors.*"[9]

This "moralistic worldview," of course, would be a "personal politics" directly opposite to that of the late-1960s Left: pro-family, pro-traditional morality, strongly against abortion and women's liberation, strongly against gay rights, strongly anti-drug, anti-pornography, and pro-chastity (and at the same time reflecting the more traditional concerns of the Right in being anti–welfare state, anti-Communist, and pro–national defense spending).

Compared to the Left, the New Right certainly had a much easier time developing a "personal politics" since it drew on the grass-roots fundamentalist and evangelical tradition of American Protestantism, particularly in the South and in rural areas. The New Right was innovative in scope and rhetoric as well as in its use of direct-mail organizing; but its genius was in repackaging the more conservative aspects of nineteenth-century politics from Knownothingism to conservative versions of populism, prohibitionism, and the Social Purity Movement. The Right's quest for Puritan values had a further advantage: The demographic time clock was such that the symbols of the baby boomers' youth, particularly "free" sex and drugs, would decline in popularity among this group as they aged and had children of their own. Hence, by the 1980s and 1990s, on many of these "moral" issues, the Right would come closer to the nation's dominant opinion than the few aging libertarians who remained.

Sin and the Republican Strategy

The Republican Party, the minority party from the 1930s to the 1960s, had experimented with some new appeals in the 1960s to improve its electoral showing. "Street crime" first became a theme of moral decay in Barry Goldwater's unsuccessful 1964 campaign. Far more successful, of course, was the Nixon-Agnew campaign of 1968 in which crime was linked with "lawlessness, looting and rioting" and drug use with student unrest and general "permissiveness" within society.[10] Drawing from George Wallace's successful populist appeal, Nixon and Agnew used "law and order" and "moral values" as codes appealing to a "silent majority" of conservative Americans. The GOP hoped to develop a successful "Southern strategy" that would wrest not only the solid South from De-mocratic hands but also socially conservative, blue-collar, ethnic voters from their attachment to the New Deal—specifically, by offsetting the economic and social welfare issues with a social/cultural appeal.

Yet although Nixon played successfully on the "permissiveness" theme against liberals, students, and the New Left, for a variety of rea-sons he and the more moderate wing of the Republican Party (Nelson Rockefeller, Gerald Ford, etc.) never fully utilized temperance/Puri-tanism as a political strategy. First, some of the major events that pro-voked the development of the New Right (e.g., the *Roe v. Wade* decision of 1973) lay ahead. Second, however, Nixon and the other Republican leaders probably did not envision a puritanical approach to sex or even a total attack on drugs to be strategically wise. Nor did they view a direct attack on the burgeoning women's movement as being in their best in-terests. For example, in endorsing the Equal Rights Amendment (ERA) in the early 1970s, Nixon and Republican office holders viewed the issue as a relatively noncontroversial bow to women voters that would have no revolutionary impact. It came as a shock to moderate Republicans, as well as Democrats, when the ERA was later blocked. In 1970 Nixon's Commission on Obscenity and Pornography issued a liberal report find-ing no proof of obscenity's harm, and in 1972 his Commission on Mari-juana recommended decriminalization (although Nixon himself refused the recommendation). Given the gains the sexual revolution was making in the early 1970s and the rise in marijuana use, it was not obvious that these were popular political issues. If a wide constituency could be mo-bilized to vote based on an anti-sexuality, anti-modernist, and anti–new social movement theme, this fact had not yet been demonstrated.

In the mid-1970s, it remained for conservative strategists such as Richard Viguerie, Paul Weyrich, Howard Phillips, and Terry Dolan to de-velop a successful political strategy that would dramatically reverse

Democratic majorities in Congress, as well as in many statehouses and legislatures, and help lead to a wide margin of victories for Ronald Reagan in 1980 and 1984. Of course, the New Right was successful on many issues, so it is hard to separate the impact of what I have identified as temperance issues (sexual behavior, drugs, family values) from that of other issues including forced busing, quotas, militant anti-communism, and even opposition to the Panama Canal treaty. Nevertheless, the leaders of the Right themselves admitted that they had intentionally targeted sexual and family issues as a way of mobilizing conservative religious voters.

Richard Viguerie, the New Right's direct-mail wizard, though not a fundamentalist himself, was among the first to realize how a political realignment could occur; he estimated that there were 85 million Americans who could form a "pro-family" coalition: 50 million born-again Christians, 30 million morally conservative Roman Catholics, 3 million Mormons, and 2 million Orthodox Jews. This "vast untapped reservoir" could be tapped if political loyalties were cast around moral issues. Indeed, it appears that political consultants, not Christian Right groups, suggested that Jerry Falwell form a group like the Moral Majority.[11] Paul Weyrich, of the National Conservative Political Action Committee, predicted that "sexuality [would become] the Achilles heel of liberal Democrats" and that "family issues will be to [the] Right what Vietnam in the 1960s and consumer and environmental issues were to the Left in the 1970s."[12]

The power strategy of the Right was based on polls suggesting that there was indeed a basis for a politics of Social Purity that closely linked issues such as sexual promiscuity, abortion, divorce, teen pregnancy, and pornography. Although certain groups on the Christian Right such as the Moral Majority and Christian Voice would eventually alienate many people, including moderate and conservative voters, and although many voters never approved of some of the Christian Right's stands (such as a complete ban on abortion), in the late 1970s and early 1980s the Right managed to position itself much closer to majority sentiment than did the remnants of the 1960s Left. For example, John Simpson concluded from his survey that in the late 1970s a plurality of Americans endorsed the Moral Majority's position on homosexuality, prayer in the schools, gender roles, and some limits on abortion. Yinger and Cutler reported similar results from their survey, finding "intolerance toward antireligious and homosexual writings, opposition to legalized marijuana, abortion, extramarital and homosexual relations, and pornography."[13]

The success of the New Right on issues of sex and moral behavior was based on two factors. One was the ability of the New Right to mobilize evangelical and fundamentalist Protestants who were either nonvoters or had previously voted Democratic, particularly for Jimmy Carter in 1976.[14] Ed Rollins, the Republican pollster, estimates that 10–12 million votes shifted to the Republicans as a result of the rise of the religious Right, a shift "comparable to what the Democrats had gotten from Roman Catholic ethnics in the 1940s, 1950s, and 1960s."[15] Second, like the Social Purity Movement, the New Right found that at a time of vast social change and economic uncertainty, advocacy of traditionalist gender roles was a popular basis for organizing, particularly among conservative women in the South and in rural areas. The New Right skillfully tied the new sexual norms of the 1960s and 1970s to male vice and homewrecking. It also made the argument that the sexual revolution and women's liberation were leading to divorce, family breakup, and increasing poverty among housewives and other women. In her book *The Hearts of Men,* Ehrenreich directly compared women's support for the New Right in the 1970s with women's support for the Temperance Movement of the nineteenth century: In both eras, many women with limited earning potential were drawn to the idea that protecting the home and traditional family was a better strategy than the call of feminists for women's independence. Thus, in the absence of available high-wage jobs and generous social welfare benefits for women, conservative women saw the traditional sanctions against male vice as their only protection available.[16] The surprising success of the "traditional values" slogan among some women may be one reason why segments of the women's movement shifted in the late 1970s from an anti-family stance to a rhetoric focused on women's safety (i.e., protection against domestic violence, rape, etc.) as well as to anti-pornography campaigns.

Some observers do overrate the success of the New Right. Programmatically, groups like the Moral Majority were not terribly successful; and soon after Reagan's election, they bitterly complained that he had abandoned their social issues to focus on budget cutting and foreign policy. They were even less enamored of the Bush administration. But whereas the New Right lost legislatively and judicially on a number of important issues such as prayer in the schools, the overturning of *Roe v. Wade,* and funding for religious education, it was successful in altering the political climate and changing the terms of the debate. David Snowball captures this development in his history of the Moral Majority:

> Although it is clear that the Moral Majority gained little by way of legislative victories, . . . the organization helped to reshape the terms of public debate. By the late 1980s, public debate seemed to center on what sorts of controls should be imposed on pornography and abortion rather than whether such controls should be imposed. The question became how much the defense budget should grow, not "Should it grow?" . . . [A]bortion is no longer de-

fended by feminists as a positive good. . . . [I]t is, at best, a necessary evil. We no longer ask, "Should the schools go back to the basics?," but rather, "What is basic?" Finally, there is no longer any credible political defense of the vision of the Great Society. . . . In each of these areas, we now seem to be debating from fundamentally different premises than when first the Moral Majority emerged.[17]

Although Jerry Falwell, Pat Robertson, and others would have preferred to achieve a complete victory on every issue, the cultural success of the New Right was so great that by the mid-1980s conservative leaders were gloating about the New Temperance. Commenting respectively on the 1986 Meese Commission's report on pornography (which reversed the Nixon Commission's findings) and the Supreme Court ruling upholding state bans on sodomy, Falwell and Robertson were ecstatic. Falwell exclaimed, "The new moralism in this country has been growing for the past two decades. The awakening is manifesting itself in the change in the national lifestyle." And Robertson remarked, "I see a definite spiritual revival that is touching the standards of conduct of the entire society, which has gone too far toward sexual freedom. . . . [T]he American people are looking for a return to moral values that strengthen the family."[18]

The reaction to AIDS by some on the Right was almost gleeful; for these observers, the plague was a God-sent message in their battle against all that the "60s" represented, including liberalism and promiscuity. As Joseph Sobran described it: "[T]here was an unmistakable feeling in the air: the romance had gone out of the sexual revolution. . . . Today more than ever, to fornicate is to swim in polluted waters. The risk is incalculable." Don Feder and Ray Kerrison also referred to "the Sexual Revolution which began in the '60s and tore down nearly every protective moral restraint. The pitch was 'You can have it all, baby, without cost.' Virtue, chastity, monogamy were labeled Victorian and junked. Today, the tab is in. It's staggering and still climbing."[19]

The success of the Right's war against sin, however, also helped promote the New Temperance among the very movements stereotyped by the Right (and sometimes the media) as being libertarian or in favor of intemperance.

The Left and Puritanism

Interestingly, the association of "free love" and other intemperant behavior with leftist political views is a relatively recent one. In fact, early countercultural activists of the 1960s and 1970s as well as feminist and gay activists of the same period often railed against the social conservatism of the organized Left, particularly the Marxist parties.[20] As often as not, the Left has embraced temperance, based not on a supra-moralism of religion but, rather, in the words of Sidney and Beatrice Webb, on "Puritanism of a *rational* kind, founded not on religion, but on hygiene and on economics."[21] In fact, an argument frequently made by leftists is that capitalism is immoral because it breaks up families, leads women into prostitution and both sexes into immorality, and "hooks" people on pleasurable commodities from whose reach they cannot escape.[22]

Of course, historical generalizations should be made with caution, but it does appear that revolutionary periods characterized by mass surges of unrest tend to be associated with popular movements challenging puritanical symbols. The French Revolution, for example, was associated by the English, and by conservatives generally, with sexual intemperance—particularly adultery, open prostitution, and nudity.[23] And the Russian Revolution dramatically liberalized the social norms of that era: Proscriptions against homosexuality were overturned; anti-abortion, anti-divorce, and anti-contraceptive laws were dropped; and, in fact, almost all laws that limited personal behavior (including age-of-consent and incest laws) were eliminated.[24] The libertarian leftism of the 1960s and early 1970s in the United States appears to most closely parallel these periods.

By contrast, the Soviet Union under Stalin sharply reversed the earlier period of liberalization:

> The revival of Puritanism [in Russia] led to not only a condemning of frivolity, promiscuity, rape [the definition of which sometimes included having several marriages in a row], libertinism, seduction, [and] perversions . . . but to [admonitions against] kissing on the street, use of drugs or alcohol, [and support for] abstinence from smoking. . . . [T]he State further moved to re-criminalize homosexuality and abortion and put in more stringent divorce rules.[25]

For a variety of complex reasons, the Puritanism associated with Stalinism became characteristic of many twentieth-century Marxist and some Social Democratic parties. As often as not, governments in Eastern Europe, China, and Cuba embraced a belief in healthism and strict social control rather than in libertarianism. In part, they were responding to the administrative dilemmas of governance, which under both communism and social democracy came to resemble the power tactics of capitalist governing coalitions. But even in the United States, where the exercise of power was never a real possibility for the Left, a strand of radicalism has always been highly moralistic and utopian in its aims to correct the behavior of the masses.

Although perhaps less significant historically than the turnabout that occurred after the Russian Revolution, the shift in the American Left's understanding of personal behavior between the early 1970s and late 1980s was nearly as dramatic. For example, most liberal and leftist political groups and publications, many members of the organized women's movement, and some members of the gay movement arguably came to endorse aspects of the New Temperance. Although many Left observers suggest that the "influence of the Right" was primarily responsible for these changes on the Left, such arguments are too simple. They fail to account not only for the Left's own beliefs in healthism and moral perfectionism but also for the quest of many movements, particularly the "identity movements," for a way to be respectable, cleansing themselves of the sexual and other stigmatized connotations of their origins. (Such phrases as "bra burners" and "promiscuous gays" come to mind in this context).

Although organized forms of liberalism and leftism have perhaps not developed the coherent moral vision of a temperant life that the Right has, they have converged with the Right in a New Temperance consensus along several lines. The Left began to embrace healthism by the late 1970s. Such moralizing about health is most apparent in admonitions against cigarette smoking and for proper dietary habits, but over the years some on the Left have also emphasized the dangers of alcohol, drugs, television viewing, and sexuality. Although many leftists initially found it difficult to appear anti-sexual, it was during the mid-1970s, when cultural feminism emerged, that much heterosexual behavior, some aspects of homosexual behavior, and many media portrayals of sex came under attack and were deemed violent, aggressive, and unhealthy. Beginning in the late 1970s, various segments of the Left also became caught up in their own vision of crime control. From domestic violence to hate crimes, from stalking to "deadbeat dads," criticism of incarceration and other forms of punishment receded, changing to a proactive call for the state to "crack down" on various types of offenders.

The Construction of Anti-Corporate Healthism

It must have seemed quite odd to an old leftist of the 1930s, or even to a short-term Rip Van Winkle from the 1960s who had been active in the Students for Democratic Society or the Black Panther Party, to read the pages of some leftist and liberal publications in the late 1970s. For example, *Mother Jones*, a leftist magazine founded in 1976, featured articles of traditional concerns to the Left, but it also included articles on the dangers of salt, cigarette smoking, artificial lighting, fatty foods, prescription drugs, television viewing, and pornography as well as on the benefits of homeopathic medicine and eating tofu.[26] Though named after radical labor organizer Mary Harris Jones, *Mother Jones* never explained the relationship between the health issues just noted and the class struggles of the coal fields.[27] Nor in retrospect can the Left's embrace of these health issues be chalked up to a lack of other important issues: Indeed, the period from the middle to late 1970s was the start of a dramatic downturn in American living standards, deindustrialization and plant closings, and a severe fiscal crisis of the state.

There are many reasons for the Left's change in focus to "personal politics." First, with the exception of the Black Movement, the Left in the 1960s was a middle-class movement; so, compared to the Left of earlier days in America (and in some other countries), it is not surprising that matters of health and style competed with an interest in the rights of workers and poor people. Second, by the mid-1970s, many issues that had united the New Left, particularly the draft and the Vietnam War, were no longer around, and a search for new causes was becoming apparent. The environmental and consumer movements, which began as liberal issues in the 1960s, had a strong impact on much of the Left by the 1970s as a new source of popular organizing issues. Finally, the appeal of the "personal politics" of feminism, the gay and lesbian movement, and the environmental movement likely combined with the countercultural lifestyle of many former hippies and leftists to produce an interest in the politics of health and lifestyle.

As noted earlier, the counterculture of the baby boom generation was also attracted both to attacks on hypocrisy within the "system" and to attacks on behavior characteristic of the conservative members of the older generation. One favorite, which perhaps made anti-cigarette smoking and anti-alcohol arguments so popular on the Left, was the comparison between the relative lack of harm associated with drugs like marijuana and the use of tobacco and alcohol by "straights." Opposition to the illegality of marijuana (and, to a lesser degree, of all illicit drugs) was one of the main generational points of agreement for much of the baby boom generation. Paradoxically, the pro-legalization argument failed to carry the day, but the Left moved to an anti-tobacco and, sometimes, anti-alcohol stance. The Left's critique of cigarettes and liquor was easily co-opted by forces as varied as Surgeon Generals and Mothers Against Drunk Driving (MADD). By the 1980s the new "substance abuse" paradigm had strongly linked tobacco and alcohol use with illicit drug use, and all drug use (including cigarette smoking) was increasingly being prohibited from schools and workplaces. Many former radicals are indeed now employed as teachers, social workers, counselors, and doctors who manage the substance abuse industry and police these very prohibitions.

But what the Left probably found most attractive about the New Temperance was the fact that corporate giants were behind the production of cigarettes, fast food, alcohol, prescription drugs, and other products criticized by the Left. Taking on the tobacco industry proved popular because a small number of large corporations could be portrayed as "villains" that profited from people's illnesses or deaths. A similar argument was made with respect to the food industry:

> The American diet is getting worse because the oligopolistic food industry concentrates on selling sweets and junk food with little or no nutritional value. . . . [T]he food industry's propaganda runs a close second to its products in nausea level.[28]

> Our ample supplies of tobacco and social tolerance of both smoking and withdrawal symptoms ("I need a cigarette") make its addictive property nearly invisible. Nevertheless, this is precisely why tobacco is one of the country's most profitable and, in turn, most politically powerful industries. Tobacco's promoters never stop working. Their activities range from contributions to political campaigns . . . and support for well-placed members of Congress to the advertisements that make most of the nation's press afraid to print stories like this.[29]

For segments of the Left, the ideal targets for attack were corporate giants that polluted the environment, produced dangerous or unhealthy products, and wielded corrupt or insidious political power. Two decades after the first such attacks by the Left, liberal columnist Ellen Goodman candidly admitted her glee over the ensnarement of such juicy villains: "Someday we are all going to miss the tobacco companies. They just don't make corporate villains like this anymore. Oh, occasionally an oil company turns a massive spill into a public-relations bonanza. But nothing rivals the . . . tobacco industry."[30]

The basic logic of the anti-corporate argument regarding tobacco, food, alcohol, and (later) pornography and television is that they "hook" consumers through glamorous advertisements and promises of joy. Then, over time, the consumers become "addicted" to these substances or pleasures—and, of course, it is in the best interests of the capitalists to keep as many customers addicted to the product for as long as possible, in order to maximize profits. Few would argue that this premise is not true: Just as a drug pusher pushes drugs, so a tobacco company pushes cigarettes; McDonald's, hamburgers; Seagram's, alcohol; and CBS, television shows.

But despite the basic truth of this anti-capitalist analysis, the anti-corporatism of the Left has failed to produce the desired results and, indeed, embodies its own logical contradictions. Several issues are raised. First, the attack on the food industry, tobacco companies, and other corporations was initially meant as *metaphor:* The American people, presumably through education about corporate profit making, would eventually see the tobacco or alcohol pushers as *paradigmatic* of capitalism as a whole. In other words, at least among the organized Left, reform of smoking or eating habits was not really a goal *in itself* but, rather, a vehicle toward a goal (namely, the overthrow of an entire system based on profit). Unfortunately, such symbolic metaphors have historically undermined broader goals rather than enhanced them. As Joseph Gusfield notes, the first Temperance Movement also drew on some radical symbols, such as "the anti–big business campaign of Populism." But by attacking only the "liquor trusts," the movement actually helped turn these anti-capitalist instincts into a purely anti-alcoholism crusade rather than an anti-capitalist movement.[31] As with the old Temperance Movement, evidence suggests that the basic message the public receives is that cigarettes or fatty foods or alcoholic beverages are "bad." The public may or may not come to believe that the corporate chiefs of *these* industries (much less those of other industries) are corrupt. Propaganda initially based on anti-corporatism has turned primarily into agitation about the harmfulness of the particular products. Neither the early temperance movements nor the more recent ones ever succeeded in doing more than focusing the public on the unhealthy aspects of a substance or product, as opposed to revealing the broader morality of profit-making business.

In fact, as with the Temperance Movement of old, since many conservatives and moderates agree with objections raised against the sale of tobacco and alcohol, and are even critical of profit making from unsavory items such as pornography or violent movies, the leftist critique of these industries is popular precisely because it brings about *convergence* with nonradical, even conservative parts of the public. By attacking *only* these unsavory items, the health advocates are implicitly supporting the other products of capitalism, thus presumably implying that there are "good" and "bad" things to buy. In fact, reformist campaigns against such products almost inevitably create "good guys" to counter the "bad guys." Hence, in a 1979 issue of *Mother Jones,* half of which was devoted to the ills of smoking, the "good guys" were often other capitalists, such as broadcasters who wanted to do exposés on cigarettes. Or in the two 1994 issues of *The Nation* that attacked cigarette companies and smoking, the "good guys" turned out to be people like Everett Koop and President Clinton for taking on the "tobacco cartel."[32] Both the temperance campaigns of the nineteenth and early twentieth centuries and the anti-corporatism of the New Temperance suggest a basic argument not with capitalism but only with "irresponsible" capitalists.

Another logical criticism is that if tobacco companies, food companies, pharmaceutical companies, and the like cannot be trusted with the nation's health, why not take a socialist position and call for their nationalization? After all, socialist theory would postulate that worker and consumer exploitation arises from the extraction of profits, not only from the product itself. Moreover, if the incentive to "hook" people on tobacco, alcohol, television, or drugs relates to profits, why not eliminate the profits and the incentive to sell more of the product? Christopher Hitchens, a leftist critic of the anti-tobacco agitation, shares my skepticism about health activists. Indeed, he suggests that they are no longer anti-capitalist in any serious sense:

> Much of this militant [anti-tobacco] prohibitionism is fueled by a stern sense that those who practice it are standing up to the big, ruthless corporations. . . . I am, of course, shocked as anyone else to find out that big corporations can behave unethically when it comes to research and marketing. . . . Try a simple thought experiment. Would great and courageous social reformers . . . relax their attitude one bit if I grew my own tobacco and rolled my own, handmade cigarettes? The question answers itself.[33]

The failure of reformers to propose nationalizing these industries feeds the suspicion that they do not like the smoke, drink, drugs, fast food, and other products they are criticizing. Under the guise of anti-corporatism is an embedded critique that judges the *consumer* as much as the producer: "The naive indignation about the tobacco industry is no more than a populist decoration for a campaign which actually targets the consumers rather than the producers."[34] In other words, rather than advocating nationalization of the evil industries, the liberal and leftist position on a variety of subjects—from smoking to television—has merely embraced the public health education approach of haranguing the citizenry. As I noted in Chapter 4, the healthist view of the consumer is really quite negative. What do these activists really think of people who, after decades of health messages, continue to smoke cigarettes, eat fatty food, drink alcohol to excess, and so on? The best that can be said is that they are seen as judgmental dupes who have no power of their own to stop their unhealthy behavior. This view of life, encapsulated in the popular new jargon of addiction and self-esteem, is curiously contradictory. Though the Left historically has spoken of "empowerment," "self-determination," the "people's will," and so on, it often embraces a view of corporations as intelligent (if devious) but of the average person as rather dull and unable to make sound decisions about daily life. Further, the issue of health and habits, cultural likes and dislikes, raises the question of who should decide which consumer goods are to be produced. As sometimes charged by the Right, leftist supporters of healthism and temperance often do appear to be elitists when they discuss public habits and culture. Although it is unlikely that a middle-class Left would have such power, one does wonder whether, for example, soap operas or action films would be banned under their aegis as retrograde and unenlightening to the public.

Ultimately, healthism has led the Left into a mild liberalism of "corporate responsibility," a vague term implying minor limits on only the most untrammeled corporate power. For example, the alcohol industry is called upon to take responsibility for drunk driving, or the television industry is urged to better police its violent shows. Like other vague residues of the social movements of the 1960s, these stances can be seen as the triumph of an expressive politics, of form over substance. By retaining the trappings of the anti-capitalist language of their youth, many ex-radicals have more easily reconciled their overall peace with capitalism as a system by righteously condemning tobacco companies or the entertainment industry.

Sex, Violence, and Feminism

I think words like purity, morality, and decency are very nice words. I wish the women's movement would reclaim these words.

—Radical feminist Susan Brownmiller[35]

And yet it was feminism—not the new right, certainly not the as-yet-unknown AIDS virus—that first displaced the counterculture's vision of sex with a considerably harsher view.

—Radical ("pro-sex") feminist Ellen Willis[36]

Just as a Rip Van Winkle of the SDS would be surprised upon waking up twenty years later to find that leftist anti-capitalism had become only a critique of the "bad guy" industries, many of the early activists of the women's liberation movement would be surprised to awaken in the 1980s or 1990s to find that, in general, feminism was now focused on the "male predator" rather than on overturning the social system. Although the move of some feminists from a social-structural critique to a moralistic crusade against male vice has been opposed by a number of prominent activists in the wings of the movement, often the most publicized feminists have not only focused their anger on male vice but have also been critical of heterosexual sex, and have viewed gender relations in a neo-Victorian light.

Interestingly, accounts of the early history of second-wave American feminism from the mid-1960s to the mid-1970s agree that activists were strongly wedded to sexual freedom rather than to sexual control.[37] Kate Millet was typical of early leaders of the women's movement in calling for an "end of traditional sexual inhibitions and taboos, particularly those that most threaten patriarchal monogamous marriage: homosexuality, illegitimacy, adolescent, pre- and extra-marital sex."[38] Indeed, Barbara Ehrenreich, Elizabeth Hess, and Gloria Jacobs argue in *Re-Mak-*

ing Love that the women's movement, rather than opposing the sexual revolution, was radical in its insistence that women enjoy sex:

> The feminist reclamation of sex made women's liberation, at least for a brief few years in the early seventies, as much a movement for sexual liberation. Clearly, women had been deprived, sexually stunted in service of the vaginal and phallocentric sex imposed by men. They needed more sex, but they needed sex in a variety that went far beyond the traditional in-and-out, man-on-top intercourse. Clitoral sex, Alix Shulman pointed out, demanded a wider range of options, including oral sex, lesbian sex, and positions for intercourse that were more favorable to clitoral stimulation. All the old prohibitions and taboos would have to give way to the needs of the sexually liberated woman.[39]

Although the women's movement of the 1960s and early 1970s had much to say that was critical of men's sexual behavior and sexism generally, Ehrenreich and leftist feminists such as Ellen Willis, Deirdre English, Alice Echols, and Lynne Segal argued that it is "to falsify [the] past" to claim, as many cultural feminists later did, that the sexual revolution was "male," with only male interests at stake.[40] In fact, the stereotype of "bra burners" cultivated by the media, though intentionally dismissive, was closer to the mood of the late 1960s than the stern attitude toward sex that some authors and activists embraced later on and retrospectively applied to the sexual revolution.

Nor was the feminist movement of 1966–1975, in either its more liberal or its more leftist variant, primarily about male violence. For example, the demands of the massive August 1970 march by the National Organization of Women (NOW) in New York City focused on twenty-four-hour child care, abortion on demand, and equal employment and educational opportunities.[41] As Lynne Segal notes, in the 1970s the British women's movement focused "on child care, family allowances and welfare, women employees organizing, and [the] demand for women's control over sexuality and fertility."[42] Rape was first introduced as an important women's issue during speakouts in New York in 1971, although it did not become a prominent rallying point until some years later. The issue of battered women did not emerge until the mid-1970s.[43] And issues such as incest, child sexual abuse, and date rape did not arise until well into the 1980s.

Of course, all social movements change their focus over time, and few people would dispute the importance of the seminal work on combating violence that has been revealed by feminist authors and activists. But a movement focused on criticizing sexual excess or male aggressiveness has a very different implication from a movement focused on, say, "wages for housework," comparable worth in pay, welfare rights, or access to birth control. The post-1975 history of the women's movement includes several complex developments: the detachment of most activists from a leftist perspective; the defeat by the Right of many proposed reforms (most prominently the ERA in the 1970s); and the influence of cultural feminist writers who have countered gender-equality arguments with what has been criticized as an "essentialist" argument in which women exclusively represent purity, motherhood, and peacefulness whereas men exclusively represent power, aggression, and anger. Rather than calling for gender equality, then, cultural feminists sometimes assert the eternal superiority of broadly defined "female" values and culture.

Although a historical account of the debates within the women's movement is beyond the scope of this book, I can point to some important differences between the women's movement that originated on the Left in the 1960s and the more conservative women's movement that came later. First, the earlier movement aimed at changing society by altering the *organization* of the social structure. That is, it understood patriarchy and capitalism to be socially embedded in the economic, political, and legal orders. Of course, early (second-wave) feminism also recognized personal issues and problems; but the movement's discussion of the "personal" (even in early consciousness-raising groups) was intended to bring about broader social change, not to be an end in itself. As segments of the movement developed a more cultural feminist orientation, the power arrangements of society were often elided. In other words, sexism or patriarchy came to be identified more with *individual* men and their behavior than with the social structure. Hence an attack on a pornographer or an abusive husband or a sexual harasser came to be viewed by some as "political," although it is unclear how punishing individual offenders necessarily advances broader economic or social transformations.

Second, the earlier women's movement was more optimistic about human behavior and more concerned about creating conditions for both sexes to change collectively than with relying on state power to police human behavior. But as a parallel to what has occurred in other social movements (e.g., racial minorities' and gay activists' support for severe punishment of hate crimes), the more recent position in American feminism is one of support for the identification and punishment of miscreants. The state, once identified as the seat of patriarchal power, now often assumes the mantle of a neutral agent, protecting women and other victims of crime and violence.

First introduced in the early 1970s was a "politics of rage" within the women's movement, which was often separatist, hostile to the Left, and highly personal in its attacks on women accused of pursuing "male" politics. By the late 1970s a body of work associated with Susan Brownmiller, Adrienne Rich, Andrea Dworkin, Robin Morgan, Catherine

MacKinnon, Mary Daley, Rita Mae Brown, Sheila Jeffreys, and others was providing a new theory for the movement. Cultural feminism saw sexuality as a primary sphere of male power, which in turn was produced and reproduced through sexual acts, sexual overtures, and the consorting of women who accommodated male lust and desire. For some theorists, rape was indistinguishable from ordinary sex:

> Violence is male; the male is the penis; violence is the penis.[44]

> Rape is male biological destiny.... [T]he human male is a predator and the human female serves as his natural prey.[45]

> All men are potential rapists. ... [E]very man benefits from the actions of every rapist.[46]

Although many feminists (even those within the cultural feminist orbit) would not agree with these more extreme formulations, several political implications drawn from them helped spur a feminist New Temperance. First, the association between sex and rape was extended to pornography. In simple terms, it was claimed that "pornography is the theory, rape is the practice"—in other words, that the violent, sexist, and patriarchal psychosocial development of men was predicated on their exposure to sexual and violent material in books, film, art, speech, and so on. Second, heterosexual relations were so dominated by men that relations between women became superior ("Lesbianism is the practice and feminism is the theory"). Many feminist activists were put on the defensive if they were partnered with or having sex with men. Yet some lesbians criticized the new "political lesbianism" as patronizing and de-sexing of lesbian sexual relationships. That is, some feminists appeared to accept lesbianism as a political act but to frown on *actual* sex.[47] Third, feminists criticized some behaviors that were associated with male violence and aggression (e.g., promiscuous, underage, public, or sadomasochistic sex) even when such behaviors were practiced by women, and even when the criticism explicitly pitted cultural feminists against gay male activists. And, fourth, since domination of women was associated with the practice of violence, a crusade against all forms of individual male violence seems to have taken primacy over other issues. Metaphorically at least, causes such as those directed against "incest and marital rape strike blows at the fundamental institution of male supremacy itself, the heterosexual family," as Sheila Jeffreys put it.[48] The focus on eternal, essential male vice, coupled with a fixed notion of the victimized female, arguably replayed the moralism of the Social Purity Movement of a hundred years earlier.

In the late 1970s and early 1980s, groups such as Women Against Pornography (WAP) emerged and marched along with the New Right, pressing city councils and state governments to censor pornographic books and other media. (They succeeded only briefly in Indianapolis and Suffolk County, New York, before courts overturned the anti-pornography laws that ensued.) At the same time, however, a number of leftist feminists formed groups such as Feminists Against Censorship Today (FACT) and "No More Nice Girls," a pro-choice organization that linked sexual liberation with abortion rights. Yet as noted by Ellen Willis, one of the leaders of leftist "pro-sex" feminism, although such organizing helped halt further resolutions supporting censorship in the women's movement, these groups "got little media visibility" in comparison with the anti-pornography movement.[49] In the early 1980s, Willis and others also connected the new sexual conservatism with the Social Purity and Temperance movements, and warned that such strategies would lead to a political convergence and cooperation with the Right: "[T]he [women's] movement's attacks on sexual exploitation and violence, male irresponsibility, pornography, and so on, have often reinforced right-wing propaganda by giving the impression that feminists consider the loosening of controls over sexual behavior a worse threat to women than repression."[50] In a related context, Willis noted:

> Whatever its intent, the effect of feminists' emphasis on controlling male sexuality—particularly when that emphasis is combined with a neo-Victorian view of women's nature and the conviction that securing women's safety from male aggression should be the chief priority of the women's movement—is to undercut feminist opposition to the right. It provides powerful reinforcement for conservative efforts to manipulate women's fear of untrammeled male sexuality, intimidating women into stifling their own impulses toward freedom so as to cling to what little protection the traditional roles still offer.[51]

By the 1990s, a variant of many cultural feminist ideas has succeeded in having a major policy impact, at least where such rhetoric can be utilized to support conventional morality. For example, widespread campaigns have been launched on local, state, and national levels to protect women and children from graphic sexual representations. From the 1986 Meese Commission's citation of radical feminist rhetoric, to the Parents Music Resource Center's reference to violence against women as a reason to censor rock music lyrics, to the efforts at censoring the Internet in 1995, right-wing, centrist, and liberal politicians have all used pro-women rhetoric as a justification for repressive policies.

A strengthening of police apparatus, including centralized information systems and stiffer sentencing, has emerged in both the United States and Great Britain as a result of an informal alliance between the ostensibly opposed camps of women's groups and social conservatives.[52] Examples include mandatory arrest of domestic abusers, community notification about the presence of alleged child molesters, the public stigmatizing of some sex offenders, laws against stalking, laws against ritual abuse, and laws permitting the expansion of the statute of limitations for charges of sexual abuse. In 1994, the Clinton administration's Crime Bill, which promised to build more prisons and to put more police officers on the street, also garnered some feminist and liberal support because of its violence-against-women provisions. In addition, a variety of repressive actions taken against gays and other sexual minorities have obtained some tacit support. For example, many of the most repressive actions ostensibly taken against HIV/AIDS, such as closing gay bathhouses and increasing harassment of prostitutes, have met with neutrality and even support within the women's movement. Publicizing the names of "johns" involved in prostitution, prohibiting sexual "cruising," and posting the names or taking away the licenses of "deadbeat dads" are additional examples of current social-control efforts that are gaining the support of some liberal and cultural feminists.

Key to the success of the new pro-temperance feminism, as opposed to the older leftist or more libertarian feminism, has been its very ability to shed the ideological baggage of the Left that some activists saw as limiting its appeal. Alice Echols, whose historical account associates the rise of the women's movement with the New Left and criticizes its subsequent detachment, attacks the apoliticism of groups like WAP. For example, she disapprovingly quotes activist Judith Bat-Ada calling for "a coalition of all women [against pornography] . . . regardless of race, color, creed, religion, or *political persuasion*," arguing that Bat-Ada sanctions a "grand and virtuous sisterhood to combat male lasciviousness"[53] by making no allowances for class and racial differences, avoiding any suggestion of unity with oppressed men, and relying on the patriarchal state. Though Echols is correct from a leftist perspective, this is precisely the *point* of consensual issue organizing, particularly where the politics of "motherhood and apple pie" is concerned. To gain the support of *all* women, to unify *across class* and *across political lines:* This is exactly the goal of respectable temperant politics. By choosing conventional issues drawing on long-term cultural distaste and opposition (pornography, violence against women, etc.), mainstream temperant politics achieves a better fit between the women's movement and the conservatism of the American political system. Along the way, of course, the residues of anti-capitalism or anti-statism are usually shed at the doorstep of the statehouse or city hall where such lobbying occurs.

Like the left's campaigning against cigarette smoking, alcohol, and unhealthy diets, campaigns against violence and pornography can be seen as ways of achieving feminist respectability. As the "sex radical" editors of *Powers of Desire* note in comparing the late nineteenth century to the 1970s and 1980s, "[S]exual politics makes strange bedfellows. . . . Then, as now, a moral crusade offer[s] the Left a chance to cleanse itself of the taint of sex radicalism and free love."[54] The politics of respectability develops coalitions with dominant powers based on conventional morality both because such coalitions are a time-tested way of achieving reforms in the conservative political process and because they allow middle-class radicals or former radicals to prove that they support dominant values (after all) and are deserving of legislative success as well as political, professional, and bureaucratic leadership positions within the system.

De-Sexualizing the Gay Movement

We demand . . . the right to make love with anyone, anyway, anytime, . . . the right to treat and express our bodies as we will and the right to express our own individuality.
>   —Gay Activists Alliance (late 1960s)[55]

Many [are now] . . . prepared to describe homosexuality as falling within the moral boundaries of American society only if it approximated a middle class romantic ideal. In this regard they have enlisted AIDS in their campaign to construct an image of "the respectable homosexual" to legitimate a sexual ethic of monogamy and romance where Eros is justified only in this context.
>   —Steven Seidman (1992)[56]

Perhaps no movement coming out of the 1960s was as libertarian about personal behavior as the gay rights movement, which emerged after the Stonewall riot in 1969. First, looking back on centuries of oppression by governments throughout the Western world, gay activists were more suspicious of state regulation than were other activists associated with the Left (e.g., socialists and feminists). Second, at least initially, the experience of oppression based on sexuality, so basic to personal life, led gay activists to speak in terms of *human* liberation rather than about fixed sexual orientation. The right not only to practice any sexual act but to conduct oneself in any fashion that was not harmful to others was championed by the movement. As Dennis Altman points out in his provocative *The Homosexualization of America,* the gay rights movement merged with other liberatory trends in the 1960s and 1970s to influence the behavior of young people who did not identify as "gay." The movement also challenged the "natural" connection between sex and procreation, sex and monogamy, sex and marriage, and sex and privacy, which had all come under question as elements of the sexual revolution and counterculture of the era. Ultimately, the gay movement frightened social conservatives not only because it flouted their obvious hostility toward homosexual acts, but also because it was profoundly influencing young people of all sexual proclivities and seemed to undermine marriage, the family, religion, and the social order.[57]

By the late 1970s, as with the women's movement, a combination of right-wing gains, the collapse of any broader Left, and the need to consolidate and unify a separate gay movement united by sexual orientation but cutting across class and other political lines considerably deradicalized the movement. The model of pursuing rights as an "ethnic minority" model based on a fixed gay or lesbian orientation rather than on the liberatory goals of freedom of sexual behavior has been critiqued by radical gay author Jeffrey Weeks as follows: "The early theorists of gay liberation echoed [Herbert] Marcuse and the Left, and saw gay liberation as leading to 'the end of the homosexual,' breaking down the separate construction. . . . [N]ow in a great ruse of history, it was the less radical elements in gay liberation who took up the idea of a gay 'minority' which ultimately made for a better fit with liberal pluralism."[58]

The gay movement moved from a call for sexual and personal freedom to a construction of people "who have no choice" but are simply biologically or otherwise driven into a fixed sexual orientation. Rather than becoming "liberated," then, gay behavior was arguably somewhat remedicalized into something innate or at least inalterable. Moreover, in response to hostile attacks, "liberation" evolved into reformism, a more narrow justification for gay, lesbian, and bisexual rights, along the lines of the American right to privacy (which similarly became the major justification for abortion rights). As Susan Johnston points out, in many ways the right to privacy contradicts the sex radicalism of the gay, lesbian, and other sexual minority movements: "The rhetorical strategies in response to the Right's anti-gay campaigning ultimately reinforce rather than disrupt the Right's agenda. The rhetoric on both sides depends on liberal political theory, but Liberal Political Theory cannot depathologize homosexual sex and therefore cannot produce rights for sexual minorities. . . . [T]hey are different sides of the same discourse."[59]

Johnston argues that liberal political theory, the finding of a civil right for private behavior, contradicts the whole notion of queer rights as moving "out of the closet." The right not only to have sex with any person but to *identify* oneself publicly as being gay is at the heart of queer politics. Acceptance of the belief that sexuality or some other manifestation of identity should remain a private right exercised at home behind closed doors reinforces the conservative view that the problem with sexual radicals is that they want to be public about sex. Much right-wing rhetoric, in fact, suggests that if gays and other sexual minorities would just stop making their sexuality so visible, and instead be temperate and private, they would not require "special rights."

The use of both a minority model and a liberal civil rights model led many gay leaders to embrace the New Temperance even at a time (in the 1970s) when many male homosexual communities were still associated with open sexuality. To those who are leading reform groups, forming pressure groups in legislatures and Congress, and investing in the political process, it is very inconvenient to see embarrassing behavior on the streets or sexual displays on the news. Weeks notes that by 1978 gay leaders were seeing "widespread promiscuity as weakening the respectability and political pull of the community."[60] But beyond promiscuity, the way gays looked, how public their sexuality was, and what other practices they engaged in concerned gay leaders. In fact, by the 1990s, the public persona of homosexuality had gradually begun to parallel the informal rules of the old 1950s-style pressure groups such as the Mattachine Society, as described by Tobi Marotta: "Homosexuals who looked and acted 'straight' [heterosexual], preferred monogamous couplings, and confined their sexual activity to the bedroom were said to deserve rights and status; those who enjoyed promiscuity, pornography, sex role deviation, and cross-dressing were said to have problems; and those who pursued sex in public places, intimacy with minors, and fetishistic sexual activity were alternatively pitied and denounced."[61]

Of course, the AIDS crisis, to put it mildly, further undermined efforts to present gay sexual behavior in a positive light. Here, seemingly from "nature," was a justification for the more rabid critics of sexual freedom to say "we told you so!" The gay movement has struggled over the last decade and a half against a whole range of proposals for violating the civil liberties of a great many people—not only gays but also drug users, prostitutes, people of color, and all people who are potentially HIV-positive. But of interest here is the fact that, under the pressure of public panic about AIDS, the voices from the gay movement most often heard in the mainstream media (as a parallel to the way debates within the women's movement have been covered) were those of gays who were the most puritanical about sex. An example is Randy Shilts, the author of *And the Band Played On* and, before his death, one of the most-quoted spokespeople on AIDS and the gay community. Shilts's description of San Francisco gay life conveyed shock and horror over the gay community's failure to protect itself, becoming a victim of its own sexual irresponsibility. This account was widely pronounced as gospel by the media, but it leaves out Shilts's own participation in San Francisco's gay politics as well as his own role in spreading panic about the gay bathhouses.[62] Two other widely quoted gay activists were Larry Kramer, playwright and founder of the Gay Men's Health Crisis in New York City, who attacked gay irresponsibility and promiscuity, and Michael Callen, a gay activist who cowrote the alarmist 1982 article "We Know Who We Are," which blamed the AIDS epidemic on promiscuous gay sex.[63]

Influenced by AIDS and the temperant visions of the time, "the new orthodoxy became that gay promiscuity was a sign of self-hate and immaturity," and widespread 12-step recovery language found its way into the gay community as a criticism of both "sexual addiction" and open displays of sexuality.[64] As parodied in the irreverent 1995 film *Jeffry*, about gay life in the 1990s, the conventional wisdom of the time regarding gay presentation of the self combines recovery language, respectable comportment, and a de-sexualization of looks and behavior. In one scene from the movie, an inspirational New Age speaker played by Sigourney Weaver convinces a crowd of gay men that low self-esteem is the cause of AIDS, and that individual will power can overcome the disease and the inner weakness that causes it. In another scene, three gay men parody the "we are like everyone else" message, mimicking the strong masculine voice with which activists must speak to the press and joking that their own "gay occupations" (waiter, interior designer, hairdresser) cannot be revealed to the public because as activists they must appear to be doctors, lawyers, or construction workers. In still other scenes, the film satirizes the new injunctions against public kissing and handholding, wearing leather and "looking gay," and being promiscuous or "on the make."

The de-sexing of homosexuality was in part strategic, since the AIDS crisis had perhaps given the heterosexual public far more details about gay sex than they cared to know. Demanding civil rights for average-looking, (presumably) monogamous, middle-class doctors and lawyers was a far better political strategy than demanding sexual rights for effeminate hairdressers or rowdy, threatening-looking men in leather. Yet this strategy came at the cost of adopting a new standard of sexual and social life that was conventional. As Robert Padgug comments in "Gay Villain, Gay Hero":

> The nature of the gay community, the institutions that provide its cohesion, and the way gay people deal with one another have all changed considerably. At the same time, gay sexuality has increasingly been reconstructed under the impetus of AIDS along the lines of sexuality found in the majority heterosexual world. This has, for example, meant a new emphasis on "dating" and on longer-term, more monogamous relationships among gay men. The new sexuality is perhaps symbolized by the "wedding" ceremony that brought together thousands of gay and lesbian couples to reaffirm their commitment to each other on Oct. 10, 1987. . . . [C]hange has also meant a decline in the various forms of sexual experimentation, spontaneity, unorthodox relationships, community "flamboyance," willingness to

cross social boundaries, and sense of "celebration"—the "Dionysian" aspects of life—that made the gay community so interesting and creative in the 1970s.[65]

It is, of course, difficult to speculate exactly how the New Temperance would have developed by the late 1980s and 1990s without the AIDS virus as a powerful catalyst. But observers such as Altman, Seidman, and Weeks suggest that the trend toward sexual Puritanism started well before AIDS. In their view, a middle-class-sanctioned "sexual choice but only within defined limits" is not a surprising result given the already limited strategy that gay leaders had developed by the late 1970s. A liberal construction of homosexuality was adopted by a variety of opinion leaders by the 1980s, paradoxically often helped by the AIDS crisis, which generated sympathy for gays. The new liberal view supported gay rights, but only for those who were willing to "reaffirm a sexual ethic that binds sex to romance, love, intimacy and monogamy."[66] Long-term gay couples who could qualify for domestic partnership benefits were contrasted with homosexuals leading "the fast lane, free-wheeling sexual lifestyle," which, of course, was held responsible for AIDS. By the mid-1990s, Ann Landers could reassure her readers that "most gay males are indistinguishable from straight males" and that it was only the "lunatic fringe, extremists and nut cases who impede progress, block acceptance and make life hard for everybody" (the latter presumably being effeminate, overly sexual, and otherwise stereotypical gays).[67]

Convergence in the Politics of Danger

There is always a minister of health, but virtually never of pleasure. There is a gross national product, but not a gross national pleasure."

—Lionel Tiger[68]

In a society that holds up an increasingly punitive work ethic above any ethic of love or compassion, it is risky indeed to assert *pleasure* as a legitimate social goal. But to remain silent is to concede to a particular political mentality and view of the world.

—Barbara Ehrenreich, Elizabeth Hess, and Gloria Jacobs[69]

A convergence, if not on all issues, then on many, now characterizes the partisan political spectrum, as exemplified by the centrist politics of neoliberalism and President Bill Clinton. The "new consensus" on sex, drugs, and personal behavior, of course, parallels the widely trumpeted new consensus on issues such as welfare reform, crime, foreign policy, and a balanced budget. One way of framing the New Temperance is that it elevates the politics of danger—crime, disease, danger, family break-down—above any possible sense of a politics of pleasure. The "excesses" of the past, whether in terms of welfare benefits, the underclass, the "60s," liberalism, or leftism, are now to be regretted by all "responsible" politicians.

Without question, the Right advanced the politics of danger in the mid-1970s, and it bears chief responsibility for prosecuting the Temperance Wars, including the war against drugs. In concise form, the New Temperance marks a victory for conservative politics. That is, the middle 1960s to early 1970s politics of the New Left, the counterculture, the women's movement, the gay and lesbian movement, and other movements paradoxically produced a stronger right-wing counterreaction in the political sphere than participants of these movements would ever have imagined. Skillfully using the symbols of home and family, and wielding a kind of "apple pie authoritarianism,"[70] the Right outmaneuvered leftists and liberals in the political process, and placed the nascent social movements of the 1960s on the defensive. Key among the Right's symbols have been the dangers posed by sex, substances, and "permissiveness." By the 1980s, remnants of the leftist social movements as well as the Democratic Party strategically saved a few vestiges of power here and there (primarily in areas such as the academy, journalism, and social services) and prevented a few of the social gains won by the new social movements, such as abortion and gay rights, from being totally extinguished. As noted earlier, the political process favored the Right on issues of personal behavior, for reasons having to do with the demographics of the electorate as well as with the historical, cultural, and religious symbols to which most Americans adhere. These conservative beliefs favor a politics based on fear of danger, crime, disease, and social breakdown over a politics of pleasure.

Yet I am also struck by the degree to which the New Temperance had become a consensual movement by the 1980s and 1990s. Perhaps, as both Tiger and Ehrenreich have noted, the politics of pleasure is just not politically popular.[71] And as Douglas and Wildavsky have observed, "[T]he language of the political process accepts no risks," so in a sense the *possibility* of danger arouses more emotion than the possibility of personal pleasure.[72] The Right has frequently made use of, and even directly quoted, cultural feminist thought to justify anti-pornography ordinances and increased police action against male predators. Similarly, some feminists have quoted right-wing theorists such as George Gilder to support their view of the innate violence of men.[73] In the campaigns against substance abuse, not only do conservatives and liberals compete about who is "tougher on drugs," but liberals and leftist critics continue to call for more repression of smokers and drinkers (particularly teens), citing the hypocrisy of the "drug war." In turn, some on the Right have used the liberals' anti-smoking war as a favorable example of how improper behavior can be changed.[74] Somewhat logically they ask, If the behavior of smokers can be changed, why can't the same be true of sexual and other behaviors, which liberals sometimes assert are immutable?[75]

One symbol of the new consensus around health and danger was the popularity of Surgeon General Everett Koop. A conservative anti-abortionist, Koop was appointed by Ronald Reagan in 1981 as a sop to the New Right. Yet over the decade, Koop received praise from many liberals, primarily because of his opposition to tobacco smoking and the tobacco companies, and his willingness to speak out against the dangers of AIDS.[76] Praise for Koop can benignly be interpreted as representing the new minimalism (it doesn't take much for a politician to win some liberal praise these days). But more important, liberal activists seem not to notice that they are embracing a model of social control, which, buried behind its righteousness, is not very "progressive" in its vision. Koop's opposition to smoking, like that of Mormon Orrin Hatch, for example, proceeded from the conservative American tradition, and, of course, was linked with the war on drugs and alcohol. Whereas Koop's medical training led him to endorse the provision of condoms to those "who will not abstain" from sex, his overall approach to the AIDS crisis was to engage in the gloom and doom of vastly overstated predictions coupled with denunciations of promiscuity and teen sex. So, even though he never really strayed very far from traditional American conservatism, his popularity suggests just how powerful *danger* can be as a political metaphor, compared with pleasure. Radical English gay writer Dennis Altman has suggested that the response to AIDS in the United States was a particularly American one. Criticizing the exaggeration and sensationalization of the disease by gay activists as well as by the Right, he points to the contradiction implicit in the paranoia about the medical establishment, on the one hand, and the activists' all-abiding faith in science, on the other. He also noted "how demands of gays to get government out of their lives . . . became a sad irony [when] in the name of health, gays now demand government action."[77] Oddly enough, the conservative Koop and some AIDS activists came together in a politics of apocalyptic doom, whereby virtually any observer who questioned predictions about the spread of the disease was subject to criticism or even picketing.[78]

By the 1990s, the politics of danger had completely succeeded. Little, if any, difference seems to exist between conservative and liberal parties regarding campaigns to cleanse television, film, rock 'n' roll, even cyberspace, of sex and violence; campaigns against "deadbeat dads" and other child custody violators; campaigns of punishment and identification of rapists, child abusers, Satanists, and people charged with ritual abuse; campaigns against pornography; campaigns against underage sex, teen pregnancy, and promiscuity; campaigns for anti-crime and anti–domestic violence legislation; campaigns against public sex, prostitution, and cruising; campaigns against substance abuse (particularly drunk driving and underage smoking and drinking); and campaigns warning children about the dangers of almost everything from suicide and AIDS to high cholesterol and cigarette smoking.

Even when liberals dissent from the politics of danger, they often focus on tenuous or tendentious aspects of an issue rather than confronting the politics of danger head on. Those on the Right suspect that liberals endorse abortion rights, gay rights, and condom distribution in the schools because, somewhere in their souls, they *actually are* pro-sex and pro-pleasure. But even so, liberal columnists and politicians have spent a great deal of time denying it, claiming that they are only combating danger. The right of a young woman to have sex is central to abortion rights, but liberals affirm their desire to prevent youthful sex. Instead of defending the right to sex, they engage in Talmudic arguments about the developmental stage at which the fetus reaches personhood. In short, *danger* is the trump card of the liberal abortion argument: Either women will die during back-alley abortions or unwanted children will be foisted on the country.

Similarly, the stance of many liberal activists and educators is that they favor abstinence among teens, but since kids are "going to have sex anyway" they also favor the distribution of condoms in schools to prevent the AIDS virus. Yet when conservative activists point to the failure rate for condom use, a series of technical arguments ensues about whether the actual condom failure rate among kids is 5 percent or 12 percent. In a way, conservatives' criticism of a sole focus on condom distribution is well taken because the liberal advocacy of condoms is so totalistic as to imply that latex is *the* answer to the AIDS epidemic. But this advocacy both overstates the risks of HIV for youngsters through constant pronouncements against the dangers of sex and minimizes the importance of other issues related to the epidemic, from finding a cure for AIDS to structural changes in the health-care system. Except among a few radical activists, an argument for the right of teens to have sex is rarely made. Such a right, of course, would be accompanied by risks. And the risks would be present with condoms or without condoms; but liberals and educators do not confront this fact. Rather than accept the existence of these risks (as would be consistent with Douglas and Wildavsky's argument about the politics of risk),[79] liberals present condoms as a sort of technical solution to sexual disease and reproduction. The politics of danger can offer no justification for teen sex other than that "it is inevitable, anyway." Little wonder, against this tepid justification for AIDS prevention and sex education, that right-wingers have an easier time mobilizing people; as far as some parents are concerned, they at least appear to believe strongly in something.

The politics of pleasure holds so little sway not only for demographic reasons (its constituency would likely be young and non-middle class, hence less likely to vote) but also because it seems frivolous. Whereas the marketplace constantly bombards us with visions of pleasure, whether it is to be had through owning a car or boat, smoking a cigarette, or associating sex with the "right" kind of running shoe, the political realm appears to function in almost the opposite way. Yet it would seem politically odd to assert the right to experience the joy of food or sex or any other daily pleasure.[80] Who cares? And what constituency directly comes forth in support of pleasure? Pleasure gets defined as *personal*, whereas danger and disorder are defined as *public*. A long tradition of the state's political involvement in regulating order and policing the dangers of life provides legitimacy for reformers who seek state action in these areas. But rarely does legitimacy exist for movements that are liberatory in nature. Apparently only corporations (tobacco, alcohol, etc.) have the legitimacy to lobby for intemperance.

Ironically, the politics of danger, despite its popularity, rarely assists a politics of the Left, at least in this country. If law-and-order and control are the proper responses to danger, as our traditions seem to suggest, the Right (or some tempered version of it) is really much better equipped than the Left, both ideologically and culturally, to mete out punishment. I do not deny that the dangers and risks of life are real and apparent; rather, my point is that the issues raised by the politics of personal "deviancy" and responsibility ultimately do not jibe well with a left-wing structural analysis of power in our society.

seven

From Loyalty Oaths to Urine Tests

I have argued throughout this book that the political strategies and so-cial movements that led to the New Temperance of the late twentieth century contrasted sharply with, and repudiated, the brief liberatory im-pulses in American culture associated with the "60s." The movements and political strategies of the current period, particularly the drug war and the various campaigns against sexuality, seem historically consis-tent with the old temperance movements of the nineteenth and early twentieth centuries. I have suggested that, although both the older and newer versions of these movements and campaigns target behavior that certainly can be dangerous or unhealthy, they all tend(ed) to exaggerate the risks of life while de-contextualizing them from their social environ-ments. Further, I have stressed the class basis of both the New Temper-ance and the older temperance movements. As in the nineteenth and early twentieth centuries, today's campaigns for "correct" behavior res-onate more with the middle class than with the classes above and below it, helping it to develop internal cohesion and identity. Finally, I have ar-gued that a political convergence has taken place on several fronts as the successful Republican and New Right strategy against sin and vice has, in turn, influenced many former radicals and liberal activists to turn against the 1960s cultural revolution of "sex, drugs, and rock 'n' roll."

In this chapter, I suggest that, symbolically, the New Temperance has served as one vehicle for conquering the remnants of the "60s" chal-lenge to American society and its dominant norms and political struc-ture. As was true of other periods in this century (e.g., the 1930s), the ideas and movements that arise in times of social disorder not only frighten elites but pose serious problems of legitimacy for established power. Although some tactics are useful in adapting to and co-opting these problems, other strategies serve to suppress the remaining mem-ory of dissent. Later in the chapter I also question how well the state can totally administer the behavior of citizens: Can behavioral control and repression be considered "successful" even on their own terms?

Demonizing the 1960s

It is not coincidental that advocates of the New Temperance have so strongly attacked behavior that they claim was at the heart of the "excesses" of the 1960s. The war on drugs and on many forms of sexuality has been fought as much for its *symbolic* value (i.e., as part of a strategy of eradicating the mythologized "60s") as for any of its more manifest purposes. Writing late in his life, Richard Nixon forcefully pointed us back to Woodstock as a symbolic reason for continuing the war on drugs: "Even today, when most of the prestige media have managed to crowd onto the anti-drug bandwagon, they could not help indulging in a revolting orgy of nostalgia during the twentieth anniversary of Woodstock. The smarmy retrospectives glossed over the fact that Woodstock's only significant legacy was the glorification of dangerous illegal drugs. . . . *To erase the grim legacy of Woodstock, we need a total war against drugs.*"[1]

Similarly, former British Prime Minister Margaret Thatcher was fond of attacking the sexual doctrines of the 1960s, holding promiscuity and free love responsible for the AIDS epidemic and the widespread child sexual abuse reported during the 1980s: "We are reaping what was sown in the 1960s. The fashionable theories and permissiveness claptrap set the scene for a society in which the old virtues of discipline and self-restraint were denigrated."[2]

The historical events of the "60s" (in actuality including much of the 1970s) have been repainted in dangerous and frightening hues. Consider this vitriolic comment by conservative historian Joseph Conlin regarding the "60s" lifestyle: "[L]ife in the New Age communes of the 1960s and 1970s . . . [was like living in] 'garbage dumps' and 'hells': children smeared in their own filth for days, hysterical under the LSD given to pacify them. . . . [V]enereal infection, pneumonia, influenza, and the unprimitive affliction of hepatitis reached disastrous proportions."[3]

For many people alive at the time of the 1960s counterculture, this sinister and bizarre reconfiguration of history has a clear agenda of vilification. Of course, not *everything* that occurred in this (or any other) time period was positive or worth repeating. But the presence of a few dirty and sick children on a commune somewhere by no means sums up the reality of this period, any more than conservatives of the time were correct in summing up the French Revolution as primarily about terrorism and guillotine practice. The popular movie *Forest Gump* similarly portrays 1960s "long-hair radicals" as violent and misogynist, and the movie hero must save his girlfriend from their abuse. Perhaps there were a few more people of this sort than I was ever aware of in the late 1960s, but it is still absurd to portray "60s"-style radicalism in this way. If anything, the image of the peaceful hippie flashing a peace sign would be closer to the mood of the times. In short, the retrospective portrayal of the "60s" has little to do with veracity. Rather, it is an attempt to take the essence of the social and cultural revolution of the 1960s and convert it to one primarily of sin and vice. The editors of *The 60s Without Apology* made a similar point more than a decade ago:

> Trashing the 60s has become a strategic feature of the current struggle for hegemony. Attacks on "permissiveness," the defense of the old-fashioned nuclear family . . . [and] a general turn away from the cultural "styles" of the 60s . . . are parts of a whole ideological conflict for which Gramsci's term *hegemony* remains the most convenient shorthand, a conflict which includes contests over interpretations of history, and above all of that crucial period both sides call "the 60s." . . . But visions of history play an enormous—if incalculable—role in people's political practice in the present and this all the more when the interpretation . . . [is] of [the] immediate past.[4]

The demonization of a historical period, however, is not a new phenomenon in America. Each period of social unrest in the twentieth century—1900 to 1914, the 1930s, and the 1960s to the early 1970s—has been followed by a period of social and political repression. In these latter periods—the 1920s, the late 1940s to the 1950s, and the late 1970s to the 1990s—political leaders, corporate elites, and the dominant media have sought to actively repudiate the periods that preceded. Most important, those *in particular* who were charged with having participated in the disruptive events or could be associated with them (sometimes just by race, religion, personal style, or appearance) were called forward to disown or repudiate these events.

In the public mind, a major threat during the first few decades of this century was centered on Central and Eastern European immigrants who constituted a disproportionate number of the radicals in groups such as the Socialist Party and the Industrial Workers of the World (IWW). The specter of political and labor unrest merged, again in the public mind, with racist and xenophobic fears about the lifestyle of Germans, Italians, Russians, and others, particularly during World War I and in the aftermath of the Bolshevik Revolution of 1917. Beginning with the repression of those who refused to go to war, or to support it, and culminating in the brutal Palmer Raids, Prohibition, and passage of the anti-immigration laws, the threat to power was symbolically constructed as "alien," as a foreign culture whose germs and ideas would prey on American culture and destroy it. These "germs" had to be purged and expelled (in fact, thousands of suspicious-looking "aliens" were literally put on boats back to Europe). But such violent repression could not be mounted against all foreigners, much less all suspicious-looking people. Instead, "aliens" were pressured to eschew association with things foreign, to swear allegiance to Americanism, and to commit themselves to assimilation (i.e., to the idea of the "melting pot"). Germans and Russians, for example, had to cleanse themselves by swearing citizenship, dropping their native language in public, leaving the traditional fraternal or other civic organizations organized around their distinctive cultures, and opposing any radical, "alien" ideas.

Social unrest in the 1930s centered on the class struggles of workers, unemployed people, and poor people during the Great Depression. Although considerably vitiated by the 1940s through absorption in the New Deal and the Popular Front strategies of the Communist Party, the specter of radicalism remained after World War II, as reflected in massive labor unrest in 1946. The anti-communism of the late 1940s and 1950s, now known as "McCarthyism," was directed not just against the foreign Communist menace (recall those irrational fears of Reds pouring in from Mexico or Canada). Indeed, it was also intended to cleanse the American political system of any radical taint from a leftward direction. The powerful social-control apparatus put in place in the late 1940s—resulting in the expulsion of Congress of Industrial Organizations (CIO) unions as red-dominated, the purges of federal workers, the hounding of Hollywood writers and academics—was specifically aimed at forcing former, current, and potential leftists to *take sides*. The loyalty oath and the "Are you now or have you ever been a Communist?" questions of the House Un-American Activities Committee (HUAC) were intended to achieve submission from all potential opposition to the social order. And the key point was to repudiate the ideas and actions of the 1930s through "naming names." By naming the names of those who had signed petitions or demonstrated during the 1930s or 1940s, a person displayed not only compliance with power but also that he or she had "outgrown" the taint of communism or radicalism.

I don't mean to imply that repression, whether of individuals or of the masses, was the only tactical strategy for containing the remnants of radicalism. Repression is not the only tool, or even necessarily the most effective tool, against dissent. For example, the expansion of social welfare programs and relatively high-wage contracts in the postwar era considerably tempered unrest. Similarly, the reaction to the "60s" has been multifaceted; in the areas of civil rights, gender equity, multiculturalism, and environmentalism, it has included considerable compromise and co-optation in both the political sphere and the private sector. Yet just as the previous conservative periods put in place a powerful repressive surveillance system, the post-1960s period has done the same.

I make no claim of originality in drawing a connection between the mandatory drug testing of the current period and the McCarthyism of the 1950s. As early as 1986 a leader of the Civil Liberties Union called drug testing a "form of social McCarthyism aimed at getting rid of people who won't buy the line. It's a step away from an authoritarian society."[5] In addition, writer Ellen Willis has observed a link between the drug test and the loyalty oath: "The purpose of this '80s version of the loyalty oath is less to deter drug use than to make people undergo a humiliating ritual of subordination: 'When I say pee, you pee.'"[6]

What is puzzling, at first glance, about the power strategies adopted in the 1980s and 1990s is that, unlike the Palmer Raids or the HUAC hearings, they often seem to occur in the "nonpolitical" realm. Mandatory drug tests as well as other proposals to sort out and contain "deviants" have been implemented by corporate and private health providers, as have an increasing number of surveillance strategies, from identification of alcohol users and testing for HIV to scrutiny of personal life both on and off the job. The social control of the 1980s and 1990s particularly reflects Foucault's discussion of direct control over *bodies*, the surveillance of which has become more and more detached from political classification and discussion and placed in the hands of professionals and personnel officials.

The urine test—along with mandatory sentencing and other severe behavioral controls central to the drug war—is a power strategy that mirrors the "personal is political" radicalism of the 1960s. It takes seriously the proposition that those who resist the dictates of power, whether or not such resistance is framed as "political" in the conventional sense, are enemies and are undermining production, public order, and rationality. Like the loyalty oath and the "naming of names," the policing of everyday life—which in schools, for example, focuses on behaviors such as smoking, speech, and sexuality—requires Americans, from an early age on, to comply with the norms of the powerful without asking questions, and to accept the right of the state and corporate power to hold their bodies captive. Ultimately, it is not important whether drug testing finds traces of a drug in a student's urine or if locker searches turn up cigarettes or guns or pornographic literature. Rather, it is the *policing itself* that makes the point about who is in control.

Another key point about the role of the New Temperance in symbolically eradicating the "60s" is its constant use against members of the baby boom generation, particularly those who might be charged with having some relationship to the social movements of that period. It is not coincidental that Democratic Party politicians from Gary Hart to Bill Clinton have come under relentless questioning about their sexuality, prior drug use, and past participation in political demonstrations (although some Republicans such as former Supreme Court justice nominee Arthur Ginsburg have been caught in the net as well). Reminiscent of McCarthyism's "Are you now or have you ever been a Communist?" questions, political leaders (and many potential civic, corporate, and bureaucratic leaders) are now asked "Are you now or have you ever been a '60s'-style person?" That is, did you use drugs, engage in nonmarital sex, attend anti-war rallies, or burn a flag?

As in the ritualized hearings of the 1950s, most members of the 1960s generation either admit guilt and purge themselves of sin or minimize their past guilt ("I didn't inhale") and promise future clean living. To some extent, liberals and former leftists have been forced, far more than conservatives and moderate politicians born before the baby boom, to actively *repudiate* the 1960s. And like many liberals in the late 1940s and 1950s who dissociated themselves from communism, they have, for the most part, happily obliged. Some sociologists studying the drug war, for example, have observed that, in the election campaigns of 1986 and 1988, liberal Democrats hammered home the attack on drugs far more than Republicans did, and charged government leaders with being "soft on drugs."[7]

The reason that Bill and Hillary Clinton, Gary Hart, George McGovern, Tom Hayden and Jane Fonda, and other leaders or public figures must constantly answer McCarthyite questions about the 1960s, and reveal their views on issues like drugs and sex, is that their opinions on these issues and their distance from the tradition of the 1960s are considered a measure of their respectability and readiness to accept political, corporate, and civic leadership. Conversely, there is little reason to question the Bob Doles and Dan Quayles whose loyalty to dominant norms has never been in doubt. But among those who have had any association with the dreaded "60s," only a repudiation of both the politics and the culture of the times is deemed acceptable by the media and political elites as a measure of their potential to serve as responsible leaders.

Novelist Sol Yurick captures the sense of this constant need to repress the 1960s: "[T]he 60s, like some compulsive recurrent nightmare[,] still persists in the consciousness of the ruling elites. They must exorcise and reexorcise it, demand acts of contrition, to ask of its adherents that they confess that they were possessed by the devil. . . . We are asked to admit, once and for all, . . . [that we] *were wrong, to make penance and obeisance, to hypostatize those sins into those devils now on trial.*"[8]

There is, however, an irony in the efforts of the powerful to repress the symbols of previous social unrest: Since each period of turmoil in American history never quite repeats the past, and since the symbols and issues associated with these periods (e.g., the 1930s versus the 1960s) are often dramatically different, the dominant media and leadership are stuck in a retrospective campaign. For example, whereas loyalty oaths and propaganda about communism were still a major focus of American life in the early 1960s, the civil rights, New Left, feminist, and other new social movements initially had few links either to 1930s issues or to Marxism. The next period of social unrest is unlikely to occur in the same fashion as the 1960s did, and the "personal politics" of sex and drugs may have little to do with the issues or symbols of the next period. Despite the constant calls to repudiate the past, the radical counterculture is long dead and hardly poses a social threat. Not knowing how to prevent future challenges, political and social leaders hope that the *idea* of political protest and social unrest can be expunged from society, but such hope is likely an unrealistic one.

The Limits of the Totally Administered Society

Social scientists and other authors have long warned us about the specter of a bureaucratized society whose expanded police power would be utilized to increasingly scrutinize and control every human action. In passages from the work of Max Weber and the Frankfurt School theorists to that of Michel Foucault and George Orwell, the power of elites to manage daily human life down to the most micro-level (as in "the totally administered society" described by Theodor Adorno)[9] seems exemplified by the New Temperance. As I discussed in Chapter 3, the irony of total administration—of state intrusion into the most private aspects of life—is that people have often come to *identify with* powerful social control as being in their own interest. They often *want* the state to expurgate drugs or cigarettes or to prosecute criminals or pornographers. But, of course, this identification, at least in America, is highly ambivalent. Those who support the drug war often refuse to accept regulation of their guns or tobacco habits; those who oppose controls over sexuality sometimes are happy to have the state control others' gun ownership or speech habits. As revealed by the public's reactions to the Rodney King beating in 1991 and to the government attack on David Koresh's Branch Davidian cult in 1994, actions by the state can suddenly blow up in officials' faces and unite popular opinion against the power of the state.

This is actually the good news. There is a strong possibility that, despite the increased technical surveillance available to the state and other authorities, the ability of elites to totally control people's lives may be exaggerated. The limits of state power and the New Temperance can be shown in this anecdote about Iran noted by drug legalization advocate Arnold Trebach:

> In Iran, there is a story of the roving executioner of the revolution, Ayatollah Khalikhali. Khalikhali had a power that many people here dream of. If he found you with drugs, he put you against a wall and shot you. According to wire reports, within a seven-week period, he killed 176 people. Khalikhali

was photographed standing amidst stacks of opium bags and drug products. Yet, he was criticized because drug use was still rampant. His defensive response was "If we wanted to kill everybody who had five grams of
heroin, we would have to kill five thousand people." And, then, he added
this classic phrase, "And this would be difficult."[10]

The irony of the Ayatollah's inability to either suppress or eradicate all
personal behavioral deviance, despite his access to the most drastic
tools, is heartening. If even Iran must stop somewhere, presumably a society based on democratic and civil liberties rhetoric must be limited in
its reach. State and corporate control over behavior is ultimately limited
in at least two ways. On the one hand, there is ideological opposition to
force being applied against *specific* private acts (drug use, sexual behavior, etc.). On the other hand, there is *general* public opposition to the use
of *too* much force, whatever the cause—particularly when such force is
no longer theoretical but has become personal (as when it is you or your
neighbor against whom force is directed) or when television forces you
to watch it again and again (as when the Rodney King beating and the
burning of the Branch Davidian compound were repeatedly aired).

Another matter paralleling the critical issues of civil liberties and social control that I have been raising concerns the pragmatics of repression. Does it work? Despite the acceptance of a simple minded behav-
iorism by many observers across the political spectrum (i.e., acceptance
that some combination of punishment and role modeling will either
force or influence people to act "right"), there is fairly mixed evidence
regarding the success of behavioral change, whether through old-style
Puritanism or the New Temperance. Otherwise, how do we explain the
following facts about America? We have more jails and prisons *and* more
crime than any other country in the world; more substance users *and*
harsher laws against all drugs; more dieters *and* more overweight people; more puritanical views about sex *and* more rape and pornography.
One explanation is, of course, that we need the prisons because of so
much crime, and that we need harsh laws to control so much sexual
abuse, drug addiction, and so on.

The problem with this explanation is twofold. It fails to own up to the
historic failure of repression of human urges to "cure" any of these problems, and it fails to accurately reflect the time sequence between disorder and control. The wisdom of public exhortation summed up in the
phrase "just say no" is basically the wisdom that developed in Massachusetts with the Puritans. And it has failed. More prisons have not
stopped crime, more drug laws have not stopped drugs, and more laws
on pornography have not stopped dirty books. Our political leaders can
offer us only more of the same, again and again. There's crime, so let's
build more jails. There's drug use, so let's pass more laws. There's teen

sex, so let's have more prohibitions and/or more education. Neither repression nor a public health campaign (nor some combination of both) necessarily fends off sin and vice.

What if the reason for all the crime and jails, the heavy-duty laws and the drug use, is not as it seems? What if repression *produces* the very dangerous classes it supposedly seeks to punish? What if banning drugs *encourages* people to get high, resulting in millions of drug offenders? What if the state builds more and more prisons and then (surprise!) begins to fill them up with more and more prisoners? What if exhortations against uncontrolled sexual behavior and food intake lead people to become obsessed with these very drives? One half of the equation produces the other: The obsession with personal misbehavior may produce the very behavior that is prohibited.

For example, some researchers report that when former President Bush held up a bag of crack in a televised speech against drugs, millions of people were prompted to want to take the drug.[11] This is an interesting example of the failure of prohibitionism. By constantly bombarding young people with the message that using drugs (or smoking a cigarette, taking a drink, or having sexual relations) is prohibited, we may be conveying the opposite message. America's obsession with the control of behavior thus has a flip side: By engaging in constant attention to these behaviors, we reveal a cultural obsession suggesting that such activities are *central* to pleasure and the essence of life. For example, in America we constantly call our children's attention to the dangers of substances, sex, and even food. But in other countries where wine and other alcoholic beverages are used regularly at meals with no special attention paid to them, alcoholism is far less widespread.[12] And where food is savored over long meals as a pleasure, there is both less dieting and less obesity.[13]

From an empirical viewpoint, the assumption that prohibition follows misbehavior is often also not supported, thus overturning the expectation that a rise in misbehavior triggers the need for more social control. For example, scholarly works by William Chambliss and Katherine Beckett on the rise of street crime and drug use as political issues show *no* correlation between increased crime or drug and public concern. If anything, the reverse is true: It is *political and media attention* to these issues that leads to increased concern and increased crime fighting and repression.[14] How does crime control *produce* crime rather than the opposite? One answer is "seek and ye shall find." Chambliss reports that just as it becomes commonplace for young African-American men to be stopped by police, it becomes commonplace to have more and more arrests, and hence more and more criminals. Initially, police may pull cars over for minor traffic infractions. But conflicts between police and citizens often ensue, even before a vehicular search is conducted. Criminals, then, are essentially *produced* by constant overwhelming scrutiny, which in turn encourages resistance to authority and self-identification with that which is being policed. Can those of us who do not live in America's inner cities even imagine being constantly subject to police scrutiny and harsh treatment? Can we imagine not resisting such authority and fighting back? Police power may also lead to an acceptance of how such power defines us: "Yes, I am a drug dealer" or "Yes, I am a gun-toting person who is 'bad'" is not a totally irrational response to continual victimization.

Of course, it is not realistic to believe that we can have a society without rules and laws. But the New Temperance suggests as much about the limitations of state power as about its success in repressing the radical visions of the 1960s. The New Temperance, though often well meaning, conveys a utopian view of life suggesting that power can be used to promote conformance to a set of established rules, or that all human behavior can be shaped. But the very idealism of temperance is what undermines it, because such moral perfectionism leads to repression and punishment for transgressors as well as to our frustration when humans act so imperfectly. As Alvin Gouldner warned: "It is when man [*sic*] is at his most purely moral that he may be most dangerous to the interests and the most callously indifferent to the needs of others. Social systems know no fury like the man of moral absolutism aroused."[15]

My own view (though it is hard to make predictions) is that the New Temperance will come to an end. Its end will not be announced but, rather, will be dwarfed by new movements and new periods of unrest that, in turn, will move American society out of its current obsession with personal behavior. Like the earlier fervor to ban alcohol in America, the force and focus now directed at issues such as illicit drug use may be looked upon by future Americans with the same curiosity and head scratching we now exhibit when contemplating the days of Prohibition. Perhaps, as with Prohibition's repeal under the weight of the Great Depression, American culture will come so close to a precipice that (as in those earlier days) the government might even sanction some new form of drugs to be dispensed to everyone, if only to provide some political relief.

Notes

CHAPTER 1

1. Associated Press, "New Age on Campus: Can the Keg," *Maine Sunday Telegram*, March 13, 1994, p. 4B.

2. See D. Hamilton, "Is a Waft of Fragrance Poisoning Your Space?" *Los Angeles Times*, December 15, 1994, p. E1; and Associated Press, "Support Group Helps People with 'Messy' Problems," *Maine Sunday Telegram*, February 20, 1994, p. 10B.

3. For a powerful study of police practices in Washington, D.C., where ghetto areas are designated "war zones" against drugs and virtually any African-American male in a vehicle is subject to search, see W. Chambliss, "Policing the Ghetto Underclass: The Politics of Law and Law Enforcement," *Social Problems*, 41:2 (1994), pp. 177–194.

4. D. Hoey, "Plan Enlists Community in Drug War," *Portland Press Herald*, October 3, 1994, pp. 1A, 9A. (The community in question is the affluent suburb of Cape Elizabeth, Maine.)

5. M. Wines, "In Baptist Talk, Clinton Stresses Moral Themes," *New York Times*, September 10, 1994, p. 1A.

6. Donna Shalala, secretary of Health and Human Services, cited in J. Stacey, "The New Family Values Crusaders," *The Nation*, July 25/August 1, 1994, p. 120.

7. Marion Barry, cited in K. Pollit, "Subject to Debate," *The Nation*, January 30, 1995, p. 120.

8. E. Goodman, "Teen-Age Moms Don't Do It Alone," *Boston Globe*, February 21, 1995, p. 87.

9. "Fallen Angel," *Casco Bay Weekly*, May 12, 1994, pp. 1, 8–11.

10. Letter to the editor, *Casco Bay Weekly*, February 15, 1996, p. 8.

11. It is admittedly difficult to talk generically about a Left and a Right, for two reasons. First, differences exist *within* conservative, liberal, and leftist circles, and each has some libertarian dissenters. Second, since America in the 1990s lacks much of an organized Left, it is extremely difficult to characterize it. Although it is relatively easy to identify the Center and Right, American socialists, anarchists, or Communists are hard to find. I must at times use liberal or left-liberal magazines such as *The Nation* and *Mother Jones* to represent a "Left," although they might better be called "liberal." In Chapter 6, I attempt to situate the development of a temperance ideology in a Right-Left convergence in the decades of the 1970s through the 1990s.

12. Many authors have been writing and talking about these developments under different names. In 1987, I referred to them collectively as the "new temperance" (see D. Wagner, "The New Temperance Movement and Social Control

at the Workplace," *Contemporary Drug Problems*, 14:4 [1987], pp. 539–556; and
D. Wagner, "The New Temperance and Social Work," *California Sociologist*, 10:2
[1987], pp. 65–82). A year earlier, R. Goldstein used the "new sobriety" label in
"The New Sobriety: What We Risk When We Just Say No," *Village Voice*, December
30, 1986, pp. 23–28. The "new puritanism" label has more recently been used in
both "The New Puritanism," *Salmagundi*, Special Issue (Winter-Spring 1994),
pp. 101–102; and E. Willis, *No More Nice Girls: Countercultural Essays* (Hanover,
N.H.: Wesleyan University Press, 1992). Finally, the "healthism" label was used by
I. Illich, ed., in *Disabling Professions* (London: Marion Boyars, 1976). Nevertheless, I consider "temperance" to be the best analytic construct because it links
the "behavioral wars" to historic continuities with older social movements and
political strategies. Other labels imply a religious/national explanation (puritanism) or a medicalization model (healthism). Moreover, for many people the
term *sobriety* connotes only alcohol; *puritanism* connotes mostly sexual prudery, but not issues linked to substances or food; and *healthism* seems to apply
best to dieting/exercising issues.

13. I don't mean to imply that the United States is the only nation that has had
strong movements against drugs, alcohol, or other temperance issues. Indeed,
such movements have also occurred, for example, in Canada, Britain, some
Nordic nations, and Russia, for example. Generally, however, few nations other
than the United States have experienced such sustained and broad anxiety-based
movements concerning so many different areas of human behaviors.(Southern
and Central European countries, by contrast, seem most non-Puritanical.)

14. See Chapter 2 for a more in-depth discussion of the Temperance Movement (against alcohol), the anti-smoking movement of earlier times, and the
Vice and Vigilance, Social Purity, and Social Hygiene movements. Also note that
the health spa in Battle Creek, Michigan, run by Dr. Kellogg is portrayed in the
1994 film *The Road to Wellville,* featuring Anthony Hopkins as Kellogg.

15. In Joseph Gusfield's classic *Symbolic Crusade: Status Politics and the American Temperance Movement* (Urbana, Ill.: University of Illinois Press, 1963), the
author argues that this middle-class unity was one of the key functions of the
earlier Temperance Movement. The status and class politics of temperance
united the members of the white Protestant middle class in a way that other issues divided them. Hence the anti-alcoholism movement, for example, was
more successful than other reform issues of the late nineteenth and early twentieth centuries. Much of my analysis is indebted to Gusfield's sociological study of
the (first) Temperance Movement.

16. See B. Ehrenreich, *Fear of Falling: The Inner Life of the Middle Class* (New
York: Pantheon, 1989). Along with Gusfield's *Symbolic Crusade* (see Note 15),
Ehrenreich's analysis of the psychology and sociology of the middle class has
been a major influence on my thinking in this book.

17. In this connection, see Chapter 3. "Medicalization" arguments seem to me
to be narrowly focused on the role of medical doctors and other experts in defining "deviancy," whereas "moral panic" arguments go perhaps to the other extreme by zeroing in on the media and popular contagion. Foucault's argument
that moralization is a power strategy, available to both elites and others, serves
as an effective theoretical bridge in this context.

18. "Culture wars" seems a popular appellation for the liberal/conservative divide on such social issues as abortion, sex education, condom distribution in schools, prayer in the schools, and gun control. See S. Roberts, "The Culture Wars of 1990," *U.S. News and World Report*, 108:25 (June 25, 1990), pp. 22–25; and J. Hunter, *Culture Wars: The Struggle to Define America* (New York: Basic Books, 1991). I do not mean to minimize the importance of the aforementioned social issues or to imply that liberals and conservatives are in agreement when in fact they are not. My point is simply that political disagreements on some issues can obscure long-term convergences in broader worldviews between sectors of the Left and Right (and Center).

19. See S. Peele, *The Diseasing of America: Addiction Treatment Out of Control* (New York: Houghton Mifflin, 1989), ch. 2; and T. Duster, "The Legislation of Morality: Creating Drug Laws," in D. Kelly, ed., *Deviant Behavior*, 3rd ed. (New York: St. Martin's Press, 1989), p. 32.

20. Peele, *The Diseasing of America*, p. 251.

21. Ibid.

CHAPTER 2

1. The new revisionist history in the New Left, feminist, and various postmodern and poststructuralist scholarship has often exposed the realities of life beneath the official pronouncements. Thus, for example, new scholarship has been declaring Victorian times to be much less "Victorian" in the sense of sexual prudery than was previously assumed. See, for example, F. Barret-Ducrocq, *Love in the Time of Victoria* (New York: Penguin, 1989); J. D'Emilio and E. Freedman, *Intimate Matters: A History of Sexuality in America* (New York: Harper and Row, 1988); and M. Foucault, *The History of Sexuality*, Vol. 1 (New York: Pantheon, 1978). Although these new approaches add a needed corrective to the old generalizations, they should not obscure the fact that the Victorian era was an extremely harsh time in which to be judged a "deviant" (a homosexual, an illegitimate child, a drug addict, etc.); and it is for this very reason that historians must locate sexual and other "deviant" activity in the "underlife" of the nineteenth century, hidden from public and official view.

2. B. Ehrenreich, *The Hearts of Men* (Garden City, N.Y.: Anchor Books, 1983).

3. See Chapter 5 for further discussion of how in the 1960s and 1970s previously "deviant" or intemperate behavior, once associated with lower-class and minority groups, became prevalent in the middle class as well. It was during this period that the sexual revolution occurred, strongly reshaping norms about premarital and extramarital sex, and that increasing numbers of middle-class people began using drugs.

4. In this connection, consider the portrayal of wife swapping in Alan Pakula's *Consenting Adults* (1992). In the tradition of *Fatal Attraction*, intemperance (here, the desire of two neighboring men to sleep with each other's wives) leads not only to divorce and family breakup but to death and the false imprisonment and near conviction of the hero, played by Kevin Klein, for murder. The film carries a none-too-subtle message about any type of risk, portraying risk taker Kevin Spacey as both psychotic and psychopathic.

5. J. Gusfield, *Symbolic Crusade: Status Politics and the American Temperance Movement* (Urbana, Ill.: University of Illinois Press, 1963), p. 4.

6. T. Duster, "The Legislation of Morality: Creating Drug Laws," in D. Kelly, ed., *Deviant Behavior*, 3rd ed. (New York: St. Martin's Press, 1989), p. 33.

7. R. Troyer and G. Markle, *Cigarettes: The Battle over Smoking* (New Brunswick, N.J.: Rutgers University Press, 1983), p. 6.

8. P. Conrad and J. Schneider, *Deviance and Medicalization: From Badness to Sickness* (Philadelphia: Temple University Press, 1992), p. 1.

9. M. Foucault, *Power/Knowledge: Selected Interviews and Other Writings 1972–77* (New York: Pantheon, 1980), pp. 42–43.

10. Gay Activists Alliance manifesto, cited in T. Marotta, *The Politics of Homosexuality* (Boston: Houghton Mifflin, 1981), p. 144.

11. The trend toward a genetic or "born that way" basis for being "gay" is much disputed, particularly by radicals in the gay, lesbian, and sexual minority movements; see, for example, L. Van Gelder, "The 'Born That Way' Trap," *Ms.*, May/June 1991, pp. 86–87. And for a recent critique from the Left of the struggle for gay rights, see S. Johnston, "On the Fire Brigade: Why Liberalism Won't Stop the Anti-Gay Campaigning of the Right," *Critical Sociology*, 20:3 (1994).

12. A good source of information on the first Temperance Movement is James Timberlake's *Prohibition and the Progressive Movement 1900–1920* (Cambridge, Mass.: Harvard University Press, 1966), which clarifies the groups of supporters and opponents involved. For works from a feminist perspective on this movement, see B. Epstein, *The Politics of Domesticity: Women, Evangelicalism, and Temperance in 19th Century America* (New York: Columbia University Press, 1981); and R. Bordin, *Woman and Temperance: The Quest for Power and Liberty* (New Brunswick, N.J.: Rutgers University Press, 1990). See also Note 27.

13. See D'Emilio and Freedman, *Intimate Matters*, p. 153.

14. The transition from limitation or moderation of alcohol consumption to complete prohibition is given considerable attention in Gusfield's *Symbolic Crusade*. Here, "assimilative" reform (whereby the reformer seeks change by persuasion) is contrasted with "coercive" reform (whereby people are forced to behave properly). Gusfield identifies this transition as a major historical change in the Temperance Movement.

15. Troyer and Markle, *Cigarettes*, p. 3.

16. Cited in Timberlake, *Prohibition and the Progressive Movement*, p. 52.

17. Cited in ibid., p. 87.

18. Cited in G. Dillow, "The Hundred Year War Against the Cigarette," *American Heritage*, February/March 1981, p. 7.

19. Timberlake, *Prohibition and the Progressive Movement*, ch. 3.

20. E. Goldman, "The Hypocrisy of Puritanism," in A. Shulman, ed., *Red Emma Speaks: An Emma Goldman Reader* (New York: Schocken Books, 1982), p. 157.

21. For an interesting discussion of the origins of tobacco smoking and its association with the "dandies" of the upper class, see R. Klein, *Cigarettes Are Sublime* (Durham, N.C.: Duke University Press, 1993). It was not until late in the nineteenth century that mass production of cigarettes occurred; prior to this time, tobacco was quite expensive and had to be hand-rolled. Interestingly, as

with many other behaviors we shall consider in this book, the pathologization of cigarette smoking in America coincided with its widespread adaptation by the poorer classes.

22. Cited in Dillow, "The Hundred Year War Against the Cigarette," p. 11.

23. Cited in S. Peele, *The Diseasing of America: Addiction Treatment Out of Control* (New York: Houghton Mifflin, 1989), p. 41.

24. A good discussion of the forces leading to the repeal of Prohibition can be found in J. Blocker, *American Temperance Movements: Cycles of Reform* (Boston: Twayne Publishers, 1989), pp. 125–129 especially.

25. In this connection, see Troyer and Markle, *Cigarettes*, pp. 40–41. See also Klein, who, in *Cigarettes Are Sublime*, more generally discusses the association of cigarette smoking and combat; indeed, smoking has historically been a major way for soldiers not only to counteract fear, anxiety, and boredom on the battlefield but also to mark off time.

26. Cited in Dillow, "The Hundred Year War Against the Cigarette," p. 15.

27. See Blocker, *American Temperance Movements*, p. xi. Blocker quotes this stereotype with disapproval, as his book is one of several recent works that are sympathetic to the Temperance Movement. Interestingly, early histories of temperance and Prohibition such as Gusfield's *Symbolic Crusade*, Timberlake's *Prohibition and the Progressive Movement*, and A. Sinclair's *Prohibition: The Era of Excess* (Boston: Little, Brown, 1962) were extremely critical of the temperance warriors. By contrast, such works as Blocker's *American Temperance Movements* and Bordin's *Woman and Temperance* are sympathetic, representing, I would suggest, the time in which each group of authors is writing.

28. "Promise Keepers," a major movement involving Christian men throughout the United States, emerged around 1992 and since that time has held large rallies in which the participants pledge themselves to marital fidelity, good parenting, chastity before marriage, and Christian values.

29. The best sources for the identification of key actors in the Social Purity Movement are E. Bristow's *Vice and Vigilance: Purity Movements in Britain Since 1700* (Dublin: Gill and MacMillan, 1977), D. Pivar's *Purity Crusade: Sexual Morality and Social Control 1868–1900* (Westport, Conn.: Greenwood Press, 1973), and J. Walkowitz's "Male Vice and Female Virtue: Feminism and the Politics of Prostitution in 19th Century Britain," in A. Snitow, C. Stansell, and S. S. Thompson, eds., *Powers of Desire: The Politics of Sexuality* (New York: Monthly Review Press, 1983), pp. 419–438. For discussion of this movement's activities in America, see especially Pivar's appendix A (pp. 281–286). The composition of the Vice and Vigilance Movement is well laid out in P. Boyer, *Purity in Print* (New York: Charles Scribner's Sons, 1968), ch. 1. And for information regarding the Progressive leadership of the Social Hygiene Movement, see A. Brandt, *No Magic Bullet: A Social History of Venereal Disease in the United States Since 1880* (New York: Oxford University Press, 1985), ch. 1.

30. D'Emilio and Freedman, *Intimate Matters*. See also Brandt, *No Magic Bullet;* and J. Weeks, *Sexuality and Its Discontents* (London: Routledge & Kegan Paul, 1985).

31. For a history of American censorship up to the 1940s, see Boyer, *Purity in Print*.

32. Cited in Bristow, *Vice and Vigilance*, p. 118.

33. See Boyer, *Purity in Print*, p. 6.

34. Ibid., ch. 1.

35. Ibid., p. 12.

36. In the late 1970s and throughout the 1980s, some members of the women's movement allied with conservative leaders in supporting laws against pornography and participating in demonstrations and other actions. See Weeks, *Sexuality and Its Discontents*, pp. 228–236; and S. Seidman, *Embattled Eros: Sexual Politics and Ethics in Contemporary America* (New York: Routledge, 1992), ch. 3. For a feminist critique of the politics of Women Against Pornography (whose leaders included Andrea Dworkin, Catherine MacKinnon, and Adrienne Rich), see Willis, *No More Nice Girls*, particularly the chapter entitled "Lust Horizons: Is the Women's Movement Pro Sex?" (pp. 3–14). See also Chapter 6 of the present volume.

37. Cited in Boyer, *Purity in Print*, p. 14.

38. Cited in ibid., p. 17.

39. The activities of the Catholic League of Decency in the 1930s led to voluntary production codes in American cinema, to which Hollywood adhered until the 1950s (see D'Emilio and Freedman, *Intimate Matters*, pp. 282–284). Concern about media portrayal of violence is also not new. For example, a law enforcement campaign (also during the 1930s) forced censors to change film plots that portrayed gangsters in a positive fashion. For more on this topic, see R. Toll, *The Entertainment Machine: American Show Business in the 20th Century* (Oxford: Oxford University Press, 1982), p. 162.

40. There is a long history of struggle aimed at banning popular sports and leisure pursuits such as cockfighting, boxing, bearbaiting, and horse racing. For further information on this topic, see W. Rybczynski, *Waiting for the Weekend* (New York: Penguin Books, 1991), pp. 98–104.

41. See Pivar, *Purity Crusade*, ch. 2; and Bristow, *Vice and Vigilance*, ch. 4.

42. See Pivar, *Purity Crusade*, pp. 141–143.

43. See, for example, Emma Goldman's piece, "The Traffic in Women," in Shulman, ed., *Red Emma Speaks*.

44. Further discussion is provided in D'Emilio and Freedman, *Intimate Matters*, p. 216.

45. See Pivar, *Purity Crusade*, pp. 281–284, for a list of the leaders of the American Purity Alliance in 1895. Among these leaders were Elizabeth Blackwell, Anthony Comstock, Mrs. Dodge, Julia Ward Howe, Dr. Kellogg, and the WCTU's Frances Willard. The alliance membership encompassed temperance editors as well as representatives of women's suffrage groups, the YMCA, and major Protestant denominations.

46. Cited in Bristow, *Vice and Vigilance*, p. 143.

47. See the discussion of this issue in Pivar, *Purity Crusade*, pp. 140–143.

48. Bristow, *Vice and Vigilance*, p. 189.

49. Cited in D'Emilio and Freedman, *Intimate Matters*, p. 209.

50. Ibid., pp. 202–203.

51. Brandt, *No Magic Bullet*, ch. 1.

52. Frances Willard, cited in D'Emilio and Freedman, *Intimate Matters*, p. 218.

53. Pivar, *Purity Crusade*, pp. 243–244.

54. Cited in Bristow, *Vice and Vigilance*, p. 38.

55. A critical comparison between the treatment of VD and that of other diseases is made by T. Rosenburg in *Microbes and Morals: The Strange Story of VD* (New York: Viking Press, 1971), p. 256.

56. Bristow, *Vice and Vigilance*, p. 147.

57. Brandt, *No Magic Bullet*, p. 12.

58. In *No Magic Bullet*, pp. 10–13, Brandt reaches no firm numerical conclusions, but he does suggest that a range of 10–20 percent of men would be more accurate. Rosenburg, in *Microbes and Morals*, puts the figures even lower, at 3 or 4 percent.

59. Brandt, *No Magic Bullet*, p. 22.

60. Cited in ibid., p. 50.

61. Cited in D'Emilio and Freedman, *Intimate Matters*, p. 206.

62. Boyer, *Purity in Print*, p. 26.

63. Dr. Prince Morrow, cited in Brandt, *No Magic Bullet*, p. 19.

64. See the related discussions in R. Bayer, *Private Acts, Social Consequences: AIDS and the Politics of Public Health* (New York: Free Press, 1989), p. 182; S. Sontag, *AIDS and Its Metaphors* (New York: Farrar, Strauss and Giroux, 1989), p. 81; and Brandt, *No Magic Bullet*. The last of these sources provides an extended discussion of World War I and VD in chapters 2 and 3.

65. This phrase is taken from *Private Acts, Social Consequences*, p. 15, where Bayer notes that the theory of public health often contrasts sharply with that of civil liberties. For a critique that makes a similar point from a leftist perspective (arguing that public health creates a fictional "public"), see A. Sears, "AIDS and the Health of Nations: The Contradictions of Public Health," *Critical Sociology*, 18:2 (Summer 1991), pp. 31–50.

66. Foucault, *The History of Sexuality*, Vol. 1.

67. Consider, for example, the KKK's opposition to domestic violence, child molestation, and drunkenness directed against white Protestants (along with nonwhites, Jews, and Catholics), as noted in E. Pleck, *Domestic Tyranny* (New York: Oxford University Press, 1987), pp. 109–110. Pleck also observes that issues of domestic violence have been pursued as strongly by the Right at various points in history as by feminists and the Left.

68. In this connection, see, for example, Gusfield's *Symbolic Crusade*, Pivar's *Purity Crusade*, Epstein's *The Politics of Domesticity*, and Ehrenreich's *The Hearts of Men* (pp. 149–151). Of course, labeling something a "displaced" symbol is not without its own subjectivity. Early intellectual critics, such as Gusfield, saw temperance as entailing displaced symbols pertaining to status and ethnic conflicts. And feminist writers such as Epstein and Ehrenreich stress the displacement of women's anger about their social repression and status in the family by attacking alcohol and prostitution.

69. For discussions of the Progressive mentality, see, for example, R. Wiebe, *The Search for Order 1877–1920* (New York: Hill and Wang, 1967); G. Kolko, *The Triumph of Conservatism* (Chicago: Quadrangle Books, 1967); and J. Ehrenreich, *The Altruistic Imagination: A History of Social Work and Social Policy in the U.S.* (Ithaca, N.Y.: Cornell University Press, 1985).

CHAPTER 3

1. P. Berger and T. Luckmann's *The Social Construction of Reality* (Garden City, N.Y.: Doubleday, 1966) built upon the sociology-of-knowledge perspective pioneered by Karl Mannheim. Other influences include phenomenology, symbolic interactionism, and ethnomethodology.

2. The sometimes problematic relationship between social constructionism and deconstructionism is explored in chapters 17–20 of J. Holstein and G. Miller, eds., *Reconsidering Social Constructionism* (New York: Aldine de Gruyter, 1993).

3. See ibid. for a lengthy discussion of the difference between contextual constructionists and strict constructionists.

4. J. Best, ed., *Images of Issues: Typifying Contemporary Social Problems* (New York: Aldine de Gruyter, 1989).

5. H. Becker, *The Outsiders: Studies in the Sociology of Deviance*, 2nd ed. (New York: Free Press, 1973).

6. J. Best, "Rhetoric in Claims-Making: Constructing the Missing Children Problem," *Social Problems*, 34 (1987), pp. 101–121, and *Threatened Children: The Social Construction of a Moral Panic* (Chicago: University of Chicago Press, 1990).

7. National Safety Council, *Accident Facts* (1992), pp. 8–11.

8. Ibid., p. 34.

9. Ibid., p. 51.

10. U.S. Environmental Protection Agency, *Vehicle Related Air Toxic Study* (Washington, D.C., April 1993).

11. Robert Rickles, New York Commissioner of Air Resources, cited in R. Buel, *Dead End: The Automobile in Mass Transportation* (Englewood Cliffs, N.J.: Prentice-Hall, 1972), pp. 60, 73.

12. U.S. Environmental Protection Agency, *Vehicle Related Air Toxic Study* (Washington, D.C., April 1993).

13. Buel, *Dead End*.

14. Bristow, *Vice and Vigilance*, p. 128.

15. Benjamin Rush, cited in D'Emilio and Freedman, *Intimate Matters*, p. 68.

16. Bristow, *Vice and Vigilance*, p. 134.

17. Ibid., p. 140.

18. Bristow, *Vice and Vigilance*, p. 128.

19. Foucault, *History of Sexuality*, Vol. 1, p. 28.

20. Maurice Bigelow, cited in D'Emilio and Freedman, *Intimate Matters*, pp. 206–207.

21. Bristow, *Vice and Vigilance*, pp. 146–147.

22. See, for example, S. Restivo, "Modern Science As a Social Problem," *Social Problems*, 35:3 (1988), pp. 206–225.

23. P. Jenkins, *Intimate Matters: Moral Panics in Contemporary Great Britain* (New York: Aldine de Gruyter, 1992).

24. Best, "Rhetoric in Claims-Making," p. 117.

25. Ibid.

26. On the repression and firing of thousands of gays, lesbians, and others classified as sexual deviants by the government in the McCarthy period, see

D'Emilio and Freedman, *Intimate Matters,* pp. 283–293; and P. Conrad and J. Schneider, *Deviance and Medicalization: From Badness to Sickness* (Philadelphia: Temple University Press, 1992), p. 201. On the link between communism and pornography in the 1950s, see D'Emilio and Freedman, *Intimate Matters.* And on the link between McCarthyism and fears about rock music, jazz, and drugs, see H. Gray, "Popular Music As a Social Problem: A Social History of Claims Against Popular Music," in Best, *Images of Issues,* pp. 147–151.

27. See Holstein and Miller, *Reconsidering Social Constructionism.*

28. C. Reinarman and H. Levine, "Crack Attack: Politics and Media in America's Latest Drug Scare," in Best, *Images of Issues,* pp. 115–137.

29. S. Woolgar and D. Pawluch, "Ontological Gerrymandering: The Anatomy of Social Problems Explanations," *Social Problems,* 32:3 (1985), pp. 214–227.

30. C. W. Mills, *The Sociological Imagination* (London: Oxford University Press, 1959), pp. 3–4.

31. See, for example, T. Szasz, *The Manufacture of Madness* (New York: Harper & Row, 1970); I. Illich, *Medical Nemesis* (New York: Pantheon, 1976); N. Kittrie, *The Right to Be Different* (Baltimore: Johns Hopkins Press, 1971); and M. Foucault, *Madness and Civilization* (New York: Random House, 1965), and *The Birth of the Clinic: An Archaeology of Medical Perception* (New York: Pantheon, 1973).

32. The work of Elliot Freidson on the sociology of medicine and the professions appears to have been influential in bringing together several strands of sociological thinking in the 1970s. In particular, see *The Profession of Medicine* (New York: Harper & Row, 1970) and *Professional Dominance* (Chicago: Aldine Press, 1970).

33. Conrad and Schneider's *Deviance and Medicalization* is perhaps the clearest sociological treatment of *medicalization.*

34. Widespread opposition to the medical model emerged in the 1970s among feminists, gay activists, and leftists as well as among social scientists who saw as central the established professions' ontological construction of certain behavior as pathological. (This category included not only homosexuality but also other forms of sexuality and aspects of women's lives ranging from premenstrual syndrome to postpartum depression.) However, although opposition to medicalization has taken on a "rights" or civil libertarian framework with respect to some forms of behavior, this opposition may be ambiguous given its potential support of a more moralistic/legal social control over other behaviors. For example, some critics of the medicalization of alcoholism or addiction may want to see legal social control, and many feminists have criticized the medicalization of domestic violence, preferring prison or arrest rather than a treatment model.

35. S. Cohen, *Folk Devils and Moral Panics: The Creation of the Mods and Rockers* (Oxford: Blackwell, 1972), p. 28.

36. See, for example, S. Hall, with C. Critcher, T. Jefferson, J. Clarke, and B. Roberts, *Policing the Crisis: Mugging, the State and Law and Order* (New York: Holmes & Meier, 1978); N. Parton, "The Natural History of Child Abuse: A Study in Social Problem Definition," *British Journal of Social Work,* 9 (1979), pp. 431–451, "Child Abuse, Social Anxiety, and Welfare," *British Journal of Social Work,* 11 (1981), pp. 391–414, and *The Politics of Child Abuse* (London: Macmil-

lan, 1985); G. Pearson, M. Gilman, and S. McGiver, *Young People and Heroin* (Aldershot: Gower, 1987); I. Taylor, "Violence and Video: For a Social Democratic Perspective," *Contemporary Crises*, 11 (1987), pp. 107–128; and A. Vass, *AIDS—A Plague in Us: A Social Perspective* (London: Venus Academica, 1986).

37. In the 1991 and 1992 editions of *The Readers Guide to Periodical Literature*, I located approximately 150 terms relating to deviancy, unhealthy behavior, and medicalized popular vocabulary. These terms did not appear in the 1970 and 1971 editions.

Of course, any such review is necessarily somewhat subjective; hence another observer might question some of the terms I selected or add terms not on my list. (For example, I excluded medical diseases unknown to me that someone else might recognize and argue to be socially constructed.) Incidentally, the 1950s and 1960s editions of the *The Readers Guide to Periodical Literature* revealed no correspondingly large increase in the number of terms related to personal behavior, whereas the *New York Times* index for the 1970s and 1980s did show a parallel increase.

38. J. Kroker, cited in R. Michalowski, "(De)Construction, Postmodernism, and Social Problems: Facts, Fiction, and Fantasies at the 'End of History,'" in Holstein and Miller, eds., *Reconsidering Social Constructionism*, p. 390.

39. See P.A.J. Waddington, "Mugging as a Moral Panic: A Question of Proportion," *British Journal of Sociology*, 37:2 (1986), especially p. 258.

40. One issue I have not discussed at length here but that merits some mention is the fact that Soviet and other socialist societies of the twentieth century, at least from the advent of Stalinism on, adapted a very harsh and strict version of Puritanical temperance. Antonio Gramsci believed that the techniques of "Fordism," in which he included Puritanism, were being adapted by the Soviets and, in the hands of the working class, could lead to progress. In stressing the bourgeois origins of temperance, I see no necessary contradiction in the Soviet-style states' acceptance of a temperance ideology. Rather, they simply adapted the power strategies of Western capitalism and state authority to their own bureaucratic elites' needs and to their process of industrial accumulation. In my view, this is one of the many ways in which the Soviet-style states failed to move beyond capitalism as a structure and ideology.

41. See M. Douglas and A. Wildavsky, *Risk and Culture* (Berkeley: University of California Press, 1982), for a discussion of taboos and pollution rituals in other societies and an explanation of how external events shape indigenous people's perceptions of their ruling elites.

42. Max Weber, cited in Gusfield, *Symbolic Crusade*, p. 28.

43. Cited in Foucault, *The Birth of the Clinic*, p. 34.

44. Werner Sombart, cited in S. Ranulf, *Moral Indignation and Middle Class Psychology* (New York: Schocken Books, 1964), p. 41.

45. Gusfield, *Symbolic Crusade*, pp. 5, 8.

46. Of course, there was a period, particularly the Gilded Age (in late-nineteenth-century America), when some American capitalists exulted in their wealth and engaged in the "conspicuous consumption" noted in Thorstein Veben's famous work, *The Theory of the Leisure Class* (New York: Viking, 1967 [orig. 1899]). In the 1980s, too, some well-known figures, such as Malcolm Forbes and

Nancy Reagan, came close to adopting this style. But such instances were quickly and severely criticized in the media, whereupon many displays of wealth and greed again became hidden. I would argue that the open appeal to luxury and overconsumption has been rare in the history of Anglo-American society, as compared with other societies, and is more commonly concealed by the affluent.

47. As described later, there are additional reasons as to why "bringing down the big guys" occurs. In any case, it is an extremely popular sport among the public to find moral fault with political and other leaders in society. This aspect of temperance movements reflects a populist impulse.

48. For Foucault's description of how the Europeans lumped together a large percentage of the population (by means of what he called the "Great Confinement") and later separated them into categories, see his *Madness and Civilization*. In the United States, the Poor Laws of the mid–nineteenth century similarly lumped together "rogues, vagabonds, idle persons begging, persons using subtle crafts, juggling, unlawful games or plays, feigning themselves to have knowledge of physiognomy, palmistry or pretending that they could tell destinies or fortunes, . . . common pipers, fiddlers, runaways, common drunkards, common night walkers, pilferers, wanton and lascivious persons, in speech, conduct or behaviour; common railers or brawlers, such as neglect their callings or employments, misspend what they earn and do not provide for themselves and for the support of their family, . . . [and] persons unfit to go at large and under distraction" as eligible for the houses of correction. (This Connecticut legal statute is cited in A. Deutsch, *The Mentally Ill in America* [Garden City, N.Y.: Doubleday, 1949], p. 52.)

Initially, the colonists and early American institutions hoped to divide the "deserving" from the "undeserving" poor, but they never fully succeeded in separating the "deserving" groups (aged people, widows, and orphans) from the "undeserving" ones until the passage of the Social Security Act in 1935. Then, finally, the "deserving" poor were removed from local institutions such as the almshouse and local outdoor relief. See M. Katz, *In the Shadow of the Poorhouse* (New York: Basic Books, 1986) for a good historical account.

49. M. Foucault, *Power/Knowledge: Selected Interviews and Other Writings 1972–77* (New York: Pantheon, 1980), p. 15.

50. See, for example, D. Rothman, *The Discovery of the Asylum* (Boston: Little, Brown, 1971), where Foucault's European view is reinforced by an explanation of how America, from the Jacksonian period on, separated deviants through categorization.

51. Foucault, *Power/Knowledge*, p. 15.

52. Ibid., p. 41.

53. Of course, this strategy is not always effective, in that it works with some groups but not others. Many people, particularly youth, racial minorities, and the poor, resist such identifications by subverting them, and by rooting for the "bad guys." Artists, too, are frequently hard to control and may be disloyal to bourgeois norms. From rap songs to films (*Pulp Fiction* comes to mind), there are cultural representations that resist moralization and, hence, tend to enrage political leaders.

54. A. Gramsci, "Americanism and Fordism," in Gramsci, *Selections from the Prison Notebooks* (New York: International Publishers, 1983), pp. 277–320.

55. Ibid., p. 302.

56. See ibid. Note, though, that Gramsci himself does not separate these functions.

57. Ibid., pp. 302–303.

58. Ibid., pp. 304–305.

59. For an example of this argument from a conservative standpoint, see J. Burnham, *Bad Habits: Drinking, Smoking, Taking Drugs, Gambling, Sexual Misbehavior, and Swearing in American History* (New York: New York University Press, 1993). Many leftist perspectives on sexuality (see D'Emilio and Freedman, *Intimate Matters;* S. Seidman, *Embattled Eros: Sexual Politics and Ethics in Contemporary America* [New York: Routledge, 1992]; and J. Weeks, *Sexuality and Its Discontents* [London: Routledge & Kegan Paul, 1985]) emphasize the role of advertising and marketing in sexualizing the society. Also on the Left, see D. Forbes, who, in *False Fixes* (Albany: SUNY Press, 1994), emphasizes capitalism's promotion of an "addictive paradigm" of relations that links drugs to other compulsions such as shopping, sports, and consuming. A recent Volkswagen ad readily illustrates how capitalist advertising can associate pleasure with health. A man is shown working out at a gym, measuring out some cereal, and engaging in other healthy activities, while a voice-over states, "You eat right," "You work out," "You live right." (pause) "So where can you let loose?" The rhetorical question is answered by a change of scene in which the man appears driving his VW Jetta.

60. Douglas and Wildavsky, *Risk and Culture*, pp. 7–8.

61. Ibid., p. 36.

62. Ibid., p. 47.

63. Ibid., p. 59.

64. D'Emilio and Freedman, *Intimate Matters*, pp. 23–24.

65. See Gusfield, *Symbolic Crusade*, pp. 44–45; and J. Blocker, *American Temperance Movements: Cycles of Reform* (Boston: Twayne Publishers, 1989), p. 22.

66. For example, I have found in my work with the homeless and formerly homeless that subjects were very aware of the popularity of "recovery" jargon among professionals and, indeed, often embraced this terminology as a status enhancer. In this connection, see D. Wagner, *Checkerboard Square: Culture and Resistance in a Homeless Community* (Boulder, Colo.: Westview Press, 1993).

67. See the related discussion in E. Bristow, *Vice and Vigilance: Purity Movements in Britain Since 1700* (Dublin: Gill and MacMillan, 1977).

68. Ibid.; see also Jenkins, *Intimate Matters*.

69. This point is made in J. Walkowitz, "Male Vice and Female Virtue: Feminism and the Politics of Prostitution in 19th Century Britain," in A. Snitow, C. Stansell, and S. S. Thompson, eds., *Powers of Desire: The Politics of Sexuality* (New York: Monthly Review Press, 1983), as well as in Bristow, *Vice and Vigilance.*

70. M. Robinson, "Puritans and Prigs," *Salmagundi*, Special Issue (Winter-Spring 1994), pp. 101–102.

71. See K. Roiphe, *The Morning After: Sex, Fear, and Feminism* (Boston: Little, Brown, 1994), p. 34. Roiphe, a twenty-something author who has criticized aspects of current feminist activism, has in turn been criticized by many feminists.

However, much of her book, if read as a critique of the exaggeration of the dangers of male predators, is at odds neither with the recent work of leftist feminists such as Ellen Willis and Lynne Segal (see Chapter 6 of the present volume) nor with that of the leftist British theorists of moral panic noted earlier. I suspect that much of the criticism aimed at Roiphe originates from the fact that she does not come out of the Left or the modern women's movement and thus seems to be taking a critical tone toward the women's movement as an outsider.

72. See D'Emilio and Freedman, *Intimate Matters;* Snitow, Stansell, and Thompson, eds., *Powers of Desire*; and the essays in K. Peiss and C. Simmons, *Passion and Power: Sexuality in History* (Philadelphia: Temple University Press, 1989).

CHAPTER 4

1. S. Peele, *The Diseasing of America: Addiction Treatment Out of Control* (New York: Houghton Mifflin, 1989), p. 34.

2. Lester Grinspool, cited in C. Caldwell, "Smoke Gets in Your Eyes," *American Spectator*, May 1992, p. 28.

3. L. Kantor, "Many Abstinence-Based Programs Are Harmful," in K. Swisher, *Teenage Sexuality: Opposing Viewpoints* (San Diego: Greenhaven Press, 1994), pp. 161–162.

4. For examples of liberal anti-tobacco rhetoric, see E. Goodman, "Smoking Acquires Conservative Chic," *Boston Globe*, February 26, 1995, p. 75, and "Tobacco Lobby Makes an Offer," *Portland Press Herald*, June 28, 1994, p. 9a; and A. Cockburn, "The Other Drug War, Where Tobacco Firms Are the Pushers," *Wall Street Journal*, September 27, 1990, p. A19. For an example of liberal anti-fat sentiment, see Ralph Nader's testimony on frankfurters in H. Levenstein, *Paradox of Plenty: A Social History of Eating in America* (New York: Oxford University Press, 1993), p. 171; also note the phrase "heart attack on a plate" (referring to fettucine Alfredo), which was coined by the Center for Science in the Public Interest in 1994. The phrase "deadly miasma of contagion and death" is taken from S. Watney, "Photography and AIDS," in C. Squires, ed., *The Critical Image: Essays on Contemporary Photography* (Seattle: Bay Press, 1990), p. 174.

5. For recent critical discussions of the cholesterol-fat issue, see J. Bennett and T. DiLorenzo, *Unhealthy Charities: Hazardous to Your Health and Wealth* (New York: Basic Books, 1994), ch. 5; M. Stacey, *Consumed: Why Americans Love, Hate, and Fear Food* (New York: Simon and Schuster, 1994); J. Brody, "Low Fat Diet Might Add Only Months to Lifetime, Study Says," *New York Times*, June 26, 1991, p. C5; and J. Brody, "A Closer Look at the Effects of Eggs Suggests That Some People Can Safely Increase Their Consumption," *New York Times*, January 11, 1995, p. B7. For low correlations between high cholesterol and other dietary hazards, on the one hand, and people who are not middle-aged men, on the other, see C. Tavris, *The Mismeasure of Women* (New York: Touchstone Books, 1992), pp. 102–103. See also Levenstein, *Paradox of Plenty,* p. 208; and "Medical Researchers Say Health Advisories Go Too Far," *New York Times*, May 14, 1995.

6. See Wagner, *Checkerboard Square.* Although the study was focused on a group of homeless people in only one city, it involved intensive participatory re-

search over a long period of time. I argue against the idea that homelessness can be attributed to substance use and abuse; rather, my point is that substance use can be an *effect* of the situation of homelessness and poverty.

7. These slogans from Maryland's campaign against early sex are cited in J. Gross, "Sex Educators for Young See New Virtue in Chastity," *New York Times*, January 16, 1994, pp. 1, 19.

8. Although one can argue that the rationalistic, logical, and "power over nature" faith is also a masculine cultural trait, support for temperance measures has historically been high among women—sometimes even higher than among men. This support is probably best explained in terms of the cultural association between male violence and intemperant forms of behavior, particularly alcohol or drug use. One may also argue that white Protestant Calvinism, with its logical rationalism, differs sharply from the belief systems of the African-American and indigenous American cultures. Whether it differs from the belief systems of other ethnic groups, such as Asians, is less clear.

9. W. Bennett, "Teaching Moral Values Can Reduce Chemical Dependency," in C. Cozic and K. Swisher, eds., *Chemical Dependency: Opposing Viewpoints* (San Diego: Greenhaven Press, 1991), p. 235. (The quotation is excerpted from Bennett's book *First Things* [1990].)

10. "Battling the Enemy Within," *Time*, March 17, 1986, pp. 52–53.

11. M. Falco, "Drug Abuse Is a Serious Problem," in K. Swisher, ed., *Drug Abuse: Opposing Viewpoints* (San Diego: Greenhaven Press, 1994), p. 18. (The quotation is excerpted from Swisher's *The Making of a Drug-Free America* [New York: Random House, 1992].)

12. Robert DuPont, cited in Cozic and Swisher, *Chemical Dependency*, p. 16.

13. T. Duster, "The Legislation of Morality: Creating Drug Laws," in D. Kelly, ed., *Deviant Behavior*, 3rd ed. (New York: St. Martin's Press, 1989), pp. 13–14.

14. Noted in B. Alexander, *Peaceful Measures: Canada's Way Out of the "War on Drugs"* (Toronto: University of Toronto Press, 1990), p. 192.

15. R. Dennis, "The Economics of Legalizing Drugs," *The Atlantic*, November 1990, pp. 126–132. Dennis indicates that three-quarters of all violations of drug laws involve marijuana.

16. See the article by Quayle in *American Psychologist*, cited in C. Reinarman, D. Waldorf, and S. Murphy, "Cocaine and the Workplace: Empirical Findings and Notes on Scapegoating and Social Control in the Construction of a Public Problem," *Research in Law, Deviance, and Social Control*, 9 (1987), pp. 16–17.

17. These figures are taken from Peele, *The Diseasing of America*, p. 25.

18. P. Stark, "Increased Regulation of Prescription Drugs Is Necessary," in Swisher, ed., *Drug Abuse*, p. 146. (Reprinted from Stark's article in *USA Today*, July 1991.)

19. See the citation of *Newsweek's* "Kids and Cocaine: An Epidemic Strikes Middle America" (March 1986) in J. Orcutt and J. B. Turner, "Shocking Numbers and Graphic Accounts: Quantified Images of Drug Problems in the Print Media," *Social Problems*, 40:2 (1993), pp. 190–206.

20. Ibid., p. 201.

21. For further information on anti-depressants, see P. Kramer, *Listening to Prozac* (New York: Penguin Books, 1993).

22. Gerald Klerman, cited in ibid., p. 274. See also p. 370.

23. Reinarman, Waldorf, and Murphy, "Cocaine and the Workplace," p. 18.

24. Orcutt and Turner, "Shocking Numbers and Graphic Accounts," pp. 190–206.

25. Falco, "Drug Abuse Is a Serious Problem," p. 9.

26. J. Henningfield of the National Institute on Drug Abuse (NIDA), cited in Peele, *The Diseasing of America,* p. 163; originally reported in *New York Times,* August 24, 1989.

27. Alexander, *Peaceful Measures,* p. 194.

28. This study was performed by Arnold Trebach, president of the Drug Policy Foundation. See A. Trebach and K. Zeese, *Drug Prohibition and the Conscience of Nations* (Washington, D.C.: Drug Policy Foundation, 1990).

29. S. Murphy and M. Rosenbaum, "Myths About Crack" (letter to the editor), *New York Times,* February 8, 1990, p. A28.

30. E. Nadelman, "The Case for Legalization," in J. Inciardi, ed., *The Drug Legislation Debate* (Newbury Park, Calif.: Sage, 1991).

31. Dennis, "The Economics of Legalizing Drugs," p. 128.

32. See Reinarman, Waldorf, and Murphy, "Cocaine and the Workplace," p. 8. The extremely high figures regarding "lost productivity" are very suspect. Many drug users begin taking drugs in an attempt to better tolerate their work environments and cope with busy schedules. One can argue that the absence of drugs may actually result in a *loss* of productivity. Moreover, it would be absurd to assume that all absences, late arrivals to work, and illnesses among drug users are due to drug use.

33. C. Faupel and C. Klockars, "Drugs-Crime Connections: Elaborations from the Life Histories of Hard-Core Heroin Addicts," *Social Problems,* 34:1 (1987), p. 57.

34. Study by Phillipe Bourgeois, cited in L. Tiger, *The Pursuit of Pleasure* (Boston: Little, Brown, 1992), p. 118.

35. S. Peele, "Control Yourself," *Reason* 21:9 (1990), pp. 23–24.

36. Ibid.

37. Jack Henningfield, cited in A. Levine, "America's Addiction to Addictions," *U.S. News and World Report,* February 5, 1990, p. 62.

38. Everett Koop, cited in Klein, *Cigarettes Are Sublime,* p. 10.

39. K. H. Ginzel (a University of Arkansas pharmacologist and toxicologist), "Cigarette Smoking Is Harmful," in Cozic and Swisher, eds., *Chemical Dependency,* p. 59. (This article originally appeared in *Priorities* [Fall 1990], published by the American Council on Science and Health.)

40. See T. Sterling, "Dubious Figures Cast a Cloud over Anti-Tobacco Lobby," *Vancouver Sun,* September 2, 1993, p. 26. For recent estimates and state-by-state listings of smoking deaths, see "Maine Makes Top 10 in Smoking Deaths," *Portland Press Herald,* June 27, 1994, p. 3A.

41. P. Berger, "Furtive Smokers—and What They Tell Us About America," *Commentary,* June 1994, p. 23.

42. Douglas and Wildavsky, *Risk and Culture,* ch. 3.

43. Klein, *Cigarettes Are Sublime,* p. 185.

44. C. Hitchens, "Smoke and Mirrors," *Vanity Fair,* October 1994, p. 90.

45. See, for example, T. Hall, "Smoking of Cigarettes Seems to Be Becoming a Lower-Class Habit," *Wall Street Journal,* June 25, 1985, pp. 1, 17. Hall points out that many young people and minorities smoke only a few cigarettes a day. For information regarding people who go back and forth between abstinence and heavy and light smoking, see, for example, G. Marlatt, S. Curry, and J. Gordon, "A Longitudinal Analysis of Unaided Smoking Cessation," *Journal of Consulting and Clinical Psychology,* 56:5 (1988), pp. 715–720. And for discussion of the connection between stress and smoking, see Klein, *Cigarettes Are Sublime,* p. 14.

46. The 33 percent death rate of smokers is cited in M. Straus, "New Theory and Old Canards About Family Violence Research," *Social Problems,* 38:2 (1991), p. 184. Straus invokes this argument—that we regard smoking as being a killer despite the fact that a majority of people do not die from it—in support of the society-wide acceptance of all correlational data.

47. W. Kip Viscusi, cited in D. Warsh, "Cigarettes and Other Risks of Modern Life," *Boston Sunday Globe,* November 22, 1993.

48. Ginzel's estimate of 10 percent is cited in "Cigarette Smoking Is Harmful," p. 58, whereas the 5 percent estimate is given by R. Sobel, an author with a less pronounced anti-smoking stance, in an earlier book entitled *They Satisfy: The Cigarette in American Life* (Garden City, N.Y.: Anchor Books, 1978).

49. N. McWhirter, "Computer Blows Out Smoking-Related Death Figures with No Real Human Facts," *Detroit News,* October 18, 1992, p. 4C. See also N. McWhirter, "Researchers May Be Blowing Smoke in Our Faces with 'New' Data on Tobacco," *Detroit News and Free Press,* August 29, 1993, p. 22; Sterling, "Dubious Figures Cast a Cloud over Anti-Tobacco Lobby," p. 26; and T. Sterling, W. Rosenbaum, and J. Weinkam, "Risk Attribution and Tobacco-Related Deaths," *American Journal of Epidemiology,* 30:4 (1993), p. 457.

50. McWhirter, "Researchers May Be Blowing Smoke in Our Faces," p. 22.

51. Caldwell, "Smoke Gets in Your Eyes," pp. 25–28. See also Associated Press, "Teen Smokers' Behavior Differs from Nonsmokers'," *Portland Press Herald,* April 25, 1995, p. 5A.

52. D. Goff, D. Henderson, and E. Amico, "Cigarette Smoking in Schizophrenia: Relationship to Psychopathology and Medication Side Effects," *American Journal of Psychiatry,* 149:9 (1992), pp. 1189–1194.

53. Ibid.; see also "When Smoking Is Okay," *Psychology Today,* September/October 1993, p. 10.

54. Alexander Glassman, cited in ibid.

55. These studies are cited in Peele, *The Diseasing of America,* p. 99.

56. See Kramer, *Listening to Prozac,* especially pp. 235–236, 369.

57. In particular, see the chart entitled "The Effects of Nicotine," provided by John Anderson of the *Washington Post,* in P. Hilts, "FDA Panel Rules That Nicotine Is Addictive," *New York Times,* August 3, 1994, p. 1. See also D. Forbes, *False Fixes* (Albany: SUNY Press, 1994), pp. 86, 185; Hitchens, "Smoke and Mirrors," pp. 90, 95; and Klein, *Cigarettes Are Sublime.*

58. R. Siegal, "It's a Drive As Natural As Food or Sex," *Los Angeles Times,* March 15, 1990, p. B7.

59. The phrase "scaring the bejeezus" is taken from McWhirter, "Researchers May Be Blowing Smoke in Our Faces," p. 22. The reference to altering the harm of

cigarettes is to the exploration by scientists and government agencies of the possibility of gradually reducing nicotine levels to wean smokers from heavy use. See P. Hilts, "Visions of Nationwide Withdrawal," *New York Times*, April 27, 1994, p. B7.

60. See C. Nathanson, *Dangerous Passage: The Social Control of Sexuality in Women's Adolescence* (Philadelphia: Temple University Press, 1991), p. 25.

61. D. Rhode, "Adolescent Pregnancy and Public Policy," in A. Lawson and D. Rhode, eds., *The Politics of Pregnancy* (New Haven: Yale University Press, 1993).

62. M. Males, "School Age Pregnancy: Why Hasn't Prevention Worked?" *Journal of School Health*, 63:10 (1993), p. 429.

63. This quote by Ben Wattenberg, a conservative writer, originally appeared in the *San Diego Union-Tribune* and is cited in Swisher, ed., *Teenage Sexuality*, p. 96.

64. This quote by Ronald Reagan, from the *New York Times* (March 9, 1983), is cited in Nathanson, *Dangerous Passage*, p. 61.

65. This quote by Democratic Secretary of Health and Human Services Donna Shalala is cited in J. Stacey, "The New Family Values Crusaders," *The Nation*, July 25/August 1, 1994, p. 120.

66. This quote by liberal columnist Ellen Goodman first appeared in "Countering the Culture of Sex," *Boston Globe*, February 16, 1995, p. 19; emphasis added.

67. C. Tucker, "Restraint Best Taught by Peers," *Portland Press Herald*, April 30, 1994, p. 7A.

68. S. Fields, "Family Breakdown Causes Teen Pregnancy," in Swisher, ed., *Teenage Sexuality*, p. 55. (This article was originally published under the title "Teenage Girls Tragically Think Babies Will Ease Their Plight," in *Insight*, June 15, 1992.

69. Nathanson, *Dangerous Passage;* M. Argyle, *The Psychology of Social Class* (London: Routledge, 1994); C. G. Mascie-Taylor, *Biosocial Aspects of Social Class* (Oxford: Oxford University Press, 1990); and E. Lauman, J. Gagnon, R. Michael, and S. Michaels, eds., *The Social Organization of Sexuality: Sexual Practices in the United States* (Chicago: University of Chicago Press, 1994).

70. Nathanson, *Dangerous Passage*, p. 35.

71. M. W. Edelman, "Reducing Teen Pregnancy Would Decrease Childhood Poverty," in C. Wekesser, ed., *America's Children: Opposing Viewpoints* (San Diego: Greenhaven Press, 1991), pp. 149–156. (This chapter was reprinted from Edelman's book *Families in Peril: An Agenda for Social Change* [Cambridge, Mass.: Harvard University Press, 1987].)

72. Data from the Alan Guttmacher Institute cited in J. Rosoff, "For Most Teens, Chastity Isn't a Choice" (letter to the editor), *Wall Street Journal*, July 13, 1994, p. 12.

73. See, for example, L. Dash, "When Children Want Children," *Society*, 27 (July/August 1990), pp. 17–20. In addition, note the studies performed by Arline Geronomius et al., summarized in A. Cockburn, "Beat the Devil," *The Nation*, February 28, 1994, p. 259, and "Beat the Devil," *The Nation*, April 25, 1994, p. 549.

74. Fields, "Family Breakdown Causes Teen Pregnancy," p. 55.

75. Tucker, "Restraint Best Taught by Peers," p. 7A.

76. C. L. Allen, "Reducing Teen Pregnancy Would Not Decrease Childhood Poverty," in Wekesser, ed., *America's Children*, pp. 162–164.

77. See N. Farber, "The Significance of Race and Class in Marital Decisions Among Unmarried Adolescent Mothers," *Social Problems,* 37:1 (1990), pp. 51–63. Farber's very interesting study indicates that when middle-class girls *do* have children, their own families often encourage them *not to marry,* a phenomenon that greatly irritates moralists. Many middle-class (and working-class) parents assume that their children are not ready for commitment, and that marriage as well as childrearing will prevent them from returning to school or pursuing career options. Yet Farber found that, compared to their affluent counterparts, poor girls were more often raising kids "out-of-wedlock" because they lacked suitable male partners (e.g., because the fathers were in jail, had been abusive, had committed rape, or had denied paternity).

78. Again, refer to the Geronomius et al. studies summarized in Cockburn, "Beat the Devil," February 28, 1994, p. 259, and April 25, 1994, p. 549. See also D. Rhode, "Adolescent Pregnancy and Public Policy," in Lawson and Rhode, eds., *The Politics of Pregnancy;* C. Brindis, "Antecedents and Consequences: The Need for Diverse Strategies in Adolescent Pregnancy Prevention," in Lawson and Rhode, eds., *The Politics of Pregnancy;* Nathanson, *Dangerous Passage;* and B. Leadbetter's review of *The Young, Poor and Pregnant: The Psychology of Teenage Motherhood,* by Judith Musick, in *Social Service Review,* 69:2 (1995), pp. 370–374.

79. Males, "School Age Pregnancy," p. 429.

80. See F. Furstenberg, J. Gunn, and S. Morgan, "Adolescent Mothers and Their Children in Later Life," *Family Planning Perspectives,* 19 (July/August 1987), pp. 142–151.

81. These studies are cited in Cockburn, "Beat the Devil," February 28, 1994, p. 259, and April 25, 1994, p. 549. See also D. Rhode, "Adolescent Pregnancy and Public Policy," in Lawson and Rhode, eds., *The Politics of Pregnancy;* Brindis, "Antecedents and Consequences: The Need for Diverse Strategies in Adolescent Pregnancy Prevention"; and Allen, "Reducing Teen Pregnancy Would Not Decrease Childhood Poverty."

82. Brindis, "Antecedents and Consequences: The Need for Diverse Strategies in Adolescent Pregnancy Prevention."

83. J. Shapiro, "Teenage Sex: Just Say 'Wait,'" *U.S. News and World Report,* July 26, 1993, p. 57.

84. Gross, "Sex Educators for Young See New Virtue in Chastity," p. 1.

85. In part, European attitudes represent the greater acceptance and availability of contraception as well as the greater acceptance of sex education. In some countries, the more accepted role of sex seems to have resulted in *lower* rates of teen pregnancy; for example, according to data from the Alan Guttmacher Institute, very low teen pregnancy rates are recorded in Denmark and Sweden. (In 1988, for example, the rate in Denmark was 9 pregnancies per 1,000 women and in Sweden, 11 per 1,000, compared with 53 per 1,000 in the United States and 27 per 1,000 in the United Kingdom.)

86. W. Bennett and E. Koop, "Statement on AIDS Education," jointly released on January 30, 1987; cited in Nathanson, *Dangerous Passage,* pp. 64–65.

87. A. Novello, "AIDS Is a Serious Problem for Women," address presented to the National Conference on Women and HIV Infection on December 13, 1990;

reprinted in M. Biskup and K. Swisher, eds., *AIDS: Opposing Viewpoints* (San Diego: Greenhaven Press, 1992), p. 35.

88. Sontag, *Aids and Its Metaphors*, p. 78.

89. "The New Sexual Leprosy," *Time*, July 28, 1980, p. 76.

90. Rosenberg, *Microbes and Morals*, p. 175.

91. Douglas and Wildavsky, *Risk and Culture*, pp. 28–31.

92. Watney, "Photography and AIDS," p. 174.

93. S. Murray and K. Payne, "Medical Policy Without Scientific Evidence: The Promiscuity Paradigm and AIDS," *California Sociologist* (Winter/Summer 1988), pp. 16–17.

94. The survey on which this information is based, performed in 1984 by McKusick et al., is cited in ibid., pp. 27–35. For other critiques of AIDS moralism, see D. Altman, *AIDS in the Mind of America* (Garden City, N.Y.: Doubleday, 1986); and M. Caldwell, "The Literature of AIDS," *Dissent*, 37 (1990), pp. 342–347. See also Bayer, *Private Acts, Social Consequences*. Though an advocate of more interventionist public health measures, Bayer does not dispute the lack of proof that HIV was spread in bathhouses; but he does seem to support their closing as a symbolic measure.

95. See the related discussion in V. Jenness, "From Sex to Sin to Sex as Work: COYOTE and the Reorganization of Prostitution as a Social Problem," *Social Problems*, 37:3 (1990), pp. 403–420.

96. For a good discussion of how the major media shifted from treating AIDS as a "gay problem" or "deviant problem" to projecting a "widespread outbreak" among heterosexuals, see E. Albert, "AIDS and the Press: The Creation and Transformation of a Social Problem," in Best, ed., *Images of Issues*, pp. 39–54.

97. J. Seale, "How to Turn a Disease into VD," *New Scientist*, issue no. 1461 (1985), pp. 38–41.

98. C. Cole and H. Denny, "Visualizing Deviance in Post-Reagan America: Magic Johnson, AIDS, and the Promiscuous World of Professional Sport," *Critical Sociology*, 20:3 (1994), pp. 133–134.

99. A. Humm and F. Kunreuther, "The Invisible Epidemic: Teenagers and AIDS," *Social Policy*, 21:4 (1991), pp. 40–47.

100. Dr. Karen Hein, director of Montefiore Hospital's adolescent AIDS program in New York, cited in S. Nelson, "Condom Use Will Help Prevent AIDS," in Biskup and Swisher, eds., *AIDS: Opposing Viewpoints*, p. 121. (Nelson's article was reprinted from *Glamour* magazine, February 1992).

101. E. Maticka-Tyndale, "Social Construction of HIV Transmission and Prevention Among Heterosexual Young Adults," *Social Problems*, 39:3 (1992), pp. 238–249.

102. Ibid., p. 246.

103. A. Brandt, "AIDS and Metaphor," *Social Research*, 55 (1988), p. 429.

104. For medical data on heterosexual transmission of AIDS, see, for example, N. Padian et al., "Male-to-Female Transmission of Human Immunodeficiency Virus," *Journal of the American Medical Association*, 6 (1987), p. 789; and N. Hearst and S. Hulley, "Preventing the Heterosexual Spread of AIDS," *Journal of the American Medical Association*, 259 (1988), pp. 2428–2430.

105. See Lauman, Gagnon, Michael, and Michaels, eds., *The Social Organization of Sexuality: Sexual Practices in the United States,* pp. 18–19, 173–74, 225, 392. See also D. Haney, "Backlash Emerging over Risk of AIDS," *Maine Sunday Telegram,* April 17, 1994, pp. A1, A6.

106. See Lauman, Gagnon, Michael, and Michaels, eds., *The Social Organization of Sexuality: Sexual Practices in the United States,* p. 393. The data presented here are based on male-to-female transmission (the reverse would lower the odds greatly) through vaginal intercourse, assuming a 10 percent condom failure rate per exposure. Other data suggest even lower transmission rates: In particular, see Padian et al., "Male-to-Female Transmission of Human Immunodeficiency Virus"; and Hearst and Hulley, "Preventing the Heterosexual Spread of AIDS."

107. Lauman, Gagnon, Michael, and Michaels, eds., *The Social Organization of Sexuality: Sexual Practices in the United States,* pp. 173–174.

108. R. Nixon, "Zero Tolerance for Drugs Can Reduce Chemical Dependency," in Cozic and Swisher, eds., *Chemical Dependency,* p. 231. (This chapter was Reprinted from Nixon's book *In the Arena: A Memoir of Victory, Defeat and Renewal* [1990].)

109. J. Sobran, "School Curricula Should Not Provide Homosexual Propaganda," in Swisher, ed., *Teenage Sexuality,* p. 190. (Sobran's article was reprinted from *Human Life Review,* Fall 1992.)

110. G. Nahas, cited in Cozic and Swisher, eds., *Chemical Dependency,* p. 16.

111. H. Fingarette, "Alcoholism Is Not a Disease," in Cozic and Swisher, eds., *Chemical Dependency,* p. 102. (Fingarette's article was reprinted from the *San Diego Union,* January 29, 1989.) I should note that, although the comment quoted here has validity for many problem drinkers, it does not differentiate those who have experienced serious physical withdrawal associated with the most serious forms of alcoholism and drug addiction from those for whom physical addiction is less provable.

112. Peele, *The Diseasing of America,* p. 50.

113. Nelson, "Condom Use Will Help Prevent AIDS," p.118.

114. See R. Blendon, K. Donelan, and R. Knox, "Public Opinion and AIDS: Lessons from the Second Decade," *Journal of the American Medical Association,* 267:7 (1992), pp. 981–986. Although hysteria did occasionally grip the public, opinion surveys generally show that concern about AIDS was not only relatively realistic but also strongest among those most at risk.

115. For example, Undersecretary of Health and Human Services John Bowen and scientist Stephen Jay Gould predicted that AIDS would "dwarf the Black Plague" and kill off one-quarter of the world's people. Although such claims were presumably well-meaning, the empirical evidence to support them have been difficult to come by. Sontag, among others (as discussed in Chapter 6), has cited a particular American fascination with apocalyptic thinking of this sort. (See her *AIDS and Its Metaphors.*)

116. *New York Times* sportswriter Robert Lipsyte, "What Price Fitness?" *New York Times Magazine,* February 16, 1986; cited in Levenstein, *Paradox of Plenty,* p. 241.

117. Goodman, "Countering the Culture of Sex."

118. H. Piper, "Light-Up Time," *Baltimore Sun*, March 20, 1994, p. 24.

119. Dash, "When Children Want Children," p. 17.

120. The Denver study is cited in Fields, "Family Breakdown Causes Teen Pregnancy," p. 54. And the Atlanta study is cited in D. Besharov, "Improved Education Could Reduce Teen Pregnancy," in Swisher, *Teenage Sexuality*, p. 110 (reprinted from *The American Enterprise*, March/April 1993).

121. T. Levin, "Boys Are More Comfortable with Sex Than Girls Are, Survey Finds," *New York Times*, May 18, 1994, p. A20.

122. Nathanson, *Dangerous Passage*, p. 62; original emphasis.

123. Edwin Lemert, cited in Gusfield, *Symbolic Crusade*, p. 26.

124. Historians and sociologists often dichotomize "political" resistance from what many view as self-destructive behaviors (e.g., alcoholism) among the poor and others. Such a dichotomy is difficult to argue cogently, however. Historically, the "crowd" (from the storming of the Bastille to the 1960s ghetto riots in America) often does include people who are inebriated or otherwise discreditable. Sometimes these may well be the folks who throw the first rocks; at other times, they might be the ones who nobly stand up to powerful armed forces. Without wishing to glorify the excessive use of alcohol and other substances, I note the crucial contradiction between the Left's efforts to improve the behavior of poor and working-class people, on the one hand, and its tendency to urge the same groups to engage in social unrest, on the other. Of course, social unrest itself may flow from anger and outrage, which are usually bottled up when social control works effectively but which alcohol and other substances tend to bring out. In the face of increasing efforts to render America a totally administered society (see Chapter 7), one wonders, should these efforts ever succeed, whether social unrest of the type the Left has traditionally supported (strikes, riots, militant protests) would occur.

125. Klein, *Cigarettes Are Sublime*, p. 86.

126. Ibid., especially pp. 14, 117.

127. Ibid., pp. 189, 201. For example, the proportion of female smokers is highest in the Nordic countries and lowest in Spain and Portugal. And during the last two decades in the United States, the number of female smokers has begun to catch up with that of male smokers after historically trailing far behind.

128. Piper, "Light-Up Time," p. 24.

CHAPTER 5

1. See B. Ehrenreich, *Fear of Falling: The Inner Life of the Middle Class* (New York: Pantheon, 1989), pp. 75–78. The present chapter is generally indebted to this seminal work.

2. Margaret Mead, cited in ibid., p. 75.

3. Ehrenreich, *Fear of Falling*, p. 15.

4. Ibid., p. 83.

5. Ibid., p. 14.

6. Ibid., p. 229.

7. The issue of other classes' support for temperance is important, and I do not completely agree with those who suggest that only the middle class embraces the New Temperance. Indeed, the support of other classes, particularly

the working class, is key to a number of temperance issues. For example, as noted in Chapter 3, the "mob" in the nineteenth century did at times use charges of scandal to attack elites.

The position of the working class is more ambiguous today. On the one hand, lacking the cultural power and sense of style of the middle class, it tends to be charged with "cultural lag," and on issues such as cigarette smoking and food tastes, class cues continue to separate the middle from the working class. On the other hand, there is a long history of working-class respectability, particularly among skilled workers. This tendency, in combination with the often conservative social attitudes associated with the American working class (particularly among some ethnic and religious groups), sometimes leads to attacks on those charged with "deviance," regarding drug taking or sexual behavior, for example.

Nevertheless, the working class rarely has been able to initiate new tastes and status cues. For example, even though anti-drug attitudes are quite common in blue-collar neighborhoods, the drug war is still more accurately described as having originated in decisions by elites and the middle class.

8. J. Burnham, *Bad Habits: Drinking, Smoking, Taking Drugs, Gambling, Sexual Misbehavior, and Swearing in American History* (New York: New York University Press, 1993), p. 5.

9. See J. Gusfield, *Symbolic Crusade: Status Politics and the American Temperance Movement* (Urbana, Ill.: University of Illinois Press, 1963).

10. Burnham, *Bad Habits*, p. 9.

11. Gusfield, *Symbolic Crusade.*

12. Almost all data on the heavy and consistent use of substances (drugs, alcohol, tobacco), on youthful sexuality, even on poor diet and obesity, and crime and aggression, reflect a disproportionate representation of the poor and ethnic minorities. In this connection, see also Notes 17, 24, 25, 41, 52, and 53.

13. See especially Gusfield, *Symbolic Crusade.*

14. For further discussion of the effects of Prohibition on the various social classes, see especially A. Sinclair, *Prohibition: The Era of Excess* (Boston: Little, Brown, 1962); and J. Blocker, *American Temperance Movements: Cycles of Reform* (Boston: Twayne Publishers, 1989).

15. For a good historical account, see H. Levenstein, *Paradox of Plenty: A Social History of Eating in America* (New York: Oxford University Press, 1993), pp. 28–29.

16. The influence of World Wars I and II on cigarette consumption is discussed in R. Klein, *Cigarettes Are Sublime* (Durham, N.C.: Duke University Press, 1993); R. Sobel, *They Satisfy: The Cigarette in American Life* (Garden City, N.Y.: Anchor Books, 1978); R. Troyer and G. Markle, *Cigarettes: The Battle over Smoking* (New Brunswick, N.J.: Rutgers University Press, 1983); and S. Wagner, *Cigarette Country: Tobacco in American History and Politics* (New York: Praeger, 1971). In *Bad Habits* (pp. 61, 73), Burnham argues that alcohol consumption and sexual habits, as well as smoking habits, converged during and after World War II.

17. For a discussion of differences among class approaches to food and exercise, see Levenstein, *Paradox of Plenty;* p. 86. For related information concerning smoking, including the decline in smoking among the professional classes that

began in the late 1940s, see H. Diehl, *Tobacco and Your Health: The Smoking Controversy* (New York: McGraw-Hill, 1969), pp. 128–129.

18. See, for example, H. Becker, *The Outsiders: Studies in the Sociology of Deviance*, 2nd ed. (New York: Free Press, 1973); H. W. Morgan, *Drugs in America: A Social History 1800–1980* (Syracuse, N.Y.: Syracuse University Press, 1981); and D. Musto, *The American Disease: The Origins of Narcotic Control* (New Haven: Yale University Press, 1973).

19. See especially E. Freedman, "'Uncontrolled Desires': The Response to the Sexual Psychopath, 1920–1960"; and J. D'Emilio, "The Homosexual Menace: The Politics of Sexuality in Cold War America," in K. Peiss and C. Simmons, *Passion and Power: Sexuality in History* (Philadelphia: Temple University Press, 1989).

20. Jerry Falwell, cited in Ehrenreich, *Fear of Falling*, p. 168.

21. R. Larkin and D. Foss, "Lexicon of Folk-Etymology," in S. Sayres, A. Stephanson, S. Aronowitz, and F. Jameson, eds., *The 60s Without Apology* (Minneapolis: University of Minnesota Press, 1984), p. 360; original emphasis.

22. Ehrenreich, *Fear of Falling*, p. 61.

23. Midge Decter, cited in ibid., p. 74.

24. I am relying here on available data about alcohol consumption, illicit drug use, rates of cigarette smoking, food habits, teen pregnancy, and sexual partnering. (a) Regarding drugs: In the 1960s, when the "tune in, turn on, and drop out" mantra was being widely publicized, experts noted "the recent spread of narcotics and hallucinogenic drugs into the middle and upper classes of America and Europe"; but they also cited data showing that only marijuana had obtained high rates of usage among middle-class youth, and that middle-class students had only minimal involvement with "hard" drugs as "compared to [the pattern of drug usage in] the ghetto areas of large cities." (For a sense of what drug expert opinion was at this time, see the papers in D. Malikin, ed., *Social Disability: Alcoholism, Drug Addiction, Crime and Social Disadvantage* [New York: New York University Press, 1973].) In addition, James Inciardi, a noted drug researcher, cites an extensive 1969 New York study of narcotic use "whose results were some of the highest correlation coefficients ever encountered in social science research" among poverty, unemployment, illegitimacy, welfare assistance, "delinquency," and use of drugs (J. Inciardi, *The War on Drugs: Heroin, Cocaine, Crime and Public Policy* [Palo Alto, Calif.: Mayfield Publishing, 1986], p. 162). (b) Regarding sexuality: Research indicated that rates of early sexual intercourse and number of sex partners varied by social class in the direction of more temperant behavior in the higher classes, at least until the 1970s (see, for example, M. Weinberg and C. Williams, "Sexual Embourgeoisment? Social Class and Sexual Activity: 1938–1970," *American Sociological Review*, 45 [1980], pp. 33–48).

Of course, these conclusions are generalizations, inasmuch as the patterns of democratization were different in each area mentioned. It certainly began to *appear* to people—most especially with drugs and sexuality—that the middle class young were leading the way toward intemperance and hedonism.

Part of the difficulty here, in addition to the obvious problem of obtaining "good" data about personal habits that have been stigmatized, is the tendency to mistake experimental and visible manifestations of drug use and sexual abandon for long-term patterns. In retrospect, it appears that the highly visible drug use and sexual behavior of middle-class "baby boomers" was time-limited for most, whereas data on long-term use of drugs and alcohol, and even on early sexuality and number of sexual partners, indicate that these behaviors are still more common below the middle-class level.

25. (a) Regarding drugs: See the NIDA data indicating that drug use in all classes peaked in the late 1970s (National Institute on Drug Abuse, *Drug Use, Drinking and Smoking: National Survey Results from High School, College and Young Adult Populations 1975–1988* [Rockville, Md.: NIDA, 1989]) and certainly reached higher levels among middle-class youth in this period than in earlier ones. (b) Regarding sexuality: Many reports indicate the reality of a cross-class sexual revolution (see, for example, R. Levin and A. Levin, "Sexual Pleasure: The Surprising Preferences of 100,000 Women," *Redbook*, September 1975; and Lauman, Gagnon, Michael, and Michaels, eds., *The Social Organization of Sexuality: Sexual Practices in the United States,* especially pp. 199–200, 542. (c) Regarding food: Research indicates that dietary norms converged to the greatest extent in the 1950s and 1960s but, after the recession of 1973, began to diverge again (Levenstein, *Paradox of Plenty,* p. 222).

26. These data are cited in K. Butler, "The Great Boomer Bust," *Mother Jones,* June 1989, p. 35.

27. L. Rubin, *Families on the Fault Line* (New York: Harper Collins, 1994), p. 32.

28. See, for example, B. Bluestone and B. Harrison, *The Deindustrialization of America* (New York: Basic Books, 1982); M. Harrington, *The New American Poverty* (New York: Holt, Rinehart and Winston, 1984); K. Newman, *Falling from Grace* (New York: Free Press, 1988); and W. J. Wilson, *The Truly Disadvantaged* (Chicago: University of Chicago Press, 1987).

29. Newman, *Falling from Grace,* pp. 35–36.

30. Butler, "The Great Boomer Bust," p. 33.

31. Ibid., p. 32.

32. Ibid., pp. 35–36.

33. Ehrenreich, *Fear of Falling,* pp. 225–226.

34. Joseph Califano, cited in Bayer, *Private Acts, Social Consequences,* p. 14.

35. It should be noted that the 1980s were not without civil rights victories that limited how far corporate power could go. By the late 1980s, despite growing concern about employer-mandated AIDS testing, the gay movement and its allies had succeeded in halting its spread; and Congress had successfully restricted the use of polygraph tests. Even the 1980s legislation protecting unpaid maternity leave has significance here, given previous employer firings and demotions of pregnant employees.

36. "Can You Pass the Job Test?" *Newsweek,* May 5, 1986, pp. 46–53.

37. Ehrenreich, *Fear of Falling,* p. 220.

38. Ibid.

39. Ibid., p. 229.

40. See Wilson, *The Truly Disadvantaged.*

41. For an excellent general discussion of the correlations among gender, income, and violence and aggression, see the works of James Messerschmidt: *Capitalism, Patriarchy, and Crime* (Totowa, N.J.: Rowman and Littlefield, 1986), and *Masculinities and Crime* (Totowa, N.J.: Roman and Littlefield, 1993). Similarly,

Peele, in *The Diseasing of America*, summarizes many studies linking alcoholism, drugs, and heavy cigarette smoking with men, low income, unemployment, and underemployment. In this connection, see also D. Cahalan, *Problem Drinkers* (San Francisco: Jossey-Bass, 1970); D. Cahalan and R. Room, *Problem Drinking Among American Men* (New Brunswick, N.J.: Rutgers Center for Alcohol Studies, 1974); G. Valliant, *The Natural History of Alcoholism* (Cambridge, Mass.: Harvard University Press, 1983); R. Crum, J. Helzer, and J. Anthony, "Level of Education and Alcohol Abuse and Dependence in Adulthood: A Further Inquiry," *American Journal of Public Health*, 83:6 (1993), pp. 830–836; and K. Thompson, "Gender and Adolescent Drinking Problems: The Effects of Occupational Structure," *Social Problems*, 36:1 (1989), pp. 30–47. For research on cigarette smoking and class, gender, and income, see T. Hall, "Smoking of Cigarettes Seems to Be Becoming a Lower-Class Habit," *Wall Street Journal*, June 25, 1985; and J. Pierce, M. Fiore, T. Novotny, E. Hatziandreu, and R. Davis, "Trends in Cigarette Smoking in the United States," *Journal of the American Medical Association*, 261:1 (1989), p. 58. Finally, for international perspectives on these issues, see C. G. Mascie-Taylor, *Biosocial Aspects of Social Class* (Oxford: Oxford University Press, 1990), p. 124; and M. Argyle, *The Psychology of Social Class* (London: Routledge, 1994), p. 11, 268.

42. See the discussion of this phrase in E. Pleck, *Domestic Tyranny* (New York: Oxford University Press, 1987), especially chapter 3.

43. E. Maticka-Tyndale, "Social Construction of HIV Transmission and Prevention Among Heterosexual Young Adults," *Social Problems*, 39:3 (1992), pp. 238–249.

44. See ibid.; and Pleck, *Domestic Tyranny.*

45. See K. Roiphe, *The Morning After: Sex, Fear, and Feminism* (Boston: Little, Brown, 1994), especially pp. 77–84. According to Roiphe, much of the anxiety on campus that expresses itself through the date rape and sexual harassment movements is reflective of class and race anxiety. Certainly when movements focus on transients and off-campus visitors to places like Columbia, Yale, the University of Chicago, and other universities near slum areas, they are open to this charge.

46. J. Best, "Rhetoric in Claims-Making: Constructing the Missing Children Problem," *Social Problems*, 34 (1987); J. Best, *Threatened Children: The Social Construction of a Moral Panic* (Chicago: University of Chicago Press, 1990); P. Jenkins, *Intimate Matters: Moral Panics in Contemporary Great Britain* (New York: Aldine de Gruyter, 1992).

47. Ehrenreich, *Fear of Falling*, ch. 1.

48. Wilson, *The Truly Disadvantaged;* D. Massey and N. Denton, *American Apartheid* (Cambridge, Mass.: Harvard University Press, 1993).

49. Of course, I don't mean to imply that mayors of other cities beset by disorders have ever approved of them; but few officials prior to the late 1970s had ever so unmitigatingly attacked poor people as lacking legitimate grievances as did the previously liberal Ed Koch in 1977.

50. Ehrenreich, *Fear of Falling*, pp. 249–250.

51. Ibid., p. 186.

52. It has become fashionable in the last two decades to deny this, and there are some good reasons to be cautious. Fund-raisers and social service agencies

seek to secure more support by characterizing a variety of ills as "crossing class lines," and the positive result has been to diminish stigma and discrimination based on race and class. Of course, I am also aware of the liberal, sometimes radical, arguments often made against the use of official statistics regarding stigmatized behavior. It is true that middle-class people are sometimes in a position to hide their "deviance"; and, on some issues, probably including illicit drugs and child abuse, the poor are the most policed social class and, hence, more subject to official reports of "deviance."

I suggest, however, that this argument has been greatly exaggerated, for two main reasons (see D. Wagner, "The Universalization of Social Problems: Does Everything 'Cut Across Class Lines'?" Paper presented at the annual meeting of the Eastern Sociological Society, Boston, March 30, 1996). First, some major social problems are hard to keep hidden or disguised. In particular, murder, or serious injury and disfigurement, rarely escape the notice of police, health officials, and social agencies. For example, in 1988, the year in which the Joel Steinberg case in New York became well known, Nat Hentoff ("Is It a Crime to Do Nothing?" *Village Voice*, November 22, 1988, p. 28) reported that while the news devoted page after page to the Steinbergs, 103 children (2 a week) died from parental abuse and neglect in New York City, nearly all in lower-class and ghetto neighborhoods. Granted, charges of neglect are correlated with higher levels of scrutiny of poor families; but it is hard to believe that affluent people are killing their children, or their wives, husbands, fathers, or mothers, and somehow bribing police or media not to report such incidents.

Second, a considerable body of data collection is now based on self-reporting. Though hardly perfect, data of this type provide relatively reliable results in that they avoid the previously mentioned pitfalls of official records. For example, NIDA, which annually performs surveys on substance use, has found since the 1970s (with exceptions here and there) that drug, alcohol, and cigarette use among youth (particularly heavy and long-term use) is correlated with low education and self-assessment of low prospects for further education, both of which, in turn, are correlated with social class. The issue of crime provides another case in point: Not only do self-reports reveal that poor people commit more criminal acts than middle-class people, but, as G. Kleck has found, when subjects are asked about their own actions, poor people actually *underreport* their actions compared to middle-class people (Kleck, cited in Argyle, *The Psychology of Social Class*, p. 250).

For related discussions of teen pregnancy and class, see C. Nathanson, *Dangerous Passage: The Social Control of Sexuality in Women's Adolescence* (Philadelphia: Temple University Press, 1991); J. Rosoff, "For Most Teens, Chastity Isn't a Choice" (letter to the editor), *Wall Street Journal*, July 13, 1994; M. W. Edelman, "Reducing Teen Pregnancy Would Decrease Childhood Poverty," in C. Wekesser, ed., *America's Children: Opposing Viewpoints* (San Diego: Greenhaven Press, 1991); L. Dash, "When Children Want Children," *Society*, 27 (July/August 1990); N. Farber, "The Significance of Race and Class in Marital Decisions Among Unmarried Adolescent Mothers," *Social Problems*, 37:1 (1990); and M. Males, "School Age Pregnancy: Why Hasn't Prevention Worked?" *Journal of School Health*, 63:10 (1993).

See also the data concerning nonmarital sexual behavior in T. Kemper, *Social Structure and Testosterone* (New Brunswick: Rutgers University Press, 1990). Kemper notes that, among men under forty in particular, the number of sexual partners is inversely proportional to level of social class. In addition, according to statistical studies performed at the Battelle Human Affairs Research Center, black males tend to have more sexual partners than white males (cited in F. Chideya, *Don't Believe the Hype* [New York: Plume, 1995], p. 30). These findings tend to support the earlier work by Weinberg and Williams on sexuality and class ("Sexual Embourgeoisment? Social Class and Sexual Activity: 1938–1970") as well as the cross-national data in Argyle (*The Psychology of Social Class*) and Mascie-Taylor (*Biosocial Aspects of Social Class*).

Regarding correlations of diet and exercise with education and race, see Center for Disease Control, "Prevalence of Selected Risk Factors for Chronic Disease by Education Level in Racial/Ethnic Groups—United States 1991–92," *Morbidity and Mortality Weekly Report*, 43:38 (December 8, 1994), pp. 894–898. For information on international studies of this issue, see Argyle, *The Psychology of Social Class*, pp. 193–194; Mascie-Taylor, *Biosocial Aspects of Social Class*, pp. 130–131; R. Wilkinson, *Class and Health* (London: Tavistock, 1986), p. 15; and Levenstein, *Paradox of Plenty*, pp. 244–245.

For cross-national data on crime, see J. Braithwaite, *Inequality, Crime, and Public Policy* (London: Routledge, 1979) as well as T. Chiricos's review of sixty-three studies on the relationship of crime and unemployment in "Rates of Crime and Unemployment: An Analysis of Aggregate Research Evidence," *Social Problems*, 34:2 (1987), pp. 187–212. For good summaries of crime rates as correlated with age, gender, and class, see Messerschmidt's *Capitalism, Patriarchy, and Crime* and *Masculinities and Crime*.

Good reviews of child abuse and class issues can be found in C. Kruttschnitt, J. McLeod, and M. Dornfeld, "The Economic Environment of Child Abuse," *Social Problems*, 41:2 (1994), pp. 299–314; R. Gelles and M. Straus, *Intimate Violence: The Definitive Study of the Causes and Consequences of Abuse in the American Family* (New York: Simon and Schuster, 1988); L. Pelton, "Child Abuse and Neglect: The Myth of Classlessness," in L. Pelton, ed., *The Social Context of Child Abuse and Neglect* (New York: Human Sciences Press, 1981); and B. McNeil, "Poverty Causes Child Abuse," in K. Koster and K. Swisher, *Child Abuse: Opposing Viewpoints* (San Diego: Greenhaven Press, 1994), p. 93.

For a good summary of data on income, occupation, and wife/partner abuse, see Messerschmidt, *Masculinities and Crime*, pp. 148–150. A recent CDC study also confirms class and age differences among women involved in domestic violence; see "Study Suggests 6 Percent of Pregnant Women Are Battered," *New York Times*, March 4, 1994, p. A12. Finally, for historical data on the relationship between social class and wife abuse (as well as that between child abuse and child sexual abuse), see the chart on page 174 of L. Gordon, *Heroes of Their Own Lives* (New York: Viking Press, 1988).

53. For a good discussion of how and why social class might structure personal behavior, see Argyle, *The Psychology of Social Class*. Also useful are the discussions of how male socialization structures aggression and "deviance" in Messerschmidt, *Capitalism, Patriarchy, and Crime* and *Masculinities and Crime*.

54. See J. D'Emilio and E. Freedman, *Intimate Matters: A History of Sexuality in America* (New York: Harper and Row, 1988), pp. xvi, 6–8, 31, 35; S. Mintz and S. Kellogg, *Domestic Revolutions: A Social History of American Family Life* (New York: Free Press, 1988), particularly ch. 4.

55. D. Schneider and J. Smith, *Class Differences and Sex Roles in American Kinship and Family Structure* (Englewood Cliffs: Prentice-Hall, 1973), cited in Burnham, *Bad Habits*, p. 183.

56. Ibid.

57. See Wagner, *Checkerboard Square*, particularly pp. 43–44 as well as chs. 3 and 7.

58. T. Hirschi, *The Causes of Delinquency* (Berkeley: University of California Press, 1969).

59. Kemper, *Social Structure and Testosterone*, p. 75.

CHAPTER 6

1. See, for example, F. Piven and R. Cloward, *Why Americans Don't Vote* (New York: Pantheon, 1989). Note, however, that widespread commentary on low voter turnout for national elections obscures the fact of even lower turnout for state and local elections—which in turn are frequently critical in terms of the issues under discussion. For example, a host of ordinances on such issues as tobacco smoking, underage drinking, drunk driving, and condom distribution in the schools, to name just a few, are implemented at the level of state or local policy, not national policy.

2. For reasons already touched upon—namely, the historical association of alcohol with male violence, and the cultural association of "promiscuity" with men in Western society—it is not clear that a majority of women office holders would necessarily hold different views on temperance issues (though they might on issues of teen pregnancy or female sexuality). The most supportable generalizations would be those pertaining to social class, age, and race and ethnicity.

3. On aspects of the "personal is political," see W. Breines, *Community and Organization in the New Left: 1962–1968: The Great Refusal* (New York: Praeger, 1982); S. Evans, *Personal Politics: The Roots of Women's Liberation in the Civil Rights Movement and the New Left* (New York: Knopf, 1979); and A. Echols, *Daring to Be Bad: Radical Feminism in America 1967–1975* (Minneapolis: University of Minnesota Press, 1989).

4. Jean Tepperman, cited in Echols, *Daring to Be Bad*, p. 222.

5. Ti-Grace Atkinson, cited in S. Seidman, *Embattled Eros: Sexual Politics and Ethics in Contemporary America* (New York: Routledge, 1992), p. 79.

6. Echols, *Daring to Be Bad*, p. 17. Many leftist and feminist observers insist that this phrase has been misinterpreted by many later activists. But I would suggest that the ambiguity is built into the paradigm. This is not to say that all actions do not have political overtones and ramifications; however, the point of the phrase is that personal politics (as opposed to the older leftist tradition of structural politics) would be liberatory. At any rate, evidence about the success of personal politics is at best decidedly mixed.

7. Jerry Falwell, cited in E. Jorstead, *The New Christian Right 1981–88* (Lewiston, N.Y.: Edward Mellen Press, 1987), pp. 31–32.

8. R. Viguerie, *The New Right: We're Ready to Lead* (Falls Church, Va.: Viguerie Company, 1980), p. 186.

9. Jorstead, *The New Christian Right 1981–88*, p. 80; emphasis added.

10. Excellent accounts of the development of "crime" and "drugs" as socially constructed political strategies can be found in W. Chambliss, "Policing the Ghetto Underclass: The Politics of Law and Law Enforcement," *Social Problems*, 41:2 (1994); and K. Beckett, "Setting the Public Agenda: 'Street Crime' and Drug Abuse in American Politics," *Social Problems*, 41:3 (1994), pp. 425–446.

11. See D. Snowball, *Continuity and Change in the Rhetoric of the Moral Majority* (New York: Praeger, 1991), pp. 50–51.

12. Paul Weyrich, cited in D'Emilio and Freedman, *Intimate Matters*, p. 348; and in Viguerie, *The New Right*, p. 152.

13. Both surveys are cited in C. Wilcox, *God's Warriors: The Christian Right in Twentieth Century America* (Baltimore: Johns Hopkins Press, 1992), p. 212. Of course, much depends on how survey questions are asked, and a case can be made that the public was slightly more liberal than these two surveys suggest.

14. See ibid. for a discussion of the significance of the Carter campaign's successful efforts to bring "born again" Christians to the polls. Ironically, these voters later swung to the Republican Party.

15. Ed Rollins, cited in Jorstead, *The New Christian Right 1981–88*, p. 144.

16. B. Ehrenreich, *The Hearts of Men* (Garden City, N.Y.: Anchor Books, 1983), pp. 149–151.

17. Snowball, *Continuity and Change in the Rhetoric of the Moral Majority*, pp. 23, 162.

18. Both quotations are cited in R. Stengel, "Sex Busters," *Time*, July 21, 1986, p. 17.

19. Both quotations are cited in M. Biskup and K. Swisher, eds., *AIDS: Opposing Viewpoints* (San Diego: Greenhaven Press, 1992), where the Sobran piece has been reprinted under the title "AIDS Is a Moral Issue" (pp. 47–54) and the Feder and Kerrison piece, under the title "Condom Use Will Not Help Prevent AIDS" (pp. 124–129).

20. See, for example, the review of sexual issues and the Left in A. Snitow, C. Stansell, and S. S. Thompson, eds., *Powers of Desire: The Politics of Sexuality* (New York: Monthly Review Press, 1983), pp. 19–21.

21. Sidney and Beatrice Webb, cited in S. Ranulf, *Moral Indignation and Middle Class Psychology* (New York: Schocken Books, 1964), p. 189.

22. The Victorian assumptions of Marx and Engels embedded in their attack on capitalism are discussed in Snitow, Stansell, and Thompson, eds., *Powers of Desire: The Politics of Sexuality*, pp. 13–16.

23. E. Bristow, *Vice and Vigilance: Purity Movements in Britain Since 1700* (Dublin: Gill and MacMillan, 1977), pp. 40–41.

24. Ranulf, *Moral Indignation and Middle Class Psychology*, p. 187.

25. Ibid., pp. 188–190.

26. A content analysis of *Mother Jones* magazine between 1976 and 1980 reveals a large number of articles relevant to the New Temperance. See, for exam-

ple, M. Jacobson, "The Deadly White Powder" (July 1978), on the dangers of salt; G. Blair, "Why Dick Can't Stop Smoking" (January 1979), one of four articles on the dangers of smoking; "They Blight Up Your Life" (June 1978 "Frontlines"), on artificial lighting; H. Drummond, "Add Poison for Freshness and Flavor" (April 1977), on food additives; "O.D.ing on Salt" (May 1977 "Frontlines"); H. Drummond, "Empires: Born, Bred, Dead of Lead" (June 1977), on cigarette smoking and lead; the July 1977 "Frontlines" on garlic and heart disease; and D. Romano, "Eating Our Hearts Out" (June 1980), on food. Two anti-prescription-drug articles are J. Bernard's "Just What the Doctor Ordered" (February/March 1976) and H. Drummond's "Down So Long, Feels Like Valium to me" (July 1977). In H. Drummond's "Growing Old Absurd" (May 1980), smoking, eating fatty foods, taking prescription drugs, and watching television are all condemned. On pornography, see L. Shapiro, "Violence: The Most Obscene Fantasy" (December 1977) and D. English, "The Politics of Porn" (April 1980). Finally, the benefits of homeopathic medicine are described in S. Craig, "Take Two Arsenic Pills and Call Me in the Morning" (May 1976); and of eating tofu, in "Tofu" (August 1976).

27. I do not mean to "pick on" *Mother Jones* magazine. I believe other left-wing publications such as *The Nation, In These Times,* and *The Guardian* have treated these issues in much the same way. The glossy appearance and higher price of *Mother Jones* suggested a more affluent audience. In addition, *The Guardian* followed a harder Left line at the time. But though the New Age and temperant concerns of the Left came a bit earlier to *Mother Jones* than to, say, *The Guardian,* my analysis suggests that by the 1980s most leftist and liberal papers had taken up similar positions on the issues under discussion.

28. J. Van Allen, "Eating It! From Here to 2001," *Ramparts,* May 1972, p. 26.

29. G. Blair, "Why Dick Can't Stop Smoking," *Mother Jones,* 4 (January 1979), p. 32.

30. E. Goodman, "Tobacco Lobby Makes an Offer," *Portland Press Herald,* June 28, 1994.

31. J. Gusfield, *Symbolic Crusade: Status Politics and the American Temperance Movement* (Urbana, Ill.: University of Illinois Press, 1963), p. 97. The basic problem with asserting that the temperance message is conducive to anti-capitalist perspectives is that it shifts concern from the morality of profit and economic organization to the quality or morality of the products manufactured.

32. See the January 1979 issue of *Mother Jones,* cited in Blair, "Why Dick Can't Stop Smoking," pp. 34–35; "Kicking Mr. Butts" (editorial), *The Nation,* June 20, 1994, p. 854; and M. Ebrahim and C. Lewis, "Will Washington Kick Tobacco?" *The Nation,* April 25, 1994, pp. 555–557.

33. C. Hitchens, "Smoke and Mirrors," *Vanity Fair,* October 1994, p. 95.

34. Ibid.

35. Susan Brownmiller, cited in J. Walkowitz, "Male Vice and Female Virtue," in Snitow, Stansell, and Thompson, eds., *Powers of Desire: The Politics of Sexuality,* p. 420.

36. E. Willis, *No More Nice Girls: Countercultural Essays* (Hanover, N.H.: Wesleyan University Press, 1992), p. 262.

37. See Echols, *Daring to Be Bad;* Willis, "Radical Feminism and Feminist Radicalizing," in S. Sayres, A. Stephanson, S. Aronowitz, and F. Jameson, eds., *The 60s*

Without Apology (Minneapolis: University of Minnesota Press, 1984); B. Ehrenreich, E. Hess, and G. Jacobs, *Re-Making Love: The Feminization of Sex* (Garden City, N.Y.: Anchor Books, 1986); L. Tiefer, *Sex Is Not a Natural Act and Other Essays* (Boulder, Colo.: Westview Press, 1995); L. Segal, *Is the Future Female? Troubled Thoughts on Contemporary Feminism* (New York: Bedrick, 1988); and Snitow, Stansell, and Thompson, eds., *Powers of Desire: The Politics of Sexuality.*

38. Kate Millet, cited in Seidman, *Embattled Eros,* p. 46.

39. Ehrenreich, Hess, and Jacobs, *Re-Making Love,* p. 71.

40. Ibid., pp. 192–193. See also Echols, *Daring to Be Bad,* p. 43; and Segal, *Is the Future Female?* p. 76.

41. See Echols, *Daring to Be Bad,* p. 4.

42. Segal, *Is the Future Female?* p. 46.

43. For further discussion of the emergence of rape as an issue, see Echols, *Daring to Be Bad,* p. 193. On the emergence of battered women as an issue, see Pleck, *Domestic Tyranny.*

44. Andrea Dworkin, cited in Seidman, *Embattled Eros,* p. 106.

45. Susan Brownmiller, cited in A. Echols, "The Feminism of Yin and Yan," in Snitow, Stansell, and Thompson, eds., *Powers of Desire: The Politics of Sexuality,* p. 442.

46. Sheila Jeffreys, cited in P. Jenkins, *Intimate Matters: Moral Panics in Contemporary Great Britain* (New York: Aldine de Gruyter, 1992), p. 58.

47. See, for example, the critique by A. Hollibaugh and C. Moraga, "What We're Rolling Around in Bed With: Sexual Silences in Feminism," in Snitow, Stansell, and Thompson, eds., *Powers of Desire: The Politics of Sexuality,* pp. 394–405.

48. Sheila Jeffreys, cited in Jenkins, *Intimate Matters,* p. 109. Of course, I understand the feminist argument that policing of male aggression and violence weakens patriarchal authority. But the question is, Can policing be considered "radical"? It seems to me that two assumptions are being made here: first, that patriarchal authority is embodied in each male even in the lowest classes, and, second, that only feminists or radicals will struggle against male violence, even though, historically, others (including conservatives) have often been involved in such campaigns. In short, I am not questioning the desirability of these campaigns per se so much as the characterization of the campaigns as having to do with "radical" or "progressive" politics.

49. E. Willis, "Villains and Victims," *Salmagundi,* Special Issue (Winter-Spring 1994), p. 77.

50. E. Willis, "Lust Horizons: Is the Women's Movement Pro-Sex?" in Willis, *No More Nice Girls,* p. 9.

51. E. Willis, "Towards a Feminist Sexual Revolution," *Social Text* (1983); reprinted in Willis, *No More Nice Girls,* p. 30.

52. In *Intimate Matters,* Jenkins discusses at length the degree to which police forces and conservative politicians in the U.K. have supported militant feminist rhetoric against certain classes of perpetrators, such as child abusers and satanists, to advance their own agenda. In *Domestic Tyranny* (e.g., pp. 10, 192), Pleck makes a similar point about domestic violence legislation in the United States. Also, for an early critique of how the battered women's movement became less radical and, hence, more approving of state control, see G. Sullivan,

"The Co-optation of Alternative Services: The Battered Women's Movement as a Case Study," *Catalyst*, 14 (1982), p. 41.

53. Echols, "The Feminism of Yin and Yan," p. 454; emphasis in original.

54. Snitow, Stansell, and Thompson, eds., *Powers of Desire: The Politics of Sexuality*, p. 419.

55. Manifesto of the Gay Activists Alliance, cited in T. Marotta, *The Politics of Homosexuality* (Boston: Houghton Mifflin, 1981), p. 144.

56. Seidman, *Embattled Eros*, p. 156.

57. D. Altman, *The Homosexualization of America* (New York: St. Martins Press, 1982).

58. J. Weeks, *Sexuality and Its Discontents* (London: Routledge & Kegan Paul, 1985), p. 198.

59. S. Johnston, "On the Fire Brigade: Why Liberalism Won't Stop the Anti-Gay Campaigning of the Right," *Critical Sociology*, 20:3 (1994), p. 5. A guiding principle of liberalism is that, given the strength of conservatism, radical agendas must be watered down. Yet gay rights may illustrate liberalism's own failure to interpret public sentiment correctly. It is possible that a broadly libertarian approach to sexuality might work more effectively in some regions of the country than a narrowly prescribed "minority only" rights approach. For example, heterosexuals and bisexuals are rarely given a direct stake in referenda or other campaigns; for the most part, they have been called on to support the gay rights agenda out of an altruistic concern for the "Other."

60. Weeks, *Sexuality and Its Discontents*, p. 48.

61. Marotta, *The Politics of Homosexuality*, p. 18.

62. See, for example, S. Murray and K. Payne, "Medical Policy Without Scientific Evidence: The Promiscuity Paradigm and AIDS," *California Sociologist* (Winter/Summer 1988), pp. 28–30.

63. On Kramer, see, for example, M. Caldwell, "The Literature of AIDS," *Dissent*, 37 (1990), p. 344; and on Callen, see, for example, R. Bayer, *Private Acts, Social Consequences: AIDS and the Politics of Public Health* (New York: Free Press, 1989), p. 24.

64. D. Altman, *AIDS in the Mind of America* (Garden City, N.Y.: Doubleday, 1986), p. 160. See also Seidman, *Embattled Eros*, pp. 173–175. Both the gay and lesbian movement and the women's movement seem to be fertile ground for the recovery movements generally, but this issue is beyond our present scope.

65. R. Padgug, "Gay Hero, Gay Villain: Homosexuality and the Social Construction of AIDS," in K. Peiss and C. Simmons, *Passion and Power: Sexuality in History* (Philadelphia: Temple University Press, 1989), pp. 304–305.

66. Seidman, *Embattled Eros*, p. 161.

67. Ann Landers, cited in W. Chapkis, "Freaks, Fairies, and Fat Ladies: A Right to Discriminate," *Critical Sociology*, 20:3 (1994), p. 152.

68. L. Tiger, *The Pursuit of Pleasure* (Boston: Little, Brown, 1992), pp. 21–22.

69. Ehrenreich, Hess, and Jacobs, *Re-Making Love*, p. 207; original emphasis.

70. This phrase is taken from Weeks, *Sexuality and Its Discontents*, p. 41.

71. Tiger, *The Pursuit of Pleasure*; Ehrenreich, *Re-Making Love*.

72. M. Douglas and A. Wildavsky, *Risk and Culture* (Berkeley: University of California Press, 1982), p. 52.

73. See, for example, the related quotes in Weeks, *Sexuality and Its Discontents*, pp. 41–42; and in Echols, "The Feminism of Yin and Yan," p. 442.

74. See, for example, S. Chapman, "Real and False Solutions for Teen Pregnancy," *Conservative Chronicle*, October 2, 1991; reprinted in K. Swisher, *Teenage Sexuality: Opposing Viewpoints* (San Diego: Greenhaven Press, 1994), p. 105. See also M. Levitsky, "Progress in the International War Against Illicit Drugs," *U.S. Department of State Dispatch*; reprinted in K. Swisher, ed., *Drug Abuse: Opposing Viewpoints* (San Diego: Greenhaven Press, 1994), p. 74. It is true, however, that of all the "behavior wars," smoking prohibitions have aroused the most dissent from the Right. In this connection, see, for example, P. Berger, "Furtive Smokers—and What They Tell Us About America," *Commentary*, June 1994; and F. King, "I'd Rather Smoke Than Kiss," *National Review*, July 9, 1990, pp. 32–36.

75. This issue is discussed later in the chapter. I have in mind the Right's attack on liberals and other activists whose support for condoms or nonmarital sex has been reduced to the plea that "they're going to do it anyway" statements. There is some consistency to the Right's temperance logic: If the paradigm of moral perfectionism can be applied in one area of human life, why not in others? Yet some on the Left deem sexuality to be an immutable imperative but would never take this position with respect to substance use or aggressive behavior.

76. For liberal praise of his anti-tobacco position, see, for example, R. Troyer, "The Surprising Resurgence of the Smoking Problem," in J. Best, ed., *Images of Issues: Typifying Contemporary Social Problems* (New York: Aldine de Gruyter, 1989), p. 161; and Ebrahim and Lewis, "Will Washington Kick Tobacco?" pp. 555–556. For praise of his AIDS policy from activists, see, for example, D'Emilio and Freedman, *Intimate Matters*, p. 357; and Bayer, *Private Acts, Social Consequences*, p. 163.

77. See Altman, *AIDS in the Mind of America*, especially pp. 13, 19, 134, 166–167.

78. Criticism of these apocalyptic predictions about AIDS often came from the political Right in the United States in response to the development of a leftist AIDS activism. See, for example, M. Fumento, *The Myth of Heterosexual AIDS* (New York: Basic Books, 1990); and Fumento, "AIDS Is Not a Serious Problem for Heterosexuals," in Biskup and Swisher, eds., *AIDS: Opposing Viewpoints*, pp. 24–31. However, others, including critics on the Left, have registered this objection as well, and to an increasing degree as the disease has failed to live up to initial predictions not only of a mass heterosexual "outbreak" but of its development into "an equal opportunity disease." Objections to the apocalyptic rhetoric of AIDS activism can be found, for example, in Altman, *AIDS in the Mind of America*, and S. Sontag, *AIDS and Its Metaphors* (New York: Farrar, Straus, and Giroux, 1989), and, more recently, in D. Kirp, "AIDS in Our Time, Part 1, After the Band Stopped Playing," *The Nation*, July 4, 1994. ACT/UP's picketing in the late 1980s of people like Michael Fumento and columnist Joe Queenan, of magazines and newspapers like *Forbes, Cosmopolitan*, and the *New York Times*, and of institutions like the N.Y.C. Department of Health (all of which were charged with underrating the AIDS epidemic or lowering the estimates of the number of people afflicted) will, I believe, go down in history as one of the stranger and more quintessentially American flirtations with apocalyptic thinking.

Of course, different sides of the political spectrum emphasized AIDS for different reasons. On the Right, the constant danger of AIDS served as an object lesson about promiscuity, gay sex, and drugs. On the Left, the effort was aimed at undermining the association of gays with the disease by claiming that "everyone is at risk for AIDS"; and, perhaps just as important, liberals have been provided with an easy way to express their "political correctness" (e.g., by wearing red ribbons) without actually having to do anything to alter the social structure. As with the Left's anti-tobacco, anti-alcohol, or anti–domestic violence campaigns, this "political correctness" in turn has facilitated an ostensible popular cause. (Who, after all, would be "for" AIDS?) Yet what has the wearing of red ribbons accomplished in the way of left-wing ideological or political transformations?

79. Douglas and Wildavsky, *Risk and Culture.*

80. This is not to say that pleasure is *never* politicized in a positive way. Two examples come to mind: the opposition to alcohol prohibition in nineteenth- and early-twentieth-century America, and the labor strikes and demonstrations in various countries (particularly those in Eastern Europe) over rations of meat and tobacco. Generally, however, these have been defensive battles against proposals to cut out pleasures already expected, and against the cutting out of goods (such as meat) that were recognized as part of the social wage. In this sense, the products were not viewed as simply frivolous pleasures.

CHAPTER 7

1. From R. Nixon's book *In the Arena*, excerpted in C. Cozic and K. Swisher, eds., *Chemical Dependency: Opposing Viewpoints* (San Diego: Greenhaven Press, 1991), p. 232.

2. Margaret Thatcher, cited in J. Weeks, *Sexuality and Its Discontents* (London: Routledge & Kegan Paul, 1985), p. 18.

3. Joseph Conlin, cited in B. Christensen, "Single-Parent Households Harm Children," in C. Wekesser, ed., *America's Children: Opposing Viewpoints* (San Diego: Greenhaven Press, 1991), p. 246.

4. Sayres et al., eds., *The 60s Without Apology* (Minneapolis: University of Minnesota Press, 1984), p. 8.

5. Cited in "Worker Drug Test Provoking Debate," *New York Times*, May 3, 1986, p. 32.

6. E. Willis, "The Drug War: Hell No, I Won't Go," in E. Willis, ed., *No More Nice Girls: Countercultural Essays* (Hanover, N.H.: Wesleyan University Press, 1992), p. 252.

7. See C. Reinarman, D. Waldorf, and S. Murphy, "Cocaine and the Workplace: Empirical Findings and Notes on Scapegoating and Social Control in the Construction of a Public Problem," *Research in Law, Deviance, and Social Control*, 9 (1987); and C. Reinarman and H. Levine, "Crack Attack: Politics and Media in America's Latest Drug Scare," in J. Best, ed., *Images of Issues: Typifying Contemporary Social Problems* (New York: Aldine de Gruyter, 1989), pp. 129–130.

8. S. Yurick, "The Other Side," in Sayres et al., eds., *The 60s Without Apology*, p. 308; emphasis added.

9. Theodor Adorno, cited in B. Agger, "The Problem with Social Problems: From Social Constructionism to Critical Theory," in J. Holstein and G. Miller, eds., *Reconsidering Social Constructionism* (New York: Aldine de Gruyter, 1993), p. 287.

10. A. Trebach, "Why Not Decriminalize?" *New Perspective Quarterly* (Summer 1989); reprinted in Cozic and Swisher, eds., *Chemical Dependency*, p. 152.

11. Cited in D. Forbes, *False Fixes* (Albany: SUNY Press, 1994), p. 96.

12. In particular, see S. Peele, *The Diseasing of America: Addiction Treatment Out of Control* (New York: Houghton Mifflin, 1989), pp. 69–73.

13. This is a major theme of M. Stacey's *Consumed: Why Americans Love, Hate, and Fear Food* (New York: Simon and Schuster, 1994).

14. See W. Chambliss, "Policing the Ghetto Underclass: The Politics of Law and Law Enforcement," *Social Problems*, 41:2 (1994); and K. Beckett, "Setting the Public Agenda: 'Street Crime' and Drug Abuse in American Politics," *Social Problems*, 41:3 (1994).

15. A. Gouldner, *For Sociology* (New York: Basic, 1973); cited in Weeks, *Sexuality and Its Discontents*, p. 211.

About the Book
and Author

The war on drugs . . . the campaigns against smoking cigarettes . . . v-chips to control what children watch on TV . . . censoring the Internet and Calvin Klein jean ads . . . bipartisan lectures about the dangers of teen sex . . . constant warnings about food and fat . . . all are examples of what David Wagner terms the "New Temperance."

Although the obsession with personal behavior in America over the last two decades has sharply reversed the liberatory trend of the 1960s and early 1970s, *The New Temperance* argues that this behavior parallels rather closely the nineteenth century and early twentieth century social movements such as the Temperance, Social Purity, and Vice and Vigilance movements.

The New Temperance questions the constant mantra in the media and in political debates about the dangers of personal behavior and challenges America's love affair with repression. Drawing on historical, sociological, and philosophical sources, the author argues the New Temperance is a strategy serving state and dominant social class interests as well as a popular social movement that develops consensual coalitions between traditionally identified elements of the Right and Left.

David Wagner is associate professor of social work and sociology at the University of Southern Maine. He is the author of two previous books including *Checkerboard Square* (Westview Press, 1993), which won the 1993 C. Wright Mills award. He is associate editor of *Flying Horse*, a literary journal for poor people, and editorial board member of *The Journal of Progressive Human Services* and *The Journal of Poverty*.

Index

BOUNDLESS

ALSO BY R. A. SALVATORE

FORGOTTEN REALMS™

BOUNDLESS

A DRIZZT NOVEL

R. A. Salvatore

HARPER Voyager
An Imprint of HarperCollinsPublishers

FIRST EDITION

Designed by Paula Russell Szafranski

Frontispiece and opener art © Aleks Melnik / Shutterstock

Library of Congress Cataloging-in-Publication Data has been applied for.

ISBN 978-0-06-268863-7

19 20 21 22 23   LSC   10 9 8 7 6 5 4 3 2 1

To Diane. And to Julian, Camillo, Dominic, Charlie, and Owen,

the next generation as this wonderful journey continues.

CONTENTS

DRAMATIS PERSONAE

In the past . . . all of them drow.

HOUSE DO'URDEN

Matron Malice: The young and ferocious drow leads House Do'Urden. Ambitious and insatiable, she is determined to climb the hierarchy of Menzoberranzan's nearly eighty houses to one day gain a seat on the Ruling Council reserved for the top eight houses.

Zaknafein Do'Urden: Former weapon master of House Simfray, Zaknafein was plucked from the battle which destroyed that house and given to the insatiable and ambitious Matron Malice Do'Urden to serve as her weapon master and consort. With Zaknafein in the fold, House Do'Urden is considered a real threat to many of those houses ranked above them.

Patron Rizzen: Malice's open consort, father of Nalfein, he is considered an incredibly mediocre companion by the ambitious Malice.

Nalfein Do'Urden: Malice's oldest son, elderboy of the house, Nalfein is everything one might expect from the loins of Patron Rizzen.

Briza Do'Urden: Malice's eldest daughter. Huge and formidable.

HOUSE XORLARRIN

Matron Zeerith Xorlarrin: Powerful leader of the city's fourth-ranked house.

Horroodissomoth Xorlarrin: Xorlarrin house wizard and former master of Sorcere, the drow academy for practitioners of arcane magic.
Kiriy: Priestess of Lolth, daughter of Zeerith and Horroodissomoth.

HOUSE SIMFRAY

Matron Divine Simfray: Ruler of the minor house.

HOUSE TR'ARACH

Matron Hauzz: Deceased matron of the minor house.
Duvon Tr'arach: Son of Matron Hauzz, former weapon master of House Tr'arach, determined to prove himself.
Daungelina Tr'arach: Oldest daughter of Matron Hauzz and first priestess of the minor house.
Dab'nay Tr'arach: Daughter of Matron Hauzz. With the fall of the house, currently in the service of Jarlaxle.

HOUSE BAENRE

Matron Mother Yvonnel Baenre: Also known as Yvonnel the Eternal, Matron Mother Baenre is the undisputed leader not only of the First House, but of the entire city. While other families might refer to their matron as "matron mother," all in the city use that title for Yvonnel Baenre. She is the oldest living drow, and has been in a position of great power longer than the longest memory of anyone in the city.
Gromph Baenre: Matron Mother Baenre's oldest child, archmage of Menzoberranzan, the highest-ranking man in the city, and most formidable wizard in the entire Underdark, by many estimations.
Dantrag Baenre: Son of Matron Mother Baenre, weapon master of the great house, considered one of the greatest warriors in the city.
Triel, Quenthel, and Sos'Umptu Baenre: Three of Matron Mother Baenre's daughters, priestesses of Lolth.

OTHER NOTABLES

K'yorl Odran: Matron of House Oblodra, notable for its use of the strange mind magics called psionics.

Jarlaxle: A houseless rogue who began Bregan D'aerthe, a mercenary band quietly serving the needs of many drow houses, but mostly serving its own needs.

Arathis Hune: Drow lieutenant to Jarlaxle and assassin extraordinaire. Taken into the band, as with many of the members, after the fall of his house.

In the present . . . many races.

Drizzt Do'Urden: Born in Menzoberranzan and fled the evil ways of the city. Drow warrior, hero of the north, and Companion of the Hall, along with his four dear friends.

Catti-brie: Human wife of Drizzt, Chosen of the goddess Mielikki, skilled in both arcane and divine magic. Companion of the Hall.

Regis (Spider Parrafin): Halfling husband of Donnola Topolino, leader of the halfling community of Bleeding Vines. Companion of the Hall.

King Bruenor Battlehammer: Eighth king of Mithral Hall, tenth king of Mithral Hall, now king of Gauntlgrym, an ancient dwarven city he reclaimed with his dwarven kin. Companion of the Hall. Adoptive father of both Wulfgar and Catti-brie.

Wulfgar: Born to the Tribe of the Elk in Icewind Dale, the giant human was captured by Bruenor in battle and became the adopted son of the dwarf king. Companion of the Hall.

Artemis Entreri: Former nemesis of Drizzt, the human assassin is the drow warrior's near equal or equal in battle. Now he runs with Jarlaxle's Bregan D'aerthe band, and considers Drizzt and the other Companions of the Hall friends.

Guenhwyvar: Magical panther, companion of Drizzt, summoned to his side from the Astral Plane.

Andahar: Drizzt's summoned steed, a magical unicorn. Unlike the living Guenhwyvar, Andahar is a purely magical construct.

Lord Dagult Neverember: Open lord of Waterdeep and lord protector of Neverwinter. A dashing and ambitious human.

Penelope Harpell: The leader of the eccentric wizards known as the Harpells, who oversee the town of Longsaddle from their estate, the

Ivy Mansion. Penelope is a powerful wizard, mentoring Catti-brie, and has dated Wulfgar on occasion.

Donnola Topolino: Halfling wife of Regis, and leader of the halfling town of Bleeding Vines. She came from Aglarond, in the distant east, where she once headed a thieves' guild.

Inkeri Margaster: A lady of Waterdeep, the noblewoman is considered the leader of the Waterdhavian House of Margaster.

Alvilda Margaster: Cousin of Inkeri. Also a noble lady of Waterdeep.

Brevindon Margaster: Inkeri's brother, another Waterdhavian noble.

Grandmaster Kane: A human monk who has transcended his mortal coil and become a being beyond the Material Plane, Kane is the Grandmaster of Flowers of the Monastery of the Yellow Rose in far-off Damara. He is friend and mentor to Drizzt as the drow tries to find peace at last along a turbulent road.

Dahlia Syn'dalay (Dahlia Sin'felle): A tall and beautiful blue-eyed elf, Dahlia strives to surprise as much with her appearance as with her brilliant fighting techniques. Once the lover of Drizzt, she is now the companion of Artemis Entreri, the two finding a better way together than either ever paved alone.

Thibbledorf Pwent: A walking weapon in his spiked and sharp-ridged armor, Pwent is a battle-hardened dwarf whose loyalty is as strong as the aroma emanating from him. He led every seemingly suicidal charge with a cry of "Me King!" and gave his life saving King Bruenor in the bowels of Gauntlgrym. His death was not the end of Pwent, though, for he was slain by a vampire, and now continues as one—a cursed and miserable thing, haunting the lowest tunnels of Gauntlgrym and satisfying his insatiable hunger by feeding on the goblins beyond the dwarven realm.

The Brothers Bouldershoulder, Ivan and Pikel: Ivan Bouldershoulder is a grizzled old veteran of many battles, mundane and magical. He's risen to a position of great trust as a commander in Bruenor's Gauntlgrym guard.

More eccentric and extreme than Ivan, the green-haired Pikel fancies himself a druid, or "doo-dad," and helped Donnola Topolino create wonderful vineyards in Bleeding Vines. His limited and stilted vocabulary only adds to the deceptive innocence of this quite powerful dwarf.

Kimmuriel Oblodra: A powerful drow psionicist, Kimmuriel serves as coleader of Bregan D'aerthe beside Jarlaxle. He is the logic foil to the emotional Jarlaxle, and Jarlaxle knows it.

ETERNAL BEINGS

Lolth, the Lady of Chaos, the Demon Queen of Spiders, the Queen of the Demonweb Pits: The mighty demon Lolth reigns as the most influential goddess of the drow, particularly in the greatest drow city, Menzoberranzan, known as the City of Spiders for the devotion of its inhabitants. True to her name, the Lady of Chaos constantly shocks her followers, keeping her true plans buried beneath the webbing of other more obvious and understandable schemes. Her end goal, above all, is chaos.

Eskavidne and Yiccardaria: Lesser demons known as yochlol, they serve as two of the handmaidens of Lolth. The pair have proven so resourceful and skilled that Lolth gives them great rein in walking the ways of the drow and making a glorious mess of everything.

BOUNDLESS

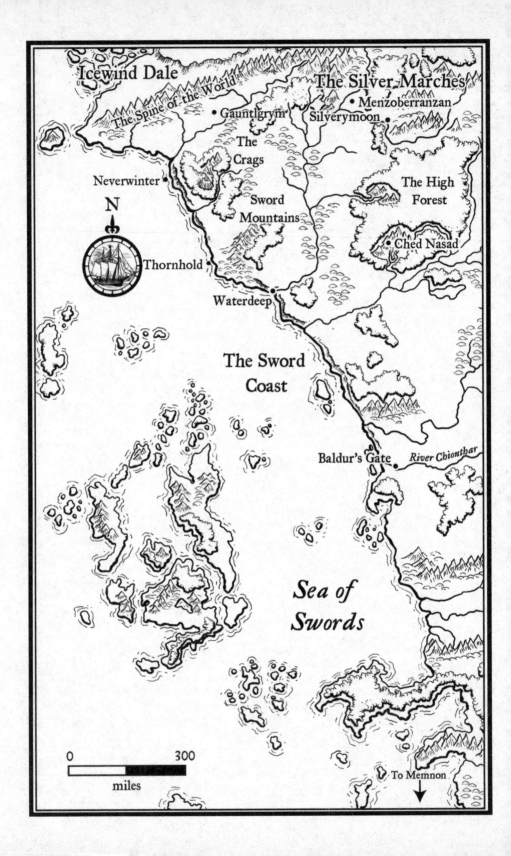

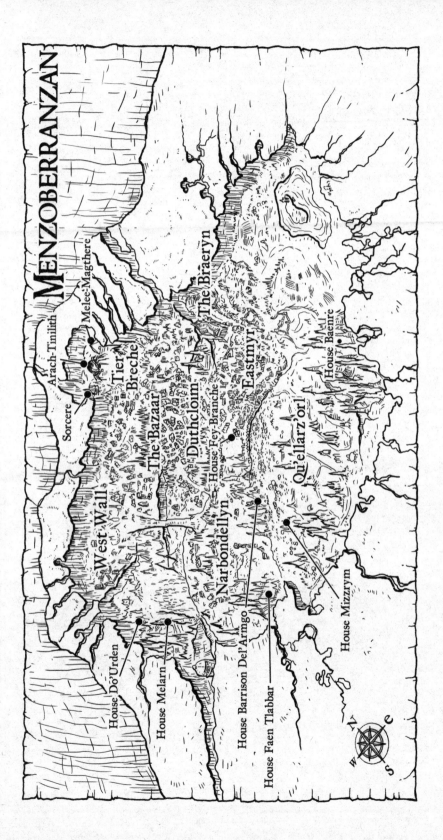

PROLOGUE

The Year of Dwarvenkind Reborn
Dalereckoning 1488

He could hear the labored breathing of his poor pony, but Regis didn't dare slow. For the shadows within the shadows were not far away, black, misshapen things, lumbering and twisted by evil and unrelenting anger.

Demons. Everywhere in the forest, demons.

The halfling weaved about the trees, urging poor Rumblebelly on. He came down around a stone, the trail bending to the south and into a clearing. He winced, noting the sheen of sweat on his pinto's brown-and-white coat.

At least now he could stop, but only briefly, and only because Showithal Terdidy, one of the leaders of the Grinning Ponies, rode into the small clearing from the other direction.

"Where is Doregardo?" Regis asked, pulling up alongside his friend.

Showithal nodded back the way he had come. "The wood's thick with the fiends," he said. "We'll not get through."

"And they're all heading in the same direction," Regis added.

Showithal nodded. "Doregardo is convinced that these monsters are guided by a greater purpose, and that they know of Bleeding Vines," he explained. "The beasts are moving in a wide arc, by all reports coming up and down the line, and will strike the town all at once."

"Then you've got to get there before them," Regis ordered. "All of you, turn about and ride as if the lives of all in Bleeding Vines depend upon your speed, for surely that is the truth."

"The farms . . . the villages . . ."

Regis shook his head. "You cannot get to them, and even if any of you did, you'd only be leading demons to new victims. The farmers will hear the monsters. They have lived in the wilds all their lives. They will shelter and hide. You must get to Bleeding Vines. All of you."

"All of *us*, Spider Parrafin," Showithal corrected.

Again Regis shook his head. "Waterdeep must be told," Regis explained. It was terribly hard for him to speak those words. He wanted nothing more than to turn about and gallop all the way back to Bleeding Vines, then ride the tram beside his beloved Donnola and his dear Rumblebelly all the way to the safety of Gauntlgrym. But he could not. Not now.

Not in this life.

In his previous life, Regis had been the tagalong, too often making victory more difficult for his beloved Companions of the Hall instead of helping them to achieve their goals—at least, that's the way he viewed it. In those long-ago years, Regis had been the least of the heroes. This time, this rebirth, he had determined to change that course. He would be no burden. He would live as a hero worthy of the friendship of Drizzt, Bruenor, Catti-brie, and Wulfgar.

Now his path was clear before him. He had to get to Waterdeep, the great City of Splendors, the Crown of the North, the most influential and powerful city in all of Faerun. The lords of Waterdeep could turn back the demon tide, and Regis had to get to them.

"If you're on to Waterdeep, then you're not riding alone," Showithal insisted, moving his own pony up beside Rumblebelly.

"Go tell the Grinning Ponies to return to Bleeding Vines," Regis ordered. "That mission, too, is critical."

A commotion in the trees to the side turned the two.

Demons.

"Go!" Regis ordered, and he slapped the flank of Showithal's pony, sending the mount leaping away, then quick-turned Rumblebelly and galloped off into the darkness in the other direction.

Heavy footsteps followed him as he wove again through the trees, and buzzing loomed overhead, above the canopy.

"I know, my friend," he whispered into poor Rumblebelly's ear. "Give me this run and you'll find a rest."

Regis didn't believe it. He knew Rumblebelly would give him all that he asked for, but understood, too, that he would likely run his beautiful blue-eyed pony quite literally to its death.

But he had no choice.

They were all around him. They were above, and, he found out to his great dismay, they were below him, for the ground to the side erupted suddenly, huge pincers snipping tree roots with ease and a massive demon clawing up from the earth. A hulking four-armed glabrezu emerged with long, loping strides, easily pacing Rumblebelly.

Behind Regis, a vulture-like fiend leaped and half flew, half ran in close pursuit.

Rumblebelly's breathing came in ragged gasps, and Regis knew that he could no longer outrun this demon.

Still, he said, "No," and he put his head lower, coaxing his poor mount ahead more swiftly, recklessly even, and hoped that he would not crash into a tree.

No halfling had ever ridden a pony better than Doregardo, Showithal Terdidy fervently believed, and his dear friend was proving it to him yet again.

Doregardo effortlessly took his black stallion through the tangle of trees, hardly slowing for the obstacles and brambles, anticipating each turn far ahead and leaning in, urging his pony ever forward, obviously confident that the animal would obey. That the mount had full confidence in him was just as obvious.

A host of demons chased Doregardo, including several he had cleverly and brilliantly pulled from their pursuit of Showithal. They would not catch Doregardo, Showithal believed.

No one could catch the great Doregardo of the Grinning Ponies.

He paced his mount down a slope into another copse of trees, the demons scrambling close behind. Despite his confidence, Showithal held his breath, and indeed grimaced when he saw those trees shaking violently and heard the growls and roars and shrieks of the fiends.

But Doregardo came galloping out the side, he and his mount showing not a mark as far as the distant Showithal could see, and there was no immediate pursuit—indeed, the battle in the copse continued.

Showithal Terdidy managed a smile despite the desperate situation. Doregardo had turned the demons back on each other, a tangling mess of clawing, biting, chaotic frenzy.

When the two rejoined in a small clearing a short time later, it was clear that Doregardo had bought them both some time.

"Our companions have all turned back for Bleeding Vines," Doregardo told his second-in-command. "We've lost none, but that will not hold true for long."

"Too many of the beasts," Showithal agreed.

As if on cue, the brush behind them began to shake violently and a pair of misshapen demons burst into the clearing. The halfling pair were already away, though, Doregardo letting Showithal lead in a straightaway run for the distant settlement, while he went back into his forest dance.

But more shadows loomed at their flanks, and a loud buzzing sound followed them overhead, and for all their efforts and all of Doregardo's brilliant maneuvering, when the pair joined once more on a wide road farther along, they knew that they were in deep trouble. They came together again soon after in another small clearing, now understanding the depth of their predicament.

"Others will make it," Doregardo said somberly to his friend.

"We'll make it!" Showithal insisted.

Doregardo nodded, but clearly he was not convinced. Nor was

Showithal, for now the moving shadows were ahead of them, left and right in the trees.

"Right, then," Doregardo remarked. "Full charge, you. Head down and gallop for all your pony's life. I'll keep our ugly fiend friends busy. My love to Spider and Lady Donnola, aye?"

He kicked his pony and started away, but barely got moving, for Showithal grabbed his reins, holding him and the pony back.

Doregardo looked at him curiously.

"You'll break me clear, only for me to be caught farther along," Showithal explained. "And you know it. Only Doregardo can get to Bleeding Vines, and only alone."

"Others will get there," Doregardo insisted.

"Perhaps, but is that a chance you are willing to take? How many will be slaughtered if they are not forewarned?"

"Warn them, then, and I will join you!"

"No," Showithal said softly. "You go, all speed."

"I'll grant you a head start."

The two halflings, friends for all their lives, comrades in arms for decades, shared a long look, one of friendship and brotherly love.

And of acceptance.

"Go," Showithal said.

Still Doregardo shook his head.

"You will make a waste of my valor," said Showithal.

Doregardo started to respond, but there was really nothing he could say. He didn't believe that either of them would get out of the forest alive, but if one had a chance, given a head start here, it would, of course, be him. "Pray Regis—Spider, makes Waterdeep," he said.

"Pray Doregardo makes Bleeding Vines," Showithal replied. "And pray he gets Lady Donnola and all the others down to the safety of King Bruenor's mighty gates."

"I will see you there, then, my friend," Doregardo said. "In Gauntl-grym, where the demon horde will falter."

Showithal nodded, but couldn't find the strength to audibly re-spond. He yanked back on the reins, then slapped Doregardo's black pony on the rump as it moved past him.

Doregardo charged away and Showithal Terdidy drew his sword.

It seemed a meager weapon indeed, measured against the hulking forms scrambling about the shadows.

So be it.

Despite the pursuit, Regis had to slow Rumblebelly as he descended a steep decline. Reins tight in his left hand, the halfling grasped the small hand crossbow hung about his neck and kept glancing back, expecting a huge demon to come leaping down upon him. They were close, he knew, and yet none had attacked thus far.

He breathed a bit of relief when the ground leveled, and cut right around a boulder at the bottom of the decline, gathering up to a gallop once more on the level trail.

But Regis was riding blind here, in an area he did not know, and the trail proved a false one, a dead end. A wall of trees loomed ahead. He had nowhere to go.

He pulled up short and swung about, his only options to go back the way he had come or to abandon Rumblebelly and run off on foot through the tangle.

Around the boulder, not too far behind, came a pair of monsters: the giant four-armed dog-faced demon, thrice the halfling's height, and another, not much smaller, that resembled a weird cross between a large humanoid and a buzzard.

Regis considered his puny weapons, fully confident that either of these monsters alone could easily tear him apart.

"We die together, Rumblebelly," he said as the pair slowly approached, their stalking angles clearly coordinated and leaving him no room to charge past them and break free. "I could not find a more valiant companion with whom to share these last, most glorious moments. What ho!"

Rumblebelly reared and whinnied as if in agreement, and as the pony came back to all fours, Regis moved to kick him into a charge.

He held, though, and tugged the reins more forcefully to hold

back the sweating steed, for across the way, the demons had turned—
not back, but upon each other!

The vulture demon, a vrock, started it, swinging about suddenly—
so abruptly that it stumbled upon its companion, giving some strange,
strained shriek, then leaping high, flapping its winglike arms, and falling down hard on the four-armed monster, snapping its head forward
to drive its pointed beak powerfully into demon flesh. It aimed for the
neck, and almost got it, which would have ended the fight immediately,
but the glabrezu turned just enough to take the hit in its shoulder.
Both of its pincer arms immediately clamped about the vrock, and the
much heavier glabrezu continued its turn, throwing itself and its attacker off balance, to fall upon the ground in a heap, where they rolled
and thrashed, punching, biting, pecking. And those great and terrible
pincers snapped and dragged, digging deep gouges in the vrock, from
which spurted green bile and black blood.

Regis didn't know how to decipher the scene before him. He knew
demons were chaotic in the extreme, knew that they would kill anything, even each other. But never could he have expected this sudden
turn, not with a plump halfling and a plumper pony right there for easy
feasting.

So shocked was he that he didn't, couldn't, respond for many moments as the two fiendish behemoths rolled and gored each other with
demonic abandon. He did wince, though, repeatedly, at the ghastly
sounds emanating from the monstrous battle, and Rumblebelly flattened his ears and backed away nervously. Regis was a seasoned
enough rider to recognize that his poor pony was near the edge of collapse here, with fright if not exhaustion.

That brought the halfling from his trance. He leaned forward and
whispered assurances in his pony's ear.

"Come, Rumblebelly," he said. "Easy now and let us get past these
beasts."

He edged his pony forward, veering to the side, and if a pony
could be said to tiptoe, Rumblebelly was doing exactly that.

Regis didn't turn to regard the rolling, battling demons. He stayed low, continuing to whisper into Rumblebelly's ear, preparing to launch the pony into a leap and run. He was about to do just that when both he and his pony jerked suddenly, startled. Regis sat up straight, while Rumblebelly desperately backed up once more, head going high in surprise and terror as a dark form flew across in front of them.

That form, the body of the vrock, hit a tree and wrapped halfway around it, sliding down to the ground at its base, black smoke rising from the corpse as the dead thing sank back across the planes of existence to the smoldering Abyss.

That left the glabrezu, rising up to its full height, battered but very much alive, and very, very angry.

The demon moved out from the side of the trail, four arms out wide as if daring the halfling to try to ride past it.

Regis knew he couldn't make it. He thought to dismount and attack, opening the way for his beloved pony.

But where might Rumblebelly go?

"We fight, my valiant steed," he said aloud, trying to exude confidence and lifting his fine rapier up into the air before him. "For Rumblebelly, for Bleeding Vines, for the Companions of the Hall!"

By the time Doregardo regained full control of his startled mount, he had put some distance between himself and Showithal, and had left his friend out of sight as his pony dodged down and around some trees, then crested a short ridge and clambered down the back side. The leader of the Grinning Ponies pulled the reins hard, his pony leaning back and skidding to a stop. Then, with legs and expert control of the bridle, Doregardo had his mount quickly into a gallop.

Horse and rider nearly got run over then as Showithal's pony charged past.

Showithal's riderless pony.

Only then did Doregardo recognize the screams behind him, the wails of his friend. He kicked his pony and leaped away, but skidded again at the sound of a last, desperate dying shriek.

Doregardo's friendship demanded that he go back for Showithal.

Doregardo's responsibility to his people demanded that he continue in the retreat, organizing and warning any allies he could find.

But it was Doregardo's pledge to Lady Donnola that left no choice in the matter. Bleeding Vines had to be forewarned or hundreds would die.

"Fare well in the Green Fields of Mount Celestia, my friend," he whispered to the night wind, and he pulled his mount around again and charged away for the halfling town.

For all his regret, and there was indeed much, Doregardo understood that he had chosen right when he was spotted by the night sentries of Bleeding Vines, hailing him and, he quickly learned, fully oblivious to the coming army of fiends.

"To arms! To arms!" the halfling sentries shouted, a call carried down the line, all about, and then through the small village as candles showed in every house.

Doregardo charged his mount straight for Lady Donnola's modest home, and met her coming out her door.

"We cannot fight them," he shouted before even properly greeting her. "To arms, nay! To Gauntlgrym, or we all shall die!"

"Them?"

"Demons, milady. Such a horde as I have never seen, and never heard in the songs of bards. Demons to rival the flights of dragons that laid waste to Vaasa in the time of the Witch King!"

Lady Donnola, who of course was well aware of Doregardo's penchant for hyperbole, arched her eyebrow at that.

"Showithal is dead, milady," Doregardo told her somberly, and it so happened that Showithal's pony was not far away, standing forlornly, untethered and unattended.

"Where is Regis?" she asked with sudden urgency.

"Determined to get word to Waterdeep."

"You just said . . ." she started to reply, but her voice trailed off.

Doregardo understood her resignation here, for they both knew that Regis would not be easily turned from such a mission when it was clearly so critical for the survival of Bleeding Vines. "We cannot fight them," Doregardo told her. "We cannot stop them. To Gauntlgrym, I beg, and let us pray that King Bruenor's defenses will hold back the horde."

"You question the might of Gauntlgrym?" Donnola retorted, shaking her head.

Doregardo didn't answer, but just sat stone-faced upon his stallion.

"That many?" Donnola asked.

"Run, lady, I beg. Do not even try to stop them or slow them. Just run."

The word went out from Donnola to her personal guards, and from them to the sentries. And so the retreat to Gauntlgrym echoed all through the small town. Halflings grabbed whatever they could carry and ran for the tunnel entrance to the dwarven city, where one tram was always stationed at the ready and another could be quickly retrieved from the mountain depths.

On Donnola's order, Doregardo rode over to the tram platform to organize the retreat at that most critical choke point.

Other members of the Grinning Ponies and the Kneebreakers filtered into the town from the surrounding hills and forests, many carrying wounds from skirmishes with the demonic horde. Any who could help did so, the disciplined group aiding the other halflings to board the carts, then sending the tram away into the dark decline to Gauntlgrym as soon as the next one's lights were spotted in the return tunnel.

Families, children, horses, livestock, pets, and treasure came with every group, all rushing to board the tram, and despite the lack of notice, the evacuation seemed to be progressing smoothly.

But then the demonic howls began to echo, carried on the wind, and a great buzzing sound filled the air as a swarm of flying chasmes bore down on the doomed village.

Doregardo shouted orders every which way, his subordinates relaying them.

"Flying monsters!" one told him.

"Call the gals and boys together," Doregardo determinedly replied. "We fight to the last, that our friends will escape."

Not a Grinning Pony, not a Kneebreaker blinked at that expected command—in many ways, it was unnecessary for Doregardo to utter it. They formed up without complaint.

Pony ears went flat all up and down that line when the dark cloud of chasmes appeared over a nearby hill, black against the starry sky, and in that moment, Doregardo feared that most of the village would be slaughtered.

That feeling only deepened when another black cloud appeared, this one right overhead, filled with flashes of lightning.

"What demon magic, this?" one of the halfling band cried.

"Nah," came a gruff response that had the halflings, Doregardo included, looking back toward the tram, to see an old dwarf staring back at them. "That's just me brudder," Ivan Bouldershoulder explained as the thunder began to rumble.

A strong wind kicked up, blowing straight in the ugly faces of the flying demons, slowing their approach. Bolts of lightning shot out of the cloud, not randomly but aimed, slicing into the monstrous flock.

"Me brudder," Ivan Bouldershoulder said with a proud smile, mimicking Pikel's strange accent.

The second loaded tram rolled from the elevated station into the dark cave, diving down into the mountain. Up came the third, rambling into place, and this one was filled with dwarven warriors, Clan Battlehammer soldiers, who leaped out and formed a defensive line, ushering fleeing halflings through.

Doregardo's chest swelled with pride and hope at the precision and discipline of his own people and their brave neighbors. Still, he knew that he and his charges would be in desperate battle soon, for the magical cloud would not be enough to fully halt the demonic aerial swarm.

Holding heavy crossbows, a host of Battlehammer dwarves ran in front of Doregardo's defensive cavalry line. As one, they fell to a knee, leaving enough space between each for a pony to pass through, and lifted their weapons at the coming threat. Down at the right end of the line, not far from Doregardo, the dwarven commander barked out her command to hold.

Despite the dire circumstances, Doregardo couldn't suppress his grin when he regarded the dwarven woman. He wasn't sure whether it was Fist or Fury, Tannabritches or Mallabritches, the twin queens of Gauntlgrym. It was one of them, though, a wife of King Bruenor himself, out here on the very front line to hold back a horde of demons.

The chasms closed. Another bolt of lightning reached out, shooting a line of destruction down the middle of the pack, blasting some to shreds, searing the delicate wings off many others so that they fell spinning to the ground. But Pikel's cloud was dissipating, and many of the demons remained.

"Let fly!" the dwarven commander yelled, and as one, the crossbowmen fired, a swarm of heavy bolts reaching into the night sky—a few converging on the same target, as the skilled Battlehammers chose their marks accordingly. A dozen more chasms fell out of the air.

"Load!" came the immediate order, already being carried out.

"For Queen Mallabritches!" shouted one dwarf near Doregardo, clarifying the commander's identity for him.

"Huzzah!" they all yelled, and the halflings joined in.

Down came the demons, and out leaped the halfling cavalry. "Fours!" Doregardo yelled, and the riders broke into diamond-shaped formations with their mounts.

"Up tall, Battlehammers," roared Queen Mallabritches, "and put the high low."

Doregardo didn't quite know what that command might mean, and he was too busy to figure it out at the moment. Leading his foursome, he charged upon a trio of chasms, the demons rearing, their long stingers twitching in anticipation of the taste of blood.

Two remained close to the ground to engage the halflings, but the third, the central one at whom Doregardo was charging, lifted up higher suddenly, while its companions sped in, viselike, at Doregardo.

He spun his pony expertly, sword going one way to fend off one chasme, the pony bucking and kicking out behind to send the other flying.

Then Doregardo understood the dwarf queen's command, for a host of crossbow bolts crackled the air above him, slamming into the rising demon as soon as it had gotten clear of Doregardo's head, killing the beast, putting the "high low," as she had ordered.

Doregardo's three companions came in hard to the fight, a pair overwhelming the chasme he had fended with his sword, driving the ugly half-human, half-insect monster down low with their long spears, then trampling it with their well-trained mounts. To the other side, the chasme stunned by Doregardo's pony lifted up as the group galloped in, but it flew too high and a volley of dwarven crossbow bolts ripped it apart.

It was a good start. But it was only a start, Doregardo knew, and his group was under assault again before they had even properly re-formed their diamond. Off to his right came calls for help from other riders as the cavalry worked hard to keep up with the more maneuverable and quicker chasmes.

But many of those demons swept right over the halflings, facing another crossbow volley in order to close in on those dwarves. Enough got through, though, and Doregardo understood that his aerial support was at its end when Queen Mallabritches commanded, "Axe!"

The halfling worked his sword across his body at one attacker, then brought it back just in time to intercept the sudden rush of another, the slashing blade halving the demon's long proboscis. Doregardo took the moment of reprieve to glance back at Mallabritches's forces to see if they needed help. His gaze went beyond the dwarven line, though, despite the heavy combat all along it, and he noted the last car of another tram disappearing into the mountain on its way to Gauntlgrym. It was replaced almost immediately by a fourth, another filled with Battlehammer warriors—and not just any Battlehammers, but the famed Gutbuster Brigade. These elite, vicious battleragers leaped from the tram before it had even climbed the platform and settled into place, hitting the ground running, rolling, bouncing—it didn't matter—contorting themselves every which way to get to the fight as quickly as possible.

That heartened Doregardo, of course, but it also frightened him. Their only course, he believed, was to cover the last fleeing villagers, then themselves retreat, with all haste, to the greater defenses of Gauntlgrym.

True to their reputation, the battleragers didn't seem as if they were in any mood for a retreat. The stubborn fools would probably remain out here in their battle lust even after all the innocents had been evacuated. If that was the case, the halfling leader decided, they would be on their own.

He turned back with his team, the diamond shifting to go out to the right, where a family of halflings ran for their lives from a pursuing flying demon.

As they moved to intercept, Doregardo noted rustling from the distant trees. The horde had come, and now it pounced upon them, misshapen humanoid forms, the wretched lesser demons known as manes, shambling out of the brush like an army of humans risen from the dead. Behind them, between them, here and there came their masters, the true demons of all types, enough of them alone, not even counting the multitude of manes and chasmes, to be considered an overwhelming force.

"Get them in quick, my riders!" he told his three companions.

They had just put themselves between the halflings and the pursuing beasts, engaging the chasme, when a cracking sound drew the cavalry leader's eyes to the tree line once more.

He worried that yet another foe was emerging. Instead he saw, standing before the advancing horde, a lone figure—a green-robed dwarf—one arm raised and waving. The dwarf was calling upon the grasses and trees, Doregardo realized . . . and the plants were listening!

Branches bent to swat at demons; grasses wrapped the ankles of the manes, slowing some, stopping others. Hope blossomed, but only for a moment, for then a hulking demon put an end to the dwarven druid's spell. A mighty balor demon, the greatest of demonkind other than the demon lords themselves, had come. All darkness and fire, the powerful creature stamped its foot, sending rolling flames outward to punish the grass and shrubs that dared try to grasp it, and it moved determinedly for the lone dwarf, its whip of fire rolling high, snapping forward and spewing deadly flames.

It cracked right above the dwarf, Pikel Bouldershoulder, who melted downward below it, and the whip spat forth a tremendous fireball.

Though it was far away, the heat of the blast washed over Doregardo. He strained to see through the smoke, to catch sight of the dwarf.

But no. He had to consider that Pikel, the sommelier of Bleeding Vines, the druid green-thumb who had fostered the wonderful vine-yard, had been killed.

And Doregardo knew that he couldn't go to Pikel, or to his body. They were out of time. He called for his group to turn, shouted a general retreat, and galloped back toward the tram station. Other diamond groups linked up with them, and they shifted their forma-tion accordingly, riding tight, fighting defensively, a host of spears and swords lifting to fend off any chasme that got too near. Back by the trams, the battleragers leaped and spun, throwing themselves upon demons and simply shaking the beasts to shreds under the ridges of their sharpened armor so effectively that Queen Mallabritches had nearly half of her contingent up with crossbows again, while the rest gathered up the fallen—more than a dozen—and dragged them for the tram.

Away went that train, and yet another came up, and more dwarves joined the fight, and there, in a semicircle right before the tram sta-tion, the halflings and the dwarves made their stand as the last of Bleeding Vines's civilians, including Lady Donnola herself, rode that tram away.

"Now we die," Doregardo told his soldiers, "so die well," and he shared a grim nod with Queen Mallabritches.

"You should go, good queen," he told her.

"Me sister'll be givin' Bruenor his heirs," she replied with a smile and a wink, and she banged her warhammer hard against her shield.

In came the manes, and the halflings and dwarves cut them down twenty to one—but there were enough of the wretched beasts to ac-cept those losses and still prevail.

Another tram rolled up, though with few dwarves aboard this time, for Gauntlgrym was obviously calling for a full retreat.

"Ponies!" Doregardo yelled, and it was echoed down the line. In such close quarters, the ponies would become a liability, but of course there wasn't a Grinning Pony or a Kneebreaker who would not sacrifice his or her own life for their beloved mounts. So they dismounted—many already had—and started to usher their horses toward the tram.

But loading a pony on a tram was no easy task in calm times, and with the battle raging all around, such an action seemed more dangerous than fighting a demon.

He had no easy answers, and lamented that his beloved mount was likely doomed. Even as those melancholy thoughts threatened to crash over him, a piping melody filled the air above the din of battle, the clashing weapons, and the demonic shrieks, and the halfling watched in amazement as a dwarf, the one and only Pikel Boulder-shoulder, stepped out from a tree—not from beside a tree, but out of a tree!—playing the pipes with surprising adeptness. The music from those pipes calmed the ponies, and they boarded the tram placidly as Pikel ran up and down the line, kicking the cart doors closed as each filled.

Away went the tram, and Doregardo took heart that his beloved pony might survive this awful day. He then turned back and launched himself at a demon mane, fully expecting that he would not.

The demon responded with a word of its own, a croaking, grating combination of hard syllables that sounded to Regis like a porcupine being rubbed across the flesh of a giant frog.

He thought to taunt the demon, but then, so suddenly, his only thought was to try, futilely, to hold on to his weapon as the stunning magic of the infernal beast's word of power slapped his consciousness.

Dazed, he nearly fell. Dazed, Rumblebelly stumbled sideways.

The dog-faced demon grinned wickedly and came forward a step—

Then thrashed, as the air before it suddenly filled with spinning magical blades, a wall of whirring weapons, cutting and biting at demon flesh. The demon's pincers snapped and swatted, and the floating magical swords clicked and sparked and some flew wide, dissipating to nothingness. Some struck true, though, and lines of blood erupted about the glabrezu, but it didn't back down, stubbornly fighting the blades, clearly diminishing them, picking them out of this wall of summoned fury one at a time.

Regis didn't know what to make of it, didn't know how this powerful dweomer might have come to be. He knew it to be a temporary reprieve, though, and could only hope that the demon would be more severely wounded by the time it got through the wall of bladed mayhem. He looked around to find an avenue of escape, and he saw her.

She came out of the trees behind him, behind his pony, startling the halfling so terribly that he nearly fell from his seat yet again. She was beautiful and terrible and powerful, but mostly, to Regis, she was beautiful.

For he knew this young woman, this powerful drow named Yvonnel, daughter of Gromph, friend of Drizzt, and relief flooded through him. He was certain he couldn't beat a glabrezu.

But Yvonnel probably could.

She walked past him without acknowledging him, her gaze locked on the demon, who stared back at her hatefully as it slapped aside the last of the magical blades. Its skin hung in tatters, one pincer chipped short, both hands bloody.

It did not seem as if it would be falling over dead anytime soon, however.

Regardless, Yvonnel did not falter in her approach. "*Ecanti'tu Rethnorel, desper nosferat,*" she said, then repeated.

The glabrezu growled.

"*Ecanti'tu Rethnorel, desper nosferat.*"

Regis didn't understand the words, and didn't even believe them to be the language of the drow, but he could sense their power.

The demon growled again, but came up straight, out of its aggressive crouch, almost leaning back.

Yvonnel kept her determined and steady approach.

"*Ecanti'tu Rethnorel, desper nosferat,*" she recited, and Regis's eyes went wide as he realized the strength in those words, as if Yvonnel's breath, blowing them out, was that of a magical dragon, one designed specifically against the life force of a demon. *Rethnorel* sounded like a name to him—the demon's name, he decided.

"*Ecanti'tu Rethnorel, desper nosferat.*"

The halfling noticed black shadows flowing backward from the glabrezu, as if Yvonnel's words had created a killing wind that struck at its corporeal form and blew back the demonic essence animating that physical body. Every syllable hit Rethnorel the way the flowing breath of a speaker might make the flame of a candle blow back.

Yvonnel was quite literally blowing out the life force of this monstrous fiend.

"*Ecanti'tu Rethnorel, desper nosferat,*" she continued, her voice growing more powerful still. She was close enough for the glabrezu to reach out with its pincer arms and cut her in half. But somehow, it could not. The fiend simply stood very still, leaning back from the drow, and it appeared to take all of Rethnorel's willpower and strength just to hold that pose.

Yvonnel recited the words of power again, then pursed her lips, leaned forward, and blew, and such a gust of wind came forth that the branches of all the trees before her shook as if in a hurricane, and the black shadows of the demon stretched back many strides from its form. Then, as if its entire life force exited with those shadows, the hulking creature lifted off the ground and flapped weirdly, like clothing hung out to dry in that same hurricane. It wobbled, it flew away, it disappeared.

Yvonnel stopped. She stood very still, clearly trying to compose herself and regain her strength.

Finally she lifted her head, nodded at her handiwork, then looked back to regard Regis.

He nearly fell to his knees under the supernatural weight of that stare, not in gratitude but in worship.

He tried to speak his thanks, but his shivering mouth would not form words.

Doregardo came back to consciousness as he tumbled over some small wall, landing hard despite a myriad of hands trying to catch him. It took him a moment to realize he had been pulled into one of the tram carts, and the hands grabbing at him belonged to a pair of dwarves and many of his own Grinning Ponies riders. He looked to them, but they didn't return the stare, all instead looking past him, and with open horror on their faces. Doregardo pulled himself up and managed to glance back, and then he understood, for there stood the greatest demon of the field, the mighty balor of fire and darkness.

Doregardo's thoughts whirled as he tried to remember how he had become unconscious. Had the balor thrown him into the cart?

But no, he realized as the tram rolled away, speeding as it turned down the steeply descending tunnel, for in that moment, another form had revealed itself: the lean body of a drow, and one he knew.

Standing on the raised platform. Not in a cart.

It was him, Doregardo thought. The halfling had been hoisted over the back wall of the last cart of the last tram by Drizzt Do'Urden. Who was still out there. Doregardo heard a whistle, clear and smooth, but didn't understand the significance in that moment of confusion and fear. For Drizzt was out there.

With the demons.

With the balor.

And then the cart made another turn, and the drow warrior was lost to Doregardo's view.

PART I

The Daggers of Bregan D'aerthe

Jarlaxle has spent many hours of late—since the resurrection of Zaknafein—relating to me tales of his early days beside my father in Menzoberranzan. His purpose, I expect, is to help me better get to know this man who was so important to me in my early years, a man whose past has remained mostly a mystery until now. Perhaps Jarlaxle sees this as a way to bridge the divide that I have unexpectedly found separating me from my father, to soften the edges of Zaknafein's attitudes toward any who are not drow.

What I have found most of all, however, is that Jarlaxle's stories have told me more about Jarlaxle than they have about Zaknafein, most especially of the evolution of Jarlaxle and his mercenary band of Bregan D'aerthe. I view this evolution with great optimism, as it seems to me a smaller example of that which I hope might come about within the drow culture as a whole.

When he started his band of outcasts, Jarlaxle did so simply to keep himself alive. He was a houseless rogue, a reality that in Menzoberranzan typically ensured one a difficult and short existence. But clever Jarlaxle collected others in similar straits and brought them together, and made of these individuals a powerful force that offered value to the ruling matrons without threatening them. That band, though, was not the same as the

Bregan D'aerthe that now controls the city of Luskan, and the distinction is not subtle, though I'm not sure if Jarlaxle himself is even conscious of it.

Bregan D'aerthe is a very different troupe now, but the change, I expect, has been gradual across the centuries. Jarlaxle, too, must be different.

And so, dare I hope that Zaknafein will find his way as well?

In the beginning, the Bregan D'aerthe reflected the savage culture of Menzoberranzan's houses, and in many ways exploited the schisms within Menzoberranzan, both interhouse and intrahouse. Great indeed were those treacheries! My own life was spared the sacrificial blade only because my brother Dinin murdered my brother Nalfein on the day of my birth. Everyone knew the truth of it, including our mother, Matron Malice, and yet there was no punishment to Dinin. Rather, there was only gain because of the clever manner in which he had executed Nalfein, away from obvious witnesses. Similarly, I would guess that nearly half the matrons serving as the heads of drow houses arrived at their station by killing (or at least by helping to facilitate the death of) their own mothers. This is the way of Lolth and so this is the way of the drow and so this was the way of Bregan D'aerthe.

As such, Jarlaxle gave his underlings free rein and little guidance as they tried to climb the hierarchy of Bregan D'aerthe. His only rule, from what I can fathom, was that members take care of the cost that any of their actions might incur upon him. His underlings would fight and cheat, steal and kill, and Jarlaxle did not care enough to get involved. A murdered associate would have to be properly replaced at the expense of the murderer, I suppose, but Jarlaxle imposed no moral code upon his underlings.

I sometimes wonder if he was then possessed of such a code himself.

I ask that honestly, for while I do not doubt that he has always held some code of honor, that is not necessarily the same thing as a moral center. Artemis Entreri held on to some misplaced sense of honor, too, but it is only in very recent times that he has allowed simple morality to even seep into his decisions.

But then, Artemis Entreri viewed the human societies in much the same way that Jarlaxle—and Zaknafein—viewed the drow: irredeemable and wretched and worthy of his extreme scorn and ultimate judgment.

What a sad waste is such an outlook!

When Jarlaxle relates those early stories of his band of not-brothers, he doesn't even seem aware of the stark differences that are representative of Bregan D'aerthe today. Then, the secret society survived by strength alone, by Jarlaxle's ability to will the disparate and rivalrous troupe through the tasks put before him by the matrons, particularly Matron Mother Baenre. From all that I can extrapolate through these stories, Jarlaxle lost more foot soldiers to Bregan D'aerthe blades than to those of enemies.

Now, though, I witness a much different structure within Bregan D'aerthe, and one very much more powerful.

For Jarlaxle has given to his followers something truly special among the Lolth-serving drow: an element of trust.

And he does so by example. Jarlaxle has entrusted Kimmuriel Oblodra with the very leadership of the band on those many occasions when he, Jarlaxle, is out on some adventure or other. He has even tasked Kimmuriel with reining in his own worst excesses—with keeping Jarlaxle himself in line!

Jarlaxle has given great latitude to Beniago in his role as High Captain Kurth, overseeing the city of Luskan. Beniago does not consult with Jarlaxle about his every move, and yet Jarlaxle trusts in him to operate the city smoothly, profitably, and, I am led to believe, with some measure of the general welfare and common good of the citizens in mind.

Perhaps most telling of all is the manner in which Jarlaxle has accepted the mighty former archmage. Gromph Baenre is not a full member of Bregan D'aerthe, from all that I can tell, but he resides in Luskan as the ultimate archmage of the Hosttower of the Arcane, and does so at the sufferance of Jarlaxle. The Hosttower itself could not have been rebuilt if not for Jarlaxle's approval, for Gromph would never have been able to go against the whole of Bregan D'aerthe and would have found no support from King Bruenor, and certainly no help in the construction from Catti-brie.

Jarlaxle granted Gromph this greatest of wizard towers, a force as singularly powerful as any castle I have ever known, even that of King Gareth Dragonsbane in Damara, or of Sorcere, the drow school of wizards in Menzoberranzan. The collection of magic, and of those who can expertly wield such magic, now residing in the Hosttower could unleash unimaginable devastation.

But it won't. Jarlaxle knows it won't. Gromph's acceptance into Bregan D'aerthe, and into the city controlled by Bregan D'aerthe, was highly conditional. His leash is short, and yet a large part of that leash lies in the realm of trust.

And that's all possible because Bregan D'aerthe has grown, has evolved. As their leader goes, they go.

And that gives me hope.

So I dare. Dare hope that Jarlaxle's influence and example will find their way into Zaknafein's heart.

Even still, I fear that Zaknafein's transformation will not come in time to earn friendship, even familial love, from Catti-brie or from our child, and in that instance, it will not be in time to earn the love of Drizzt Do'Urden.

I hope that is not the case.

But he is my family by blood. And she is my family by choice.

I have come to learn that the latter is a stronger bond.

                                                              —Drizzt Do'Urden

CHAPTER 1

THE YEAR OF THE FALSE BARGAIN
DALERECKONING 1118

Running Free

Your mood is foul, friend," Jarlaxle said to Arathis Hune in the tavern known as the Oozing Myconid one remarkable night.

"My road has been long," the weary and wary assassin replied. "And soon will be again, I am told. Every third year, it seems, someone in Ched Nasad is in need of being murdered."

"You're good at it," Jarlaxle said, lifting a glass of powerful mushroom bourbon in a toast.

"Tell it to the one who fills my purse," Arathis Hune dryly replied, and Jarlaxle returned a grin at the assassin's quip . . . as Jarlaxle was the one who filled Arathis Hune's purse.

"Nothing has been decided regarding the City of Shimmering Webs," Jarlaxle replied, after calling for a drink for his associate.

"No movement from Matron Mother Baenre?"

"None. I doubt she even cares enough to remember that she wanted to kill somebody there. Or, more likely, she put forth the whispers of dispatching assassins, and that alone was enough to elicit the behavioral change she desired. Surely, she—*we* have killed enough people there so that even a Baenre whisper—"

"*I*," Arathis Hune corrected. "*I* have killed enough people. It hasn't been 'we' in decades regarding anything to do with Ched Nasad."

Jarlaxle leaned back in his chair to take a long look at his assassin, at the deepening of the man's ill mood as soon as Jarlaxle had informed him that a journey to Ched Nasad would be unlikely. The assassin had darkened, and that after he had hinted that he really didn't want to undertake the mission.

So why had he grown so salty?

Jarlaxle's own mood was souring, too. The assassin's words about his lack of involvement in recent missions rang true enough. Bregan D'aerthe was growing strong in Menzoberranzan, but that impressive reputation—and rising number of foot soldiers—had forced Jarlaxle to all but abandon the roads beyond the city. Bregan D'aerthe was too tempting a target for the matrons of powerful houses—would he go to Ched Nasad or some other distant locale only to return to discover that the matron of House Barrison Del'Armgo or some other rival of Matron Mother Baenre had seized control of his mercenary band? Jarlaxle had spent fifteen decades building Bregan D'aerthe, whose quarters now sprawled in the tunnels of the Clawrift, the great chasm that split the cavern holding the drow city, and he wasn't about to lose it.

No, he simply wouldn't risk that. Not now. Not when Bregan D'aerthe was not yet strong enough to scare away any such attempts. And so he stayed in this city, while Arathis Hune went on the important missions far out in the Underdark.

That alone could not explain the assassin's mood, though. Jarlaxle had come to entrust Arathis Hune with these critically important kills. That confidence should bring satisfaction to Arathis Hune, he supposed, as the man maneuvered to become a powerful boss within the clandestine organization. So, again: why was he sour?

Could he know the significance of this occasion? Could Arathis Hune know why he was summoned to the Stenchstreets? If so, the man's barely disguised scowl would be understood.

It was an unnerving thought.

Jarlaxle rarely second-guessed himself, but he was doing so at that moment. This was a special night for him, more important to him than he had anticipated, because he was meeting another old friend and associate, one he had barely seen over the past thirty years. Someone, he realized, he missed fiercely.

Not that he could blame his friend for the long absence. As the weapon master of a rising drow house, he'd been instrumental in helping his matron climb the ranks of Menzoberranzan's difficult hierarchy. As such, his reputation had grown large—even though that reputation did not do justice to his true skill with his swords—and so Zaknafein Do'Urden was not often seen outside of House Do'Urden of late. He had made too many enemies, and made nervous too many matrons of houses that might be next in line or those hindering the ambitious Matron Malice Do'Urden's determined climb toward her seat at the spider-shaped table of the city's Ruling Council.

Even rarer was Zaknafein outside House Do'Urden alone, and rarer still would the weapon master venture to the Braeryn, the Stenchstreets, the underbelly of a city whose finest neighborhoods often knew murder.

Jarlaxle cherished the fact that Zaknafein would risk all that to meet up.

"I had thought you would enjoy a night of respite," Jarlaxle apologized. "If you would prefer otherwise . . ."

"A hundred years, is it?" Arathis Hune interrupted.

Jarlaxle started to respond, but held back the words. A hundred years indeed, he thought, since he had first pulled Zaknafein—then Zaknafein Simfray—from a battlefield littered with the bodies of two warring drow houses.

Arathis Hune glanced at the bar across the room, where an impressive silver-haired woman leaned back against the far wall, a drink in her hand, several men listening to her every word, clearly enraptured and hoping for a night in her bed.

"A hundred years for priestess Dab'nay Tr'arach, as well," the assassin remarked.

"Just Dab'nay," Jarlaxle corrected. "She has abandoned her familial name, and no longer openly professes herself as a priestess. But yes, ten-eighteen was a good year for Bregan D'aerthe. We doubled our number, fattened our coffers, and added some very powerful associates."

"Some?"

"Three."

"Now just that one," Arathis Hune said, nodding his chin toward the former noble daughter of House Tr'arach.

"More than one," Jarlaxle argued, but he left it at that. Duvon Tr'arach, Dab'nay's brother, had been all but lost to Bregan D'aerthe, for Jarlaxle had sold him to House Fey-Branche, to become their weapon master until one of Matron Byrtyn's own children could become proficient and veteran enough to assume the mantle. He had done so with Duvon's blessing, however, and so Jarlaxle had made it clear Duvon had a home when that time came.

And Zaknafein was simply too busy with his duties to Matron Malice, and too "hot" to be out often on the streets, given Malice's growing list of powerful enemies, to be of much use these days. But he would always be welcome among the Bregan D'aerthe.

Regardless, Arathis Hune, again, wasn't wrong. There was no doubt in Jarlaxle's mind about which addition had made that year, 1018, so special.

As if reading Jarlaxle's thoughts, Arathis Hune snorted and moved across the tavern to join Dab'nay and some others. Jarlaxle watched him all the way, though he wasn't too concerned with anything regarding the man. This rogue could be quite the charming fellow, laughed as often as he scowled, made love as often as he made mischief, and could drink more than any drow ought. While that could surely aggravate Jarlaxle, and sometimes even concerned him, in the end he trusted that he understood the assassin's loyalties enough to feel secure about Arathis Hune.

"Perhaps I have been too severe with you of late," Jarlaxle whispered under his breath. The mercenary leader nodded and took another sip of his liquor. Although it hadn't been a constant, Jarlaxle had watched a rising melancholy within Arathis Hune ever since that long-ago day when Zaknafein Simfray had been taken from the battlefield, a melancholy that seemed to diminish whenever Zaknafein was absent for extended periods. Of course they were rivals, these two magnificent killers, and so of course Hune would remain skeptical and cautious regarding Zaknafein. But this seemed even more than that, a level of jealousy that surprised Jarlaxle.

Jarlaxle didn't like to be surprised.

He sighed, took another sip, and turned back toward the door— and nearly jumped out of his chair to find a very dangerous drow standing right beside him. With a nod, Zaknafein took a seat next to Jarlaxle, looking past the mercenary to the bar and the other two powerful members of Bregan D'aerthe.

"Priestess Tr'arach and Arathis Hune? They plot your demise, of course," Zaknafein said.

"They would not be the only ones, nor the most dangerous," Jarlaxle answered, and waved to the barkeep, another man he had taken from a battlefield a century before, and whom he had only recently installed in the Oozing Myconid. He signaled for a drink for his friend and a refill of his own. "And we call her Dab'nay now. There is no Tr'arach."

"Not even the one behind the bar?"

Jarlaxle just grinned and tipped his drink in salute to the observant weapon master.

"You seem in fine spirits," Jarlaxle remarked.

"I soon will be."

"Even now."

"I am . . . relaxed," Zaknafein admitted with a shrug.

"Matron Malice has stolen all of that angry edge?"

That brought a smile to Zaknafein's face.

"She is all that her reputation claims?"

"I would have thought that you would have learned that for yourself by now."

"Truly?" Jarlaxle asked, and grasped his chest as if taken aback. Zaknafein started to respond, but held back as the barkeep came over and placed a glass before him, then refilled Jarlaxle's cup. The man met the stare of Zaknafein, who thought he detected a bit of resentment there.

"Long are the memories of foolish drow," Zaknafein said as the former Tr'arach warrior moved back across the tavern.

"I would think that a good thing."

"It would be, if they also remembered that I can still kill them, and would be glad to do so," said Zaknafein, and to Jarlaxle's wide-eyed stare, he finished, "Yes, yes, I will then offer recompense for stealing a soldier from you."

"Surely you do not wish to kill that one, or any of them, else you would have done so that long-ago day when they attacked House Simfray. That one in particular," he said, pointing at the barkeep. "You had Harbondair beaten on the bridge between the towers, an easy kill. Yet one Zaknafein did not take."

"He was riding a lizard," Zaknafein said, nodding. He didn't remember the warrior specifically, but he did remember knocking a lizard and its rider over the rail.

"His beloved mount, one he had raised from a hatchling. Your Simfray fellows gutted it above him. He rode its unwinding entrails to the ground."

"That explains the stench," Zaknafein said dryly. He lifted his glass to drink, but paused. "Should I imbibe some antivenom first?"

Jarlaxle laughed. "Harbondair could not afford to replace you, and would not dare invoke the rage of Matron Malice. And no, to answer your question about Malice, I would not cuckold my dear friend."

"You might be the only drow in Menzoberranzan who has not, and so I would hardly consider it thus." He said it with a laugh and quaffed the drink in one great gulp, then held the glass up for Harbondair Tr'arach to see.

"She is all that you claimed," Zaknafein continued. "Insatiable . . . and insane. If Malice could fight like she ruts, she'd prove the finest weapon master in Menzoberranzan."

"Well, then, you're welcome."

"From what I have seen, I did not need to join her house to learn the truth."

"What of the boy, then?" Jarlaxle asked.

Harbondair approached with the bottle, but Zaknafein just took it from him and waved the man away.

"What of him?" Zaknafein replied.

"Dinin, yes? Is he . . . ?"

"Is he what?"

Jarlaxle heaved a great sigh and sat back in his seat, staring.

"No," Zaknafein answered. "He is not my son."

"You have been with Matron Malice often. How can you know?"

"Not mine," Zaknafein insisted. "It was likely Rizzen who sired him. I had wondered if it was you, but you've already said otherwise."

Jarlaxle's expression turned curious.

Zaknafein shrugged. "He is a worthy enough boy, and one who would do Rizzen proud, surely, after the mediocrity of Nalfein. Did I tell you that Nalfein actually challenged me to serve as House Do'Urden's weapon master?"

"Truly? So Matron Malice once again has but one son?"

"I didn't kill him. I didn't even fight him, really, just disarmed him before he could even draw his weapons." Zaknafein took another drink. "His pants fell down, too. Again, and as expected, unimpressive."

"Ah, yes," said Jarlaxle, "I did hear whispers that Nalfein Do'Urden had returned to the Academy, though I didn't bother to confirm them."

"But to Sorcere, not Melee-Magthere," Zaknafein replied. "In our one-sided contest, it seems that I convinced him to try his hand at wizardry."

"And?"

Zaknafein shrugged. "He is better at that than at fighting. But then, were he not, he'd have turned himself into a squiggle newt by now."

"To feeble wizards, then," said Jarlaxle, lifting his glass for Zaknafein to tap his against it.

"To dead wizards," Zaknafein agreed.

"And this secondboy?" Jarlaxle asked as he refilled his glass. "The one you claim is not yours. Is he, too, bound for the winding corridors of Sorcere?"

"Melee-Magthere."

"Like Zaknafein," Jarlaxle slyly observed, but Zaknafein shook his head.

"He is clever enough to be a fighter, but he favors one hand. More like Arathis Hune, I expect, or perhaps like Jarlaxle."

"I have warned you many times not to underestimate me."

"And I have warned you many times not to think you've been underestimated." Zaknafein drained his glass again and quickly refilled it. "I expect Dinin is the son of Rizzen," he went on. "And if so, then that is the best that Malice will ever get from that one."

"And from Zaknafein?"

The weapon master just stared at him from over his glass as he drained it a third time, then poured a fourth. "Who would even know? Even with Dinin. Perhaps he is a cambion, or the result of some dark magic. Malice spent nearly two centuries riding partners twenty times a tenday, and yet produced nothing but a horde of exhausted lovers."

"She had already birthed two children," Jarlaxle reminded. "She is not barren."

"Would that she were," Zaknafein mumbled under his breath, and if Jarlaxle weren't wearing a tiny magical ear horn to heighten his already keen drow senses, he wouldn't have caught the remark, or the continuing, "Would that they all were."

Jarlaxle let it go at that, and sat quiet, considering his friend. Zaknafein had come into the Oozing Myconid full of cheer, but the mood could not ever hold with this one, not against the reality of Menzoberranzan.

The only answer, Jarlaxle knew, was a challenge. He grabbed Zaknafein's arm as the man lifted his glass for another drink.

"Cavern jumping?" he asked.

Zaknafein stared at him from over the rim of the glass, incredulously at first.

But a grin began to spread, and it carried him out of the tavern and partway across the city, until he stood with Jarlaxle on a high ledge along the West Wall of the cavern, not far from the balconies of House Do'Urden. Directly east of them loomed the timeclock obelisk of Narbondel, dark now as the night grew long.

"The risk," Zaknafein chuckled, shaking his head.

"That's what makes it fun," Jarlaxle answered with a wry grin of his own.

The pair stripped off their weapons, magical items, and armor, hiding them away. They now wore only the simple pants, shirts, and soft padded boots that were their custom. Here they were, out alone in the Menzoberranzan night, fully two miles from the Oozing Myconid.

The two exchanged a glance, then shrugged in unison, and Zaknafein leaped away. He fell just a few feet to another ledge, caught himself softly by absorbing the drop with a deep bend, then launched himself outward, spinning and somersaulting to come down in a run across the roof of a nearby structure. He sprang up high in a vault, his hands planting on the top sill of the jutting window of the structure's guard tower, then flowed into a cartwheel above that window, landing on the far side, letting his legs roll out under him, then tumbling right off the far side of the roof to a lower roof. He landed, flipped once, then again, came up straight, and launched himself into a gainer, backflipping to stem his momentum so that he could plant a landing on the street below.

Jarlaxle dropped down to Zaknafein's right, landing in a roll that kept him moving eastward. He went off farther to the right of a large stalagmite, while Zaknafein sprinted around the left of the imposing mound.

They came around with Zaknafein a step ahead of the mercenary, another stalagmite looming before them. Up the side ran Zaknafein, springing from a ledge, then a second, catching a third with his hand, then spinning to reverse his grip and put his back to the wall. He pulled up and tucked his legs, throwing himself right over backward, clearing that section of rock and dropping down the other side. He hand-walked to secure his landing, then threw himself outward, and on he ran.

He hurdled the low wall of a minor house, ignoring the shouts of some guards over in the darkness to his right. He sprang from the bank of a small decorative fish pond, somersaulting and stretching his legs out far before him to catch the lip of the far bank. He worked his arms, nearly pitching backward into the water, then cursed even as he regained his balance, for Jarlaxle came rushing past him.

"Just in time to catch their crossbow bolts," the mercenary taunted.

Zaknafein took it more as a prudent warning than an insult, though, and ran, dove, rolled, zigged and zagged over the next open avenue. He thought he heard a quarrel fly overhead, but he could not be sure, and he did not care.

He had been stuck by the darts before in this game he and Jarlaxle played.

When they passed the open ground, around another wall, up over the outcropping on another natural mound, Zaknafein began to perfectly mirror Jarlaxle's movements, leaping, vaulting, hurdling, rolling, to mimic the lead runner exactly. He remembered the route well enough to know where he wanted to make his move to overtake his opponent.

Getting to the door of the Oozing Myconid first wasn't critical and didn't determine the winner, but it was a matter of pride.

On they went, past Narbondel and through the section of the city known as the Narbondellyn, running, springing, climbing, flowing from one jump to a tumble to another roll, to a leap-and-spider-scramble maneuver up a nearly sheer wall. They passed the long courtyard and structures of House Fey-Branche, even going up atop the north wall of the compound at one point, scurrying along like a pair of giant rats fleeing the purring pursuit of a hungry displacer beast.

They neared the northeastern corner, where the wall cut back at a square angle. Even as the guards began to shout, Jarlaxle bent down in his run, planting his right hand on the wall's top, then flung himself around and over, landing on his feet on the eastern wall, facing into the compound, that he could wave to the shocked Fey-Branche sentries before backflipping away to the east.

Zaknafein was similarly in the air before Jarlaxle ever touched, turning about as he descended, as had Jarlaxle, to hit the ground running. Right behind his old friend, the weapon master leaped up to a wall in a narrow alleyway, splaying flat out as his feet kept moving, with his hands slapping the opposite wall to keep him horizontally aloft until he had rounded a corner.

There, still mirroring Jarlaxle, he dropped back to his feet and ran to the northeast down the bending alley. He couldn't help but smile when he heard a hand-crossbow quarrel strike the wall at the corner he had just smoothly turned. He stayed right on the mercenary's heels as the pair crossed into the Braeryn, now being seen and quietly cheered by some of those who knew about the challenge and were out spotting from the Oozing Myconid.

A clear patch of ground led them into a sprint, almost side by side as Zaknafein slightly outpaced Jarlaxle, moving up along his right flank. With two walls—the first neck high, the second waist high—the only things between them and the door of the tavern, Zaknafein went into his new move. He stepped his right foot ahead but turned it inward, to the left. Planting strongly, he half turned, then kicked his left leg out behind the right, lifting, lifting as high as he could. Up into the air he went, clearing the neck-high wall, landing on the other side facing Jarlaxle, who was using the more common reverse-grip, back-rollover maneuver.

Not slowing at all, Zaknafein leaped again, lifting in a sideways somersault up and over the second, lower wall. Landing with his feet moving, he charged across the closing ground and shouldered through the door of the Oozing Myconid to rousing cheers.

NOT SO FAR AWAY, BACK NEAR THE NARBONDELLYN, WITHIN the very compound upon whose wall the pair had run, a young matron in one of the city's oldest houses took personal interest in a courier from the Oozing Myconid.

"He is with Jarlaxle now," explained the man, a houseless rogue whose blood was too thick with mind-altering mushroom spores, fungus chews, and alcohol to be of much use to anyone—anyone but Matron Byrtyn.

Her weapon master, Avinvesa Fey, stood beside the courier, nodding and grinning.

"My sister is there as well," Avinvesa told his matron, who had acquired him from Jarlaxle's band for a hefty sum of gold and magic.

"You have no sisters," Matron Byrtyn reminded him. Formally, at least, this man's previous existence was dead and gone as far as she was concerned, and any such references to the past were simply not allowed. Avinvesa said nothing.

Byrtyn leaned back in her comfortable throne, pondering the news, and waved the two males back from her dais.

"Why would Matron Malice let him out at this time?" she asked the priestess Affyn, her third-oldest but perhaps most impressive daughter, who stood at her side this day. "She has many webs cast, and to so dangle her most precious asset openly . . ."

"If she even knows," Affyn answered. "Matron Malice is often . . . indisposed, and by all accounts, her famed weapon master is an unruly one."

"And a great friend of Jarlaxle's," Byrtyn agreed. She faced forward again and waved her hand at Avinvesa and their guest a second time, dismissing them.

"This might be a good time to be rid of Zaknafein, Matron," Affyn said when they were alone.

Byrtyn nodded, considering her options here. House Do'Urden's ambitious and aggressive moves had not put them directly against House Fey-Branche yet, but it seemed only a matter of time—unless, of course, House Do'Urden suffered the loss of an asset as great as Zaknafein. The personal tie was there, as well, for Avinvesa—formerly Duvon Tr'arach—still held an unhealthy grudge against Zaknafein, whom he blamed for the downfall of his house and family.

Never mind the fact that the only reason Duvon had survived was through the efforts of Jarlaxle and his merry band of misfits—the grudge against Zaknafein remained. Byrtyn had seen it in his eyes just then, the eagerness at the mere thought that his rival might be exposed and eliminated.

Matron Byrtyn had spent great resources on Duvon, not only in acquiring him from Jarlaxle, but in training him, outfitting him, even placing enhancements upon his strength and speed, made permanent by expensive wizards. She had turned him into a proper weapon master, perhaps even one strong enough to take out Zaknafein Do'Urden—with a little help.

"How fares Geldrin?" she asked.

Affyn was clearly caught off guard by the question, which disappointed Byrtyn. They were talking about Zaknafein and important and dangerous house business here, which included the potential loss of their current weapon master. Why shouldn't Byrtyn then inquire about her young son, recently returned from Melee-Magthere? He was, after all, the logical successor to Avinvesa, who was not of Fey blood.

"His training proceeds well," Affyn replied after composing herself.

Matron Byrtyn nodded and rubbed her chin.

"He is not nearly ready to assume a position of great responsibility," Affyn added, seeming concerned.

Again Byrtyn nodded, but she also smiled.

"Can he beat Zaknafein?" she asked, more to herself than to her daughter.

"No," Affyn answered anyway. "Geldrin? The Do'Urden weapon master would—"

"Not Geldrin, you fool," Matron Byrtyn scolded. "You think I would send my own promising son against one of Zaknafein Do'Urden's reputation?"

"Ah, Avinvesa, then," Affyn remarked. "From all the whispers of Matron Malice's latest conquests, I don't know that I would wager against Zaknafein Do'Urden, not even against Dantrag Baenre or Uthegentel Armgo. Well," she conceded, "perhaps in a fight with Uthegentel."

"Strong words, and if Matron Mother Baenre heard you speak them aloud, she would kill Zaknafein out of spite, and kill you for offering such an insult to her beloved son Dantrag."

"I can speak honestly to Matron Byrtyn," the young woman replied, swallowing hard.

"Yes, but say such things *only* to me, daughter. I'll not have Matron Mother Baenre or those vicious Barrison Del'Armgo creatures angry with us. You raise an interesting point, though: wager. There are two questions to ask before making any wager. First, can you quietly help your side of the bet along? And second, is there a way to manage and mitigate a loss?"

"It sounds as if you are considering this news of Zaknafein coming out from the walls of House Do'Urden as important, Matron."

Byrtyn didn't answer, other than to ever so slightly nod her head, deep in thought. She wouldn't get many chances against Malice Do'Urden unless and until she had to defend against that ambitious creature, she knew. Might she escalate and turn this to her advantage, and quickly, this very night?

And, more importantly, might she do so from afar, without implication against House Fey-Branche?

ZAKNAFEIN HAD STOPPED RUNNING, OF COURSE, BUT HE hadn't won the race yet. There, right before him, stood two tables, five large flagons of thick dark ale set upon each.

The exhausted weapon master lifted the first to his lips as Jarlaxle came into the room. Up it tilted as he gulped, emptying it in one hoist. He went for the second flagon.

So did Jarlaxle, having drained his first more quickly.

By the third, Jarlaxle had taken a slight lead, but neither of them got that third one down as fast as the first two.

Zaknafein grabbed the edge of the table, steadying himself, calming his belly. All five had to be downed, with no vomiting.

Jarlaxle was halfway through the fourth when Zaknafein lifted his flagon again.

But Zaknafein finished that one first, as Jarlaxle had to stop and belch several times, very carefully.

The two stared at each other unblinking as they each hoisted their last ale.

Jarlaxle went faster—too fast, and barely had he finished, one hand dropping the flagon back to the table, the other lifting in victory, when he lost the race and the contents of his belly at the same time.

Zaknafein stepped back and slowed his drinking—no need to

hurry now. He belched repeatedly with the flagon still to his lips, calming his stomach, taking his time.

Then he was done, victorious. He had beaten Jarlaxle.

"Twenty-two to twenty-two," he told his friend.

"You remembered?" Jarlaxle replied with surprise.

"For decades, it has tightened my jaw that you were leading our running competition by one race. How convenient, I always thought it, that after the forty-third run, Jarlaxle had left Menzoberranzan for nearly two years."

Jarlaxle laughed at that, for it was true enough, though he hadn't left out of convenience or regarding anything to do with their competition. Opportunities on the surface world had simply proven too enticing for him to stay.

"You know what this means?" he asked Zaknafein.

"I'll be back for another race soon enough," the weapon master assured him. Around them, the patrons cheered at that.

"I look forward to it . . . especially now that I know your closing move," Jarlaxle warned, to a series of accompanying *oohs*.

"And no doubt you'll *try* to perfect it," Zaknafein countered, along with a number of *aahs* from the onlookers.

Jarlaxle shook his head. "I'll find a better one."

"Then I will have to use a few of the other, *better* ones that I've perfected for other obstacles along our course."

The *huzzahs* had begun with Jarlaxle's promise, but they grew tremendously with Zaknafein's unhesitating rejoinder.

Jarlaxle snapped his fingers and lifted his hand up high to catch the wand the barkeep Harbondair threw to him. Zaknafein in tow, he moved on shaky legs to an empty table at the side of the room, pointed the wand at it, and issued a series of command words, dismissing the extradimensional space he had created there to return all of his and Zaknafein's items, other than the belt pouch and the portable hole, which he had given to Harbondair and Dab'nay to hold.

It would not be wise to place either of those items into an extradimensional place!

CHAPTER 2

The Unexpected Interloper

*S*ee *with your marvelous eyes, rogue. Let no one die. Seek profit ever.*

The magical whisper, for his ears only, surprised Jarlaxle, but only for a moment. He immediately tried to identify the sender—a powerful priestess, obviously—but the voice was masked.

His mind moved quickly, working to sort out the puzzle. Who knew about his "marvelous eyes," referring, almost certainly, to his magical eyepatch? That made him think of House Baenre, of course, since Matron Mother Baenre had been instrumental to Jarlaxle acquiring this most useful item.

But no, this couldn't be a message from her, or one of her daughters, he figured. Baenres never shied from announcing themselves, magically or otherwise. Nor did the city's matron mother ever deal with him, or anyone, cryptically.

Matron Mother Baenre wasn't one to allow anything worth talking about to hinge on a proper interpretation of an unclear message.

Jarlaxle lifted his glass for a drink, using that to cover a much-needed deep breath. He replayed the message in his thoughts.

Over the top of his glass, Jarlaxle surveyed the many patrons milling about the large common room of the Oozing Myconid. He closed his one exposed eye and began to sway and hum, as if falling into the melody coming from a back corner of the room, where one bard was playing a lute, another a flute, and a third singing quietly.

Those who knew Jarlaxle well, however, knew two things about that moment. First, Jarlaxle never closed his eyes in a public place, and so, second, the eye under that magical eyepatch was surely open wide and seeing as clearly as if he were wearing no covering. Jarlaxle was quite the opposite of what he then appeared: vulnerable.

With every head movement to the left, he focused on the door, for there was always considerable turnover within the tavern, patrons leaving with partners for brief sexual encounters or for stronger mind-numbing substances than could be found among the bar's wares.

He knew most of the patrons as regulars, including more than a few of his own band.

Each time he turned his head back to the right, his gaze went nearer the bar, the rogue swaying a bit more forcefully with the bardic melody. He noted Zaknafein, moving toward the bar to gather more drinks.

Jarlaxle did well to hide his grin when he considered the weapon master. He hadn't seen Zaknafein so frequently in three decades, at least, but now his friend was visiting once more. In the last two ten-days since their race from the West Wall, Zaknafein had frequented the Oozing Myconid no less than three times. It seemed like old times, and those old times, Jarlaxle thought, had been quite enjoyable.

He couldn't help but smile, too, when he recalled a journey of theirs to Ched Nasad. It had been then, in flight from the city guards, that clever Zaknafein had cut the edge of a high landing made of webbing and used that frayed edge like a rope, swinging down below. Such a daring move, and one that could have left Zaknafein as no more than a stain on the chasm floor far below.

Jarlaxle let the memory fade and focused again across the way, but not on Zaknafein. Rather, he more closely watched Harbondair Tr'arach, whose visage soured every time he glanced Zaknafein's way—at least, whenever Zaknafein wasn't looking back at him.

Jarlaxle had sent Zaknafein to get two drinks, but Harbondair put only one up on the counter, then made a show of cleaning out a glass, taking his time until, Jarlaxle noticed, Zaknafein had taken a sip from the first. Then the barkeep got the second filled and up on the bar in short order.

Interesting.

The other former House Tr'arach survivor was again at the bar by the far wall. Dab'nay laughed and flirted with a rather notorious rogue, one of the finest fighters and burglars in the Stenchstreets who was not a member of Bregan D'aerthe.

Farther to the right, another group of miserable miscreants sat around a circular table, more unconscious than not, with three of the five having succumbed to their many intoxicants and the other two looking ready to collapse. And just beyond them stood Arathis Hune, fully engaged with a very young woman of obvious charms.

Jarlaxle nodded, blending the movement in with his "dance," when he noted that his lieutenant was still very much aware of his surroundings beyond the alluring woman, the man's eyes constantly scanning, subtle movements that Jarlaxle noticed only because he knew Hune so well. Arathis Hune didn't let down his guard, which was a big part of the reason Jarlaxle had moved him so high up the mercenary band's hierarchy.

Jarlaxle continued to turn, thinking to go all the way around and back to the door, when a movement back to the left grabbed his attention once more.

A young man walked past Dab'nay, very close, over to an interior door.

She reacted, only slightly—very slightly—as if she didn't want anyone to note that she had reacted.

Then the young man disappeared through the door.

Jarlaxle kept turning back to the left, noting Zaknafein returning to the table, two drinks in hand. Jarlaxle fell back into his seat, again scanning the gathering, back to the door.

He grew frustrated. He replayed the magical whisper.

See with your marvelous eyes.

A pair of men walked into the tavern. Zaknafein took his seat and set a glass before Jarlaxle, who opened his visible eye and gathered his drink up absently, but still stared through his eyepatch toward the door.

Finally the eyepatch revealed it: one of the two drow men who had just entered was not as he appeared!

His long hair had been dyed blue, and that was a feint within a feint, since the whole of it was a wig. Jarlaxle's eyepatch could determine such things, and showed him the man's true hair: cut very short on the sides and back, with the top longer. He was also more slender and younger than he appeared, as his shoulders were padded under his shabby jerkin, and with a finer set of armor hidden underneath, as well.

This was no houseless male.

His face had been altered with makeup both mundane and magical, but the eyepatch cut through all of that, and Jarlaxle actually recognized the man.

The man who used to be known as Duvon Tr'arach.

In that moment, clever Jarlaxle figured out who had sent him the magical whisper.

And why.

"Publicly drunk?" Zaknafein asked, setting his mug back on the table.

Jarlaxle noted a slight lisp in the weapon master's voice. He watched as Zaknafein lifted his glass again, stared at it, then shrugged and raised it for another sip.

Jarlaxle arched an eyebrow and Zaknafein paused, the drink just below his lips.

"A bit pungent," Zaknafein said. "Not a fine batch." He shrugged again and took his drink, and Jarlaxle looked down at his own.

"Yours probably tastes better," Zaknafein said, suddenly slurring.

Jarlaxle caught on and smiled at his friend as he lifted his glass and tipped it in toast to Zaknafein, before taking a large swallow.

He surveyed the room again as he drank, noting Duvon, some distance away but casting a glance Zaknafein's way.

"Mine is too weak," he told Zaknafein. "Blech." He licked his lips in apparent disgust and rose, shaking his head, then moved to the bar, as if he meant to exchange the glass. He didn't, though, and instead set himself into position so that Dab'nay could clearly see his hands as he cupped them around the glass on the bar.

A risk is better made with a proper wager, his fingers signed to her, and her curious expression told him that she had noted his communication, and that he had caught her off guard.

All noble children should understand this, Jarlaxle silently and subtly added.

Dab'nay's eyes widened despite her obvious attempts to remain impassive. He hadn't just referred to her, after all, but to someone she knew (and knew about) who had just entered the bar.

Jarlaxle drained his glass and motioned for Harbondair to refill it. He gathered it up and started from the bar, trying to figure out how much the little game being played this night might cost him, and from whom he might recoup those expenses. He didn't head straight back to Zaknafein's table but took a roundabout route, bringing him right past Dab'nay and a couple of eager young men who were clearly looking to romance her that night.

"I find myself quite lonely of late, good lady," Jarlaxle said. "I will leave room in my bed for you."

One of the drow, a young man who clearly didn't know enough about the Braeryn to ensure a long and healthy life, turned briskly to square up with Jarlaxle, as if to warn him away.

"My friend, I value this establishment too much to color it with your blood," Jarlaxle calmly said, and he gave a quick glance to Dab'nay, an invitation.

"It would be better if no one died in the Oozing Myconid this night," she told her young suitor, sweetly, but with all the weight of a priestess of Lolth's voice behind it.

Jarlaxle moved along, smiling at the thought of playing with Dab'nay that night—something he had not done in a long while—and pleased that his Bregan D'aerthe associate had so clearly read the actual meaning in his cryptic hand signals.

Not for the first time and not for the last, Jarlaxle was glad of his decision that century ago to spare Dab'nay Tr'arach.

He looked down at his drink, sad that he had to cradle this one. He couldn't afford to dull his senses at that time.

"You could have brought one for me," Zaknafein said when he arrived at the table, the weapon master once more slurring his words, even wobbling a bit as he spoke them.

"You don't look like you need one, my friend," Jarlaxle replied. "Especially while in a dangerous place like this."

Zaknafein snorted and pulled himself up to his feet, then started for the bar. He stumbled, though, and went a couple of steps to the side, bumping into another patron.

That patron's companion took immediate offense.

A blade flashed—indeed, flashed more than anyone expected as a sudden, brilliant light appeared, drawing groans and shouts from stunned, blinded, and angry dark elves.

Even before countering darkness spells turned the light back to its normal dimness, Jarlaxle (who had, of course, thrown the ceramic pellet with the enchanted light stone into the midst) launched a second such ball and was on to his third trick, calling forth a minor spell from a ring he wore on his right hand.

In the eyeblink before a dozen drow darkness spells overwhelmed the magical light and filled that whole section of the tavern with darkness, Jarlaxle saw that the attacking patron, Duvon, had both swords in hand. Duvon thrust one straight ahead while bringing the second down from on high, powerfully, aiming for the hollow in Zaknafein's neck.

Zaknafein, drawing only then, sent his left-hand blade across and out, taking the thrusting blade with it, while his right rose up horizontally to execute the second block—a brilliant and beautifully fast double draw that had Jarlaxle almost laughing out loud, both in admiration for Zaknafein, and at himself for even fearing that his weapon master friend might actually be inebriated.

That laugh didn't hold as the light blinked to absolute blackness, though, for the weight of Duvon's blow drove Zaknafein's sword down and even wobbled the weapon master's knees.

Something was wrong.

DAB'NAY KEPT HER FOCUS ON THE SPELLCASTING IN THE blinking light. She tried to put aside her fears that Jarlaxle knew more than he should, and her even greater fears that she would fail him now and pay for it, severely, later on.

By the time of the second, more complete darkness, her powerful wave of healing had launched, falling over the combatants—and not a moment too soon, as both cried out as if stabbed!

And more cries followed, these mostly of protest, accompanied by angry shouting and the screeching sound as a blade slipped across metal.

Dab'nay neared panic. She started a second mass healing spell, thinking to throw it in the general direction of the fighters and hope it landed appropriately. Before she could, though, the light returned, a normal light for the tavern, and now Dab'nay scrambled to take it all in.

She was surprised to see that a block of magical webs filled the area where the fight had started, with three drow, including the first to strike, fully caught, and with Zaknafein at the near edge, working to tear himself free.

Many other blades were showing in the tavern then, however, a semicircle of drow with swords drawn and leveled at the combatants. Dab'nay considered them, and recognized them, and quickly relaxed. They were all Bregan D'aerthe fighters, and into the center of their formation walked Jarlaxle.

"Enough!" the mercenary leader demanded. "There will be no blood shed in this place this night."

"Too late," Zaknafein muttered back at him. "This is not your fight."

"How dare you stop this?" said the other combatant, clearing his mouth of the webs but not moving too forcefully to otherwise break free.

"*Delay* it," Jarlaxle corrected. "You will have your fight, fairly, in the alley behind this very establishment, three nights hence. Are we agreed?"

"Now, tomorrow, the next day, or any other," Zaknafein said.

"Agreed," said the other.

"To first blood or last blood?" Jarlaxle asked.

"Last," both replied.

Dab'nay sucked in her breath. Someone important in her life would likely die in three days.

Now she just had to figure out which corpse would be of most benefit to her.

Or perhaps not, she thought, when Jarlaxle declared, "Wrong. To surrender, and the humiliation that comes with it.

"That is worse than death."

CHAPTER 3

Those Strange Oblodran Creatures

J
arlaxle found himself at a loss as he tried to figure out who
might have instigated the conflict the previous night. The first
question in such situations was always, of course, along the
lines of "Who would benefit?"

But in Menzoberranzan, where everyone was always looking for
some way to gain, such a question only rarely narrowed the list of
suspects. In this case, Jarlaxle's list included some of his most important associates, a distinguished matron of one of the oldest and most
respected ruling houses in the city, and even the principals involved in
the fight—both of them.

He wasn't going to solve this before the contest, but getting to the
bottom of it might be the only way for him to keep two valued associates alive.

"I would ask what you are thinking, but if I wanted to know, I
would already be in your thoughts," came a voice that brought the
mercenary leader from his contemplations. He turned to view a di-

minutive drow, a tiny woman who terrified Jarlaxle perhaps more than any other drow in the city, including the great and powerful Matron Mother Baenre herself.

"Greetings, Matron K'yorl," he responded, trying to collect himself—and trying to steel himself against the strange mental intrusions for which K'yorl and her House Oblodra were famous. They were psionicists, mind wizards, not unlike the terrifying race of illithids (which were, quite appropriately, also known as mind flayers). Secretly, Oblodra was the most hated house in the city, Jarlaxle knew, but no one would dare go against them, not even House Baenre.

K'yorl grinned—she always wore that superior smirk!

"I warned you when I allowed you to build your complex here in the Clawrift that I would visit," she said, something she always brought up on those occasions when she simply showed up in the mostly natural corridors of the Bregan D'aerthe home.

"Collecting kobold servants?" Jarlaxle asked.

"Perhaps."

"Seeking my services, then," Jarlaxle stated, regaining a bit of his swagger.

"Not as long as you wear that eyepatch," the matron bluntly stated. "I do business with no one who hides his thoughts from me."

"We've done business before, great lady."

K'yorl grinned again and Jarlaxle felt a compulsion to remove his eyepatch. His hand reflexively lifted and he almost did it, catching himself only at the last moment.

Her laughter mocked him. The too-clever matron was finding her way through his magical defenses, he knew.

"Fear not, Jarlaxle Baenre," she said, and the mercenary winced at having his proper surname whispered aloud. Few knew the truth of Jarlaxle's heritage, or that the sacrifice of Matron Mother Baenre's thirdborn son, which tradition dictated, had been a farce, foiled by the strange magical mind powers of this very same K'yorl Odran.

"I find you useful, and quite a valuable plaything," K'yorl continued. "You have nothing to fear from me as long as you remain outside of the goings-on in Menzoberranzan. Jarlaxle knows everything that is happening in the city, so they say, and that includes knowing when to keep himself out of business that does not concern him."

"I do try, Matron."

"When I can confirm that with your thoughts and not merely your words, I will believe you."

Jarlaxle held up his hands and shrugged. "Soon, then?"

"Sooner than you believe," K'yorl replied.

Jarlaxle flashed his own smile, that wide grin conveying too much joy and light for the dark shadows of Menzoberranzan.

"I must be away," K'yorl said. "I came for other reasons, but thought it would be impolite to not pay a visit to the—patron?—of this cavernous household."

You came to prove that you could walk through my room's newest defenses, Jarlaxle thought, but did not say, and he hoped his eyepatch had blocked her from "hearing" that.

K'yorl's form began to flicker weirdly, but Jarlaxle had seen this before and was not surprised. Then she was simply gone, disappeared, and Jarlaxle wondered if she had actually been standing before him or not. With any other drow, he might have shifted his magical eyepatch to the other eye, that it would grant him an enchantment of true-seeing, but he didn't dare remove his protections from psionic intrusion with K'yorl about.

As if he didn't have enough to think about already, now he had to try to discern why Matron Oblodra had come here this day.

He had a suspicion, one that led him to believe that K'yorl might not be the only member of House Oblodra to have come down into the Clawrift from the house above.

"I CAN ANTICIPATE YOUR EVERY DESIRE," QUAVYLENE OB-lodra, K'yorl's oldest and most important daughter, told Arathis Hune as she lay atop him, the pair bathed in sweat. "I know just what you want. I know just how you feel, and so I can feel that way with you. That is why I like to share your bed."

She then answered before Arathis Hune could ask the question that came to him, "Because you are so careful and guarded. It must be exhausting to hide from everyone. But with me you cannot hide, and so your pleasure comes forth like a giant lake being released from pressing cavern walls. It is a ride I do so enjoy."

With the revelation that the woman, who was skilled in the divine magic of Lolth and also in the ways of Oblodran mind magic, was in his thoughts, Arathis Hune determinedly sought a mental distraction. He settled on something that he had always wondered about anyway.

"Because we do," Quavylene answered his unspoken question. "Odran and Oblodran are the same surname, from a common source. Some, like the matron, use Odran, which was the name before our family formally accepted the Spider Queen as our deity, because that brags of her near indifference to the religious order of the city and the Spider Queen herself."

"You are the first priestess of House Oblodra," Arathis Hune reasoned. "A priestess of Lolth. So Odran would not do for that role?"

"Yes. Perhaps when I am the matron, I will change my name to Odran."

"You are a priestess, a first priestess of a major house, yet do not seem so devout," he dared to say. "Doesn't that anger Lolth?"

Quavylene smiled and kissed him on his bare chest. "Oblodra is not a young house, and Matron K'yorl Odran, certainly no devout priestess of the Spider Queen, has ruled it for two centuries. None doubt that we will soon climb to a seat on the Ruling Council. The only question remaining is which house we will replace. Lady Lolth approves of us and the doubt and chaos we can bring to her city, it would seem."

Arathis Hune couldn't disagree with that. He loved sharing Quavylene's bed, but couldn't deny that she always had him nervous and off balance. How could she not when she was so often in his very thoughts?

Yet, this strange mind magic might prove very useful to him someday, perhaps soon. And, as he had noted, there were delightful perks.

Quavylene smiled as he thought about both things, and he didn't need to be a psionicist to recognize that she was entertaining a similar possibility that the arrangement could prove even more mutually beneficial.

"THE FIELD IS READY?" JARLAXLE ASKED ARATHIS HUNE AS the pair exited the Clawrift later that day.

"The betting has already begun."

Jarlaxle nodded. "Spread as much gold as you can, but quietly and in small bits. Let us not draw too much attention."

"On?"

Jarlaxle skidded to a stop and whirled on his companion, his face reflecting his shock.

"The blood in that tavern skirmish, before the healing wave closed the wounds, was Zaknafein's," Arathis Hune reminded him.

"It was not a severe wound—a clipped hand from a near-perfect parry and nothing more."

"Blood is blood."

"On Zaknafein," Jarlaxle said, to which Arathis Hune simply shrugged. "You know the identity of his opponent, yes?" Jarlaxle asked.

"I think him more than a street rogue."

"Yes. Perhaps one sent to get in a fight with Zaknafein."

Arathis Hune nodded—the thought had indeed crossed his mind. Zaknafein was well known in the Braeryn and few would dare challenge the weapon master unbidden.

"It was our former associate, Duvon Tr'arach," Jarlaxle told him.

"The weapon master of House Fey-Branche? Why would Matron Byrtyn . . . ?" He stopped as the answer came to him. Matron Byrtyn would certainly be happy with wounding the ambitious and climbing House Do'Urden, and really, even a hundred years later, did Duvon Tr'arach need a reason to try to kill the man who had almost single-handedly brought his family to ruin?

"He is more formidable than I remember," he said.

"Fine armor, fine weapons, fine training, and powerful enchantments will do that," Jarlaxle answered dryly.

"How did he know that Zaknafein would be in the tavern that particular night?"

"A good question. Who sent word of the arrival of our dear friend?"

"Dab'nay?"

"Maybe. But Zaknafein was a bit off his game that night," said Jarlaxle. "A bit too much fungus in his drink, I believe."

"So Harbondair?"

"Both?"

"And others, perhaps?" Arathis Hune said in a sly tone, hinting that he might suspect that Jarlaxle might suspect . . . him.

But Jarlaxle shrugged as if it did not matter. "It is the City of Spiders," Jarlaxle said. "Creatures who are known to kill after mating. Creatures who capture and torture victims to slow death. If Zaknafein cannot keep his guard appropriately high, he will be killed. For all of us, I say. That is the way."

Arathis Hune conceded the point.

"I am off to visit a matron," Jarlaxle went on. "You will go to the Oozing Myconid to check on the proceedings and begin shuffling the wagers? Keep it under two hundred gold pieces this night, and no wager more than five at a time."

"And a third of that more visibly wagered on the opponent?" Arathis Hune knew well the tactic. Quiet bets on the one Jarlaxle believed would win, louder bets on the presumed loser.

Arathis Hune mused that perhaps he would take some of those louder bets himself. He had too much to gain here to let this fortunate turn of events slip past—he had quietly built up enough associates to secretly filter the countering money anonymously. Even from Jarlaxle. For all of Jarlaxle's scheming, there would be a lot of gold wagered on Zaknafein Do'Urden in a battle against an unknown opponent, and perhaps even more among those who had figured out that the drow in question was Avinvesa Fey-Branche, formerly Duvon Tr'arach.

In a fair fight, the wager would be obvious.

This, however, would not be a fair fight.

Arathis Hune decided to make it less fair still. The opportunity to garner a small treasure shined too brightly, and even better, perhaps Arathis would be rid of Zaknafein once and for all.

Someone had tried to poison Zaknafein in the Oozing Myconid, not to kill him, but to slow him so that Duvon could do the deed. That had failed—of course it had failed! And it was a stupid attempt in the first place. Zaknafein was a true master of his craft as a warrior. How many hundreds of times had he poisoned himself in order to render his body immune to such parlor tricks?

No, poison wouldn't work on Zaknafein, nor would spells thrown secretly into the ring to defeat him.

But Arathis Hune thought of Quavylene Oblodra and wondered if he might have found an undetectable and effective way through the weapon master's precautions.

CHAPTER 4

Perfecting the Edges

The importance of these sudden movements kept Zaknafein practicing them over and over, a hundred times a day, every day. They were so simple, usually, and straightforward, and the gains in speed on the second turn so miniscule that many fighters paid only cursory attention.

But Zaknafein knew better. The fights sung by the bards were almost always drawn-out affairs, with great leaping pirouettes and counters to counters to counters, but the truth of staying alive was simpler, though perhaps unworthy of long verse: most fights were won or lost on the draw.

So he practiced.

He sent a small disk of a carved mushroom stalk spinning up in the air before him, relaxing himself fully as it lifted, closing his eyes until he heard the random flip hit the floor in front of him.

He opened his eyes. He looked. He found the image facing up on the disk, the left hand, so he moved suddenly, hands across his belly to grab the hilts of his swords at his hips, right forearm over left—it had to be that way to defeat the incoming attacker, as identified by the coin, and focus on countering her first, not the associate to the left.

Out came the swords in an eyeblink, rising and cutting across in a double-backhand parry. He turned his right wrist as that sword came across, bringing it vertical in its sweep, then shortening the cut, while the left went across perfectly horizontally, with full follow-through and even a step with the left foot in that direction. That left slash was designed to fend off any associates on the attack, the right was a shortened parry to deflect the thrusting attack aside and lead into a sudden reversal and thrust designed to kill.

To kill on the draw.

To be done with the fight before it had even really begun.

Three times did Zaknafein practice that draw, double parry, and thrust, right hand over left, then three times in reverse, left hand over right, left sword backing, shortening, and thrusting straight ahead.

Weapons sheathed, he retrieved the mushroom disk, shook out his neck and shoulders, and sent it spinning once more.

Then again after six more draws.

Basic movements, draws Zaknafein had executed thousands of times in his life.

From there, he went to a series of same-hand, same-hip draws, where he brought forth the sword on his left hip with his left hand, right hand for the right. This was typically a reverse draw technique, reversing the hand over the hilt, drawing and executing a flip of the blades as the elbows rolled under, creating a reverse pincer movement with the swords, crossing in the middle between the extending arms and cutting outward in a short and swift sweep. This movement was far more awkward than the first, but with repetition, endless repetition, the muscles could be trained to safely begin the turn of the blades as soon as the sword tips exited the scabbards.

Zaknafein had perfected three different executions of this technique, two to mirror the more usual cross-hand draw, one following through to the left and one to the right, but without the steps. And, if he was facing but one opponent, he would double parry with the reverse sweeps, shorten both, and thrust ahead with both following the sudden stop. He had become so skilled with this that he could even alter the angle of attack with those thrusts, every combination of putting the blades ahead, two high, two low, or one each way, alternatingly.

Few drow warriors would attempt this type of draw in a real fight. It was too easy to hook a tip in the scabbard or simply be too slow to defeat an attack by the time a parrying blade was on its way. Zaknafein, though, could execute it as smoothly as the more typical cross-hand draw, and he found the looks on the faces of his would-be killers quite amusing when he immediately defeated them in this manner.

He could almost hear them asking "*How?*" before falling over dead.

The blades came forth several times, spinning, parrying, thrusting, then snapping back into their respective scabbards.

Satisfied, Zaknafein nodded, wiped his sweaty hands on a nearby towel, and took a deep and steadying breath.

Now came the same-hand, same-hip draw, simply grabbing the hilts and lifting his arms up, drawing the swords fully downward for a double vertical block, tips facing the floor.

In this routine, that draw was a first move, only a first move, and after the block was initiated, one or both of the swords had to be moving quickly to a more normal, comfortable, and usable grip.

This was where Zaknafein could separate himself from almost all others in the opening moments of a fight. Drawing his swords in this manner was the fastest and cleanest extraction from the scabbards— there was no reversal of momentum—and so could be effective in the very last eyeblink to defeat an incoming thrust or cut.

This was also the hardest to improvise, the most limited in second movements, with both swords in a reversed grip.

Zaknafein had envisioned many ways to change that, though of course it was always easier to see it in his mind than to actually execute such a maneuver.

"A thousand times a thousand," he whispered to himself as he repeatedly tried his newest continuation of the draw. That was his mantra, a thousand times a thousand, reminding him that repetition trained muscles, and that there was no shortcut or substitute.

"A thousand times a thousand," he said when he lost control of his left-hand blade and it went flying out before him.

Undaunted, he gathered up the sword and replaced it in its scabbard, then took a deep breath and drew again, both swords.

With the right, he let go ever so slightly as it rose and came free, letting the weight of the blade drop it to be recaught with the same reversed grip, but now with his arm slicing down and back.

That was the easy part.

When he drew with his left hand, he grabbed the hilt only with his pointer and middle fingers wrapping above, his ring finger and little finger going back against the hilt nearer the crosspiece. Up went the blade and as it did, Zaknafein let go with his thumb and pressed with his lower two fingers, redirecting the momentum of the lift to send the blade spinning under and then up, then up and over and turning tip-down as he brought his hand back down behind his shoulder.

The sword blade began to sweep across to Zaknafein's right even as it stabbed downward, intending to parry an attack from the rear.

To an onlooker, it was a beautiful and swift movement, but Zaknafein growled in frustration, stopped short his final movements, and let the blade fly from his grasp out to the right and clank down to the floor.

He had not reestablished a strong enough grip on the sword to block the cut of a child, and that with three more movements necessary to complete the counterstrike routine.

Again.

JARLAXLE AND YOUNG DININ DO'URDEN CAME IN SIGHT OF Zaknafein, with the weapon master's back to them as he went through his practice routines in the house training room. His left arm up high, his sword swung through, tip-down across his back, and kept going up and around before him; his right-hand blade thrust backward suddenly, right behind the passing left-hand blade.

Jarlaxle held Dinin back and silent as he watched the weapon master finish, with Zaknafein tossing his left-hand blade to reverse his grip and back-thrust similarly as he retracted the right, then executing a rather awkward turn, coming around with a look of frustration clear on his face.

He noticed the visitors and stood up straight immediately.

"What are you doing here?"

"I came with business for Matron Malice," Jarlaxle answered, truthfully, "and decided to see how my friend fared in what might be the last days of his life."

That brought a smirk to Zaknafein's face. "Be gone, whelp," he told Dinin.

The young man, the younger son of Malice, straightened and sucked in his breath, obviously taking offense.

Zaknafein laughed at him.

Jarlaxle put his arm about the young Do'Urden's shoulders. "It is never wise to show your anger to he who made you angry," he whispered into Dinin's ear. "And less so still to do it when that person could cut you into pieces before that scowl even left your face."

"Matron Malice told me to escort you," Dinin argued.

"And so you have."

"I'll not leave you free rein of the house, rogue," Dinin said.

Jarlaxle slightly bowed, and he did respect the young one's courage (though he figured it would get Dinin killed). "Wait for me in the hall, then," he offered. "I would speak with my friend alone."

"Get out," Zaknafein added from over at the side wall, where he had collected a dry towel to wipe away his sweat.

Dinin moved back through the door, but didn't close it.

"How many imaginary foes did you just slay?" Jarlaxle asked, moving to his friend.

"None; I fear he is still alive."

Jarlaxle considered the movements he had seen. "Then you are dead," he reasoned.

"Sadly."

"Practicing your draw and strike techniques?"

Zaknafein nodded and wiped the towel over his face.

"You understand that you will both begin your fight with your blades in hand?" Jarlaxle asked.

"So?"

"You will not need to draw."

"And?"

"Do not be so obtuse. Why are you practicing something you will not need?"

"I need it often."

Jarlaxle started to sigh, but Zaknafein quickly continued, "Not in the fight two days hence, no, but do you really expect me to surrender my days of practice for the likes of Duvon Tr'arach? Should I also practice my running in case I am assailed by a sewer rat on my way to your play?"

"My play?"

"You should have simply let me kill him in the tavern, then and there."

"He is a weapon master of a powerful and long-standing house," Jarlaxle reminded. "What consequence for House Do'Urden if you had done that?"

"The same as after I kill him in the arranged battle," Zaknafein replied without hesitation.

"Not so," Jarlaxle answered, though he really wasn't sure what practical difference it might make. Either way, Duvon, or Avinvesa, seemed to be freelancing here, so his death at Zaknafein's hands, whether in a bar fight or an alley fight, could bring some troubling questions Matron Malice's way.

"You do not have to kill him," Jarlaxle added.

"Says the man who is not Duvon's target. He came to find me. He moved in order to incite an excuse to kill me, not you."

Jarlaxle had no reply to that. Instead, he said, "You would be dead, you know?" motioning his chin back toward the center of the room, where Zaknafein had been working on his drawing techniques. "The turn was awkward and too removed from the draw."

"Anything more than a second move is folly," Zaknafein dryly replied, reciting the mantra of Melee-Magthere regarding that most important beginning sequence of any close combat. The draw and a single follow were the rule of thumb. Draw and strike, nothing more, then go to an even posture with your attacker, who previously held the initiative.

"I counted a third and fourth, though that one failed. You are well beyond what is considered proper. The block, over your shoulder as it was, was brilliantly done, and the backward thrust would buy you time to disengage and come up square against whomever it was that tried to kill you. Why try to go beyond that when you are at such a disadvantage?"

"You would have me play the counter to even?"

"That is how you were taught."

"By warriors who would fall to me," Zaknafein said.

Jarlaxle conceded the point with a helpless laugh.

"Why are you here?" Zaknafein asked.

"I told you."

"You told me you had business with Matron Malice. Why are you here, in this room?"

"To greet an old friend?"

Zaknafein crossed his arms over his chest.

Jarlaxle glanced back at the opened door, then moved closer so that the eavesdropping young Dinin wouldn't see, and signed with his hand, *Do you need me to facilitate your release from House Do'Urden on the night of the fight?*

Only if you can do so without implicating yourself in that release, Zaknafein signed back.

Jarlaxle smiled too wryly.

Zaknafein didn't bother to ask.

SOON AFTER HE LEFT HOUSE DO'URDEN, BEFORE HE HAD even returned to the Clawrift, Jarlaxle was met by a Bregan D'aerthe courier who handed him a scroll.

Curious. After a magical examination to ensure that it was not trapped, he unrolled it to find a betting ledger on the upcoming fight, with a note from Arathis Hune informing him that all the seed money had already been claimed in wager.

Jarlaxle rolled the parchment and considered it. In less than half a day, all the bets on Zaknafein had been covered? Tr'arachs, he first figured. Dab'nay and Harbondair were not the only survivors of that house circulating within Jarlaxle's orbit. Certainly they all knew the true identity of Zaknafein's assailant and so would quietly cheer for Duvon to get revenge for what Zaknafein had done to their house that century before.

But would they bet on Duvon? They knew Duvon best, and so knew Duvon's limitations. Wanting someone to win and betting on that outcome were two very different things, after all.

"Tell him to seed half again more gold today, and another full amount tomorrow," Jarlaxle instructed the young courier. "Similar amounts regarded to each combatant."

The young man nodded and sprinted away.

Jarlaxle considered the parchment again, even opened it to see if the amounts of each bet listed could give him some clue as to who was thinking that Duvon—Avinvesa Fey-Branche—would win. His first certainty, of course, was that someone expected that she could influence the bout. In the first encounter, Zaknafein had battled some poison as well as Duvon, Jarlaxle was positive. So who would be able to do so again?

Or did any of these people actually believe that Duvon could defeat Zaknafein? Certainly Duvon would be superbly outfitted, and likely bolstered by magical enhancements to his body as well, but no matter how much they enhanced Duvon, could they hope it enough?

Would they also try to wound Zaknafein? Poison again? Magic? He would be guarded against all of that, of course.

Unless . . .

A hint of a smile—he would not laugh aloud when he suspected, as he always suspected, that spying eyes were upon him—creased Jarlaxle's lips as he considered someone else who might be very glad to see the fall of Zaknafein Do'Urden, and the unorthodox methods that might be available to that person to see that it was carried out.

Jarlaxle veered in his course, moving instead for the raised alcove of the great cavern known as Tier Breche, which housed the famed Academy of Menzoberranzan.

THE SWORD CAME AROUND OVER HIS RIGHT SHOULDER, rising as he swept it before him. He let go simply to reverse his grip and began his backward thrust as he turned.

Zaknafein stopped and snarled.

It was too awkward. The masters at Melee-Magthere had always taught the one-move mantra: in a sudden encounter, you had one move following a draw to make your attack, just one. After that, revert to a fighting stance and begin the formal combat.

The weapon master shook his head. He was so close here, not just to the second move, but the third and fourth as well, and with all of them stealing from his attacker any choice except retreat, and leaving that assailant vulnerable if she wasn't smart enough to immediately flee.

Too close.

But the balance was all wrong. He could get his left-hand blade around, could reverse and thrust, but that would accomplish nothing more than the initial thrust. It was a delaying tactic, designed to hold the fight static for one more eyeblink, one more turn.

He could not execute that turn successfully. It didn't work.

Zaknafein pondered the sword movements and his footwork. Perhaps if he added a step to the left . . .

"IT IS A RIDICULOUS PROPOSITION, EVEN FOR YOU," ARCH-mage Gromph Baenre answered Jarlaxle. The two sat in comfortable chairs before a blazing hearth in the chambers of the great wizard, an extradimensional mansion accessed through a secret closet in Gromph's mundane quarters in Sorcere, the drow school for wizards.

"But it can be done?"

Gromph sighed and sipped the fine—the *very* fine—liquor Jarlaxle had brought to him, the price Gromph demanded for any and every visit from the mercenary leader.

"Anything can be done," he replied. "Not everything *should* be done."

"Why should this not be done? It seems a rather minor dweomer, and of little consequence."

"Because it is not worth the trouble."

"It is simply a variation of a minor spell," Jarlaxle protested.

"Then do it yourself."

It was Jarlaxle's turn to sigh. "Why would I not ask the greatest mage in the city?"

"Should I then ask Jarlaxle when I need a rat exterminated?"

"If it is an extraordinary rat, I suppose," Jarlaxle replied, then slyly added, "or even a mundane one, if you were willing to pay Jarlaxle's fee."

Gromph snorted. "Tell me why, then."

"Because too many matrons know the properties from eye to eye."

"The Oblodrans, you mean," Gromph reasoned. "You continue to deal with those strange creatures?"

"They live in my attic, one might say."

"Then hire a rat-killer and be rid of them."

Jarlaxle arched his eyebrow at that remark, and Gromph shrugged and took another drink. Revealing his frustration, Jarlaxle knew, for even the mighty Gromph was unnerved by the foreign powers of Matron K'yorl Odran and her psionic clan.

"A spell wouldn't be of much use to you because of the time constraints. So you would have to cast it, and it would be no minor thing, as you claim. Unless, of course, you wish it to be permanent, and I warn you . . ."

"Oh no, not permanent," Jarlaxle interrupted. "Just a short duration."

"An alchemist would be a better choice than a wizard," Gromph explained. "You have heard of daylight oil?"

"Of course." In fact, Jarlaxle had used daylight oil, coating the small stones encased in ceramic balls, to break up the fight in the Oozing Myconid.

"Something akin to that, I believe," Gromph said. "A temporary dweomer once applied, one that sets in place upon the item and does not bleed onto anything it touches. Not as simple as you might think, but probably possible."

"I have fine alchemists," Jarlaxle remarked.

"And I have finer ones," Gromph said.

"But more expensive ones."

"You are paying my fee either way, rogue," the archmage said. "It was my idea."

Jarlaxle nodded and tipped his glass toward Gromph. "When?"

"When do you need it?"

"Two days."

"Double the fee."

Jarlaxle started to argue, but bit it back and nodded. He thought to offer Gromph the usual fee and tell the archmage how he could easily double it himself, but then deferred, not really wanting to involve any Baenres in this little fight he had arranged. Perhaps he would just bet that fee additionally himself.

Either way, it didn't matter. He would gain a useful item, salvage a useful ally, and make plenty of gold in the process.

CHAPTER 5

Fair and Not Square

Wearing an eyepatch that did nothing more than hinder his vision in one eye, Jarlaxle watched from afar, well past the appointed time. Growing anxious, he went into the Oozing Myconid to find an equally anxious Arathis Hune leaning on the bar, rolling an empty glass in his hand.

"Where is he?" the assassin asked Jarlaxle when he sidled up beside him.

"The opponent is out back in the alleyway."

"With a score of onlookers, and another hundred watching from nearby windows, and hundreds more awaiting the information from those appointed watchers."

"It's been a while since the last fight between such impressive combatants, for I suspect that word has leaked that Zaknafein's opponent is in fact the weapon master of House Fey-Branche."

"There have been whispers," Arathis Hune quietly confirmed.

Jarlaxle couldn't help but smile as he motioned to barkeep Harbondair for a glass of his favorite liquor. He had more than six hundred pieces of gold spread out among the streets, almost none in his own name, and the expected return would be almost nine hundred, he believed, since the odds had surprisingly shifted closer. In truth, Jarlaxle hadn't even expected to find many takers for his bets on Zaknafein, for who would bet against Zaknafein Do'Urden unless the opponent was Uthegentel Armgo, or perhaps Dantrag Baenre?

"He's out in the alleyway, no doubt pacing nervously," Jarlaxle said.

"No doubt."

"Expending his energy. Making his limbs heavier by the step . . ."

"You think this a tactic?" Arathis Hune asked. "More likely Matron Malice wouldn't let her toy soldier come out and play."

"She will let him out this night," Jarlaxle assured him. As he took a sip of his drink, Jarlaxle caught the man staring at him with obvious suspicion.

Where is your eyepatch? Hune's fingers signed.

"On my head," Jarlaxle replied aloud, drawing a skeptical stare from his associate.

Jarlaxle turned a bit to better display the back strap of the eyepatch, which was still visible, though the rest of the magical item was not.

Arathis Hune's expression turned curious indeed.

"Our Oblodran friends have come to discern which eye grants me protection from their intrusions, and which allows me the power of true-seeing," Jarlaxle explained. "Better that they do not see the item, or if they do realize that I am covertly wearing it, better that they do not easily discern which eye it is covering. They are grand with their mind magics, indeed, but not so much, not even their house wizard, with more mundane magic.

"Like seeing invisible things."

A bell chimed at the back of the bar, and Harbondair rushed to a specific point in the wine rack, removing a bottle and putting his ear to the opening for just a moment.

"Zaknafein Do'Urden approaches," he informed Jarlaxle and Arathis Hune. Jarlaxle upended his glass in one great swallow, and

Arathis Hune slid his empty glass back across the bar, turning to leave with the mercenary leader.

"How is this possible?" Arathis Hune asked. "I have never heard of such a thing."

"I know formidable wizards—the most formidable—and peerless alchemists," Jarlaxle replied. "And I have gold. It is amazing what magical or alchemical creations one might inspire with gold."

Arathis Hune blew a deep breath. "But why leave the strap visible at all?" he asked, seeming at a loss.

Jarlaxle shrugged and chuckled. "It wasn't visible when I first enchanted the item with the vanishing salve, but I dropped it, and it took me a long while to find it!"

"Vanishing salve?" Arathis Hune echoed, but then just stared blankly at his boss, finally shaking his head helplessly in surrender.

Just as Jarlaxle wanted it.

ZAKNAFEIN RAISED HIS HAND TO HIS EAR AND FLIPPED THE band over the top of it, as it had slipped down when he adjusted the item and begun pinching him just a bit. It was nothing serious, of course, just a leather tie, but any crimp, any bustle, any distraction at all at this particular time was indeed a big deal to the weapon master.

Everything had to be perfect. *He* had to be perfect.

There could be no distractions, and this gift from Jarlaxle, even properly adjusted, was distracting him.

He wanted to reach up, pull it off, and tuck it away.

But he didn't. For all of his complaining about the mercenary, Zaknafein had to admit—though only to himself—that even as he had come to quite enjoy the company of Jarlaxle, he had come to trust him more.

He closed his eyes for a few strides and composed himself, playing out his practice sessions in his thoughts, gathering his muscle memory. He felt as though he might vomit, and to him, that was a good thing.

He was on edge.

He was ready for battle.

Many eyes were upon him, he knew, before he even came around the back corner of the Oozing Myconid. Drow, many nobles among them, lined the alleyway before him, both sides, some high up on the walls of the tavern, some on the roof, peering over. The building across the way had been fashioned from a stalagmite mound, like most drow structures, offering many natural seats along its uneven wall, all of which were filled with onlookers.

He saw his opponent, Duvon—still in disguise—standing down the way, beyond another drow, a woman he did not know, but one who was commanding great attention. She lifted her right hand up high, pinching her middle finger to her palm with her thumb and showing the gap between her ring and index fingers. She moved it down to within a hand's width of her face and peered through to the southwest.

Glancing that way, Zaknafein understood. She was indicating the distant towering obelisk of Narbondel, the magical timeclock of Menzoberranzan, one that measured the days with its glow, climbing to the apex from the floor, midnight to noon, then diminishing back down the great pillar as the day grew long. The indicated distance between her straightened fingers showed how much time, how much of the glow, she would allow to dissipate before calling for an end to the betting.

And indeed, the coin began to flow all about that alley behind the tavern.

Zaknafein wondered if he might look unsure, perhaps bluffing so that those betting on him in these waning moments might find better odds.

He looked down the alleyway to his opponent, though, and found that he couldn't begin to muster such a facade. There stood Duvon, who had tried to murder him, who had arranged for poison in Zaknafein's drink, thinking the mushroom drug would slow the weapon master enough for him to make a quick and clean kill.

Whatever sympathy Zaknafein might feel, whatever kinship he might hold for the other male drow could not push through that truth.

Zaknafein walked to the near end of the alley, and there waited.

Another drow, a woman whose name Zaknafein did not know but who was often seen about the Stenchstreets, came out of an alcove to the side, holding a thin blue wand.

She held up her hand for silence, and indeed, the onlookers quieted.

"Coins away!" she declared. "No wager beyond this moment will be enforced by the rules of Braeryn."

Zaknafein heard jingling to the sides, and in the windows above, the last bets covered. He had heard of these organized fights, but had never witnessed one. He now understood, though, that this woman standing between him and Duvon held great power in the Stenchstreets, to so calm an always unruly crowd.

"Who called this fight?" she asked.

"I did, good lady," said Jarlaxle, coming out of the shadows to the right side of the alleyway, through the back door of the Oozing Myconid.

"And these are the principals?" she asked, indicating Zaknafein, then Duvon.

"They are," Jarlaxle answered.

"You are sure?"

"I am."

"And they are known by the names of?"

"Zaknafein is known in the Braeryn," Jarlaxle replied. "And of this other fellow . . ." He paused and looked at Duvon, who narrowed his eyes in reply. "We shall call him Blue, as he has not offered any name."

Zaknafein heard whispers of "Avinvesa Fey-Branche," and even "Duvon Tr'arach," all about. Others even mentioned that Jarlaxle surely knew this fellow.

Perhaps Jarlaxle was not as clever as he believed, Zaknafein mused. If the bettors knew that Jarlaxle was intimately familiar with both fighters, then how would he make his bets?

Zaknafein didn't even allow his thoughts to go down that certainly winding road. He hadn't the time or energy for any of that. Jarlaxle seemed quite pleased at this time, though that, too, offered only conflicting theories and concerns to Zaknafein.

"Blue?" the woman asked.

"A name is only important in ensuring the intent of the wager," Jarlaxle interrupted. "Zaknafein is known. The other is irrelevant."

"Will he still be irrelevant when Zaknafein lies dead, I wonder?" another voice intervened, that of Duvon himself.

That brought a smile to Zaknafein's face.

"Coins away!" the woman cried once more. "And approach, warriors, to five strides."

Zaknafein's stare never left Duvon, and was reciprocated every step, as he walked to a distance of about five strides to the woman officiating, Duvon opposite him a similar distance away from the officiant.

"What weapons you have are your own," the woman said. "What armor you wear is your own. What tricks you might play are your own, except . . ."

She paused and looked to Jarlaxle.

"Warriors, both," he said.

"Then no dweomers cast," she declared, "beyond the enchantments already upon your gear, and your noble abilities. Are we agreed?"

Zaknafein's hands rolled about the hilts of his swords, weapons he and Jarlaxle had long ago stolen from the treasury of House Barrison Del'Armgo. Fine weapons, and probably at least as good as those Duvon was now wearing. The combatants were very likely similarly outfitted, he believed.

"Agreed," the warriors said, nearly in unison.

The woman pointed her wand at Zaknafein then and uttered a command word. The weapon master felt a small blast of wind, a wave of disenchantment. Any spells that had been cast on him, of protection or enhancement of strength or speed or agility, would not survive that nullifying enchantment.

She turned and similarly disenchanted Duvon, then lifted a large and clear crystal orb for all to see.

"Should any dweomers fall upon these opponents, or within the alleyway, I will know," she promised.

Zaknafein just wanted to be done with this and on with the fight, but he supposed that this was about as "fair" a battle as any drow could manage in the City of Spiders.

Except that he was certain it wasn't going to be fair, and hoped that his opponent didn't know that he knew. He had no idea of how Duvon's allies might get a spell through to him, but Jarlaxle had given him the warning, and the eyepatch, for some reason.

The weapon master wanted to spit in disgust. He would have preferred a fight in an unremarkable chamber, with equal gear, or no gear, and no onlookers. A fight based on skill alone, his against Duvon's, and let the better warrior win.

No matter, he decided, and grasped his swords. That would happen regardless.

"To surrender or to death," the woman called as she moved toward her alcove, and the crowd backed away as much as they could. "Have at it!"

Zaknafein found himself engulfed in magical darkness even as the words left her mouth. A perfectly legal attack by the rules of the fight, since it was an innate noble ability, but having Duvon throw it so immediately did surprise the weapon master.

Duvon was charging him, he knew, the lesser fighter going for the quick kill. The risks seemed enormous to Zaknafein, his mind spinning through all the possible plays here. Could Duvon correctly guess Zaknafein's responding move and so approach correctly?

If Zaknafein went left or right and Duvon guessed opposite, his darkness would be foolishly wasted. If Zaknafein came forward and Duvon was thinking otherwise, his own darkness would work against him, perhaps catastrophically.

It was a riddle that might have ensnared a less seasoned warrior, or even a veteran who could not process the changes of a battlefield with the clarity or speed of Zaknafein Do'Urden. For Zaknafein immediately understood the risks before Duvon for leading with a summoned globe of darkness, a tactic most commonly used by a drow battling another drow only in desperation, a moment of a missed parry or thrust, in order to bring the battlefield back to even ground. Few were the drow who could not fight well in absolute darkness, after all.

Duvon would not go left, and he wouldn't go right, nor would he come straight ahead, for any of those choices might gain him a bit of an advantage if he guessed right, but could lead to utter catastrophe if he guessed wrong.

No, he had thrown the darkness to throw his entire repertoire of tricks into one sudden killing move.

Zaknafein couldn't see him, but Zaknafein knew where he was.

So Zaknafein readied himself and his swords and then didn't move.

Nor did he make a sound.

He waited, because he understood Duvon's play, and realized that the House Fey-Branche weapon master was now above him. Duvon had levitated, that second drow noble ability. He couldn't fly and couldn't continue any ascent, instead simply going weightless and leaping into the air, floating upward to the end of his enchantment.

Or until he had caught a ledge on which he could wait.

He was up there, waiting to see where Zaknafein would appear, that he might leap down from on high.

Zaknafein waited.

Zaknafein threw his own globe of darkness just ahead, hoping to overlap the two and further confuse Duvon.

And Zaknafein waited, perfectly still, listening. He was using no energy here, but his opponent, up high, had to have a precarious perch. It wouldn't last much longer.

He heard the slight scraping of a boot on stone up above, and then he leaped, levitating, up and back to the right, swords working overhead and forward in case Duvon came too close.

Zaknafein exited the top of the darkness globe just as Duvon entered, some few feet before him, just out of reach—of the swords, at least, for both combatants reached into their magical abilities and limned each other with harmless faerie fire, Zaknafein's purple, Duvon's blue. Zaknafein hit the lip of the Oozing Myconid's roof and threw himself back the way he had come, back into the globe, landing with a flurry of blows, most hitting nothing until one, then a second, struck a sword coming at him the other way.

WATCHING FROM THE SIDE, JARLAXLE SILENTLY APPLAUDED Duvon's courage and cleverness, but he was not surprised at all to see Zaknafein quickly and methodically counter. Now the battle had begun in earnest, deep within the magical darkness, swords ringing together with bangs and scrapes.

The onlookers gasped and cheered; some complained that they could not witness the swordplay.

That was a loss, Jarlaxle knew from the sheer speed of the ringing blades. Furiously the two battled, each playing through known routines, adapting and switching in an attempt to catch the other off guard.

Duvon couldn't win here, Jarlaxle felt certain. He could not beat Zaknafein in the darkness, or even in the light—but in the light, at least, Duvon likely had another devious trick to play.

Jarlaxle focused on the sounds, on the continuing direction. Zaknafein was advancing, Duvon retreating.

Now Jarlaxle understood why Zaknafein had thrown the second globe—the darkness was his ally against Duvon's as-yet unknown assistance! Zaknafein meant to finish Duvon before the magic darkness faded.

But now Duvon fully retreated into the second globe, moving through it toward the light. Finally he tumbled out of the far side, to the cheers of those gathered deeper in the alleyway.

Duvon's fabulous armor was visible now, Jarlaxle saw, for Zaknafein had cut the man's outer cloak and shirt apart. And first blood, or at least the most spilled blood, belonged to the blades of Zaknafein, who had snuck more than one cut past Duvon's defenses in the darkness.

Jarlaxle nodded in appreciation, though, when Zaknafein emerged, for Duvon had scored a hit, too.

"You have improved," Jarlaxle congratulated the former son of House Tr'arach under his breath. He considered House Fey-Branche and when Matron Byrtyn might be done with Duvon. Perhaps this one might again prove valuable to him. "I hope Zaknafein doesn't kill you."

ZAKNAFEIN MEASURED HIS THRUSTS AND KEPT HIS SIDE-long cuts short, his swords always in position to defend. Something unusual was coming, he knew. Duvon had taken a great chance in utilizing both his darkness and his levitation in that initial attempt to end it.

But now, with those tricks failing and already put back on his heels, Duvon was not panicking, and his expression showed him to be perturbed, not alarmed.

He had wanted to defeat Zaknafein on his own, by cleverness and boldness alone.

But that didn't mean that he thought he was now in danger of losing.

And he should think that, Zaknafein knew. Both of Zaknafein's swords thrust ahead, then retracted so quickly that Duvon missed them in his parry. Back in for Duvon's torso came those swords, parallel only initially, then each angling out to send them in wide. Thus the left-hand blade picked off the attempted powerful slash of Duvon's right-hand blade, a sweeping parry that the Fey-Branche weapon master obviously hoped would move both swords harmlessly aside. His second blade was lifting to come in over his parry, and Duvon had to leap back and throw the blade down fast before him simply to avoid Zaknafein's thrust.

He still got hit—painfully, if his yelp was any indication—on the left hip.

Duvon continued back another step and flung himself around to his right, thinking to turn a full circuit to come up balanced ahead and to the side.

But Zaknafein was too quick for that, and his pursuit forced Duvon to break his circuit halfway around, then simply sprint away for the natural wall of the stalagmite bordering the alley. Up he went with surprising grace and speed, just ahead of Zaknafein's blades. He leaped and somersaulted, a move that would have normally deposited him back on the ground behind Zaknafein. Not this time, though, as Duvon used his own waving blades to feign that he meant to travel such a distance, but cut short his backward spring, instead coming down at the same spot from which he had leaped, only facing his opponent now.

Zaknafein did get in a stinging hit across Duvon's shin, the drow's armor saving him from too serious a wound.

But Duvon fell into rhythm quickly, his blades working down low, defending. Zaknafein, though holding the low ground, played along, for he had the initiative here, had Duvon moving frantically side to side, had him working his blades from an awkward bend.

Finally, Duvon managed to go even higher on the stalagmite, and Zaknafein started up.

Only a step, though, and from there he pushed off and backflipped, landing toward the middle of the alleyway, facing his opponent and motioning for Duvon to come on.

Duvon glanced to the side, just briefly, but Zaknafein caught it.

Duvon leaped out at him from on high. Zaknafein felt a tickle, like a feather somehow passing harmlessly through his forehead.

That was all.

Just as Jarlaxle had promised.

Zaknafein stood very straight, blinking absently, his swords lowering.

Duvon bore down on him, swords working in circles at either side, back and up, over and down. He ended that furious rhythm perfectly as he closed the last steps, the blades coming over, halting in perfect alignment, and diving for the chest of the helpless Zaknafein. The weapon master of House Fey-Branche, the former elderboy and weapon master of House Tr'arach, cried out in victory . . .

Too soon.

For Zaknafein was not there, so suddenly, and Duvon's swords stabbed the empty air.

And a leg cracked across the front of his leading ankle, and a second leg came scissoring in hard against the back of his trailing knee, then his leading knee, too, as his legs came together.

Duvon pitched headlong to the alleyway, bouncing, then rolling about and turning, desperately coming up to his knees, facing back, weapons slashing to fend off the expected approach.

But again, Zaknafein was simply not there, not in line with Duvon's defense, at least.

No, he was up in the air, a great leap and turn, his swords presented before his chest, tips straight down. He landed behind Duvon, just behind, and kept falling, his weight driving those swords straight down, the momentum and strength of Zaknafein battling the fine armor. On the right side of Duvon's head, the sword tip was turned, but still gashed Duvon, collar to breast.

The sword on the left side caught more fully, and Zaknafein was quick to adjust his weight to drive it down, finally pushing it through the stubborn armor and into the soft flesh at the hollow of Duvon's collarbone.

Down slid the blades, a bright line of red showing on the doomed drow's right breast, blood fountaining from the wound in the left.

The onlookers screamed, cheered, yelled denials for lost bets, and above them all, Zaknafein heard the voice of Jarlaxle: "Bah!"

CHAPTER 6

Squaring Up

H e surrenders!" priestess Dab'nay yelled, rushing forward from the alley wall and already beginning to cast a spell of healing.

Zaknafein turned to regard her and smiled wickedly. His blade had cut Duvon's artery, clearly, although that would not likely prove fatal with a powerful cleric at hand. But Duvon was helpless to defend, and the tip of that sword was already at the man's lung, Zaknafein knew, and with only a slight press, he could drive it right through and down to Duvon's heart, killing him before any spell could help.

He gave a little press, and Duvon gasped.

Dab'nay skidded to a stop, and stopped too her spellcasting. "No, please, I beg," she implored Zaknafein. "He will not challenge you again. You have won. I pledge my fealty! Please." She inched forward.

Zaknafein stared at her, then snapped his free right-hand sword up suddenly, the tip coming in against Dab'nay's soft throat.

"Perhaps I should kill you instead," he said, and added with venom, "priestess."

She swallowed hard, but did not reply.

"Perhaps both," Zaknafein said.

Dab'nay merely shrugged, thoroughly defeated.

Zaknafein pulled the sword out of Duvon, who toppled over, the blood still flying from the wound. He lifted Dab'nay's chin with his other sword, smiling.

"Your loyalty is unusual," he said, "and unexpected."

Dab'nay said nothing.

"And your word is meaningless," said Zaknafein.

"Mine, then?" asked another, Jarlaxle walking over.

Zaknafein lowered his sword. "Try your spell," he told Dab'nay, the sword still dangerously close. "I dare you."

She stared at him hard, but began to recite her spell, stubbornly.

Zaknafein laughed at her.

Jarlaxle held his breath—this was a priestess of Lolth accepting the dare of Zaknafein, who loved nothing more than killing priestesses of Lolth!

"Zaknafein," he said, and when the weapon master glanced at him, he subtly shook his head, begging restraint.

Zaknafein flashed that smile, one promising that this was not over, but walked away.

JARLAXLE GOT THE WEAPON MASTER BACK IN HIS SIGHT almost halfway across the city. He slowed his approach and faded down one alleyway, though, when he realized that other eyes were on Zaknafein, and on him, at that time.

He figured it to be the handiwork of Matron Byrtyn Fey, perhaps ensuring that Zaknafein did not return to Matron Malice, whatever the outcome of the duel. He sprinted to the end of the alley and threw his portable hole out before him, then rushed through the opening and pulled the magical item out behind him, solidifying the wall once more. He was in a training gym, where only a pair of warriors stood in a face-off, though both were now looking incredulously at him.

He flipped them a jaunty salute, and then was across the gym, deploying the portable hole again, disappearing out the other side.

On and on he ran, cutting corners by moving through walls, surprising many, until he at last came out on the main street out of the Braeryn.

Where Zaknafein came strolling around a corner before him.

"What?" the weapon master asked, initially startled. But this was Jarlaxle, after all, and Zaknafein calmed quickly, a stark admission that he should not be surprised.

"Quick, follow," Jarlaxle said, and he threw the magical hole against the same wall he had just exited and moved for it, waving for Zaknafein to follow.

Zaknafein did not.

"Quickly!" Jarlaxle harshly whispered. "You are in danger."

Zaknafein crossed his arms over his chest but did not approach. Behind him, atop a low roof, Jarlaxle saw some movement, a hand crossbow raising before a drow sniper.

"Down! Down!" Jarlaxle cried, and he took a fast step and threw himself back through the hole, taking cover.

"Are you okay, weapon master?" Jarlaxle heard from the rooftop.

"He is," said yet another. "That is just Jarlaxle, as expected."

Confused, Jarlaxle peeked above the rim of the magical hole. There stood Zaknafein, arms still crossed over his chest, a hint of a smile stamped upon his face. Behind him, the drow had lowered the hand crossbow and watched closely.

Jarlaxle stood up and stepped back through the hole, then pulled the magical item from the wall, closing the opening.

"You think I would be foolish enough to come out alone this night?" Zaknafein asked him.

"These are Do'Urdens?"

"Of course."

Clever Zaknafein, Jarlaxle thought, but did not say—he didn't want to give Zaknafein an even bigger ego than he surely had after the fight. He started to smile, but could not hold it when he noted another Do'Urden, Malice's rather nasty and vicious daughter Briza, moving toward them from the side. He felt very vulnerable then, and even naked, for a priestess could use spells to see into his thoughts or detect if he was lying, and he wasn't wearing his magical eyepatch, but this imposter piece of normal leather instead!

Your head is itchy, Jarlaxle's fingers subtly flashed to Zaknafein.

"What?"

Itchy! Jarlaxle signaled more vehemently.

Zaknafein chuckled, but he did reach up to scratch the side of his head. And in that movement, he secretly slipped the eyepatch off his head, taking care to conceal the only visible part, the back band, within his closed fist. He brought the arm down between himself and Jarlaxle and dropped the item, which Jarlaxle caught.

With a subtle movement, Jarlaxle dipped the magical eyepatch into a secondary belt pouch, one he had filled with a disenchanting liquid that removed the magical invisibility salve from the item.

Priestess Briza neared, and Jarlaxle dropped a low and graceful bow, using the movement to lift his hand to his face, where he seemed to adjust his eyepatch to his other eye, as he was known to often do. Using quick hands and dipping even lower as a distraction, he actually replaced the benign covering entirely with the magical one.

"Matron Malice will speak with you," the brutish eldest daughter and first priestess of House Do'Urden told Jarlaxle when she arrived before him and the weapon master. "I think her not pleased."

She stared at him curiously then, and Jarlaxle suspected that she was trying to use some probing spell on him.

"From all that I am told, Matron Malice is only pleased in certain moments," he replied.

Briza's face tightened at the obvious reference to Malice's sexual appetite. "Men have been killed for less biting words," she reminded.

Jarlaxle merely smiled and replied, "Inform her that I will come to visit soon." He gave another polite bow and started to turn as if to leave, but found drow soldiers coming at him from every direction.

"You can tell her that yourself," Briza replied, and off they went.

"Did you really believe that you could put Matron Malice's valuable weapon master in such peril without evoking her anger?" Briza asked the mercenary leader as they walked along toward the cavern's West Wall, which held House Do'Urden.

"It was against Avinvesa Fey-Branche," Jarlaxle replied. "Do you think that Zaknafein was ever really in danger?"

"Many of the onlookers were agents of House Do'Urden," said Briza. "So, no, we would not allow that."

And many of the others were agents of House Fey-Branche, which is more powerful than House Do'Urden, Jarlaxle thought, but again did not say.

It was all such a silly game, these house rivalries and wasteful animosity, but at least Jarlaxle could usually find a way to make some gain in the battles. He just needed to figure out how to do so with Matron Malice this time.

"YOU HAVE ALREADY COLLECTED THE COIN?" MATRON MA-lice Do'Urden asked Jarlaxle when he placed a hefty bag of silver and gold at the foot of her grand seat in the throne room of House Do'Urden.

"Oh, hardly," he replied. "But it would not do to make a matron wait for her gains."

"Wise choice."

"One taught to me since I was old enough to understand who was on the other side of a snake-headed scourge," Jarlaxle replied, and bowed low.

Malice snorted but let it go. "I took a great risk in allowing my weapon master to leave the house for this little game you arranged," she said.

"Not so great," Jarlaxle assured her, but paused and rethought his direction here when she scowled at him.

"It is true that there was danger, yes," he said instead. "But I watched closely, and really, Zaknafein could not lose to the inferior weapon master of House Fey-Branche as long as there was no untoward outside influence. And I assure you, as I did when we made this . . ."

side arrangement, that I had many agents guarding against that possibility. The bet was better than the offered odds."

"Two-to-three?" she asked.

Jarlaxle stiffened a bit and shrugged. "They actually moved closer to three-to-four," he admitted.

"Unacceptable," Matron Malice replied, too calmly.

"I cannot control—"

"Unacceptable, given the risk that House Do'Urden took to allow this."

Jarlaxle nodded. "I know, Matron." He gave a sly little smile. "You will find in that sack that I covered you at one-to-one."

He caught her off guard, he realized when she sat up straight and seemed for a moment like she might topple from her throne. Which was Jarlaxle's whole point in lying to her, after all. The odds really hadn't changed as he had said, and in fact had moved closer to even, but Jarlaxle was buying goodwill here, and Matron Malice wouldn't waste her resources digging into the murk to see what odds might have been offered at the time one of Jarlaxle's unannounced agents had secretly placed her rather substantial bets.

"Matron Byrtyn's weapon master is dead?" Malice asked.

"He lived, I believe. At least, a priestess was tending him when I left him, and his wound seemed to be diminishing."

Malice let out a little growl.

"It would not have mattered," Jarlaxle quickly added, not wanting her to run down a tangent issue here. "Avinvesa will not serve Matron Byrtyn in that capacity for much longer, in any case. He is merely keeping the sword handles warm for a proper Fey-Branche noble."

"She will still retain a fine blade."

Jarlaxle shrugged, then shook his head. "If she doesn't kill him, I will buy him out of her house, I think. No doubt Matron Byrtyn lost a considerable amount of coin on this fight and so she will have little use for Avinvesa going forward."

That seemed to mollify the vicious little matron a bit, Jarlaxle was glad to note. Once again, he had to hope that Malice wouldn't take it upon herself to check the veracity of his assertion—or at least, that he had created enough plausible deniability so that his erroneous claim could be construed merely as a mistaken, though logical, assumption.

"This could have ended badly for Zaknafein, and so, for you," Malice said.

Jarlaxle shrugged. "Not too badly for me, altogether."

"You would have surrendered your band to another. I had your word. Matron Mother Baenre would not side with you."

Jarlaxle gave a little laugh. "Dear Matron Malice, if Zaknafein had fallen, I assure you that I would have lived up to our bargain to serve House Do'Urden as its weapon master. I do not wish that, no, but I thought it an easy concession to offer you, since I knew that Zaknafein could not lose. He is magnificent—I don't know that I would bet against him no matter his drow opponent."

He had hoped to lighten the mood with his sincere approval and assessment of Zaknafein, but Malice's scowl only deepened.

"You do not wish that?" she echoed in low and threatening tones.

Jarlaxle stood confused for a moment, until he realized that Matron Malice wasn't talking about Zaknafein's formal role here, but rather, he gathered, other services Zaknafein provided.

"Only the weapon master part," he blurted inelegantly.

"You will prove that," Malice replied, sounding very much like a cat with a cornered mouse.

Jarlaxle wanted to shrug, but was wise enough to keep anything that might be construed as ambivalence out of his voice or posture at that delicate moment. He couldn't deny that this woman before him was alluring, even more so given her reputation, but neither could he dismiss that Zaknafein was his friend. It didn't much matter, he supposed, because he was indeed a cornered mouse.

"Truly, Matron?" he asked brightly, eagerly. "You would so honor me?"

Her eyes never leaving the mercenary, Matron Malice began to undo her robes.

A DISHEVELED AND EXHAUSTED JARLAXLE—MALICE'S REP-
utation was not exaggerated, he had learned at last—arrived at the
court of Matron Byrtyn Fey some time later, dropping before her
throne a bag of gold and silver nearly as large as the one he had given
to Matron Malice.

He had told Malice that Byrtyn would be upset at her weapon
master's failure because she likely had lost considerable money on the
fight, but the truth was quite the opposite. Heeding Jarlaxle's advice,
Matron Byrtyn had bet quite heavily against her own combatant.

She had done so sourly, however, and still was not thrilled with
the outcome of the battle—but her anger was not directed toward Jarlaxle, who had begged her to hedge any losses in stature or in the position of weapon master by taking advantage of the probable outcome.

Especially when Jarlaxle had promised to cover her losses if Avinvesa had somehow prevailed.

"I have already begun the whispers that the fight was not fair,"
Jarlaxle assured her. "Some strange force was used to stun Avinvesa
Fey-Branche and that Oblodran agents were seen near to the Oozing
Myconid."

"Those rumors will gather no real credibility."

"They do not have to," Jarlaxle replied. "A seed of doubt is enough
for House Fey-Branche to avoid any fall of reputation. That seed is being planted all about Menzoberranzan, as we agreed."

"You should have let him die," Matron Byrtyn said with obvious
disgust.

"I, too, am amazed that his sister from House Tr'arach maintained
enough loyalty to him to bother with spells of healing," he lied. He was
doing that—lying—quite a bit this day, and to quite powerful women.
How glad Jarlaxle was that he had regained his magical eyepatch!

"He is an embarrassment to my house," Byrtyn said.

Jarlaxle pulled another bag of gold from his magical belt pouch, a
marvelous satchel that could hold a roomful of goods. He held it up
and gave it a little shake.

"Then sell him back to me. Same price as you paid for him."

Matron Byrtyn cocked her head at that. "You did quite well in your betting this day," she said.

Jarlaxle didn't deny it.

"Enough so that perhaps Jarlaxle made sure that he could not lose, yes?"

The mercenary swallowed hard. "I did nothing to impinge upon the rules of the fight," he stated flatly. "And I would say that under your divining eye."

She motioned for him to remove his eyepatch and began casting a spell. Jarlaxle did so but couldn't help but sigh as he moved to obey. The matrons were all coming to understand the powers of that magical eyepatch, and he feared that this might be a request—nay, a command—he would hear often in the future.

A few heartbeats later, Byrtyn Fey went silent and looked at him directly and intently.

"I did nothing to impinge upon the rules of the fight," he restated with confidence.

She motioned for him to expand.

"Nor did any of those under my control."

The matron stared at him a while longer, her expression skeptical. But Jarlaxle hadn't lied—for once today. All that he had done was provide a defense to Zaknafein against a cheat, which, in itself, surely wasn't cheating.

Matron Byrtyn finally gave a slight nod, though she hardly seemed satisfied, and Jarlaxle replaced his eyepatch.

"You play dangerous games, Jarlaxle," she remarked.

"The dangerous ones are the most profitable."

"One mistake will be the end of you," she promised.

"More reason to take great care, then."

Matron Byrtyn Fey was a devout Lolthian, her house one of the oldest and most respected in the city. But her smile gave it away to Jarlaxle at that time: though she was sneering at him now, she loved his games. The intrigue, the risk-taking, the ultimate stakes, the chaos. Yes, the chaos. She saw Jarlaxle as an agent of chaos, and no matron could give a higher compliment to any drow, particularly a male drow, than that.

It was in that very moment that Jarlaxle first realized the true potential here for Bregan D'aerthe, a band he had created simply out of self-preservation. Now he was beginning to fully appreciate the evolution of his gambit. The matrons, powerful matrons, knew about his eyepatch yet rarely ordered him to remove it in their presence. Matron Malice had trusted him at incredible risk—losing Zaknafein would have crippled her ambitions.

Or it would not have, if she believed Jarlaxle equally worthy, and that, too, was a startling admission from her.

Jarlaxle was still playing mostly in the Braeryn, the Stenchstreets, but he was bringing the most powerful women of Menzoberranzan, the most powerful drow in the entire Underdark, to his games.

"I will keep him," Matron Byrtyn announced suddenly, startling Jarlaxle from his contemplations.

"Matron?" Jarlaxle really didn't know who she was talking about in that moment, so overwhelmed was he with his epiphany.

"I will keep him."

Avinvesa, Jarlaxle realized.

"For now," Matron Byrtyn continued. "Until I have confirmed the particulars of the fight with more reliable informants."

"Of course," Jarlaxle said with a low bow. "And then?" he dared ask when he came back up straight.

"I will kill him, or put him to guard the wall for the rest of his miserable existence."

Jarlaxle shook the bag of gold.

"Dear Jarlaxle, you remind me that you are, after all, a simple male," she said. "How would it appear for the dignified House Fey-Branche to sell him back to you and so be inextricably tied to a band of houseless rogues?"

"I will purchase him when next I have a mission from Matron Mother Baenre to the City of Shimmering Webs," Jarlaxle answered without hesitation. "A journey to Ched Nasad will remove Duvon Tr'arach from Menzoberranzan for nearly a year, at least, and when he returns, who will know that he left on that same caravan, or that he was not in Ched Nasad for all these years?"

"His living siblings who serve in your very band will know."

"And they will say nothing to keep from losing their tongues most horribly," Jarlaxle replied. "And truly, Matron Byrtyn, in a year, who would even care, especially since your own position will have been filled for that year with a proper Fey-Branche noble son?"

Matron Byrtyn smirked but said nothing and motioned to the door, dismissing the rogue.

Jarlaxle was happy to be out of there, since he was certain then that he would indeed be able to buy back Duvon Tr'arach from Matron Byrtyn for a similar price to the one she had paid for the fighter. Only now Duvon would be coming back better trained, more seasoned, and more mature.

Yes, it would work out soon enough. All Jarlaxle had to do was figure out how to make sure Zaknafein didn't kill the returning Bregan D'aerthe soldier.

MORE THAN A TENDAY PASSED BEFORE ZAKNAFEIN AP-peared again at the Oozing Myconid, but ever patient, Jarlaxle was there waiting for him. The mercenary pulled a couple of drinks from the bar and moved across to intercept Zaknafein just as he was taking a seat in his favored area of the common room. He dropped the glass on the table before Zaknafein, then sat down opposite the man, lifting his own glass in a toast.

"To a battle well fought and a victory well earned," he said.

Zaknafein stared at him hard, but eventually did lift his glass. "They attacked, as you expected," he said quietly. "Without your mask, I would have . . ." He ended there and just sighed and took his gulp.

"You probably would have fought through the mind attack and won anyway. I just could not take that risk."

"So you—so we—cheated."

"Not so," Jarlaxle argued. "We simply stopped *them* from cheating. That is not a subtle distinction, my friend. Do you doubt that you would beat Avinve— Duvon, in a fair fight?"

"A hundred fights out of a hundred," Zaknafein replied. It was not an idle boast, Jarlaxle knew, which was why he had bet so heavily on Zaknafein and had dared to entice two matrons to do the same through him.

The two sat in silence for some time, and through another round of drinks.

"I know your designs," Jarlaxle said finally.

"Do you indeed?"

"You think to find Duvon and finish him, and perhaps to quietly kill Dab'nay, too."

Zaknafein smiled and tipped his glass to the mercenary's reasoning, but when he did, Jarlaxle noted something. He couldn't quite put his finger on it, but it seemed to him that perhaps his guess was not correct after all, at least, not wholly.

"They are valuable," he said, probing.

"He is a treacherous fool, and if I see him again—"

"You will do nothing," Jarlaxle forcefully interjected, for he sensed sincerity in that threat. Perhaps he had been wrong about Dab'nay? But yes, he was sure that Zaknafein wanted to kill Duvon, something Jarlaxle had no intention of allowing him to do.

"I am the weapon master of a noble house, one whose matron may soon enough sit on the Ruling Council," Zaknafein reminded him.

"And I am the only one who can get you out of that house safely, for these excursions such as you have found tonight. Without my imprimatur, how long would Zaknafein survive the Braeryn?"

Zaknafein snorted and downed his drink, then motioned for a third.

Jarlaxle took his time with his own drink. He wanted to stay fully within his wits this night, to watch and to make note. He took a calculated gamble then, in allowing more drinks to flow Zaknafein's way. He knew that other eyes were upon Zaknafein. Perhaps it was time to strip it all bare and bring the intrigue boiling to the surface.

CHAPTER 7

Stripped Naked

His steps uneven, his route meandering, Zaknafein walked out of the Oozing Myconid later that night.

From the edge of the bar, Jarlaxle watched him go, smiling knowingly when Zaknafein took a step a bit too far to the side, crashing into the doorjamb, against which he had not-so-subtly braced.

The mercenary leader took his time finishing his drink before taking his leave. Just outside, he went around the side of the building, then again around a second corner, back into the alleyway where the fight had taken place. There, at a specific spot, he used his portable hole and went back into the building, into a room he knew to be empty, then stepped out of sight and pulled the portable hole from the wall. He cast a spell out of a ring on his left hand, then, invisible, he slipped through the room's opened door, padded silently down the hall, and passed through the common room along the wall to once again exit the tavern.

He picked up his pace, moving swiftly down the course he knew

Zaknafein would take. There were no Do'Urden agents spying from the rooftops to protect the weapon master this night.

Logically, Jarlaxle knew that he should not be worried. With his cavern-jumping techniques and training, Zaknafein could elude almost anyone, even with a fair amount of liquor flowing through him—how many times had Zaknafein come out alone to the Braeryn, after all? For some reason, however, perhaps something he had noticed subconsciously, the skin on the back of Jarlaxle's shaved neck was tingling.

He sprinted along as fast as he could go, his magical boots keeping his footfalls perfectly silent. He thought he was nearing Zaknafein when he noted someone else, someone casting a spell and facing the alleyway that he expected Zaknafein would be traversing.

Jarlaxle ran toward the nearest building, tapped his noble house emblem, one of House Baenre given to him by the matron mother herself, and leaped from the ground, floating up to the roof. He moved across slowly and carefully to look over the alleyway.

There stood Zaknafein, unmoving.

Perfectly still. Not blinking, not even seeming to breathe.

A woman approached him, one Jarlaxle certainly recognized. She walked toward the weapon master, rolling a dagger about in her hand.

"Oh, Dab'nay," Jarlaxle whispered under his breath, shaking his head and thinking it all such a terrible waste.

"AH, WEAPON MASTER, YOU HAVE TRULY SURPRISED ME with your foolishness," Dab'nay said, standing right before the House Do'Urden swordsman. "You cannot be poisoned by an enemy, yet you poison yourself with drink!" She shook her head and sighed. "I would not have expected you to let down your guard so quickly. Did you think that there would be no consequences, no ill will, after such a fight as you waged with my brother? How many sinister characters lost coin in that battle?"

She rolled the dagger in her hand, bringing it up slowly before Zaknafein's face.

"When you are the central player in a game of gain and loss, do you not think it wise to take extra precautions?" she asked. "Or is it that you are so full of self-hatred that you simply do not care?"

She laughed at him. "And so even the great Zaknafein let down his guard and finds himself caught by my spell—an enchantment I would never even dare to cast on you were you not intoxicated. It would seem that I overestimated your skill, your mental discipline, and your quest for perfection. That disappoints me."

Dab'nay sighed again. "You are fortunate this night, Zaknafein Do'Urden," she said, lowering the blade. "For I've no desire to hurt you. None."

Up on the roof, wand leveled and ready to strike Dab'nay down, Jarlaxle nearly laughed aloud with relief.

Zaknafein's arm moved then, exactly as he practiced every day, drawing his sword and turning it to strike in the same movement, practically the same instant. The blade ended its stab right beside Dab'nay's neck, before Zaknafein, after a moment of staring the woman in the eye, flipped it and returned it to its sheath, nearly as quickly.

"If you thought you would ever get that dagger near to me, then I am the one who should be disappointed," Zaknafein answered evenly to the shocked priestess, who seemed as if she might simply fall over.

"Come with me," Dab'nay said after she had collected herself, and she led Zaknafein away.

Jarlaxle knew relief, great relief—almost as great as his shock at all of these surprising events. He didn't know what to make of it, any of it, including these two unlikely companions walking off together.

Was there anyone Dab'nay wanted to kill more than Zaknafein, given what the weapon master had done to her brother, a sibling to whom she held an unusually close bond?

Was there anyone Zaknafein wanted to kill more than a priestess of Lolth—*any* priestess of Lolth?

It didn't make sense to him.

So he followed.

He tracked them to an inn where he knew Dab'nay to stay on

those occasions when she was not in Bregan D'aerthe's Clawrift complex. He secretly followed their movements from outside the building, watching the candlelight in the room on the corner of the top floor that he knew to be Dab'nay's, and went to the roof above that spot. He waited just long enough for them to settle in, then carefully set his portable hole again, keeping it small so that he could peer through without attracting their attention—he hoped.

He heard them before he finished setting the peephole, but it didn't register clearly to him, and so his surprise was complete when he looked down to see the bottom of a bare foot, then a second, lifted into the air. Dab'nay's legs . . . and with Zaknafein between them.

A shaken Jarlaxle removed the hole and staggered away. He felt as if the ground beneath his feet had become shifting sand, all of his preconceptions of these two shattered.

He had to rethink so many things: the hierarchy of his mercenary band, the positioning of his lieutenants, his very existence. Why would Zaknafein willingly play with a priestess of Lolth, unless, of course, such play included deadly weapons?

All the way back to his quarters in the Clawrift, the unshakable Jarlaxle couldn't stop shaking his head.

"I AM GRATEFUL THAT YOU DID NOT KILL HIM," DAB'NAY said, lying beside Zaknafein on her side, propped up on one elbow.

Zaknafein couldn't deny her beauty, her delicate lines and curves, her graceful neck, her long hair cascading across it. He had to remind himself many times that she was a priestess of Lolth, and thus that beauty was more likely lure than allure.

To her thoughts, though, she had caught him helpless in the alleyway, and she hadn't struck. Why would he doubt her now?

Because she was a priestess of the Spider Queen, and keeping him alive would merely allow her to utilize him in some greater evil, perhaps? Or so that she could play with him before killing him?

Zaknafein had no intention of letting his guard down, no matter how much he—surprisingly!—wanted to.

"I am unused to priestesses caring about their brothers," he replied. "Or about any males."

Dab'nay shrugged, then shook her head, her hair falling back behind her, affording Zaknafein a full view of her naked form.

"Or about anyone, for that matter," Zaknafein pressed.

That brought a laugh. "I wish I could deny your words, but alas, it does seem that we all hold ourselves too high above anyone and everyone else. That is how Lady Lolth teaches us."

"But you do not agree with it?"

"I didn't say that."

"You didn't have to." Zaknafein grinned as he reached up to run the back of his hand gently across Dab'nay's angular cheek. She closed her eyes when he brushed her ear, just a slight breeze-like touch, then moved down the side of her neck. "But yes, you did say that."

Dab'nay's red eyes popped open and a flash of anger flared in them, one that Zaknafein, who had spent the entirety of his life under the thumb of Lolthian priestesses, certainly knew well.

But it passed, very quickly.

"How so?"

"Duvon—or should I say Avinvesa Fey?—holds no practical value to you anymore, and forevermore," Zaknafein explained. "When Jarlaxle sold Duvon to Matron Byrtyn, he offered you as well."

Dab'nay's face went very tight.

"You knew that, of course," said Zaknafein. "And you knew why Jarlaxle had tried to do that. Having a priestess of Lolth in the midst of his mercenary band raised his profile higher than he was comfortable with. Rightly so. Noble Dab'nay Tr'arach could have brought ruin to Bregan D'aerthe."

"But she did not."

"No," Zaknafein agreed. "And Matron Byrtyn didn't want you, and that at a price cheaper than that which she paid for your brother, a mere male. I am surprised that did not, and does not, infuriate you."

Dab'nay merely shrugged again.

"That bothered me more than it bothered you," Zaknafein went on. "But then I came to understand that there was likely a good reason for it, and one that you understood." He stroked the woman's face and neck again. "You are not in Lolth's favor. You weren't then, when Duvon was sold, and you are not now."

"She still gives me her gifts. My spells do not fail me."

Zaknafein shrugged as if that did not matter, for of course, it did not. A priestess had to do a lot more than simply fall out of Lolth's favor to lose her spells, particularly the lesser enchantments which taxed the limits of Dab'nay's mediocre powers. She would have to enrage Lolth to the point where the goddess left her helpless to face the executioners of her wrath.

That wasn't the way the Spider Queen played her chaos game.

"I was often wicked to Duvon when he was a child," Dab'nay admitted. Her gaze went past Zaknafein, and she wasn't looking at anything in particular in the room, he knew. Her mind's eye was far away, on a long-ago day in House Tr'arach.

"Even more than I had to be. I enjoyed it: the whippings, the sheer dominance I exerted over him. It is a heady elixir, this power. I was told not to care about his pain, his screams, his heart, and I wanted to believe that, and so I did. And it made it all so easy."

"But you grew closer," Zaknafein reasoned.

"Hardly. I fully expected him to die on the field when we raided House Simfray. I expected him to die at the edge of your blades, Zaknafein." She looked him right in the eye. "I even hoped for it."

"But now you are grateful that I did not kill him?"

Dab'nay gave yet another shrug. She was struggling here, Zaknafein recognized. And why shouldn't she be? Her heart was leading her in a direction diametrically opposed to everything she had been taught to believe and practice—something he knew a great deal about.

"Something changed after that disaster at the compound of House Simfray," she admitted.

"I do not consider it such a disaster."

That brought Dab'nay's eyes to meet Zaknafein's gaze.

"I suppose that I do not, either, when I step back and look at it these hundred years removed," she admitted. "I have learned much with Bregan D'aerthe. Or perhaps it would be more accurate to say that I have unlearned much. To my surprise, Jarlaxle kept Duvon in line, and it wasn't just that my brother was afraid of Jarlaxle."

"He was happy," Zaknafein concluded.

Dab'nay nodded. "And now, he is again Duvon," she admitted. "And you would have been justified in killing him. You still would be, and perhaps that is your wisest play."

"But you don't want me to."

"I beg you not to."

"And again, I am left asking, 'Why?'"

"Because something even greater has changed within me," she said. "Outside of my house, outside of the daily rituals of the Spider Queen and the constant reminders of the inferiority of males, and the constant reinforcement of the selfish nature of drow, I have come to see the world—not just Duvon, but the world around me—quite differently." It was her turn to reach out and gently stroke Zaknafein's face. "I find men much more pleasurable when they lie with me of their own accord and desire."

Zaknafein grabbed her by the wrist and pulled her hand away, holding it fast. "And again, I am left with the truth that you still retain great powers from Lady Lolth."

"Not so great," Dab'nay humbly admitted. "Never that. Never spells powerful enough to require divine permission or interest. But yes, she still grants me my spells," she conceded. "Why wouldn't she?"

"You just said why."

"Do not lie to yourself or deceive yourself, ever-angry Zaknafein," she said. "Jarlaxle, too, is in the favor of the Spider Queen and always has been."

"I've never seen him pray to her or to anyone else."

Dab'nay offered no answer, other than another shrug.

"You promise that there will be no retribution against me by Dab'nay?" Zaknafein bluntly asked.

Another shrug. "That would depend upon whether or not you anger me," she said coyly. "Or maybe if you fail to please me when we are at play."

"I am your servant again?"

"Willingly!"

Zaknafein found himself matching her grin.

"Still, you did try to cheat in my fight with Duvon, and so would you have stayed his blade if your cheating had borne the expected results?"

She appeared honestly perplexed by that. "My cheating?"

"You do not admit that you would have preferred that Duvon win?"

"I would have preferred that you did not fight, and not only because I lost a large bag of gold."

"You bet on Duvon."

"I did."

"But you know him well, and you know that he could not defeat me."

"That, too, is true."

"Because you cheated?"

"I did nothing."

Zaknafein stared at her doubtfully, then came to understand her dodge. "Because you knew that someone else was cheating."

Dab'nay shrugged and did not deny it.

"Who?"

"The attack upon you in the fight was not divine, nor arcane," Dab'nay stated.

"It was similar to that which you tried this very night in the alleyway, I think."

"No. It was no spell of Lolth's giving, and none cast by a mage." When Zaknafein didn't seem to understand, she stated it more clearly. "Who among us is in bed, quite literally, with an Oblodran?" Dab'nay asked.

"The mind magic," the weapon master whispered, more to himself than to Dab'nay. He hadn't even considered a psionic attack, for the Oblodrans were not ones to bother with such matters as duels in the Braeryn, certainly.

"Who?" Dab'nay asked again.

Zaknafein could only shrug, as he had no idea.

"Ah, of course, you have not been in the Clawrift in decades," Dab'nay said. "An easier clue, then, my lover. Who among Bregan D'aerthe would most benefit from the death of Zaknafein Do'Urden?"

"I am not of Bregan D'aerthe any—"

"Oh, but you are," Dab'nay insisted. "You are still the favorite of Jarlaxle, and you know it. And for one other, that remains unacceptable."

Zaknafein tried to keep his expression blank as he considered the reasoning. He found himself wincing more than once, though, and more than twice, as he tried to process the dire implications here. This could cost him his life, of course, but worse, to his thinking, this could force him to stay inside House Do'Urden!

"Why do you tell me this?" he demanded.

"Because I lost a large bag of gold." Her expression was grim, one Zaknafein was far more used to seeing from a priestess of Lolth, and in that moment, had he been wearing a sword, he might have struck Dab'nay down.

A moment later, though, she merely shrugged again, a reminder to him that this was the way of the drow, even among allies, and despite himself, Zaknafein was glad that he didn't have a sword in hand. He wasn't going to stay mad at Dab'nay because she had tried to profit over some inside information. Would he have done anything differently if their roles had been reversed?

JARLAXLE WAS SURPRISED TO SEE ZAKNAFEIN RETURNING to the Oozing Myconid that night, but when he noted the man's scowl as he approached the table, he was able to guess the reason.

"You knew," Zaknafein said with a growl, standing, pointedly not sitting, right beside the mercenary leader.

"I know much."

"No games, Jarlaxle."

"My friend, it is all a game. Would you care to narrow the horizon of your question?"

"I would care to take you out in the alley and cut you apart."

"I wouldn't care much for that."

"Jarlaxle!"

Jarlaxle held up his hands for Zaknafein to see, showing him that they were empty, then slowly rose. "Let us go in the back."

Zaknafein started to argue, but then motioned for Jarlaxle to lead and followed the man into a room just off the common room. No doubt, ears were pressed against the door, but Jarlaxle produced his portable hole and motioned for Zaknafein to go in.

The weapon master hesitated, eyeing Jarlaxle with open suspicion.

Jarlaxle heaved a heavy sigh, then placed his belt pouch to the side and entered the hole, and when Zaknafein finally entered behind him, he pulled in the edges, creating an extradimensional pocket.

"Be quick," he said. "I do not wish to have my pouch stolen."

"You knew—you *know*—who did it," Zaknafein stated.

"Did what?"

"Attacked my mind in my fight with Duvon Tr'arach," Zaknafein spat. "Arathis Hune."

"Quavylene Oblodra, more likely."

"Hired by Arathis Hune," the weapon master said through gritted teeth.

"That would be my guess, yes," Jarlaxle confirmed.

"Where is he?"

"Nowhere that matters to you, Weapon Master of House Do'Urden."

Zaknafein stared at him with his jaw hanging open.

"I'm sorry for being so formal, but you leave me no choice. If you strike at Arathis Hune, then House Do'Urden will have struck hard at Bregan D'aerthe, and Matron Mother Baenre will likely have a word, or more like a scourge, with Matron Malice in that event."

"Do not play that game!"

"It is all a game."

"Shut up!" Zaknafein growled in frustration. "Just shut up. Why haven't you punished him? Why is he still alive?"

"Because he is valuable to me."

"He tried to kill me."

Jarlaxle's shrug deflated Zaknafein, visibly so.

"We are drow, my friend Zaknafein. We are all drow. You are drow. This is our lot, this is our way. So, we are ever on our guard, and so we survive."

"And if treachery is revealed?"

"By whom? To what court? Would you have me take your charges to the Ruling Council? I am sure the matrons will give it proper consideration."

"Don't be foolish. He tried to have me killed, and so I will kill him myself."

"No."

"*No?*"

"We've been through this. He is valuable to me, and I need him now, with you spending your days in the service of Matron Malice. You cannot kill him."

Zaknafein stared at him hard.

"Are you intending to kill every drow who might use your own demise as a manner of personal gain?" Jarlaxle asked. "If so, you'll be dead or you'll be alone."

"Does that include Jarlaxle?"

"Fair point, my friend. You'd then be alone, except for my wonderful company."

"Which is what you'd have to say to stay alive, isn't it?"

"Ah, Zaknafein, I promise you, if we two were trapped in a cave alone and starving, I would not kill you. But if you died first, I cannot promise that I wouldn't eat you."

Zaknafein just shook his head, the hints of a smile impossible to stymie.

"You will find no allies, not even me, if you pursue this to your desired end," Jarlaxle warned in all seriousness. "Let it go." Jarlaxle rose and moved toward the common room, aware the whole time of Zaknafein's eyes on his back.

PART 2

Every
Front

If I am to believe the wisdom of Grandmaster Kane, then I am made of the same stuff as all around me, then we are one. All of us, everything.

Is this observation merely a philosophical bend or the truth of it? For surely this is not how the matrons of Menzoberranzan view the world, nor the dwarves of Gauntlgrym, nor even my beloved wife, who foresees her future in the Grove of the Unicorns within the House of Nature, wherein resides the goddess Mielikki.

So is it that Grandmaster Kane has seen the truth, beyond the religions and dogma of the material world? Or is it that his truth is not in opposition to the others; that his truth is, perhaps, a different angle viewing the same image?

It gives me great pleasure and satisfaction to recognize that this ancient human who has taken me as his student would not bristle at my question. Nay, he would celebrate it, indeed demand it of me, for this oneness of all he envisions requires inquisitiveness and curiosity, open heart and open mind. I cannot deny the power of Kane's truth. I have seen a blade pass through him without disturbing his mortal flesh.

He can walk through a stone wall. In the body of Brother Afafrenfere, he vanished to sparkling nothingness before the breath of a dragon, only to soon reconstitute in the mortal corporeal form and slay the beast.

It occurs to me that a wizard or high priestess might do the same with their varying spells, and I know that Kimmuriel can replicate much of what Grandmaster Kane accomplishes with the use of his strange mind magic.

Yes, perhaps Kimmuriel Oblodra and Grandmaster Kane are more alike than either of them would wish to admit. Neither consciously calls upon the elements or some godlike being for his powers. For Kimmuriel, it is the power of a trained mind, and so it is with Grandmaster Kane.

I wonder, then, are their philosophies joined? Or are they accessing some hidden power from different directions?

I do love these puzzles, I admit, but also, I am troubled by the seeming contentment and acceptance shown by my mentor. Once more, if I am to believe the wisdom of Grandmaster Kane, then I am made of the same stuff as all that is around me, then we are one. All of us, everything. Is it sentience and reasoning that gives us form? What then of the stones and clouds? Is it our sentience that gives them form?

I am not sure that even Grandmaster Kane could answer those questions, but there is another inescapable question to his philosophy that seemed not to bother him at all: If we are all one, all of the same stuff, and our ultimate fates are thus joined, then to what point do we make determinations of good and evil? Why should I care for such concepts if we are all of the same stuff, if we are all to be joined in the eternity of everything? Am I to meld with ogre pieces, then? Or demon bits?

But Kane cares about this question, and his answer is simple, and one I find satisfying. To him, the universe bends toward goodness and justice, and the ultimate reward for us all is that place of brotherhood and tranquility. There is indeed a philosophical and moral compass to it all, say the sisters and brothers of the Yellow Rose, and so such gains are not merely temporary conveniences but lasting measurements in a universal scale.

Perhaps they're correct. Perhaps it's all for nothing, and there is no ultimate reward or punishment beyond this mortal coil. These are answers for those who, to our experience, are no more, who have returned to whatever eternity or emptiness there might be for us all. For now, says Kane, and so say I, we must follow that which is in our heart and soul. A belief in universal, eternal harmony and oneness does not discount a belief in goodness, in love, in joy, in friendship and sisterhood.

I found my peace here in this monastery nestled in the Galena Mountains of Damara. True peace and contentment, and in that light, when I return home to Longsaddle or Gauntlgrym, on those occasions when I am beside Catti-brie or any of the others, I know that I will be a better friend.

—Drizzt Do'Urden

CHAPTER 8

Commander Zhindia

W e will meet with them?" Kyrnill Melarn, the first priestess of House Melarn, asked Matron Zhindia. They and their charges, the 350 soldiers of House Melarn—half that number of goblin and kobold slaves, and more than a hundred driders—had come out of the Underdark in the midst of the rocky and hilly region known as the Crags, just a few miles from the now ruined halfling city of Bleeding Vines and the back entrance to the dwarven complex where Bruenor Battlehammer was king.

More important than where he ruled was the fact that Bruenor was the best friend of the heretic Drizzt Do'Urden, whom Zhindia meant to capture or kill, along with Drizzt's father, Zaknafein, who had been mysteriously taken from his grave and returned to life.

To Zhindia, that act of soul-stealing had been the greatest insult to her dear Lady Lolth imaginable.

"We must," Zhindia told the priestess. "They are our fodder to bring the dwarves out of their holes."

"Why do we need them?" Kyrnill asked, turning about to view the other "soldiers" House Melarn had brought to the surface with them: a pair of gigantic golems fashioned in the shape of spiders. The truly monstrous beasts, retrievers, were among the most prized constructs of the lower planes, used by demon lords and demon goddesses, created with single-minded purpose at tremendous expense and sacrifice. A retriever was built to bring back, dead or alive, a single being.

Only the most valuable of outlaws would warrant such an expense as this, and the Spider Queen, the goddess Lolth, through her yochlol handmaidens, had clearly agreed with Zhindia's estimation that Drizzt and Zaknafein qualified in that regard.

"Can the dwarves stop our . . ." Kyrnill fumbled around for a word to properly describe the powerful creatures before them, and finally settled on "blessed spiders? Can anything?"

"Never be imprudent," Matron Zhindia scolded her. "We are entrusted by our goddess with the most precious constructs of the Abyss. Arrogance is uncalled for."

"What can stop them, other than the completion of their mission?"

"They are not invincible. No," she said, staving off another protest, "I do not underestimate their power. They were created by the greatest of the demon lords, and so they are mighty allies to be treasured, and beyond the power of anything else we can bring to bear against our enemies. But they are not immortal, and never think of them as such. Yes, they will capture or kill Drizzt Do'Urden and Zaknafein, no doubt, but then they will be gone, back to the Abyss, and we will still be here facing a formidable and entrenched enemy."

"But you will have achieved greatness, my matron," Kyrnill said, bowing. "You will have done what the Baenres failed to do, and when we return . . ."

"When we have defeated the two heretics, then conquered the dwarven city and all lands about it, we will return in true victory. Only then will I enact that which Lolth most deserves: that her most devout and loving matron becomes, at long last, matron mother of Menzoberranzan. The time of the Baenres is nearing its end. It is past time to return to pure devotion to the Lady of Chaos, past time for the drow to become the unquestioned rulers of the Underdark, with tendrils ever rising to the surface to remind the heretics above that we, not they, are the chosen beings of the true god.

"But first," she continued sharply, "we must protect what we have. The retrievers have sensed that Drizzt and Zaknafein are nearby, down below. Without my control—and indeed it wavers!—they will run straightaway for the tunnels to crash against King Bruenor's walls."

"And they will knock those walls down."

"They will, if we are clever. Our allies among the humans and dwarves, with the army of demons seeded by House Hunzrin merchants, will wound the dwarves and show us their strengths and weaknesses, and through those weaknesses, the abyssal retrievers will deliver a scalding blow to King Bruenor and his friends."

"Forgive my imprudence," Kyrnill begged with another bow.

Matron Zhindia gave an atypical smile, since it was an honest one. First Priestess Kyrnill, who had been matron of House Kenafin and could have fought for the same position when that house had merged with House Horlbar, had never really offered sincere and honest respect to her rival, Zhindia. Things had changed, though, since Zhindia had properly and mercilessly punished Ash'ala, Kyrnill's third daughter. Ever since they had left Ash'ala in the milk bath, being slowly eaten by maggots, Kyrnill had at long last come to understand the true balance of power here. That was one of the reasons Zhindia had decided to be so cruel, of course. Ash'ala had surely deserved her gruesome and painful fate, but equally important to Zhindia, the ever-dangerous First Priestess Kyrnill needed to see it.

"It is easy to become arrogant, even complacent, with such power in our grasp," Zhindia said, a rare offer of understanding. "We must all properly guard when the future seems so wonderful."

THE TWO DWARVES SIGHED IN UNISON AND SHOOK THEIR heads in unison, their reactions, mannerisms, and appearances so similar that any casual onlooker would surely think them father and son.

"Tweren't it our gripe with that Athrogate fool that he be friendin' dark elves?" Frenkyn, the younger of the two, asked sarcastically.

Bronkyn sighed again and scratched his head, his yellow hair tightly bound into scalp braids in neat little rows hanging down past his shoulders to blend in with his enormous yellow beard.

Conversely, Frenkyn let his yellow hair hang loose and bushy, but still reached up almost at the same time as his uncle Bronkyn to similarly scratch at his scalp.

Down the ridge before them stood two humans, Margaster women, alongside a handful of drow, with horrid creatures—half drow and half spider—all around the drow women and filtering back through the many shadows of the forest. Scores of these horrid mutants milled about, and even for the dwarves, who were consorting with demons themselves, the cursed behemoths seemed simply . . . wrong.

"I'm thinkin' we shouldn't've listened to them damned Margasters," Bronkyn admitted. "Even though we got us Thornhold."

"And are to be gettin' Gauntlgrym," Frenkyn said with a wide grin.

Bronkyn shrugged, not willing to count on that just yet. "Now half our boys are half demon, and we're to have all o' the north hating us."

"Only if we don't win," Frenkyn reminded him.

Bronkyn had to nod, for there was the truth of it. For all their proclamations otherwise, to the supposedly noble lords and ladies of the Sword Coast, *might for right* was a quaint and public concept, whereas *might makes right* was more akin to the reality. And looking at the army of demons all around the destroyed halfling village—and now with the drow and their freakish drider monsters, and all the money moved and stashed between the Margasters and Lord Neverember—winning certainly seemed in the cards.

And by his deal with Inkeri Margaster, Bronkyn Stoneshaft would then become second king of Gauntlgrym, with all the power of the fire primordial, all the influence of the greatest magical forge in Faerun, and in friendship to Lord Dagult Neverember of Neverwinter and Waterdeep—Luskan, too, for that city was sure to soon fall.

It was worth the terrible feeling in his gut as he looked at his allies.

Win first and worry about getting rid of the demons after, Bronkyn silently told himself.

THE TRAM TO BLEEDING VINES SAT QUIET ON THE RAISED platform across the dark underground pool from the castle walls of Gauntlgrym. Beyond loomed the vast entry cavern, like a dark forest with its stalagmite and stalactite trees. Fortified dwarven positions in some of those hollowed-out structures occasionally sent a torch flare flying, lighting one area or another just long enough for the crews of the many side-slinger catapults to sight in on the area, or to throw missiles at any intruders.

Mostly, though, the giant cavern was quiet, unnervingly so. The demons were out there, in great numbers. Every dwarf in the place could sense them, like crouched lions ready to spring.

Waiting and plotting.

And the waiting was the worst.

"How much can you give me?" King Bruenor asked. He walked with Jarlaxle and Zaknafein along the bank nearest the city wall of the underground pond.

"What would you have me say, my friend?" Jarlaxle replied. "I've not many soldiers, and I don't know if their tactics would play well with those of your dwarves."

"I'll be takin' whatever ye're givin' me," said Bruenor. "Just send yer boys in up above at Bleeding Vines to sting the damned monsters."

"I will see what I can do," Jarlaxle promised.

"And tell them wizards at the Hosttower to get the durn gates to the Silver Marches burnin' with their magic soon," Bruenor replied after a long stare at the drow mercenary. He had been around Jarlaxle long enough to trust the eccentric fellow, but also to know that Jarlaxle would always put Jarlaxle first. Still, he had to take the drow's weaselly promise for what it was. "I ain't got enough to chase 'em out, but give me those gates and I'll be bringing in the boys from Mithral Hall, Felbarr, and Adbar, and then ye'll see some demon splattering, don't ye doubt!"

Jarlaxle laughed and nodded, glancing at Zaknafein, who didn't seem to understand. The problem was not the language, for with Catti-brie's help, the weapon master had already become quite proficient in the common tongue of Faerun's surface races, but the meaning behind the words.

"Three dwarven citadels in a land called the Silver Marches," Jarlaxle explained. "Good Bruenor here was king of Mithral Hall, twice, before reclaiming this most ancient dwarven homeland of Gauntlgrym."

Zaknafein arched a white eyebrow at that.

"If the teleport gates are opened to the appointed location in the tunnels between those three citadels, King Bruenor can bring in ten thousand heavily armored dwarven soldiers in short order."

"We'd sweep the dogs all the way back to the Sword Coast and drown them in the ocean," Bruenor declared, and Jarlaxle nodded, not doubting the claim.

"It will still be a while, from everything Gromph has told me," Jarlaxle replied. "The magic is growing, but given the danger of the primordial, it has to be carefully cultivated."

"Aye, me girl's said much the same," Bruenor muttered, and began ascending the stair to the bridge that crossed over the pond to the tram platform. "So we got to hold.

"So we'll hold," he said with firm finality.

"It is so strangely quiet," Jarlaxle remarked when he came up beside the dwarf on the bridge, the two and Zaknafein looking out at the dark forest of stone trees.

"Oh, they're out there, don't ye doubt," Bruenor assured him.

"My son is out there," Zaknafein added.

"I don't doubt that, either," Bruenor said with a chuckle. "Trust him. He's been out there many times all around the world and against anythin' ye can think ye might be fightin'. Trust him," he repeated.

Zaknafein stared at the orange-haired dwarf curiously, seeming off guard here, and it occurred to Jarlaxle that Zaknafein had not thought for a moment that this person, a dwarven king, would offer him words of comfort regarding Drizzt. But Jarlaxle knew, of course, that Bruenor was more friend to Drizzt than Zaknafein had ever been, and indeed, more father to Drizzt than Zaknafein had ever been. Not through any fault of Zaknafein's, no, but because Drizzt and Bruenor had spent centuries together, supporting each other, defending each other, counting on each other.

His friend was looking at him now, and Jarlaxle nodded at Zaknafein. Drizzt could handle himself.

No, what worried him were their opponents.

"I do not doubt that they're out there, good dwarf," Jarlaxle said, "but these are demons. *Demons.* Chaos embodied. Always hungering for blood. They are out there, but what are they doing? Why is it so quiet?"

"Yeah, been wonderin' the same," said Bruenor. He looked at Zaknafein and offered a warm smile, white teeth shining in the torchlight from within the tangle of his orange beard. "Yer boy probably killed the lot o' them!"

"Wouldn't be the first time," Jarlaxle dryly added, and the three looked back to Gauntlgrym's huge antechamber.

"Nah," Bruenor decided. "They're still out there. Demon scum. I can smell 'em."

"YOU MUST PRESS THEM WITHOUT PAUSE," THE SHARP-featured drow matron told the trio of leaders in Bleeding Vines, under the shadows of the trees across from the two tunnels that led into the mountain.

Bronkyn stared at the white-haired woman, shaking his head repeatedly in disbelief. She was handsome enough, he thought, as elves went, though she needed a lot of fattening up, but aside from that, the thick-limbed dwarf didn't really know what to make of her. Her gown, certainly of fabulous and expensive materials and design, had so many spiders on it that it made Bronkyn's head spin, and he was pretty sure that some of them, at least, were *actual* spiders, living and crawling, and not just decorative stitching or brooches. The Margasters had warned him that this one was particularly fervent about her so-called Spider Queen, but really, to Bronkyn, this devotion seemed a bit much.

Even the way she talked grated on him, every bitten-off word making him feel like someone was running the bark of an old and gnarly oak tree down the back of his neck. It seemed like this drow woman could barely get the words out of her mouth, so tight was her jaw, and when they did come out, they carried the hissing timbre of an open fire in a downpour.

Truly, he wanted to just punch her, but Inkeri and Alvilda had warned Bronkyn that she was important to their cause—indeed, that this Matron Zhindia of House Melarn gave them a chance to defeat Gauntlgrym and take the whole of the coastal lands north of great Waterdeep as their own.

"We will, Matron," Inkeri promised. "With these magnificent baubles your associates have given us, we will keep the dwarves caught in their hole." She looked to one of Matron Zhindia's entourage as she spoke, one Bronkyn knew well: Charri Hunzrin, who had delivered many of the magical phylacteries to Clan Stoneshaft.

He didn't much like that one, either.

"Bah, but it's a killing field in that cavern," Bronkyn interjected. "They'll take us down ten to one."

"That is the beauty of our demon allies," Matron Zhindia told him. "Let Bruenor's dwarves kill the manes and other minor demons. The greater demons will simply open magical gates to the Abyss to bring more in."

"Aye, but ye're not to be replacing Stoneshafts, so I ain't to be sendin' too many o' me boys into King Bruenor's flesh grinder."

The drow woman snorted at him, clearly derisively, and snapped her critical gaze over the two Margaster women.

"And that's what I be wonderin', and needing yer answer about," Bronkyn went on. "So ye tell me and tell me now. Some o' me boys got yer demon friends in their gems and jewels, and them demons come forth with power and rage. But they lose—I seen some lose—and then go all smoky and melt away. And sometimes me dwarf gets back up, wobbling but livin', and sometimes me dwarf don't. So what's it about? What happens to me boys when the demon loses?"

"Ask the ones who got up," Matron Zhindia told him coldly.

"I'm askin' yerself," he said, just as cold.

"It is what you said, dwarf. Some will survive the shock of the destruction of their demon companions and some will not."

"Then ye'll understand me when I say that I ain't for sendin' the whole o' Clan Stoneshaft down to that cavern full o' catapults, crossbows, and ballistae. We got plenty o' demons that ain't paired with me dwarfs to send down, but—"

"But?" Matron Zhindia interrupted sharply. "We have Bruenor and his friends caught in a hole."

"Good place for them," said Bronkyn.

"Yes—until they get their portals opened to the Silver Marches to the east, and all the dwarves of the north join together against you," she snapped.

"Against us," Bronkyn corrected.

But Matron Zhindia shrugged and grinned that awful grin. After all, she had somewhere to run where Bruenor's dwarves would not dare to chase. Could Clan Stoneshaft claim the same?

"Press them," she said, more to the two Margasters than to Bronkyn.

"Bronkyn Stoneshaft leads these forces," Inkeri informed her, and Zhindia looked back to the dwarf, barely containing her sneer.

"So, them spiders crawling on ye," Bronkyn asked, barely containing his snarl, "ye keep 'em for snacks?"

"Snacks?" Matron Zhindia echoed, seeming sincerely confused, and beyond her, both Margaster women were looking at Bronkyn pleadingly, shaking their heads, begging him to quickly change the subject.

The dwarf chortled. "I'll be sendin' down the demons, whole hordes o' the beasts, but I'm not bringing me flesh 'n' blood boys into that murder zone 'til we've softened Bruenor up a bit."

"Snacks?" Zhindia asked again.

Bronkyn hawked in his throat and sent a wad of spit to the ground, then walked away, barking orders for his charges to ready an assault.

Behind him, Matron Zhindia turned her scowl upon the two Margasters.

"Clan Stoneshaft will press Bruenor hard," Inkeri promised. "The greater demons have been creating portals to bring in minions since we destroyed this halfling village. They are legion."

"And they are all hungry," Alvilda added with a grin.

"You two will lead," Matron Zhindia said. The Margasters looked to each other, but were shaking their heads in unison when they looked back at her.

"We are fast to Waterdeep," Inkeri explained. "There is too much happening all at once and it is imperative that we remain available to Lord Neverember to help him keep the lords of Waterdeep in their palaces and safely away from the battlefield."

"If the brunt of that city came against us, our fight would be lost," Alvilda added.

Zhindia's lips curled in an awful smile. "Do not be so certain of that," she said evenly.

Again Inkeri and Alvilda exchanged looks, both intrigued. The unexpected arrival of House Melarn, with its small army of mighty driders, had unnerved them. Driders and something more, so they believed, though whatever upper hand Zhindia might be holding was only vaguely hinted at by this supremely confident drow matron. Perhaps it was merely a bluff, but if so, Zhindia had surely perfected the art. Her confidence was infectious.

But it had also unnerved them more than a little.

"No matter, then," Zhindia went on. "Dismiss this fool dwarf and his charges to their coastal home, where they can serve as vanguard." She looked around. "My house will take control of this field of battle."

"Bronkyn wants Gauntlgrym above all else," said Alvilda.

"Then perhaps he should act as if the gain is worth the price" came Zhindia's curt reply.

THE DROW RANGER ARRIVED AT THE TOP OF THE EGRESS tunnel, where the Gauntlgrym tram exited the mountain to roll to the platform in the station at Bleeding Vines—a station that, like almost everything else about the halfling village, had been destroyed. Drizzt wasn't too concerned with that at the moment, for he knew that the dwarves would help Regis and Donnola and their citizens rebuild it into something magnificent.

If they could survive.

Drizzt stared at the village upside down, standing on the ceiling, as it were, for he had not gone past the ending point of the magical reversal of gravity, which allowed the tram to roll "downhill" up the mountain on the ceiling of the tunnel. That point had been clearly marked simply by the rolling turn of the tracks as they descended from the ceiling to put the tram back upright in the area unaffected by the magical inversion.

What a marvelous creation this had been, he thought. And now these demons were intent on tearing it all down.

What could they do about it? Drizzt wondered, considering his options here. Should he go out and try to decapitate the attackers? Certainly he and his allies had to take down the major demons among their enemies, or that foul crew would continue gating in lesser fiends to throw against them, an inexhaustible supply.

That thought crystallized a few moments later when a horde of enemies came into view, crossing the broken village and heading straight for the tram tunnels. Hardly thinking of the movement, purely on instinct, the drow ranger leaped forward past the inversion line, caught a handhold, and hooked his feet on the descending tracks as he started to fall. He pulled himself up and over the tracks, wedging himself in against what was now, again, the ceiling. Drizzt called upon his training, monk and ranger, and his innate drow abilities then, and all but melted into the stone, contorting himself perfectly to fully disappear from any view below.

And not a moment too soon, for the demons—misshapen humanoids ambling like the undead, flying chasmes, powerful birdlike bipedal vrocks, and all other manner of misshapen beast—swarmed below him. If the situation hadn't been so dire, with Gauntlgrym certainly about to enter another ferocious fight in the entry cavern, Drizzt might have thought the next moments amusing, as the demons, clearly unaware of the permanent gravity inversion in the tunnel, began flailing and falling . . . up!

Even the flying chasmes, with their bloated human faces and proboscis-like noses, veered and swerved and collided with the walls and ceiling and floor, so disoriented did they suddenly become.

It didn't deter their forward progress, though. The line of charging demons went on and on, and while the larger and greater fiends seemed to figure out the strange enchantment, the lesser monsters kept stepping into the tunnel and falling upward to crash against the ceiling.

Any bit of damage on them might help down below, Drizzt thought, and as the horrific procession went on and on, he could only hope that the unexpected fall would truly wound many.

Because if not, there were a great many foes to face.

Perhaps too many.

He watched as they charged past him for a long, long while, and an equal number, he realized, were likely heading down through the tunnel to the right side of the broken tram station as well, one that was not enchanted with reverse gravity, one that let the tram simply roll back down the mountain to the Gauntlgrym station far below.

Drizzt crept out of the tunnel, crawling along the ceiling, then crossed behind the station ruins to the other tunnel and started down. He glanced back before the village went out of sight, though, and then so much of this sudden onslaught came clearer to Drizzt Do'Urden.

Driders.

If driders were here, then drow were here, and if drow were here, then there was little doubt in Drizzt's mind as to their role as leaders in this demonic invasion.

Which raised the question: why hadn't Jarlaxle known?

He couldn't worry about that then, however, for the demons were far away now, far below him in the tunnel and likely nearing the entry cavern outside Gauntlgrym. The battle was possibly already joined.

Drizzt blew the whistle hanging about his neck and started running down the tunnel. Soon he was caught by Andahar, his great unicorn steed, and he leaped up atop the wide and strong back and grabbed a handful of shining white mane. Down they charged into the darkness of the mountain depths.

"IT'S NOT AS CONFUSIN' AS IT SEEMS," BRUENOR EXPLAINED to Jarlaxle and Zaknafein when the three of them scaled the tram station to look out over the vast underground chamber. "We got throwers—side-slinger catapults, mostly—aiming down every straight run. Throwing scattershot, flamin' if we want it, but against demons, probably not, eh?"

"There don't seem to be many such straight avenues," Zaknafein replied.

"More than ye think," Bruenor assured him. "We cut 'em, but so they're hard to see, and we got others with walls shaped to bank the shot around corners."

Zaknafein looked to Jarlaxle, and Bruenor gave a great laugh when Jarlaxle just shrugged and nodded.

"Ain't no one better at makin' killin' zones, elf. No one," the dwarf king insisted. "We got every spot on the floor sighted, ready to light it, ready to melt it."

"How many dwarves are out there?" Zaknafein asked.

"A dozen catapult flingers, half again that ballista crews, half-a-hunnerd crossbow boys, all set up high, and always a dozen Gutbusters covering any retreat," Bruenor said. "We got tunnels cut about the ceiling to get most of 'em to this side o' the lake, and a hunnerd guards on th'other side o' that wall behind us in the throne room, ready to come out and lend a boot. And I can get another five hunnerd up here in short order, don't ye doubt." Quite satisfied with himself, Bruenor crossed his arms defiantly over his burly chest.

"You'll need them," Zaknafein said before he had even completed the action.

"Eh?"

"What do you know?" Jarlaxle asked.

"Shh," Zaknafein bade his companions. "I hear them."

No sooner had he said that than the far side of the cavern erupted in flames and shrieks, and elongated shadows of misshapen monsters flickered and flitted about the patches of fiery, and then magical, light.

"Lot of 'em," Bruenor agreed. "What d'ye got for me, elf?"

Jarlaxle looked to Zaknafein.

"Cavern looks like a challenge," Zaknafein said slyly. "Lots of uneven walls and millions of ledges, wide enough for those who can sense them." He gave Jarlaxle a wink and drew out his swords. "Do you think you can still vault and hurdle, flip and spin?"

Despite the obviously grave situation, the shouts and explosions growing nearer by the moment, a wide smile spread over Jarlaxle's face. "I'm older now, so it will hurt in the morning, I am sure. But I can sure keep up with you."

"Not on your life."

"It may just be," Jarlaxle said with a laugh.

"Boys," Bruenor interrupted. "We got a fight out there."

"Obviously. Your best killing lane, King Bruenor?" Jarlaxle asked.

"Eh?" Bruenor shook his head, then pointed out into the cavern to the left-hand side of the tram station. "Long and wide run, and with lots o' crews . . ."

The dwarf paused and shook his head again, for the two drow were already gone, over the station wall and down to the stone below. Bruenor caught one last glimpse of them: Jarlaxle running up the side of a stalagmite to the left, Zaknafein doing likewise to the right. The dwarf started with surprise as both leaped off toward each other, turning flips and spins that Bruenor couldn't quite follow, crossing paths in midair, then each replacing the other as they ran on.

"It all started when me girl found Drizzt on the side of a hill in Icewind Dale," Bruenor muttered, and he called for his guard commanders, pulled a mug of ale from his magical shield, drained it in one swallow, then sent both the tankard and a loud belch flying.

CHAPTER 9

Epler Veien

The Melarni have marched," Kimmuriel told Gromph, the two of them in the archmage's suite at the Hosttower. "In force, all of them, and House Hunzrin beside them, I expect."

"When?" Gromph demanded. "And where have you been?" He was feeling especially edgy this day, with whispers all about Luskan of an approaching hostile fleet and the news from the south of the advance of demon hordes.

"I was sent to speak with priestess Ash'ala."

"That was tendays ago."

"What she hinted to me required confirmation, and so I sought confirmation, but not any that could be found on this plane of existence."

"You went to the illithid hive mind," Gromph stated.

Kimmuriel nodded.

"Over the disposition of puny Matron Zhindia Melarn?" the great wizard asked incredulously. "Does she make you so unsettled that you run to the mind flayers? Would you like me to find her and destroy her?"

Kimmuriel's expression did not change in the face of Gromph's sarcasm, or the great wizard's boast, which, under normal circumstances, would be a perfectly reasonable one.

"Well?" the agitated Gromph prompted.

"*Arachna'chinin'lihi'elders,*" Kimmuriel replied. "Matron Zhindia is not alone."

Gromph stared curiously at the diminutive psionicist for a few heartbeats, replaying the strange word in his thoughts. It was in an old language, older than he, older than Menzoberranzan. His eyes widened as he at last deciphered it.

"A *retriever?* Zhindia has been granted a retriever?" Gromph paused and took a deep and steadying breath, then shook his head. "You are certain?"

Kimmuriel didn't blink.

"Then it was not Lolth who brought Zaknafein back from his eternal sleep, no," Gromph reasoned. "And now the Spider Queen will have him back, and she has chosen Matron Zhindia Melarn as her spear?" He shook his head again. "Zaknafein, yes? It must be Zaknafein."

"It is an old word," Kimmuriel replied. "Perhaps I misspoke."

"Then take better care," Gromph scolded. "Do not throw such a prospect as a retriever—"

"*Arachna'chinin'lihi'eldernai,*" Kimmuriel corrected, the proper way to pluralize the demonic constructs.

"*Eldernai?*" Gromph echoed breathlessly. "Plural?"

"Two," Kimmuriel confirmed.

"Then Lolth is truly with her," said Gromph. "And we must consider that our lives and allegiances—"

"We do not know that it is Lolth at all," Kimmuriel interrupted.

"Then who?" Gromph said dismissively, but the question slammed back against him before Kimmuriel had even responded.

"There is another demon lord, who titles himself the Prince of Demons, who is not pleased," the psionicist reminded him.

Demogorgon, the archmage realized, brought to the material plane by Gromph, and destroyed in its corporeal form through the power of Menzoberranzan channeled through the might of the illithid hive mind—channeled, in no small part, by these very same two drow.

"You assume the targets to be Zaknafein and, possibly, Drizzt Do'Urden, of course," Kimmuriel said. "But there are others who have gained the enmity of demons powerful enough to create retrievers. I find it unlikely that Drizzt is so hunted, though Matron Zhindia surely loathes him, since Lolth had him in the tunnels of Damara and did not destroy him. Perhaps they are both for Zaknafein."

Now it was Gromph's turn to shake his head. "You cannot aim two such beasts at the same target, for they would attack each other for interference, so singularly are they focused on one task alone."

Gromph played all angles out in his thoughts. Matron Zhindia was leading this charge—that was the only thing giving him hope here that he was not one of the targets. Zhindia hated Drizzt and Jarlaxle, and the human Entreri, for they three had attacked her in her house and had murdered her only daughter—with Entreri's awful dagger, so said the whispers, and so she could not be resurrected. But would Zhindia, would Lolth, waste a retriever on the likes of a mere human?

Gromph didn't think that likely.

"It is not Artemis Entreri," Kimmuriel said to him, an unsubtle reminder that the psionicist was reading his thoughts.

"We must learn who, then," Gromph demanded, growing angry. "It must be confirmed. Did you learn *anything* among the mind flayers?"

"The hive mind does not exist to answer my questions on my time-table," he replied.

"Press them."

"Press? One does not press illithids."

"Need I remind you that it was Kimmuriel who brought the power of the hive mind to bear against Demogorgon? It is quite possible that these unstoppable golems are here for you."

Kimmuriel shrugged again.

"You will flee to the illithids if that is the case!" Gromph accused.

"As would, as *will*, Gromph if he learns similarly."

"This is no play in which I wish to partake," the archmage said.

"We must learn the alliances behind this rise of darkness. Who granted the *arachna'chinin'lihi'eldernai*, and why?"

"Whoever it was, and for whatever target, our world has changed, Archmage," Kimmuriel stated, and to that Gromph could only nod his agreement. If either of these beasts had Gromph as its target, he would spend the coming decades, centuries even, in constant flight, plane-walking, unless and until he was caught or somehow found a way to defeat that which was virtually unbeatable and unstoppable.

PENELOPE HARPELL CRAWLED ONTO THE SIDE OF HER large bed in her comfortable chambers at the Hosttower.

She paused and stared at her lover's naked back, huge and strong, thick but hard as granite, and with clear defining lines separating the many muscles. It seemed to Penelope that if he stood and bent forward, arms wide to either side, you could put the whole world on that back and he would hold it aloft. The woman waited a moment longer before she crawled up behind him as he sat on the bed, near the bottom, legs crossed before him and seemingly unaware that she had returned.

Wulfgar had a lot on his mind, she knew. The news from the south, from Gauntlgrym, where his adoptive dwarven father was king and where many of his dearest friends resided, was not promising. And Bleeding Vines, the village he had helped build with his friend Regis, had been utterly sacked, the vineyards torn asunder, the tram station to the Causeway ruined.

And Wulfgar had been here through all of that sudden assault and the ensuing press on Gauntlgrym, visiting Penelope, wanting to share her bed. All seemed relatively secure in Gauntlgrym at the moment, at least, and Bruenor had sent word through the magical portal for Wulfgar to remain in Luskan as Bruenor's emissary. That, too, had weighed heavily on this warrior, Penelope understood. He wanted nothing more than to go through that gate and join the fight on the front lines beside his friends. He wouldn't disobey King Bruenor on this, however, and so he had returned to Penelope.

That thought, that Wulfgar had sought comfort and distraction with her, sent shivers down the woman's spine, particularly now as she looked at his huge and chiseled body, a body that was somewhere around twenty years of age, though the man's consciousness was much older than that, older than Penelope by far. She was closer to fifty than forty, with gray beginning to show in her dark hair and a few more lines in her face, particularly around the eyes from all the squinting she did when studying spellbooks and old scrolls. She was still quite strong and healthy, though thicker than she liked in a few places, and not as firm in others as she had once been. She didn't really care too much about all that, but it felt good to know that she could still turn the eye of a man like Wulfgar.

He kept coming back to her bed, eagerly, happily.

She crawled over to kneel behind him and brought her hands to either side of his neck, digging in her thumbs to massage the corded bands of muscle that ran to his shoulders.

"My magnificent man," she said, "why are you here in my bed once more?"

"Why wouldn't I be?" he responded, bringing his left hand up and across to place it atop her right.

"Is there a woman on the Sword Coast who wouldn't open for you? Is there a young and pretty girl who would not love to be safely en-wrapped in your strong arms?" As she asked, she ran her hands down over his shoulders to his giant biceps. "And yet you are here, with me."

Wulfgar gave a little laugh. "Penelope Harpell, the grand dame of the Ivy Mansion, doubts herself?" He swiveled his head to let her see his incredulous look. "Few things surprise me, woman, but yes, I am surprised."

"Not a doubt," she returned with a playful slap on his shoulder. "Merely simple honesty." She shuffled around the side of him to better look into his crystal-blue eyes—ah, those eyes! Even Wulfgar's eyes spoke of the startling and wonderful contrasts of this man. He was dark and he was light, hard and strong but oh so gentle.

"You are a young man," she said, "and I am not a young woman."

"I was a century and four years when I was killed by a yeti," Wulf-gar reminded her with a sincere and warm laugh.

"Yes, but you were reborn, and given youth and strength and all the beauty that comes with them. You could have almost any woman, but here you are. Why?"

"*Epler veien*," Wulfgar answered after a brief pause.

"*Epler* . . ." Penelope, too, paused, and considered the root of the language—she knew most of the dialects in the north, and recognized this as an Uthgardt barbarian phrase, certainly. She became even more confused as she did sort it, though, and it showed on her face.

"Trail apples," Wulfgar said.

"You think me deer poo?"

"I think you honest," Wulfgar replied. "Not just to others, but to yourself. I think you wonderfully and refreshingly selfish."

"The compliments just flow from your pretty lips," Penelope answered with a grin and a shake of her head. She leaned back from the side of his shoulder and looked at him a bit sidelong.

"Perhaps *selfish* is the wrong word, but I do not mean it as an insult," Wulfgar told her. "Quite the opposite. Penelope Harpell knows what she wants and moves to get it. You are honest with yourself and brave enough to proclaim that honesty to all around you. You tear free the bindings of convention and tradition and . . . signs."

"Signs?"

"Aye," said Wulfgar, nodding and gaining clarity in his own thoughts now. "Signs. They are everywhere, written or spoken, rules and laws, and some matter, and some are there because they are there, because somewhere, sometime, someone put them there."

"Like trail apples."

Wulfgar laughed. "Exactly. And no one has had the courage or the sense to tear them down. But you don't step in them, no. There is no pretense to Penelope. There is no hidden Penelope. Do you not understand, my beautiful and wonderful friend? You are not just who I desire, you are what I desire of myself."

Penelope spent a heartbeat trying to digest that. "Am I your lover or your teacher?" she asked.

"Yes, and more!" Wulfgar proclaimed. He playfully reached down and touched the inside of Penelope's knee as she knelt beside him, then ran his fingers lightly, so lightly—perhaps they weren't even touching her, but just calling to her skin!—up the inside of her thigh.

"You are my truth," he said earnestly. "You are my hero."

Penelope swung around before him and straddled him, never letting go of his intense gaze. She gasped as he thrust forward to join them together.

"But there are so many pretty girls," she said, and now she was just playing with him. "Do you not wish to . . . ?"

"Have you ever told me that I should not?"

Penelope pulled her head back and stared at him slyly.

"Are you jealous?" Wulfgar asked with a playful grin.

She returned the look. "Only if I am not there with you," she teased, and came forward to kiss him, and they held the kiss all through their lovemaking, a long and single kiss, then melted together to the blankets to fall asleep in each other's arms.

RINGING BELLS AWAKENED WULFGAR AND PENELOPE SOME-time later.

"What?" the big man asked, and when he realized the location of the bells, right outside Penelope's door, he laughed. "Of course," he said to her as she pushed herself up on her elbows and shook the hair out of her face. "You would not accept a simple knock upon your door."

"That is not my doing," the woman assured him. She rolled over on her back, sat up, and pulled the bedcovers up.

"May we enter, lady?" Gromph Baenre asked from beyond the door.

Wulfgar was confused. Penelope's chambers, like those of many of the great wizards housed here at this most unusual abode, were extraplanar, pockets of extradimensional space much larger than the physical area they inhabited at the Hosttower.

But it sounded to him as if Gromph was right outside the physical door—despite the fact that this physical door was not even on the same plane of existence as the archmage at the time.

Or was it?

"Wizards are confusing creatures," the man grumbled.

"Enter," Penelope answered, and waved her hand. The door swung open, revealing two of Wulfgar's least favorite people: Gromph Baenre and Kimmuriel Oblodra. With only a very few exceptions, wizards unnerved Wulfgar because he didn't understand them, but compared to Kimmuriel, Gromph would be a welcomed dinner companion.

The two walked right up to the foot of the bed, Kimmuriel looking straight at Wulfgar and offering a clearly derisive snort.

"We've trouble brewing," Gromph said.

"We've heard," said Penelope.

"You've heard of Bleeding Vines and the press on Gauntlgrym, but we are speaking of a different event," Kimmuriel corrected.

"There is a fleet bound for Luskan, a great war armada," Gromph explained. "Port Llast was sacked, we believe, though there has been no word directly from the town, and the fleet sailed out from there to the north."

"For Luskan," Penelope said.

"So it would seem. High Captain Kurth is rallying the ships to sail out to meet the challenge, that we might at least learn their intent," Gromph went on. "We suspect they mean to attack straightaway, but we need to know more about their disposition, and their strength."

Penelope nodded.

"I will discern all of that," Kimmuriel explained. "And I would take you, Wulfgar, with me, to guard over me."

"Of course," said Penelope, clutching the blankets tight to her chest. She looked to her lover and promised, "We will stop them."

"Not you, lady," Gromph told her. "Him. You go home to Longsaddle."

Penelope scoffed openly at that, staring at the man angrily. "Gromph does not—" she began to say.

"Go to Catti-brie, lady," he interrupted, "and keep her safe."

"She can well keep herself safe," Penelope angrily replied, and would have gone further, except that Wulfgar put his hand on her shoulder to quiet her.

"What do you know?" Wulfgar demanded.

"This darkness is more than you comprehend," Gromph explained, speaking more to Penelope than to Wulfgar. "A great evil is come, and it is aimed and with purpose, and that purpose is for chosen people. I think it is aimed at the man Catti-brie loves most, but I cannot be certain. If that is the case, then she, too, might be in great danger, and so I bid you to go to her."

"Catti-brie is more powerful than I," Penelope replied. "If she cannot defend herself, then what am I to do?"

"Put the eyes from the Ivy Mansion all about," Gromph told her. "And if the darkness approaches, then send her away, far away, to the ends of Faerun, to another plane, even."

"What are you babbling about, wizard?" Wulfgar demanded. He moved forward, the blankets falling away, showing the muscles of his arms and chest tight with tension.

Gromph ignored him. "Would you have Drizzt breath his last knowing that Catti-brie died before him? Knowing that their child was killed because of him?" he asked of Penelope.

The tone of his voice surprised the woman, for it was filled with unexpected humanity.

"Lady, go to Catti-brie and make sure that she is safe," the archmage stated flatly.

Penelope turned to Wulfgar, both wearing expressions of confusion and trepidation.

"We must go," Kimmuriel said to him. "We must learn the truth of this armada that sails against Luskan. The ships are readying."

Wulfgar nodded.

"You're going to die out there," Penelope whispered.

"This is my truth," Wulfgar quietly replied. "I hate the signs. I love you because you ignore the signs, but this, this I cannot ignore. The sign of friendship is one I welcome and must not, cannot ignore." He pulled her face up to look her in the eye. "Nor can you."

CHAPTER 10

Clandestine

With the strange young drow woman's magical prowess, Regis, Athrogate, and Yvonnel covered the many miles to Waterdeep in only a few days, with Athrogate, still sorely wounded, riding the entire way on a conjured magical disk.

Now the city—not the most populous of the Realms, but considered by most to be the greatest in Faerun—lay in sight, off in the distance to the southeast, with its great towers and palaces, and bridges, and giant statues.

Regis took a deep breath, signifying the importance and danger of his chosen mission.

"You are certain of this?" Yvonnel asked him.

"The lords of Waterdeep have to know. I do wish you'd come in with me."

"My life is complicated enough already," Yvonnel replied. "I am not even sure of what role I have played in all of this, or of what my role might be going forward. Having me there would more than com-plicate your message, my friend; it would give those who oppose you weapons to use against you with those who might otherwise be sym-pathetic to your pleas."

Regis nodded. They had already discussed this extensively. Still, he had witnessed the power of Yvonnel Baenre quite clearly—the woman had used a simple word of power to dissolve a major demon! And Athrogate—how could Regis look upon his battered dwarven friend and not recognize that without the amazing magical healing of Yvonnel, Athrogate would be long dead? Even now, for all her efforts, the mighty dwarf slept most of the day, with groans and not snores, and whenever he had to get off that disk, it took Regis's shoulder to hold him upright.

"You will heal him again this day?" he asked.

"Every day, or he will die," Yvonnel answered. "He was stung by the barbs of the lower planes. The poison is thick. Truly, I am sur-prised that he survived."

"If ye're thinkin' me dead, then make yer bet. I'll be takin' yer coin, 'cause I ain't dead yet," Athrogate said, his voice weak and shaky, but his tone defiant. Usually there was a laugh to accompany the black-bearded dwarf's silly rhymes, but not this time, Regis noted. Not at all. The dwarf was deadly serious and had told Regis that he wasn't dying until he had found revenge for his beloved Ambergris.

Regis heard it in Athrogate's voice now and realized that he cer-tainly wouldn't be betting against this tough old dwarf!

"How will you know which of the Waterdhavian lords to trust?" Yvonnel asked, taking him back to the matter at hand. "And which of them might betray you to Lord Neverember or these other conspira-tors?"

"We have spies in place in Waterdeep," Regis replied. "I know where to find them, one in particular. I've no doubt that he has already sorted friend from enemy."

"Artemis Entreri?"

Regis nodded.

"Your friend?"

Regis chuckled. "I don't think I'd ever call him that, but in this matter, I can trust him. At least, I hope I can."

"And if not?"

Regis shrugged. "A fine Companion of the Hall would I be if I wouldn't even have the courage to try."

Yvonnel looked at him curiously, obviously not getting the reference.

"Here's to hoping that someday we'll be sitting by my hearth in Bleeding Vines rebuilt, and I can tell you all the stories, lady. All of them."

"Ye tell her about me Ambergris, Amber Gristle O'Maul," Athrogate said from the floating disk.

"You'll tell her those tales," Regis replied.

"Aye," the dwarf said unconvincingly. He heaved a sigh. "And if I can't, yerself'll tell 'em, eh, Rumblebelly?"

Regis couldn't help but smile at the nickname, his own nickname and the one he had given to his pony, a nickname Bruenor had given to him years and years before on the banks of Maer Dualdon in Icewind Dale.

"I will," he promised, then said to Yvonnel, "Keep him alive. Make him well." He slid from his mount and handed the reins to the drow woman. "And keep him well, too. He's been a fine companion."

The striking Yvonnel—whose eyes were now purple to match those of Drizzt, Regis noted—offered a nod.

"And where will you go?" Regis asked.

Yvonnel looked to Athrogate. "We'll find our way. Eventually back to Drizzt, I hope. But we may be doing some good out here."

"Thornhold!" Athrogate said, coughing some blood as he did.

Yvonnel patted her hand in the air to calm him. She had warned him not to become too agitated, and not to speak loudly or harshly for a while. She turned back to Regis and shrugged deferentially, making him think that they would indeed revisit the old and battered keep where Amber had died, where Athrogate had been so wickedly wounded.

The halfling nodded his farewell, took a deep and steadying breath, then turned to the southwest and the distant waiting city. He thought of his friends, caught in a hole beneath the mountain. He thought of Donnola and Drizzt and Bruenor and Wulfgar and Catti-brie. He remembered why he had agreed with the proposition of Iruladoon, the magical afterlife forest where he, Bruenor, Catti-brie, and Wulfgar had been given the opportunity of rebirth. On that occasion, when the choice was laid bare, Regis hadn't hesitated, and had been glad for the ability to live his life once more, primarily because he vowed that this time would be different, particularly in his relationship with his beloved friends. This time, he wouldn't be the tagalong. This time, he had vowed, determined, and trained all of his second life to ensure he wouldn't be the one the others had to look out for. No, this time, Regis would more than earn his place among the Companions of the Hall.

Now that meant he had to go into a nest of powerful vipers, the Margasters and their allies. Demonic villains, literally.

"They need me," he whispered under his breath, and he straightened his belt and took his first bold step toward Waterdeep.

DAHLIA MOVED CAREFULLY ABOUT THE GRAND HALL, BAT-ting her eyes at the gentlemen and offering polite but somewhat icy nods to the ladies at the ball. From her years in Thay, the graceful elven woman had this act perfected, and so she blended in seamlessly with these lords and ladies, all of whom she considered rather dull and contemptible. Had any of them truly earned their place in these exclusive circles?

Birthright and nothing more, she was certain for most at least, and to Dahlia there was little worse than station without merit. But she knew how to play this game, and how to use her charms to garner whatever information she might need. Information was power, and Dahlia liked power, particularly now with word from Jarlaxle of the brewing trouble. Entreri had tasked her with sorting out where the lords and ladies might stand on Lord Neverember and King Bruenor.

Dahlia hoped to gain a lot more information than that, particularly when noting how many young men here, and more than a few young women, kept looking her way hungrily.

She painted on a pretty and demure smile when a young lord and lady approached her, the man holding an extra glass of fine Feywine.

"I'm not sure I've had the pleasure," he said, and he introduced himself and his friend—pointedly calling the lady his *friend*, and not *wife* or *companion*. Dahlia was pretty sure what he wanted.

"Dahlia Syn'dalay of the Shakebrook Syn'dalay," she replied, honestly, for she was certain that none here would know of that distant, tiny elven clan. She said it with the practiced haughtiness of a finely bred elf, which she was, or would have been, had she not been kidnapped by the horrid Netherese at the tender age of twelve.

Certainly, in her sleeveless and backless crimson gown, she looked the part of one who would be invited to such a ball as this. She was tall for an elf, nearly six feet, with black hair that she dyed with streaks of cardinal red. For most of her life, she had kept her head mostly shaven, with a single braid running down the back and over her shoulder, that she could chew on it when she was concerned or confused, but now she had let the hair grow quite long on the right side, and had grown it out, too, on the left, though she kept that much shorter, so as not to cover her left ear, which was nearly fully lined with small diamonds.

Those diamonds meant a lot to her, and not for reasons monetary.

Displaying those diamonds meant a lot to her, and not for reasons of vanity.

She wasn't wearing any studs in her right ear these days and hadn't since she had come to understand the truth of her relationship with Artemis Entreri. Indeed, the thought of adding a stud for him had not, other than initially, crossed her mind.

For those studs meant something, signifying lovers she meant to kill, so that she could transfer them to her left ear, with their diamond match, to show off how many lovers she had already killed. She had once worn as many as five at one time in that right ear, but now there could be only one, and for a man she had no intention of ever harming, a man who understood her because his youthful experiences had been so awfully similar to her own.

Artemis Entreri had overcome those demons, finally, and was helping Dahlia do the same. So she hoped.

"Well, milady Syn'dalay, truly I am so very pleased to meet you," the man said, and at that moment, Dahlia realized that she should have been more attentive so that she might actually remember the names of her conversation partners.

"Yes, well, that is the whole point of such gatherings, is it not?" she purred back, leaning forward as she took the offered drink from him. She watched his eyes as she did and decided to find a way to get his name, because she knew that he would do much to make her happy. Yes, it would be very important to this young lord to make Dahlia Syn'dalay like him.

His companion knew it, too; Dahlia could tell by her not-quite-hidden scowl as she watched his eyes following Dahlia's bow, a scowl she extended to Dahlia, knowing very well that the elven woman's forward bend was neither unconscious nor unintentional.

For the first time that night, Dahlia was enjoying herself—not because she had any intention of even kissing this pompous fool, but because she did so enjoy the play of confounding, frustrating, and angering these powdered and perfumed empty souls.

So, she set about the task immediately, or started to, when out of the side of her eye she noted the entrance of another quite striking figure.

He was almost exactly half her height, though his grand blue beret made him seem a bit taller. While he appeared to be in fine physical health, there wasn't much girth to him, but somehow, the halfling seemed much larger than that, with his perfectly trimmed mustache, curling upward just beyond his ample lips, and a hint of a beard running down the center of his chin. He wore the fashionable beret and a cape to match, thick and luxurious, along with a fine leather vest over his red shirt, a bandolier of hand-crossbow quarrels crossing from his left shoulder to his right hip. A brilliant rapier sat on his left hip, and a three-tined dagger showed fantastic craftsmanship, with the outer two swordbreakers shaped as cobras about to strike. His black boots with silver buckles were so shiny that Dahlia fancied she might comb her hair in her reflection in them.

Yes, he was quite the dashing figure, his cloak flung back over his left shoulder to give a full view of that marvelous rapier and his vest undone just enough to hint at another weapon he carried beneath it: a hand crossbow of drow design.

"Spider Parrafin," Dahlia muttered, for she knew this newcomer. In fact, she knew him better as Regis, friend to her former lover, Drizzt, and his gang, the Companions of the Hall. "What are you doing here, you little troublemaker?" she muttered under her breath, but not quietly enough, apparently, for the man standing before her said, "Your pardon? Troublemaker? Why yes, I suppose—"

"Shut up," said the woman with him, and he did.

"Oh, I am terribly sorry," Dahlia said. "I did not mean . . . there are these voices that will not leave me alone. Well, one voice, low and grating, and telling me to do all kinds of awful things . . ."

The man blanched, the woman gasped, and both fell back a step.

"These are strange times," said the woman, clearly trying to pull the man away.

"Who are you visiting in Waterdeep, good Lady Syn'dalay?" the man asked, determined to continue his acquaintance with the elf.

Dahlia suppressed her grin, thinking she had stumbled onto a fine and possibly beneficial tangent here. "Just some friends. I thought they would be at the ball, but alas, I see none. I am afraid that I know no one here, to my surprise."

"What friends?" both asked together.

"Why do you ask?"

The way they looked at each other told the perceptive Dahlia quite a bit. These two had heard rumors of some strange happenings, she realized, and she could well guess which house of Waterdeep they might now be thinking of as Dahlia's hosts.

"No reason at all," the woman replied to her. "It's just that perhaps we might know them and so could suggest some course of action for you to see about this . . . affliction."

"Oh, it's no affliction!" Dahlia said dramatically. "And nothing new. I was kicked by a headstrong pony—but then, I repeat myself— when I—" She paused, recognizing that the man was about to speak.

"Not the Margasters, then?" he asked, and again Dahlia did well to hide her grin, for that was exactly what she had wanted to hear.

"Kicked when I was young," she finished, "and these voices have followed me ever since. I do believe the little beastly thing kicked a spirit into my head!" She ended with a laugh, then paused and said, "Margasters?" as if she had never before heard the name.

The young lord and lady again looked to each other, the woman rolling her eyes, the man wearing a disappointed expression indeed.

"Well, do enjoy the ball, with your voice . . . er, friend," the woman said, moving away and tugging her companion with her, leaving Dahlia's path open to Regis.

Dahlia watched them a few moments longer, rolling her eyes rather crazily when the woman glanced back her way. She knew that she shouldn't be standing out like this with her feigned troubles, but sometimes she just couldn't resist.

Finished playing, she moved toward Regis, who was at the cloakroom just inside the main hall, handing over his sword belt, bandolier, and finally, with apparent great remorse, his precious hand crossbow.

He turned before she arrived, his face brightening when he recognized her, but Dahlia quickly lifted her hand to rub her eye, the Bregan D'aerthe signal to feign that they were not companions or known to each other.

"A so pretty elf at a Waterdeep ball," Regis said loudly at her approach, and he bowed gracefully. "I am not used to such unexpected pleasures." He took her hand and kissed it, looking rather stupid in the process, she thought.

"And what is your name, beautiful lady?"

"Dahlia Syn'dalay," she replied.

"Spider—" he started to answer.

"Parrafin," she finished for him. "Yes, of course I know of you and the Grinning Ponies who protect the Trade Way. Who has not heard of the dashing halfling?"

She tried not to laugh at Regis's confused expression.

"In truth, my heroic one, I came here hoping to meet you," Dahlia said. "Perhaps we can go find a quiet place to discuss our evening's plans? To see if they, perhaps, coincide, I mean."

The man collecting cloaks and weapons put on a knowing grin, even tossed a wink to Dahlia over the halfling's head.

Regis spun about to collect his weapons. "I have only just arrived," he said, feigning some disappointment. "But how can I refuse one of your obvious charms?"

Touch one of those charms and I'll kill you, Dahlia thought, and meant, but did not say. She wasn't very fond of halflings in general and had little love for the Companions of the Hall on top of that.

"We'll soon return," Dahlia told the man, retrieving her own cloak, and she grabbed Regis's arm and pulled him hurriedly out of the room.

Through the large anteroom and down a side hallway, several smaller rooms had been set up for the party, some as bedrooms, others as conversation sitting rooms, complete with a bartender and tables set apart for private chatter. Dahlia really didn't trust these second rooms, as Artemis Entreri had come to an earlier ball with another Bregan D'aerthe associate and had dropped some rumors in them, just to see if they had spread—which they had. Those sitting rooms were not secure from curious eavesdroppers.

The bedrooms, though, likely were—one Waterdeep family had been caught eavesdropping on a dalliance years earlier and was still shunned to this day for their voyeurism and troublemaking. After all, the Waterdeep noble families, indeed noble families everywhere, really weren't that different from the drow of Menzoberranzan or the Red Wizards of Thay, Dahlia knew: you could do anything you could get away with, but anyone interrupting and gossiping about that secret play would never again be allowed in "polite" company.

She yanked Regis roughly into one of the bedrooms and pulled the door closed behind them, even as the halfling was crying out, "Lady, you are quite the aggressor!"

"What are you doing here?" Dahlia demanded when the door was closed.

"I—"

"Who told you to come here this night? Are you trying to expose me, you fool?"

"Lady, no. There is much . . . I mean, I had no choice."

"Explain," Dahlia demanded, crossing her arms and glaring down at the little halfling.

Regis glanced around nervously.

"No one can hear," Dahlia said.

So Regis did explain. He told her about Thornhold and the demons, about the attack on Bleeding Vines and Gauntlgrym, and of how he and the other Grinning Ponies had decided that they needed to get to Waterdeep to beg intervention, or all might be lost, even Luskan, with an invading fleet sailing north along the Sword Coast.

Dahlia couldn't hold her anger at him as he explained, her arms gradually slipping down to her sides.

"I only came in here because I thought I might find you or Entreri in attendance," Regis finished. "I don't know which lords I might trust, and a wrong word would be disastrous."

Dahlia nodded. He had done everything correctly, she knew, and indeed, his caution was merited.

"Tell no one," Dahlia warned him. "Go back into the ball and play the night away however you might—with no intoxicating drink or smoke!"

"I have already taken appropriate precautions, lady," he said with a sly grin, then on impulse, he whispered, "For the love of pink pearls," the trigger words for his pouch, which was really a pouch of holding with a large extradimensional pocket. He reached in and pulled out a small flask, then a second.

"This will prevent you from being poisoned, even with alcohol or some other intoxicating thing," he told Dahlia, handing it over. "And this one . . ." He grinned wickedly and held the flask aloft, swirling it, showing her the pink ovoid floating within the somewhat translucent purple liquid. "This one will let you scan the thoughts of another, preferably one who has had a bit too much to drink."

That, too, he handed over.

"You may find it of some use, though you'd likely not need it to discern the thoughts of any man you might be speaking with."

"Playing on my vanity?" Dahlia replied. "Such a charming one."

"Speaking simple truth, and don't pretend you don't know it, and know how to use it," said Regis, and when Dahlia cocked an eyebrow, he quickly added, honestly, "Because I do the same thing, as does my lovely wife, Donnola."

That brought a chuckle, at least.

Dahlia glanced around, although they were in a small, enclosed room and there was obviously no one else about, then moved near and whispered an address into Regis's ear. "South Ward," she explained. "Tonight, after midnight. And take great care in making your way. It would be better if you were not dead quite yet."

Regis nodded, then closed his eyes and silently repeated the address to commit it to memory, exactly as his years at House Topolino in Aglarond—where paper trails meant hanging thieves—had taught him.

When he opened his eyes again, Dahlia was already gone, back to the ball.

With a shrug, the halfling followed. He had hours to kill, so he might as well enjoy himself and learn what he could in the meantime.

"YOU ARE AWAKE."

"Aye, ye might be callin' it that. Wish I weren't." The sound of his own voice, shaky and breaking, reminded Athrogate of just how miserable and weak he felt, as if every joint in his body had been driven through with a stake, as if his skin had been taken off and then put back on, but with biting midges lining the inside of it. He was too hot and too cold, all at the same time, and the mere thought of food made him want to vomit.

"I will soon have more spells to offer to ease your pain," Yvonnel said.

With great effort, the dwarf propped himself up on one elbow and looked around. He was still on the magical disk and it was moving, following Yvonnel as she moved slowly along the road, Regis's pony in tow. North, Athrogate realized, since the water was on the left.

"Still at the coast?" he asked, sinking back down as he did, for the sensation of motion as the ground rolled past the disk had his belly roiling. It took him a long while to settle himself enough to add, "Thinked we'd be turnin' inland for the Crags and Gauntlgrym."

"There is an army of demons surrounding the place," Yvonnel replied. "We'll do no one any good there, particularly with you in such a state."

"Bah!" He sensed the disk stopping. Then Yvonnel towered over him, staring down.

"Good Athrogate, I warn you that you are not yet healed, and far from recovered," she said. "I am doing all that I can, and will continue to do so, of course, but do not misperceive that your survival is assured."

"Good," he muttered as soon as he had deciphered the highbrow and somewhat obtuse remark.

Yvonnel grabbed him by the collar and forced him to look at her. "I could let you die," she said calmly, "if I truly believed that you wanted to die, or that your immediate belief that you would prefer death weren't solely because of the great pain of losing one you loved."

"Bah, what d'ya know?" the dwarf asked.

"More than you can imagine," the drow woman replied. "You think me young, but I have memories longer than the oldest person you will ever meet. Older than Jarlaxle by a millennium."

Athrogate harrumphed.

"Look at me, dwarf," Yvonnel quietly demanded, and he did, though with a scowl he simply could not wipe off his face. "I do understand your pain. It is pain I have known many times."

To his surprise, Athrogate found that he believed her.

"It will ever be there, but it *will* diminish, and it will diminish more for you, particularly for you, if you know that you dealt with this in a way that honors the memory of your beloved Amber."

"Ye think ye know her, then?"

"I wish I had," she said with sincerity. "I know of her, though. I know what others say about her. I know what you have said about her. Amber was no coward, and if she were here now and Athrogate were the one who had been killed . . ."

"If only that!"

Yvonnel smiled and nodded, conceding the point to him. "She would have said exactly that to my point," she said.

The words hit home. Athrogate couldn't dispute them.

"And she, I believe, would come forth from the dark shade within her heart to honor the loss of Athrogate. She, if she was all that you and others claim, would accept my help and fight her way back to health, if only so that she could inflict great pain upon those who took you from her."

Athrogate had no answer to that. Clever woman, he thought, to so turn the tables on him!

Yvonnel leaned in very close. "I'm going to get you healthy and strong once more," she whispered. "If you're so content with the thought of your own death, then be not afraid of punishing the monsters who took your love from you."

"Aye, lass, ye make a good argument."

"And I'll be there right beside you, Athrogate. What say you then? For Amber Gristle O'Maul of the Adbar O'Mauls?"

The dwarf smiled, widely and warmly, then closed his eyes as Yvonnel began a spell, one that sent waves of warm healing through him and sent him falling, falling, into a deep sleep.

"WE'VE BEEN IN THIS WRETCHED CITY ALMOST ENTIRELY since I returned from the Underdark," Artemis Entreri told Regis when the halfling joined him and Dahlia at his apartment in Waterdeep's South Ward much later that night. "And neither of us has any idea of which are friend and which enemy."

"And we haven't the time to figure it out," Regis replied. He tried to hold his voice steady, tried to remind himself that everything was at stake here, and that the very reason he had decided on this second chance at life was to succeed in exactly this position. Still, he couldn't deny the intimidation of Artemis Entreri. Regis knew everything that was said about the man, of how he had grown and become a better person, an ally.

But Regis kept nervously fidgeting with the remaining stub of his left pinkie finger, lost in this life, the result coincidentally mimicking almost exactly the stub he had worn for most of his first life, after this same Artemis Entreri had cut off that finger to send it as a message to Drizzt.

Was there any amount of time and any number of deeds that could fully erase that? Regis wondered.

"So you decided to openly proclaim your presence?" Entreri asked, barely containing a sneer. "Yes, I know all about your play at Never-ember's palace, and of Spider Parrafin's drinks with a pair of Water-dhavian nobles in the Driftwood Tavern in Neverwinter City."

"How could—"

"And if I know, do you not believe that half of Waterdeep knows? Or at least, half of those who would wish to know? What were you thinking walking into that tavern openly? Are you fool enough to believe that the names Spider Parrafin and Regis are not realized to be one and the same?"

"I . . . I had no reason to disguise myself at that time," the halfling tried to explain. "I was not known to be in the city, and since my purpose there was to legitimately sell wine from Bleeding Vines, there seemed no reason for any cover. We had no idea at that time how deep—nay, how demonic this conspiracy lay."

"But now you do," Entreri retorted, "and you still walked into the ball tonight openly as Regis Topolino, or Spider Parrafin, or whatever you fancy to call yourself at this time."

Regis felt sick to his stomach, but he fought it away. "Strong words from Barrabus the Gray," he said back, drawing a snort from Entreri.

"Do not even pretend you understand that," Entreri warned, hold-ing fast his aggressive upper hand and not wanting to discuss that long-past time in his life, when he had been enslaved. "I'll ask again: why would you enter that ball this night?"

"Because I expected I would find you," Regis replied, "or her, or another of our operatives in attendance. There was no ball in Delthuntle that did not include a member of House Topolino in my years there."

"But openly?" Dahlia interjected.

Regis shrugged at her. "How else might I have gotten an invitation if not as Regis of Bleeding Vines, friend of King Bruenor Battlehammer?" He turned determinedly back to Artemis Entreri. "None mentioned the battles in the north. None blinked an eye when they learned of my identity, even though Bleeding Vines is likely under siege as we speak."

"Bleeding Vines has been wholly sacked," the assassin replied.

Regis was beginning to reply before Entreri had even finished the sentence, but the weight of that statement stole the breath from the halfling.

"Lady Donnola is alive and well," Entreri quickly added, and there seemed to be something unusual in his voice. Sympathy? "Almost all of the town got down the tram to Gauntlgrym, and so survived, but Gauntlgrym now is under attack itself."

Regis fought frantically and futilely to find his voice.

"The lords of Waterdeep surely know what is happening in the Crags," Entreri went on. "But they don't want anyone, particularly one like *you*, to know that they know."

"But why?"

"Because then they would have to do something about it," Dahlia said, and Entreri nodded.

"You poor little fool," Entreri added. "You still hold out hope for the valiance and altruism of the ruling nobles of Faerun."

"That would include King Bruenor," Regis reminded.

"Bruenor is not typical of the class," said Entreri. "Understand that first and foremost."

"I am no inexperienced waif."

"Then quit acting like one."

"You seem to believe that I had many options before me!"

"That is a reasonable point," said Dahlia.

Entreri thought on that for a moment, then nodded. "So you came to inform and mobilize Waterdeep."

"I had hoped to discern ally from enemy first, through your information."

Entreri nodded. "Would that it might be so simple. We know the main enemy."

"Margasters, and likely Neverember himself."

"Lord Dagult remains in Neverwinter, from all that I can tell. But yes, the Margasters are deep in this. Do not underestimate them."

"I don't. I have seen their treasury."

"And that is but a part. As far as I can tell, they have bought the acquiescence, if not alliance, of several other noble houses, and half the city guards."

"We don't know that," Dahlia said.

"I prefer to assume it," Entreri replied. "We know it to be true of some, at least, and I do not believe they'd leave things to half measures."

When Dahlia didn't dispute that, there followed an uncomfortable silence, the weight of dread palpable in the room, until Regis broke it with a meek "What do we do?"

"We know the serpent's head," Artemis Entreri quietly replied, and he gave that look, that awful look—awful to Regis even though he knew he wasn't the target of it!—that had become so synonymous with his reputation through the decades.

"I see no reason to appeal to the good nature of the proper authorities, then," the halfling agreed, mimicking the assassin's deathly even tone so completely that it drew an arched eyebrow from Entreri.

Regis took that as a compliment.

But he found his moment of pride short-lived when the room's door burst open and what looked like a rolling ball of abyssal sludge rambled into the room.

CHAPTER 11

Skitterwombles in
the Sarcophobulous

"Yeah, but ye don't understand," Ivan Bouldershoulder told Queen Mallabritches Battlehammer. "This is the sarcophagus of Thibbledorf Pwent. *The* Pwent."

"Sarcophobulous!" giggled Pikel, who was standing on the ladder opposite. "Hee-hee-hee."

"Oh, but we're understandin' well enough," Queen Tannabritches replied. "We're understandin' a pair o' dwarfs standin' on ladders in our husband's throne room, not twenty steps from the Throne o' the Dwarven Gods, tryin' to tear down a monument King Bruenor put there. What's not for understandin', ye durned Bouldershoulder skitterwombles?"

"Why we're doing it," said Ivan.

"Skitterwombles in da sarcophobulous, hee-hee-hee," Pikel proclaimed.

The other three sighed in unison.

"Because ye're hopin' Bruenor'll put his fist in yer eye?" Mallabritches guessed.

"Bah!" Ivan snorted.

"Ye're bats!" Mallabritches declared.

"Nah, but we're thinking Pwent might be," Ivan replied, and the Gauntlgrym queens looked at each other curiously. Before either could respond, the throne room, which was just inside the wall before the entry cavern's dark pond, shook under the weight of an explosion out in that vast cavern, and a sentry dwarf kicked open the outer door.

"Fightin'!" he yelled. "Demons come chargin' back! To arms!"

"Bruenor's out there with Jarlaxle and Drizzt's da," Tannabritches told her sister, and the two rushed to gather their weapons and armor.

"Well, let's go smack some demons," Ivan said to Pikel, but Pikel shook his head and waggled a finger back at his brother.

"Uh-uh."

"Ye heared 'em!"

Pikel didn't seem to be listening, instead working at one of the latches at the back of the sarcophagus, which they had loosened from the wall.

"Ye really think it?" Ivan asked.

"Ayup-yup."

The fastened sarcophagus shifted just a bit as Pikel wedged his hand in behind. Ivan crinkled his face, thinking his brother was about to grasp the butt end of a rotting body.

"Nope," Pikel said.

"Nope? What? He ain't in there?"

"Nope," the dwarf repeated, wagging his green-haired head.

"Well, where?" Ivan demanded.

In response, Pikel gave a great open-mouthed hiss, bringing his one hand to his mouth, two fingers pointing down to mimic vampire fangs.

"Stop with that!"

"Hee-hee-hee. Nope."

Ivan sighed. "Ah, ye dumb Pwent, what're ye about?" he whispered. He grasped the outer supports of the ladder and slid quickly down the fifteen feet to the floor, while Pikel relatched and reset the sarcophagus. Old Ivan Bouldershoulder scratched his yellow beard, not really knowing how he was going to tell his friend Bruenor that they might have yet another problem.

Another explosion shook the room. Ivan gathered up his axe.

First things first.

FROM THE HIGH DECK OF THE TRAM STATION ACROSS THE underground pond, Bruenor watched the unfolding battle in the huge and high-ceilinged cave. At this point, the action was all far in the back, with flames exploding and lightning bolts flashing, the bits of sudden light inevitably showing the misshapen forms of demonic foot soldiers. Horns blew notes of coordinated defense for the dwarven strategic positions, and shouts echoed, begging reinforcements at one stalagmite or another, or calls for retreat at positions sure to be quickly overrun.

Bruenor tried hard to put those horns and shouts out of his mind. His forces had practiced and practiced for this day. They knew their roles, when to fight, how to fight, when to fall back, which positions to let go and which to hold to the last dwarf.

Bruenor, too, had a role, right here, at the last line of defense before the wall of Gauntlgrym itself.

Thibbledorf Pwent was lost to him. Athrogate and Ambergris were lost to him. Dagnabbet was queen of Mithral Hall and could not get to his side until those magical gates were at last opened.

Drizzt was out there, somewhere. Wulfgar wasn't here but in Luskan. Nor was Regis, who had ridden for Waterdeep. Nor Catti-brie, very pregnant and home in Longsaddle. The dwarf king felt very much alone.

He glanced to his right, where Jarlaxle and Zaknafein had gone over the wall.

"So it's come to this," he muttered, but he didn't let any doubts diminish his stubborn and unyielding determination. He was Bruenor, King Bruenor, who had gone forth into Keeper's Dale to turn back an army.

He was King Bruenor, who had reclaimed Mithral Hall and brought it to new heights of prosperity and acclaim, who had reclaimed Gauntl-grym and control of the godlike primordial, which powered the most magical forge in Faerun.

He was King Bruenor, who had united, or would soon unite, the Delzoun dwarves into a singular force.

Unbeatable.

Still, he felt much better when two old friends rushed up to join him on that tram platform centered on the outer wall, across the small pond from Gauntlgrym proper.

"Dere! Dere!" Pikel implored his brother, pointing to a patch of ground between the tram wall and the lake, over to the right, near where the two drow had gone out.

"Me brother wants ye to . . ." Ivan began, but stopped as Pikel interrupted with "Me brudder!"

"Aye, he wants ye to bring in yer dwarfs through the gate to the right," Ivan finished, pointing to the spot Pikel had indicated. "He's got a bit o' surprise to hold any demons chasing them in, one that'll serve 'em up for yer crossbows and catapults."

Bruenor looked from one Bouldershoulder to the other, finally nodding to assure them that he trusted them.

"And here, if I might," said Ivan, hoisting a large bandolier full of heavy crossbow quarrels of unusual design. He pulled one from the chain and held it up for Bruenor to see. "Old design," he explained. "One made by Cadderly."

"Cadderly! Boom!" said Pikel.

"Aye, boom," Ivan agreed, pointing to the open center of the large bolt, which held a tiny flask filled with some liquid and supported only by thin lines of metal from the front half to the back. "When it hits, it folds. When it folds . . ."

"Boom!" Pikel happily explained.

"Oil of impact," Ivan remarked. "Sure that it'll be leavin' a mark."

"Spread them around, good dwarf," Bruenor told Ivan.

"Dere! Dere!" Pikel reiterated, pointing his one arm frantically at the spot to the right.

"Aye, dere," Bruenor played along, using the dwarf's own word.

"Hee-hee-hee."

"Look for the light!" Bruenor shouted to his commanders along the wall. "Tell yer boys all about the cavern that we got friends directing their fire!"

"Where're ye needin' us, me king?" came a call from behind, a woman's voice, and Bruenor spun about to see his two queens, aptly nicknamed Fist and Fury, hustling up to join him on the platform. Battle-scarred and full of as much fight as Thibbledorf Pwent at a goblin inn, the powerful and battle-ready sister queens surely bolstered Bruenor's spirits.

"Right with meself," he told them, and indeed he needed them, and the Bouldershoulders as well.

King Bruenor Battlehammer nodded and puffed out his muscular chest. He was not alone.

FLIPPING AND SPINNING, WALL TO FLOOR, FLOOR TO WALL, Jarlaxle and Zaknafein crossed paths with every dart and tumble, the swords of one always covering for the movements of the other. They passed demons large and small, scored hits big and little, and were always gone before anything could touch them, running free, as Zaknafein put it, around the next stalagmite, somersaulting, vaulting, flipping, and sprinting, a growing horde of angry demons in hot pursuit.

"Bleeding line," Jarlaxle called, coming down one expanse, a straight and wide run culminating in a pair of thick stalagmites with walkways built up high.

Zaknafein reached into his pouch and produced a handful of pellets, ceramic balls specially coated with enchanted oil to harness the energy within. He dropped them behind him, confident one of the horde not far behind would crush the casing, releasing the magic.

Up to the right he ran, gaining height on the slope of a mound, then leaping and spinning from it to land in a dead run, crossing Jarlaxle's path as the mercenary leader similarly rushed the other way.

That avenue behind them lit up as the pursuing demon horde trampled the pellets, releasing the brilliant magical light enclosed within. The response was almost instantaneous, dwarven side-slinger catapults letting fly and ballista bolts vibrating the air above the heads of the leading drow pair.

Behind the companions, demon minions died by the score under the barrage.

Around a huge mound the drow pair went, then across a side channel, and around another, turning now and heading generally back toward Gauntlgrym, looking for another suitable causeway for carnage.

FROM A SIDE POSITION, NOT FAR FROM THE RUNNING PAIR, Drizzt watched his father and friend with mounting admiration and joy—joy to see his father so willingly risking his life for the cause of the goodly folk of the Crags!

With Taulmaril the Heartseeker in hand, the ranger measured the progress of the two running drow, marveling at their coordination and movements, immediately deciphering the elements inciting their seemingly random flips and crosses. Drizzt passed behind a stalagmite mound, the pair coming into view as they rounded a wider turn before him, then noticed an intercepting group of flying chasme demons.

Away went his arrows, streaking silver with the power of magical lightning, skimming just behind Zaknafein and Jarlaxle to catch the distracted demons right in their bulbous faces.

Down went the chasmes, spinning and crashing, one after another. And as the last of his barrage flew away, Drizzt turned and twisted the magical bow, breaking it down once more so that it would fit into his belt buckle as he sprinted away.

Around another bend came Jarlaxle and Zaknafein, and this time, a third companion jumped into their midst, twirling past Zaknafein as he leaped, landing right before Jarlaxle, and sprinting along to keep up with the running pair.

"Orbs!" Jarlaxle called as they rounded another bend, coming in sight of the outer defensive wall, to the left of the tram station. He and Zaknafein somersaulted past each other, both pulling forth handfuls of the light-encasing ceramic balls, while Drizzt rushed off to the side, finding a shadowed cubby along a stalagmite mound and drawing forth his magical bow from the buckle of his belt once more.

On came the pursuing demons, ravenously, too focused to realize that they were once again crushing light pellets, revealing their position.

Catapult balls and ballista bolts charged down the avenue at them, laying waste, melting and impaling, and the carnage was made worse by the drow ranger with the recurved bow off to the side, as Drizzt Do'Urden let fly arrow after arrow, missiles made all the more powerful by the stalled horde of demons, for the arrows of Taulmaril blew through their first targets to score deadly hits on the next in line, and even the third on many occasions.

Demons melted under that withering barrage, and it took a long while for them to catch on to the presence of Drizzt and his bow.

When they did, the chase took on a new dimension, but Drizzt was ready for them.

"Guenhwyvar, I need you," he beckoned to his magical statuette, and the gray mist collected behind him as the loyal panther came to his call, forming right before a charging vrock and taking down the vulture-like demon as easily as a real leopard might take down a rooster.

On ran Drizzt, scimitars drawn. He noted another area lit up by magical ceramic balls, and the whole of the cavern then shook with the booming resonance of side-slinger catapults. He jumped to the top of a low wall, noted a marilith demon—six-armed, and with each hand holding a sword—and moved to intercept.

Drizzt veered right for her, leaping to a low stone, flipping from it to drive in hard at the creature, his blades neatly ringing against her multipronged attack. Out went his right-hand blade, Icingdeath, driving wide three of the marilith demon's swords, then past them and back again, picking off the attacks as the demon swept its various weapons back in.

Down and over went the scimitar, and Drizzt turned and kicked out, high and fast, his foot slamming the demon in the face, dazing it.

With a hiss of protest the marilith lifted all six arms high and wide, like a crowning eagle about to devour its prey.

But then the creature was flying backward, hit by a living missile of muscle, claws, and fangs.

Drizzt couldn't wait, and on he ran, firing shot after shot to light up the path before him and clear it of demons, and soon enough, Guenhwyvar was running beside him. He was separated again from Jarlaxle and his father, but they didn't need him, and indeed, in watching their precision, he feared that his presence might trip them all up.

They knew he was here, too, now, running and shooting, leaping along the stalagmite mounds and turning too often and too fast for any of the invaders to take up a serious chase.

And if they did, Drizzt knew this cavern better than any. He knew where the dwarven crossbowmen perched, and knew, too, the lanes for the catapults and ballista.

The demons were about to pay a steep price for chasing him.

DEMON FIRE ROARED THROUGH THE CAVERN. FORMATIONS of chasmes flew for the stalactites, many hollowed and set with crossbowmen and spotters. Rushing at them, demons faced withering fire, bolt after bolt taking the flying monsters down.

But there were too many, and for all the carnage in the hall, almost all of it inflicted upon the invaders, the dwarves were forced back, again and again, scrambling along ceiling tunnels to the next defensive position, and as those positions tightened, more dwarves were forced all the way back beyond the tram wall, sliding down smooth poles within constructed chutes.

"Farthest third's lost," McCorbis Gemcutter told his king and two queens up on that wall.

"Did they all get out?" Bruenor asked.

The dwarf, bleeding from a host of scratches and bruises from scrambling fast along the tight stone tunnels, offered only a shrug. "Didn't see none die, but I heared some screams. Dwarf screams."

Bruenor nodded grimly and patted the dwarf on the shoulder, then looked out at the cavern as the battle inched closer.

"We'll be holdin' them here, don't ye doubt," Queen Tannabritches said.

"Aye, and then we'll drive 'em back across the hall and up the tunnel and might that I'll run a tram over 'em in the Causeway just for the fun of it!"

From somewhere not far to the side, a crossbow clicked.

"Hold yer shots, boys!" Bruenor yelled, then added to those near, "Might be more of our own coming in." He looked to his queens and nodded, and the two darted away to spread the word.

They had barely gone a running stride, though, when there came a blinding flash followed by a thunderous retort out in the cavern, up high along the ceiling. Stones fell and dwarves fell behind them from on high.

"They're findin' the crawl tunnels!" Bruenor cried. "Get yer bows up and ready! Ivan!" He looked back and to the side to see the Bouldershoulder brothers standing by the dark pond between the tram platform and the right-hand wall.

"We'll have boys comin' in fast," Bruenor shouted to them.

Ivan pointed straight ahead to the gates on that side of the wall, before which he and Pikel had just been walking. "Them," the old yellowbeard yelled back to Bruenor. "Bring 'em in through them doors!"

Ivan spun and gave a shrill whistle and Bruenor looked back across the small pond to see dozens of dwarves readying heavy crossbows.

Another huge explosion rocked the cavern, and fires blew out from one hollowed stalagmite mound, side-slinger catapults falling from its sides in flames.

"Juicers!" Bruenor called.

His well-trained forces were already on it, rolling the heavy crushing machines over the pond's bridge, then down a forking trail to the main gate's doors. The machines were nothing more than huge flatnosed rams, with long poles extending out the back to be held by a team of running dwarves. It was hard to get one of those things rolling with any speed, but harder still to stop it once one had.

"Yer brothers and sisters'll be coming fast," Bruenor shouted to the dwarves lining the parapets. "With demons right behind and demons flying above. Ye give them dogs a fast trip to the hell what spawned 'em!"

ZAKNAFEIN RAN UP HIGH AND LEAPED OUT, THROWING HIS arms and legs wide to shorten the jump, which landed him several strides from a powerful boar-like demon. The ravenous beast leaped at him in blind fury, too hungry to even realize the second form, the one taking advantage of Zaknafein's shortened leap.

Jarlaxle flashed between the demon and Zaknafein, cutting from left to right before his friend, his swords working furiously as he crossed, and as soon as he went beyond weapon's reach, he began pumping his arm, first throwing a sword, then creating dagger after dagger in his hand from his magical wrist pouch, a line of stinging missiles streaming out at the demon.

The strange creature, which ran hunched, almost on all fours, squealed with each hit, but somehow managed to keep its focus on Zaknafein and charged ahead.

But Zaknafein wasn't there, flipping an easy cartwheel to his left but turning in midspin, landing, planting, and coming right back in. He caught the demonic beast as it turned, getting in behind its thrashing tusks, his fine swords quickly finishing the task Jarlaxle had started.

As the demon fell aside, already melting and smoking as its vile life force sank back to the lower planes, Zaknafein noted that Jarlaxle's expression was hardly one of victory.

"Our game nears its end," Jarlaxle said, nodding his chin over to the left, deeper into the cavern, behind Zaknafein.

When the weapon master turned, he understood, for the demons were organizing well, driving the dwarves from one entrenchment after another.

Crossbows clacked on the outer wall—the tram wall.

"Left of the tram, Bruenor said," Zaknafein reminded him. "Let's bring the dwarves a host to slaughter."

"They're already fighting at the wall," Jarlaxle said. "The dwarves might be in full retreat."

"How much do you trust this King Bruenor?"

Jarlaxle gave a little grin. "Let's bring them a host."

Off the two ran, deeper into the cavern, a circling route that would turn them back to the tram wall, all the way over to the left side of the vast chamber. They took care not to fully engage any monsters anymore—their goal was to taunt, not to get bogged down in any fights.

They cut fast corners and leaped up high. Zaknafein slid down on his knees under the wind-whipping cut of a giant hammer, wielded by the thickly muscled arms of a huge and squat beast that came out from one side alley swinging.

Jarlaxle leaped instead, actually touching down briefly atop that hammer and diving away into a somersault and roll that brought him right back to his feet in a dead run.

"You have your toy?" Zaknafein cried when a host of chasmes and other flying fiends appeared overhead, diving at them.

Down went Jarlaxle, tumbling and coming around with a strange-looking wheel-like object in his hand and a sly smile on his face. "Sometimes I have too many toys to remember," he said, working fast to take four feathers off the object and stick the tips of their shafts into holes set equidistantly within the inner wheel of the object.

"Akadi," he said—the command word and also the name of a powerful aerial being—as he started to run off once more, Zaknafein pulling him along.

Jarlaxle took care to hold the item far from him as the feathers spun faster and faster, creating a small vortex. He struggled to hold it, and seemed to struggle with something more, Zaknafein noted, as if Jarlaxle was afraid of the power he now held.

"Do it!" the weapon master yelled, and Jarlaxle growled and clenched hard, yelling the command word more insistently, demanding everything the item could offer.

Now he held the bottom tip of a tornado, and he swept it above and about, sending the aerial demons flying and spinning every which way. He lowered it back the way they had come, thinking to scatter the nearest pursuers, but as soon as the item went sidelong, the enchantment simply ceased. But it had been enough to gain them some time.

"Run!" Zaknafein cried, and they did. A horde of demons, lesser fiends by the score and even a few powerful beings like vrock and glabrezu and other misshapen monsters huge and terrible, came on in thunderous pursuit.

DRIZZT DOVE TO THE FLOOR AND ROLLED, APPEARING DESperate to get aside from the demonic flames flowing out from what seemed to be the powerful commander of this assault, a hulking bipedal monstrosity creating a field of flames about itself and wielding a shining red sword and a whip that crackled with lightning.

A balor. The same balor he had fled outside the tram station up above.

Drizzt knew this type of demon quite well, for he had battled them, and one in particular, Errtu, on several occasions. He knew their flame shields rolling out from their massive bodies, curling and puffing with every stamp of the monster's foot. He knew their terrible whips.

He knew.

But this particular balor didn't know him, it seemed, for he could hear its victorious laughter as he rolled and squirmed through the flames.

Because if the demon did know who it was dealing with, it would know those flames couldn't touch Drizzt Do'Urden, not while he was holding Icingdeath, a blade that hungered for the very life force of these beings of fire.

He didn't want the balor to figure that out, though, because he understood balors. Such cruel beings would play with their prey before the slaughter.

So, Drizzt rolled and screamed. The whip cracked very near and really did sting him, so he screamed again, then curled up. Knees, elbows. And face on the hot floor. He heard the monster's approach—so confident, the great demon didn't even try to mask it. Up went its huge foot to smash down on Drizzt . . .

. . . and the drow ranger swiftly rolled to his back and planted the pommel of Icingdeath against the floor, holding on to it with all his strength and determination when the fiery demon stomped upon it.

How the balor roared!

How the balor thrashed!

It hopped, howling as Icingdeath ate at its life essence, and kicked out with all of its gigantic strength, sending Drizzt spinning across the floor.

The drow rolled, contorting his body perfectly to take the momentum of that throw and transfer it as he came up, leaping high and spinning a circle kick that drove his foot into the face of the pursuing behemoth.

A balor would normally walk right through such a kick from a puny elf, but this was no ordinary strike. Drizzt's training with Grandmaster Kane had taught him to harness his own life energy and guide it through his limbs to devastating effect. So when his foot hit the demon's face, it snapped its head back, sending it staggering backward a limping step, its red eyes unfocused, its tongue lolling out between jagged knifelike teeth.

Drizzt would have liked nothing more than to charge in and engage, but the demon was not alone, far from it, and so many others appeared not so far away.

His hesitation cost him.

The balor extended its giant bat wings and puffed up its chest, throwing forward one arm, reaching to full length with that awful whip. Drizzt felt the sting as he fled, sharp and full of fire, and full of poison.

BRUENOR WATCHED NERVOUSLY FROM THE RIGHT-HAND side of the defensive outer wall, far down from the tram station and above the gates Ivan had designated. A large group of fleeing dwarves came into view, running hard and with a horde of monsters close behind. The dwarf king winced every time a straggler got pulled down, to be devoured by the demons.

"Ye give 'em cover," he shouted to the archers. "Shoot higher than a dwarf and lower than a demon! And kill them damned overgrown houseflies!"

Crossbows began to sing out from the wall, but the volley seemed a pitiful thing against the sheer volume of the demonic press.

"Run, me boys!" Bruenor shouted at the retreating forces, banging his many-notched axe against his shining shield. "To me! To me! For all yer lives, to me!"

A chasme demon, ahead of the horde and ahead of the fleeing dwarves, dove down from the darkness above at the dwarven king.

But Bruenor saw it. With pure nerve, he held his posture, seeming oblivious, until the last second, then exploded in a fast turn, right arm coming about with all the speed and power the dwarf king could muster. And his axe, that legendary weapon, enchanted anew in the fire of the Great Forge of Gauntlgrym, sheared right through the demon, human face to insect arse, splitting it neatly down the middle.

The dwarves cheered. The crossbows fired anew.

"Run, Battlehammers!" a score of voices, then a hundred voices, implored their fleeing kin.

Bruenor glanced below inside the wall, noting a team in place to swing wide those doors. He looked back a bit from the wall to see Pikel Bouldershoulder standing resolutely, eyes closed and muttering something. "Trust the fool doo-dad," Bruenor quietly reminded himself.

The retreating dwarves neared the gates, and the crossbow volleys became more pointed and devastating, several archers working together to send a barrage into any major demons they could pick out among the charging monsters.

"Gates!" Bruenor yelled, but no sooner had the word escaped him than a cry came out from way down at the other end of the wall, far to the left, warning of a second horde of demons coming in strong.

Bruenor chewed his lip, thinking that it had to be Jarlaxle and Zaknafein bringing the monsters to slaughter. But he couldn't be there, not now with a large group of fleeing Battlehammers about to be overrun. He nodded as he reminded himself once more to trust in his forces, for that far end of the wall, left of the tram station, was the most fortified position of all, thick with artillery and commanded by capable generals.

Below him, the gates swung open and in swarmed the fleeing Battlehammers. The archers leaned over the parapets, plunking the leading demon pursuers, desperate to give some daylight. Still, they'd never get the gates closed in time, and many a dwarf cried out in concern.

But Bruenor just smiled, readied his axe and shield, and watched the first foray. He glanced at Pikel, who had his eyes opened wide now, his one arm up and fingers waggling. He watched the plants sprouting from the sand and through cracks in the stones, coming out to the call of the powerful and unusual dwarven druid.

Those plants surprised the fleeing dwarves but did not trip them up.

Those plants weren't even noticed by the ravenous horde—until they began to grab at demon legs, holding fast.

"Well, get 'em!" Bruenor heard Ivan Bouldershoulder yell, and the air filled with the clanking of a hundred heavy crossbows, launching large and very special quarrels at the slowed demons.

Every bolt that hit—and almost all did—collapsed upon itself, the center vial shattering in the impact, the two heavy ends crashing together with the magical oil in between.

A hundred thunderous explosions sent demon bits flying and blew the front ends of the quarrels right through the struck beast, usually to take down a second, third, or even fourth behind it.

Again those crossbows sang, and unearthly howls and shrieks filled the cavern, and the smoke of melting demon corpses filled Bruenor's nostrils.

Such a beautiful, awful smell, at once the sweetest and most horrid stench in all the world.

The fleeing Battlehammers turned as one, Ivan's brigades rushing to join, archers reloading for a third devastating volley.

"Close the gates!" yelled Mallabritches when that third went off, cutting into the horde outside and thinning those demons inside so much that there was little doubt that Ivan and the others could tear them apart in short order.

So yes, the logical move was to close the gates, secure the wall, put the horde back outside and cut them down from the parapets.

But King Bruenor had another idea.

"Battlehammer!" he yelled, and to the surprise of all, mighty King Bruenor leaped down from the wall—not inside to join with Ivan Bouldershoulder, but outside, among the disoriented and blasted demons.

Despite the unexpected move, Queens Fist and Fury were quickly down to flank him, demon body parts flying every which way from each swing of that mighty axe. A score of shield dwarves, Gutbusters all, the elite guard of King Bruenor, rushed over the wall and surrounded their rulers, hungry for battle.

And Ivan Bouldershoulder and his boys ran over those demons caught inside the wall, and didn't slow in coming through the gates, old Ivan himself the tip of that flying wedge of destruction.

At the opened gates, Ivan's archers trained their crossbows and explosive quarrels higher, and soon enough, shattered chasmes and other winged menaces swirled down like the whipping snows of an Icewind Dale blizzard.

JARLAXLE LEANED FAR TO THE LEFT, HOOKED HIS FINGERS on a jag in the stone, and pulled himself around the base of a mound, rolling his feet and flipping over to keep his momentum as he cut the sharp turn. He had not time to slow, nor did Zaknafein, who cut in behind the nearly horizontal Jarlaxle, leaped up upon the wide base of the stalagmite, kicked a forward flip to a higher spot, then a second, coming over the edge, straightening his legs to catch the downward slope and running down it with that same amazing agility that had marked his son's reputation.

He hit the floor behind the rising and running Jarlaxle, but with more momentum behind him, enough so that he was quickly sprinting beside the rogue.

Now they were in the last stretch of their run, the outer wall of Gauntlgrym in sight, with explosions and the screams and shrieks of battle echoing before them and to the left.

Jarlaxle wondered if the dwarves had been pressed too hard in other areas—was the coordinated defense that had been promised on this side of the tram already compromised? The mercenary put it out of his thoughts. He had no time for that. He had no time for anything but moving forward.

He and Zaknafein ran on, a full sprint here, the last couple hundred strides to the wall.

And then what? For there was no opened gate before them, no ropes or ladders hanging down to help them up to safety.

Trap doors opened on the wall face, revealing the gleaming barbed tips of huge ballista bolts. Two other flaps of the wall fell away, showing side-slinger catapults stacked atop each other, ready to let fly.

And dwarves appeared atop the wall, heavy crossbows leveling.

"Don't wait for us!" Zaknafein screamed, to which Jarlaxle gasped, "What?"

Atop the wall, some dwarves let fly, aiming up high, quarrels whipping out, some hitting demons, others stalactites, and all collapsing and exploding, powerfully, beautifully.

"Let 'em fly, boys!" came a cry from the wall.

Zaknafein yelled, expecting to catch the coming barrage square in the face. He thought it ridiculous that he had returned to this life, to his son, only to be killed so quickly. And for dwarves? Still, these were Drizzt's friends, he reminded himself. If his last act in this rebirth was to aid in that defense, then so be it—he would have to trust Jarlaxle and his son that the sacrifice would be worth it.

He yelled again when he heard the crossbows and ballistae from the wall firing, expecting to die.

But then, so suddenly, he was flying, falling, across a sudden pit, slamming into the other side and clawing at the floor to hold his precarious perch.

"Let go, you fool!" Jarlaxle yelled behind him. Then Zaknafein understood, and as the ballista let fly, two huge spears soaring forth with a heavy and sharp chain bound between them, and as the side-slingers, one, two, three left, and one, two, three right, flung their pay-loads, Jarlaxle and Zaknafein fell into the magical hole, Jarlaxle taking the back lip of the hole with him, Zaknafein inadvertently taking the front lip with him, as they tumbled down together, turning the pit into an extradimensional space.

They were away from the carnage, though they heard it, the demonic shrieks of surprise and pain. And they smelled it, as demon corpses melted to the abyssal fumes that would take the host's life essence back to the lower planes.

In the darkness, though, they couldn't see it.

THE CARNAGE AND CHAOS INTENSIFIED WHEN THE FIRST juicers rolled across to that left-hand slaughter lane. The artillery and crossbow barrage had already destroyed so many demons, and had created confusion among the remaining fiends, which turned many of them upon each other.

The juicers did good work taking care of the rest.

But there were always more.

With Bruenor, Fist, and Fury taking the lead, the dwarves weren't about to surrender their advantage. They came on in perfect support and coordination, the juicers slicing lines through the demon block, the dwarven wedge formations catching the remnants and cutting them apart.

And right there was the king, at the angle of one such wedge, willing his charges on behind him, his mighty axe, so steeped in the power of Gauntlgrym's forge and with a wielder so steeped in the strength of the magical Throne of the Dwarven Gods, chopping through any defense the demons tried to offer.

AS THE DWARVES PRESSED DOWN THE LANE, PASSING THE unseen haven of the two drow, Jarlaxle peeked out of his portable hole. The demon horde had already been decimated, and those remaining, surprisingly, had turned tail and were fleeing back across the entry cavern, back the way they had come, the dwarven forces in hot pursuit.

"When did demons learn to retreat?" Zaknafein asked, but Jarlaxle could only shrug.

THE BALOR'S LAUGHTER RECEDED AS THE RANGER SPED away, winding through the stalagmite maze. It thought the poison would kill Drizzt, surely, and had Drizzt been a lesser being, had he not been trained by the Grandmaster of Flowers, it might well have done so. Even as he ran, the drow flexed and unclenched his muscles, feeling the poison in the wound, pushing it back out of his flesh. By the time he had made his third turn, the poison had been defeated, and on the ranger ran.

When he reached the far edge of the cavern, Drizzt, too, was surprised by the sudden and violent turn of events over by the outer wall, by the sheer carnage so suddenly inflicted on the demon invaders. He moved off to the side as far as he could manage, finding a sheltered hole beside the entrance of the Causeway from which he could launch a barrage of lightning arrows. He let the first of the demons move past, minor fiends and mostly the misshapen, zombie-like manes.

Whenever a major demon approached, Drizzt noted its turn to the right, moving across the cavern to the exit Causeway, which made sense because just a few dozen strides in there, the creatures would be effectively running downhill, instead of making the steep climb all the way to the surface of this tunnel.

They herded all of the minor demons, their fodder, into this uphill one, though, likely to split the dwarven pursuing force.

A wise move, but Drizzt couldn't quite understand it all. They were retreating. These were demons, and they were running away and taking their fodder, which they considered expendable, with them.

The drow ranger eased out of his sheltered cubby, into view of the next approaching manes . . .

. . . who seemed not to notice him and kept their course for the tunnel.

Purely on a hunch, Drizzt took a chance, leveling Taulmaril and letting fly at the group, blasting a hole in one mane, and then the second behind it, both falling to smoking husks.

Even with this attack, the rest kept up their determined march for the Causeway entrance and the rising tunnel beyond. Drizzt's immediate reaction was to take advantage of this unusual and unexpected circumstance, and he put Taulmaril to devastating effect, blasting away at the moving horde. Manes fell two or three at a time; chasmes spun down from above, shattered by the enchanted missiles of the bow known as the Heartseeker.

Drizzt kept firing, and even moved into the cavern's tram entry tunnel, climbing up behind the manes and other minor demons, throwing lightning arrow after lightning arrow through their ranks, expecting them to turn.

But they still did not.

Something was very wrong here.

He came back out of the tunnel into the cavern to see another group of demons approaching, and with fierce fighting—no, not fighting, but slaughter—close behind, the dwarves rolling out in pursuit, chopping the monsters down.

Across the way seemed quieter now, but a second group of dwarves was coming on strong, Drizzt noted, mostly from the explosive crossbow quarrels blasting off stones and through the straggler demons.

The fact that he couldn't figure out why they were retreating chilled Drizzt.

He knew it was reckless, but he blew the whistle hanging about his neck to summon Andahar anyway. He leaped up and the unicorn sprang away, up the tram tunnel. Drizzt led the way with a barrage of arrows, then collapsed the bow back into his belt buckle and drew out both scimitars. He did not need to guide Andahar with his hands, for the magical steed understood his telepathic commands. He closed on the back rows of fleeing demons, who remained heedless of his approach, and he urged Andahar right through them, trampling the monsters directly in line while Drizzt's blades destroyed those to either side.

He knew it was risky, perhaps even stupid—would the monsters suddenly turn on him and catch him in between two demon hordes?—but he had to find out what this was all about.

Andahar charged up the slope. More demons fell to the horn and hooves and flashing scimitars. A commotion far up ahead had Drizzt squeezing his legs and leaning back while telepathically screaming at the mount to stop.

With his keen vision, Drizzt could see that something was happening—he just wasn't sure what. The manes and other minor fiends were now scrambling to the sides of the tunnel, but he couldn't quite make out why.

He pulled Taulmaril again and let fly a lightning arrow, straight up the tunnel, aiming for nothing but distance.

Drizzt's eyes widened, and he suddenly understood.

For there, far ahead but coming down at him with speed, he saw the beast, a monstrous spider, skittering down the tunnel along the ceiling. He knew instinctively that this wasn't merely a giant spider, or even one of the guardian jade spiders he had seen in Menzoberranzan. No, from the way the demons were avoiding this animated catastrophe, he knew. This was a demon lord, likely, or some other horror from the lower planes.

He let fly another arrow, then a third, aiming higher. The first hit the ceiling just before the charging monster, which didn't slow, while the second caught the spider right in the face, or seemed to by the flash of explosive lightning. But again the spider didn't slow, and if the magical arrow had done it any harm at all, Drizzt couldn't see it.

"What monster is this?" he whispered, and he let fly again and again, the arrows rushing up the tunnel to score two more hits.

Or maybe not. He couldn't tell, and the creature never slowed.

The spider rushed down the tunnel and Drizzt spun Andahar about to flee . . .

Too late, he realized.

JARLAXLE AND ZAKNAFEIN SPILLED OUT OF THE EXTRA-dimensional hole onto the floor of the cavern before the dwarven wall, and amid the carnage, demon bits, and limbs and blood and brains.

"Warn me when you throw that!" Zaknafein scolded, still gasping for breath and certain that he had cracked more than one rib when he had flown across the sudden pit to slam into the opposite wall of it.

Jarlaxle wasn't really listening, but rather was taking in the lay of the battle. The dwarves were far away by then and moving farther. He could see the light of their torches and hear their calls of victory.

Zaknafein moved past him. "Are you coming?"

But Jarlaxle shook his head. "No reason," he said, and motioned for Zaknafein to follow him the other way back to the wall, where rope ladders were dropped for them by the remaining sentries.

Up and over they went, and back into the complex proper through the throne room, where Jarlaxle heard a whisper in his head, and recognized the call. He pulled Zaknafein with him into a side chamber to find Kimmuriel Oblodra waiting for him.

"What do you know?" he asked. "What word from Luskan?"

"None yet," Kimmuriel answered. "The armada approaches. But that is not why I have come to you."

"Pray tell, then," said Zaknafein, drawing a scowl from the psionicist, who rather petulantly tightened his lips and crossed his skinny arms over his chest.

"Leave us," Jarlaxle ordered Zaknafein immediately, and with a snort, the weapon master went back out into the corridor.

Jarlaxle looked at his lieutenant curiously. "You're not really here, are you?"

"In thought," the specter answered.

"Where in body?"

"On a ship out of Luskan, sailing to learn of our enemies."

"But you find the need to speak with me before you have the answers," said Jarlaxle, in a tone that made clear his intrigue and worry. It was not like Kimmuriel to travel side streets when on an important mission.

"You should know what soon comes against you," the psionicist explained. "Matron Zhindia Melarn has taken the field with the demon horde."

"At which I am not the least bit surprised," Jarlaxle replied.

"She brought friends. Tools of great power. Two of them, with specific goals."

"Demon lords?"

"Demon constructs."

Jarlaxle's face screwed up in confusion as he scoured his own thoughts for any hint of what that might mean.

"One for Drizzt and one for Zaknafein," Kimmuriel added.

Jarlaxle paused another moment before his eyes went wide and his jaw went slack.

He hurried to find his oldest friend.

CHAPTER 12

Icy Waves and Demon Fire

Though the twilight air was not especially warm, the cold water splashing high and washing back across the deck felt good on Wulfgar's bare arms and face. He found it invigorating and bracing, putting him in the exact frame of mind he would need to fulfill his duties this day. The droplets flew up above him, catching the last rays of sunlight glinting across the water before them from the right, the western horizon, which now seemed to be swallowing the sun.

He was on a swift ship, *Joen's Heirloom*, in full sail with following seas out of Luskan Harbor, slashing through the swells to meet an incoming flotilla of invaders, mostly human but with other, more notorious creatures, including one ship, so the scout ships had reported, crewed entirely by vicious gnolls.

The hope was to parlay, with Luskan showing a powerful force of its own, nearly a hundred vessels representing all five of the city's high captains. And including quieter, but more powerful reinforcements still, like the drow man standing not far from Wulfgar on this very deck.

"We'll not strike any sails," he heard Calico Grimm, the ship's captain, tell that unusual drow, and in a tone too sharp, Wulfgar thought.

"He's busy," Wulfgar called back over his shoulder.

"Busy?" The captain's confusion didn't surprise Wulfgar. Kimmuriel was simply standing there, propped and secured against the rail of the higher prow deck. To all appearances, he was just standing and watching, but Wulfgar knew better. Kimmuriel's consciousness wasn't in his body at that time, but was far away, reporting to Jarlaxle. He had bidden Wulfgar to watch over him, over his helpless physical form at least, while his spirit was far afield.

When Wulfgar didn't respond, the captain snorted, and Wulfgar turned again to make sure that the foolish Grimm didn't strike the strange drow. They certainly didn't need that out here on the open waters! Calico Grimm was a tough one, aye, but he'd do better than picking any fights with this particular dark elf. Even not counting Kimmuriel's position of power within the Bregan D'aerthe, whose complete domination of Luskan was an open secret among all the crews, this drow was not one to be trifled with. Wulfgar would rather anger Jarlaxle, or even the great Gromph Baenre himself, before engaging in any conflict with Kimmuriel and his strange and unsettling psionics.

Wulfgar could understand a fireball, and while ducking under one wouldn't be a pleasant experience, against Kimmuriel, such an explosion would happen inside one's mind, an illusion become all too real, and with no place to hide and no cover to shield.

It was cold on the water, but for the first time today, he shuddered.

"Have I asked you to do so?" came an unemotional response from Kimmuriel, an apparent reply to Calico Grimm's first declaration.

Wulfgar swiveled his head to regard the drow. Was there any other kind of response from this one? With a helpless shake of his head, confident now that Kimmuriel was back in control of his physical body, and therefore, of the situation around him, Wulfgar looked back out over the prow, squinting against the spray, pondering, and not for the first time, whether Kimmuriel was actually alive or just an animated construct, or even some emotionless undead thing.

"You're demanding parlay," Calico Grimm said.

"I am saying that it is wiser. We do not know the disposition of this fleet, or what intent brings them so far to the north."

"You know what happened in the Crags, in Port Llast," Calico Grimm reminded.

"I do."

"They've gnolls sailing with 'em," added Bonnie Charlee, the first mate, a woman covered in battle scars, the grease of rope lines, and sea spray.

"I admit, it does not look like a happy enjoining," said Kimmuriel.

"Eh?" asked the captain.

"Says they're going to be shootin' at us," Bonnie Charlee remarked.

"I will discern their intent before we ever get close enough for any meaningful exchange of words or missiles," Kimmuriel assured the pair.

"And how do you propose to—" the captain started to ask.

"Just believe him," Wulfgar interjected. He swung around a guide rope to turn back facing the trio. "Believe him," he repeated. "We'll know all about this approaching fleet long before they learn anything much about us."

Calico Grimm and Bonnie Charlee exchanged looks and a shrug.

"If they're wanting to talk, then we'll do it one boat out to one boat," Calico Grimm told Kimmuriel. "And no other is striking sails or unloading catapults. If it comes to a fight and they lose, they run. If we lose, we lose our home behind us. Don't you forget that when you're asking for a parlay, eh?"

"Eh, indeed." Kimmuriel snorted dismissively.

Wulfgar glanced back to the approaching fleet, then turned back to see Kimmuriel walking toward him, the captain and his first mate staring angrily at the psionicist's back and both looking like they were about to say something unpleasant.

Wulfgar slowly shook his head at them, and to his surprise, the two remained quiet.

The four watched the approaching sails draw nearer, then Kimmuriel announced, "I go."

"You go where?" Calico Grimm asked.

The drow closed his eyes and seemed to shrink within himself.

"To parlay," Wulfgar answered for him.

"Eh now, what d'ye mean by that?"

"Patience, captain," Wulfgar said. "When the drow speaks again, we will know much more about those who sail against us."

BREVINDON MARGASTER PACED THE DECK OF THE SQUARE-masted caravel, wondering how it had come to this, and wondering, too, if he could end the path he was on simply by removing the magical necklace, a phylactery that contained the spirit of a most wicked cambion.

It seemed so simple, after all. Remove the necklace and toss it into the sea. He could do it, then go to his sister, Inkeri, and take her necklace, and those of the other Margaster nobles, and similarly be rid of the demons.

So simple.

But his hands did not move, and his doubts crept higher.

What would happen to him, to them all, when the lords of Waterdeep learned the truth of the Margaster family? How might anyone protect them when all the powers of the north came to realize that the Margasters had been washing money with Lord Neverember, stealing millions from the city? Brevindon had thought the whole thing funny at first—wasn't the back-dealing and double-crossing all just a game, after all? Everyone was corrupt, of course, so what harm could it be? Also, Lord Dagult Neverember, who had hatched the schemes with Inkeri, was one of the most respected and powerful men on the Sword Coast. Like many Waterdhavian men his age, Brevindon had grown up idolizing the handsome Dagult. Every woman wanted him; every warrior wanted to train with him.

What did it matter, then, if the Margasters threw in with Neverember in creating a new power about Neverwinter City, perhaps to rival Waterdeep itself in the coming years? Why would that be any worse than the current lords ruling, essentially, the entire Sword Coast north of Baldur's Gate, with the sole exception of Luskan, which was in control of pirates, or worse, if the rumors were true?

The justifications rang hollow to him and Brevindon blew a heavy sigh, wondering how it had come to this point. How was it that he was leading a fleet of scoundrels and scallywags, unrepentant murderers one and all, and with a boatload of gnolls along for the ride? How had it come to pass that the army thrown against King Bruenor would be led by demons, actual demons, pulled from the Abyss to rain carnage on the enemies of Neverember?

Brevindon couldn't even remember who had given the order, or when it had been decided that they would march against Gauntlgrym. One little step had led to another, to another, to another, and, seemingly suddenly, here they were.

The fleet had just left the unfortunate settlement of Port Llast, which was mostly in ruins now, the surviving citizens put to work in their quarries in service to the House of Margaster.

You cannot do great things if you fear small . . . inconveniences, said a voice in Brevindon's head, the voice of Asbeel, the cambion contained within the phylactery hanging about the Margaster nobleman's neck.

No, not contained, he thought. Perhaps initially it had been so, but that word wouldn't properly describe the phylactery or the relationship between Asbeel and Brevindon anymore. Asbeel was in Brevindon's thoughts at Asbeel's preference, not Brevindon's. In the phylactery, Asbeel could hide from him, but the enchanted bauble was no longer a two-way barrier.

Was there anywhere Brevindon could now hide from Asbeel?

No, the voice in his head answered the thought.

Brevindon gave a helpless laugh.

When Luskan is ours, you will begin to see the gain and glory of it all, impatient host, Asbeel telepathically imparted.

Brevindon tried to mentally agree, or pretend to agree, or something, anything, to keep the beast from looking deeper into his thoughts.

And, of course, he knew that Asbeel had felt that effort as well. Before the demon could respond, however, a shout rang across the ship.

"Sails to the north!" came the cry from the crow's nest high above. Brevindon was glad for the distraction, any distraction.

"Many sails!" the man above yelled. "The Luskan fleet, to be sure!"

Brevindon smiled, reminding himself that Luskan was under the control of the dark elves, friends of Bruenor, and so enemies of Lord Neverember.

This was a fight, he told himself resolutely, against enemies worthy of feeling the sharp edge of his weapon.

But then he winced yet again, considering the new black blade slung across his back: a curving, viciously serrated bastard sword with a handle of jagged spikes that cut into his hands when he wielded it, biting barbs digging deep into his flesh. The torturous sword healed him as fast as it wounded him, leaving him with no injury but in constant torment.

A reminder to be done with his enemies quickly, Asbeel had told him.

Brevindon had not yet wielded the finished sword in battle—its enchantments and magical edge had only been completed in the town of Port Llast after the sacking—but he could well imagine its horrible power. Merely thinking of an enemy while holding the sword in hand brought a coating of biting red fire to the metal, and though the sword was not telepathic in any meaningful sense, Brevindon could certainly feel its hunger. It had been designed for one purpose alone: to inflict horrible pain. Fashioned with a purpose, the weapon ever sought to satisfy that hunger.

Your imagination is not strong enough to truly understand the pleasure, Asbeel's telepathic voice rang in his head, melodic and high-pitched, the voice of an elf, but twisted and grating.

Brevindon tried hard to focus on the task before him, on reminding himself that Luskan was under drow control and so this was not an unwarranted attack, and to turn his thoughts from the sword.

Asbeel's sword. The awful, terrible, diabolical sword.

LIKE A GHOST, KIMMURIEL'S DISEMBODIED THOUGHTS soared across the cold water, closing fast on the incoming enemy fleet.

With a quick perusal, he became confident as to which was likely the command ship, so much larger and finer was it than the others. He gave it a wide berth, circling up high. One man, dressed in expensive armor and with a large black sword strapped to his back, was clearly giving the commands here.

Kimmuriel went past him, to the wheel before the aft deck, to a chubby and greasy little human who looked quite simple-minded.

All the better.

A moment later, the psionicist blinked through human eyes, and was surprised at how dark the evening had become, absent his keen drow vision. It didn't much matter, for the pilot stood within earshot now of the ship's captain. Kimmuriel soon enough confirmed from the imprisoned mind of the man he had possessed that the captain was indeed the fleet commander.

That man—well dressed, Lord Brevindon by name, he knew from his hostage—snapped his head about suddenly to regard Kimmuriel, or at least, to regard the man Kimmuriel had possessed.

Surely Brevindon couldn't know.

The captain waved away a nearby woman moving to ask him something, then painted on a wicked grin, drew the terrible sword over his shoulder, and took a step toward Kimmuriel.

Kimmuriel looked into his thoughts.

The drow psionicist floated out of the possessed pilot just before Lord Brevindon, his jaw clenched in apparent pain, cut the man nearly in half, that wicked sword driving through the poor fool's shoulder, down across his chest, and out just above the opposite hip. Knowing now the truth of the commander and his minions, including a sorceress who appeared human but certainly was not, Kimmuriel didn't look back but soared across the waters and into his own corporeal body with all speed.

"Well?" Calico Grimm demanded of him the moment he blinked his eyes and moved.

"There is no parlay," Kimmuriel replied.

"So we fight," the captain said, turning to Bonnie Charlee and nodding. The woman leaped away to order full sails.

"Or run," Kimmuriel quietly replied.

"Eh?" Calico Grimm said. "What, ye ain't got the spine for a good fight, skinny one?"

Wulfgar shook his head, unsurprised by the sardonic drow's typically cynical suggestion.

Kimmuriel's snort in response was all that he needed to reply. The captain took it as if the drow was simply answering a challenge against his courage, of course, but Kimmuriel glanced at Wulfgar and knew that the veteran warrior understood the true context of the dismissive response.

Kimmuriel really didn't care if they fought the incoming fleet or not. Kimmuriel had spent years living among the illithids—he wasn't much concerned about getting killed in such a crude battle, after all.

THE CREWS OF ALL THE BOATS AROUND HIM WERE SINGING, off-key and different songs, and different words, even, to those songs they were trying to coordinate, but their energy was infectious and exhilarating, and with the spray in his face and battle against a worthy foe so near, Wulfgar could not wipe the smile from his face.

He was a warrior to his bones, in this life and in his previous. He lived and thrived on the edge of fear, because nowhere else could he feel himself so very much alive.

Almost nowhere else, he corrected himself in his thoughts, and he imagined then that he was in the arms of Penelope. He wished she were here and was glad she was not all at the same time, and so he told himself, vowed to himself, that he would survive this fight and return to her.

The first skirmish began far to the side of *Joen's Heirloom*, where a stroke of lightning and the flash of a fireball erupted, two ships closing to melee range and each leading with a blast from a wizard.

"Do you wish to die out here, friend of Drizzt?" Kimmuriel asked him, and he spun on the strange drow, as surprised by Kimmuriel actually beginning a conversation with him as he was by the ridiculous question.

"You know many who wish for death?" Wulfgar replied. He saw immediately that his sarcasm was lost on the drow. "No, of course I do not," he answered more seriously.

"It would not be an honorable death for you?"

"Yes, of course," a confused Wulfgar answered.

Kimmuriel nodded, then pointed past the large man to a fine ship, the largest and most decorated vessel in sight. "Their commanders, I believe," he said. "We should go—"

"Fireball! Wizard!" came cries from behind.

"Drow, where are you?" they heard Calico Grimm shouting.

"Keep the course to that ship and perhaps we'll find victory," Kimmuriel told Wulfgar, and the drow turned and walked back amidships, where Grimm and Bonnie Charlee and others were scrambling, trying to find some cover. Following their looks, Wulfgar understood their fears, for on a ship closing from starboard stood a man in fanciful robes, waggling his fingers dramatically, wisps of flame wafting from them.

Back amidships, the captain continued screaming at Kimmuriel, a loud reminder that the drow was brought along on the word of High Captain Kurth specifically that Kimmuriel could provide the needed magical defense of the ship. When Kimmuriel didn't respond, the volatile Grimm began hurling insults against Kurth for foisting the drow upon him.

Taking it all in, Wulfgar relaxed, seeing Kimmuriel's posture. He had been thinking of going low over the side to the slack anchor line, down near the water and thick in the prow spray as protection from the incoming fireball, but now he decided against that course and simply stood his ground instead.

Because he knew what Kimmuriel was capable of.

Calico Grimm ranted and yelled, even shoved the drow, who fell over limply to the deck—which only made the captain grow more incensed, to the point where he drew out his saber.

"Do not!" Wulfgar yelled, at the same time another crewman called out for everyone to take cover.

Indeed, across the way, the wizard went into the last moments of his spellcasting, his hands aflame, creating another fiery bomb. He moved to throw it across the water to ignite *Joen's Heirloom*, but then he suddenly froze in place and simply held the pose.

He was still holding his fireball when it exploded, engulfing his own ship in biting flames.

Wulfgar laughed.

Kimmuriel stood back up and straightened his clothing.

"Well now," Calico Grimm said, as much of an apology as the man would ever give.

"You should have some faith," Kimmuriel told him, to which the captain snorted. "And you should repent your actions."

"What're ye meanin' by that?" asked Bonnie Charlee.

Kimmuriel stared hard at Calico Grimm.

"Well?" the first mate demanded.

"Repent," Kimmuriel ordered.

Calico Grimm snorted, but then his face contorted weirdly, a look of utter surprise, a combination of shock and terror. The look of a man who was not alone in his own mind and body.

Calico Grimm spun about and sprinted away, past his surprised companion, running face-first into *Joen's Heirloom*'s mainmast. He dropped to the deck hard, blood flying from his nose, a pair of teeth falling out onto the boards.

Bonnie Charlee gasped, then looked past the groaning captain to the laughing Wulfgar, who merely shrugged in response. Clearly agitated, outraged even, the woman put her hands to the hilts of the daggers on her belt, and she turned to follow Kimmuriel as he moved back toward Wulfgar.

The big man shook his head. Bonnie Charlee wisely did not draw.

It would have been the last thing she ever did, Wulfgar knew, unless one counted her gasping for her final breaths as she sank under the waves after, for some reason she could not understand, she had decided to jump into the middle of the ocean. Wulfgar found himself pleased that Bonnie Charlee hadn't so foolishly tossed her life away.

And he found himself hoping that Calico Grimm, when he recovered from his face-plant, would.

By the time Kimmuriel arrived at the prow beside Wulfgar, it was clear that the lead enemy ship had noted their approach and was turn-ing to meet the charge.

"His sword is a demon blade," Kimmuriel warned. "Do not be struck."

"Whose?"

"Their commander. A Margaster, but much more than that."

Wulfgar nodded and brought his warhammer, Aegis-fang, into his hand, slapping the heavy weapon easily against his other palm.

"Mage ahead!" came a cry.

"Let them blow themselves up, then," said Wulfgar.

But Kimmuriel shook his head. "Such a possession as I performed before might overwhelm a stupid human, but not the spellcaster on the ship before us."

"You already know about him . . . her?" Wulfgar asked, changing the pronoun when he noted the woman at the prow of the ship, deep in concentration.

But then she wasn't, and she staggered back a step, blinking in confusion.

"I have bought you moments, Captain Grimm," Kimmuriel called back. "If you slow, the wizard will strike at you."

Grimm spat out blood, but yelled to his pilot, "Bring her along-side! Thump her hard and tangle the sails, and let's be done with these dogs!"

"Brace!" came the shout all along *Joen's Heirloom*'s deck, and the crew knew to a man and woman exactly what was expected of them. This swift schooner had been built for ramming and tangling. She was reinforced in all the critical areas, and the crew had been selected for their skill in close combat, as the pilot had been chosen for his tal-ent and his nerve. He showed both then, guiding *Joen's Heirloom* in at full sail right alongside the enemy ship, close enough so that the tips of their longest spars crossed, tangling rigging. At that precise moment, the crew dropped the sails and the pilot cut hard to starboard, crunch-ing the ships together, tearing rigging and sails and locking them in place, the momentum of both pulling them in a dancer's turn and sending a swirl of watery swell outward.

Both crews were quick to their respective rails, crossbows leveling and firing. A hulking ogre charged across the enemy's deck, leaping over the rail, flying for *Joen's Heirloom*.

A spinning warhammer met the brute in midair, smashing it with tremendous force, enough to stop its breathing and its momentum. It flew in short, slamming against the side of *Joen's Heirloom*, somehow managing to catch the rail with one outstretched hand.

But Wulfgar was there above it.

The ogre groaned and tried to pull itself up.

"Tempus," Wulfgar whispered, the command word to return that warhammer to his grasp.

He let the ogre climb up just high enough, then drove the warhammer through its skull. The weapon tangled in the bone, so he let it drop into the sea with the dead behemoth.

"Ha!" he heard across the way, and looked up just in time to see an enemy leveling his crossbow.

Wulfgar stared him down, and moved with the speed of a viper when the quarrel flew his way. He wasn't quite quick enough for a full dodge and took it in the side, a painful bite and somewhat serious wound, but Wulfgar was in his battle lust now, and the pain angered him more than it hindered him.

"Ha!" the archer across the way said again.

"Tempus," Wulfgar replied, followed by a "Ha!" and throw of his own.

The archer ducked, but Wulfgar had aimed low, expecting the dodge. The man got behind his ship's rail, which hardly mattered against the brute force of Aegis-fang, which broke through, slammed him, and sent him sprawling.

More than a dozen feet separated the hulls, and many planks were being set by both sides. But Wulfgar didn't need that. A single running stride and leap sent him flying, calling to his god as he went to once again magically retrieve his warhammer.

The poor wounded archer shrieked and clawed to get away.

Wulfgar paid him no heed, for he hadn't the luxury. As soon as he skidded down on the deck, a handful of enemies charged at him.

He set Aegis-fang in a wild spin, halting the charge, driving them back. On one swing, he let the hammer fly, striking dead one woman, throwing her broken body across the deck. Even as he let go, the barbarian half turned the other way, then leaned back to avoid the stab of a long pike. He caught the weapon shaft cleanly and with a sudden and brutal jerk launched the wielder into the air and over the rail.

Up went Wulfgar's left arm, bent at the elbow to catch the downward cut of a battleaxe, the handle slamming his forearm—which didn't budge. He slapped that arm down and around, rolling his shoulders to slug the man with a right cross and with such force as to send that one, too, tumbling away.

He knew that the remaining rogues were rushing in at his exposed back, but a roar brought Aegis-fang back into his hand, and this time when he turned and swept the weapon powerfully about, he caught both in its sweep and sent them tumbling.

By then, the planks were set and fighters charged back and forth, deck to deck, the melee growing wild all about him. Now the enemies couldn't come at Wulfgar all together in coordinated fashion, so he waded along, easily destroying any who moved to intercept. For no shield short of Bruenor's magnificent spiderweb buckler could hope to stop the pounding hammer, and no parry from a less-than-exceptional warrior could deflect the strong man's aim. It didn't take the fighters on the other ship long to realize that, and so the path became clear for Wulfgar.

And not just for him, he noted, for his own crewmates were taking great pains to avoid a different warrior, one dressed in the magnificent armor of a Waterdeep nobleman and wielding a bastard sword with a curving black blade licked with fire. He knew in a moment who this was, and though it was unlikely that the man knew him by name, there was little doubt that this man, Brevindon Margaster, had seen the devastation Wulfgar had inflicted on his crew.

The two stalked toward each other, each occasionally flicking out his weapon left or right to stop or even kill a lesser fighter. Slowly they closed, though, until they were but a few strides away, when both, as if some silent understanding had passed between them, leaped into the air and roared, coming together in a sudden whirlwind of fury.

Kimmuriel had warned Wulfgar that this one was more than he seemed, and Wulfgar was glad he had heeded the message, for in those first moments of combat, the barbarian came to realize that this foe was far more akin to Drizzt or Entreri than to what he'd expect from a pampered Waterdhavian lord. The man's sword worked in a blur, every movement sending it at Wulfgar in a different angle, sometimes a slash, sometimes a stab, sometimes a punch from the hilt.

The big man soon found himself blocking more than attacking, the barrage coming at him relentlessly, and his opponent crying out as if in pain incessantly. Wulfgar realized the source soon enough, as blood flew from the man's hand—from both hands when he gripped that awful spiked hilt with his second hand as well. The sword was wounding him, and in turn inciting his rage, a fury that he threw into every strike.

Had Kimmuriel not warned him, Wulfgar expected that he would have been cut a dozen times already!

Now he had the measure, and he fell into a rhythm of blocks, spinning his warhammer before him, sending it out with one hand, then both, deflecting a cut from the left, using it to keep the sword to his right by lifting it vertically before him and dodging left behind it, then clasping it wide-gripped horizontally up high to intercept a powerful downward chop.

And there was his opening. With remarkable agility for a man so large, Wulfgar turned that block into a sudden punch, sending the hammer's head out to connect heavily with the shoulder of his opponent.

The man staggered back several steps, grimacing, his torn shoulder curled before him.

Wulfgar waited until he started to straighten, then hurled Aegisfang into his chest, throwing him away.

"Tempus!" Wulfgar roared in victory, thinking the fight at an end, but even as the hammer reappeared in his waiting hand, Brevindon

Margaster pulled himself up from the deck, glaring hatefully at Wulf-gar, standing as if he was hardly injured.

And there, before Wulfgar's eyes, the man began to change. He began to shrink in on himself, going from the muscled body of a human to a lithe and more elf-like form. His face grew very red—at first Wulfgar thought it was the blood of rage. But no, his skin itself became a reddish-brown hue. He pulled off his now ill-fitting breastplate and tossed it aside, and finally, most tellingly, a pair of leathery wings sprouted from behind his shoulders, rising wide and ominously.

His crew cheered. They had known.

The crew of *Joen's Heirloom*, the few on this ship at least, recoiled in horror.

Wulfgar glanced to the side, thinking to retreat. He saw, though, that there was nowhere to run, for this demon's minions were winning on *Joen's Heirloom* and seemed as much in control of that ship now as this one.

So Wulfgar took up Aegis-fang, thinking to at least kill this demon creature.

I am with you, came a voice in his head. *Fight without fear. Strike when it is time and fear not your opponent's blade.*

Wulfgar wasn't sure what that meant, but he had witnessed enough of the strange powers of Kimmuriel Oblodra to know that the drow had put something devious in motion.

The barbarian leaped ahead, roaring to his god, closing on the demon with a series of short and powerful chops of his warhammer. He drove the creature back on its heels and might have bowled it right over and buried it then and there, but those wings thrashed at the air and kept the demon aloft, even lifted it from the deck at one point so that its block of Wulfgar's strike sent it farther backward than the barbarian had intended, causing him to overbalance forward.

He tried to retreat, but too late, and that awful flaming blade got in over Aegis-fang's block and drove hard into his forearm . . .

And did nothing, startling both Wulfgar and the demon.

No, not nothing, Wulfgar realized, for he felt the energy of that strike thrumming within him, and so solved the riddle. For this was a trick Kimmuriel had used before, and very recently with Drizzt in Menzoberranzan, creating a telekinetic barrier that absorbed the power of every strike, magical or physical, holding it in stasis, ready for the magically armored person to release it back.

Grinning fiercely, Wulfgar charged in ferociously, not even trying to defend, accepting the demon's strikes in order to get in some of his own. He didn't release the mounting energy, not yet, wanting to utterly destroy the being when he turned its own strikes back on it.

That would come sooner than he had expected, he realized when a crossbow quarrel slammed him in the back—but did not penetrate. The demon's crew was charging him, striking with clubs and gaffs, swords and spears. Wulfgar swatted them aside with Aegis-fang, trying to keep his focus on the demon, but it got around him with a flying leap, landing back amidships near the mainmast.

Wulfgar turned and charged, desperately so, for he understood that he could not hold this energy within him much longer. Perhaps not at all, for he could feel his blood beginning to churn, and he understood instinctively that if he didn't throw forth the kinetic power, it would implode within him, obliterating him wholly.

So he charged at the demon, ignoring the others, and leaped headlong, launching a powerful swipe.

But the demon dodged.

Aegis-fang struck the mainmast and Wulfgar had no choice but to release the gathered energy.

The explosion rocked both ships, the warhammer exploding through the thick oaken beam with ease, separating it so cleanly from the trunk that it fell straight down upon the deck, like a giant spear, blasting through, tearing lines on both ships, crashing down to the hull's shell and more.

No one on that deck, not even Wulfgar, was still standing against the shock of that blast, but the demon, up in the air, had escaped its effects.

The mast leaned to the right, away from *Joen's Heirloom*, creaking and groaning. Rigging lines snapped, a spar fell free, and the mast went over more, tilting the ship to port.

Men and women slid down the sloping deck, some grabbing at the rail, but that, too, was soon swamped. Wulfgar caught the base of the mast and there held—until the demon swooped down and drove its sword across his back.

He wasn't protected by Kimmuriel's telekinetic barrier any longer and felt his skin tearing, felt the fiery bite of the jagged blade, felt the lethal demonic poison.

He was sliding, but hardly knew it.

Then he was in the water. Somewhere he sensed the profound chill, though consciously, he hardly registered it.

CHAPTER 13

In the Shadows

Regis wasn't sure if the intruder was a living being or some sort of trap, or maybe even a combination of both. It looked like a pile of feces held together with webbing, unrolling like a cut sod strip. With every circuit, the intruder also flapped out its sides, widening, filling the room.

The halfling wasn't sure where to go. He started up from his chair, moving left, then right, then realized to his horror that he had been too slow. Dahlia, too!

Artemis Entreri hit him squarely in the chest, a powerful grab and throw that sent Regis tumbling to the back of the room, rolling head over heels to crash into the outer wall right under the window. At first he thought the assassin had turned on him, but then Dahlia, too, came flying, thrown sidelong by the man, who leaped upon the table as the monstrous thing rolled in, and sprang away, the only way he could go, straight up, as the beast or trap or web or whatever it was rolled under him. Entreri caught a beam and lifted himself up high, just getting above the enveloping sludge.

Over the table went the abyssal thing, and the wood of the chairs and table began to smoke and dissolve immediately.

"Out! Out!" Dahlia yelled at Regis, and she smashed out the window and shutters with her metallic staff.

"Go!" Regis bravely told her, drawing out his rapier, though what that might do against this sludge thing, he had no idea. It didn't matter anyway, for Dahlia was having none of his silliness. Faster than Regis could register, she grabbed him by the shoulder and shoved him out the window. For the second time in a matter of seconds, someone had thrown him, and even as the halfling caught the ledge at the last moment, avoiding a fifteen-foot drop, he was beginning to resent being tossed about so. He started to yell at the woman, but when he heard the screaming, he realized that Dahlia had done him a great favor.

He quickly slid his rapier away and lived up to the nickname he had been given as a child, moving like a spider across the wall, and noting as he did that other shadowy figures were moving about both exits of the alleyway.

The sludge thing wasn't alone.

"LEAP!" DAHLIA YELLED BACK TO ENTRERI AS REGIS WENT crashing out the window. Seeing her lover's predicament, dangling and hardly yet in control, the sludge rolling out beneath him, Dahlia jumped back toward the center of the room and took up her enchanted staff, Kozah's Needle. She swatted at the thing, releasing the pent-up lightning energy within the powerful weapon, blasting the muck and webbing—but if she was harming the thing, if the thing was even alive, it did not show.

Worse, the impact sent sludge flying, the same acidic substance that had melted the table. Dahlia fell back, stung about her face and hands, her vision blurred.

"Artemis!" she yelled from the window.

"Go!" he shouted back, and with both hands on the beam now, the assassin began to rock back and forth.

Dahlia understood immediately, for she had witnessed the graceful acrobatics of Artemis Entreri enough to hold confidence that he'd come sailing through the window right behind her.

She didn't have a choice anyway, for the sludgy sod continued unwinding, nearly filling the room already. Dahlia had nowhere to go but out.

"Now!" she yelled back to Entreri, throwing herself through the broken window. She might as well have been speaking to the sludge, though, she realized in that last terrible moment, for as she exited, she glanced back to see Entreri in his last swing. But just before he let go, the sludge creature snapped upward, its entire perimeter rising about the room like some giant snare trap. Entreri leaped and was lost from Dahlia's sight immediately, engulfed by the sludge monster, enwrapped and dropped to the floor within a cocoon of stinking feces, sludge, and webbing.

Dahlia tried to grab at the windowpane, tried to catch herself and get back in to save the man she loved.

But she couldn't quite reach it, and she fell away, clawing at the side of the building to somewhat lessen her fall, spewing curses and denials all the way down to the ground. She landed hard, but managed a roll to absorb the impact and avoid too much damage. She thought to go right back up the wall to the room, but before she could begin the climb—hands scraped and raw from the fall, her knee bruised, one eye swollen and closed, the other still blurry—she heard closing footsteps and swung about to see armored soldiers coming at her, three left, two right.

She was too bruised, too disoriented, and too blind at that moment to even begin to flee, so Dahlia slipped her hand to a trigger on Kozah's Needle and broke her metallic staff into two pieces, one in each hand. A second movement had those two falling in half, joined end to end by a length of fine and strong metal chain.

In the same singular, fluid procession, she sent those nunchaku into wide and flamboyant spins, moving them all about, hoping to keep the soldiers at bay long enough for her to recover from the drop.

But the three to her left commanded all of her attention, and when she at last had driven them back enough to spin about, the other two were simply too close!

Except then they weren't, one flying backward, then the other, thrown to the ground and each with a leering, undead apparition looming behind, the specters clutching garrotes as they choked the life from the soldiers.

Dahlia didn't understand the shocking scene in that moment of confusion, but neither did she hesitate, diving out to the left, rolling to the ground, then back upright just before the kicking feet of the two desperate soldiers as they thrashed about.

The other three came at her, the middle one slumping as she did, to her knees, then facedown to the ground, a small dart sticking from the back of her neck.

A quick glance past that fallen soldier answered Dahlia's questions, for there, perched on a balcony of the next building, peeking out from behind some drying laundry, she spotted the blue beret of Regis. Somehow that little fool had taken down three of her attackers in short order, leaving two for Dahlia, who had shaken the sting from her eyes now and had her nunchaku spinning once more.

REGIS GLANCED AT THE BROKEN WINDOW OVER TO THE side, then down at Dahlia and past her to the far end of the alleyway. He knew that more enemies were coming, likely from every direction. They had to move, and quickly.

"Time to be a hero," the halfling whispered and drew out his rapier, the magnificent blade that had once belonged to the great Pericolo Topolino. He glanced down, then widened a grin as he considered the clothesline strung around this balcony.

He jumped up, caught it, cut the line with a deft flick of his blade, and swung down, the gallant halfling hero swooping down to rescue Dahlia.

He came in far too high, fumbled and flailed, and got his rapier nowhere near either of the opponents facing Dahlia. He swung past, nearly falling from the rope as he tried to better angle his return pendulum swing.

But no, on this second swing he did no better, and the return angle scraped him against the building, stealing his momentum, leaving him hanging some ten feet from the ground and far to the side of Dahlia's fight. The halfling did manage to invert, hooking his leg within a spiral of the rope. He replaced his rapier on his belt and fumbled with his hand crossbow, trying to set a bolt—which was no easy task, hanging upside down!

"Hang on," he quietly implored, glancing nervously to Dahlia. Then he nearly laughed aloud, realizing that the woman needed no further help from him. She rolled between her assailants, nunchaku spinning to whack at their weapons and shields, then coming in close to clang together, each rap of the metallic poles causing an arc of energy, the magic of Kozah's Needle creating and holding the lightning.

Above her head went those strange weapons, spinning furiously as she cut fast and turned to the left, her left arm coming down suddenly in a powerful backhand that sent her nunchaku slamming against the nearest soldier's shield. And there, Dahlia released the energy, a sudden shock and blast that folded the shield and sent the poor soldier flying hard across the narrow alleyway to slam into the wall.

Regis yelped, trying to warn Dahlia of the remaining soldier's short charge.

Dahlia was continuing her turn, however, and that kept the left nunchaku sweeping before her again, the right one going into a sudden vertical spin that brought it down and around, coming up under her armpit, where she clamped her upper arm tight about it, holding it fast, her right wrist down-turning, straining to tear it free.

As she came fully around, square to the charging soldier and, more particularly, that soldier's leading shield, Dahlia jerked the trapped nunchaku free, snapping it forward like a serpent's strike. This one, too, released its pent-up charge as it connected with the shield, but so powerful and focused was the strike, so direct the release of lightning, that the nunchaku drove right through that shield, right through the forearm holding the shield, and right through the soldier's armor, stopping the burly warrior in his tracks—indeed, sending him flying backward.

Regis rolled over, unhooked his leg, and scrambled down the side of the building. He sprinted past Dahlia, who watched him curiously, and to the two warriors who had been garroted by the specters, the creatures still tugging at the cords around the necks of their victims—cords that had been the snake side-blades of Regis's darkly magical dirk.

Regis knew the deeper secret of those specters, and he exploited that now, poking each in turn with his rapier, the single touch making the monster vanish.

Neither of the prone soldiers moved at all—the halfling had no idea if they were unconscious or dead, nor did he have the time to check.

"Run!" he told Dahlia, who was back beneath the broken window, her staff returned to its full length. "No!" he added, when it seemed like she meant to go back up.

As if to accentuate the halfling's point, at that moment, a thick and short demonic beast appeared at the window to throw a heavy block down at Dahlia. The agile elf woman dodged aside, just barely, as the block crashed into the cobblestones.

"I can't leave him!" she yelled at Regis.

"Neither of us is any good to him dead," the halfling replied.

Shouts came at them from both sides of the alley. More demons appeared at the window, raining stones.

Across the way the pair sprinted, Regis leaping upon the building wall and scrambling up, Dahlia setting her staff between two cobblestones and vaulting high to land on the first balcony.

Arrows and hurled stones chased them up the side of that building. Regis made the roof first and pulled Dahlia up behind, tugging her along as he ran off.

"Yasgur's," Dahlia told him, the name of a safe house all in Bregan D'aerthe and House Topolino knew, and she turned aside, running across the roof, leaping to the next in line, then to the end of that one, where she planted Kozah's Needle again and in a great running vault cleared the wide street to crash down on a distant roof, where she collected herself and ran on.

Regis thought the leap impressive, but couldn't really stop and marvel at it, for he too was running for his very life. He heard the shouts below and behind, the heavy footfalls of armored boots on the cobblestone streets.

He couldn't outrun them. He thought to use his beret, a magical cap of disguise, but it was early in the morning and the streets were deserted. What guise might he don to fool them?

He came over the peak of one roof and realized that he was running out of room, for the buildings were farther apart now and he couldn't keep going roof to roof.

He moved to a nearby chimney, too tight for him to squeeze in. He pulled the magical pouch from his belt and lay it atop the brickwork, opening it as far as he could.

A moment later, that pouch fell down into the hearth of a private Waterdeep home.

WITH HER VAULTING SKILLS AND STAFF, DAHLIA WAS FAR afield of the pursuit in short order. She came down to the street and turned back, thinking to circle in behind the soldiers and get back to the room and Entreri. She did get close, and at an angle that allowed her to see the now darkened window.

Could she get there?

She was picking her course, determined to try, when she spotted the procession.

Dahlia fell back, trying to catch her breath. Below her, marching along the alley, went a host of soldiers—Margaster soldiers, she presumed—along with a quartet of short and thick demonic, dwarflike creatures, each holding a pole of a litter bearing the thing that had unrolled upon them in the room, now balled up like a fecal sculpture of a closed tulip.

Dahlia knew what was inside that foul, deadly flower.

FORESBY YOUNG HAD A LOT OF WORK TO DO THAT DAY. THE architect had been commissioned to redesign a warehouse space for a merchant guild and they wanted to see the drawings later that same tenday.

He went into his workshop, which had once been the den (and would be again once his wife's patience had run out, he knew), and spread out his parchment upon his drawing table. He thought a fire might be in order here. He was always inspired by the dancing flames of a good fire, even on hot days in the summertime.

He took a log from the pile and bent low to toss it in, but paused. "What?" he asked, placing the log on the floor and reaching in among the remains of the previous day's burn, where sat a leather pouch of some sort.

"Now, how—" he started to ask as he pulled it open, but the end of the question came out as a gasp as a small dart flew out of the pouch and stabbed him under the chin.

Foresby tried to scream, but no, he was already falling backward to the floor, and was fast asleep before he even plunked down.

Out of the pouch, the wonderful pouch of holding, crawled Regis, taking in a big gulp of air after the stuffy confines of the extradimensional pocket.

He looked around, noted that dawn had come, then tapped his beret.

A few moments later, a young human girl walked out of the house of Foresby Young. She trotted, she skipped, she giggled and played the silly games young humans often played, all the while making her determined way to the house of farmer Yasgur.

Where Dahlia waited.

BUZZING . . . STINGING . . . LITTLE BURSTS OF FIERYPAIN-brightandorangeflashing . . .

They're climbing up under my pants, biting, a thousand wasps, a thousand thousand countless. Too many.

Gackgadsgod, ah! In my mouth! They're in . . . Why can't I move? Why can't I see? O the pain, the little pains, too many little pains altogether.

Wasps! Not wasps!

Fierypainbrightandorangeflashing . . . kill me. Kill me, please.

Dahlia . . . Dahlia . . .

PART 3

Cultural
Boundaries

So many guiding sayings follow us our every step, but are they wisdom or boundaries? Snippets of value to be heeded or the lesser ways of lost times, best forgotten, or at the very least updated?

So many times, I find these traditions, or ancient wisdoms or ways, to be the latter. The very notion of the wisdom of the day seems . . . malleable, after all, and if we are to be tied to the ways of our ancestors, then how can we hope to improve upon that which they have left us? Are ritual and tradition so very different from physical structures? Would the dwarves stop mining when they reached the boundaries of the tunnels in their ancient homelands?

Of course they would not. They would dig new tunnels, and if in that work they were to discover better materials or designs for their scaffolding, they would use them—and likely would go back to the older tunnels and better the work left behind by their fathers' fathers' fathers' fathers.

Why, then, would this be different in matters of tradition? Certainly among my own people, traditions are limiting, terribly so. Half the population of Menzoberranzan is trapped into lesser roles, their ambitions caged by words older than the oldest dark elves, words inscribed millennia past. Part of the reason in this case is obvious: Lady Lolth and her decrees.

Indeed, religion, to those of the faith, any faith, is often unbending and not subject to the scrutiny of reason or to pleas against simple injustice. The Word is eternal, it is claimed, and yet, on many occasions, it is obvious that it is not.

Why, then, do these so-called wisdoms hold on so tightly?

The whims of an unavailable, and conveniently unassailable, deity are only part of the answer, I believe. The other part goes to the darker corner of the ways of every reasoning race. For those traditions kept past all plausible rationales or obvious moral failings, those held most fervently, too often serve those who gain the most by keeping them.

In the city of my birth, those in power do not have to compete with half the population. The matrons need not worry about a patron, surely, and indeed, by tradition, can use their male counterparts as they please. Even those acts as personal as lovemaking are determined by the demands of the women of Menzoberranzan—and let there be little illusion about the "love" in such an act—and a man who will not comply could face harsh retribution for his insolence. Only women can serve as the head of a house. Only women can sit on the Ruling Council, and even the highest-ranking man in the city, typically the archmage of Menzoberranzan, is, by tradition, by edict, by the demands of those merciless rulers, still counted more lowly than the lowest-ranking woman.

The drow are not the only people cornered and held fast by such systemic indecencies—far from it! In Wulfgar's tribe and throughout many of the peoples all about the north, tradition demands patriarchy instead of matriarchy, and while the men are not as brutal in their control as the drow women, the result, I expect, isn't much different. Perhaps the treatment is softer—I recall Wulfgar's shame, so profound that it led him to run away from us, when, in a fit of demon-induced memories, he struck Catti-brie. I could never imagine Wulfgar beating a woman intentionally, or demanding sexual pleasures from her against her will, but even in his contrition there remained inside him for many years that soft condescension. He must protect the women, he thought, which might be a noble undertaking, except that it came with an unspoken—but surely evident—belief that they were not capable of protecting themselves. He placed them on a pedestal, but as if they were fragile things—he simply could not bring himself to under-

stand the true competence of a woman, even one as powerful, intelligent, capable, and proven as Catti-brie.

It took him years to brush it aside and fully recognize the value, the equal worth and potential, of Catti-brie and of all women. So ingrained were the teachings of his earliest years that even when he was faced with so much clear and convincing evidence of the error of his ways, it took a great effort on his part to free himself.

Yes, to free himself, for that is what it is to fully accept that that which you have been taught so thoroughly, the designs of the entire society around you, might be in error.

Wulfgar let go of the nonsensical sexism of his people, and the greatest beneficiary of that dismissal was, in fact, Wulfgar himself.

Dare I hope the same from Yvonnel? For this is Jarlaxle's hope, I know, and his quest, and one in which he continues to use me as his shining example. I can only laugh.

And can only hope that the powerful matrons of Menzoberranzan don't grow so tired of Jarlaxle's games that they come and kill me to take from him his preeminent symbol.

There are people all about free of such sexism, of course, but they, too, are chained by their ways. In the Delzoun dwarf tradition, the gender of a dwarf is unimportant against the weight of merit. There is in Mithral Hall now a queen, Dagnabbet, daughter of Dagnabbit, son of Dagna. It matters not. Her rule will be judged by her actions alone. In every aspect of dwarven life, from combat to cooking to mining to ruling and everything in between, merit and competence are all that matter.

If the person in question is a dwarf.

I cannot complain—far from it!—of the treatment I have received from the dwarves in my many decades on the surface, but that was more the matter of Bruenor's personal compassion. For he is a true credit to his people. A friend is a friend and an enemy is an enemy, and not the size of one's ears, the color of her skin, or the height he stands makes a lick of spit difference to King Bruenor Battlehammer.

Were it not for him, though, the dwarves of Icewind Dale would not likely have ever accepted a lost and wandering dark elf into their homes as kin.

Unless there was another like Bruenor who first happened upon me on the slopes of Kelvin's Cairn. I cannot dismiss that possibility, for within every people, every culture, there exists the rainbow span of qualities, prejudices, compassion, kindness, and cruelty.

It is an absurd belief of the humans that the drow are simply evil—oh, many drow have earned that reputation, to be sure! But so have many humans. They make war on each other as commonly as drow houses battle in the shadows, and on a scale so great that one battle might leave more broken victims, including those who have no part in the fight, than exist in the entire city of Menzoberranzan. I have witnessed Prisoner's Carnival, where the magistrates torture fellow humans with as much skill and glee as any whip-wielding priestess of Lolth. I have seen the elves of the surface turn refugees away from their shelter, leaving them to the mercy of those pursuing them. Even the often carefree halflings are not exempt from the darker shades of the heart.

Yet for all of this, I remain confident of a better tomorrow. Bruenor and the other dwarven kings and queens do not hold their people clenched within as tight a fist as their predecessors did. Regis and Donnola do not rule Bleeding Vines, no. They are called the lord and lady of the village, but they are more the overseers of the business of the place, and, amazingly, they serve at the sufferance of their villagers. For Donnola has changed the tradition of the Topolino clan. And now the people of Bleeding Vines have been given a great gift: their voice.

Because that's what tradition does: it robs an individual of their voice. It eschews the solo and focuses solely on the chorus—and woe betide the singer who goes against the conductor!

No, Bleeding Vines is more of an orchestra, each instrument having its say but playing in harmony, creating a whole. If the people there choose others to lead, then Donnola and Regis will step aside.

This is the tomorrow I hope for, because, I believe, only in a culture where the demands of all the people are heard can the needs of the people be met.

This is the sound of tomorrow, and so tomorrow will be better than today.

—Drizzt Do'Urden

CHAPTER 14

THE YEAR OF THE FALSE BARGAIN
DALERECKONING 1118

If Only

D ab'nay stirred from her deep slumber, rolling about in the thick, warm furs. She didn't open her eyes, because she wanted to focus entirely on the softness and comfort. She knew where she was, on a quiet ledge on Menzoberranzan's eastern wall, a safe place where few drow happened by, mostly because the area was thick with the stench of monster slaves. There were goblins here, and kobolds, but they remained down below in their filthy hovels, and none would dare climb up to challenge a priestess and a weapon master.

So here, ironically, Dab'nay and her lover could find moments of reprieve.

At last she stretched and opened her eyes, and as they adjusted to the low light on this darker end of Menzoberranzan, she made out the silhouette of Zaknafein, sitting on the edge, legs dangling over, taking in the view of the city. She crawled up behind him and draped her arms around his neck and shoulders.

"It is beautiful, yes," she said. Far away, nearly a mile and a half, the giant pillar of Narbondel showed the early-morning glow, a slight orange-red hue amid a sea of faerie-fire-decorated stalagmites and stalactites, mostly blue and purple, but with every color of the spectrum represented. All of the giant cavern seemed a living, breathing thing, the lights shifting hue and intensity to fit the aesthetic demands of each house's demanding matron. The greater houses up on the Qu'ellarz'orl carried the most magnificent designs within their accent lights.

Such a serene facade for the always tumultuous City of Spiders, the city dedicated to the Lady of Chaos. It occurred to Dab'nay that anyone who entered the great cavern from this end without understanding the drow would look upon Menzoberranzan with a first impression that would likely get them murdered or enslaved.

Exactly as the matrons wanted it.

Never before had Dab'nay considered that the appearance might be tactical and not simply pretty dressing. But now, here, it all made sense.

"It should be beautiful," Zaknafein replied, rather sourly.

"Think of the power concentrated there, among those lights and shadows," Dab'nay said, snuggling a bit closer. "Who but the gods and great lords of the lower planes could come against us and survive?"

"The power to build whatever we choose," Zaknafein agreed, "except that we are so busy killing each other that we dare not look beyond our own walls. Walls that we have built against each other more than any outsiders."

"'So busy killing each other,'" Dab'nay slyly echoed, smirking. "Something that Zaknafein is quite adept at doing, I seem to recall."

The weapon master shrugged and glanced back at the woman. "If not, then I would be long dead. And does it matter? If I didn't kill them, I'm sure they could find others to offer their blades for the task."

"How many others feel the same, I wonder?" Dab'nay asked.

"Not enough," he said. "And so it perpetuates until, perhaps, we kill enough of each other to allow some other people to come in and pay us back for our viciousness."

"*Our* viciousness? It was their viciousness that put us here in the first place!"

Zaknafein's little responding laugh was so full of resignation that it gave Dab'nay pause.

"It was Corellon Larethian who betrayed us," Dab'nay reminded him. "Corellon, who is god to the elves of the surface worlds, who gave us to Lolth—gave us, as if we were rothé cattle."

"Yet you love Lolth," Zaknafein retorted.

Dab'nay knew that her hesitation was likely quite telling, but she was truly taken aback and couldn't react fast enough. "Love" was not the word she would use to describe her feelings for the Spider Queen. She feared Lolth and understood her duty to Lolth, and so she was devoted to Lolth, because to be otherwise in Menzoberranzan was to be abandoned and likely soon dead.

"Do not most people of all races love their goddesses?" she asked, trying to find some way around this uncomfortable line of discussion, particularly with one as blunt and cynical as Zaknafein Do'Urden.

"Do they? Or do they love having their fear of death assuaged?"

"Devotion is more than fear," she insisted.

"It can be, but with the notion of gods and an afterlife, I expect it most usually is not," Zaknafein answered. "The fear of death is too pervasive, as is the fear of never again seeing those we love." He gave another of his helpless chuckles, dripping with resignation and venom. "But then, we are so afraid that we don't dare love, do we?"

Dab'nay buried her face in Zaknafein's hair and did not answer. Not with words, anyway, but he felt her sobs, surely, and that should be sufficient.

"We're all trapped," he whispered—to the city and to himself, she knew, and not specifically to her. "We have been ruled by fear for so long that we are afraid of being afraid."

"Lolth taught us that we are superior," Dab'nay did say then, because she was indeed afraid at that moment, afraid that even such a conversation as this would throw her from the favor of the Spider Queen. A priestess without that favor—even one without official title anymore—would be vulnerable indeed. "Would you rather we grovel beneath the evil elves, or crouch in the mines of smelly dwarves, or beg for acceptance from the short-lived, stupid humans?"

"No, of course not," he replied, and Dab'nay thought she heard a hint of sarcasm creeping in. "Better that we hold fast to a grievance that has been passed down through generations, about an incident that may or may not have actually occurred and perhaps or perhaps not in the manner in which we've been taught."

"Blasphemy," she whispered in stern warning.

"Is it, though? Would it be against the edicts of the Spider Queen for Matron Mother Baenre or any other matron to so tilt the very history of the elven races to her own benefit?" Zaknafein answered.

It was a question that Dab'nay had privately considered many times, and one that she expected almost every other drow had asked of herself or himself many times.

"Prisoners," Zaknafein whispered. "All of us, in jails of our own making."

"Is life so bad for you, Zaknafein?" she asked, and she squeezed him tighter and nuzzled his neck. "To think so now, at this particular moment . . . well, truly, you wound me."

That brought a smile from him, she was glad to see. Both fell silent then and just stared at the dancing and glowing faerie fires of Menzoberranzan, enjoying the beautiful stillness.

Even though they knew it a lie.

ONLY A COUPLE OF DAYS LATER, ZAKNAFEIN DUCKED DOWN a dark alleyway in the Braeryn. He thought himself a fool for coming here, on word from Dab'nay alone, and figured that he was walking to his doom.

But the prize was simply too great to ignore.

At the end of a straight avenue between two structures, he moved cautiously around a stalagmite that formed the right-hand corner of the alley bend, and peered ahead. This second juncture was also empty, with the path varying in width but not enough to create any hidden alcoves. Zaknafein didn't know this place, but he had already circled the buildings and stalagmites forming this alley network and was confident that if the prize was waiting, it would be around that second bend.

He crept down silent as death. He peered around.

Arathis Hune stood only ten strides away, leaning on the alley's back wall, a doorway to his left for a quick exit.

Zaknafein could turn this into an ambush, he knew, considering the man's posture. Arathis Hune wasn't holding weapons. He was expecting someone, but not Zaknafein. No, he was expecting Dab'nay, and so he had no reason to be overly on his guard.

If he came around in a full charge, Zaknafein would hold all the initiative, and he was superior to Arathis Hune and so would likely end the fight before it could ever truly begin.

But Zaknafein shook his head and walked around instead, openly, his weapons sheathed, to face his foe.

Arathis Hune's expression revealed his surprise. He came up off the wall to stand straight, hands going to his sides.

"What are you doing here?"

"You were expecting someone else?" Zaknafein replied.

"Or I was expecting no one at all."

"You come here to ponder the meaning of life?"

Arathis Hune scowled at him.

"Or perhaps to consider the deceit that guides your every move? The treachery that fills your heart? The inability to determine friend from foe?"

Zaknafein kept walking as he spoke, finishing within three strides of the man.

"What spittle falls from your lips, Zaknafein?" Arathis Hune demanded.

"You deny it?"

"Probably," Arathis Hune answered with a snicker. "What am I denying?"

"My fight with Duvon Tr'arach," said Zaknafein, "was not fairly waged."

"Wagered? The betting was open and, for many of us, quite profitable."

"*Waged*," Zaknafein reiterated. "Duvon cheated, or someone cheated for him."

"Not very well, then," the man returned dryly.

"From what I have heard, Arathis Hune did not fare so well in his betting," Zaknafein said.

"Ask Jarlaxle about the bags of gold I returned to him."

"Jarlaxle's gold. What of your own?"

"Why would that be of concern to Zaknafein?"

"Because someone cheated on behalf of Duvon."

"Are you accusing me?"

"I am."

"You know the workings of Menzoberranzan, weapon master, and so I urge you now, as your friend, to caution. One does not make such accusations without—"

"Do not think to act my better and teach me the ways of our people. I'm well aware of what I say. But know this: I am making the accusation only to you, openly and alone, standing right here before you."

"An accusation I deny."

"Of course you do, but it is my experience that most cheaters are also liars."

Arathis Hune snickered. "A hundred eyes were on that fight. What might I have done—"

"Quavylene Oblodra," Zaknafein interrupted.

Arathis Hune's expression changed rather dramatically at that moment and he suddenly seemed quite uninterested in replying.

Both realized there was nothing left to say.

Both drow drew out their weapons, two swords for Zaknafein, a sword and a long dirk for Arathis Hune.

Zaknafein started forward quickly, bringing up his opponent's blades. He cut fast to the right and leaped up onto the alley's side wall, then immediately sprang back the other way in a sidelong somersault, landing with solid footing and soft legs that bent to absorb the weight of the landing and to redirect him forward to finish the charge he had started.

Now, though, Arathis Hune wasn't quite as square with him, having followed the break to the side with both his eyes and posture.

He had to cross-block with his sword, coming across right-to-left to intercept the downward chop of Zaknafein's right-hand blade, then making a slight turn to catch Zaknafein's sword before sliding fast and hard back the other way.

He surprised the weapon master then, though, by not completing the returning block with that sword against Zaknafein's second, thrusting blade. Instead, Arathis Hune ran his right hand under the engaged swords, his dagger neatly catching Zaknafein's sword, which he turned inward and across as he turned his hips the other way.

Arathis Hune had escaped the initial engagement, and now ran two strides to leap up against the rear wall of the alley, angling so that his second spring brought him to the wall to Zaknafein's left, and there angling so that his third leap, adding a tight somersault, landed him beside the spot, but now to the side, and ready to take the initiative.

Except Zaknafein wasn't there.

For as Arathis Hune had begun his retreat, Zaknafein had instantly measured the likely angles and jumps he had planned, and so Zaknafein had rushed and jumped out to the right-hand wall, up high, catching a ledge, springing again even higher from that point, tossing his right-hand sword up high while catching the top of the door frame with his right hand to begin a swing that sent him against the back wall to rebound high and into a backward somersault.

He noted Arathis Hune's progress as he executed that move and tucked his legs to properly time his own landing.

He came down an eyeblink after Arathis Hune, appearing suddenly before the puzzled man. Zaknafein caught his descending sword up high even as his left-hand blade worked fast to properly align his opponent's blocking sword and dagger, keeping them too low for a deflection of the higher strike.

Just like that, Zaknafein had him.

"THE DO'URDEN WEAPON MASTER COULD HAVE GAINED A great advantage by charging straight in instead of engaging his enemy with banter," Matron Soulez Armgo told her visitor. The two women stared into a scrying pool of still water to watch the events unfolding in the prescribed alleyway.

"Zaknafein would not do that," Dab'nay Tr'arach replied to the powerful matron. She shifted nervously, wondering, and not for the first time, if she had made a terrible mistake here. "He is too honorable."

"Too stupid, you mean. He will not survive for long. Matron Malice has undeniably caught herself a fine fighter, but unless he becomes a great killer, he'll just be another rotting corpse soon."

Dab'nay started to reply, but caught herself and just nodded. She tried not to wince and thus betray her emotions toward Zaknafein, but inside, the woman's stomach was twisting with anxiety. It was more pain than she had imagined possible when she had taken the deal offered her by Matron Soulez and had quietly arranged this fight.

She focused on the images revealed in the magical pool, then, watching her magnificent lover in a great struggle with an able opponent for the second time in a tenday.

As great as Zaknafein had been against Duvon, now, with more room and fewer observers about, she saw him in all his glory, leaping, spinning, landing in line for the next attack. She began to breathe a bit easier, growing confident that Arathis Hune could not defeat Zaknafein.

But then the image, unexpectedly, blinked out to blackness.

ZAKNAFEIN WENT FOR THE KILL, HIS CAUGHT SWORD AIMED perfectly for the assassin's skull.

But then Zaknafein got hit—he felt as if a large rothé had kicked him. His sensibilities flew from him, his thoughts scrambling and flying off in shocked tangents. He tried to bring his swords up defensively, only to realize that he wasn't even holding the weapons anymore.

The realization hit him starkly, as he understood then that he was hopelessly, helplessly vulnerable. He stumbled aside, toward the back wall of the alley, but couldn't even control his muscles enough to hold his balance, and down he crumpled, expecting Arathis Hune to come up over him and cut him apart.

Only after he had settled, seated against that wall, did he realize that his opponent, too, had been hit. Arathis Hune was facing the alley entrance, taking staggered steps, trying to hold his footing, but futilely, for he toppled hard to the stone.

Zaknafein heard the sharp thump as Arathis Hune's face hit the cavern floor. He could make no sense of that, of any of it, until he glanced past Arathis Hune to see a familiar figure walking calmly down the alleyway.

Jarlaxle bent before Arathis Hune and retrieved the man's weapons, then tossed them back the other way down the alley. Then Jarlaxle took Zaknafein's swords, rolling them about in his hands, holding them at the ready.

Zaknafein was still groggy, still trying to get his sensibilities in line with the events unfolding before him, whatever they might be.

"It was not . . ." he heard Arathis Hune say, the man's voice slurred and his speech broken, as he, too, had not yet recovered from whatever it was that had struck the fighting pair.

"I care not," Jarlaxle sternly replied. "My thoughts on this have been made clear to both of you."

"Zaknafein attacked me," Arathis Hune replied, his voice growing steadier.

"Go and retrieve your weapons and keep moving," Jarlaxle ordered. "Out of the alley, out of the Braeryn. You and I meet tomorrow when Narbondel's light begins to glow once more."

Arathis Hune started to reply, but Jarlaxle interrupted with "Go!"

Zaknafein managed to pull himself to a seated position, looking back down the alley, watching his enemy depart and another drow, one he did not know, coming forward, passing the assassin without any acknowledgment at all, as far as Zaknafein could determine.

"And you," Jarlaxle said to the unknown associate. "What am I to do with Zaknafein?"

"You've already done it," Zaknafein reminded him. "For Zaknafein is Do'Urden and not Bregan D'aerthe."

Jarlaxle sighed.

"You are the betting king," Zaknafein told him. "Another match, then. Put that foul Hune in the alley and do not bet against me. On this one, I promise, do not bet against me."

"We've already had this talk," Jarlaxle countered.

Zaknafein looked past him to the newcomer drow, a very young man, he seemed, who stood a few steps behind Jarlaxle and appeared rather bored with this all.

"You are both valuable to me," Jarlaxle said, drawing his attention again. "More valuable than a few sacks of gold coins. We three have many years of growing power ahead of us, my friend, and you trying to kill each other would put a serious damper on my plans."

"To the Abyss with your plans! He tried to have me killed. By *cheating*. If Arathis Hune had gotten his way, I would be dead by Duvon's hand."

Jarlaxle shrugged. "We are drow. This is our way. We kill when we see gain. But for one of you to die—that would be to no one's advantage here. Arathis Hune does not appreciate the true power of Bregan D'aerthe quite yet, perhaps, but he will come to see the benefit for us all with Zaknafein on our side."

"You're a clever fool," Zaknafein said. He didn't try to keep his anger out of his tone. "And a bigger fool when you believe you are at your most clever."

"Again, we are drow. Have you not figured out what that means?"

"Tell me, Jarlaxle, what does that mean? That we should expect deception and treachery? That none are worth trusting?"

"Yes, to both!"

"Yet you ask me to trust you," Zaknafein said, and Jarlaxle, for once, seemed at a loss for words.

Behind Jarlaxle, the young man snickered.

"Who are you?" Zaknafein demanded angrily.

"This is Kimmuriel," Jarlaxle answered.

No one you want to anger, Zaknafein heard in his mind, and it all came together for him then. He had heard the name Kimmuriel before, in connection with House Oblodra, those of the mind magics.

Mind magics, like the unseen blast that had sent both Zaknafein and Arathis Hune spinning to the ground.

Like the kind Hune had used against him in the duel against Duvon.

Zaknafein turned his glare over Jarlaxle again, now focusing on the mercenary leader's eyepatch and wondering if there was some way he might borrow it—just long enough for a single strike.

DAB'NAY KEPT GLANCING AT THE BLACK SCRYING POOL, betraying her nervousness. She had arranged the fight, indeed, in order to garner the favor of Matron Soulez, who was trying to protect Uthegentel. The hulking weapon master of House Barrison Del'Armgo had long been watching Zaknafein, reportedly. Dab'nay knew Uthegentel only from afar, but even that cursory understanding of the man made it clear to her why Soulez was so interested in being rid of Zaknafein. Not only would that wound the ever-ambitious Matron Malice Do'Urden and likely halt her ascent, but it would stop the valuable Uthegentel from battling the man, a fight Uthegentel would likely, but not certainly, win.

What a disaster Uthegentel falling to Zaknafein would be for Soulez Armgo!

Dab'nay looked to the matron, who was also staring at the darkened pool and seeming none too happy.

"What do you think happened, Matron?" Dab'nay dared to ask.

Matron Soulez snapped her glare over to the priestess. Despite her station, Soulez wasn't much older, Dab'nay believed. But there was no question of their relative power. Dab'nay struggled with the basics of the religion, while Soulez was a powerful high priestess, and now a matron. And Soulez played the game of Menzoberranzan better than almost anyone—her house was not as openly ambitious as House Do'Urden, but the Armgos were likely to sit their matron on the Ruling Council sooner, and certainly Soulez was destined for a higher seat on that council than Malice Do'Urden could ever hope to achieve.

If the two houses ever went to war, Malice would likely be dead within an hour.

If Zaknafein were no longer in the picture.

He might add another hour.

The pool began to shimmer once more, finally, and the alleyway came back into focus.

The empty alleyway.

"There is no blood," Dab'nay observed.

"You will go and find out what happened," Soulez told her. "Immediately."

Dab'nay shuffled nervously from foot to foot. She had no idea which of the two remained alive, if not both. She had no idea whether someone had intervened—perhaps someone who had learned of her visits to House Barrison Del'Armgo, and so had figured out her role in arranging this fight.

Arathis Hune would certainly murder her if he learned of that. Zaknafein might not kill her, she thought, but in a way, that might be even more painful.

Because, she realized now, she did love him.

And yet she had arranged for him to very possibly be killed.

Dab'nay looked from the image in the scrying pool over to Matron Soulez. The woman had offered her so much—too much for her to refuse. No matter who won the fight, Dab'nay would climb within Bregan D'aerthe through simple elimination of one higher up than she, but Soulez had also promised her a place in House Barrison Del'Armgo.

She would become a priestess in a powerful house, and one that Dab'nay could not help but respect, mostly because of how expertly Matron Soulez had kept it away from the attention that could lead it to disaster.

One reason it kept such a low profile—and also a reason behind so much of its power—was how Soulez's house used its men, specifically drawing strength from warriors and wizards, and not from its clergy, which was sparse and mostly unimpressive. The arrogant matrons of the other houses could not comprehend, or would not admit, the power of Barrison Del'Armgo without the appropriate balance of priestesses.

And yet, despite its seemingly low ranking among houses, Barrison Del'Amargo was dismissed at the other matrons' peril.

With all that, the path for Dab'nay was alluring. If she could be brought into the house, her competition in the altar room would be akin to that she had known in House Tr'arach, an even lesser house. Other than Matron Soulez, and perhaps her promising young daughter Mez'Barris, there was little divine power to oppose her.

Yes, Dab'nay would like that. And she would know safety for the first time since her days in House Tr'arach.

She looked back at the scrying pool. A big part of her hoped Zaknafein had won the fight and Arathis Hune was dead.

But a bigger part hoped that the two had killed each other.

She didn't want to admit that, not even to herself, but she told herself repeatedly that there was no place for love in Menzoberranzan, and even less place for honor. Even if Zaknafein had not been killed by her interference, how long might he survive?

And how long would she survive, she wondered as she departed House Barrison Del'Armgo, a question that would be raised again not long after when she went to the Oozing Myconid and learned from barkeep Harbondair that both Zaknafein and Arathis Hune had walked out of that alleyway due to the interference of Jarlaxle himself.

Dab'nay retired immediately to one of her many rooms scattered throughout the city, and there she remained for several days, even summoning her own food and drink so that she would not be near to any potential assassins. She played through every scenario she could think of, given the disaster of the failure in the alleyway. Would Zaknafein try to kill her? Would Arathis Hune? Would Matron Soulez? She had to be prepared for the first two, but not the latter, and certainly not the possibility of both (or all three) at once. That compounded her nerves, for the two men would approach revenge very differently.

And who could know how the cunning matron would play it.

For the moment, though, it was the two men that preyed on her thoughts, especially when she considered that perhaps they would both come to see the role she had played, and figure out why she had done so, and so come after her in unison.

Few in the city could survive a determined murder attempt by those two.

Many times over the next half tenday, Dab'nay told herself that she was being foolish, that her role in the fight had been a minor thing, after all, and that it was more likely that both Zaknafein and Arathis would thank her than blame her for the chance at killing the other.

Still, when the soft knock came on her door on the fifth day of her self-imposed exile, poor Dab'nay nearly jumped out of her slippers.

She moved to the door and listened.

"Don't bother opening it," came a voice from behind her, and she whirled about to see Jarlaxle sitting on the edge of her bed. "I only bothered to knock to announce that you had a visitor."

"Well met, then," Dab'nay replied, trying to stay calm. "I was about to have some supper—I have gotten quite good at summoning feasts that are as tasty as they are filling. Would you care to join me?"

"How could I possibly refuse?" asked the ever-cagey mercenary.

Dab'nay had not been lying about her growing proficiency in summoning food and drink, and she conjured up a feast worthy of the station of her guest, to which Jarlaxle added his own touch by producing a bottle of vintage Feywine from his magical pouch.

"You have not been about of late," Jarlaxle remarked almost as soon as they had started their meal. "I grew worried that perhaps I had lost a powerful ally. Bregan D'aerthe is not rich in those with divine powers, of course."

"Just that, of course," Dab'nay replied, a bit more testily than she had intended. As she considered her reflexive response, and Jarlaxle's answering dumbfounded expression, she really didn't care at that moment. Perhaps it was past time that someone put this arrogant rogue in his place.

"Do you need a proclamation of mutual interest and benefit?" Jarlaxle asked.

"I do not even know what that means," she answered. She knew what she really wanted but wasn't about to say it. The proclamation that Dab'nay desperately wanted was one of friendship and loyalty.

She wasn't going to get it, though, and knew that she couldn't.

Rarely would a drow in Menzoberranzan leave themself that vulnerable.

"I am glad that you are well, Priestess Dab'nay. Truly." He lifted his Feywine in a toast to her.

She accepted that, even tapped her glass against his, and told herself that she should be satisfied with that, for it was more than most would get from any dark elf. She believed it, too, and would have believed Jarlaxle if he had indeed called her a friend, just as she believed that Zaknafein truly cared for her.

As she took her sip, she was glad the glass was hiding her frown, for Dab'nay realized that the cruel little woman she had thrown in with, Matron Soulez Armgo, would never see her that way.

Never.

"How fare your two lieutenants?" she asked.

"Three."

That was a surprise to Dab'nay, and her heart flitted a bit. Was he offering her such a position?

"I have found a third," Jarlaxle went on. "A new companion to us all, and one whose value cannot be underestimated."

Dab'nay stared at him blankly.

"You will meet him soon enough, I expect."

"Who?"

Jarlaxle held up his hand and shook his head. "It is not my place to introduce him when he is not beside me."

Dab'nay took another drink, this time to hide her scowl.

"As to Zaknafein and Arathis Hune," Jarlaxle said, "they are well. Zaknafein is back by Matron Malice's side, and there to stay for some long while, I would think. She'll not risk him again anytime soon. Whispers say that Mali— Matron Malice is preparing another ascent among the city hierarchy."

Dab'nay knew that his slip of the tongue in referring to Matron Malice as simply Malice was Jarlaxle's way of taking a measure of her. She was a priestess of Lolth, and no true priestess of Lolth would let such a break in etiquette go unscolded.

But Dab'nay remained impassive.

"Arathis Hune is out of the city," Jarlaxle went on, apparently satisfied with her lack of response. "His mission might take him all the way to Ched Nasad."

Dab'nay searched Jarlaxle's red eyes for a hint of deception. Wouldn't that be a convenient story to get her off her guard, so that Arathis Hune could kill her quickly?

He continued, "When do you expect to be returned to the Oozing Myconid?"

"That I might meet your new lieutenant?" she answered coldly. "Do you expect me to bow?"

"To no one!" Jarlaxle was quick to reply. "Of course not. Ah, dear Dab'nay, I hear the anger behind your words. And I understand it. But I am surprised to have to explain this to you: You will never assume a position in the top ranks of Bregan D'aerthe. Not openly, at least. Do you think that Matron Mother Baenre and the others of the Ruling Council would ever allow such a thing of a priestess of Lolth? As far as they are concerned, as far as they must *ever* be concerned, you are an associate, an independent priestess who sometimes works with Bregan D'aerthe, and always with fine recompense."

"As one can discern from my lavish surroundings," Dab'nay replied sarcastically.

Jarlaxle rose to leave. He paused and looked around the large and somewhat well-furnished room, which they both knew was one of several Dab'nay owned. "Better this than where Dab'nay found herself after the disaster of House Tr'arach's attack on House Simfray."

"A battle my house won."

"A battle you lost," Jarlaxle corrected. "To the death of Matron Hauzz."

"Only because—" she started to argue, her ire flaring.

Jarlaxle stopped her with an upraised hand. "It was a drow house war," he said. "There is no 'only because.' House Tr'arach found disaster because greater forces than House Simfray were allied against them."

"Including you."

"Including me. Which is the only reason you survived. Or your brother, for that matter."

The two stared at each other for a long while, then Jarlaxle tapped his forehead in a semi-salute and departed through the room's door—which was locked, but which opened to his verbal call before he ever touched it!

Dab'nay sat there for a long while, not even bothering to get up and shut the door, pondering the conversation. Jarlaxle had openly placed a limitation upon her ascent within his mercenary band, but strangely, she was not angry, and was not even glad then that she had thrown in her lot with Matron Soulez. It took her a while to sort through that seeming paradox. If she couldn't climb the ladder of Bregan D'aerthe, shouldn't she logically want to join House Barrison Del'Armgo?

But Dab'nay couldn't deny the truth of Jarlaxle's reasoning. Were he to elevate Dab'nay or any other priestess within his band to a position of official leadership, particularly now that Bregan D'aerthe was growing quite powerful, some of the matrons would likely see them as a threat, perhaps even as a potential new house, and one more dangerous because it was mobile, ethereal even, and with business connections to the greatest houses in the city.

She couldn't sort through it. Not then.

Nor was she sure how she felt about Zaknafein being trapped within House Do'Urden. She missed his caress and his kiss, but perhaps it was for the better. At least with him in there beside Malice, the cruel Soulez could not soon try to arrange his demise once again.

Dab'nay got up and went to close the door, carefully checking the hallway.

She hoped that Arathis Hune was really out of the city, and hoped, too, that he would stay away for a long, long time.

CHAPTER 15

Every Angle

The young drow warrior peered over the edge of the balcony, trying to stay out of sight. He didn't want the man in the mostly empty chamber below him to know he was there. To him, it was like watching a woman undressing or a priestess at prayer. If the target knew he was there, watching, the thrill would not be the same, nor would the insights he hoped to gain.

Dinin Do'Urden, secondboy of the house, had gone to great lengths to manipulate this area of the balcony ringing House Do'Urden's training gymnasium so that he might watch the display below unnoticed.

Now, finally, his efforts had paid off.

Below him stood Zaknafein, the drow whose reputation was spreading far and wide across the winding ways of Menzoberranzan. Stripped to the waist, sinewy muscles glistening with sweat, the man had already completed the more energetic part of his daily training ritual.

Now he stood calmly, his back not quite square with Dinin's position. His arms hung loosely at his sides—he was affecting a posture of

relaxation, a normal pose in an unthreatening situation. Before him
and to the right, a large rat sat up on its haunches, chewing some tidbit
it had found.

Dinin didn't understand that. There were not supposed to be rats
in House Do'Urden; how might one have gotten into this room?

The vermin squeaked and skittered, and then Dinin understood
the creature to be somehow a part of this practice session, for Zaknafein exploded into action.

Up came his hands before him, taking with them his swords from
their scabbards. His left-hand blade rolled over as it rose, right over his
shoulder, to stab, point-down, behind his back, immediately sweeping
across and up over the back of Zaknafein's right shoulder.

Even as that sword crossed by, the weapon master sent a backhand
stab out behind him with his right blade. And with all that, he was
turning, the left blade coming back across before him.

Dinin's warrior instincts informed him that Zaknafein would go
right around with that blade, a complete circuit that would have it
cutting across as he turned around and backed away, disengaging from
the imaginary assassin who had tried to stab him in the back.

But no!

Zaknafein stopped the blade's swing, reversed his grip, and thrust
it back, as he had with the right, and he came around behind it, now
with his right-hand blade recovered and cutting a wide and wicked
down-angled slash.

Dinin had seen Zaknafein hundreds of times, had even sparred
with him.

But never like this.

Zaknafein sheathed his weapons and threw a crumb across the
floor to the rat.

Once more, the rodent sat up and began to eat, and once more,
Zaknafein assumed his relaxed posture, exactly as before, except that
now Dinin could see the man more from the front.

The rat squeaked and moved, and the weapon master's blades
seemed to simply appear in his hands, the left going up and over with
startling and beautiful fluidity. Dinin's gaze locked on Zaknafein's left

hand, on the intricate work of the weapon master's fingers in that brilliant and exact sword roll.

Not a wasted movement. None.

Dinin tried to keep up with the routine: the sweep; the thrust; the second, unexpected thrust; and the final, devastating slash. Every movement bled into the next. Every turn, twist, or shift of balance in completing one move angled, positioned, and set Zaknafein to execute the next.

Another crumb flew out toward the rat. Zaknafein was using the living creature because its timing could not be predicted. The rat, not Zaknafein, would dictate the furious start.

Dinin thought it perfectly brilliant. Instead of dictating the beginning of his practice, which of course was no option for a man defending against an actual ambush, this superb weapon master was letting a creature—something wholly chaotic—do it. Even more remarkable, the fighting sequence on display before Dinin was designed for a specific and singular situation, for one unexpected strike from one angle alone.

How many hundreds of hours had Zaknafein toiled at perfecting these few sequential movements? How many other similar routines had he devised and perfected for other specific threats?

Up there on the ledge of the training gymnasium, Dinin Do'Urden came to understand the truth of Zaknafein. Dinin thought himself a promising young drow warrior, and he had witnessed many of Menzoberranzan's finest swordsmen at play, even a real duel between masters on two separate occasions. He understood the arts martial and the beauty of the sword dance.

But this? This was something more. This was a level of perfection and danger Dinin had never imagined.

Again Zaknafein went through the routine, and again after that.

He'd do it a dozen more times, Dinin understood. Two dozen, perhaps. A hundred, perhaps!

Dinin shook his head and slipped back silently, exiting the gym through the small secret door he had fashioned. Walking alone out in the corridors of the house, he could only shake his head, his thoughts lost somewhere between the sheer beauty of what he had seen and his sudden and intense dislike of weapon master Zaknafein. At one point, he stopped, closed his eyes, and replayed the sequence: the rolling sword, the thrust, the thrust and turn, the slash.

How much would he have to sacrifice to even approach that level of precision and speed? Could he even attain such mastery if he gave every hour of his life in the pursuit?

Dinin appreciated Zaknafein.

Dinin was in awe of Zaknafein.

Dinin hated Zaknafein.

DAB'NAY NEARLY GASPED ALOUD WHEN ZAKNAFEIN EN-tered the Oozing Myconid, more than seven tendays since the fight she had arranged against Arathis Hune in the alleyway. She couldn't deny her happiness at seeing him, but neither could she ignore her profound trepidation.

Her heart pulled her toward the weapon master.

Her head told her to run.

It was rare with Dab'nay—or with any dark elf—that her heart would win out, but this time she did not heed the sound warnings and flee, and instead found herself standing beside the seated weapon master.

Zaknafein looked up at her and offered a smile, warm and inviting, and she thought it sincere. He motioned for her to sit beside him, so she did.

"I was hoping to find you here," he confided.

"You didn't come here at the request of Jarlaxle?"

Dab'nay raised two fingers and motioned to Harbondair.

"I haven't seen or heard from Jarlaxle in . . . since that day in the alleyway when he interrupted my victory."

"Victory?"

"Oh yes," Zaknafein assured her. "And Arathis Hune knew it. He has left Menzoberranzan, I am told."

Temporarily, perhaps, Dab'nay thought but didn't say.

Harbondair arrived with a pair of drinks and set them down before the patrons. No sooner had he turned and started back to the bar, though, than Zaknafein pushed his glass away.

Dab'nay looked at him curiously. "Surely you do not believe . . ."

Zaknafein reached across to her, took her drink, and slid his in its place. He sat back in his chair, arms crossed over his chest in that typical and powerful Zaknafein pose, one hand coming up just enough to motion for her to go ahead and partake.

Dab'nay looked down at the swirling amber liquid in the glass, then over at Harbondair, who was not looking their way.

She shrugged and waggled the fingers of one hand over the glass, casting a minor spell, then grabbed the glass, lifted it in a toast, and brought it to her lips.

No sooner had she set it down than Zaknafein slid the other glass before her and motioned for her to purify that one, as well.

"That was mine," she protested. "Do you think Harbondair would deign to poison me?"

Zaknafein arched his eyebrows and offered a sly grin but made no move to uncross his arms again and take the glass back.

Dab'nay started to laugh, but bit it back, realizing the implications of Zaknafein's continued doubts. He knew that Harbondair wouldn't poison Dab'nay, but did the barkeep, perhaps with Dab'nay's help, expect a switch of glasses?

The woman laughed and cast another spell, noting the intensity of Zaknafein's stare as she went through the precise motions and uttered the exact syllables. When she finished, she started to slide the glass back to him, but to her surprise, he stood up.

"Let us be gone from this place," he said.

Dab'nay started to motion to his drink but changed her mind when she noted Zaknafein's hateful stare toward the bar. She rose to follow, and well enough, she decided. She had not been in Zaknafein's arms for far too long.

Some time later, they lay beside each other, the soft glow of candlelight catching pinpricks of sparkle in the beads of sweat they both wore.

"I missed you," Dab'nay said.

"I trust it was worth the wait."

"*You* were worth the wait," she corrected, and ran her finger playfully along the top of Zaknafein's nose.

"I came forth from House Do'Urden three times in the days after the fight. But alas, you were not to be found."

"I didn't know—I still do not!—what happened in the alleyway," she replied. "And when you did not return immediately, I became afraid. I thought it best that I tend to other matters."

"One thing I have been curious about," Zaknafein said. "Tell me, however did you coax Arathis Hune into that alley that night?"

"Same way as I lured you," Dab'nay replied, hardly considering the response, though it was not entirely true. Zaknafein had gone there expecting a fight with Arathis, but Arathis had gone in anticipation of a rendezvous with Dab'nay and a different weapon master, one regarded by most as the greatest warrior in the city.

She caught a hint of doubt in Zaknafein's eyes as he stared at her. Just a flash, an instant, that either passed as soon as it had begun, or had been suppressed before it could be revealing.

LATE ONE NIGHT MANY DAYS LATER, DAB'NAY SAT ALONE in one of her apartments, reading through some histories of Menzoberranzan that Jarlaxle had given to her. She was lonely, and more than that, she was bored.

She hoped that Zaknafein would come out again soon. She hoped that Jarlaxle would start some mischief or other—something, anything, to bring some excitement to her life.

Most of all, she wished that Matron Soulez would have given her enough credit for her efforts bringing Zaknafein and Arathis Hune to battle to follow through on her promise and formally allow Dab'nay into the ranks of her promising house. Yes, that would be grand, she thought. House Barrison Del'Armgo was full of men, and having so many about to serve her every need seemed much more enjoyable than this lonely existence, where she was always looking over her shoulder.

The knock on her door startled her, an insistent sharp rapping. Not Zaknafein's knock, she knew.

Dab'nay silently placed her book down beside her, then rose and scanned the room, noting her escape routes. Taking great care, she padded to the door and listened.

"Do not make me wait, priestess," came a voice from the hallway, a woman's voice, and one that Dab'nay recognized.

She sucked in her breath, near panic, her thoughts swirling with great hopes and great fears. What was Matron Soulez doing outside her door at this hour? How did the matron even know where to find her?

Dab'nay's sensibilities told her to flee, to run out one of the secret exits in the room, through the narrow tunnel walls, and out of the building altogether. She almost did it, even took a step toward the hearth, with the fake shelves beside it.

She held back, however, and shook her head at her own stupidity. This was a matron, and a powerful one at that. Soulez would not be here knocking on Dab'nay's door if the entire area within and about the small inn weren't teeming with her agents. Fleeing was not an option.

And even if she did somehow get away, there were few places she could hide where Matron Soulez couldn't find her—the knocking on the door of her secret apartment was evidence of that.

As if on cue, another sharp knock had her nearly jumping out of her soft slippers. Without hesitation this time, she yanked the door open.

"Your pardon, Matron," she said, and she began smoothing the ruffled material of her robe.

Matron Soulez pushed past her into the room. Dab'nay managed to glance both ways along the corridor and was happy to see that the powerful woman at least seemed to be alone.

"What have you learned?" Soulez asked impatiently. She scanned the room briefly, then took the largest and most comfortable chair as her own.

"Jarlaxle intervened," Dab'nay replied, closing the door.

"Yes, of course. But what have you learned? You have seen Zakna-fein Do'Urden, yes?"

Dab'nay nodded. "Yes, and I retain his confidence."

Soulez gave her a look that seemed more scowl than intrigue. "If only someone who held confidence with Zaknafein would find a way to use that to be rid of him," she said. "A great gift that would be for me."

Dab'nay tried to digest that.

"Arathis Hune returns to Menzoberranzan on the morrow," Soulez said.

"You would have me arrange another . . . meeting between those two?"

"Do you think that you retain the confidence of Arathis Hune as well?"

"I . . . I . . ." Dab'nay really didn't know what to make of that statement.

"You only gave Zaknafein that which he desired, foolish girl," Soulez scolded. "Arathis Hune could not defeat him in that alley, given the way you arranged the meeting. Zaknafein came in aware of an impending fight, and his opponent did not."

"But Zaknafein did not use that advantage."

"Because he did not need it," Soulez replied. "Arathis Hune serves best from behind his foe. He could not beat Zaknafein in such a fight as you arranged. He knows it, Zaknafein knows it, and you know it."

The look Zaknafein had flashed at her when she had answered his question as to how she had persuaded Arathis Hune into that alley came back to Dab'nay then, that instant of surprise from the cunning weapon master.

"If that is true, then at least Jarlaxle would have lost his oldest lieutenant, one he has trusted since before the Tr'arach-Simfray war," Dab'nay said.

"Wounding Jarlaxle would please me, yes. But I care nothing for Arathis Hune. My desire is to halt the ambitions of Matron Malice Do'Urden. Her actions are complicating my own ascent."

"What are you saying, Matron?"

"The task before you is to rid me of Zaknafein, however you might. Another fight with Arathis Hune? Yes, that would be fine, but it will be no fair fight this time. I'll not depend upon the blade of Arathis Hune to defeat the great Zaknafein."

Dab'nay swallowed hard and had no response.

"Zaknafein has been about again of late and Arathis Hune will soon enough return. I am possessed of great patience, child, but I have already waited many months. When you are ready, I will grant you those resources that you need to properly complete your task."

"Yes, Matron," Dab'nay said, because, after all, what else could she possibly say?

"SO HERE WE ARE," JARLAXLE TOLD ZAKNAFEIN AND Arathis Hune, the three of them sitting in his chambers in the Claw-rift beneath House Oblodra. "I trust that enough time has passed to dull the edges of your common hatred."

"You underestimate my determination," said Zaknafein, glancing at his enemy.

"You overestimate the amount of time," Arathis Hune added, meeting that stare with his own.

"And you both disregard the cost of your feud," said Jarlaxle. He motioned down the hallway and a fourth entered the gathering, a smallish man dressed in finery worthy of a noble house. His face was clean-shaven, his hair cut short and neatly trimmed.

"Because of your . . . stubbornness, I have found the need to bring in another confidant," Jarlaxle explained. "One who will quickly climb above the both of you in the hierarchy of the band, I'm sure."

"Good for him. I am of House Do'Urden now, by Jarlaxle's de-mand," said Zaknafein, as if that explained, and so justified, his disre-garding the remarks.

"And that might prove temporary, and you might indeed need me again someday, Zaknafein."

The weapon master shrugged.

"Do you wish full dismissal from Bregan D'aerthe?"

Zaknafein glared at Jarlaxle but did not answer.

"If so and I grant it, and then you continue your pursuit of Arathis Hune, you will be doing so merely as an agent of House Do'Urden," Jarlaxle explained. "The implications of that are perhaps more dire than you recognize in this moment, so I will give you all the time you need to sort it out."

"What do you want from me, Jarlaxle?" Zaknafein demanded.

"And from me?" Arathis Hune agreed.

"You don't like each other," Jarlaxle said. "I understand. Just do not kill each other! That is all. No fighting."

"Then keep us apart," Arathis Hune demanded. "Surely your many plots are wide-flung enough that I never need see the likes of Zaknafein again."

"Nor I him," Zaknafein agreed.

"Insufferable," Jarlaxle remarked, looking to Kimmuriel, who seemed wholly bored with all of this.

The mercenary leader heaved a great sigh and waved them all away.

HOWEVER SHE MIGHT PLAY THIS, IT WAS GOING TO BE DELI-cate, she knew, and all of this was getting very dangerous for Dab'nay. She feared that she was in way above her abilities with Matron Soulez, never mind Zaknafein and Arathis Hune.

That point was hard to ignore as she lay there next to Zakna-fein this quiet night. She looked to the bottom of the bed, where the weapon master had hung his weapon belt, those beautiful sword hilts glimmering in the candlelight.

She leaned over to study Zaknafein's breathing. So rhythmic and even. Surely he was asleep. Dab'nay could be done with all of this so easily. After all, Zaknafein was the one Matron Soulez wanted dead.

And now, so easily, Dab'nay could grant Soulez her wish to be rid of him. Dab'nay would be brought into House Barrison Del'Armgo as a full priestess, perhaps even with a path to becoming a high priestess someday. Too, she would be a noblewoman again, and not a houseless rogue. Given Zaknafein's unending hatred of the Spider Queen, she figured that Lady Lolth would certainly bless the move as well!

All she had to do was collect one of those swords and stab it through Zaknafein's heart as he slept.

She stared at the weapons.

She hated them and hated what they might do.

If she took one, she would be stabbing herself in the heart no less than Zaknafein.

But what choice did she have? She had put herself in an untenable situation, one that was very likely going to get her killed if anything at all went wrong along the way.

Dab'nay buried her face in Zaknafein's hair.

The sword called to her.

She didn't look back at it. She couldn't.

CHAPTER 16

Deaths Deserved, Deaths Undeserved

The three drow warriors raced around a corner, hand crossbows drawn. Up went the weapons, and two let fly at the same time that the third drow yelled for them to hold, seeing a figure coming their way.

That lone figure executed a brilliant and swift dance, spinning about, his *piwafwi* cloak flying wide to harmlessly catch the quarrels. He came out of that spin in a leaping charge at the trio, boldly one against three.

Out came four swords from the two in front to meet him, while the third, still back a few steps, yelled, "No! No! Zaknafein!"

The two in front stabbed their nearest blades in unison, each sweeping across with the other in perfect harmony, a tremendous and practiced defense that would have killed or at least halted almost any drow warrior.

Their opponent did not fit that description.

He slid down low to his knees, engaging their thrusts with uplifting blades that brought those two swords up high enough to intercept their slashes.

And up the attacker popped to his feet, his blades angling perfectly, each coming to a stop with its tip under the chin of its respective target, drawing blood, lifting the drow to their toes.

"Your weapons on the ground or your blood on the ground," the attacker said. "I care not which."

Four swords clanged to the stone.

"Idiots," said the drow behind them, the noble secondboy of House Do'Urden. Then to the attacker, he added, "Are you quite done with your play, weapon master?"

Zaknafein stared at Dinin from between the two trapped soldiers. With an amused grin, he turned his wrists, sending the pair staggering backward, extending the superficial wounds, and as he let them disengage, he held out the side of his *piwafwi*, showing the hanging darts.

"You might have just stopped down the hall," Dinin Do'Urden said dryly.

"I do not live my life on uncertainties like 'might have,'" Zaknafein replied.

"You did not recognize us?"

"Oh, of course I did. That doesn't mean I trust you."

Dinin blew a sigh. "The house is almost clear," he said to change the subject. The four Do'Urdens and a host of others had come into House Ben'Zarafez, a weak house whose high ranking was based on inertia from its long-ago glory days, along with the way its matron had wisely sidestepped any ascending houses who desired to pass her by. That desperate situation had come to an end when the same matron, Decliz Ben'Zarafez, had secretly plotted to hire on a host of mercenaries, a pitiful attempt to try to sneak some true power back into her overranked house.

The fallout had been swift and severe, leaving House Ben'Zarafez without its mercenaries and with its external spy networks destroyed.

Leaving House Ben'Zarafez an easy target for Matron Malice.

Perhaps a war had not been necessary, since Matron Decliz, wounded as she was, would have certainly allowed House Do'Urden to step above her house in rank, but this had apparently proven too tempting an opportunity for Malice to show her power for her to accept any such agreement.

Besides, she had told the Do'Urden attack force, this would be good training for the certain wars against more imposing houses, like House DeVir, coming up in short order.

Here they were, then, sweeping through the middle levels of the central and largest stalagmite of the three mounds that comprised the main structures of House Ben'Zarafez, finding minimal resistance and rolling over it with not a single loss of a Do'Urden soldier yet reported.

"The house was almost clear before we came into it," Zaknafein quipped in reply, and truly, he expected that they would have found more resistance if they had attacked the Oozing Myconid than they had encountered here.

"We are nearly to Matron Decliz's chamber," said Dinin.

Zaknafein hardly heard him, as he was focusing on the warrior to his right, who held his hand up to his throat to stem the bleeding and glared at Zaknafein with open contempt.

"Well, strike then if you wish," Zaknafein said to the man.

The look of hatred turned to one of fear. "Weapon master, no, of course not," the warrior said, falling back a step and holding his hands up submissively.

"If you ever deign to look at me again in that manner, then strike and strike to kill," Zaknafein warned him. "Because if you don't kill me, I will kill you."

The terrified soldier seemed as if he would simply topple over.

When Zaknafein looked back to Dinin, he found the young noble staring at him incredulously, shocked even. So was the other soldier, farther to the left. When he thought about it, Zaknafein understood the surprise, for his words to the poor soldier had been quite harsh and extreme, no doubt.

Uncharacteristically so.

But so be it, he decided. This unpleasant business had left a most foul taste in his mouth.

"Matron Decliz has been severely weakened," he told Dinin. "Her defenses will be minimal, no doubt." He wanted to tell Dinin to take his two soldiers and go get her, and he almost did so. But the thought of Matron Malice's reaction to such a thing was not a pleasant one. She didn't want her young son going into battle against any house matron, of course. She had tasked Zaknafein with that role specifically—that was part of the reason she had paid so dearly to bring him into her house, and that was also the message she wanted to filter out into the streets after events such as this, to build the reputation of Zaknafein and thus build the status of House Do'Urden.

Zaknafein certainly didn't mind the task, either. Killing priestesses of Lolth remained one of his few joys in life.

But alas, he knew that Matron Decliz wouldn't be alone.

"Follow on a count of two hundred," he told Dinin, and he moved back down the hallway to the stairs that would bring him to the highest level of the hollowed-out stalagmite mound.

He had already discerned and disarmed the two traps on the curving staircase, so now Zaknafein sprinted up, taking three steps at a time. He came to a landing set with a heavy door.

He brought the monocle Matron Malice had given him up to his eye and carefully scrutinized the edges and the lock. Finding no trap, he lifted his hand and whispered a command word into an onyx ring.

He heard the tumblers clicking, but the door did not open. Zaknafein shook his head and snorted, thinking that Matron Decliz was just delaying the inevitable.

Into the ring he uttered a different command, this time sending forth a wave of dispelling energy to defeat the magical hold on the portal. Then he issued the first command again, expending the last of the three spells Malice had put into this ring, another dweomer to open portals. This time, the door flew open, revealing a curving hallway.

Zaknafein didn't hesitate; sprinting along, he went up on the wall around the bend, coming back down to the floor with a spinning and tumbling maneuver that had him flinging himself onward, straight at the two guards standing before the matron's chambers.

He could see the fear on their faces, could see the hesitation as they lifted their swords in what they knew would be the last moments of their lives.

For even if they defeated this invader, they understood that a host was following close behind.

Zaknafein darted left to fully engage the one on that side, throwing his right sword back the other way to pick off a thrust by the other. The guard before him used a thrust-and-slash combination that he easily blocked, ducked, then blocked again, and on that interception of the second thrust, Zaknafein turned his blade over that of the Ben'Zarafez soldier, then up and over again, and around a third time, each circling move twisting the soldier's arm a bit more as the overmatched drow tried desperately to disengage.

For the blade of Zaknafein moved too quickly for that guard to pace it, and so, predictably, the soldier tried to simply back away.

But Zaknafein's right hand picked off another stab from the other soldier, went up to intercept and defeat a downward slash, and whipped across underneath that blade to send the man falling away to the wall, leaving the weapon master free to advance in concert with the first soldier's retreat.

The man was against the matron's door then, and out of room to continue his retreat. He tried to maneuver as Zaknafein bore in with sudden ferocity, but Zaknafein had him cornered, and every movement of that guard's sword was met with a ringing rebuttal.

Zaknafein pounded him relentlessly, numbing his arms under the weight of his blows. In those first furious instants, the weapon master saw at least three opportunities to slip a blade past the awkward and desperate defenses and kill the Ben'Zarafez soldier, but he didn't take them.

Out from the wall came the other soldier, swords leading.

Zaknafein noted his every move.

Down and across went the weapon master, to his knees and turning underneath the stabbing swords of the guard to the right. This one, too, he could have gutted, but no, instead he came up inside the man's reach and still turning, going right around to come out of the spin by driving his pommel hard into the poor guard's face, snapping the man's head to the side. Over he tumbled, facedown to the floor.

Zaknafein was back the other way before the unconscious man hit the stone.

His blades worked in a blur, picking off every thrust and cut, and indeed, hitting the man's swords two or three times for every parry, overwhelming him with sheer speed.

The poor guard just threw his swords aside and his hands up high. He fell to his knees, begging for mercy.

Zaknafein gave him what he wanted . . . of a sort. He kicked him in the face, knocking his head back against the wall, and he, too, slumped down. He wasn't unconscious, like his companion, but neither was he about to get up anytime soon.

Zaknafein kicked in the door.

This was the throne room of the house, the inner sanctum, the place of House Ben'Zarafez's greatest power. Yet so depleted was the house that there sat Matron Decliz, alone and clearly frightened. She was not surrounded by other priestesses or nobles of the house. It was just her.

And she made no move to strike at him with spells or her snake-headed scourge, which lay lifeless on the table before her.

Zaknafein glanced out to the sides and behind, ensuring that the two guards were not about to jump into the fight anytime soon. Satisfied that they were finished, he moved cautiously into the room to the table opposite the matron.

"You are that Zaknafein creature, no doubt," she said.

He didn't answer, moving cautiously, looking all about for traps or hidden doors, trying to sense other people in the room who might be waiting invisibly for him to let down his guard.

"Long ago, I could have petitioned the Ruling Council to strip my house of its rank," Matron Decliz said, and she gave a resigned shrug when Zaknafein focused again on her. "Every ascendant house learned the truth easily enough, after all."

"What truth is that, Matron?"

"That House Ben'Zarafez is little more than an illusion."

"And thus you simply allowed them to pass above you, accepting the demotion."

She nodded. "I knew it was only a matter of time before one too desirous of a victory would deny the ruse and put an end to House Ben'Zarafez. I even came to predict that it would be Matron Malice—that one is ever hungry, from all that I have learned of her."

Zaknafein kept his expression impassive. He wasn't about to give away anything here.

"Where are your children, Matron Decliz?" he asked.

"There are only two."

"I know. Why are they not with you?"

"I removed them from the house. I took away their surname." She offered a pathetic little shrug, but one that touched Zaknafein. She cared enough about her children to remove them to safety? Such actions were hardly commonplace in Menzoberranzan.

"And your priestesses?"

"None remain. There is only me."

"You expect me to believe that?"

She chortled. "I expect you to kill me. That is why you are here, yes?"

"Take up your weapon. Gather your spells."

The matron stood up and glanced at her scourge, but left it lying on the table as she stepped away from her seat.

Zaknafein's thoughts swirled here. He considered Dab'nay—might Jarlaxle be interested in gathering up another priestess, and perhaps a few soldiers as well?

"Raise your swords, weapon master," Matron Decliz told him.

"You ask for a merciful death?"

She laughed at him, harshly, mockingly. "It is time for me to go to Lady Lolth," she said, and Zaknafein found his sympathy fast flying. "It is a journey I eagerly accept. If you wish to torture before the killing blow, then do your worst, filthy male. The Spider Queen favors me. I have prayed."

"Then why is your house so pathetic and falling?"

"Lolth appreciates how long beyond our time House Ben'Zarafez has managed to survive," the matron explained. "She appreciates my cunning. She has told me this through her handmaidens."

"Such devotion," Zaknafein replied sarcastically.

"Is there any other purpose?"

"Yet you removed your children," the weapon master countered in an effort to dissolve her ridiculous claims.

But Matron Decliz laughed at him all the louder. "I gave them to Lolth, idiot," she said.

That was the last word Matron Decliz Ben'Zarafez would ever utter, for before another could leave her mouth, before she could even gasp in surprise, Zaknafein was there, right before her, his sword expertly taking out her throat.

He stared at that bloody sword when the woman crumpled to the floor before him. She hadn't even enacted any defensive spells. The cut had been so easy!

He shook his head, trying to make sense of all this. What god would expect such things from devout followers? What god would ask for the sacrifice of the children? And Zaknafein knew that Matron Decliz's son was only a decade old.

Sounds from the hall spun him around, to find that horrible witch Briza playing with the two guards he had downed. She had one up against the wall, the poor man trying to cover himself as her scourge, its barbs a pair of living, venomous snakes, hissed and bit at him. The other guard kept trying to rise, but Briza kicked and laughed at him, stomping him flat to the floor.

The rest of the house was almost certainly cleared by then, Zaknafein knew, and he knew, too, that Briza would torture these two through the night. And then she would kill them—there would be no reprieve for any of House Ben'Zarafez, no bartering for slavery, no selling them to Jarlaxle for Bregan D'aerthe. In the name of Lolth, none of House Ben'Zarafez would survive this night.

That was the rule in Menzoberranzan for a house going to war against another: there could be no witnesses, because no witnesses meant there had been no war in the first place.

But neither could Zaknafein stomach the taunting serpents of Priestess Briza. The poor victim's wails of agony assaulted the weapon master's heart. His own misplaced sense of mercy toward the two had precipitated this predictable situation.

Zaknafein moved to the doorway. "Matron Decliz is not quite dead, I believe," he said to Briza. Her red eyes sparkled and she verily ran past him, eager to claim the greatest prize of all.

No sooner had she stepped into the room than Zaknafein took her place in the hall. He stared at the three priestesses who had accompanied Briza, warning them back with his scowl, then put his swords to sudden and violent work with expert precision, ending the torment of the doomed Ben'Zarafez guards.

The priestesses gasped, one yelped, and behind him in the room, Briza spun about to glare at him, offering an almost feral growl. Zaknafein turned slowly and matched that stare, unblinking.

Briza swung back around and leaped ahead, guessing his ploy, he knew. The pool of blood had widened around the body of Matron Decliz, with the woman quite obviously dead before Briza had gone to her. The first priestess of House Do'Urden stormed back to the door, scourge in hand.

"She is dead," she stated.

"Ah, I thought she had a bit of life left," Zaknafein replied with a purposely unconvincing shrug.

Briza stared at him hard, then glanced to the guard slumped against the wall, then to the one on the floor, both gone from this life.

"You play dangerous games, weapon master," she whispered, as if she believed that lowering her voice would somehow unnerve the man.

Zaknafein tried not to smile. In that moment of outrage, he hoped she would make a move at him, and resolved that if she did, he'd kill her and be done with it, then kill the three priestesses of her entourage for good measure. Because they did this, all of them. All of the priestesses who listened to the murderous call of the Spider Queen, that most horrible goddess. The house guards hadn't deserved death, let alone torture—this was not a war.

No, it was murder, and now he was a murderer, a killer fighting for no noble cause, no higher purpose, and not out of necessity to protect himself or any loved one.

Zaknafein had trained for all of his life to be a warrior, a great warrior.

He didn't feel like one in that dark moment.

TWO HOURS LATER, ZAKNAFEIN SAT AT HIS TABLE AT THE Oozing Myconid, cradling a very potent drink. He knew that he would be punished by Malice when he returned to House Do'Urden, something he should have done immediately after House Ben'Zarafez was declared dead by Briza.

So be it.

He needed the reprieve offered by this place, a filthy little tavern with terrible food and worse liquor, but one outside the rules of the wicked matrons and their horrid goddess. Upon arriving, though, he found his relief short-lived, as he was met by word of the impending return of a particular agent of Bregan D'aerthe.

He lingered longer than he had intended, into the early morning hours, when finally Jarlaxle entered the tavern.

"Matron Malice will be pleased," the mercenary leader said, taking a seat opposite Zaknafein. "I heard that your victory was without cost."

Zaknafein could hardly agree with that sentiment, but he didn't bother replying.

"Why are you here?" Jarlaxle pressed. "Won't she wish to secure her house fully, fearing some retribution after such a raid?"

Zaknafein lifted his glass in a toast. "Here's hoping that the whole lot of them gets murdered," he said, and he gulped down the contents.

Jarlaxle's expression reflected sincere concern, but still, Zaknafein thought it might be grand to punch him right then.

"What?" the mercenary leader asked.

"You bought him back."

"Who?"

Zaknafein's expression hardened.

"Yes," Jarlaxle admitted with a shrug.

"And I cannot kill him, I suppose."

"I would greatly prefer that you do not. The coin to repurchase Duvon Tr'arach was not insubstantial. Matron Byrtyn Fey drove a ferocious bargain."

"Then why didn't you let her keep the fool?"

"She was done with him and I feared she would sacrifice him to Lolth, and that, I believe, would be a waste. He is not without talent."

Zaknafein snorted.

"He gave you a finer fight than even you expected! Admit it, my friend."

"In Menzoberranzan, the second-best swordsman is usually as dead as the worst of the bunch," Zaknafein dryly replied.

"I did not wish to see him dead," Jarlaxle admitted.

"So you bring him back that he will try to kill me?"

"He will not," Jarlaxle insisted.

"Ah, yes, Jarlaxle of Bregan D'aerthe. So sure of himself, the puller of strings." He waved for another drink, then turned back to lock stares with Jarlaxle. "Until a puppet's dance goes awry, and then there is blood."

"Duvon will not seek revenge," Jarlaxle reiterated.

"If he does, your money will be wasted, do not doubt."

"I do not."

Zaknafein laughed, and it wasn't meant to comfort the man sitting across from him.

"And what of you, then?" Jarlaxle asked.

"I would have you pay for my drinks this night."

"Indeed, and fair enough. But what of you, Zaknafein?" he repeated.

"What of me?"

"Duvon returns. Perhaps it is Zaknafein who will seek to finish that which Duvon started on that long-ago day."

"Not so long ago."

"Zaknafein?"

The conversation paused as Harbondair moved between the two, placing a glass before each and offering a quick and less-than-friendly look at Zaknafein as he did.

"I will not kill Duvon," Zaknafein promised, and Jarlaxle lifted his glass to toast to that.

But Zaknafein wasn't finished.

"The other one will satisfy me," he added.

The unexpected request put a blank stare on Jarlaxle's face and he slowly lowered his glass. "Other one?"

Zaknafein glanced over his shoulder at the man walking away from them, the barkeep who had tried to poison him that night when Duvon had attacked.

"Harbondair?"

"Harbondair Tr'arach," Zaknafein reminded him.

"He is a good barkeep."

"When he isn't trying to poison his patrons, you mean. Besides, how hard is it to serve this swill?"

"Yet you trust him enough that you come in here and drink that which he placed before you," Jarlaxle reasoned.

"Because he is afraid of me and has no support should he anger me. That will change when Duvon returns, perhaps."

"No, it will not. I will not—"

"I gave you a choice," Zaknafein interrupted, and lifted his glass to his lips. After a small sip, he stated flatly, "You choose or I will. Or perhaps I'll just take both."

"You forget your place in Bregan D'aerthe."

"I forget nothing. You owe me this."

Jarlaxle glanced from Zaknafein to Harbondair and back again. He shook his head, but then blew a heavy sigh, tremendous disappointment clear upon his face.

"It still seems a waste."

"With House Ben'Zarafez defeated, Matron Malice will lie low, and so you will find me at your side more often."

"If I grant you this, you will need to learn how to properly prepare drinks," Jarlaxle warned.

Zaknafein offered no smile at the poor attempt at a joke.

"Do not kill Duvon," Jarlaxle flatly ordered, and he rose and left abruptly.

Zaknafein nodded as he watched the door close behind the departing mercenary leader. Then he went back to his drink, which he knew was not poisoned.

He remained in the Oozing Myconid throughout the night, sitting, just sitting, with his back against a wall. When all the patrons had departed, he focused his gaze upon Harbondair, who was clearly growing increasingly uncomfortable.

"Would you like another drink?"

"No."

"Some food, perhaps?"

"No."

"The morning is come," Harbondair said. "I must take my leave."

"Who is stopping you?"

"Well, I am to lock—"

"You know who I am; you know who I, who we, serve."

"Yes, but—"

"Take your leave."

The man moved deliberately, his gaze never leaving the seated Zaknafein until he was through the door.

Zaknafein lifted and drained his glass—the same one he had been sipping with Jarlaxle hours before. He rose and threw on his *piwafwi*, then moved to the door.

A glance left, a glance right, and off he sprinted, up the side of a stalagmite mound, leaping, spinning, somersaulting, to hit the ground in perfect balance and at a full run. At the next bend in the lane, he went up the side of another mound, then backflipped off of it, turning as he soared to land on the roof of a lower structure. Three running strides took him across to a parallel road, and there, without even looking, he leaped and twisted again, dropping lightly to the street, facing back in the direction of the Oozing Myconid.

Facing Harbondair.

"Draw your weapons," Zaknafein told him.

"I . . ."

Out came Zaknafein's swords. "Now! Or I will take my time with your flesh."

Harbondair drew out a sword and a long dirk with unsteady hands. "I wish no fight with you," he said.

"Truly?" Zaknafein taunted, and he held his swords out wide to either side.

As he expected, Harbondair took the bait and charged ahead. He stabbed hard, and with surprising accuracy, but Zaknafein seemed to somehow melt away, falling to the side, supported strangely by one turned leg. He came out of the bend with a hop and a somersault, landing facing the man in a low crouch, from which he exploded up and forward, his left-hand blade working furiously in a slap-and-roll movement to take the sword from Harbondair's grasp and send it flying, his right-hand blade coming under the man's dirk arm and lifting it up high.

Zaknafein turned under it, dropped his right-hand blade, and slapped his free hand over Harbondair's fist. With tremendous strength, the weapon master bent the barkeep's hand at the wrist, turning it down painfully—so painfully that the dirk fell free.

And in that instant, Zaknafein jerked the man's arm up higher, rolled back underneath it, and came face-to-face with the horrified barkeep, his sword coming in across Harbondair's neck, pinching the tender flesh. With that blade and his free arm, Zaknafein guided the man across the road to slam hard against the side of a building.

"Please, please," Harbondair gasped.

"Do not beg," Zaknafein told him.

Harbondair closed his eyes.

"You poisoned me that night when Duvon first returned to the tavern," Zaknafein said.

Harbondair's eyes popped open wide. "No, no!"

"Admit it," Zaknafein said calmly, too calmly, and the barkeep began to slump, and would have fallen over if Zaknafein had not been holding him so tightly.

Harbondair was fighting back tears, Zaknafein knew. He stared at Zaknafein, trying to slightly shake his head, but carefully, so that his own movements didn't do the sword's work.

"I am a patient man," Zaknafein whispered.

"I did," Harbondair blurted. "Just to slow you. I feared for Duv—"

Zaknafein pulled him from the wall and slammed him back against it, hard.

"You poisoned me again this night," he said.

"No!" the barkeep gasped.

"Why not? Would it not have served your purpose to simply kill me? Or did you fear that you could not?"

"I would not. I have no call," the man sputtered.

"I killed two men who did not deserve to die this night," Zaknafein explained, his voice going suddenly somber, and truly, it pained the weapon master to even speak of it. "And so . . ."

He stepped back, retracting his sword as he let go of Harbondair.

"They didn't deserve it, but you do," Zaknafein said.

Harbondair just stared, frozen by uncertainty.

Zaknafein shook his head. "But no. I cannot bring them back. For you, then, I grant reprieve, and I'll not ever threaten you again, barkeep . . . unless you force my hand."

Harbondair didn't move, didn't even appear to be breathing, and clearly did not trust anything he heard.

But Zaknafein simply bent over and retrieved his dropped sword, then slid it and the other into their scabbards.

"Fare well, Harbondair Tr'arach," he said, and he walked away.

The ghosts of the dead Ben'Zarafezes followed him through the mostly deserted streets of Menzoberranzan. Soon, behind him, the light of Narbondel just began to hint of the coming day, while before him loomed the city's West Wall and the compound of House Daermon N'a'shezbaernon, House Do'Urden.

As he walked those last steps to the lair of Matron Malice, he considered the difference between Jarlaxle and the others, between Bregan D'aerthe and those who followed the edicts of evil Lolth. He remembered the fateful battle with House Tr'arach that century before. He had tried to keep as many of the invaders alive as he could. Harbondair had been one of them!

This time, though—and in all these new battles in which Zaknafein found himself—he could not hope to offer mercy. To do so would leave witnesses of the aggression of Matron Malice. In their adventures at removing rivals and houses above them in rank, House Do'Urden could take no prisoners.

Zaknafein had never felt so trapped by the misery of Lolth.

Perhaps, he thought, that was why he had not killed Harbondair this night. Maybe he just needed to show mercy to someone, anyone, and know that there wasn't someone directly behind him who would spoil that clemency.

Even if that meant sparing someone who had once tried to kill him.

CHAPTER 17

Trapped

M y patience thins," Matron Soulez told Dab'nay nearly a year to the day after House Do'Urden's elimination of House Ben'Zarafez. "Matron Malice has been quiet long enough for her to be up to trouble once again, and I would not prefer that."

Dab'nay nodded but said nothing. House Do'Urden was nearing the upper echelons in rank now—soon fifteenth, by her calculations—an amazing climb since the addition of Zaknafein a century and a year previous. That number was significant, Dab'nay knew, because in that range, Matron Malice would become an attractive ally for the ruling houses, mostly so that she would choose her conquests to climb higher among her enemies. At the point where House Do'Urden moved into the top fifteen houses, Matron Soulez's plans for House Do'Urden would become much more complicated.

"Your gain will be considerable, both in my house and in Jarlaxle's little gang, when they are both dead," Matron Soulez added.

"Not so easy a task," Dab'nay replied.

"Oh, this time, it will be," Soulez replied. "Do your part, priestess, and I will do mine. How blessed will you be to call Soulez Armgo your matron mother?"

"Blessed beyond my furthest dreams, Matron," Dab'nay replied, and it was a sincere response.

She was surprised, then, at how difficult this task was proving to be for her, emotionally. Because it involved something—someone— else she coveted, more than she had ever thought possible.

The choice was made for her, however. If she didn't do as Matron Soulez had demanded, Dab'nay held no illusions that she would survive the year.

"YOU WILL WATCH THEM," THE WITHERED, ANCIENT MA- tron Mother Baenre told three of her children. "Closely."

"The Armgos?" asked Triel, Matron Mother Baenre's eldest daughter and the second-oldest child of the great woman, behind only Gromph, and who stood beside Matron Mother Baenre this day, a rarity. "Is that even their name? Are they even considered a singular family?"

"They are," Matron Mother Baenre answered curtly, her desiccated lips curling to show her old and worn teeth. When she had been younger, Yvonnel the Eternal, the Matron Mother of House Baenre and of all Menzoberranzan since beyond the memories of the oldest drow, had been considered quite beautiful, on par with Quenthel, her third daughter, who also stood before her. Other elder matrons and priestesses often remarked that Quenthel looked very much like a younger Yvonnel.

A pity that Quenthel couldn't think like Yvonnel, Triel often thought, but would not say to anyone other than Gromph. Quenthel was Triel's closest advisor, mostly because the clever Triel could manipulate her quite easily. Quenthel served as a fine buffer between Triel and two of their other sisters, Bladen'Kerst and Vendes, a pair of the cruelest and most dangerous priestesses in the city.

"Are they, these Armgos, even given a rank?"

"Forty-three," answered Gromph, "though many put it at forty-seven."

"And yet there are not fifteen houses in the city who could stand against the legions of House Barrison Del'Armgo and survive," Matron Mother Baenre added. "Perhaps not ten."

"So you would have me watch them?"

"I would have *you*—all three of you, and with any support you might need—watch them," the old matron mother clarified.

"What are we looking for?"

"Matron Soulez Armgo will move against some powerful house, not in a full war, but to show that she can," Gromph answered.

"So intelligent for a man," Matron Mother Baenre said in open admiration of her son. "Yes, she will."

"Matron Malice Do'Urden," Gromph added.

"That would be my guess."

"And what would you have us do, more than watch?" Triel pressed.

"It will not be a war," her mother replied. "It will not be anything of monumental or highly visible scale. Matron Soulez will seek to slow the ambitions of Matron Malice, likely. She is not pleased that House Do'Urden finished off House Ben'Zarafez. Matron Soulez was holding Matron Decliz as her big play. There were even whispers that Matron Decliz Ben'Zarafez would have invited House Barrison Del'Armgo to join with her, instead of simply letting them move beyond the rank of Matron Decliz's house, as so many others had. And truly, were that the case, would any house lower than House Ben'Zarafez pose a threat to Matron Soulez?"

To the left of Triel, Quenthel began to nod, while Gromph on her right tried hard to look very bored, as if he had already sorted all of this out long ago.

"She will go after Malice's pet weapon master, no doubt," Triel reasoned. "The one who runs with Bregan D'aerthe."

Matron Mother Baenre shrugged, a curious motion from her, and one that had her old shoulders crackling loudly. "Do not be so sure of anything, for that will blind you to anything else."

"Yes, my matron mother," Triel said with a deep and respectful bow. "And you would have us interfere with Matron Soulez's plans, should we uncover them?"

"Make it harder for her. Make it cost her."

Yvonnel the Eternal waved her three children away, and they went out into the great Baenre compound, moving far from any curious eavesdroppers.

"It will be the weapon master," Gromph said when they were alone.

"To hear you credit me so!" Triel replied, gasping as if she might swoon. "The great archmage!"

Gromph scowled at her, then at Quenthel when she giggled at Triel's sarcastic taunt.

"Matron Soulez Armgo's most precious toy is not so different from Matron Malice's," Gromph explained.

"Uthegentel," Triel agreed, nodding. "That beast."

"Except that Soulez does not play with her toy as Malice does, by all whispers," Quenthel added.

"When you speak of matrons, you title them as such," Triel scolded. "If Sos'Umptu heard you, she would demand a grueling penance."

"Sos'Umptu isn't here, though, is she?" Quenthel answered. They were speaking of yet another sister, the most devout Lolthian of the lot, and one who was likely to someday lead Arach-Tinilith, the drow academy for priestesses. At the very least. Of all the daughters of Matron Mother Yvonnel Baenre, Sos'Umptu was the least seen about the house, and the most knowing and powerful in the ways of Lolth. She was far down in the birth order, but many quietly whispered that she, not Triel, would succeed the Matron Mother.

"But I might tell her," Gromph warned, and his expression, that typically bored and angry affect he always wore upon his face, showed that he was not casting idle threats.

The subject of the conversation reminded Triel in no uncertain terms that she should not take this task lightly. Matron Mother Baenre was testing her here, and to fail would be dire.

"I will set eyes all about the city," she told her two co-conspirators. "I will seek word of this weapon master Zaknafein, or anything else concerning the Armgos. We three should speak daily."

"My days are filled with duty—important duty to the city and not the house," Gromph reminded.

The other two scowled at him.

"Yes, I know," he replied to those looks, and he heaved a great sigh. "When the expected incident occurs, my actions alone will determine the outcome." He sighed again.

Triel wanted to argue with him, but in truth, she suspected that he was right. Even so, she was the first priestess of House Baenre, the oldest daughter. Not that it mattered for Gromph, for even the youngest daughter outranked him, whatever titles he might don. The archmage's actions might certainly prove crucial, but they would be directed by Triel, and that was something she was determined never to let her older brother forget.

"YOU CANNOT KNOW TRUTH FROM LIES," DAB'NAY WHISpered, leaning over the table so that her voice was very soft, but so that Zaknafein surely heard every word.

The weapon master rolled his glass about in his fingers, digesting the news. Jarlaxle had assured him that Arathis Hune had learned his lesson and any old feelings had been buried, and while he trusted Jarlaxle—as much as one could trust the mercenary—he didn't disbelieve Dab'nay's information. Her brother Duvon was out of House Fey-Branche now and back with Bregan D'aerthe. And that one, ever a stubborn fool, had likely not forgotten the beating Zaknafein had put on him in the alley behind this very tavern.

Duvon was whispering into Dab'nay's ear, no doubt, and finding her less than receptive. It would make a great deal of sense for him to turn to Arathis Hune for support.

"They will coax you, unexpectedly, and when you are there, you will find an enemy where you expected a friend," Dab'nay told him.

"And then?" he asked as Dab'nay settled back into her seat.

"Stay alive, my only friend," she bade him. "I need you to stay alive."

Zaknafein turned his eyes to his glass and didn't respond, nor did he look up when Dab'nay rose and left the Oozing Myconid. He simply sat there in silent bitterness.

Having at last been allowed out of House Do'Urden after months of what he considered imprisonment, he had come to the tavern in search of companionship, only to find that the intrigue concerning him out here in the wild streets of Menzoberranzan had grown more dangerous.

How sick he was of all of it, how ready to simply draw his blades and go to battle against anyone and everyone until he was mercifully struck down.

He closed his eyes and let the dark moment of anger pass, that internal primal scream that, for but an instant, could overwhelm his every joy.

A steadying breath had him leaning back in his chair, sipping his drink. He wouldn't dare partake of too much liquor, he thought, and the notion had him glancing across the floor to where Harbondair was wiping clean the bar. The man noticed Zaknafein's stare and returned it with a nod, holding up a bottle.

Zaknafein shook his head and Harbondair nodded again, miming a snap of his fingers to indicate that all Zaknafein had to do was ask and more would be rushed over.

The weapon master was glad that he hadn't killed this one, and not because of the excellent service Harbondair had since provided. No, Zaknafein's sense of relief went much deeper than that. He rose from his chair and moved over to take a seat at the bar, which was mostly empty.

"Something else, perhaps?" Harbondair asked.

Zaknafein held up his hand. "I must be back to House Do'Urden soon. It would not do for me to stagger across the balcony."

"Or into Matron Malice's bedroom, eh?" the barkeep quipped with a sly grin, and Zaknafein was happy to return it.

"To Matron Malice," he said, hoisting his drink, "the untamed."

Harbondair tapped the bottle against the glass.

"She is all that they say?"

"And more," Zaknafein replied. "She inflicts more wounds than a displacer cat."

"Claw or suction?"

"Yes!" Zaknafein answered, and both laughed.

When that died away, the two former enemies stared at each other from across the bar, very close.

Zaknafein felt comfortable with this new relationship he had formed. It surprised him to realize that he trusted Harbondair, but he did. Whatever plot Dab'nay had warned him of did not involve this man, he was certain.

"How fares Duvon Tr'arach?" Zaknafein dared to ask.

The question seemed to surprise the barkeep.

"He is a better man than he was when he entered House Fey-Branche, by all accounts," he at last replied.

"And why do you suppose that might be?"

Harbondair shrugged. "He has seen the inside of a noble house, with the constant plotting and backstabbing and frontstabbing, but without the disaster of our own old house. I think perhaps that the experience widened Duvon's perspective and has given him a better appreciation of Bregan D'aerthe."

Zaknafein nodded, and certainly understood. How he wished that Malice would set him free, as Matron Byrtyn had released Duvon.

"And what of Harbondair?" Zaknafein asked.

"Still you doubt?"

"I did not say that."

"Implied," the barkeep replied. "What of me? I am content, perhaps more so than I ever was in the centuries I toiled in the house of Matron Hauzz."

"The priestesses would call that blasphemy."

"The priestesses know blasphemy, I agree."

It was a simple answer, but one with several implications. Harbondair was very good at that, Zaknafein had come to learn. The man could distill a lifetime of frustration and subjugation, along with a giant pile of utter contempt, into four words: "*The priestesses know blasphemy.*"

Zaknafein appreciated that talent.

He was glad he had chosen mercy with this one, indeed.

Zaknafein meandered back across the city soon after, to House Do'Urden and Matron Malice, and there he remained as the tendays slipped past.

And every day, he rose from his bed and thought that he was a day closer to death.

And that, at least, was a good thing, after all.

"Wherever is your friend?" Matron Malice asked him one day, months later.

The question was cryptic and unexpected, but Zaknafein knew at once that Malice had to be referring to Jarlaxle, who had not been about House Do'Urden in many months, perhaps more than a year.

"The last I heard of him, he was out of Menzoberranzan."

"He has returned, two tendays ago, so say the whispers, but he has not returned to Zaknafein," Malice remarked, seeming intrigued.

"He knows that you will not let me out, so I am of no use to him."

"Part of your value to me is that you remain of use to him. I would keep Bregan D'aerthe friendly to House Do'Urden."

Zaknafein shrugged helplessly.

"Finish your lessons with Dinin and you may have a night free," Malice agreed. "One night."

"One night and more if Jarlaxle has work for me?"

Matron Malice scowled, and Zaknafein suppressed his grin, knowing she would concede.

KYORLI SEEMED VERY MUCH LIKE AN ORDINARY RAT, EX-cept that his fur was much cleaner than one might expect for a critter running about the sewers, sludge, and gutters of Menzoberranzan. To Gromph Baenre, however, Kyorli was much more than that. He was his familiar, a companion, even. He was eyes where Gromph could not go, or where the archmage didn't want to be seen.

In the second alley behind Narbondel, not far from Gromph's own private mansion, Kyorli once again showed the archmage his worth. As soon as the rat spotted the approaching drow, it had telepathically contacted the great wizard, who then wasted no time in teleporting back to the spot. Gromph silently nodded his appreciation to Triel, who was not there, for his sister had uncovered much in the tendays since their meeting with Matron Mother Baenre, including, most importantly, this particular location.

Matron Mother Baenre had privately told Gromph that if he was going to interdict an Armgo plan, as they had discussed, he should do so with a potent reminder that he was indeed the archmage of Menzoberranzan. Gromph would be Matron Mother Baenre's unsubtle reminder to House Barrison Del'Armgo and that upstart Matron Soulez that they were not a threat to the great Baenres.

As soon as he had learned of the location, Gromph had familiarized himself with every entrance, every hiding spot, every crevice, along the backs of the three structures that formed this alleyway. Any ambushers had four ways to get into the alley's wide end: one from the street and one from each of the three buildings, through secret doors.

Except that those doors weren't secret to Gromph, and he had already drawn his glyphs and runes about them.

Now, invisibly, he moved about the alley, enacting the magic. One, two, three, and it was all he could do to keep from laughing at how beautifully diabolical and insulting his little extradimensional tunnels might prove.

As he finished the third, he heard movement from down the alley and turned to regard the approach of a man, moving stealthily and cleverly among the shadows. Gromph knew him, though not by name.

He had seen this one with Jarlaxle.

Bait, he figured, and as the assassin moved into the alleyway's cul-de-sac, Gromph slid past him and moved out the other way, down a mostly natural bending corridor, open to the cavern roof, and out onto the street, not far from Narbondel, and not far from his home.

He telepathically bade Kyorli to stay nearby so that he could watch the entertainment through the eyes of his rodent friend.

A FEW DAYS AFTER HIS UNEXPECTED AND SURPRISINGLY good talk with Matron Malice, Zaknafein got his chance, and out he went, into the city, to the Braeryn and the Oozing Myconid. His disappointment grew as he searched the tavern, to find that neither Jarlaxle nor his lieutenants, or even Duvon Tr'arach, were anywhere about. He made his way to the bar and waited for a quiet moment when he was able to speak with Harbondair alone.

"I have heard tell that Jarlaxle has returned to the city," he said.

"Aye," the barkeep quietly replied. "I've heard the same, and with a waiting word that he has been expecting you. A messenger came to me quietly a short while before you arrived, with news that you had left House Do'Urden this night and were likely on your way to the tavern."

"Jarlaxle has been looking for me?"

Harbondair shrugged.

"He informed me that Jarlaxle waits for you now in the second alley behind Narbondel," Harbondair explained. "You know the place?"

"He told you this?"

"Not Jarlaxle," Harbondair clarified. "The messenger. I have not seen Jarlaxle, or that strange Oblodran person who is often by his side, or Arathis Hune, in months."

"Then who told you? Who is this messenger?"

"An associate, I would expect."

The hairs on the back of Zaknafein's neck tingled. Jarlaxle rarely sought clandestine meetings with him and would normally just be in the tavern openly inviting Zaknafein to join his table.

"What of Dab'nay?"

"She spends almost all of her time in the house of Matron Soulez Armgo. She, too, has not been about in tendays, at least."

"When did Jarlaxle return?"

Another shrug. "I heard he has been back in the city for two tendays."

"And you have not seen him?"

"Jarlaxle is ever occupied. Probably in the bed of some matron or ten."

Zaknafein nodded and offered an appreciative smile to Harbondair, who moved off to serve another customer. The weapon master sat at the bar for a long time, slowly sipping his drink and digesting the information. Something seemed wrong to him here—somewhere in the back of his mind, much of what he had just been told seemed . . . off.

He watched Harbondair as the man went about his business, and Zaknafein became convinced as he did that the barkeep had been honest with him.

But honest in reporting what he had been told, not in any truth or treachery behind it.

"The second alley behind Narbondel," Zaknafein whispered under his breath, using the verbal cue to better recall that location, a place where he had met Jarlaxle and other Bregan D'aerthe associates before, though long ago.

Out he went, called more by his suspicions than his sense of duty.

As he neared the appointed rendezvous, he circled the area, looking for agents. He knew their haunts, particularly in areas like this, where Bregan D'aerthe often met. He found no one about. Again the hairs on the back of his neck tingled. He recalled then his last conversation with Dab'nay, where she had warned him of a trap, though in vague terms.

Nevertheless, Zaknafein started into the alley. Its sides were lined with boxes and huge sacks, offering plenty of cover for would-be ambushers. He silently vowed to kill Harbondair if this turned out to be a trap, but then reconsidered almost immediately. The man had been sincere, he believed, and had passed along only that which he had been instructed.

He wouldn't kill the messenger. But he'd certainly consider killing the messenger's messenger.

The alley continued down a dozen strides, bent to the left, then back to the right, he recalled. Still, he didn't have his weapons drawn as he made his way.

He was Zaknafein—his swords in their scabbards were as good as drawn.

He moved along the bend, then rushed around the sharp right-hand corner to find the alley dead-ending and empty.

Except that it wasn't.

"I knew it would be you!" came a familiar voice, and Arathis Hune leaped down from on high, weapons drawn, landing just a couple of strides from Zaknafein, who easily spun and blocked, his blades appearing in his hands as if they had been there all along.

Zaknafein could have moved right in then, pressing the man, as his parry had left him in an advantageous position. With his skill, he might have put Arathis Hune on his heels and kept him there until the end.

But . . . something was wrong here.

He did not advance.

This was not the trap.

CHAPTER 18

The Words He Knew

Priestess Mez'Barris Armgo stared out to the west from the balcony of the family's sprawling compound. Not counting the extradimensional spaces in some of the other powerful houses, Xorlarrin and Baenre mostly, House Barrison Del'Armgo was the largest compound in the city, and certainly greater than the house's ranking would suggest.

For all that room, though, Mez'Barris remained in the very same chair where she had watched the Armgo war parties depart. She stared longingly toward Narbondel now, its light diminishing to nothingness beyond the same boulevard where she had watched Uthegentel move out of sight.

It pained her to see him heading out there, with the dangerous Zaknafein Do'Urden in his sights, and with that incompetent fool Dab'nay beside him. How could her mother have sent him with her? Why not Mez'Barris?

True, Parsnalvi, the house wizard, was also flanking Uthegentel, and with an enchanted item that had only one specific purpose, but still . . .

Sometimes young and promising Mez'Barris simply could not understand her mother.

She didn't ponder that for long, though, as her thoughts kept going back to the image of Uthegentel, the house weapon master. He was not an Armgo by birth. Mez'Barris could only guess at his heritage, though she was confident that it was not wholly drow. Certainly not! The man stood well over six feet tall, a height that few drow women could attain. He was stronger than the women, too—another anomaly among the drow—and was easily the strongest dark elf in the city. Even with magical assistance, other men could not match him, and even with Lolth-blessed spells of physical enhancement, other women couldn't, either.

And there was more to him than simple size and strength. As Mez'Barris considered this, she shivered at the mere thought of him in his fine black armor and carrying that mighty black trident—armor and arms suitable for a weapon master of a noble house.

Of House Baenre, even, for that noble rank is where Matron Soulez expected Barrison Del'Armgo to soon enough be.

Uthegentel, so fast, so strong, so invincible, would be a big part of that ascent, they all knew. There was something special about him, and surely the growing reputation of this Zaknafein Do'Urden paled against the reality of Uthegentel. Uthegentel was possessed of too much energy for his mortal body, and it seemed to Mez'Barris that sparks of the stuff, the very energy of life, shot from him whenever he moved, little lightning pricks to tease and nip. For all his huge chest and shoulders, and thick arms wound tightly with muscles, the man moved with the grace of a dancer, so very light on his feet.

Yes, he was more than a mere man, more than a mere mortal, and Mez'Barris was glad indeed that her mother had not taken him as her patron. Glad and shocked, for Matron Soulez had demanded that none in House Armgo ride the man except for Mez'Barris. Oh, indeed, she sometimes rented him out for breeding services, as she had with Matron Malice Do'Urden to produce that Briza creature, but that didn't bother Mez'Barris. She could not feel envy toward those who paid for the magnificent specimen with coin.

Mez'Barris took all of that in stride, as well as the teasing she endured from the other priestesses, both here and out in the city.

"How can you be with a man who is stronger than you?" most women asked, seeming sincerely aghast at the thought. "It isn't natural! Are you sure that you don't simply prefer the bed company of women?"

Mez'Barris was sure. Yes, it was unusual, almost unheard of, for a drow woman to be attracted to a man so physically superior to her, but Mez'Barris couldn't deny the thrill she felt when Uthegentel so easily tossed her up upon his hips, holding her aloft while he took her, never tiring. He threw her about as if she were a child, but he knew how to throw her indeed!

She would take their barbs and simply smile, and never let them all know the power of her lover, and the thrill he could give to her beyond anything any of them—she was sure—had ever known.

BEFORE ARATHIS HUNE PUT ON A MASK OF RAGE, ZAKNA-fein thought he saw a flicker of surprise.

The two fell into a fighting rhythm, blades clanging, each quick-stepping sidelong to take a good look at the battleground, to seek advantage.

"'They will coax you, unexpectedly, and when you are there, you will find an enemy where you expected a friend,'" Zaknafein yelled at him, rolling his left hand in and over to send his sword down hard to block the thrust of Arathis Hune's.

His opponent leaped back as if expecting a counter, but it did not come. Perhaps that explained the curious look on Arathis Hune's face, Zaknafein thought, but perhaps not, and so he repeated, "'They will coax you, unexpectedly, and when you are there, you will find an enemy where you expected a friend.'"

"'Stay alive, my only friend,'" Arathis Hune replied, his red eyes sparkling with recognition.

Zaknafein nodded, and together, the men answered, "'I need you to stay alive.'"

So they knew.

Movement to the side had the combatants suddenly charging at each other, then stopping fast and going past, very near. They hooked arms, the momentum spinning them sidelong, where Zaknafein leaped out for the right-hand side of the alley, bracing and vaulting into a somersault that landed him on both his feet, squared up to a secret door that suddenly opened before him.

Zaknafein heard the telltale clicks and spun sidelong, throwing his cloak out wide before him to catch the flying quarrels. He managed to glance over his shoulder, to see Arathis Hune similarly dodging against a different concealed door directly opposite the one that had opened before Zaknafein. And from it came a handful of drow warriors.

From both, Zaknafein saw, looking back to his own portal.

But no . . .

Zaknafein paused, mouth hanging open, for the group charging him simply disappeared, vanished, as if they had been no more than an illusion. He spun again, thinking to go to his now companion, but saw a third door opening, this one from the building at the end of the alley, and out charged another handful—or was it the same one? He couldn't be certain!

But then, those attackers too were gone, simply vanished, and farther on, Arathis Hune too was suddenly standing alone.

"BE DONE WITH THIS PUNY DO'URDEN AND COME BACK TO me," Mez'Barris whispered to the night. The priestess squirmed uncomfortably and shook her head, still surprised that her mother, Matron Soulez, had allowed Uthegentel to be involved with this mission. True, it should not be more dangerous—indeed, not even nearly as dangerous—as many of the other battles House Barrison Del'Armgo had waged of late, with overwhelming odds in their favor this night, but there was a different play here, Mez'Barris knew.

This fight involved Zaknafein Do'Urden, a man Uthegentel had been watching and planning to battle for more than a century, since the time when Zaknafein had been the only notable member of a minor house named Simfray. Mez'Barris understood her lover well. If he had a weakness, it was pride. There was no way he would stand behind the others of his war party and allow Zaknafein to be killed, no chance, even, that he would allow others to engage the weapon master of House Do'Urden beside him.

This was a kill Uthegentel craved, and with witnesses, that the word could go out far and wide of his singular and glorious victory.

With Zaknafein properly dispatched, only Dantrag Baenre himself would stand between Uthegentel and his desire to be named as the uncontested champion of Menzoberranzan.

"Be done with this puny Do'Urden and come back to me," she whispered again, and almost as if in answer, a drow warrior appeared, then another, a third, fourth, and fifth, materializing in midstride at the front of the Armgo compound. She tensed, worried they were under attack as two fell prone, hand crossbows presented, while the other three moved with perfect precision to follow those shots into battle.

Just as these skilled warriors had been trained . . . at House Barrison Del'Armgo.

The five skidded to a communal stop, all glancing about in confusion, which mirrored her own.

Out of her chair now, Mez'Barris recognized them, warriors of her own house, one of the three supporting strike teams that had gone out with Uthegentel's group of seven.

"What is it?" a voice asked behind her, and she glanced back to see the priestess Ahlm'wielle, her cousin.

"What?" she asked back.

"You gasped, loudly," Ahlm'wielle replied.

Mez'Barris pointed over the balcony to the strike team, who were all up now and moving back into the compound, shaking their heads. "Something is amiss."

"One of the war parties has returned?" Ahlm'wielle asked incredulously, but she quickly shook off any concern.

"It is still seventeen against two," Mez'Barris said to calm herself.

Ahlm'wielle wagged her finger and shook her head, correcting Mez'Barris with "Eighteen against one."

Mez'Barris started to agree, but stopped when, out of the corner of her eye, she saw a second Armgo war party appear, again as if they were charging into battle and had taken a wrong dimensional turn.

Then a third party joined the other two, fifteen Armgo warriors now, all confused, all out of the battle.

Mez'Barris leaned over the rail, peering all about for the fourth team, Uthegentel's team.

"Eight against one," she whispered to herself, trying to calm her very real and growing fears.

It didn't sound quite as good to her.

"A RUSE!" ZAKNAFEIN CRIED AS HE COMPLETED HIS TURN, to see a handful of warriors charging down the alley. Zaknafein surely recognized one in particular, a giant of a drow with spiked white hair and golden pins stuck through his cheeks. Yes, he knew of Uthegentel— everyone in Menzoberranzan knew of the beastly weapon master of House Barrison Del'Armgo—and that clarified all of this to him. For Dab'nay had played a role in this, he believed . . . or she had used her connections with House Barrison Del'Armgo to warn both him and Arathis Hune.

But why? How did it make sense that she had warned them both in such a manner that might have them killing each other before the ambush had even begun?

He didn't have time to sort any of it out, for in came four warriors, with Uthegentel hanging back. Two charged right in at Zaknafein and Arathis Hune, the other two flanking left and right to box in the intended victims.

Zaknafein and Arathis Hune turned back-to-back—they had practiced this technique many times, as had all of Jarlaxle's band—any enmity between the two forgotten . . . for the moment, at least.

Zaknafein's turn had him intercepting the back two, the ones who had flanked, for with his two long blades, he was better able to parry against enemies coming in from either side. He heard the clash of metal behind him before he blocked, Arathis Hune working his sword and dagger to halt the charge of the middle pair.

Out went the weapon master's sword to the right. Out went his left-hand blade, and he followed that parry with a quick step and turn, nudging Arathis Hune as he went, signaling the man.

Arathis Hune, too, went left, the pair circling, and so the warrior chasing Zaknafein from his right side had to halt and scramble to get his blades in line to meet the new foe. Similarly, the Armgo warrior pressing Arathis Hune from his right side now got a face full of Zaknafein, the weapon master first thrusting long to push his initial attacker back, then coming in with fury on the new opponent. Zaknafein worked his blades hard, down-angling the stabs to force the man further off balance. He almost had him but had to relent and quarter-spin back the other way to engage the charge of his initial opponent.

Round and round went the pair, building a rhythm, coming almost all the way back to their original back-to-back position—almost, but not quite, for there, they suddenly reversed, and this time, Zaknafein's abrupt shift caught that original opponent clearly off guard, and the weapon master was sure he had a clear hit.

But he heard a stumble behind him, and a cry from Arathis Hune, and had to cut short his attack to help his ally. Zaknafein lifted an enemy blade just in time for the tumbling Bregan D'aerthe assassin to go rolling out of the melee. Arathis Hune came right back to his feet, blades at the ready, but none of the four attackers had pursued.

Zaknafein recognized it first, and fast, and a good thing that was! He put his legs underneath him and leaped straight up into the air, way up high, tucking his legs to avoid two stabs and a vicious slash. Up above the blades of his three immediate enemies, the fourth still falling away from Zaknafein's reversal, Zaknafein kicked out left and right. One of his targets got his sword up fast, cutting a gash in Zaknafein's shin, but the weapon master accepted the sting gladly, for both of his boots found their marks, kicking each of the two in the face.

One went flying away, straight to the ground, where his head cracked loudly on the alleyway stone, blood flowing immediately. The other staggered back, dazed, his sword wet with Zaknafein's blood, but his nose pouring his own.

The third of the group stood alone against Zaknafein, his friend fast returning. But not fast enough. Zaknafein feigned to the right, the obvious move with another enemy closing so fast from the left, but with stunning courage, the confident Zaknafein went left instead, his blades working furiously, batting aside his surprised enemy's thrusts and stabs, working over and down in a sudden and brutal frenzy.

He got the man in the chest, a deep stab, just as the other, his initial opponent, came in at his back.

Without missing a movement, Zaknafein let go of his blades, caught them in backhand grips, and began stabbing them out behind him in rapid and brutal succession.

The poor enemy behind him had never seen such a technique or such fury and had to parry and dodge as surely as if the weapon master had been facing him.

So strong was Zaknafein's grip, so sure and quick and balanced his reverse stabs, that no parry could move the blades far enough to one side or the other to slow his rhythm. And finally, inevitably, the Armgo drow missed a parry and caught the sword tip in the gut.

Zaknafein whirled about, the bloody-nosed fellow coming in fast to join his gut-stabbed companion. Before he ever got there, though, the Armgo drow found himself alone, as Zaknafein worked his right-hand blade over and down, taking the cringing and wounded drow's swords low with it. Over that descending blade went Zaknafein's right hand, the weapon master stepping forward and putting all of his weight behind a heavy pommel punch to the face.

Three down.

Zaknafein leaped ahead and dove into a roll, coming around as he did to return to his feet facing his last opponent. As he rose, he noted Arathis Hune engaged with Uthegentel, the assassin twisted and low, pulling the front of that mighty black trident down with him.

So Uthegentel hit him across the face with the butt end of the weapon. It didn't seem so solid a blow to Zaknafein, but Arathis Hune went flying back and to the ground. He tried to rise, staggered, then simply fell over.

Zaknafein focused on the drow nearest, not wanting to battle this one and that powerful weapon master together. The Armgo warrior fell back, though, blood still dripping from his nose, wanting nothing to do with Zaknafein.

As he moved toward the alleyway exit, Zaknafein noted two more enemies and realized that he was doomed. He should have focused on the man standing there, he realized, but he could not, for he knew the other.

Dab'nay Tr'arach.

She had indeed betrayed him.

He'd deal with her later, he thought, but winced as he did, for not only was Uthegentel Armgo now closing on him, but another Armgo warrior might get back up to join in, and worse still, the man standing beside Dab'nay was certainly a wizard, given his decorated robes, and almost certainly a high-ranking wizard in a house known to have powerful arcane spellcasters.

Zaknafein hated priestesses of Lolth above all, but loved to fight them.

He hated fighting wizards.

Wizards cheated. They could melt him or shock him to death or freeze him or send him to some far-off horrid plane before he ever got close enough to strike.

Even worse, now he couldn't go after that one, accepting (and hopefully avoiding) a single spell before closing to melee range.

No, Zaknafein had a bigger problem, in the form of the biggest drow he had ever seen.

Uthegentel's approach surprised Zaknafein, for it was not bullish. He came at Zaknafein in measured steps, that huge trident handled like a short spear in his right hand, left hand out wide to complete the balance of his crouched stance. It didn't take Zaknafein long to understand why the powerful drow kept that second hand free, for Uthegentel put the trident through a series of spins and handoffs back and forth, the long weapon rotating in a blur before him, creating a wall of defense.

In the few heartbeats it took Zaknafein to figure out the unorthodox maneuver, the big man almost got him, stopping the blur suddenly, and in perfect alignment to thrust that three-tined weapon fast for Zaknafein, center torso.

Zaknafein had no time to dodge to either side, couldn't back up fast enough to escape the extended reach of the weapon, and simply wasn't strong enough to block the trident cold. The veteran weapon master, ever a student of the arts martial, understood all of that without thinking it. His muscles understood it; every bit of him understood it. His swords, weapons stolen from the armory of Uthegentel's own house, came up vertically before him, perfectly aligned to take the trident between the tines, and as the immensely strong Uthegentel drove through the block, Zaknafein kept his feet planted but fell back, bending at the knees.

Down, down, he went, so low that his shoulder blades nearly touched the ground. Uthegentel retracted, obviously to re-angle the trident downward at the low-bending weapon master, but before he could even do that, Zaknafein came back up a short way, then stopped abruptly and, with perfect muscle control, transferred his momentum fully into his legs, leaping out backward, backflipping to land on his feet.

And, angled forward, he came right back in with blinding speed, leaping up and stomping down on the trident to drive it lower, his left foot lifting and kicking out ahead to slam Uthegentel in the face.

The bulky Armgo weapon master staggered back a step, but shook it away, seeming more surprised than hurt, and with fantastic agility and speed, Uthegentel got his trident up in time to fend off Zaknafein's ensuing sword barrage.

But Zaknafein had the advantage now and pressed ferociously. On his heels, Uthegentel cut a powerful two-hand parry, then kept the trident in his right hand, his left going to his belt and producing a net.

Zaknafein had heard about this second weapon, a net magically strengthened and enchanted to attack its target on its own.

Uthegentel swept his left hand across and Zaknafein could sense the net as if it were a sentient animal, biting at him. But he didn't relent—he couldn't relent. On he pressed, swords banging against that trident in rapid succession, Zaknafein pushing ahead.

Again Uthegentel swept the net across, this time letting it fly.

Zaknafein hit it a dozen times, his blades angling perfectly to stop the magical item from widening to grasp at him. The net flew past harmlessly, and Zaknafein went right back in at the hulking drow, furiously striking, stabbing, slashing—anything to keep Uthegentel back on his heels. He didn't know if he could finish Uthegentel then, but he certainly had stolen the advantage.

But then . . . he missed, Uthegentel cleverly dipping his trident, then coming back in behind Zaknafein's left-hand slash across to stab hard.

Zaknafein's right-hand sword swept in to deflect as he spun desperately, dropping his left foot back and circling backward right around, and again, his balance perfect, he regained the upper hand.

"Enough!" he heard from the alleyway, from the wizard.

Expecting a devastating spell, Zaknafein went tumbling away defensively, throwing his magical *piwafwi* cloak about him as a shield.

But the wizard wasn't casting a lightning bolt or missiles of magical energy, and wasn't aiming at Zaknafein anyway. He held a small rod out before him horizontally in both hands, then simply snapped it in half, releasing the encapsulated dweomer.

Uthegentel roared in protest, but his voice warped as his physical form wavered, flapping like laundry in a strong wind.

The wizard likewise distorted and twisted like some empty fabric, and both were gone, *poof,* leaving Zaknafein, four wounded Armgo soldiers, Arathis Hune (who was still inexplicably facedown on the ground), and a shocked and clearly terrified Dab'nay standing in the alleyway's open exit.

The priestess shook her head slowly, staring at him, mouthing something he could not hear—but Zaknafein was confident that she was not trying to cast a spell. Her shoulders trembled slightly, perhaps from sobs.

"Well, we won and you are deserted," Zaknafein said to her, flipping his bloodied swords, deftly rubbing them across the clothes of the nearest body to clean them, then returning them skillfully to their sheaths. He glanced to the side to see a wounded Armgo warrior crawling for one of the alleyway's exits. "Did you really believe that you could succeed at this, priestess?"

"Yes, Dab'nay the Unthinking," Arathis Hune chimed in. Zaknafein hid his smile, but he was not surprised. "Did you expect a different outcome? Do you think Jarlaxle would elevate fools to his side? We knew. Of course we knew! And if you ever hoped to ascend in Bregan D'aerthe, you should have anticipated that Zaknafein and I would be three steps ahead of your deceptions.

"First," he continued, "I knew that you have been bedding Zaknafein for a long time, but for your own gain. Second, that gain is a product of elimination, both of us out of your way, and how convenient that Jarlaxle is not around. For with him near, we could not engage, of course. And where is Jarlaxle this night?"

Dab'nay's gaze never left Zaknafein, her stare locking his and holding it fast.

"Third," Arathis went on, quite confidently it seemed, "you have been courting the favor of the particularly vicious Soulez Armgo. What gain might Dab'nay find by eliminating one of us, when eliminating both would put her by Jarlaxle's side in Bregan D'aerthe? Jarlaxle who is, by the way, out of the city on business with the Armgos, of course!"

Zaknafein saw a slight shake of Dab'nay's head, but it was clear that the woman was defeated here, wholly so, emotionally so. She didn't even have the heart to argue, it seemed to the perceptive Zaknafein.

"Three steps ahead," Arathis Hune reiterated lightly, tauntingly. "And now your intended victim will put the blade to you."

Zaknafein noted a flare of sudden confusion in Dab'nay's red eyes. He wasn't surprised by it.

HER OVERRIDING FEELING WAS GUILT, NOT FEAR. DAB'NAY fully expected that she was about to die—her feeble repertoire of spells couldn't begin to protect her from either of these skilled killers, let alone both.

Strangely, though, she almost welcomed that. All of this had churned at her for so long, tearing her apart inside. She didn't want Zaknafein dead! She didn't even want Arathis Hune killed. But her situation had been wholly untenable.

So she had chosen. The only choice she could make, she had believed.

But she had chosen wrong, and so now would pay.

She noted Arathis Hune rising farther down the alley, behind Zaknafein. She noted the stealthy approach of the man and thought it curious, then more curious still when he angled not for her, but for Zaknafein's back, his dagger bared and in hand!

And Zaknafein was staring at her.

"Six steps," the weapon master corrected Arathis Hune, and Dab'nay gasped aloud at the speed of Zaknafein's arms coming up, swords with them in backhand grips. At first she thought he had tossed the left-hand blade, spinning, but then realized that he was simply flipping it over in his grasp as it went, up and over his left shoulder, even as his right-hand sword stabbed out hard behind him.

She saw Arathis Hune dodge slightly, but still come in for Zaknafein's back.

But that left-hand sword of the weapon master! Somehow, he had brought it over, turned it over, and now swept it across behind him to intercept the assassin's dagger.

Dab'nay could hardly keep up with Zaknafein's movements, his sword coming back up over his right shoulder, high over his head and around, even as he began his leftward turn. She expected that high blade to come sweeping all the way around—Arathis Hune did, too, she realized from his movement—but no! Instead, Zaknafein flipped it again as it passed before him and expertly turned it to stab straight out behind him with a backhand grip, as his other blade had done earlier.

And he was still turning, and now it was his right-hand blade that went up, then came slashing down as he completed the move, the brilliant move, a move that should have been two extensions too long, but had been executed so perfectly, so swiftly, that even the uncommonly skilled victim appeared mesmerized.

Arathis Hune did manage to throw himself back to his right and down, saving himself from decapitation.

But he staggered, for the blade had hit, and he clutched at the side of his neck, where a fountain of blood had already begun to spurt.

"Six steps ahead, not three," Zaknafein said again. "You forgot to mention the first of them: that it was Arathis Hune who used the Oblodran mind magic in an attempt to allow Duvon Tr'arach to defeat and kill me. Jarlaxle's actions in giving me his eyepatch showed me the truth of that treachery.

"Fifth, this last planned assassination that you would have me believe was the act of Dab'nay alone." The weapon master laughed, as if the very notion was absurd. "You knew of Dab'nay's efforts with the Armgos because she is not the only member of Bregan D'aerthe who has recently parlayed with them. For why would they wish Arathis Hune dead? What gain to them? And if you knew, as you just said, that it was they, the Armgos, who had arranged for Jarlaxle to be out of town, then you knew Jarlaxle was away. So why did you come here?

"And finally, you betrayed yourself in this beyond doubt, assassin. In our fight with the foursome. For Arathis Hune does not stumble."

Arathis Hune stared at him, eyes wide. He slumped down to one knee, then had to put his free hand to the ground for further support, for as tightly as he might hold the wound, he could not fully stem the spurting blood.

Dab'nay could save him. She slid her thumbs across her fingers anxiously as she considered a spell of healing. But still, she stared at Zaknafein, trying to take some measure of the man.

She began to cast her spell, but stopped as Zaknafein approached, blade leveled at her throat.

She expected to die.

"Webs over webs over webs," he said, bringing the sword tip to the tender flesh of her throat.

Dab'nay swallowed hard. Back behind Zaknafein, Arathis Hune slumped to the ground, the blood pooling.

Zaknafein retracted his sword and spun it over, sliding it and its partner blade into their respective sheaths once more. "I cannot pay the price of your head," he said. "Jarlaxle will sell you to the Armgos—he is likely doing so even now, in his current dealings with Matron Soulez. I wonder if she will buy you only to blame you for her losses this night."

"Then kill me," she whispered.

Zaknafein started to reply, but stopped and simply shook his head, his expression empty.

"I am sorry," she whispered, the words barely audible. "I have not your courage."

She noted Zaknafein's wince but couldn't begin to decipher it.

The weapon master ran past her, down the alleyway and out into the Menzoberranzan night.

Dab'nay took a deep and steadying breath, then rubbed her fingers, thinking to heal Arathis Hune.

Too late.

CHAPTER 19

When the Blood Dried

H e died," Matron Soulez scolded Dab'nay, who was now officially Dab'nay Armgo, and a priestess of House Barrison Del'Armgo, and no longer affiliated with Bregan D'aerthe, formally or otherwise.

For all the good that did her.

Dab'nay licked her lips, but didn't verbally respond, not quite sure what Matron Soulez would want her to say. One of the four warriors of the group to which she had been assigned had indeed succumbed to his wounds, because after Dab'nay had checked on the dying Arathis Hune, she had discovered that for this one, too, it was too late for any healing spells to make a difference.

However, Dab'nay's instructions upon journeying out with that group had been explicit and unbending: she was to heal Uthegentel alone. Her limited repertoire of spells was to be used on the prized weapon master, Matron Soulez had told her repeatedly. The others were expendable, and now, one had been expended.

"Our great weapon master has taken the measure of Zaknafein, and one of Jarlaxle's lieutenants is dead," she meekly replied to Matron Soulez's unceasing scowl.

"Never speak of that fight," Matron Soulez told her in a tone brooking no debate and promising the severest of consequences should she disobey.

Dab'nay lowered her gaze to the floor and gave a slight nod. She understood, surely. By all estimation, Zaknafein had been gaining the upper hand on Uthegentel. Barring something dramatic, Zaknafein Do'Urden would have won that contest. Matron Soulez didn't want that to become public knowledge, of course.

"Leave us," Soulez told Dab'nay when another priestess, Mez'Barris, entered the room.

"He is angry about the extraction," Mez'Barris informed her mother as soon as Dab'nay was gone.

"Of course he is. And you should take care of your desired patron, that his arrogance doesn't get him killed. He might have lost, likely so, according to the five who witnessed the fight. We have underestimated this Do'Urden weapon master. I hope the same does not hold true for that Matron Malice creature."

"Uthegentel is young," Mez'Barris protested. "Zaknafein was finished with Melee-Magthere before he was ever born. He hasn't the man's experience, surely not in actual combat."

Matron Soulez laughed at her and waved her silent. "One day, my beautiful Uthegentel will be done with Zaknafein," she agreed. She noted that her daughter wanted to reply but couldn't seem to speak her mind here.

"You think that we should be rid of Zaknafein now, by any manner we can find," Matron Soulez reasoned.

"He makes Matron Malice's family far more formidable," Mez'Barris replied.

"Perspective, my daughter. We are not ready to war with House Do'Urden."

"We would destroy them!"

"Of course, but in so doing, we would be telling Matron Mother Baenre and the others on the Ruling Council the truth of our power.

So many think to cow their enemies by showing their full strength. But they are wrong. Never forget that, my daughter. Revealing the great power of your army reveals, too, the limitation of that power and hints at how others might work around it to wound you.

"We will let Matron Malice keep her plaything, for now, but let us make it clear to Zaknafein that his friend Jarlaxle did little to stop this lethal ambush, though Jarlaxle knew about it."

"Jarlaxle did not know until the battle was over," Mez'Barris replied, but Matron Soulez's sigh and scowl reminded her that the truth was what they made others believe, not what had actually transpired.

That, more than anything else, was the way of the drow.

"Jarlaxle and his band of rogues are far too cozy with Matron Mother Baenre, and Jarlaxle's personal friendship with Zaknafein is . . . troubling. I'll not have Matron Mother Baenre interjecting herself into any fight we might find with House Do'Urden." She paused and snorted, her lips and eyes narrowing. "And we both understand how badly Matron Mother Baenre, mother of that pathetic Dantrag, would like to see our beloved Uthegentel removed from the conversation."

"YOU'VE LONG BEEN TOLD THAT THERE WOULD BE A PRICE," a clearly unhappy Jarlaxle said to Zaknafein a few tendays later, after returning to the city to learn that his oldest companion and trusted lieutenant was dead.

"So was he, and that did not deter his blade," replied Zaknafein, nursing a heady ale. "Only my own blade did that, and from behind, as one would expect from a true coward."

"You believe that your sense of honor serves you well here? I am amazed that you are still alive."

"Sense of honor and a lot of preparation against those I know do not share it," Zaknafein clarified.

Jarlaxle bit back his retort and thought back to the times he had witnessed Zaknafein's peculiar practice sessions, where the weapon master had worked tirelessly at that one seemingly too-long combination involving the over-the-shoulder parry, followed by the repeated backward thrusts to cover the sweeping killing blow.

"Still, I warned you, both of you, that such a battle would prove expensive to the winner," Jarlaxle insisted.

"Take it out of the gold you received for Dab'nay Tr'arach," came the sarcastic reply. "Pardon, I mean Priestess Dab'nay Armgo."

Jarlaxle had no immediate answer. Zaknafein wasn't supposed to know that.

"We cannot go to war with House Barrison Del'Armgo," he said at length. "They are far more powerful—"

"*We?*" Zaknafein interrupted simply, and the question rang with a finality to both of them.

The weapon master finished his drink in one great gulp, then pulled himself up from the table and left the Oozing Myconid, never to return.

PART 4

The
Afflicted

I have learned so much from Grandmaster Kane in such a short period of time. I have learned to control my body, even to view my body, in ways I never before imagined. It is a vessel for my consciousness, and one that I can explore more deeply than ever did I know. I can manipulate my muscles to turn my hands into daggers, to stand strong against hurricane winds, even to the point where I can work my muscles individually to expel the venom of a snake or the poison of a dagger from the wound that introduced it.

I have learned angles of attack and defense superior to those taught to me in my years at the drow academy, or even under the tutelage of my father. Perhaps even more importantly, I have learned to anticipate the exact deflections of blocking angles, so that a simple turn of my hips will allow the striking sword to pass harmlessly, guided by a subtle block by my own scimitar, or even by my hand.

My time with the Grandmaster of Flowers has been such a marvelous exploration, within and without. The world around me, my friends around me, my wife, my coming child are all different to me now, and in a more marvelous way by far, as if the negative impulses of jealousy, fear, and reactive anger have no way through the budding embarrassment I feel for even considering them. The journey is grander, lighter, and more profound all at once.

This, the larger picture of the world and multiverse about us, is the secret to Grandmaster Kane's always-calm demeanor, and his always-glad and always-humble aspect. He has come to know his place, and not in any diminishing way. Nay, far from it!

So, as I consider my time with Kane and the lasting effects of those experiences, I can say without reservation that the most important and precious thing I learned from him was gratitude.

I am grateful every day—to strive for that in every moment is to seek perfection of the soul, in much the same way I have spent my life seeking perfection of the body, of the warrior. Now I have learned to join those two things . . . no, four things—mind, body, heart, and soul—into a singular endeavor. To raise a hand in deflection of an incoming spear is to understand the movement and to hone my muscles to the required speed and reaction, of course, but such training without discipline and an understanding of the moral implications of such battle, even the spiritual repercussions of such a fight, makes one . . . Artemis Entreri—and worse, the Artemis Entreri of old.

There need be a reason, more than a simple justification, and when you understand that all is one, those reasons crystallize more completely and give strength to your battle, strength at once physical, intellectual, emotional, and philosophical.

The complete warrior is more than one trained in exact and perfect movements. I have known this for a long time. Once I told Entreri that he could not beat me, not ever, because he did not fight with heart. Now, after seeing Kane, after being humbled by this man who has become so much more than human, I better understand my own words to Artemis Entreri on that long-ago day. They are sentiments that Kane could have very recently spoken to me, leaving me with no honest recourse.

Yes, I am grateful to Kane, Grandmaster of Flowers of the Monastery of the Yellow Rose, and that which inspires my greatest gratitude is the widening perspective regarding everything about and around this consciousness I call self, regarding life itself, regarding reason itself, that reminds me to be grateful, and to learn, ever to learn.

This is our way.
This is our purpose.
This is our joy.
Our eternal joy.

—*Drizzt Do'Urden*

CHAPTER 20

THE YEAR OF DWARVENKIND REBORN
DALERECKONING 1488

Flotsam

G et up!" he heard from far, far away. "Wake up, ye shark food! Get up!"

Cold water splashed his face and ran up his nostrils, and he was vaguely aware of his own choking, that he simply wasn't getting enough air.

His sensibilities returned a bit more and he felt himself swaying, rolling with the undulations of the cold water about him. He crashed into something hard, shoulder and head, but it was a dull thump, again as if it had happened far, far away. He became aware of the sensation of falling, slowly, so slowly.

Something, someone, grabbed him roughly by the hair and yanked him back up, and again he felt the water splashing about his face and up his nose and in his mouth, and again he heard the pleading, and understood now that it was a woman's voice.

Then he was rising, and what he felt more keenly was the water running off him, the change of pressure on him as he came out of the liquid and the rolling waves splashing at him lower and lower on his body. He sensed that he was up in the air—was he dead?

That thought brought Wulfgar back to his senses, and he opened his eyes to find himself floating above the ocean, just above the side of a small dinghy, where a woman, Bonnie Charlee, grabbed at his legs to pull him into the boat. As soon as he was over the craft, he fell, and fell hard, crashing down into the small boat. It should have hurt more than it did, he somehow understood, but his body was numb, his feelings still distant. He rolled over, barely aware of his groaning, and there saw another person in the boat: Kimmuriel.

"Ye couldn't've let the fool down a bit easier, then?" Bonnie Charlee scolded.

"I could have let you hang over the side, holding him by the hair until he drowned," Kimmuriel answered, and Wulfgar thought the words and the dispassionate tone so perfectly typical.

Wulfgar tried to sit up, but his arms would barely answer his call, and the moment he moved, a burning agony across his back had him once more on the deck, facedown, writhing.

"Ah, but he's going to bleed out and be dead," Bonnie Charlee cried. "Be quick and get me that tar."

Wulfgar was lying in a way that left him staring at Kimmuriel, and the psionicist gave a little snort and made no move at all. He heard Bonnie Charlee's harrumph as she moved over him, collecting the patch bucket they kept in all the small boats.

"We've got to heat it," she said, looking all around.

"Look in the pail," Kimmuriel told her, and when she did, she paused, then glanced up at the strange drow. "It is not so difficult a task," Kimmuriel added.

Bonnie Charlee dipped her hand into the goo and brought forth a blob, which she smeared across Wulfgar's back. "Ye'll have quite the scar, Wulfgar of Icewind Dale," she said, "but at least ye won't bleed out in me dinghy, what."

"We'll need him to row as soon as he's awake," Wulfgar heard Kimmuriel say, but he didn't see the drow then, for his eyes were clenched tightly as he fought against the pain of the warm tar covering his deep, open wound, pulling at the edges of his torn skin.

"Row? He'll be lucky if he can stand," Bonnie Charlee replied.

"I . . . can stand," Wulfgar said through gritted teeth, and he pulled himself up to his elbows. He felt as if a sword were still stuck into his back, stabbing and burning with every twist. He knew he was poisoned, for he could feel the sickly stuff coursing through him, but still, with great determination, he got one foot under him and pressed upward, coming shakily to his feet in the middle of the small boat. He noted then the parade of sails gliding away from him, heading east for Luskan.

"First wave'll knock him over the side," Bonnie Charlee said, shaking her head. "He's not rowing."

"What happened?" Wulfgar asked, only vaguely aware of the events that had put him into the sea.

"You missed," Kimmuriel dryly answered.

"Sank their ship, though," said Bonnie Charlee. "Margaster ship, I'm thinkin', and a fine one. So fine. Now . . ." She shrugged and nodded her chin off to the side, and out there in the darkness, Wulfgar could make out the low-riding hull of an overturned ship.

"They took the *Heirloom*, though, so might've been better if ye hadn't sunk their boat."

"Where's Calico Grimm?"

Bonnie Charlee shook her head.

"He is not our concern," Kimmuriel interjected. "We are for Luskan, with all haste. Sit and take up the oars, Wulfgar."

"He canna'!" said Bonnie Charlee.

Wulfgar fell as much as bent down to the bench seat, and he winced against the pull and pain as his arms went out to either side to grip the oars. He paused then, feeling something very uncomfortable, as if Kimmuriel was trying to get into his mind and possess him. Purely on instinct, he fought back with all his willpower.

Let me in, fool, Kimmuriel's thoughts said to him. *You'll not row in such pain.*

Wulfgar didn't know what to make of that, though despite his stubbornness and pride, he couldn't disagree with the drow's remark. In that moment of doubt, Kimmuriel slipped into his mind, and before Wulfgar could expel him, the big man found sudden relief, all of the pain simply dissolving.

"What?" he asked aloud.

"The pain is in your mind," Kimmuriel said.

"In my back!" he corrected.

"Your wound is still there," the drow answered. "Do you feel it?"

That gave Wulfgar pause.

"The abyssal poison is still there, and yes, it will kill you if we cannot find you some help. Do you still feel it?"

He didn't. Like the burning pain that had been in his back, like the numbness in his arms, the poison seemed to him to be no more. Somehow, Kimmuriel had blocked it all.

"Row!" Kimmuriel scolded him.

Wulfgar took up the oars and gave a great pull, the small boat leaping away across the dark water.

Bonnie Charlee crawled over and sat down before him. "Sorry about yer hammer," she said. "We saw ye caught in the rigging of the broken mast, but yer weapon fell away to th'ocean floor."

Wulfgar returned her concern with a comforting smile, and more comforting than that, the barbarian lifted one of his large hands and whispered the name of his warrior god. Bonnie Charlee fell back, and nearly over, when Aegis-fang appeared in the man's hand.

"Well now, there's a trick," she gasped.

"It speaks to the skill of the maker," Kimmuriel said.

Wulfgar looked to the drow curiously, for that was as close to a compliment as he had ever heard from Kimmuriel—and one to a dwarf, no less, to Bruenor, who had crafted the weapon for Wulfgar those years and years before.

"Now, if you would be so wise as to put the weapon down and take up the oar instead, perhaps we will survive this night," Kimmuriel added. "And do take care when you put it down so that you do not drive it through the hull."

Wulfgar offered a sour look at the ever-insulting drow, then took up the oars with fervor, growling with every powerful stroke. The small boat raced past the wreckage of many ships, past many men and women in the water clinging to flotsam and jetsam.

"If you stop for one, we'll be overrun," Kimmuriel told Wulfgar and Bonnie Charlee. "The water is not that cold and they will survive the night. Their only chance is for us to get to Luskan and send out ships."

The drow was correct, Wulfgar knew, but rowing past stranded sailors (though he knew not which side most of these folks had been fighting for) pained him deeply. He grew less concerned soon after, though, when, at a gasp from Bonnie Charlee, who sat facing him and therefore looking forward past him, he slowed and glanced over his shoulder.

An orange glow brightened the eastern horizon, and it wasn't the dawn.

"It would seem that our enemies are wasting no time," Kimmuriel said from the front of the boat.

Wulfgar bore down and pulled harder, each great row lifting the prow from the water. The tide had turned and was heading back in, so again, they had following seas. Still, they had a long way yet to go, and after a while, even mighty Wulfgar needed to rest. He lifted the oars and swung about on the bench to view the city, close enough now that he could make out the general outlines of some of the taller structures.

A good portion of Luskan was in flames, and the armada of enemy ships sat near in the harbor, catapults and wizards letting fly flaming pitch and magical fireballs.

"Well, what do we do now?" Wulfgar asked.

"Is the city even fighting back?" wondered Bonnie Charlee.

"Some are, some aren't, no doubt," Wulfgar replied. "It's Luskan, after all." He looked straight at Kimmuriel as he added, "Though I'd venture that the supposed leaders of the city are risking themselves in battle."

Kimmuriel didn't answer, not even an arch of a thin white eyebrow.

Wulfgar hated him.

A separate response came to Wulfgar's doubts a moment later, though, in the form of a huge explosion near the northern edge of the city's silhouette, a vast fireball stealing the night, then rolling up like a living mushroom, spewing smoke and roiling flames. Bright flashes of lightning followed quickly, sharp and punctuating, as if the rising fireball itself were some strange and magical thunderstorm.

When that ball rolled higher, illuminating the distinct structure below it, the three on the boat knew exactly the source, however, with bolts of destruction flying from the branching arms of the Hosttower of the Arcane, thundering down to the field below to obliterate the invading forces.

"Your warhammer may kill a demon or a gnoll," Kimmuriel remarked. "How many do you think Gromph and his fellow wizards are melting right now before our eyes?"

Wulfgar didn't turn away from the spectacle to bother looking at the strange drow.

"Make for the mouth of the River Mirar," Kimmuriel said.

"The Hosttower?" asked Bonnie Charlee.

"No. The Dragon Reach and Closeguard Island."

"It's overrun, no doubt," the woman replied.

Kimmuriel shook his head. "Doubtful. There is no easy way into Ship Kurth. Not at this time."

"Easier than the Hosttower," Wulfgar argued.

"Our enemies now know that," Kimmuriel said. "But they would not have, and they would have continued across the bridge to the second island and the magnificent Hosttower, obviously the prize structure of the city."

"You assume much," said Wulfgar. "And if you are wrong . . ."

"There are ways into Ship Kurth" was all that Kimmuriel would offer as an explanation. "Do as I command."

Bonnie Charlee started to argue with the psionicist, but Wulfgar quickly raised a hand to stop her. Kimmuriel didn't need them, he knew. The drow could magically walk away from this boat, and could sink it as he left. Or, even worse, he could get into Bonnie Charlee's mind and convince her to dive overboard and swim as far under the water as she could, and there take a deep breath.

Wulfgar didn't know Kimmuriel very well, but well enough, he thought, to believe that the drow would have no qualms at all about doing exactly that—to Bonnie Charlee, at least, though the barbarian figured that his own friendship with Drizzt, and so with Jarlaxle, might stay the psionicist's devilishness from him.

His reasoning didn't convince him, though. Not with this one.

Wulfgar obediently put his oars into the water and pulled for a spot just to the right of the Hosttower, the channel called the Dragon Reach.

GROMPH BAENRE TOOK A DEEP BREATH, BLOWING OUT THE exertion of releasing what might have been his greatest fireball of all. He pondered that as he looked to the field about the Hosttower, littered with the smoking remains of the pirate horde—demons, gnolls, humans, goblins, even ogres. An impressive force, though stupid and ill-guided. They had crossed right past Ship Kurth, the seat of power of Luskan, to attack the Hosttower.

And now they were dead, or soon to be, every one.

Gromph considered his fireball, enhanced by his growing proficiency in the magic of psionics. Kimmuriel and the mind flayers had given him access to deeper concentration, and that purer focus was leading to some very impressive spells indeed. Never had the great Gromph imagined that his arcane powers could improve any further!

Still, he remained somewhat humbled. He had felt the power of the illithid hive mind flowing through him not so long ago, a force so magnificent that it had held in check the combined martial and magical power of all of Menzoberranzan. Then he had helped direct that barrage into a singular strike, through the body of Drizzt Do'Urden, to obliterate the physical manifestation of Demogorgon, the Prince of Demons.

Such power! True and pure! Gromph wanted to feel that again, and next time, he wanted to be the one creating it.

A lightning bolt flashed down from just above him, from his favorite nondrow Hosttower associate, the cloud giantess Caecilia. That lovely behemoth had surprised Gromph repeatedly since the beginnings of this new order of mages, and now again. She had claimed that her magic was all divination, illusion, and harmless conjuring. But when Gromph glanced down at the newest hole on the field, where her lightning bolt had struck—a deep scar, and one lined by a trio of corpses of minor demons who had almost made it to the base of the gigantic, treelike structure—he was positive she was much more powerful than she had let on.

More lightning rained down from above, many of the Hosttower's wizards vying to kill the last remaining enemies on the field. Gromph glanced to the southeast, across the city, to see the fires and the continuing battles. He moved to a crystal ball set on a pedestal. The magic of the scrying device carried to every chamber in the Hosttower, allowing Gromph to communicate with any of his associates or with all at once, as he did now. "Enough," he told them. "Many more will soon come against us, I expect. Conserve your power. Caecilia, I would speak with you."

He ended the magic without waiting for a response. He answered the knock on his door without question, expecting the cloud giantess. Instead, he found a Netherese man wearing a look of great concern.

"I did not summon you," he told Lord Parise, another of the Hosttower's associates.

"Summon?" the former leader of the Shade Enclave in the Netherese Empire asked in confusion. "No . . . I must speak with you."

"You have finished your studies regarding the gate?" Gromph asked him, hoping it to be the case. He and his wizards had one more duty to perform under their agreement with Jarlaxle and King Bruenor: to complete the magical portals tying Gauntlgrym with the three dwarven strongholds of the Silver Marches.

"I was interrupted," Lord Parise replied, but as he began to elaborate, he was interrupted again as Caecilia came bounding down the stairs in the central trunk and turned into the entry hallway to Gromph's personal wing.

Gromph smiled as he regarded her. She used spells to keep herself small enough to easily navigate the corridors of the Hosttower, but though the dweomers shortened her, they did so in a distorted manner, reducing her height much more than her girth, so that she looked like a blue-skinned halfling viewed through a curved window that made all of her features thicker. Still, the effect wasn't all that unpleasant, Gromph thought, and besides, of all the wizards at the Hosttower, Caecilia was the finest—other than Gromph himself, of course.

She also knew her place, and remained back when she noticed Gromph conversing with the Netherese lord.

"You were saying?" Gromph prompted.

"I told you that I had found some runes on the portal's top piece, tiny but definite," Lord Parise explained. "I was down there trying to make some sense of them yet again—they're not in old Dwarvish, I now know—but before I could properly decipher them, I found a visitor."

"A visitor?"

"At the portal."

"From Gauntlgrym," the archmage reasoned, since that was the only open magical connection to the portal beneath the Hosttower.

But Parise shook his head. "Not one who came through the portal, no."

Gromph arched an eyebrow at that. No one was supposed to be anywhere near that Hosttower portal without Gromph's express permission, which he had not given to anyone. He considered the possibilities, then said, "Catti-brie?"

Again Parise shook his head. "You should come with me, Archmage. She was quite insistent that she speak with you, and you alone."

"'She'?"

"From your homeland, I am sure."

Gromph sighed at that. He thought at first that it must be his daughter, Yvonnel, but Parise knew Yvonnel, so why would he be so obviously unnerved? Had one of Gromph Baenre's sisters come to speak with him? And why there, at the portal?

He pushed past Parise, heading for the spiral stair. "Follow," he instructed both the Netherese lord and the cloud giantess, and down he led, more angry than intrigued.

That anger turned to something different, though, when he passed through the last doors to the small side room holding the magical teleportation device.

"You should move more quickly," Matron Zhindia Melarn greeted him.

It took all of Gromph's willpower to stay an assault, with words or perhaps even a spell. What was this creature doing here at this time? And she was not alone, flanked by a trio of other drow women. One he thought her first priestess, who had previously been a matron of her own house, Kenafin. The other two were Hunzrins, including First Priestess Charri. This was no minor entourage.

"You might have noticed that I and my associates were a bit busy."

"Indeed," answered Zhindia. "And I will forgive you for so incinerating my forces. The demons will gate in new ones in short order."

"*Your* forces?"

"Of course."

"You play dangerous games. This is Bregan D'aerthe's city, with the blessings of Matron Mother Baenre."

Matron Zhindia sighed and snapped her fingers, and two more drow women suddenly appeared beside her, noticeably naked and quite beautiful. Too beautiful, and that, along with their absence of clothing, allowed Gromph to recognize them for what they were: Eskavidne and Yiccardaria, handmaidens of Lolth.

"You see, Archmage, I would argue that Bregan D'aerthe is the one playing dangerous games, along with your sister, the matron mother. Jarlaxle and his rogues—pray tell me that you have not joined with that wretched troupe—have the blessing of Matron Mother Baenre, but I, you see, have a greater imprimatur still."

"What do you want?" Gromph asked sharply, using anger to cover his nervousness here, and he was indeed uneasy. He loathed Matron Zhindia above all others, mostly because she was always so ill-tempered. But now, with the formidable power standing before him, he saw she was here with the blessing of the Spider Queen, and his distaste was being quickly replaced by a touch of fear.

"I am not holding you responsible for the misdeeds of your sister or of Jarlaxle," Matron Zhindia said.

Fear was in turn replaced with loathing. But Gromph held his tongue, though he could hardly believe that this fool was speaking so of the matron mother of Menzoberranzan. Even for Zhindia, such a remark was remarkable.

She went on. "And I will not allow my minions to cross the second bridge again to assault your . . . whatever this ugly thing might be."

"Because you have seen what will happen to them."

Matron Zhindia laughed at him. "Because this is not your fight," she corrected. "You are not even of Menzoberranzan anymore. Consider that your good fortune. So I allow you to remain out of it, wholly so. Let Lolth decide who shall reign, the current matron mother, or the one who delivered to her Drizzt Do'Urden and Zaknafein."

Gromph chortled loudly. "All of this over those two insects? Madness."

"But not your madness," Zhindia very sharply replied, poking a finger Gromph's way, "as long as you prove that it is not."

"What does that—"

"Shut down the teleportation portals," Matron Zhindia demanded. "Close this one, and do not let the dwarves connect to their other fortresses."

Gromph balked.

"You can do it from here, from this Hosttower, which is tied to the primordial that powers the magical gates," Zhindia insisted.

"He can," said Yiccardaria before Gromph could deny it.

"That is my offer, this one time only," Zhindia told him. "Shut down the portals, go into your tower, and let this play out. When I am victorious, and I shall be, there will be no repercussions against you and your"—she glanced past him to the grayish-skinned human and the cloud giant—"wizardly order."

Gromph narrowed his eyes and stared hard.

"Decide, Archmage," Matron Zhindia insisted.

Gromph glanced back at his fellow wizards. His thoughts spun as he tried to make sense of any of this. He realized, though, that he was not being asked to choose between Matron Mother Baenre and Matron Zhindia. Not yet. Not with this particular task.

If he did as she asked, then surely Jarlaxle would be unhappy with him, and King Bruenor would be truly outraged, but even if their side won, what would Gromph care? They wouldn't war with him, particularly since he would still hold the key to the entrapment of the fire primordial.

But if he didn't do as they asked and Matron Zhindia proved victorious . . .

Gromph turned back to Matron Zhindia, then looked to the handmaidens. "Lolth will demand her word be kept?" he asked.

Both laughed, for it was quite an absurd question, given the ways of the Lady of Chaos.

"She will not be displeased with you, certainly," Matron Zhindia answered for them.

Gromph thought it over for another few moments, then nodded his agreement.

CHAPTER 21

Bad Spideys

J ust looking at it, Drizzt knew that he could not defeat this monstrous spider creature. He had delayed his retreat from it, certain that his bow, a weapon that had never failed him, would stop or at least slow this beast. The arrows had shown no effect at all, however, and in his shock, the drow ranger had erred, had underestimated the giant arachnid's speed, and now it had him.

But . . . it didn't.

It instead ran right past him, or above him, at least, rambling down the tunnel's ceiling as if it hadn't even noticed Drizzt or the lightning arrows.

Drizzt stuttered over some words, trying futilely to make sense of it. Then he kicked Andahar into a run, following the spider creature down, down, back to the entry cavern. Every now and then, he met a demon coming up the other way, but a few arrows from Taulmaril took these lesser monsters down, or wounded them enough for Andahar to run them down, stomping out the last of their life force.

In the main cavern, Drizzt saw that the spider kept up its pace, moving up high into the shadows, weaving in and out among the stalactites up there. Drizzt thought he should ride ahead to warn the dwarves, and he started to do just that, but an ungodly shriek, a high-pitched squeal—from the side and not above—had him pulling up on Andahar's reins.

A second giant arachnid came into view, this one scrabbling fast across the floor, heading straight for Drizzt. Living in Menzoberranzan, Drizzt had encountered thousands and thousands of spiders, but he had never heard one shriek. A hiss, perhaps, but nothing like this— this was a scream, unearthly, more demonic than arachnid.

And it was heading straight for him.

Or perhaps heading past him, Drizzt thought, or wanted to believe, given his previous encounter.

He trotted Andahar to the side, around a stalagmite, but still in view of the avenue with the charging spider.

The beast veered, again heading straight for Drizzt.

Drizzt went back the other way around the stone mound, and the beast changed course, correcting as if locked onto Drizzt.

And it was exactly that, he sensed. It then occurred to him that the previous beast might have been focused on something, or someone, else. When this spider screamed again, Drizzt was certain that it was because it had recognized him and its prey was in sight.

He thought to gallop for the dwarven complex, but he wasn't sure the dwarves could hold back even the other creature that was charging their way. No, something was very wrong here, in both the sheer power of these creatures and in their apparent single-mindedness, for why hadn't the other monster attacked Drizzt in the tunnel?

He put up his bow and let fly a long shot, the lightning arrow lighting up the mounds in a weird and beautiful way as it passed. It struck the spider squarely in the face, but this beast, like the other, did not slow.

"What are you?" Drizzt whispered, and then he gasped as the spider returned the volley with a ray of its own, a raging line of fire shooting down the avenue straight for the drow.

Andahar reacted before Drizzt could, leaping aside, back toward the entry tunnels. Drizzt didn't even try to slow the unicorn or pull it up once it had avoided the attack, rather, urging it on faster even, as the spider gave chase.

"Bruenor, retreat!" Drizzt screamed as loudly as he could. "Run!"

And Drizzt and Andahar did the same, galloping away from Gauntlgrym. On impulse, Drizzt turned left as they neared the cavern wall opposite the dwarven complex, thinking that the tram exit tunnel might be a better choice. That brought him perilously near the spider, though, and he braced himself, expecting another fire bolt.

Andahar entered the incline at a full gallop, running between the tram tracks. Just a short way in, those tracks climbed steeply away from the floor and rolled over to invert along the ceiling. Drizzt guided the steed perfectly into the reverse gravity field, but he heard a sizzling sound behind him and glanced back to see the spider still in full charge, still not far behind, its giant mandibles arcing lightning back and forth between them.

"Run, Andahar," he whispered, bending low beside the unicorn's bobbing head.

"WE GOT 'EM RUNNIN', BOYS!" BRUENOR ROARED, LEADING the charge across the front of the outer defensive wall, then down the avenue deeper into the cavern. The demons fled before them, those that could get away. The rest were trampled by the famed Battlehammer juicers, or, if they avoided that fate, overwhelmed by hordes of angry warrior dwarves, the Gutbusters in their ridged and spiked armor tearing them apart.

Soon enough, all of the area around the wall was cleared, the demons in full flight, and Bruenor and his charges in pursuit.

A flash far across the naturally pillared cavern seemed comfortingly familiar to the dwarven king, a missile he had seen a thousand times before.

"Drizzt's got 'em, boys!" Bruenor yelled, and he got slapped on the back of his head for that remark.

"Gals!" Queen Mallabritches corrected.

"Bah! But ye're all boys to me!" Bruenor said, and when both Mallabritches and Tannabritches giggled at that remark, Bruenor stuttered for a response.

Finally, Bruenor threw up his hands in surrender to his playful, if annoying, wives, and turned back just in time to see the most tremendous conflagration of a roiling and rising wall of flame he had ever known, one whose burning licks climbed high into the cavern.

"What in the Nine Hells?" Tannabritches gasped.

Bruenor feared that the old dwarven cliché might prove accurate this time. Surely he had never seen such a display of lightning power from anything short of an actual thunderstorm.

"Bwoona! Bwoona!" he heard when he regained his sensibilities, and he thought he heard something else, the shout of a friend, a call of "Run!"

"Pikel, what?" he asked, turning to see the green-bearded dwarf hopping his way, calling his name as only Pikel could.

"Bwoona! Bwoona!"

"Me brudder's got somethin' he's needin' to tell ye," said Ivan, huffing and puffing and struggling to keep up with the animated Pikel.

"Bad, bad, bad!" Pikel exclaimed.

"Hold!" Bruenor shouted to his forces, a cry echoed by his queens and then down the line.

"Bad spideys," Pikel explained.

His face scrunched with confusion, Bruenor looked to Ivan, but the old yellow-bearded dwarf could only shrug and shake his head.

The answer came a moment later, and not far across the cavern, though way up high, in the form of a cry from some of the dwarves still in their stalactite artillery position, followed by another tremendous explosion. Bruenor and the others looked on in horror as that distant stalactite crumbled and tumbled, falling the fifty feet and more to the floor, a quartet of poor dwarves falling with it, along with their ballista, and something else.

Something huge and radiating evil.

"Bad spidey," Pikel said again. "Oooo."

Now Bruenor and the others surely understood, as a giant arachnid construct flung aside broken stones and pulled itself from the rubble, shaking off massive boulders as if they were no more an inconvenience than a pile of dry leaves.

"Run away!" Bruenor and almost every other dwarf in that corridor yelled in unison, and as one, the dwarves turned and fled—except for the juicer team.

"No!" Mallabritches yelled at them as they charged at the giant spider, but the team, Gutbusters one and all, knew their role here, and that role was to hold back the enemy so that their king and queens could get away. They roared as one, the juicer rolling and bouncing along, part battering ram, part rolling pin. Demon husks flew aside or got crunched beneath the heavy contraption, the Gutbusters cheering and singing.

Bruenor, being dragged away by his royal guard, glanced back to watch the last charge to the spider, and saw the beast's eyes glowing.

"No!" he yelled, figuring that something terrible was about to happen, but his voice could not rise above the chorus of Gutbuster glee.

A ray shot forth from the monster, a long and narrow multihued cone that widened just enough to encompass the juicer and the crew behind it.

For a few heartbeats, Bruenor wasn't even sure what had happened, for the juicer kept moving, but awkwardly, and the Gutbusters kept singing, but their chorus had hollowed greatly.

The contraption bounced and jerked from side to side, and then ran straight on, and Bruenor then understood, to his horror.

Of the ten Gutbusters on the juicer, four had been left behind, turned to stone and knocked over, and at least one seemed to have lost an arm, which was still attached to the juicer's handle!

"By the gods, oh Moradin, where ye be?" Bruenor gasped, and he winced when juicer and spider collided.

The angled cow-catcher lifted the beast onto its back legs, and for a moment, Bruenor thought his team might drive it right over—he almost called for another charge!

But no, the giant spider went up high, above the front of the war machine, and from there, it spat again, this time a fountain of gooey webbing falling over the remaining Gutbusters. They thrashed and fought against the bindings, but they couldn't get through before the spider's eyes began to glow once more.

Bruenor didn't see it, for he and his escort had turned the corner and were running along the outside of the wall then, toward the break across the cavern. He heard nothing, no lightning bolt, no rush of flames.

But he knew in his heart that none of those Gutbusters were coming home.

He had crossed the bridge over the small pond and was just about to the door when the cavern lit up in a sudden and shockingly bright flash. A moment later came the retort, a grumble of thunder that sounded more like the exploding volcano he had witnessed from this very mountain than the crackle of a lightning stroke.

"What in the Nine Hells?" Tannabritches asked again.

"Indeed" was all that Bruenor Battlehammer could answer, and into his hole he ran.

UPSIDE DOWN AND GALLOPING ALONG THE CEILING NOW, Drizzt heard the thunder of a lightning bolt and braced, expecting to be incinerated. But good fortune was with him, for the spider hadn't anticipated his rise and inversion, and the blast, the most stunning and tremendous bolt of lightning he had ever witnessed, shot past beneath him.

On ran Andahar, up the mountain tunnel. Drizzt could hear the spider's skittering behind him, but it was fading as Andahar outpaced the arachnid behemoth. Drizzt looked back one last time, trying to sort out his plan. Perhaps he would go out and come right back in down the other tunnel, though it still troubled him to bring this thing anywhere near his friends until he better understood its power.

When he looked forward again, despite the pursuit, he slowed his mouth and nearly shouted out, "Run," because there before him were a host of dwarves, set in battle formation, weapons raised.

He held that cry when he realized the truth, but he did keep Andahar at a trot as he navigated the unicorn through a forest of immovable dwarves. They had been turned to stone. Right here, in the tunnel, standing on the ceiling that was magically the floor, one of Bruenor's brigades had met a sudden end.

Drizzt fought hard to keep his breath steady, to keep his mind focused on the task at hand and the course he needed to take.

He came out of the tunnel soon after, Andahar running down the corkscrew tram rails, then leaping free of them onto solid ground right beside the destroyed tram station of Bleeding Vines. Drizzt saw no enemies, but he knew that he was not alone, for he could hear them out there in the tree line.

Not slowing, he broke left past the other tunnel, then kept going, out to the west. He heard some movement, even the click of a crossbow, but didn't get hit as he moved away at great speed.

Behind him came the spider behemoth, nearly pacing him. Many times through the rest of that night did Drizzt look back to see the silhouettes of great trees shaking behind him, some even falling down, as the spider bulled its way in pursuit.

Andahar wouldn't tire, and as long as the monster gave chase, Drizzt had no intention of stopping.

"WE'LL HOLD THE WALL!" BRUENOR GROWLED AT JARLAXLE after the drow mercenary had delivered the bad news.

"You'll not," Jarlaxle warned.

"Give me your horse," Zaknafein told him, for the third time. "I will lead the beast away."

"Ye're not even knowin' if the eight-legged beast's here for yerself!" Bruenor scolded.

"Aren't we?" argued Jarlaxle.

"I'm thinking yer Matron Baenre's no fan o' meself," Bruenor reminded. "Should I get on the hellhorse with ye, then? Should we all just run?"

"If we can," said Jarlaxle, but that brought only a profound scowl from Bruenor.

"Ye're not much knowin' Battlehammers, are ye, sneaky one?"

Jarlaxle answered with a shrug. "It will take a demon prince or a god to stop these beasts, my friend," he said.

At that moment, an explosion rocked the great entry hall and throne room of Gauntlgrym, and shouts of "Breach!" filtered in from the door, soon followed by fleeing Battlehammers.

Bruenor didn't see it, though. At Jarlaxle's mention of divine beings, the dwarf had rushed over to the great seat of the complex, the Throne of the Dwarven Gods, and leaped upon it, praying for insight and guidance. Once before had the gods granted him great power and strength. Perhaps now they would again.

But no, he knew immediately, even such a moment of giant strength would not protect him from this horrid creation of the Abyss. The mortal creatures within Gauntlgrym could not fight it.

Bruenor's eyes popped open and he nodded.

"We need a plan," Jarlaxle told him, standing right before the throne.

The wall of the room shook.

"And quickly," the mercenary added.

"Give me your horse," insisted Zaknafein, who stood to the side, weapons drawn.

Bruenor hopped off the throne, still nodding.

"Bruenor?" Jarlaxle asked.

"What do ye know, me love?" asked Queen Mallabritches.

"Aye, what did ye see in that mind o' yers?" Queen Tannabritches agreed.

"What'd ye say it'd take to beat that thing?"

"A demon prince. A god," Jarlaxle answered.

"Get me five juicers and five teams," Bruenor told his queens.

"Here?" both asked skeptically, for the wall was shaking again and it hardly seemed like they had the time.

"Nah, down below," Bruenor answered, and he looked directly at Jarlaxle as he finished, "I got a plan."

"GIVE ME YOUR HORSE," ZAKNAFEIN TOLD JARLAXLE AGAIN a moment later, when they were somewhat separated from the others. "If I am to do right by my son, that means getting his friends out of jeopardy."

"You believe you can outrun that thing?"

Zaknafein shrugged. "I think I can try, and that running out there in the wide open might prove better than letting it corner me—us—down here in tight tunnels."

"Bruenor said that he had a plan," Jarlaxle reminded him.

"You hold great faith in that, it would seem." Zaknafein could tell by the way Jarlaxle then looked at Bruenor that perhaps the faith was not as deep as he had presumed. He saw trepidation on Jarlaxle's face.

"Earlier, we asked him to trust *us*," said Jarlaxle.

"Earlier, the ones we were putting most in danger were ourselves."

"Drizzt would trust Bruenor," Jarlaxle said bluntly. "Will Zaknafein?"

"Will Jarlaxle? I know you. I've known you longer than anyone around here, and so my guess is that you've some way out if the dwarf fails."

"Truly? I am wounded."

"You might be," said Zaknafein. "You keep that horse ready, and if you leave and cannot take me with you, you'd do well to drop it for me so that I have a chance to get out as well."

"Wouldn't I do better in making sure that you can't escape? I mean, given your attitude."

"Good point," Zaknafein replied. "But you've known me long enough to realize that I'll possibly find a way out anyway, and in that event, you also know me well enough to be certain that I will find you."

Jarlaxle gave a great, exaggerated sigh. "Ah, Zaknafein, it is so good to have you back."

"More than you know, Jarlaxle. If it weren't for me being here, that spider thing would likely be chasing you."

Bruenor came bounding back toward the pair then, so Jarlaxle just ended with a "Hmm."

CHAPTER 22

. . . Mentormentor . . .

I cannot see her eyes!" Alvilda Margaster yelled at her cousin Inkeri. "Her beautiful gray eyes, so shining and pretty!"

"This you think is important at this time?" Inkeri replied with a great huff. "The whole of the north is open before us."

"She's my baby girl."

"Shut up!" Inkeri yelled at her.

Shut up! commanded another voice in Alvilda's own head, a voice like the growl of an angry giant with a mouthful of biting wasps.

"Take me," Alvilda heard herself saying, but in that demonic voice, not her own.

"Yes," said Inkeri, and she quickly pulled off her necklace, a golden chain set with a large opal, and held it out with one hand while beckoning to Alvilda with the other.

"Give me your necklace," Inkeri demanded.

"I give you nothing," Alvilda argued, or started to, for the words ended in a strangled garble. They had already swapped necklaces multiple times before, always at Inkeri's insistence. She knew not what game her cousin was playing here, but the demons contained within the respective phylacteries were not alike, and the one Alvilda currently held was more powerful by far.

"Give me your necklace or be killed," Inkeri warned.

Alvilda, her thoughts suddenly jumbled, a pain as profound as a spear tip stabbing her between her eyes, didn't even hear the command. But it didn't matter, for she had no control of her body then as the beast within her moved her hands for her, pulling the necklace, this one a golden chain set with a large ruby, over her head.

Alvilda felt the connection break, but by the time she realized it, her own body had tossed the item to Inkeri, who now stood holding both, and still presenting the opal to her.

Alvilda shrank back from it.

Inkeri flipped the ruby necklace over her head and set it around her neck. "Do you think it wise to betray us, sister?" she warned, using a term that used to be one of endearment and their special bond. Alvilda was her cousin, not her sister, though they had been raised side by side.

"You gave her the bracelet," Alvilda accused, holding fast to her outrage.

"And the being within it will protect your baby Sharon in these dangerous times."

"No!" Alvilda yelled back. "No, a hundred times no! It took her eyes."

"It did not take them," said Inkeri.

"Who is it? What fiend?" Alvilda demanded.

"I do not know," Inkeri admitted, but in that other voice, the giant's voice, the voice that had been in Alvilda's head when she had worn the necklace. "It does not matter."

"How can you say that?"

"Put on the necklace," the demon within Inkeri warned, and to accentuate the point, Inkeri began to thicken then, her limbs becoming huge and powerful, her hair growing wildly and turning orange, her face becoming that of an orangutan.

"And if I do not?" Alvilda stuttered.

The words were barely out before the creature standing before her, no longer Inkeri but a greater demon known as Barlgura, rushed forward with frightening speed and grabbed her like a child's rag doll in one massive, and massively powerful, hand. It lifted the necklace up to place over Alvilda's head, and the woman reflexively tried to block it.

Barlgura squeezed powerfully, taking the breath from Alvilda, who crumpled to her knees and curled forward, trying to alleviate the pain. She felt a rib snap. She felt her heart being squeezed.

The necklace went over her head, and Inkeri—and suddenly it was Inkeri again—let her go.

"This is no game, sister," Inkeri told her as she slumped there on her hands and knees, gasping against the waves of pain. "And no time for weakness. We have started a war against powerful enemies, and with powerful allies who are less merciful than those we battle. You cannot change your mind."

Alvilda looked up at her pitifully. "Sharon is my little girl," she whispered, and every word hurt.

Shut up! demanded a voice in her head, one that sounded like the growl of a starving feral dog.

Alvilda closed her eyes. She knew this demon, her new possessor, a six-limbed glabrezu, with four arms, two of them ending in pincers that could cut a man in half. She had seen Inkeri transform into the fiend on more than one occasion, and never with pleasant consequence. Indeed, every time Inkeri had let the glabrezu come forth, she had not, by her own admission to Alvilda, been able to coax it back into the phylactery until it had torn some person asunder.

"Sharon's bracelet protects her," Inkeri said calmly. "And the necklace hanging about your neck protects you. Do not make me repeat this lesson."

Alvilda watched as Inkeri left the drawing room of House Margaster. For all of the other problems, she wasn't angry that Inkeri had swapped necklaces with her. The one she had been wearing contained a beast more cunning and powerful than this one, she was certain.

Perhaps she could control this one.

She felt inside the laughter of the dog-faced glabrezu at that absurd notion, and the voice now in her head promised, *I can make you kill your little girl.*

She cried out, her sobs drowned by the demon's laughter.

"YOU BE TELLING LADY DONNOLA THAT I'M EXPECTING A hundred bottles of your finest for this," the grizzled farmer Yasgur scolded Regis and Dahlia as they sat at his old dinner table in the ramshackle front room of his old farmhouse. The place was impressive, or had been in its heyday, as Yasgur had been in his heyday, only a few years before. Even now, with his health declining, though the lanky man had barely entered middle age, Yasgur was considered by his neighbors to be quite the character, and not always in a positive way. His relationship with Donnola Topolino exemplified that, but even more, it was rumored that he wasn't on bad terms with the current rulers of Luskan.

Any time anyone inquired about such things, Yasgur always and only replied, "Neighbors are customers."

Dahlia looked to Regis, who shrugged, unsure of how to proceed.

"I'm sure that Lady Topolino will repay you handsomely with wine as soon as she can," Dahlia said, and Regis had to admit that it wasn't a lie, after all.

"Hundred bottles," the thin, large-nosed man insisted. "Going to throw me a party they'll be talking about a century after I'm dead and buried! Invite every bard on the Sword Coast to come and play, and aye, but we're going to play!"

"Two hundred bottles, if you invite us!" Dahlia said, and Yasgur wheezed and whooped so forcefully that the two guests feared he might fall over dead.

He winked at the woman. "Don't even make it your best. With that many, no one will know anyway."

"The best for me and you, then," Dahlia promised with a return wink.

Yasgur laughed, or wheezed, again, and left the two alone.

Dahlia smiled at him as he departed, then turned back to find Regis staring at her with his jaw hanging open.

"When we get Entreri back, Yasgur there is in for some trouble," the halfling said flippantly.

But Dahlia scowled at him and seemed in no mood for humor. The mere look had the hair on the back of Regis's neck standing up, and he marveled at (and was terrified by) how quickly the elven woman had changed moods, from playfully teasing Yasgur to a chilling darkness.

"We'll get him back," Regis said to her, because he needed to say something. "If they still have him . . ."

He paused as Dahlia's eyes widened, then went dangerously narrow.

"They have him," Regis stuttered. "I am certain. We will bargain . . ."

"With what?"

"That is what we need to figure out!" said the halfling, perhaps too enthusiastically, given the returned scowl.

Dahlia dismissed him altogether, then, taking one last bite of the stew Yasgur had given them, pushed back forcefully from the table. "Bargain," she snorted.

"These types love money above all else," Regis stammered.

"When they're dead, we'll take him back," Dahlia told him. "Simpler."

Regis had to merely nod, for what else could he do? Dahlia was already out the farmhouse door.

MUCH LATER THAT NIGHT, ALVILDA MARGASTER PADDED silently through the family's great mansion, easing up to the door of the bedroom where her daughter, Sharon, slept. Nervously, the woman put her ear to the door, hoping to hear the rhythmic breathing of sound sleep.

She grimaced, unsurprised, to hear the child's voice muttering "—mentormentormentormentor—" in a long, unbroken chain.

Alvilda sucked in her breath and tried not to cry. She pictured her dear Sharon, with her curly red hair and those sparkling gray eyes that smiled when she laughed and always seemed to be looking for a reason to dance.

At least, they had once been gray, Alvilda reminded herself.

Go and kill her, said the voice in Alvilda's head. The woman reached up and grasped the bauble hanging on the chain about her neck, wanting nothing more than to tear it off and cast it away.

But she could not.

Her skin is so soft. It will be easy and then you will worry no more, her demon told her. She hated this demon even more than the other—how she hated this one!—for the glabrezu monstrosity seemed to want nothing more than death and wanton carnage. Its every whisper to her was a coaxing to murder.

So soft . . . the voice said.

Alvilda pictured her little girl lying there among the pillows. *Yes,* she thought, *how easy it would be to kill . . .*

With a start, the woman rushed away from the door and down the grand, sweeping staircase and along to the main sitting room below, where Inkeri sat before the hearth, sipping some strong liquor.

"I want that necklace back!" Alvilda demanded, approaching.

Inkeri, who had started to point to the small table before the liquor cabinet, pulled back her hand and looked curiously at Alvilda. "Well met to you, too, dear sister."

"I want that one back," Alvilda stated, holding out her hand. "And I'm not your sister."

"The ugly ape?" Inkeri asked skeptically, fingering the ruby on the gold chain.

"If you think it so ugly now, then why did you demand it from me?" Alvilda asked.

"If you think it not ugly, then why did you so readily give it over?" Inkeri countered.

Alvilda glared at her, and Inkeri sighed. "I took it because this is not *a* barlgura," she said. "Not any barlgura. No, this is Barlgura himself, the fiend for whom this type of demon is named. He holds trust with the great Demogorgon, who was destroyed by the drow of Menzoberranzan."

Alvilda stared at her in confusion.

"Not Matron Zhindia Melarn," Inkeri explained. "The other drow. Those who once opposed Zhindia, but who will soon learn better. Sharing my body with Barlgura requires all the politesse I can find, dear sis— dear cousin, and more than you could manage."

"You were angry when the other demon—when this demon— failed you when you thought you had the halfling thief caught in Neverwinter," Alvilda accused.

"Do you find your familiar demon too weak, dear cousin?"

Alvilda blanched at that, and even more when the glabrezu added in her thoughts, *Yes, dear cousin, do you? Pray tell.*

Truly Alvilda felt trapped here, more than she had ever believed possible. And since she felt it, so too did the demon, and in her mind, she heard its laughter.

"I don't like this one," Alvilda said.

"I doubt it much likes you," Inkeri replied without hesitation. "It is a demon, after all. Do you fancy that Barlgura was much impressed by you, or that the great fiend cared at all about you, or about me, other than for what you or I could bring to it?"

"This one wants me to kill my girl," Alvilda pleaded.

"That's because it is stupid," Inkeri replied, but not in her voice. In the voice of a giant, rumbling and grating and hissing all at once, and on the edge of a shriek with every syllable. The woman began to laugh, mocking her, Alvilda knew.

"It compels me!" Alvilda cried.

"Then go," said Inkeri, in her own voice once more. "Go and kill your helpless little child."

Alvilda gasped—the demon within her urged her to obey, and she even took a step toward the stairs. But there she stopped, seeing Sharon, her precious little Sharon, coming down.

Not walking down the stairs, she noted.

Floating down the stairs.

"You cannot, but it will be entertaining to watch you try," Inkeri teased from her chair. "She is more powerful than you, silly Alvilda."

The woman hardly heard Inkeri, held fast by the specter of her white-eyed tiny child floating down the stairs like some ghost or vampire.

"You cannot, Mummy," the little girl said in her tiny voice. "Don't worry."

"Cannot?" Alvilda breathed.

"Kill me, Mummy."

Back behind Alvilda, Inkeri laughed. The demon inside Alvilda laughed. Sharon came to the doorway and looked at her Auntie Inkeri, and she too began to laugh, an innocent childish giggle that seemed so horribly out of place coming from the cherubic face of the little red-haired girl who had only white where her beautiful gray eyes used to be. She nodded at Inkeri and kept floating, right out of the room to the entry foyer.

Alvilda rushed to get in front of her, her back against the door. "Where are you going?"

"I am already there, of course."

"What? You cannot leave."

"I am not," said the child, but she moved for the doorknob.

Alvilda desperately grabbed the child's arm.

"Careful, cousin," Inkeri warned, her voice and expression telling Alvilda that she was thoroughly enjoying this.

The warning was not without merit, Alvilda knew, but she grasped Sharon's arm tightly anyway.

The white-eyed girl looked up at her, smiling, but it seemed to Alvilda to be a wicked smile indeed.

"Should I make you a cocoon, Mummy?" Sharon sweetly and innocently asked.

Alvilda blanched. A cocoon. Like the eternal torment Sharon had put upon the human assassin, Artemis Entreri.

"Don't leave," Alvilda pleaded. Her hand grasped nothing at all then, so suddenly, as Sharon became less than corporeal and simply walked right through Alvilda and then through the closed front door.

The woman gasped and cried out, then fell to the floor, sobbing.

Her guilt closed in all around her, more profoundly than Alvilda had ever thought possible, so much so that the waves brought as much confusion to her as guilt itself!

And in that moment of darkness, she heard a discordant and sweet sound: her child's laughter.

What do we care? the vicious glabrezu demon asked in her head. *The creature will be unharmed and will return, you fool. If you lose your heart, I will devour you wholly and abuse your mortal form until the skin has fallen from your bones. Then I will find another host. One strong enough to kill the child.*

Alvilda Margaster hardly heard the last threat, for that one word, *creature*, assaulted her. *Creature.* The ugly demon had called her beautiful Sharon a *creature.*

"Collect yourself, sister," Inkeri warned. "Our battle has only just begun, and I've no room for weaklings."

That threat Alvilda Margaster heard quite clearly.

"THAT HAT YOU WEAR," DAHLIA SAID. "IT CREATES DIS-guise?"

Regis tapped his beret and almost instantly appeared as a human child. Another tap and he was a dwarf, full beard and all.

Dahlia motioned with her hand.

Regis stared at it, at her, doubtfully.

"Give it to me."

"Not in your future, lady," the halfling answered.

Dahlia shook the red-streaked black hair from her face and narrowed her eyes into a threatening glare at Regis. She directed his gaze with her own, to the house at the end of the lane, and pointed up at it.

"Artemis, the man I love, is likely in there," she said. "With your hat, I can get in there to save him. Are you sure that you wish to deny me that?"

"I am sure that I am going in there beside you," Regis said. "And that I know better how to utilize my beret, and that I am no liability when swords are drawn."

Dahlia turned back upon him, her scowl unrelenting.

"Do you doubt it?" Regis said into that threatening visage, not backing down at all. "You would have died in the alley. My blades and resourcefulness saved you then, and my potions healed your wounds at Yasgur's farm. I need prove nothing more to you, Lady Dahlia."

"That is a house full of demons," Dahlia warned.

"All the more reason for you to want me by your side."

Dahlia's scowl softened, and she even managed a nod and a bit of a grin.

"How best do we manage to get in?" Regis asked.

Dahlia's smile widened and she took off immediately, sprinting down the lane, full charge.

"Oh," Regis gasped, his feet moving to keep up before he had even digested the implications.

LITTLE SHARON WALKED THE DARK STREETS OF WATER-deep's night. This was a city controlled by great and powerful lords, many of them paladins sworn to uphold justice and goodness. But it was still a city, a place of many men and women of all the races. And, as in any city, the night did not belong to the paladin lords.

Many sets of eyes turned to follow the red-haired little girl as she wandered on her merry way, most simply caught by the unusualness of the spectacle—this was no halfling woman, clearly, but a human child.

And for others, the most important added word in that sentiment was a *helpless* human child.

Outwardly, Sharon paid the leering scoundrels no heed, and didn't need to look at them, with their greasy fingers and snot-covered faces and ragged clothes, to know their intent, or even to know which might act upon that bad intent. For she could look much deeper than that, could hear their inner voices as clearly as they could hear their own.

All of those voices, every impulse, every desire, every doubt, every intent.

She knew, then, the approaching danger when a couple, a human

man and a woman, moved down one alleyway as she passed it, knew that they'd turn, knew that the man was reaching for her from behind.

Sharon turned to smile at him.

"Ah, her eyes!" cried the woman, middle-aged and scrawny. "Blind!"

"Then we might just let her live," said the man, grabbing Sharon hard by her collar. "If she plays nice with us."

"Oh, I see you," Sharon told him.

He picked her right off the ground, moving her very near his face and into the cloud of his smelly breath. "Do you, then? Then might we kill you when we're done, aye."

In response, Sharon produced a cloud of her own. She coughed, and from her mouth came a swarm of flying insects, wasplike, but with tiny human heads. Most converged on the man's face, while others flew to the woman, and there, they began viciously stinging and biting. The man dropped Sharon immediately and began slapping at his face, then fell to the ground thrashing and rolling and crying in pain.

Sharon watched him with great satisfaction, and noted the woman running away, getting stung and bitten at every step. She was not as irredeemably bad as her partner, Sharon knew, for guilt had weighed on her and only fear had overruled that guilt, not desire.

No, this filthy monster on the ground was the worse, by far, and Sharon let her minions know it.

"Finish your work quickly, my little friends," she whispered, magic carrying the command to every wasplike creature she had loosed.

Sharon nodded, satisfied by a good night's work, then started back for House Margaster. She was still in sight of the thrashing man when the wasp creatures left him, flying up under the eaves of the nearest building to begin their nest that they might complete their task.

CHAPTER 23

Sinking Ship Kurth

W e promised King Bruenor that we'd open those portals," Lord Parise said when he was alone with Gromph and the giant Caecilia soon after. Matron Zhindia and her entourage had already departed through Underdark routes to the south, where the press on Gauntlgrym continued. "It would seem that he doubly needs us to fulfill that promise now."

Gromph lowered his gaze and softly chuckled. "The two naked women who appeared at Matron Zhindia's side were not drow, and not mortal," he said, looking back up and alternating his gaze between the Netherese lord and the cloud giant. "Probably not even women, as I doubt that gender terms apply to such creatures."

Lord Parise gave a slight shudder at that—no doubt, the sight of the beautiful creatures had stirred him a bit, Gromph thought, while Caecilia just crinkled her thick-featured face in disgust.

"They were yochlols, handmaidens of Lolth herself," the archmage explained. "Beings of great power, greater still because they act as the voice of the Spider Queen goddess when they are among my people. It was not Matron Zhindi—"

"This is the first time I have heard you refer to her by her title when not in her presence," Caecilia interrupted, and the importance of that point had Gromph nodding his agreement as he continued, "Matron Zhindia is not the one who ordered me to keep the portals closed. Not truly. If there were yochlols beside her, then we know how she discerned our work here, its relationship to the primordial, and so its potential for the battlefield at Gauntlgrym. And she knew exactly what to do about it."

"So we take the side of those who would bring chaos to the north?" Caecilia asked, seeming quite unhappy with that notion.

"We take no sides."

"Is not our inaction a form of alliance?" Lord Parise reasoned.

"It is self-preservation," Gromph corrected. "It is our statement that the work of the Hosttower of the Arcane is paramount in our thoughts. Is that not why we are all here? Why do we care whether it is King Bruenor or Matron Zhindia or no one at all on the throne of Gauntlgrym?"

"King Bruenor serves as a great barrier between Luskan and Waterdeep," Caecilia argued. "Will the lords of Waterdeep remain impassive toward Luskan and her drow leaders without that barrier in place?"

"Again, why would we care? Let the lords of Waterdeep sail to Luskan harbor and lay waste to whoever might be then claiming lordship over the city. The Hosttower stands apart, powerfully defended and without political aspirations."

"And with the archmage of Menzoberranzan serving as its archmage," said Lord Parise.

"Former," Gromph corrected. "And, since you seem to have not noticed, I am the only dark elf in residence here, and in alliance with many who are favored by the lords of Waterdeep. Again, let the political warfare and nonsense play as they will."

"Matron Zhindia will have Luskan," Parise said.

"And likely Gauntlgrym," added Caecilia.

Gromph shrugged as if he hardly cared. "Perhaps, but never underestimate Jarlaxle, and doubt not that he, too, will fall into alliance with Matron Zhindia if he sees that as his best play. Ever has that one found his way to his most comfortable position. Perhaps Clan Battle-hammer will be routed from their new home, but not without a ter-rific defense, I am sure, one that will leave the invading forces greatly diminished, and one that may well turn the eyes of Waterdeep upon the demonic army that leads the assault. Would you like us caught up in that greater war as well, should it come to be?"

The Netherese man and the giant woman looked at each other, seeming at a loss.

"It pains me to fail King Bruenor and those who have been great friends to the Hosttower," Lord Parise admitted.

"Me as well," said Caecilia. "Though I doubt one would ever ex-pect to hear such things from me regarding a dwarf, of all people!"

"The gates remain inoperable," Gromph stated.

"For now?" Lord Parise asked more than demanded.

Gromph considered it for a moment, then offered a conciliatory nod. Who knew, after all, where the winds of war might blow?

"STAY CLOSE AND WE'LL GET YOU THROUGH," WULFGAR whispered to Bonnie Charlee. They had set the boat ashore on the island not far from the Hosttower of the Arcane, to find the fields scarred and littered with the remains of the invaders, both the corpses of mortal beings and the smoking husks of demonic things sent back to the lower planes.

"Go and hide, human," Kimmuriel told her. "If we are set upon by enemies, you will be the first to die."

"Do not listen to the blabbering fool," Wulfgar immediately added. "Stay close. You pulled me from the cold waves. I'm not about to forget that."

As he finished, the pain in his back became suddenly acute, nearly dropping him to his knees. He looked to Kimmuriel, who merely shrugged, and the pain diminished.

The lesson was clear.

Kimmuriel scoffed and walked away, the other two close behind. They moved onto the bridge to Closeguard Island, a stepping-stone to the mainland. As they came over the high point of the structure, they saw that a battle continued on Closeguard, before the only grand house on the island.

"House Kurth is besieged," said Bonnie Charlee.

Kimmuriel moved to Wulfgar. "Run off, woman," he told Bonnie Charlee, and he reached for the barbarian.

Wulfgar stepped back from his touch and stubbornly shook his head. "She comes with us."

Kimmuriel paused and just stared.

"Her, too," Wulfgar restated.

Then it was the psionicist who shook his head. "I have been asked by Jarlaxle to offer protection to you. He said nothing about vagabond flotsam."

"Flotsam, am I?" said Bonnie Charlee.

"Jetsam, then; it matters not," Kimmuriel said, and waved at her dismissively. He held his hand out to Wulfgar once more.

"You would leave her here? How will she cross that bridge full of invaders to get to the mainland?"

"The Hosttower is right over there," Kimmuriel indicated, pointing back behind Wulfgar to the massive treelike structure. "She should go and beg Gromph for help. Or back to the boat, and let her row to a safe landing. I am not here to play nursemaid to wayward pirates." He held out his hand to Wulfgar once more. "Come, let us go and see what High Captain Kurth can tell us."

But Wulfgar stepped back and resolutely shook his head. "I'll not leave her."

"Then I'll leave you."

"As you will," the barbarian said.

"You understand what that will mean for you?"

"I do."

With a shrug, Kimmuriel closed his eyes and became something less than substantial, his ghostly form drifting the remaining length of the bridge to Closeguard Island, then moving, unnoticed by those outside the great house, right through the wall of Ship Kurth.

"Idiot," Bonnie Charlee muttered.

"He is many things, but I wouldn't name that among them," said Wulfgar, his teeth gritting, for the pain in his back had already returned.

"Not him. Yerself!"

Wulfgar looked at her curiously.

"Ye had yer way out of the fight and into Ship Kurth, and there's no better place to be, save the Hosttower itself, in such a war as has come to Luskan," the woman explained. "Ye don't even know me."

"I'm not about to desert you here. You pulled me from the cold water. I'll not forget—"

"Was the drow that made me do it, and don't doubt that I'd be leaving yerself here if that skinny one'd given me the same choice!"

Wulfgar paused and stared hard at the woman. "Where will you go?" he asked.

"Bah, but where will *we* go?" she corrected, drawing a long knife from her belt. "Think we can get into that Ship Kurth there? I'd like to give that skinny drow a few wads of spit."

She started past Wulfgar, moving along the bridge with determined strides. The fighting continued on Closeguard Island, all along the street before the grand facade of the large structure known as Ship Kurth.

Wulfgar caught up to the woman before she made the end of the bridge, and pulled her off to the side, to cover behind a wagon. A hulking gnoll spotted them, though. The large creature, half human and half canine, reared up tall on its legs and howled, then charged at the pair.

Two strides later, it was dead, a flying warhammer caving in its chest.

Several other gnolls had watched, Wulfgar noticed, but none approached and all went back to the fight on the street.

"Brave beasties, eh?" Bonnie Charlee remarked.

"Vicious, yes," Wulfgar replied. "I've not much experience with them, but they fight like hyenas, I am told."

"Hyenas?"

"Doglike," the barbarian explained. "Pack hunters of the desert. Powerful and vicious, but too cunning to get caught in a fight they would likely lose."

"When we go near that door, they'll swarm, then, for sure," said Bonnie Charlee.

"And I'm not even sure that door will open for us," Wulfgar added.

"Well, then, back to the boat!" Bonnie Charlee stood and started for the bridge, but Wulfgar caught her by the arm and pulled her back beside him.

"Just watch a bit," he told her. "There is more to Ship Kurth than you might believe."

"It is the high captain's house," the woman answered. "Beniago Kurth is the leader of Luskan. What more?"

"Beniago *works* for the leader," Wulfgar corrected, and he gave Bonnie Charlee a skeptical look, for how could she not know the worst-kept secret in all of Luskan? "So does Kimmuriel. And that leader brings more to a fight than any high captain could ever imagine."

Before them along the road, flaming bottles sailed at House Kurth, striking the walls and spilling oil that caught the siding and began to burn.

A responding barrage of arrows and even a few lightning bolts sent many gnolls running and several others spinning down, yelping, to the street, but there was little doubt that the gnolls had gained mightily in that last exchange.

"So it would seem," the woman said sarcastically.

Her words were cut short by a jolt of thunder, a sudden and powerful flash behind them, back on, or above, the outer island.

They turned, as did the gnolls, to see a black and roiling storm cloud over the Hosttower of the Arcane.

"Well now," said Bonnie Charlee as that cloud began to speed their way.

"Did I mention that the true leader of Luskan is also a friend to the archmage of the Hosttower?"

"Might that ye should've," said the woman, and she dove under the wagon as the great darkness suddenly loomed above, lightning crackling in the clouds. A bolt snapped down, shattering a pile of crates to reveal a group of hiding gnolls. The archers from House Kurth made short work of them.

The wind mounted, the flames swirling about the sides of the building, seemingly making it worse. But then came the cloudburst, a sudden and torrential downpour.

"Now!" said Wulfgar, grabbing Bonnie Charlee's arm and tugging her out from behind the wagon, the two quickly in a dead run for House Kurth, Wulfgar groaning and lurching with every stride.

"Wulfgar of Gauntlgrym!" the big man yelled, waving his arms and hoping the archers would hear him well enough through the furious wind to not cut him down in the street.

More than his words, though, his actions saved him, for when some gnolls yelped and yipped at him from across the way, several leaping up from behind a natural berm and lifting spears, Wulfgar yelled out "Tempus!" at the top of his lungs and sent Aegis-fang flying their way.

How those gnolls barked and scattered. Not fast enough for one, though, who got hit on the side of the hip and thrown into the air, twisting before landing, broken.

Back at House Kurth, archers rushed onto the balcony, shooting wildly—for what might they hit in winds suddenly so strong that they could hardly stand?

"Wulfgar of Gauntlgrym!" the big man shouted again.

The archers on the balcony began cheering for him, urging him and Bonnie Charlee on.

The two made the door easily, no pursuit coming from across the road, to be met by Kurth soldiers, ushering them in. They entered the foyer, dripping rain, fully soaked.

"I'm glad you heard me," Wulfgar said.

"Heard?" the nearest soldier asked. "We were looking for you. Lord Beniago told us of your approach."

Wulfgar started to respond, but just sighed and let it go.

"Maybe the skinny one's not as bad as I thought," Bonnie Charlee quietly admitted.

The two were escorted to the private chambers of Lord Beniago soon after, and given blankets to put on so they might get out of their drenched clothing.

Beniago came around his grand desk and half sat, half leaned upon it. "Leave us," he told his soldiers, who quickly obeyed, one dropping Wulfgar's wolf-skin shawl and the other clothing to the floor beside the door.

No sooner had the soldiers shut the door than Kimmuriel walked out of the shadows to the side of the room, and it was clear to Wulfgar that more than shadows had been concealing the mind wizard.

Almost immediately, the pain in Wulfgar's back subsided.

"It would have been so much easier if you had just come in with me," the drow said.

"And Bonnie Charlee would be dead," Wulfgar answered. "Or running for her life."

Kimmuriel shrugged. "No small amount of coin convinced the cloud giant Caecilia to provide the storm," he said. "Coin you will repay."

"Coin from the coffers of Ship Kurth," Beniago reminded him.

Out of the corner of his eye, showing his displeasure, Kimmuriel noted the man, a tall and lanky red-haired human, in appearance at least.

"King Bruenor will happily repay Ship Kurth," Wulfgar said, looking straight at Beniago. He knew the truth of the man, of course, that this was no human at all but another drow of Bregan D'aerthe, who had been magically disguised to serve as puppet leader of Luskan for Jarlaxle. "Should I have him deliver it to Ship Kurth or Illusk?"

"Illusk?" Bonnie Charlee asked under her breath, and wisely so, for Wulfgar had just revealed quite a bit.

"Ship Kurth will soon enough be no more, it would appear," Beniago replied.

"Not so. You're winning well in the streets, and the second island is cleared of enemies."

"The city is full of attackers, and with power behind them you cannot comprehend," said Kimmuriel.

"We are putting up a good fight, but it is all for show," Beniago admitted. "We cannot hold, and have no intention of trying. The way to refuge is already cleared and waiting." He looked right at Bonnie Charlee as he spoke, and in a way that set the hairs on the back of Wulfgar's neck standing up.

"I told you not to bring her in here," Kimmuriel said. "Now she knows."

"Knows what?" Bonnie Charlee asked innocently.

"Does it matter?" asked Wulfgar.

"Yes," both Kimmuriel and Beniago answered together.

Wulfgar looked over to see Bonnie Charlee nervously licking her lips and glancing up at him. She now had no weapons on her, just a blanket wrapped around her shivering form—she probably thought that a bad thing, but given the two standing against her, Wulfgar figured that her inability to do something rash and threatening might just save her life.

"She's with me. Under my protection," he said.

What followed was the closest thing to a laugh Wulfgar had ever heard from Kimmuriel. Wulfgar focused on Beniago, who, despite the clandestine nature of his rule and identity, had been doing some important and good work for the citizens of Luskan. He saw no compassion there, however.

"I am the son of the King of Gauntlgrym," Wulfgar declared.

"You are not in line to the throne of Gauntlgrym," Beniago corrected.

"I don't have to be," the big man retorted. "Bruenor is my friend, as is Drizzt. When I say that Bonnie Charlee is under my protection, I speak for them, as well."

"That hardly matters," said Beniago. "King Bruenor knows that some things must be kept secret. At all costs."

"Give me a sword and fight me fair, then!" Bonnie Charlee snarled at him.

"Your gear is right there by the door," said Kimmuriel.

"Do not," Wulfgar told her, but she growled and went for the items, defiantly shrugging off the blanket and pulling on her shirt and pants, then taking up her knife and spinning about.

Beniago was still half sitting on the desk, Kimmuriel standing impassively beside it.

"I ask again," Wulfgar pleaded to them. "None of this is her fault."

"You were warned," Beniago said.

Aegis-fang appeared in Wulfgar's hand.

Beniago started at that, but quickly relaxed and nodded his chin to the side.

Carefully, Wulfgar turned to see Bonnie Charlee with her knife reversed, its tip pressed in against the front of her throat. Sweat surely mixed with the raindrops falling from the woman's unkempt hair. Her hand trembled as if she was trying to fight the press—or, Wulfgar knew, as if she was trying to fight the possession in her mind, the quiet voice telling her to kill herself.

Wulfgar dropped Aegis-fang to the floor.

"You can call it back with a word," Beniago said.

"I won't," the big man promised. "Bonnie Charlee is under my protection, and that of Gauntlgrym."

Beniago sighed. Over to the side, the woman gave a little squeak and a bit of blood started to show.

"When this is over, Gauntlgrym will rebuild *Joen's Heirloom*," Wulfgar blurted. "King Bruenor will spare no expense, for I, his son, will be among that crew. She'll be the finest, fastest, and meanest ship on the Sword Coast, and with a crew bolstered by battleragers and maybe even with Drizzt himself."

"Impressive," said Beniago, who seemed not impressed.

"Bonnie Charlee will captain that ship," Wulfgar finished.

"Sailing in support of Ship Kurth, I suppose," said Beniago.

Wulfgar shook his head. "No, but neither sailing against the interests of Ship Kurth. Let her go. It is in your interests. She will become a major power about the seas, and one whose ship will never be hostile to you."

Beniago looked to Kimmuriel "Do you think she understands?"

Kimmuriel gave that curious almost-laugh again. "She understands more than she ever wanted to understand," he replied, calm and superior. "It is quite disconcerting, perhaps even mind-breaking, to so quickly learn that your own body can be turned fully against you to cause great harm."

The psionicist waved his hand, and Bonnie Charlee suddenly slumped forward, released from the possession, her dagger hand dropping to her side. She gave a few gasps, and was fighting hard, Wulfgar could see, to not let them see her cry. He understood. Could anything be more invasive and traumatizing than having your body stolen from your control and turned back on you?

He shook his head. He could only imagine her torment. One day, he would pay back Kimmuriel Oblodra, he thought.

"Quite unlikely," Kimmuriel answered aloud, staring straight at him.

Beniago hopped up from the desk. "Go dry your clothes and rest," he told the two humans. "We may be leaving soon, perhaps at any time. When we go, you can follow."

"Both of us," Wulfgar stated, and Beniago nodded his agreement.

"But when the time to leave is upon us, we will go, and if you are not prepared for that journey, you will be left behind."

CAECILIA RODE HER BLACK CLOUD BACK TO THE HOST-tower to find Gromph waiting for her just outside her private chambers.

"A horde approaches," she informed him. "Your friends at Ship Kurth will be overrun."

"Of course," the archmage agreed. "Three of the city's high captains joined with the invaders even before they arrived. The flotilla that came against Luskan was larger after the sea encounter than the original force sailing to attack us."

Caecilia wore a confused look.

"They are scoundrels," Gromph explained. "The attackers offered them a better position, no doubt."

"Or perhaps they were not overly thrilled with being ruled by dark elves?"

"There is that," Gromph admitted. "I tell you without bias that the city was thriving under Jarlaxle's quiet rule, but sometimes that is not enough. And not all of the captains were doing well, of course, since High Captain Kurth has greatly curtailed their piracy."

"Because they could earn more simply through the opened trade avenues, if I understand correctly."

"Sometimes that is not enough," repeated Gromph.

"Shall I make a new storm to bite at those advancing on Ship Kurth?"

Gromph paused, then shook his head. "I do not know how far they will go. If we interfere too overtly, perhaps they will come against us once more."

"The field about our tower is littered with their dead."

"But they know that wizards tire. No, let the city sort out around us, however it may fall."

"And your friend in Ship Kurth?"

"Any who should concern us are in no danger," the archmage assured her.

Caecilia gave a little snort, but tried to cover it when she saw the scowl on Gromph's face and realized he knew she was mocking him. "Such a drow thing to say," she admitted. "If all of Luskan other than those you deem valuable to you were to be slaughtered, would you even care, Archmage?"

"Should I?"

Caecilia blew a long sigh and let it go. Curiously, though, as she walked through the door leading to her extradimensional mansion, she realized that she actually didn't believe Gromph.

Had he been so battered by the distorted culture of Menzoberranzan that he thought it a sign of great weakness to admit compassion?

How many others? the cloud giantess wondered. How many other dark elves had been similarly broken?

"BEEN AN INTERESTING DAY," WULFGAR SAID TO BONNIE Charlee when they were left alone in a sitting room at Ship Kurth. They sat across from each other at a small table, still wrapped in their blankets as their clothes dried by the flaming hearth.

"Aye, that's a word," the woman replied. "Might be others I'd use, but *interesting* works."

"Calico Grimm?" Wulfgar asked as he replayed the last few frantic hours. "How'd he go?"

Bonnie Charlee shook her head. "The red elf with the sword got him. Cut him in half."

"You'd been with him long?"

"Long enough to know enough about him to hold back me tears, aye."

Wulfgar took a while to digest that. "And what now for you?"

"I'll tell ye when I find that I have some say in that," she replied, then added with obvious intrigue, "Did ye mean what ye said?"

"What I said?"

"The *Heirloom?*"

"Ah, well . . ."

"Might not even be destroyed," Bonnie Charlee said. "When ye broke their ship, they took ours—they hadn't any other. She's in Luskan Harbor right now, not to doubt."

"Then we might take her back."

"And I'll be captain and yerself'll sign on for the fight?"

Wulfgar shrugged. "I never know where my road will take me anymore, lady . . . err, Captain Charlee. Or would it be Captain Bonnie?"

Bonnie Charlee grinned and shrugged.

"I did mean it about the ship," Wulfgar added. "When this is sorted, I expect you'd make a fine captain and a worthy ally, and yes, I would hope to sail with you, sometimes, at least."

That brought a smile to the beleaguered woman's face.

"We should get some rest," Wulfgar offered, motioning to the pillows that had been spread on the floor before the hearth.

"Aye," the woman agreed, and she quickly added, "Rest."

Before either of them even got out of a chair, the door opened and a tall drow woman entered. "Time to go," she told them.

Heeding the warning of Beniago, Bonnie Charlee rushed to grab her clothes, Wulfgar stiffly following.

The big man froze when he felt the drow woman's hand on his back, and before he could ask her intent, he felt the warmth of magical healing flowing through him.

"Be quick," she said. "You'll find more healing when we're safely away from here."

They went out into the hall and joined a procession of fast-fleeing others, and back behind them, in the direction of the street, they heard the slamming of a ram on the front door and the crackling as flames again bit at Ship Kurth's walls. Through a secret door in the wall they went, and down a long spiral staircase into a wet and dark—very dark—brine-smelling cave.

"Close it for good!" Beniago yelled out from some corner of the cave, and behind and far above, they heard the thump of a huge stone, the ground jolting beneath their feet. The secret door was no longer a door.

Few torches were burning, and those were far apart—another reminder to Wulfgar that Ship Kurth's crew were drow who didn't need much light.

They moved down a descending corridor and into a tunnel that was quite tight for the hulking barbarian.

"We're under the bay," Bonnie Charlee whispered from behind Wulfgar. Even as she spoke, the torches were extinguished and the parade moved in complete darkness, feeling their way in a long single-file line. She was right, and they were crossing to the mainland, he believed.

No, not *to* the mainland but *under* the mainland, he soon corrected, when they came into a wider area lit by magical faerie fire, an area of worked rooms and corridors, fine masonry covered in old sculptures and decorations.

Bonnie Charlee gasped and nearly leaped upon Wulfgar, for more than two-thirds of the people who had come with her had shed their human disguises.

Beniago, still a red-haired human in appearance, moved over to the pair. "Illusk," he explained. "The haunted city beneath Luskan— old Luskan, if you will."

"Haunted by drow?" Wulfgar asked.

"By more than us, though the spirits here seem content to leave us alone."

"The true power of Luskan, then. Bregan D'aerthe's secret home."

"One of them, and now you know," said Beniago. He looked directly at Bonnie Charlee, a very clear threat, as he added, "You both know."

"And so we're sworn to secrecy," she said.

"Need I even warn you of the consequences again?"

"Was the worst-kept secret in Luskan afore," the woman replied, regaining some swagger, apparently—and that impressed Wulfgar more than a little, given that they were wholly helpless here if the drow decided to be rid of them. Who would even know?

"But still a secret, and one we prefer to keep," said Beniago.

Kimmuriel walked over then and stared hard at Bonnie Charlee.

"Will you tell?" Beniago asked the woman, and before she could answer, she gasped.

Wulfgar looked from her to Kimmuriel, to see his concentration. He was in her thoughts again, the big man knew, listening to her unspoken response, her honest response, before she could properly filter it.

"A pity," Kimmuriel said, and walked away.

"What does that mean?" asked Wulfgar, thinking his friend doomed.

"It means he doesn't get to kill her, I suppose," said Beniago. He dipped an unexpected bow to the woman. "Welcome to Illusk, Bonnie Charlee. Perhaps you will indeed one day captain *Joen's Heirloom*."

The woman seemed completely at a loss, of course, and she looked pleadingly to Wulfgar.

"The drow never trust anyone who is not drow," Wulfgar started to explain.

"Or anyone who is," Beniago quickly added, and he just shrugged as both looked at him. "Now, Kimmuriel is finished with you and priestess Dab'nay is waiting. That wound is abyssal, and will fester and perhaps even kill you without her aid."

CHAPTER 24

The Eyes of the World

The dark, beautiful woman held the bird-shaped figure up high in her cupped hands, its crystal body catching and shimmering under the afternoon sun. Yvonnel whispered to her latest creation and tossed it up into the air, where it took wing and flew off.

"If them things're living, will they start laying eggs?" Athrogate asked from his seat on a large rock at the side of the small meadow. Feeling much better now, the dwarf rolled Skullcrusher, the two-handed mace that used to belong to his beloved Ambergris, around in his strong hands.

"They would make the world more beautiful, would they not?" Yvonnel answered.

"Bah, but the sun shining through 'em hurts me eyes."

Yvonnel laughed at the idea that a dwarf, any dwarf, would be complaining to a dark elf about bright light.

"How many ye got out there now?" Athrogate asked. "First ones dead, or whatever, or are all about?"

"All. Dozens, though I've lost the exact count."

"And ye see through 'em? All of them? Sounds like ye're to be getting dizzy."

"They tell me when I need to see through them," the drow replied. "I do not intend to be surprised out here, dwarf, and there is much afoot that would destroy us. We will know every approach."

"And everyone hiding," Athrogate agreed, and he turned to the side, leading Yvonnel's gaze to a nearby hillock, one that he had just left. "We'll pull 'em in, all of 'em, and kill them what need killin'!" He rambled on a bit, but paused, noting that the woman wasn't listening. Yvonnel stood with her eyes closed, a clear clue to Athrogate. He jumped up from the rock and slapped Skullcrusher across his open palm.

Yvonnel's violet eyes popped open and she turned a smile on the dwarf. "Demon," she said. "A demon in a dwarf's body."

"A dead demon, then," said the dwarf.

"But a living dwarf," Yvonnel warned.

The two stared at each other hard. She was clearly referring to their last battle, one in which Athrogate hadn't stopped his bashing quickly enough and so had destroyed a bauble-wearing, demon-possessed dwarf.

"Do not make that mistake again," Yvonnel told him.

"Mistake?"

"Dwarf, I can send you away. And I could have let you die. Grant me this one favor in return."

"Nah, ye need me," Athrogate said, that toothy smile showing again between the thick black bushes that comprised his beard. "And ye love me, too, though ye're tryin' hard to hide it."

"It is difficult to suppress such powerful feelings, but if I must," the woman answered with equal sarcasm, drawing a "Bwahaha!" from Athrogate, who smacked the powerful mace across his hand again.

"Ye want to see if ye can save a dwarf, then fine," he said more seriously and ominously. "I can wait a few heartbeats before smushing the fool's head to bone dust."

"Athrogate . . ."

"Ye do what ye need to do," he answered, "and I'll do what meself's needin' to do." He brought the mace up higher and kissed it. "I ain't forgettin' nothing."

"Being intelligent is no insult to your lost love."

"I ain't forgettin' nothing," Athrogate repeated, his face a frozen grimace. "Nothing."

Yvonnel sighed heavily. "Let us be away, dwarf, if you wish to accompany me."

Athrogate hopped up from the stone. "I'll tell our guests."

"*We'll* tell them," Yvonnel corrected. "Our hunt will take us right past the cave."

Athrogate softened his visage when he entered the shallow cave. A dozen humans, including three children, were scattered about the floor inside, huddled in whispered conversations, mostly worried about the farms they had abandoned or about what they might do if the demons ever found them. Yvonnel and Athrogate had rescued them, brought them to this place, and guarded over them. With her magic, Yvonnel was feeding them.

Athrogate couldn't stay mad at her regarding the disposition of a demon-possessed dwarf when looking upon this group. The drow woman had nothing to gain from saving these people, and in fact had put herself in harm's way in extracting most from farms that were soon after overrun. Even though most of Athrogate's experiences with drow had been with Drizzt and Jarlaxle, these continuing unexpected revelations about the race as a whole, particularly coming from, purportedly, a priestess of Lolth, had him shaking his head.

"Set guards about the entrance," Yvonnel told them. "If danger approaches, you will be warned, as will I, and I will send word as to where you should flee."

Most nodded, but more than one, Athrogate noted, grimaced, or muttered something surely unflattering under her breath. The farmers didn't really know what in the world was happening around them, and some here didn't trust Yvonnel, obviously, even though, by all appearances, she had rescued them.

That was the problem with the reputation of the drow, Athrogate mused. They were known to wrap webs over webs over more webs, and you never quite understood their real purpose until it was too late. Certainly, Athrogate occasionally flashed on doubts about Yvonnel, but he had a prior understanding of her from people he trusted and so those doubts could not take hold. These folks had likely never encountered any drow before, or if so, likely not one who would help them—unless, of course, it was Drizzt.

The dwarf looked to his companion then as she started back out of the cave, heading off to destroy another demon. He reminded himself that he owed her his life, and though he would have been perfectly fine with his own death after the loss of his beloved Ambergris, it was no small thing that he was able to help save these farmers (and there were many more out there who needed him) or that he was getting the chance to pay back those who had so wronged him and his love.

So, when he caught up to Yvonnel and she again asked him to do her this one favor, instead of immediately growling and snarling, Athrogate offered, "We'll see."

THE DAWN'S LIGHT SHOWED DRIZZT THAT HE HAD NOT ES-caped his pursuer; indeed, his attempt to throw the giant spider off his trail had only allowed the thing to close the great distance he had put between it and himself, for it could not pace Andahar.

But Andahar could not remain on this plane forever. The unicorn was a magical item, and an enchantment with a specific duration. Without the unicorn, Drizzt couldn't hope to outrun the spider, and after shooting it and its fellow arachnid in the caverns outside Gauntlgrym, he was fairly certain that he couldn't possibly defeat the spider, either—not unless he could find some weakness.

To do that, he needed time. To buy time, he needed to get far, far away.

But how?

A large tree just beyond the nearest ridge shuddered suddenly and fell over with a crash, and Drizzt didn't need to wait to figure out what had caused it. He swung his mount around and galloped away at full speed, trying to get every last stride out of Andahar before the magic expired, taking the unicorn from him for far too many hours.

But where to go? Not Longsaddle, certainly, nor Luskan. Not Waterdeep, even, for how many would be killed by the monster chasing him even if the city found the power to destroy the thing?

When he crested the next hill, the drow paused for just a moment to survey the area and figure out where he was.

He had come a long way through the night, and could see the ocean far in the distance.

ATHROGATE LOCKED HIS GAZE UPON THE PONY HE AND Yvonnel had taken from Regis. He hated using the animal as bait here, but the effectiveness of the ploy couldn't be denied.

The pony nickered and stamped its foot.

Athrogate clenched his hands more tightly on Skullcrusher.

A shadow to the side caught the dwarf's wary eye, a dark form moving through the trees, circling to the back of the pony.

The demon, a misshapen black-and-green humanoid creature with one arm twice as long as the other, both hands ending in three long claws instead of fingers, burst from the brush, sprinting at the animal.

Athrogate was already in the air, flying to intercept.

The demon didn't slow, veering to charge the dwarf instead, its unbalanced face seeming little more than a mouth that stretched halfway around its head and a pair of too-large eyes. Green spittle flew from that mouth, and green ooze dripped from every bit of the creature—every part of it reeked of disease.

A lesser fighter would have fallen away in terror. A less sturdy person would have simply melted before the reeking horror.

A less angry dwarf, even Athrogate, might have flinched.

The collision was not demon and dwarf, as the diseased abyssal creature had clearly wanted. No, it was demon and Skullcrusher, Athrogate whipping the huge mace across before him, swatting the monster in midleap and sending it flying to the side. Acidic green mucus flew from it, leaving a trail and splattering Athrogate's weapon and arms.

The magic of Skullcrusher would not allow the mighty weapon to be damaged by the stuff, though, and the anger of Athrogate would not allow him to be daunted by a few minor burns. He charged in pursuit of the demon, raining blows upon it before it regained its footing.

The creature fought back wildly, leaping side to side, clawing with its hideous hands, even spitting acid in the dwarf's face.

That only brought a roar of outrage, though, and the dwarf pounded in even more recklessly and viciously, sending Skullcrusher into a series of short downward strikes, pounding at the upraised arm of the demon, then, eventually, at its head. Athrogate accepted the clawing of the creature's other arm, the three hooks tearing into his flesh deeply. He just yelled louder, as if using his voice to drown out the pain.

His voice and a memory.

He was fighting for Amber here, and no wound would slow his strikes.

Down went the demon to its knees, and it slumped forward.

Athrogate changed his angle of attack, batting the monster's face with a great two-handed swing that sent its head snapping out to the side and sent the beast spinning down to the ground.

Athrogate swung again, but too high as the thing dropped, and the momentum of his fury sent the dwarf stumbling over the prone monster, finally floundering in a bush a few strides beyond it. He twisted and clawed his way back out, turning with murderous intent.

But where the demon had been now kneeled a dwarf on all fours, shaking her head groggily.

"Ah, but no ye don't," Athrogate whispered, and he advanced with a low growl, lifting Skullcrusher up over his head for a killing blow.

He staggered just before he finished the dwarf, though, as a bolt of golden light slammed him in the chest, knocking him back a stride. A second, similar bolt struck the kneeling dwarf, and she crumpled down to the ground.

It had not been an attack, on either, Athrogate understood as the nature of the enchantment registered. He had been struck with some weird healing magic, one that projected force along with the warmth to soothe the pain and salve to wash away the biting acid.

He looked across the small lea and saw Yvonnel standing there beside the pony. "The necklace!" she yelled at him. "Take the necklace!"

Athrogate's first thought was to cave in the kneeling Stoneshaft dwarf's head, and he even moved to that effect, but Yvonnel's order to him wasn't mundane. It too was magical, carrying great weight, and delivered so closely after the powerful healing spell, it surprised the dwarf. Before he even consciously registered the movement, Athrogate found himself holding a silver chain festooned with a large milky-blue moonstone.

He heard a voice in his head, growling and sinister, a liquid voice full of phlegm and disease, one demanding entrance.

But a second voice was there as well: the commanding tones of Yvonnel, telling Athrogate to drop the phylactery.

Athrogate, too willful and angry to be possessed to any extent by either the demon thing or the priestess, settled it his own way. He tossed the bauble into the air, took up his huge mace, and batted it far and high. It went into a nearby tree, crackling along the branches, and there it hung, out of sight.

The kneeling dwarf gasped repeatedly. Athrogate turned on her, his anger unsated, but he found Yvonnel there, standing between him and his prey.

"Move yerself," he told the drow woman.

"The dwarf is no longer possessed," Yvonnel told him.

"She'll be dyin' with a better chance o' seein' Moradin, then."

"Do not, I beg."

"Beg?"

"For yourself, Athrogate." Yvonnel moved aside just a bit, giving Athrogate a better view of the battered dwarf woman, her light hair streaked with blood, her breathing still coming in raspy heaves. "You know nothing of her, of—"

"I know she's one o' them!"

"One of what? A Stoneshaft? Yes, but did she have a voice in the decisions? And once the necklace was put upon her, did she even know what it contained? You do not know that she welcomed the possession.

You do not know that she didn't fight it with every bit of courage she could muster."

"So ye're thinkin' I should just pretend that this one, that all o' them, played no role in me Amber's death, eh?" the dwarf growled, and he couldn't even pry his clenched teeth apart as he finished, "They cut off her head."

"I know," Yvonnel said, her voice thick with sympathy. "I know, and I understand your pain and your rage. But there is more at stake here than just this one woman's life."

Behind Athrogate, a branch cracked and fell. Both Athrogate and Yvonnel stared at it, at the rotted wood and dead leaves, and the silver chain with the moonstone bauble wrapped about it, hissing.

"Do what you will," Yvonnel stated and rushed past Athrogate to the phylactery. She began to chant before she got there, an old, harsh language that Athrogate had heard enough times now to understand that she was banishing the demon that lurked within that gemstone, damning it back to the Abyss, where it belonged. He had witnessed this before, against beings more powerful than this one, he was sure, and so he had no doubt of the outcome.

He swung back around, his knuckles whitening from the grip on his mace, his teeth grinding. He lifted the weapon, but dropped it back down, then took up a fistful of bloody hair and yanked the woman's head back so he could look her in the eye.

Athrogate winced. He saw fear there, and something deeper, like some violation spilling out through her wounded eyes.

"Dwarf?" Yvonnel asked.

Athrogate glanced back at her over his shoulder. "She makes one move, says one thing, I'm not likin', and her head's getting split."

He let go and walked off, back toward the hillock and the refugees, muttering curses with every step.

DRIZZT KNEW THAT HE WAS RUNNING OUT OF TIME, AND he had not put nearly enough ground between himself and the pursuing arachnid to keep ahead of it without Andahar. From a high hilltop he spotted the monster—or at least, he spotted the line of devastation it was leaving in its wake, winding like a river of destruction through the forests in the east.

He looked down to his left, to a small hamlet of farmhouses, and wondered if he should go down and warn them.

"Or are there even farmers remaining there?" he whispered. The forests and fields were full of demons, after all.

That notion almost had him turning Andahar down that way, but he held back. The spider would likely run right past the hamlet if Drizzt went nowhere near it, since the other one had paid him no heed when he hadn't blocked its way.

Drizzt turned his mount the other way and galloped off, trying to focus on the road ahead. The unicorn was a magical item, not a living creature, he had to remind himself repeatedly. He could push his own body beyond its limits, but not so with the magic here—twelve hours, no more, and once that time had elapsed, either in a single summoning or in several smaller stints over the course of a day, Andahar would be lost to him for nearly a full day.

So he galloped full speed, knowing the mount wouldn't tire and knowing, too, that every yard of distance he put between himself and the spider gave him a better chance of surviving a day without the unicorn.

Despite his own terrible predicament, he continued to think of that other spider as well, the one that had so fully ignored him, the one so obviously focused on some other target.

He was pretty sure that he knew who that target might be.

"SO IS IT THE PONY OR THE HALFLING?" YVONNEL ASKED. She was in a fine mood, then, convinced that the dwarf woman now in the cave with the other refugees was not complicit in the darkness that had come to the Crags. She had used powerful spells of divination on the dwarf, Leerie by name, to detect any lying during her questioning, and though dwarves were by nature hard to read and re-sistant to magic, Yvonnel had been confident enough in the interview to allow Leerie into the cave unattended.

Not that she was in any shape to cause harm to the sturdy farmers after the beating Athrogate had put upon her.

"Aye," Athrogate answered, and he, too, seemed a bit lighter.

Because he hadn't crushed Leerie's skull, Yvonnel knew.

"Aye?" she echoed. "One or the other?"

"Both," Athrogate explained. "Bruenor gave the name to Regis long ago—was always hungry with a belly always growlin'. Regis passed it on to the pony."

Yvonnel sighed, finally catching on to the contraction in this language new to her. "And here I thought dwarves the most ridiculous in their naming conventions," she mumbled.

"Aye," laughed Athrogate. "Once knew a priest named Cordio Muffinhead . . ." He started to elaborate, but stopped when a crystal-line bird flew to a nearby branch, chirping a warning.

"Bah, but I'm ready to bash another one!" the dwarf declared and leaped up, taking up Skullcrusher.

But Yvonnel, listening to the warning ward, was shaking her head. "No demon," she said, and she cast the crystalline bird into the air. She motioned for Athrogate to follow and ran off after her magical creation.

They didn't have to go far, for they had barely come upon a well-worn trail when the rider came into view and was immediately recog-nizable to the pair, as was his distinctive mount.

Drizzt recognized them in turn. He galloped Andahar right up to them, skidded to a stop, and leaped from the unicorn, staring incredu-lously at Athrogate for many heartbeats before wrapping the dwarf in a great hug.

"How did you survi—?" he started to ask, but stopped and noted the dwarf's companion, who was as powerful a cleric as he had ever known. "My friend," he said instead, "it warms my heart to see you alive."

Athrogate didn't disagree, but still wore his dour expression.

"We will hoist a mug in toast to Ambergris," Drizzt said quietly. Not wanting to waste a precious moment of Andahar's remaining time, Drizzt dismissed the unicorn.

"Aye, to me Amber," the dwarf cheered.

Yvonnel began to join in, but was cut short by the drow warrior. "But first, you must be gone from here, both of you. Run, and do not look back."

"We been killin' demons," Athrogate replied.

"And gathering refugees," added Yvonnel. "Including a dwarf who was possessed, but is now free and repentant. I believe that we can help—"

Drizzt was shaking his head. "I am pursued by a beast beyond us, beyond us all. It is cutting a line of devastation behind me in its pursuit. If you encounter it and are lucky, it will ignore you, but if not, it will surely destroy you."

"Bah!" The dwarf snorted.

Yvonnel, though, wasn't so quick to dismiss the words. She knew all about Drizzt and all about his friends, and the enemies they had overcome. She had orchestrated Drizzt's explosive leap into the face of Demogorgon! So to see him so clearly unsettled . . .

"Where?" she asked.

Drizzt glanced back the way he had come. "Not far. But you have time to turn aside from its path as long as I am not with you. It will turn as I turn. It hunts me and me alone."

"What is it?" Yvonnel pressed.

"There's no time—"

But then Drizzt remembered who he was talking to. She was possessed of the intimate and complete memories of her namesake, Yvonnel the Eternal, who had lived for two millennia as the drow voice of the Spider Queen, and who knew more about the creatures of the lower planes than any drow now alive. And maybe—just maybe—she knew of a way to defeat it.

"A demon, I believe."

"A spider?"

"Yes, and there are two." Drizzt paused at Yvonnel's gasp. "One for me, and one charging for Gauntlgrym, last I saw. I thought it best to steer this one away, because I feared that Bruenor and the others could not defeat two of the beasts. Its eyes throw fire and lightning and turn people to stone. I have seen them shot with my own bow, dropped under tons of stone, but with not a hint of injury . . ."

"Retrievers," Yvonnel explained. "They are retrievers."

"You do know of them," said Drizzt.

"Then ye know how to beat 'em," added Athrogate.

"Yes," she answered Drizzt, "and no," she said to the dwarf. "I fear that Gauntlgrym cannot defeat even that single one. A retriever's limitation is also its strength. It is a golem singularly attuned to one target and it will pursue that target until it captures or kills it. The other creatures of the material plane can barely touch a retriever— they are but witnesses in a play that does not include them. Part of the golem's magic is that it and its target alone fully share their place of existence."

"But I was the one who shot the beast pursuing me."

"With a bow that shoots arrows of lightning. You will not harm it. It is beyond you."

"Then what?" Athrogate demanded, growing agitated.

"Run, Drizzt Do'Urden," Yvonnel told him. "Keep running. Run as far as you can run. I will seek a solution, but there is little I can promise."

"Bah, but I ain't about to move aside so some fat spider can kill me friend!" Athrogate protested, and he slapped Skullcrusher across his palm for emphasis.

"Then your friend will watch you be destroyed," Yvonnel calmly replied.

"What is its weakness?" Drizzt asked the woman.

"It has none. Every bit is armored. It is fast and it is strong. You'll not kill it with magic, surely."

"One of my blades is a frostbrand. It feasts on creatures of fire."

Yvonnel shrugged, for she did not know if that would matter. "I will learn what I may," she answered. "And I will find you when I do and help in any way that I can. Someone, something, very powerful is determined to get you, Drizzt Do'Urden, and to get whoever is the target of the second golem."

"Demogorgon?" Drizzt asked.

"Lolth?" Yvonnel responded.

"But Lolth had me, in a tunnel, and she did not take me," said Drizzt. "And if the other golem is for Zaknafein . . . we suspect that it was Lolth who returned him to my side."

"It was not Lolth who did that," Yvonnel stated flatly.

Drizzt began to respond, but stopped and regarded the powerful priestess curiously.

"It was not Lolth," Yvonnel repeated. "And keeping you alive then only to hunt you now would be very much in character for the Lady of Chaos. Run on, Drizzt Do'Urden. Stay ahead of the beast. I will learn what I may."

Drizzt reeled from the woman's declaration, his mind spinning. "My time with Andahar is nearing its end. The magic will soon enough expire. I cannot outrun the retriever without my steed."

"Then go and hide. Find a narrow tunnel through which the beast cannot easily follow. It will dig its way in pursuit, but not so easily."

Drizzt tried to figure how much time he had left, even while he worked to pinpoint exactly where he was and what places might be near enough around for him to reach on Andahar. Although . . . would it even matter? If he could not fight the monster, if it was indeed quite above him, would *anything* matter?

Yes, he realized and quickly decided. Some things mattered, even to the doomed. He unfastened his sword belt.

"Should we run and hide?" Athrogate was asking Yvonnel.

Yvonnel considered it for a moment, then said, "Yes. And I will have my magical spies watching carefully."

"Spider's that bad?"

Yvonnel, stone-faced, nodded. "They don't rest. They don't stop. They are almost impossible to defeat, if it's possible at all. They are the most dependable hunters in all the planes of existence, and Lolth, or Demogorgon, or both, has apparently spared no resources in their hunt."

"Bah, but I ain't for buying that, eh, elfie?" the dwarf said, turning back to Drizzt.

Drizzt moved under a spreading elm tree and dropped his weapons to the ground.

"Eh?" Athrogate said again. "Put yer belt back on, elfie, and let's kill us some spider. Doubt ye can eat the damned thing, though."

Drizzt bent low and set his backpack atop the sword belt and weapons he had just placed down. He looked up to regard the dwarf, offering a smile. He was glad indeed to see his friend finding a way to his typically ridiculous humor. "Not this spider, Athrogate."

He took off his cloak and bracers, and the quiver that supplied an endless stream of arrows to Taulmaril, and placed them, too, on the pile.

"Ye're not wantin' to kill the thing?"

"Oh, me friend, I am . . . I be wantin'," Drizzt replied, faking a dwarven brogue. "But we cannot. When I saw you two, I did hope that we might defeat the beast, for Yvonnel's power is as great as any I have witnessed. But she knows better, and she just told us that we three together would have no chance of defeating this abyssal golem."

"Then run, because it's coming," the dwarf said somberly. "Why're ye strippin'? Think yer horse-thing'll run faster?"

"I will ride," Drizzt replied, not quite answering the question. He pulled the whistle still hanging about his neck up to his lips and blew, summoning Andahar. "Andahar has little left to offer me, but enough, I hope, to get me to my destination. You and Yvonnel stay far afield of the beast. It will follow me."

"Elfie . . ."

"For your sake, my sake, and the sake of the refugees you harbor. I do not know if it will take note of you. I have already seen instances where these monsters have turned on those in their way, and where the monsters have simply run by. If it turns on you, it will kill you, and Yvonnel, and all those you protect."

"And what're ye meanin' to do, then? Ye got a plan?"

"Keep safe my possessions" was all that Drizzt was willing to answer. He pulled off his boots and mithral shirt and dropped them on the pile, leaving him with only his breeches and the whistle on the silver chain hanging about his neck. "Get all of this to Bruenor and Catti-brie if I do not return. I go hopeful of victory, and certain, even failing that, this monster will not take me to its master, nor will it remain to wreak destruction upon those I love."

The large unicorn came galloping up beside Drizzt, who caught Andahar by the mane and gracefully swung up onto the steed's back.

"Trust me," he said to Athrogate, and he offered a smile and a wink, then galloped away.

Athrogate stared down the trail where Drizzt and the unicorn had run. "Drizzt'll find a way," he muttered.

Yvonnel could only hope that he was right. She wondered, too, if Bruenor still sat on the throne of Gauntlgrym, or if there even still was a throne of Gauntlgrym.

CHAPTER 25

She Is My Friend

They probably could have walked right in through the front door, Regis thought as he and Dahlia crept through a darkened, empty sitting room on the lowest level of House Margaster. The mansion was not overtly defended, and why should it be, given that it was a noble house in a city utterly dominated by such houses, and by law. The house was not without its guards, of course. The intruding pair had seen a couple of them resting by the carriage under the awning in a side drive off the semicircular entry road to the mansion.

Regis moved across the room to the corridor door and listened carefully, then cracked it open just a bit. He fell back inside, softly closing the door and motioning to Dahlia that there was another pair of guards just on the other side, down the hall between this door and a second one.

Dahlia pointed to him and indicated for him to move quickly, then headed for the second door.

After a deep breath, Regis took up his hand crossbow and slipped out of the room, trying to plot his hoped-for sequence of events.

Two guards loomed before him: a thin man animatedly gabbing, waving his hands and dancing about, and a thick woman leaning against the wall, trying to appear interested—but doing a rather lame job of it, Regis thought.

He crept another step, hoping to get very close, but the man, in his dancing, caught sight of him and whirled.

The hand crossbow fired, the bolt catching the man in the chest. He grabbed at it and fell back a step, stumbling. He started to yell out but only slurred a garbled word, the sleeping poison already doing its work.

Regis hadn't stopped to admire the shot or its effects, though, leaping down the corridor so that as soon as the woman realized what was happening, she turned to find his fine rapier's tip ready at her throat, the halfling standing with the index finger of his other hand held up across his pursed lips.

The woman lifted her empty hands in surrender, but it didn't really matter, for Dahlia, too, was now moving.

Regis yelped and leaped back when his companion surprisingly struck, her nunchaku exploding into the guard's skull, spraying Regis with blood, bone, and brain. She crumpled to the floor as if she had been stomped by a tarrasque.

"Why did you do that?" Regis stuttered.

"Shh!"

"She surrendered," Regis whispered.

"So?"

"She might have had information," the halfling said, but for Dahlia's sensibilities and not his own. Whether she had information or not, he wouldn't have so wounded the guard. He looked down at the fallen woman, who was groaning, and thought that perhaps a heavy bandage might save her.

"Do not even think it," Dahlia warned him as if reading his mind, which, he realized, wasn't likely a difficult trick at that time.

"We cannot let her—"

"Yes, we can. We're here for a reason."

Regis tried to steady himself.

"You think she would have shown you quarter if the roles were reversed?"

"It matters not. We're supposed to be better, else what's the point?"

"The point is that we're here to rescue Artemis Entreri, who was taken from us by these people, or have you forgotten?"

"I have not!"

"Then shut up," Dahlia told him. "And put aside your mercy or it will get you killed." She started away.

"Get *us* killed," Regis meekly corrected, at which Dahlia spun on him with a narrowed gaze and a wild-eyed sparkle.

"No," she said with a calm that raised the hairs on the back of the troubled halfling's neck. "Get *you* killed."

Regis swallowed hard and followed Dahlia down the hall, fumbling to reload his hand crossbow, which was not typically lethal, at least.

Dahlia fell back against the corridor wall before entering the next open room, and Regis followed suit, both watching as another house member, a small girl with curly red hair, crossed that room before them.

They held their breath, even more when the child turned to look at them directly and flashed a strangely unnerving smile. Regis gasped, noting her eyes: pure white, only white.

The child kept walking across the room, out of sight, and Regis caught his breath and turned fast to Dahlia, fearing that even a small child would not be spared her violent wrath.

He found her against the wall, trembling, wholly unnerved.

"Dahlia?"

The woman began to pant. She shook her head—to clear it, he figured—then motioned for him to move off, and quickly.

Regis poked his head into the room to see the child exiting through another door, and to see, more importantly, a pair of house guards standing stiffly and breathlessly to either side of her as she passed.

And as she passed, the two large and well-armed guards took deep breaths indeed, their terror clear to see before one reached back and gently closed the door.

"I have an idea," Regis told Dahlia. He closed his eyes and concentrated for a bit, then tapped his beret and before Dahlia's eyes, became a close replica of the young girl he had just seen.

Dahlia looked as if she would fall over backward.

"I'll clear the way," Regis happily informed her.

"Just go," she said, waving her hands at him, trying to usher him away quickly. Regis stared at her in disbelief. He had never seen Dahlia so obviously discomfited.

"It was just a child," he said, but Dahlia was shaking her head emphatically.

"Just go. Just go. Just go."

Regis tried to figure out what was bothering her so. The little girl had seen them, if she even could see through those pupil-less eyes. Certainly it seemed as if she had seen them. But still, Regis had felt only a sense of warmth and comfort when he had looked upon the child, and that image of her lingered in his thoughts so completely that he had used his beret more powerfully than ever before.

How had that happened?

And why had the two guards, and now Dahlia, been so clearly flummoxed and upset, even terrified, by the sight of the child?

The reactions truly perplexed the halfling, who felt only good things—of course, that led him to wonder why he was feeling anything at all positive toward anyone wandering about a house of enemies and demons.

He didn't have time to play out his thoughts now, though, so he pushed along, moving through the rooms and along the corridors, and fortunately, as he went deeper into the house, he heard fewer and fewer people, and saw no one at all.

THE LECHEROUS DRUNK STUMBLED OUT OF THE ALLEYWAY, his wife in tow. Still scratching at the many wounds on his face from those nasty wasps, the man nodded toward a tavern at the end of the road. He fished in his one remaining pocket and pulled forth a piece of silver, then used it to scratch at his face and started along.

"We no' got enough for me to drink," the woman complained.

The man turned and lifted the back of his hand to her, and she ducked, turning away. The drunk nodded and started back around, but noted the look of confusion suddenly coming over his wife. He followed her gaze behind him and upward to the eaves of a building and a large ball of earthen material, and more alarmingly, to the wasplike creatures buzzing about it.

"Eh, be quick away!" he told his wife.

But he wasn't quick enough.

The large ball dropped from the eaves right behind him and began to unroll all about him and then over him, muffling his screams when it snapped shut around him, a cocoon of biting insects, relentless and vicious.

The woman shrieked and wailed. Others came to look.

But none approached, and so the old lecher lay there, writhing under a living, punishing blanket, screaming in torment until he expired from sheer agony, leaving him to scream eternally in the nether realms under the damning judgment of the little girl.

REGIS PUSHED OPEN A DOOR JUST A BIT, REVEALING THE second floor drawing room, a large, comfortably decorated chamber. To his left, the fireplace burned brightly, the light dancing upon the strange item hanging from the ceiling before it.

Entreri's cocoon.

The halfling-turned-little-girl gasped and turned back, motioning for Dahlia to hurry and join him. He entered the room, moving tentatively toward the strange wrapping. It didn't seem alive anymore, at least on the outside, and had taken on a crust more like that of a giant wasp's nest than the sod-like aspect it had originally worn.

"It might be him," Regis whispered when Dahlia hustled up beside him.

"It's him," the elven woman said definitively. "Help me cut it down."

Regis reverted to his normal form and pulled forth his dirk. He paused for a heartbeat and studied the weapon, noting that the side prongs, the snake-shaped swordcatchers, hadn't yet fully regrown. If they found a fight, he wouldn't yet have his garroting specter allies.

Before he could say anything, Dahlia grabbed him and hoisted him up high. He tried to avoid touching the demonic cocoon, but had to lean against it to gain enough leverage to finally cut the rope from which it hung.

Down it crashed, flopping over, but it did not fall open, and neither Dahlia nor Regis could find any seam.

"Cut it," the woman told him.

Regis carefully set the tip of his magical dirk against the strange substance. Trying hard to govern his movement, for he certainly didn't want to cut the man inside, he pressed and slid the weapon.

Its edge was fine, but it didn't even leave a mark on the unusual material.

Regis looked up at Dahlia and shrugged helplessly.

She took the dirk from his hand and fell over the cocoon, cutting, and when that utterly failed, she began stabbing the thing furiously, desperate to free the man she loved.

She couldn't make a mark in it.

"Well, isn't this convenient," Regis heard from the door, and he and Dahlia spun about to see a pair of Margaster women, Inkeri and Alvilda, enter the room.

FALLING? ROLLING.

Whydothestingsstillhurt? Somanybutnotnumb!

Paindiminishes . . . whynot?

I can't move . . . can't. Why still alive?

Alive?

Waspsupmynose . . . crawling biting . . . Mouth . . . Can't close my mouth.

No sound, no moving, no anything, nothingnothingnothing. Pain. Just
pain. Stingsandbites. Crawling little legs and stings.
Calmcalmcalm . . . calm . . . relax.
Whydothestingsstillhurt?
Calmcalm . . . calm. Think.
Pain!
Justicedeath?

SHARON STROLLED UP TO THE FALLEN COCOON ON THE
cobblestones outside the alleyway and nodded. She was neither pleased
nor distressed by her work.

For it wasn't really *her* work.

It was the man's own doing, after all, and now he had come to
face the truth of himself, in a most brutal and painful manner.

Sharon heard the woman sobbing behind her, at the edge of the
alley, so she turned and offered a smile, then skipped away, back to
House Margaster.

"I DO LOVE WHEN MY DINNER IS DELIVERED WITHOUT MY
even asking," Inkeri Margaster purred.

"Get him out of there!" Dahlia demanded, stamping her staff on
the floor, deftly working its mechanical-magical controls to break it
into three sections, a tri-staff. She grabbed the middle piece and
brought it up before her.

Inkeri laughed at her.

Regis licked his lips nervously. He thought he knew what to expect from Inkeri, for he had watched her turn into a glabrezu demon
in the caves beneath Lord Neverember's palace in Neverwinter City.
He pulled out the hand crossbow chained to his vest and raised it, first
at Inkeri.

He swung his arm, though, doubting he could affect the glabrezu,
hoping that he and Dahlia could defeat it, and instead let fly at Alvilda, a woman he had left unconscious once before.

She gasped when the dart struck her, and fell back. At the same time, Dahlia sent the two end sections of her tri-staff spinning, and she flipped the center section back and forth so that the outer two would occasionally collide, for that was how Kozah's Needle built its powerful lightning energy.

But at the same time, Inkeri shifted, so suddenly, and not into a four-armed glabrezu demon, as Regis had expected. Instead, the woman thickened, a carpet of orange hair sprouting all about her, her facial features turning apelike. Before Regis and Dahlia could even digest that transformation, the demon that was Inkeri leaped, easily clearing the twenty feet to crash between the two intruders, sending both Regis and Dahlia tumbling aside.

"Finish the other!" Dahlia yelled at Regis. The skilled warrior woman landed in a controlled roll, coming right back to her feet, her tri-staff working defensively as the massive Barlgura moved in for the kill. Her hands worked furiously, over and under, the end poles cracking at the demon's reaching claws, every strike eliciting a howl from the pained demon.

But she wasn't going to beat it, Regis believed, and he rushed at Alvilda, looking down desperately at his dirk once more to see if the snakes had regrown.

Regis didn't want to kill Alvilda. He had met her, dined with her, drank with her, conversed with her, and though he had never had any intention of actually sleeping with her, and his meeting with her was strictly for information gathering, he had come to like, or at least to genuinely not dislike, the funny and boisterous woman.

So he hoped that the drow sleeping poison would put her down before he arrived with his rapier.

But no, two other things happened instead. The room's door opened and the little white-eyed girl walked in, smiling still.

And Alvilda became human no more, her bones cracking and body reshaping, her shoulders widening and climbing higher, her nose and mouth coming forward into a snout, fangs growing, giant pincer claws tearing through her clothing as two lower arms sprouted.

Regis nearly fainted. He tried to call out to Dahlia, but only a squeak came forth. He looked to his rapier, so pitiful a weapon now, and he knew he could not possibly defeat this hulking monster.

DAHLIA PRESSED, HER TRI-STAFF BITING AT THE HULKING Barlgura, lightning arcs burning its orange hair and keeping it on its heels. She wasn't doing much real damage, but she pressed on, trying to find some opening, some way.

The demon leaped into the air, up and over her, and as she tracked it, she took up Kozah's Needle in one hand by the end and snapped it, whiplike, the other end piece delivering another shock.

Barlgura disappeared, turning invisible so suddenly that Dahlia had to remember what she was doing for a second. But she quickly regained her composure and rushed to keep up with the leap, trying to guess where it would land. She heard the thud as it came down a few strides ahead, only to hear that it had leaped again. And this time she wasn't able to track it.

She spun a circuit, working her staff to try to hold it at bay, and she did connect as she came around, scoring a hit, but too close! For the demon reappeared right near her, one massive fist coming in to slam her.

She put her arm up to block, felt the bone in her forearm snap, and found herself flying backward. Somehow she managed to align her body correctly to absorb the impact of her landing, but she still rolled about, grimacing in pain, trying to get up and get set.

For the demon stalked in.

GROGGY FROM THE POISON, ALVILDA FELT THE DEMON RIS-ing within her, taking control. It felt different this time, for she found herself in a strange fugue, as if she was perpetrating the actions but was not, a weird duality that sparked in her the thought that the demon was not a separate being.

That she was the demon.

She looked at the advancing halfling, whom she knew by the name of Regis Topolino of Bleeding Vines—such a pitiful thing indeed. But then the door opened, and Alvilda could not ignore the child who entered.

Her child.

Her beloved little Sharon.

Sharon looked at the halfling and smiled, and despite his obviously desperate situation, Regis, Alvilda sensed, calmed quite profoundly at the presentation of the little girl's judgment.

Sharon's *pleasant* judgment.

Alvilda didn't understand, but she fought back suddenly to stay the demon's killing pincers.

She heard the growl of the glabrezu. It reverberated through every bit of her body and mind. The most profound rage, murderous, wicked, demanding.

"It's okay, Mummy," Sharon said, and the words hit Alvilda like a bolt.

And she woke as if from a dream.

The glabrezu growled.

Alvilda Margaster, the mother of the child in the doorway who had been so corrupted, growled louder.

The hulking glabrezu demon leaped.

The blood drained from the halfling's face.

But the demon went over Regis, landing in a barreling charge, pincers clamping about the waist and neck of Barlgura!

THE ROOM SHOOK, THE HOUSE SHOOK AS THE POWERFUL demons grappled, the glabrezu's pincers cutting deep lines, Barlgura's fists pounding at the dog-faced fiend.

Not about to miss the opportunity, Dahlia snapped her tri-staff into the face of Barlgura, even taking out a long fang with one crack. When the two tumbled aside, she brought the staff back in and began that spinning motion once more to build up a powerful charge of lightning, then sealed it together into a singular quarterstaff once more. Her broken left arm throbbed with agony, but she couldn't let it slow her. Not now.

Up came Barlgura, dragging the glabrezu with it, both massive hands clasped upon the pincer about its throat. Corded muscles bulging under the strain, Barlgura pulled that pincer open, and kept pulling, snapping the base of the claw and drawing a shriek from the glabrezu.

The fight was going to be over soon, so Dahlia struck hard and true, driving the butt of her staff right into the face of Barlgura, then brilliantly twisting the staff down to loop it under the heavy necklace of her adversary, where she released all of the energy, a lightning bolt that snapped the demon's head back from the sheer force and blew apart the metal chain holding the phylactery ruby, leaving Barlgura momentarily dazed.

The ruby flew aside and Inkeri Margaster reflexively grabbed control of the stunned demon creature, the hulking form shifting suddenly to that of the human woman, albeit briefly.

But long enough for the flailing glabrezu to whip its arm with the broken claw up and across, one blade of the pincer slashing across the woman's already-torn throat.

Inkeri and Barlgura started to shift back to the demonic form, but too late, and the beast fell to the side, the head nearly severed, caught halfway between human and demon.

The glabrezu leaped about to face Dahlia, but both the demon and the elf jumped back and paused when the little red-haired girl walked up between them.

"Give me your necklace, Mummy," she said sweetly.

The glabrezu shuddered, the two beings within fighting for control.

The little girl climbed right up and, with surprisingly dexterous and clever fingers, removed the silver chain hung with the milky-blue moonstone.

The glabrezu shuddered, the little girl fell back, stumbling to the floor, then came up beside Dahlia, who started to shy in fear—until she noticed a second little girl still standing in the doorway, smiling.

The little girl beside her held up the phylactery.

"Kill it, Mummy," she whispered.

The demon form shrank, became Alvilda, then the glabrezu again, then Alvilda once more, and in that moment, the moonstone on the silver chain suddenly sparkled, receiving the spirit.

Alvilda Margaster fell back.

The little girl beside Dahlia became Regis once more. He immediately went to his magical pouch, pulling forth a jar filled with some dark liquid. Off came the cap and he dropped the phylactery in, then quickly replaced and sealed the top.

Dahlia moved to finish Alvilda, but Regis grabbed her by the arm. "No!"

"You cannot—"

"No, I beg," the halfling said. "She's no threat." He pulled at Dahlia's arm with all his strength, holding her back.

Dahlia growled. "What about her?" she asked, nodding to the door and the child. Out in the hallway, they heard sounds—house guards, no doubt.

"They're all afraid of the child, but it won't last," Regis reasoned. "Come on! Run!"

Regis jumped over to the fallen cocoon. Scared but out of options, he bent low and rolled it up onto his shoulder, then moved on shaky legs toward the room's large window, which overlooked the house's main door, one story below.

Dahlia helped him as much as she could manage through the pain, and when they got to the window, she didn't wait to search for a latch, just poked Kozah's Needle through it and released whatever remaining lightning it could offer, enough to shatter the window into a spiderweb design, glass raining on the cobblestones below.

That brought a howl from the corridor beyond the room. "The front door!" more than one voice yelled.

Regis quick-stepped forward to the sill and kept shoving. "Forgive me," he whispered, and he let the cocoon tumble out, then rolled over the sill behind it, wincing when he heard the sickening splat below.

A frantic Dahlia came down behind him, cursing and promising great pain, but the cocoon remained intact.

"The coach! Quickly!" Regis told her.

He began to hoist the cocoon once more. "Oh, but you're going to pay me back," he mumbled, thinking of the dangerous man inside. "If you're still alive."

Strangely, he actually hoped that Artemis Entreri *was* still alive—more than he had ever imagined he would hope for such a thing.

Dahlia drove up, leaped down from the bench, and pulled open the door of the fancy carriage, then helped Regis bundle Entreri inside. Regis beat her back up to the bench and snapped the reins, the team surging down the cobblestoned drive as the front door banged open and the shouts began behind them.

FALLING . . . FALLING . . . FALLINGFALLINGFALLING!

No sound, no moving, no anything, nothingnothingnothing. Pain. Just pain. But justthebitesjustthebites. Whyjustthebites? Stingsandbites. Crawling little legs and stings.

Calmcalmcalm . . . calm . . . relax.

Whydothestingsstillhurt?

Calmcalm . . . calm. Think.

Pain!

ALVILDA MARGASTER SAT ON THE FLOOR AGAINST AN overturned chair, trembling and crying.

"Don't be afraid, Mummy," Sharon said, and Alvilda glanced over at her, then gasped.

Her little girl had gray eyes again!

But back behind Sharon was yet another doppelganger, the same little girl, red locks bouncing, skipping out the door.

"Don't be afraid, Mummy," Sharon assured her. "She is my friend."

"She is a monster," a shocked Alvilda responded.

"No, Mummy. She teaches me. She shows me. She is my friend."

Alvilda stared at her, dumbfounded, horrified.

"Like you told me for Uncle Brevindon."

"Uncle Brevindon?"

"Yes, Mummy."

"That he was . . ." Alvilda paused in shock, thinking of what she had heard at Sharon's bedroom door. "That she is your *mentor*?" Alvilda asked, remembering the mumbling.

"Yes!" Sharon announced. "She shows me when I'm good or bad. I want to be good, Mummy."

"Mentor . . . tormentor," Alvilda whispered under her breath, dumbstruck and confused. She looked to the door, her jaw hanging open.

REGIS DROVE THE CARRIAGE MORE SLOWLY ALONG THE streets of Waterdeep, trying not to draw attention. The Margasters had been left far behind.

Where to go? the halfling wondered. Should he take the cocooned Entreri to the Waterdeep lords? Which lords? Who in this city could he trust?

"Yasgur?" Regis asked as they turned down a main boulevard, the city gates in sight.

"I am with you," they both heard, a child's voice wafting on the night breeze. Regis stood, Dahlia turned and rose, and both looked back over the carriage roof. In the distance, they caught sight of a small curly-haired girl in a flowing white gown floating down the road.

Dahlia fell, gasping, clutching at her arm, but obviously more disturbed by shock than by pain. "The whip, the whip," she implored her companion.

"She won't hurt us," Regis said, but he was more surprised than Dahlia by the confidence in his words. Still, he believed it, and he hesitated.

Frustrated by his slow response and with a growl against the pain,

Dahlia tugged the reins from his hands, held them loosely in the hand of her broken arm, then pulled the whip from the halfling's grasp and applied it liberally to the two black horses pulling the coach.

Away they rambled, out of Waterdeep and along the north road.

"Give them over," Regis implored her. "You cannot with your arm."

Dahlia stared at him incredulously and threateningly, but in truth, she was in no condition to argue. Pained, distressed, the elf woman surrendered the reins, then sank back against the bench seat and fought hard to slow her breathing. She clasped her good hand over her broken arm to try to keep it steady as the carriage bounced along.

She still managed to chastise Regis every time he let the team slow.

PAIN . . . BITINGSTINGING.
Crawling. On me in me.
Pain! Calm.
Pain. Calm.
Calmcalmcalmcalmcalm. Aplacetohideaplacedeep . . . calm.
Fallaway, away, leave . . . go . . .

CHAPTER 26

Down Below

"Matron Zhindia Melarn will win," Sos'Umptu Baenre told her sister, Matron Mother Quenthel Baenre, on the morning of the day when the Ruling Council was set to convene.

"A guess or a certainty?"

"Gromph sees it," Sos'Umptu reported. "He disabled the magical portals of Gauntlgrym because he knows. The powers arrayed against King Bruenor and Luskan are too formidable, and Matron Zhindia is accompanied by a pair of handmaidens *and* a pair of retrievers."

The matron mother sighed and nodded, those last tidbits already known to her. "Matron Zhindia will win, House Melarn will know all glory, and they will return here at the head of a demon army."

"You think she would dare threaten House Baenre?" Quenthel tried to speak confidently, tried to show incredulity at the mere mention of such a thing. She felt as if she had fallen short of that mark, though, and when she looked at Sos'Umptu, she saw that her sister shared her doubts. Sos'Umptu was one of the most powerful drow in

Menzoberranzan. She was the high priestess of the Fane of the Goddess, a public cathedral she had created that was exerting more and more influence among the commoners and lesser houses of the city. She remained the mistress of Arach-Tinilith, the drow academy for priestesses, and was still first priestess of House Baenre, at least until Quenthel could finish grooming her daughter Myrineyl to assume the position. And Sos'Umptu sat on the Ruling Council as the Ninth Seat, an unprecedented move by the matron mother to pack the Council in her favor.

"I do not think that she will have to," Sos'Umptu replied. "Her heroics on the surface and in Gauntlgrym will move her house above all of our allies, and her obvious blessing by Lady Lolth may cause them to reconsider their alliances. The order in Menzoberranzan will be shaken to its core, even more so because the heretics Drizzt and Zaknafein were allowed to walk free from your own dungeons."

"They were freed on the word of Yvonnel," Matron Mother Quenthel reminded her. She regretted the words as soon as she had spoken them, for they made her seem small indeed, diminished. How could anyone walk free of the dungeons of House Baenre without Quenthel's command, after all?

"And where is she now?" Sos'Umptu asked with a shrug. "Hardly relevant."

"So what would you propose?"

"Join in Matron Zhindia's campaign," said Sos'Umptu.

Matron Mother Baenre felt very insignificant, so suddenly. How quickly could the tides turn in the City of Spiders! Just a few months before, after the fall of Demogorgon at the city's gates, House Baenre had seemed more secure than ever in its perch atop the hierarchy. House Melarn, ever a thorn, had been battered and moved down the ranks. Quenthel had orchestrated the Ruling Council to keep her closest allies in positions of great power, and had even reconstituted House Xorlarrin under Matron Zeerith, giving her an ally as powerful as the city's Second House, Barrison Del'Armgo, and Matron Mez'Barris, perhaps her only true rival.

Despite all of that, though, Matron Mother Quenthel Baenre understood her vulnerability here. This great house, the ruling house of Menzoberranzan for millennia, was in a dangerous generational transition now. All of Matron Mother Yvonnel Baenre's female children were gone except for Quenthel and Sos'Umptu. And of the two remaining sons of the great Yvonnel, Gromph, though perhaps an ally, was no longer even of the city, and Jarlaxle hadn't ever really been a part of House Baenre in the first place.

When she looked across the room at the only other person present, Quenthel was reminded of this fact quite poignantly, for there stood Minolin Fey Baenre, a weakling priestess who was only a member of this court because she had carried the child of Gromph.

For several years now, Matron Mother Quenthel had known that she had to bide her time until the many promising young Baenre nobles could more fully step into their roles. Thus she had weakened the Faerzress to bring demon hordes into Menzoberranzan, deflecting any potential power grabs by rival houses. Thus she had funded the Fane of the Goddess and elevated Sos'Umptu to a position of great power. Thus she had reconstructed House Do'Urden into a reincarnation of House Xorlarrin, returning her most important ally, Matron Zeerith, who hated Matron Mez'Barris profoundly.

Would that rivalry even hold, though, if Zhindia Melarn returned to Menzoberranzan after such a tremendous victory on the surface, with the heretics given to Lolth, Gauntlgrym conquered (after King Bruenor had taken it from Zeerith Xorlarrin in the failed attempt by Matron Mother Quenthel to have the Xorlarrins secure the complex for use as a satellite city to Menzoberranzan, no less), and with a horde of demon allies?

"Should we summon Gromph?" Sos'Umptu offered.

"No," the matron mother retorted without hesitation. "If he has surrendered to Matron Zhindia, then he cannot be trusted."

Mistress Sos'Umptu nodded obediently, then, despite her legendary composure, winced noticeably when Quenthel added, "Not that I ever trusted our murderous brother anyway."

Gromph, after all, had tried to assassinate Quenthel on more than one occasion when their sister Triel had sat on the house throne as Matron Mother Baenre.

"No," Quenthel said again, nodding, for many things were becoming clear to her. "No, you," she said, motioning to Minolin Fey, "go to House Barrison Del'Armgo and inform Matron Mez'Barris that I would speak with her privately this day, before the Council sits."

Sos'Umptu and Minolin Fey exchanged skeptical looks.

"We will march," Matron Mother Quenthel told them. "We will all march." To Minolin Fey, she said bluntly, "Go!" and the woman scampered out of the room.

"What are you thinking, Matron Mother?" Sos'Umptu dared to ask when the sisters were alone.

"Long ago, our mother, the great Yvonnel the Eternal, the first and greatest Matron Mother Baenre, intervened in a relatively minor affair involving the attempted assassination of a weapon master of a relatively minor house by the matron of another supposedly minor house."

Sos'Umptu showed no recollection.

"You were not included in the discussion or the planning," Quenthel said to her. "It was all left to Gromph, Triel, and myself. The weapon master we saved was Zaknafein Do'Urden. The plotting assassin was no other than Matron Soulez Armgo, mother of Matron Mez'Barris."

"I still do not understand."

"A strange coincidence, given where we are now, wouldn't you agree?"

"You think it more than that?" Sos'Umptu replied, her doubts clear. "You think it all fated? All of it? With such foresight as to know that Zaknafein would sire the heretic Drizzt? That is—"

"No," Matron Mother Quenthel interrupted. "But perhaps it was done with some knowledge that the spark resided in Zaknafein before Drizzt, perhaps."

Sos'Umptu was shaking her head.

"Matron Mother Yvonnel's prayers to Lolth led us to that place that long-ago night to interfere with the Armgo plans. I know this, intimately."

Sos'Umptu bowed her head respectfully then, catching the reminder that Quenthel had been given the memories of Matron Mother Yvonnel Baenre. Not told the memories or even shown the memories—an illithid had imparted them into Quenthel's mind and so they were her memories as surely as they had been Yvonnel's.

"Or perhaps it is merely coincidence," Matron Mother Quenthel admitted. "But still, to see where this has led us with Zaknafein and with Matron Mez'Barris is quite remarkable."

"We are neither a populous nation nor a large city," Sos'Umptu reminded her. "What may seem like coincidence may be no more than simple proximity."

"You counsel wisely, as always," the matron mother said. "Still, here we are. We cannot allow Matron Zhindia to win and return triumphant in unshared glory."

"So House Baenre will march?"

"Menzoberranzan will march," the matron mother corrected. "In all her power."

THE BARBARIAN BIT DOWN ON THE CLOTH-WRAPPED STRIP of metal, making no sound but a growl as the dark elf priestess squeezed hard against the scarred line, balls of white pus popping forth between her pinching fingers. Wulfgar's shoulder, neck, and arm muscles corded and flexed to their limits.

Dab'nay quickly cast a spell, sending purifying healing into the opened wound. Then she backed up, one hand on Wulfgar's shoulder as she helped ease him forward so that he could properly vomit into the bucket she had put before him.

For all his size and strength, Wulfgar suddenly seemed very frail, and his oily spit subsequent to his puking came with growls of complete frustration.

"I am doing all that I can for you," Dab'nay snapped at him.

He nodded, then vomited again.

"And only because Kimmuriel ordered me to do so," she added.

Wulfgar spent a moment composing himself, clearing his mouth and making sure that there was no more vomit on its way. "Just get me to the Hosttower, I beg, and to the portal, that I might rejoin my friends in Gauntlgrym."

"You cannot," Dab'nay told him.

The door opened and Beniago entered the room. "The portals are closed," he said, and it was clear that he had been listening. He motioned to Dab'nay, who gladly took her leave.

"Then Gromph will send me."

"He will not. It was he who closed the portals. He has declared the neutrality of the Hosttower in this fight."

"Then another wizard!" Wulfgar said with as much strength as he could muster.

"None will oblige you," Beniago told him. "The Hosttower is neutral."

"Kimmuriel, then!"

Beniago shrugged.

"Is there no way for me to get to Gauntlgrym?"

Another shrug from the drow who remained in his disguise as a red-haired human. "Can you even stand?" he asked with a chuckle.

"Soon enough," Wulfgar promised.

"Then you could go through the Underdark tunnels or overland, but either way, you would almost certainly be killed before you reached the dwarven complex. And even if not, how would you get in? Gauntlgrym is surrounded by an army of demons and hostile drow."

"Kimmuriel could get me in!"

Beniago shrugged again, then stepped aside as Kimmuriel walked through the door.

"You are alive because of me," Kimmuriel stated.

Wulfgar stared at him hard, but couldn't disagree.

"I did not keep you alive because I care at all that you are alive," the drow added.

"Jarlaxle told you to protect me."

Kimmuriel snorted. "That matters not. You remain here now and I have sent a priestess to tend you because I desire your assistance."

"Then promise me that journey to Gauntlgrym."

"No. But you will help me."

Wulfgar narrowed his eyes even more.

"I suspect that you wish to kill Brevindon Margaster and the demon that holds him even more than I," Kimmuriel said.

That had Wulfgar leaning back and widening his eyes in surprise. "You are surrounded by powerful allies, powerful warriors."

"I doubt any of them could deliver the physical blow I desire."

Wulfgar considered that for a moment, then nodded. "Lead on."

But Kimmuriel was shaking his head. "There is much to settle about us in Luskan," he explained. "When it settles as I foresee, I will call upon you. Until then, heal. I doubt you will survive our attack."

That had Wulfgar looking back curiously.

"The death of this demon leading the attack on Luskan will be worth your sacrifice, should that come to pass," Kimmuriel said. "I am sure you agree with that."

After a moment of consideration, Wulfgar answered, "I do."

"Ah, a true warrior, as I suspected. To die does not frighten you—"

"I have died before," Wulfgar interrupted.

Kimmuriel looked at him in shock for just a moment, and Wulfgar smiled when he plowed ahead, for such a detail simply wasn't going to be important enough to the drow for him to bother asking for an elaboration.

"Your honor is far more important, and losing that honor would be worse than death," Kimmuriel said. "So, I offer you the chance to strike a great blow for your friends in the south, and yes, for Jarlaxle and we drow who rule in Luskan. But at great risk. You have felt the bite of Brevindon's blade."

"Give me one strike," Wulfgar replied. "I will not miss him a second time."

"It will not be on a ship that you stupidly sink beneath us, at least," Kimmuriel said dryly as he walked out of the room.

Wulfgar sat alone, trying to find his center, trying to expel the fever, the pus, the pain. When the door opened yet again, he looked up to see Bonnie Charlee entering.

"I will kill Brevindon Margaster and the red-skinned demon elf he harbors inside," Wulfgar told her determinedly before she could even begin to ask the many questions obviously stirring within her.

"Ye seem certain," she replied.

Wulfgar nodded, and the motion induced another round of vomiting.

SHE WAS IN HER OWN THRONE ROOM, BUT MATRON Mez'Barris couldn't help but squirm a little at the array of power that had come in to see her after her refusal to meet the matron mother in her home ground of House Baenre.

Five matrons, Quenthel Baenre included, and their entourages of powerful drow priestesses, wizards, and warriors, stood before her—or in Matron Zeerith Xorlarrin's case, sat before her on a floating and decorated magical disk, and in Matron Mother Baenre's case, sat upon an ornate purple-and-black throne, some portable seat more impressive than the throne of House Barrison Del'Armgo.

Mez'Barris licked her lips, pondering the offer put before her. "If I die, someone will replace me," she told Matron Mother Baenre.

"If I die, you know who will replace me," Quenthel replied.

Mez'Barris considered it for just a moment, glancing at priestess Sos'Umptu, who stood resolutely beside her sister. But no, she realized, Sos'Umptu did not want the mantle of Matron Mother.

"Yvonnel," Mez'Barris answered, barely able to spit the name of Gromph's powerful and unusual daughter, a drow child still, but in the body of a young woman and with the command, wisdom, intelligence, and experience of her namesake.

"Yvonnel," the Matron Mother confirmed.

"Is she even in Menzoberranzan?"

"She will be a thousand times your nightmare," Quenthel continued, ignoring the question. "For she is staked in this and will remember your refusal. She will not tolerate you, Matron Mez'Barris, nor the continuing games of your house."

"Are you threatening war, Matron Mother?"

"Not I. I have no such desire. But I am certain of the path Matron Mother Yvonnel would pursue."

Mez'Barris glanced around at her house nobles.

"A thousand times your nightmare," the matron mother reiterated. "And perhaps I have more to offer."

Soon after, a vast army marched out of Menzoberranzan, aided by magic to speed their way to the lower gates of Gauntlgrym. Such an army had not marched from the drow city in more than a century, the last march of the great Yvonnel the Eternal, Matron Mother Baenre, in her desire to conquer Mithral Hall.

The drow academies lay silent; the drow houses, noble and common, lay silent.

The tunnels of the Underdark cleared before them, for none of the denizens of this dark place wanted to face the full power of Menzoberranzan bared.

CHAPTER 27

The End

The vampire Thibbledorf Pwent sat on the Throne of the Dwarven Gods in the empty entry hall of Gauntlgrym. The dwarves had rushed through to the deeper chambers, dropping the entry block wall behind them. Now that wall was shaking, bits of stone falling from it from the battering on the other side.

"Ah, me gods, what've ye given me here?" the dwarf asked. "Take me home, Moradin. Ye got me caught twixt me heart and me hunger. Aye, the hunger. She's always there—or better called the thirst. Sweet blood."

Over to his right, the wall collapsed and the giant spider golem crashed through, skittering across the floor, turning up sideways on the wall to fit through the door leading to the lower levels.

Thibbledorf Pwent shook his head, not even knowing what that might mean. What monster, this?

He saw the demons pouring in behind. Surely Bruenor and the others had known this would happen, that the wall could never hold against such a horde. Why had they run?

To his surprise, there came the sound of terrific fighting, suddenly, in the chambers just beyond the entry hall.

Pwent hopped up from the throne, his corporeal form beginning to dissolve into mere smoke even as he landed. Off the vampire flew to investigate. It didn't take him long to understand that the dwarves now fighting demons furiously in the corridors and chambers beyond had let the spider monster pass.

But why?

Down flew Pwent, quickly catching up to the giant arachnid golem as it scrambled along the descending ways of Gauntlgrym, moving down walls in the high-ceilinged lower caverns with spidery ease, spitting a spindle of webbing at one point to accelerate its descent. Not a dwarf stood against it, not a crossbow quarrel or catapult payload flew to intercept the spider's run.

As they came into the lower chambers and tunnels, the sounds of the demon battle fading far behind, Pwent realized the spider's destination, and in gaseous form, he actually flew ahead of the monster into the most coveted chamber, wherein sat the Great Forge of Gauntlgrym.

It was empty of dwarves.

By Moradin's hairy beard, me king, what're ye doing? Pwent thought.

He noted that the door to the primordial's chamber was more than open; in fact, it had been removed, revealing the short tunnel from the forge room to the large pit which held the godlike beast.

Pwent hesitated, but the spider did not, scrambling down that corridor, squealing loudly as if in sudden and hungry pursuit.

Pwent followed, but before he ever entered that chamber, he heard a tremendous rumble, shouting dwarves, and a screeching spider, and as he entered, he was greeted by the blinding flash of a monstrous lightning bolt.

THIS IS MADNESS, ZAKNAFEIN'S FINGERS SIGNALED IN THE intricate drow hand code to Jarlaxle, who stood beside him at the far end of a most wondrous chamber, a long cavern bathed in an orange

glow from the roiling fires and lava of the primordial beast that powered the forges of Gauntlgrym. Trapped in a deep chasm along the
back half of the room, to Zaknafein's right as he looked back to the
corner where sat the entry door, the godlike beast's movements kept
the chamber constantly vibrating. Water elementals swirled about just
below the lip of that gorge, constantly reinforced by sheets of water
raining down from the ceiling above.

As we asked King Bruenor to trust us, so we should trust him, Jarlaxle's fingers moved in reply. *He has earned that much, many times over.*

Zaknafein glanced past his friend to the dwarf in the one-horned
helm, small buckler on one arm, many-notched axe in the other. He
tried to dismiss his doubts—how might they trust a dwarf? And a surface dwarf at that!

The world seemed so mixed up to poor Zaknafein then. All of his
life had been spent in learning the truth of the world, but that, he
was beginning to understand, was the truth of the drow world only.
And it was a truth distorted by ill intent. All that he had learned—
nay, more than learned, had come to *know* as truth—seemed to him
then like a knot beginning to loosen, as if his world was on the edge
of fully unwinding.

A crash down the way, beyond the door at the far end of the left-
hand wall, demanded his attention.

"So be it," the drow weapon master muttered, and he prepared
to die.

Bruenor had lured the spider here and had set the wall to the right
with a line of strange and huge wheeled contraptions—*juicers,* Bruenor had called them.

The whole thing seemed ridiculous to Zaknafein. Comical, even,
except that his life was among those on the line here.

Into the room crashed the spider, taking pieces of the door and
wall with it. It slid a bit as it scrambled to turn, and Zaknafein had a
fleeting moment of hope that it would pitch over into the fiery chasm.

But no, on it came, straight for him, staring at him, he knew.

One of its eyes flared and a beam of greenish light shot down at
Zaknafein, and for a moment he felt his heart stop.

In shock, though, and not from the beam, for the invisible wall of force Jarlaxle had enacted before them did its job and stopped the monster's ray.

But the spider came on, its focus fully on Zaknafein.

Then did the dwarven teams along the wall leap into action, taking up the poles of the juicers and driving the heavy contraptions forward, broadsiding the massive demonic golem. With roars and cheers, the dwarves pressed on, lifting the side of the spider with the angled front plates of the war machines. Four of the spider's legs waved up above the front of those contraptions, trying to gain a hold, the mighty retriever teetering on the very edge of the chasm!

But there the dwarves stalled, the spider holding fast to the floor and now regaining its stability and fighting back. Another of its eyes arched with tingles of sudden power. The chamber shook with a thunderous retort.

The farthest juicer shattered and smoldered, its team down and writhing, the target of the monster's lightning bolt, and the abyssal nightmare quickly gained the advantage, turning to bring its eyes up over the top of the juicer wall, several of them glowing with mounting magical power.

"For my son!" Zaknafein cried, sprinting and feeling his way around the wall of force, swords in hand.

He charged at the retriever, his distraction complete, and the beast turned on him suddenly, eyes sparkling with eagerness and power.

A blast of webbing flew forth from one, but Zaknafein fell to his knees and bent backward, sliding right beneath the sticky trap. The weapon master came up into his continuing run, determined to close those last few strides.

"Me king!" came a bellow before him and to the left, and despite his focus, Zaknafein couldn't help but gawk for just an eyeblink, seeing the strangest dwarf he had ever imagined, a veritable ball of spikes and edges, running, leaping, flying even—flying?—across and above the struggling juicer teams, launching himself with some magic Zaknafein did not understand right into the side of the retriever's head, spiked fists driving hard.

"WHERE DO YOU INTEND TO GO?" REGIS ASKED, THE CAR-
riage still bouncing along. He had just been awakened from a short
nap, having handed the reins to Dahlia, by a particularly powerful jolt.
"I doubt we'll be able to find our way into Gauntlgr—"

The carriage jerked to the side. Dahlia yelped and slapped herself
on the cheek.

"What?" Regis asked, trying to help her slow the team. He looked
down as he grabbed the reins and saw a dark spot on the bench seat,
an insect Dahlia had slapped, now spinning about as if trying to fly.

"Ow!" Dahlia called again, and again, and Regis had to pull with
all his strength to stop the carriage from pitching into a ditch at the
side of the road.

He glanced at Dahlia as soon as he could, and found her slapping—
even with her broken arm—at several wasplike insects buzzing about
her face. For a moment, he figured that they must have ridden over
a ground-wasp nest, but then he caught a clear glimpse of one of
the insects, a face more human than bug, and he knew they were in
trouble.

Then he heard the humming of a swarm behind him, right behind him, and he feared they were doomed.

He fumbled unsuccessfully with the reins, for the wagon had run
into mud at the side of the road. "Run!" he yelled, and scrambled down
from the bench seat.

Dahlia leaped down opposite him and quickly broke her staff into
a pair of nunchaku, spinning them about like horsetails fending off
flies, banging them together to build that magical lightning charge.
She grimaced in pain with every contact, her broken arm throbbing.

The swarm suddenly grew loud as the carriage door on Regis's side
fell open and a cloud of the tiny creatures flew out.

The blood drained from Regis's face, but they went right by him,
sweeping over the horses without a single sting, flying in at Dahlia.

She cried out and spun, clacking the nunchaku together to release
arcs of lightning, getting stung or bit or both repeatedly, then finally
falling and rolling, flailing desperately. She managed a larger burst of

lightning, a shock that widened out from her and blasted her as well as the attacking creatures, leaving a rain of them falling dead about her, and leaving her shaking wildly, smoke wafting from her clothes.

The remaining wasplike monsters flew away.

Regis ran to her and helped her up to her knees, where she remained for a long while, sobbing, aching, her face swelling, eyes puffy.

"We have to go," he implored her.

She nodded, cringing in pain, and struggled to her feet, cradling that agonized arm.

"They came out of the carriage," Regis explained, and moved with her to the open door.

Inside, the cocoon enwrapping Entreri lay still, though it had tumbled from the seat and was half on the floor, including the end from which it had been hanging from the ceiling.

Dahlia wailed, for that end of the strange sarcophagus, lying near the door, continued to spew the wasplike beasts. She had been stung or bitten a dozen times and the excruciating pain remained, but it was clear now that these little monsters had been feasting on her beloved for days!

She crashed her nunchaku down on the end of the wrap, one after another, pulsing forth the last bolts of lightning, frying the little monsters before they could get clear, charring the end of the cocoon. Her rage overcoming the pain, Dahlia grabbed the cocoon and dragged it out of the carriage to flop limply onto the ground, then began tearing at the burned top of it. She pulled a knife from her belt and stabbed at it repeatedly, viciously, frantically.

"No! No!" she cried every time she paused to inspect it to see that she had caused no real damage.

"Dahlia," Regis quietly called to her. "Dahlia. We have to leave."

"Help me!" she yelled at him.

"Dahlia, not now. We have to leave."

She looked up at him and sneered, but her anger mellowed when she came to realize that Regis wasn't even looking at her as he spoke, but was staring back the way they had come. Dahlia snapped her head around.

The little white-eyed girl was floating down the road toward them, smiling.

So horribly smiling.

"Help me," Dahlia cried, grabbing at the cocoon and trying to hoist it back into the carriage.

"He's gone, Dahli—"

"Help me!" Her voice promised murder, and it was no idle threat.

The two bundled the cocoon into the carriage again and scrambled to the bench, where Dahlia grabbed the reins and whipped the team until they dragged the carriage out of the mud and thundered down the road once more.

The woman passed out soon after, exhausted and agonized.

They had already put Waterdeep far behind them and the team was tired, but Regis kept them rolling to the north.

WHAT MAD DWARF WAS THIS, ZAKNAFEIN WONDERED, FOR the fool—the dear, brave fool—threw himself right into the retriever's face, giant mandibles snapping closed about him, and took the full blast of the demon golem's next magical beam—a bolt that began to turn him to stone.

Zaknafein couldn't question it, and could only hope that what was now a statue of a dwarf would block any more magical rays.

But no! For even as Zaknafein closed those last steps, his swords slashing hard at the nearest spider leg, the strange dwarf became a cloud of gas.

Then became a dwarf again, flesh and not stone.

"Me Pwent!" Zaknafein heard King Bruenor yell from not far behind.

"Me king!" the dwarf, Pwent, yelled in response, punching at the golem's eyes with his spiked gauntlets, drawing shrieks of protest from the spider as it worked furiously to expel him, and drawing cheers and cries of "Press harder!" from the scores of dwarves manning the juicers.

Pwent fell fully into his battle-rage, pounding with abandon, ignoring the mandibles as they clenched about him once again. Zakna-fein furiously attacked the nearest leg, trying to break its hold.

"Ah, ye dog!" the dwarf yelled.

Zaknafein glanced up. Lightning arced between the spider's eyes and the weapon master could feel the buildup of another explosive bolt. He saw it on the dwarf's face, and knew it, too: this brave fool was doomed.

Just before the bolt came forth, though, a glob of goo flew between the dwarf and the spider's face, green and glutinous, binding the dwarf to the monster arachnid, both his arms fully encompassed.

Zaknafein spun his head to see the source, Jarlaxle, with King Bruenor and his two queens running right beside him.

A king running in to near-certain death for the sake of his friends.

That thought stunned Zaknafein. What matron mother would do that?

And to Zaknafein's further surprise, King Bruenor seemed no dwarf then, but a giant, and one growing larger with every stride.

Zaknafein had to dodge to the side when Bruenor charged in, shield-rushing the first juicer in line, hitting it with tremendous force—more than the press of all the other dwarves pushing it.

Up higher went the retriever, and the dwarves pressed on all along the line, turning the monster up on its side and then over.

Down it tumbled, the wild Pwent still attached, several juicers fall-ing over behind it. One struck the spider monster as it tried to catch the wall, another coincidentally intercepting a line of webbing the spider managed to pull forth and launch.

Zaknafein twisted and contorted, his swords falling free, to leave him hanging by his fingers on the edge of the chasm.

IS THIS DEATH, THEN?

So this is death-mystery-obliteration-annihilation, the final fall, the ring around the rosy, the crack of the neck at the end of the rope, the head falling from the axeman's blade, the last breath of crushed lungs, the last link of guts removed. Fouler than life, ohfieohdamnohcurseyoualleternally! The piffy end of the dream, not great, all whisper of curses.

Foulfoulfoulfoulbloodycursesall!

Damn life! Touched briefly, too briefly, so briefly! Joy of Calihye, warmth of Dahlia, embrace of Jarlaxle, respect of Drizzt? Oh fie, I know not, ohfieohdamnohcurseyoualleternally!

Life, the dream, pfft, gone . . . and filledfilledfilled by stench, nostrils thick. Just stench, always stench. I deny the stench, but no, and now I am guilty? How am I? What justice? Coldhearted world of pale pains, moonlit monochrome with sunlit days too short. Eyeblink of light. Just an eyeblink. Snap! An image, a moment. Stolen!

Ohfieohdamnohcurseyoualleternally!

Too long . . . too long! Heartbeats of sparkles, hours of hate and guilt. So much blood, warming my wrist, my arm, caked on my eyes.

So much poison, so much pain.

One hope, one ask, just one, but no, I cannot die to escape the pain— nay! Nay, now I know, no escape, and now there is only hopelessness-deep-emptiness-darkness-darkness-evermore. Beyond the bites of a thousand-million-thousand wasps, little fires, unceasing pain . . .

The sting, the burn, the images flashflashflash. Calihye! The victim, the victim, the victim. Dahlia! The victim, the victim, the victim. Jarlaxle! The victim, the victim, the victim. So many, the victims. My victims, so many!

You knew! Drizzt, you knew. Ohfieohdamnohcurseyoueternally!

But no.

No.

No!

I cannot!

Would that I had used my dagger upon myself! No existence . . . no existence . . . that, so I learn too late, my only heaven.

Ohfieohdamnohcursemyselfeternally—

. . .

HANGING FROM THE LEDGE, ZAKNAFEIN LOOKED DOWN through the heavy mist to the orange glow of the lavalike primordial.

He saw one of the juicers, breaking apart from bouncing off the wall, hit the lava, immediately bursting into flames. He saw the spider golem hit, on its back, shrieking and scrabbling and trying to throw a web out.

Some darkness that he thought a cloud of smoke rose up, but then took form as a large bat, flying up from the pit.

The spider almost righted itself, but a tendril of lava rose beside it, near enough for Zaknafein to feel the sudden and sharp increase in heat, then broke like a wave over the abyssal monster, also splashing the rising bat.

The shrieking stopped immediately, drowned out under the heavy molten substance, and the lava flattened as if digesting the golem.

Zaknafein tried to hold, tried to dig in a boot to help him climb.

He felt a hand clamp over his own left, then another over his right, and he looked up to see not one but two rescuers, the queens of Gauntlgrym grabbing him and hoisting him.

Back on his feet on the ledge, Zaknafein digested the scene around him, with dwarves scrambling every which way to help their injured, and there were many. To his left, Jarlaxle rushed at him, but then stopped abruptly and fell back a step.

Zaknafein understood when he heard the shriek behind him, then turned and ducked fast as the large bat, one wing licked with flames, fluttered past, then down to the right and out of the chamber.

"Thibbledorf," he heard Queen Mallabritches say.

"The Pwent," added her sister, Tannabritches.

It was all beyond Zaknafein, but he was surely impressed by the dwarves' display of camaraderie and desire, nay desperation, to help their fallen.

"It was coming for you," Jarlaxle said, moving beside him as he turned back.

"The bat?"

"The spider," Jarlaxle explained. "I've no doubt. I watched it closely when it entered the chamber, and its reaction was most telling when its many eyes settled upon Zaknafein."

Zaknafein glanced back behind him to the orange glow. "Well, it's gone now."

"So it would seem."

Zaknafein bent over and looked down into the chasm again, then closed his eyes and took a deep breath. He began to nod before he opened his eyes, then said to Jarlaxle, "It was coming for me, and it is gone. I feel it inside, a lightness, though I didn't even notice any heaviness there before."

Jarlaxle reached out and patted his friend on the shoulder. "We should go up top and kill some demons. The dwarves are driving them back out of Gauntlgrym."

Zaknafein nodded, but glanced around. "First we help the wounded," he said.

HE GOT MORE OUT OF ANDAHAR THAN HE HAD EXPECTED, but was still far from the place he had hoped to be when the unicorn began to suddenly slow, indicating that it was time for Drizzt to dismount. Despite his straight and hours-long run from Yvonnel and Athrogate, the last high ground had shown Drizzt that the demon golem wasn't all that far behind. He thought that a good thing, since it meant that the retriever had likely ignored his friends, but now that Andahar's magic was expiring, he knew that his plans were in jeopardy.

He slid down from the unicorn and dismissed Andahar, wondering if he'd ever see the fine mount again. Then Drizzt collected himself and took his bearings. He had many miles left to run.

So he did. He took his first step, ramping himself up to speed, trying to gauge how fast he might go without tiring long before he arrived.

He thought of the Monastery of the Yellow Rose, of Grandmaster Kane, of his training there where he had learned to better join mind and body.

He did that now with every stride, concentrating on the movement of his muscles, not just of his legs. No, he went to the deeper level, contractions and stretches, and felt the interplay of his hips, hamstrings, ankles, feet—all of it, even the movement of his arms.

And with each step, his stride improved. Soon he was working less and running faster, his breathing perfectly coordinated, his arms pumping for maximum momentum in the desired direction.

He fell within himself, into a mantra, as a mile passed, then three, then five, ten, a dozen. Had he relinquished his concentration at all, he would have marveled at how long and fast he had run, for in that trance, Drizzt had simply blocked out the pain and the exhaustion. They did not exist to him, at least not consciously.

He paused only once, atop a nearby hill, both to look ahead (and take heart that his destination was in sight) and to look behind, to see that the incessant spider had greatly closed the distance and was now not far behind.

Drizzt looked to his destination, then back to the spider. Yes, he could beat it to that place, he was confident.

Now he wanted to make sure that he *barely* beat it to that place.

He took a deep breath, trying once more to block the exhaustion— it occurred to him that in his trance he might run and run and run until he simply fell over dead.

It didn't matter. In the wide world, to his friends and all of those he loved, to the goodly people of the northern Sword Coast regions, it didn't matter.

He crossed a known road, moving to rocky ground, backdropped by the rolling waves of the ocean. He moved more slowly then, looking behind more often than ahead, letting the retriever draw near and picking his careful way among the rocks to keep himself concealed from any who might be ahead of him.

The golem drew closer. Drizzt finally spotted it, and it him, and the spider monster hissed and shrieked loudly and charged.

Drizzt sprinted across the last expanse, to the outer wall of the ruined keep known as Thornhold, the spider quickly closing behind him. Up the wall he went, brilliantly and swiftly, and at the top, despite the shouts arising from the remaining Stoneshaft dwarves at the place, he didn't hesitate, flipping right over.

"Here now!" one sentry shouted, charging at the half-naked, seemingly unarmed drow, spear lowered for a skewer.

An upraised backhand slap from Drizzt's right hand and a slight turn, right shoulder dropping back, sent the strike harmlessly wide. The dwarf didn't slow, trying to barrel the lighter drow over or tackle him, but that shoulder turn had also strengthened the drow's own strike, a stiff-handed stab that caught the poor fellow right in the throat, halting him as surely as if he had run into a stone wall. He dropped the spear and staggered backward a step before dropping to his knees, gasping desperately.

Drizzt hoped he hadn't killed the fellow, but he hadn't the time to make sure he was okay, for the spider was on the wall and more dwarves were charging at him along the parapet from the other direction. He backflipped off the parapet, straightened feet-down and half twisted before he landed the twenty feet below, then came down not flat on his feet, but with his legs turned just enough to transfer the energy of the landing into a sidelong roll, which became a backward roll, which became a second backward roll and a third, where Drizzt pressed up as he rolled past his shoulders, extending and lifting into the air to land gracefully on his feet looking back at the wall.

The parapet crumbled, dwarves tumbled, and over the top came the retriever.

Drizzt turned and sprinted for the keep, moving right past the door, which started to open just ahead of a tremendous lightning blast from the closing arachnid.

Drizzt skidded to a stop and threw himself to the ground just ahead of the bolt, so near that he could feel his long hair lifting up and dancing wildly. The lightning blew the door from its hinges, so up and in he went, fast-hopping past a trio of Stoneshaft dwarves lying just inside, their clothes smoking from the blast.

FROM FAR AWAY ALONG THE NORTH ROAD, BUT WITHIN sight of the keep, two pairs of eyes watched the spider eclipse the wall.

"Ah, but he's takin' them dirty dwarfs with him," Athrogate muttered. With her magic, Yvonnel had brought him in pursuit of the spider, both of them wanting to witness the last play of Drizzt Do'Urden. Behind the spider, they were confident that the single-minded golem would not turn, after all, and when it was done its task, Yvonnel had assured Athrogate, the beast would not remain on this plane of existence.

Both winced and Athrogate sucked in his breath sharply at the sudden flash and booming thunder, thinking it might already be over.

FAR AWAY ALONG THE SOUTH ROAD, ANOTHER PAIR OF EYES watched the giant spider crossing the rocky ground, then climbing the wall of Thornhold.

"The world has gone mad," Dahlia said to Regis, slurring every word through her swollen lips.

"It's broken," Regis agreed. "It's all broken."

"We will live evermore in the stench and shadows of demons," said Dahlia, speaking as much to herself, and, her turn of the head showed, to the bag of demonic despair in the carriage, as to the half-ling. "More and varied creatures than we have ever seen, even in our nightmares."

After a long pause, Regis straightened in his seat and stated, loudly and evenly, without a whisper of a shake in his voice, "No. I'm not giving up."

AS SOON AS THE DROW PAIR EXITED THE CHAMBER, MOVING side by side into the forge room, they learned that going to the higher chambers would not be their next move. Bruenor had gone out before them and now stood by the Great Forge, which had been closed. The dwarf king appeared more than a little concerned.

He looked up at Jarlaxle and Zaknafein and began motioning immediately for them to come to him, and as if to accentuate his point, the whole chamber suddenly shuddered, a deep grumble from far, far below.

"What do you know, King Bruenor?" Jarlaxle asked.

"Ye've got to go to Luskan, and quick," Bruenor answered. "Get me to the magical gates."

"They ain't workin'," Bruenor answered. "At all. And we shut down the forges so that damned spider didn't break 'em open and let tendrils of the fire beast out—seen that before and not wanting to see it again. But now we can't get 'em restarted."

"What do you suspect?"

"Holding the primordial in the pit starts in Luskan, under the tower Gromph now rules," Bruenor explained. "That tower's not givin' us the magic we need. If it keeps slowin', won't matter if the demons get in or not, for the whole place'll blow up, don't ye doubt."

Jarlaxle looked to Zaknafein, conveying his clear worry here, for he understood all about the connection between the Hosttower of the Arcane and the fire primordial.

Another dwarf ran up to Bruenor and pulled him aside for a whispered conversation. A few moments later, that dwarf ran off, signaling for others to follow.

"What're ye knowin', Jarlaxle?" Bruenor asked directly.

"I do not understa—"

"Why's the Hosttower shuttin' us down?"

"I did not know it was, but I will go, as you wish—"

"And why're they here?" Bruenor added.

"The demons?"

"The drow."

"What drow?"

"The drow army," said Bruenor. "Big force, and with banners o' many houses, nearin' our lower gates."

Jarlaxle's jaw hung open, a rare sight indeed. Bruenor gestured for him to follow and led him and Zaknafein to a nearby room, heavily fortified and guarded. Inside they found dwarven clerics, many standing before crystal balls. They went to a nearby one and the priest working the divining magic motioned for Bruenor to glance into the sphere.

The king looked back up with something that sounded half sigh and half growl, then glanced at Jarlaxle and pointed at the magical item.

And Jarlaxle knew they were doomed, for in the crystal ball he saw the march of Menzoberranzan, the banners of House Baenre, the procession of House Barrison Del'Armgo—the presence of those two longtime enemies marching together alone told Jarlaxle that the bulk of the city had come through the tunnels.

And that, in turn, made him believe that he knew well why the Hosttower of the Arcane, and particularly its less-than-dependable archmage, was now apparently compromising King Bruenor's position.

"Well?" King Bruenor asked.

"Well what?" Jarlaxle innocently replied.

"Why're they here, elf?"

"I know not."

"When you asked me to trust King Bruenor, I had not realized that such faith would prove so unrequited," Zaknafein interrupted before Bruenor could respond.

Bruenor stuttered over that response, and stared hard at Zaknafein, who merely shrugged in reply.

"Maybe we should all go to Luskan," Jarlaxle suggested. "At *least* to Luskan."

"Or maybe we should go and hunt some priestesses," Zaknafein declared. "You did not really believe that our lovely sisters in Menzoberranzan would allow an opportunity as great as this to merely pass them by, did you? A waiting demon army, a compromised dwarven stronghold . . ."

Jarlaxle sighed at his friend's unending and, sadly, usually on point cynicism.

THROUGH THE CORRIDORS AND ROOMS OF THE KEEP, THE tunnels and chambers of the catacombs below, and back through the keep above once more, Drizzt led the retriever on a grand chase, the spider leaving a trail of destruction and dwarves turned to stone in its ruined wake.

As he neared the exit of the structure, Drizzt found a small cubby, a crack in the stone, and placed his necklace and whistle within, offering a last smile to Andahar and hoping that no evil thing would find the wondrous unicorn.

Back out into the courtyard he ran, but he stopped there and did not go on to the wall.

Out came the spider, cracking the jamb and stones around the door in its rush, bearing down on Drizzt, who stood calmly, centered, arms by his side.

The retriever reared, front legs waving to defend any strikes, eyes glowing with power and then releasing a bolt of brilliant violet over its target.

Drizzt didn't move—he knew there was no point, and was glad that he had angered the golem so much that capturing him was not enough.

The ray came . . .

And then he was gone, breaking apart into floating shards of light, like a thousand tiny flower petals floating down on a gentle breeze. His breeches flapped and shuddered, then also vanished into nothingness, disintegrated by the retriever's final and most powerful ray of all.

The demon arachnid ran in tight circles, its senses, so attuned to the life force of its victim, showing it the truth: that this creature called Drizzt was no more.

The beast shrieked, victorious, its life's mission completed. It began a tight spin on the spot where its prey had dissolved, eight legs skittering in the closest thing to happiness such a fiend might know. And there, it too dissolved, its massive corporeal form fast reducing to a smoky whisper that traversed the planes.

It had done its foul job.

ABOUT THE AUTHOR

Thirty years ago, R. A. Salvatore created the character of Drizzt Do'Urden, the dark elf who has withstood the test of time to stand today as an icon in the fantasy genre. With his work in the Forgotten Realms, the Crimson Shadow, the DemonWars Saga, and other series, Salvatore has sold more than thirty million books worldwide and has appeared on the *New York Times* bestseller list more than two dozen times. He considers writing to be his personal journey, but still, he's quite pleased that so many are walking the road beside him!

R. A. lives in Massachusetts with his wife, Diane, and their two dogs, Pikel and Dexter. He still plays softball for his team, Clan Battlehammer, and enjoys his weekly *DemonWars: Reformation* RPG game. He can be found on Facebook at https://www.facebook.com/RA Salvatore-54142479810/, on Twitter at @r_a_salvatore, and at RASalva Store.com.